STALIN

68: Stalin adopting Lenin principles
43: Reading t Lenin
102: Stalin using L's tactics
104: NEP
108: Economic policy: Great leap
110: Abandonment of NEP
112: Collectivisation
115: " as Stalinist policy
118: Comparison of S.ism + Bolshevism in reaction to famine
122: S's violence
125: S view of cash

STALIN

NEW BIOGRAPHY OF A DICTATOR

Oleg V. Khlevniuk

Translated by NORA SELIGMAN FAVOROV

Yale UNIVERSITY PRESS

New Haven and London

Yale University Press gratefully acknowledges the financial support given for this publication by the Smith Richardson Foundation.

Published with assistance from the foundation established in memory of Calvin Chapin of the Class of 1788, Yale College.

Yale University Press books may be purchased in quantity for educational, business, or promotional use. For information, please e-mail sales.press@yale.edu (U.S. office) or sales@yaleup.co.uk (U.K. office).

Set in Utopia, Bodega, and Aller type by Integrated Publishing Solutions, Grand Rapids, Michigan.
Printed in the United States of America.

ISBN: 978-0-300-16388-9 (cloth)
ISBN: 978-0-300-21978-4 (pbk.)

Catalogue records for this book are available from the Library of Congress and the British Library.

In memory of
my wife Katya
(1961–2013)

CONTENTS

PREFACE

For more than two decades, I have been studying this man and the causes and logic underlying his actions, which upended or utterly destroyed millions upon millions of lives. This work has been stressful and emotionally draining, but it is my vocation. Lately, the paradoxical turns of recent Russian history, the large-scale poisoning of minds with myths of an "alternative" Stalin—one whose effective stewardship is held up as a model worthy of emulation—have given my research more than scholarly relevance.

The literature on Stalin and his era is impossibly vast. Even scholars of Stalinism freely admit to not having seen the half of it. Within this vastness, serious, meticulously documented research coexists with slapdash pen-pushing carelessly cobbled together out of anecdotes, rumors, and fabrications. The two camps—historical scholarship and lowbrow (usually pro-Stalin) ramblings—rarely cross paths and have long since given up the idea of reconciling.

Scholarly biographies of Stalin have gone through the same stages as the historiography of the Soviet period overall. I have a high regard for some classics written at a time when Soviet archives were completely inaccessible. Two authors who stand out are Adam Ulam and Robert Tucker.[1] Back in the 1970s, historians of the Stalin period resembled specialists in antiquity: they tended to know the few available documents and memoirs inside out and had little ability to expand their number. This dearth of documentation encouraged the painstaking study of these sources and elegant and thoughtful extrapolation. The situation was bound to change after the archival floodgates were opened in the early 1990s, and it took us some time to get our heads above water. The eventual appearance of new works informed by archival materials—including scholarly biographies of Stalin, as well as other investigations of the man and the political system—signal that historians have begun to cope with the inundation.[2]

The opening of the archives gave rise to a new genre of Stalin biography that one might call "the archival exposé." It's trailblazers include Dmitri Volkogonov, a former party loyalist who became a driving force for perestroika, and the Russian playwright Edvard Radzinsky. This genre favors personal accounts over "dry" statistics or administrative paper trails and page-turning narratives over painstaking research and historical contextualization. For many readers, the archival exposé has played an important role in shaping Stalin's image.

One of the most successful Western authors working to feed appetites for newly available details about the Stalin era is Simon Sebag Montefiore. A notable feature of his method is the citation of a broad spectrum of sources, not only from memoirs and interviews, but also from the archives. Montefiore struck a sort of middle ground, striving to instill some scholarly discipline into the "archival exposés" genre while producing readable history capable of attracting a wider audience than more scholarly texts.[3]

In today's Russia, on the other hand, Stalin's image is primarily being shaped by pseudo-scholarly apologias. An extremely diverse array of authors, all with their own motivations, contributes to Stalinist mythology. Most of these authors blend a lack of the most elementary knowledge with a willingness to make bold assertions. Their apologias typically cite fabricated sources or shamelessly misrepresent real ones. The impact of this powerful ideological assault on readers' minds is intensified by the circumstances of Russian life, which include rampant corruption and outrageous social iniquities. When they reject the present, people are more likely to idealize the past.

Apologists for Stalin no longer try, as they once did, to deny the crimes of his regime. Instead they resort to more subtle rewritings of history. In their version of events, lower-level officials, such as secret police chiefs and the secretaries of regional party committees, supposedly hiding their actions from Stalin, instigated mass repression. The most cynical Stalinists take a different tack, claiming that the Terror was just and that the millions destroyed on Stalin's orders really were "enemies of the people."

Many Russian Stalinists find it convenient to draw on theories developed by various Western historians: that the Terror developed spontaneously, that Stalin was not deeply involved in it, and that he was a far more "ordinary" political leader than usually thought. It is certainly not my intention to accuse my Western colleagues of fomenting re-Stalinization. They bear no more responsibility for Russia's contemporary political battles than Marx did for the Bolshevik revolution. Still, we should be aware that our words can have bizarre reverberations.

One variety of apologia widely cultivated in Russia's intellectual and political soil is the relatively moderate idea of "modernizing Stalinism." While this ideology formally acknowledges the Terror's countless victims and the high price paid for the "great leap" strategy, it sees Stalinism as an organic and unavoidable means of addressing the need to modernize and prepare for war. Within these postulates we can detect prejudices deeply rooted in the Russian social consciousness: that the interests of the state take absolute priority, that the individual is insignificant, that the flow of history is governed by higher-order laws. According to this paradigm, Stalin was the expression of an objective historical need. His methods were regrettable but necessary and effective. Furthermore, it is inevitable that the flywheel of history will become spattered with blood.

It would be wrong to deny that the "long waves" of Russian history helped shape the path toward Bolshevism and Stalinism. A strong state with authoritarian traditions, feeble private property and civil society institutions, and the colossal reach of a colonizing power that enabled, among other things, the creation of the Gulag Archipelago, all paved the way toward the Stalinist system. But elevating these factors to some sort of "Russian destiny" leads to the dead-end theory of "inevitable Stalinism." Adherents of this theory have little interest in specific facts and prefer to recycle Stalinist interpretations of Soviet history, sometimes with a fresh twist, more often without. They adamantly dismiss questions about the price paid for transformations and military victories, alternative development paths, and the role of the dictator. They close their eyes to the fact that Stalin himself, when he brought matters to a state of crisis and ruin, was occasionally forced to soften his policies, thereby demonstrating that even within the framework of Stalinism there were multiple paths toward industrialization. They do not even try to explain how the executions of seven hundred thousand people in 1937–1938 alone, ordered by Stalin, served the goals of modernization. Overall, the theory of modernizing Stalinism makes no serious attempt to ascertain how effective the Stalinist system was or to evaluate Stalin's own role in the development of the USSR from the 1920s to the early 1950s.

Reducing history to historical imperative is the least creative way of presenting the past. Historians are compelled to deal not with simple schemes and political conjecture but with concrete facts. Working with documents, they cannot avoid noticing the intricate dance between objective factors and personalities or between pattern and random occurrence. In a dictatorship, the role of the dictator's personal predilections, prejudices, and obsessions is greatly magnified. What better medium than biography to unravel this complex tangle of problems?

Biography is a unique genre of research that can, at one extreme, be reduced to the minutia of historical context or, at the other, be bloated with novelistic details of human behavior. Context without soul and soul without context—these are the main pitfalls confronting the biographer. Navigating them was a challenge for me. In the end, I understood that it was simply not possible to squeeze into this book even a passing reference to every significant episode or aspect of the Stalin period. I was compelled to choose which phenomena and tendencies most deserved inclusion, selecting the facts and events that seemed to characterize Stalin, his time, and the system that bears his name with the greatest clarity and vividness. This selectivity was all the more necessary given the appearance, over the past twenty years, of so many new sources shedding light on Stalin and his period. These sources should be briefly identified.

First, because of the opening of the state archives after the collapse of the Soviet Union, historians now may consult original firsthand documents, whereas in the past they were forced to whittle layers of distortion from official publications. A good example is the works and speeches of Stalin himself. Most were published during the leader's lifetime, but we now have the ability to work with the originals and compare what was actually said with edited versions. Furthermore, the body of Stalin's published speeches can now be supplemented with those that did not appear in print. Among the most important documents are papers generated by governmental bodies that Stalin himself chaired, such as the protocols and stenographic records of Politburo meetings and wartime State Defense Committee decrees. These dry bureaucratic documents are tremendously important in understanding Stalin's personality and life. They took up a huge portion of the dictator's time and were the tools by which he exercised power. Many resolutions bear traces of his heavy editorial hand.

By themselves, of course, the orders issued under Stalin paint only a partial picture. Why were they adopted? What were the logic and motives behind his directives? Much more revealing is Stalin's intermittent correspondence with his Politburo colleagues, conducted primarily when he was away on vacation and requiring letters to steer the actions of his fellow leaders back in Moscow. This correspondence was most prolific in the 1920s and the first half of the 1930s, before Russia had any reliable telephone service. It is a marvelous example of how sluggish technological progress can be a historian's friend. After the war, telephone communication became more reliable, and Stalin, now securely at the pinnacle of power, felt less need for detailed correspondence with subordinates. Curt directives sufficed. Despite their fragmentary nature, Stalin's letters constitute an important documentary whole and make for fascinating reading. They represent the most candid testaments he has left to posterity.[4]

Historians have been able to glean a great deal of important information from the logs of visitors to Stalin's Kremlin office.[5] These logs recorded visitors' names and the times they entered and left the office and thus shed light on how Stalin conducted business. Comparing them with other sources (such as memoirs or the protocols of Politburo meetings) offers important clues to the circumstances surrounding the adoption of various resolutions. Still, like his correspondence, these logs reflect only a portion of Stalin's activity. In addition to his Kremlin office, he occasionally worked in his office at Central Committee headquarters on Staraia Square and received visitors in his Kremlin apartment, as well as at his numerous dachas outside Moscow and in the south. Although we know that the service responsible for protecting Soviet leaders kept records of visits to Stalin's Kremlin apartment, researchers have yet to be given access to this archive.[6] There appears to be no sign of analogous records for the Central Committee office or the dachas.

The visitor logs were kept by Stalin's secretariat and security team. It seems likely that these services also kept, for their own purposes, records of Stalin's movements, as well as accounts by security personnel of what happened during their shifts. It goes without saying that these materials would be of tremendous value to Stalin's biographers. At this point, there is no solid evidence that such records exist.

Stalin's correspondence and the log of visitors to his Kremlin office are both part of his personal archive, which was compiled under his direct supervision and apparently with an eye toward history. Many documents in this collection feature the notations "my archive" or "personal archive." An important addition to the personal archive is an assortment of materials about Stalin gathered from various repositories. This assortment, which includes books from Stalin's library with notations by him, was concentrated in the Central Party Archive. Today both sets of materials have been brought together in the Stalin Collection of the Russian State Archive of Social and Political History (RGASPI, successor to the Central Party Archive, which comprises the bulk of its holdings),[7] a key source of knowledge about Stalin now used extensively by historians.

Yet despite its importance, the Stalin Collection has serious deficiencies. It offers only limited insights into Stalin's modi vivendi and operandi. Its primary shortcoming is the absence of much of the vast array of papers that made their way to Stalin's desk on a daily basis. These include thousands upon thousands of letters, statistical compilations, diplomatic dispatches, and reports and memoranda from the various branches of state security.

The lack of access to these documents hinders historians in their effort to develop a thorough understanding of how well informed Stalin was, what he knew about a given question, and thus the logic of his actions. The documents that would enable such insights have not been lost. They reside in the Presidential Archive of the Russian Federation (APRF, the former Politburo Archive), organized into "thematic" folders.[8] While working on this book, I was able to examine a few of them. For the time being, the Presidential Archive does not accommodate systematic scholarly study. However, the very fact that these folders exist encourages hope. The history of Russia suggests that sooner or later the archive will open.

The most tempting sources for biographers are always diaries and memoirs. These contain the sorts of three-dimensional treatments of people and events that are hard to extract from official paperwork. Such firsthand accounts permit biographers to fill their works with attention-grabbing details, but historians are well aware of these sources' liabilities. Memoirists, even candid ones, are rarely disinterested, and they often muddle events and dates or simply lie. These perils are compounded in memoirs from the Soviet era. As far as we know, no member of Stalin's inner circle kept a diary, depriving us of the kind of detailed source that Goebbels's famous diaries provided to Hitler's biographers. The situation with memoirs is not much better. Only two people close to Stalin left detailed reminiscences: Nikita Khrushchev and Anastas Mikoyan.[9] While these memoirs represent major contributions, both men were silent on important topics (such as their participation in the mass repression), and there was much that they simply did not know. Within Stalin's inner circle there was a strict rule: each man was privy only to information that he needed for the effective fulfillment of his duties. In the case of Mikoyan, some elements of his memoirs were distorted by his son, who prepared the manuscript for publication. He arbitrarily and without the customary disclosures simply inserted his own additions and revisions into the dictated text, supposedly based on subsequent accounts shared by his father.[10]

We also have memoirs by Soviet and foreign officials and other prominent figures who had some—usually extremely limited—interaction with Stalin. These works make a minor contribution to what we know about his life. In additional, many memoirs (for example by Red Army marshals) were published during the Soviet era and were therefore subjected to censorship (including self-censorship). After the fall of the USSR, many other people whose paths had crossed with Stalin's spoke up. Freedom sparked a flood of memoirs from the children and relatives of Stalin-era leaders.[11]

This "children's literature," as the Russian historian Elena Zubkova so aptly labeled the genre, was mainly motivated by commerce and a passion for self-justification, and the results are indeed juvenile.[12] Many relatives of Stalin and his comrades concocted fairy tales and cock-and-bull stories, blending personal impressions with fantasy. Naive pronouncements on politics serve to show that these offspring had only the faintest idea of what their fathers were up to. Third-hand information, rumors, and gossip abound. The primary factor detracting from the potential value of this literature is that Stalin's underlings were obsessed with maintaining strict secrecy. They lived with unrelenting secret police surveillance and the constant fear of being provoked into a politically fatal slip of the tongue. It is difficult to imagine what could have compelled them to be candid within their own families. The price was too high.

In this book I have been restrained in my use of memoirs, even though many contain fascinating descriptions and anecdotes readers would certainly find of interest. Guided by the most basic rules of source verification, I have made every effort to compare memoir accounts with other materials, archival materials first and foremost. On one hand, memoirs that generally held up to scrutiny were given greater credence. On the other hand, numerous errors and flagrant fabrications were treated as clear signs of unreliability, even if some claims could not be proved false through other sources. Certain memoirs were put on my personal blacklist. While I do not condemn others for citing these works, I will never do so.

When all is said and done, however, a historian endeavoring to write a biography of Stalin is in a relatively good position. The abundance of archival documents and evidence offers opportunities for prolonged, intensive, and (one can hope) fruitful work. Significant lacunae and the inaccessibility of many materials are frustrating impediments; nevertheless, it is now possible to write a genuinely *new* biography of Stalin insofar as newly accessible archival material has forced changes in our understanding of both the man and his era.

I would like to add a few final words about the size and structure of this biography. Restraints in the former have inspired innovations in the latter. Exhaustive details had to be forsaken. References and notes had to be kept to a minimum, so priority has been given to the attribution of quotes, numbers, and facts. By no means all of the worthy works of my colleagues have been mentioned, for which I offer them my apologies. Such economies leave me ambivalent. I regret the omission of many telling facts and quotes, but I am glad for the reader. I know how it feels to gaze wistfully at stacks of fat tomes that will never be conquered.

Another aspect of the book that I hope will facilitate reading, in addition to its modest size, is its structure. A conventional chapter-section chronology did not lend itself to presenting the two interdependent strata of Stalin's biography: the sequence of his life events and the most salient features of his personality and dictatorship. This difficulty gave rise to the idea of two alternating narratives, a sort of textual *matryoshka* or Russian nesting doll. One conceptual chain examines Stalin's personality and system of rule against the backdrop of his final days. The other, more conventionally chronological, follows the main stages of his biography in sequence. As a result, the book can be read in two ways. Readers can trust my arrangement and follow the page order, or they can take one stratum at a time. I have tried to make both methods equally convenient.

THE SEATS OF STALIN'S POWER

The early morning hours of 1 March 1953 at the near dacha.
The "Five's" last supper.

On Saturday, 28 February 1953, Josef Stalin invited four of his senior associates to the Kremlin: Georgy Malenkov, Lavrenty Beria, Nikita Khrushchev, and Nikolai Bulganin.[1] During the final six months of his life, Stalin and these four men constituted what was known as the "ruling group" or simply the "Five." They met regularly in Stalin's home. The leader's other old friends—Vyacheslav Molotov, Anastas Mikoyan, and Kliment Voroshilov —were in disgrace, and he did not wish to see them.[2] Assembling a small group of supporters to act as his right hand in ruling the country was a key element of Stalin's modus operandi. He liked to name these groups according to the number of members: the Five (Piaterka), the Six (Shesterka), the Seven (Semerka), the Eight (Vos'merka), the Nine (Deviatka). These informal groups enjoyed supreme authority while formal party and state structures functioned as regular bureaucracies handling the day-to-day running of the country. Dividing government into formal and informal institutions allowed the dictator to exploit the capabilities of a vast, all-encompassing bureaucratic machine while keeping a firm hold on the true levers of power. Stalin often changed the composition of the ruling group. He maintained daily, hands-on control over this central node of power, keeping its members at his constant beck and call for meetings and "friendly" gatherings. The dictator's approach to exercising power through a combination of bureaucratic institutions and patrimonial power inspired Yoram Gorlizki to coin the phrase "neopatrimonial state."[3]

Fear was the primary force behind the dictator's patrimonial power over his top associates and other highly placed officials. With the Soviet state security system under his firm control, Stalin could arrest anyone at any moment and have the person summarily shot. He did so countless times. The entire patrimonial political enterprise rested on terror.

The most important decisions were always made through direct— ideally face-to-face—communication with the dictator. This was the fastest and most effective way for an official to achieve personal and administrative objectives. But communication required access to the seats of power, places that for countless Soviet officials and members of the top leadership took on an almost sacred aura. Some were more sacred than others. There was an unspoken hierarchy in the various settings from which Stalin wielded power, and admission to some endowed greater status than others. Stalin spent a significant portion of his life in these seats of power. Each reflected some aspect of his personality and dictatorship.

The primary and most official seat of power was Stalin's Kremlin office. This commodious, oak-paneled study was divided into two zones: Stalin's desk and a long conference table. Other furnishings included a grandfather clock (which Stalin used to monitor the promptness with which those summoned arrived) and a plaster death mask of Lenin encased in glass and displayed on a special stand. On the walls hung portraits of Lenin and Marx. During the war, they were joined by the tsarist-era military heroes Aleksandr Suvorov and Mikhail Kutuzov. Otherwise the decor hardly changed over the many years he spent there. During the war, the bomb shelter built beneath the Kremlin contained a slightly smaller but otherwise almost exact replica of this office: the same furniture, the same pictures, the same curtains (despite the lack of windows).[4]

Over thirty years, approximately three thousand different people visited the Kremlin office.[5] Stalin's closest associates, of course, were there frequently, but the visitors also included heads of government ministries and enterprises, academics, cultural figures, senior state security and military personnel, and foreign guests. The Kremlin office was the most accessible of the seats of Stalin's power.

On the evening of 28 February 1953, Bulganin, Beria, Malenkov, and Khrushchev, who had been called to the Kremlin by Stalin, did not linger in this office. Stalin immediately took them to the Kremlin movie theater, a much more exclusive place. The theater was a 7.5-by-17-meter space with twenty seats, installed in 1934 where Russia's tsars had once enjoyed a winter garden. Before it was built, Soviet leaders watched movies either outside the Kremlin, in the building of the cinematography directorate, or in a small Kremlin room that had been used for silent films.[6] Stalin enjoyed watching movies with his comrades, and these viewing sessions gradually became obligatory. Thanks to detailed records kept by Boris Shumiatsky, who oversaw the Soviet film industry, we know quite a bit about how these evenings in the movie theater were spent during 1934–1936.[7] Shumiatsky would bring the movies and listen to the comments of Stalin and his colleagues, as well as the decisions that were sometimes taken during a viewing. His notes provide a valuable window onto the rules of behavior within Stalin's inner circle and the atmosphere of these gatherings.

As a rule, the viewing sessions began late in the evening and extended into the early hours of the morning. Stalin sat in the front row, surrounded by members of the top leadership. There was always a great deal of discussion about the movies and newsreels, both while a film was rolling and afterward. Stalin always had the first word. He would issue instructions concerning the content of specific films, the Soviet film industry, and ideology in general. In the movie theater, he made on-the-spot decisions on everything from budgetary issues to the publication of policy-setting articles in the Soviet press to personnel matters. Filmmakers would occasionally be invited to viewings of their films. Such an invitation was a great honor. Stalin would congratulate them on their work and offer "guidance" on improving it. Shumiatsky's records make it clear that these get-togethers in the Kremlin movie theater were not merely relaxation for the Soviet leadership. They were informal meetings of the top level of government at which questions of ideology and cultural policy were decided. Most likely, Stalin and his colleagues also discussed other affairs of state before and after the viewings.

Shumiatsky's records end abruptly in early 1937. This was undoubtedly tied to the intensification of repression in the country. Shumiatsky himself was arrested in early 1938 and shot soon after. Stalin's movie viewing continued, but we know almost nothing about later sessions. It appears that toward the end of his life, only his closest associates were admitted to the Kremlin movie theater. The 28 February meeting of the Five was Stalin's last movie-theater get-together.

When the movie was over, Stalin, as he often did, invited the others to dine with him at his dacha near the Moscow suburb of Volynskoe. The dacha was just a few minutes away, earning it the nickname of "the near [dacha]" *(blizhniaia)*. Occasionally the seat of power would shift to one or another of the houses or dachas around Moscow or in the south, where Stalin spent lengthy annual vacations. But the "near" dacha held a special place in his heart. It was an important epicenter of his life and rule.

The first house on the site of the near dacha was built in 1933. The move there was associated with upheavals in Stalin's personal and political life. The terrible famine that swept the land in the early 1930s as a result of Stalin's policies coincided with family tragedy. In November 1932 his wife, Nadezhda Allilueva, died by her own hand.[8] Stalin started a new life in a new place.

Stalin personally oversaw the near dacha's many expansions and renovations. The huge house that resulted was an odd blend of the institutional and the pretentious.[9] All the rooms resembled one another and were, in the words of Stalin's daughter Svetlana, "impersonal."[10] The second floor, for which an elevator had been installed, was rarely used. Stalin's favorite room toward the end of his life was the so-called "small dining room" on the first floor. This roomy space contained a rectangular table three meters long, a couch, a cupboard, an easy chair, a small telephone table, and a fireplace. A pair of binoculars, hanging from a hook, and a hunting rifle were kept next to the fireplace. A large carpet covered the floor. The room led to a glassed-in veranda and a terrace. According to Svetlana, Stalin both slept and worked in this room. The large table was always piled with papers and books. Unless he had company, he ate at one of the table's corners. He kept his medicines in the cupboard. Stalin enjoyed sitting by the fire, where he would sometimes order shashlik to be roasted. He liked to receive his visitors here. It is also where he suffered the stroke that ended his life.

The dacha was surrounded by a fifty-acre park. Stalin personally oversaw the landscaping and farming that took place on the grounds. He designed a greenhouse for citrus plants, supervised the installation of a vineyard, grew his own watermelons, and kept a pond stocked with fish. He sometimes had a portion of his watermelon crop sent to Moscow stores. There were also horses, cows, chickens, ducks, and a small apiary. His bodyguards testified that Stalin devoted a great deal of time to the running of this agricultural enterprise and kept track of even the smallest details. Hundreds of orders from Stalin to the man in charge of running the estate, Lieutenant Colonel P. V. Lozgachev, have been preserved:

> 7 April 1950: a) Start planting watermelons and melons in raised beds on 10 May; b) In mid-July, trim the watermelon and melon vines. . . .
> 20 April: . . . Line the path from the kitchen to the pond with fir trees. . . . Plant corn every half meter next to the main house and between apple trees by the pond, toward the gazebo. Plant beans there too. . . . Plant eggplant, corn, and tomatoes along the edge of the garden.

Lozgachev reported that he received such instructions almost every day.[11] In essence, Stalin was the master of a small estate that he preferred to run himself, not leaving important details in the hands of subordinates. The patriarchal way in which he ran his dacha estate is consistent with his approach to running his much larger "estate," the Soviet Union. He kept track of state resources and reserves and took charge of their allocation, jotting down important pieces of information in a special notebook.[12] He immersed himself in the details of film scripts, architectural plans, and the design of military hardware. His interest in landscaping extended beyond his personal domain to the streets of Moscow: "People say that the square on the Arbat . . . has not yet been covered with paving blocks (or asphalt). This is shameful! . . . Put pressure on them and make them finish up the square."[13]

One result of Stalin's desire to shape the spaces around him was the creation of a room that served as the dacha's social nexus: a 155-square-meter hall. The room's centerpiece was a 7-meter-long table that stood on a 6-by-12-meter rug. (The area of this rug, incidentally, equaled the average living space of sixteen Soviet city dwellers in 1953: 4.5 square meters per person.) Easy chairs and couches lined the walls. Occasionally Stalin worked at the table in this large room or on the couch or easy chairs. For the most part, however, the room was reserved for meetings and festive gatherings.

A number of participants in these gatherings, which were held regularly, have left descriptions. The food was simply placed on the table, and guests helped themselves to whatever they wanted and took their plates to any free seat. Dinner stretched for many hours, ending long after midnight or even at daybreak. These meals were an opportunity to discuss and decide various matters of state. But that was not all. For Stalin, they were a way of keeping an eye on his associates and gleaning information. As one of the few forms of entertainment available to him, they also filled an important social need: they eased his sense of isolation. As Khrushchev wrote, "He felt so alone he didn't know what to do with himself."[14]

Plenty of drinking went on around this table. As he aged, Stalin moderated his own consumption of spirits, but he liked to spur others to overdo it and then watch their behavior. He had several ways of forcing his guests to drink more heavily than they might have wished. Toasts were proposed in rapid succession, and failing to empty one's glass was unacceptable. "If someone didn't participate when a toast was made, he was 'fined' by having to drink another glassful and perhaps several glasses."[15] The Yugoslav politician and writer Milovan Djilas later recalled a drinking game he witnessed at Stalin's dacha during a visit in January 1948: "Everyone guessed how many degrees below zero it was outside and then, as a penalty, downed . . . a glass for each degree he was off. . . . I remember that Beria missed by three and claimed that he had done so on purpose to get more vodka."[16]

The alcohol loosened inhibitions. "The atmosphere at these dinners was unconstrained, and jokes, many of them obscene, evoked raucous laughter."[17] In addition, there were other, more "cultured" amusements. Sometimes they sang revolutionary and folk songs in which, the wife of Andrei Zhdanov recalled, Stalin would join with a quiet tenor.[18] Zhdanov entertained his comrades with lewd ditties.[19] "Such songs could be sung only at Stalin's. You couldn't possibly repeat them anywhere," Khrushchev recalled.[20] For a while a piano stood in the large room. Some remembered Zhdanov playing it, although there is no clear record of what he played or how well. After Zhdanov's death in 1948, Stalin ordered the piano moved to an adjacent room. More often, music was provided by a radiogram (a combination radio and phonograph), on which Stalin played records, both Russian folk songs and classical music. Sometimes he enjoyed listening to his impressive collection of some 2,700 albums, on his own or with guests. Occasionally there was dancing. According to Khrushchev, Mikoyan was considered the best dancer. Everyone did the best he could. Even Stalin "would move his feet around and stretch out his arms."[21]

There probably was no dancing during those early hours of 1 March. This was a quiet get-together, limited to Stalin's most trusted associates. "We would go to Stalin's place quite often, almost every evening," Khrushchev recalled of that period. These dinner gatherings with the aging and unbalanced Stalin were not easy on his guests. In Khrushchev's words, "We were supposed to work at our jobs and the posts to which we had been elected and, besides that, attend Stalin's dinners like some sort of characters in a play and entertain him. That was a difficult and painful time for us."[22] But Stalin's comrades were not about to complain, and they assiduously fulfilled their dinner duties as a condition of their inclusion in the ruling circle. As usual, the gathering adjourned toward morning (Khrushchev places its conclusion around five or six a.m.). They parted on a good note. As Khrushchev described it, "Stalin was a bit tipsy and seemed very well disposed toward everyone." He led his guests into the vestibule, "joked a lot, waved his hands around, and as I recall he poked me in the stomach with his finger and called me Mikita. When he was in a good mood, he always used the Ukrainian form of my name—Mikita. . . . We too were in a good mood when we left because nothing unpleasant had happened at the dinner, and not all these dinners ended that well."[23] We have no reason to doubt Khrushchev's account. Dmitri Volkogonov claimed that Stalin was irritable and threatened his guests, but he does not cite any specific sources.[24]

Stalin was equally capable of rewarding his underlings with his amiability and menacing them with threats. For almost two decades he used both the carrot and the stick (in Russian, the knout and the ginger cookie, with a good deal more of the former) to keep not only his close associates in hand, but also the many millions who lived in the USSR and, later, the entire "socialist camp."

Over his seventy-four-year life, the Soviet dictator fought through a stormy historical landscape to become an important factor in events not only in Russia, but also the world. Among scholars, there is more agreement than controversy on the historical and ideational antecedents that shaped him, including traditional Russian authoritarianism and imperialism, European revolutionary traditions, and Leninist Bolshevism.[25] These influences, of course, do not diminish his major personal contribution to the formation of a uniquely Soviet totalitarian system and ideology. Ideological doctrines and prejudices were often decisive in Stalin's life and actions, but instead of receiving them passively, he adapted them to the interests of his own dictatorship and emerging superpower. His personality also played no small role in the political course he forged. He was cruel by temperament and devoid of compassion. Of all the available methods for resolving political, social, and economic conflict, he favored terror and saw no reason to moderate its use. Like other dictators, he was stubborn and inflexible. Concession and compromise were seen as a threat to the inviolability of his power. He made limited and half-hearted reforms only when socioeconomic crises were reaching the breaking point and the stability of the system was imperiled. His theoretical dogmatism lay at the root of the violence that defined his regime.

Underpinning Stalin's worldview was an extreme anti-capitalism. His hostility toward this system was unequivocal, and he rejected even the limited concessions that Lenin made in instituting the New Economic Policy (NEP). Stalin grudgingly allowed a few capitalist economic vehicles within the Soviet system, such as money, limited market relations, and personal property. After millions had died during the famine of 1932–1933, he agreed to allow peasants limited freedom to produce and sell outside the collective and state farm system. But to the end he believed that the concessions that had been forced on him by hard circumstances would soon be reversed and the socialist economy would be transformed into a money-free powerhouse where people would work as ordered by the state and receive in exchange the natural goods that the state decided they needed.

In Stalin's worldview, the state the Bolsheviks created was an absolute. All existence was completely and unconditionally subordinate to the state, and its highest personification was the party and its leader. Personal interests were recognized only to the extent that they served the state, which had the unquestioned right to demand from people any sacrifice, including their lives. The state was unrestricted in its actions and could never be wrong, as it represented the ultimate truth of historical progress. Any action by the regime could be justified by the greatness of its mission. Mistakes and crimes by the state did not exist; there was only historical necessity and inevitability or, in some cases, the growing pains of building a new society.

The primary tool used to compel submission to the state and suppress the individual and the social was the so-called "class war" against foreign and domestic "enemies." In this war, Stalin was the foremost theoretician and a ruthless tactician. With the successful advance of socialism, he asserted, the class war would only intensify. This idea was a cornerstone of his dictatorship. As a means of interpreting reality, the class war theory was also a powerful propaganda tool. Inadequate political and economic outcomes, the hardships endured by the populace, and military failures could all be explained by the underhanded scheming of "enemies." As a method of state repression, class war gave the Terror the breadth and brutality of an actual war. The Soviet dictator has earned the distinction of being the organizer and director of one of the most powerful and merciless terror machines known to history.

Stalin had no trouble reconciling Marxist and Bolshevik-Leninist dogma with great-power imperialism. In November 1937, he told his associates the following: "The Russian tsars did many bad things. They plundered and enslaved the people. They waged wars and grabbed territory in the interests of the landowners. But they did do one good thing—they created a huge state that stretches all the way to Kamchatka. We have inherited that state. And for the first time we, the Bolsheviks, have brought together and consolidated this state as a single, indivisible state . . . for the benefit of the workers."[26] These candid words are all the more telling as they were spoken at a dinner celebrating the twentieth anniversary of the October Revolution, the country's main revolutionary holiday. In the international arena, Stalin's expansion of the empire makes him a worthy heir to the Russian tsars. Only the ideological façade was different. At the Berlin train station on the eve of the Potsdam Conference in 1945, U.S. Ambassador to the Soviet Union Averell Harriman asked Stalin how it felt to arrive in the capital of a defeated enemy as a victor. Stalin replied, "Tsar Alexander made it all the way to Paris."[27] Yet Stalin arguably outdid the tsars. The Soviet empire expanded its sphere of influence to encompass huge swaths of Europe and Asia and transformed itself into one of the world's two superpowers.

Did Stalin look back on his triumphs after parting with his guests for the last time in his life on 28 February? Did his thoughts take him to earlier times—his childhood, youth, the revolution? Like the lives of his fellow revolutionaries, Stalin's life was cleanly divided into two parts: before and after the revolution. Conceptually and chronologically, these two periods were approximate halves of his life. The first thirty-eight of his seventy-four years were lived before the revolution, and twenty of them were spent actively working toward it.

1 BEFORE THE REVOLUTION

According to his official Soviet biography, Stalin was born in 1879. In fact Ioseb Jughashvili (his birth name) was born one year earlier. Stalin knew, of course, when and where he was born: in the small Georgian town of Gori, in a far corner of the vast Russian Empire. A Gori church register (part of Stalin's personal archive) provides the exact date: 6 December 1878. This date can also be found in other documents, such as his graduation certificate from the Gori Theological School. In a form filled out in 1920, his year of birth is again given as 1878. But the year 1879 began to appear in paperwork completed by his various helpers, and that date was used in all encyclopedias and reference materials. After he had consolidated power, a grand celebration was held in honor of his fiftieth birthday on 21 December 1929. There was confusion over not only the year of his birth, but also the day, given as 9 December (Old Style) instead of 6 December. This inaccuracy came to the attention of historians only in 1990.[1] The reason for it has yet to be determined. One thing is clear: in the 1920s, Stalin decided to become one year younger. And he did.

Legends surround Stalin's parentage. Sensation seekers proclaimed Ioseb (who later became Iosif once his interactions began to be primarily in Russian) to have been the illegitimate son of a prosperous merchant, a factory owner, a prince, and even Emperor Alexander III, who supposedly was attended to by Ioseb's mother while the emperor was visiting Tiflis. The historical record suggests more prosaic origins. Ioseb was born into a humble Georgian family. His mother, Ekaterine or Keke (Yekaterina in Russian) Geladze, the daughter of serfs, was born in 1856. In 1864, after the abolition of serfdom, her family moved to Gori, where, at the age of eighteen, she was given in marriage to the cobbler Besarion or Beso (Vissarion in Russian) Jughashvili, six years her senior. Their first two children died in infancy; Ioseb (Soso) was the third.[2]

Few pieces of documentary evidence survive from Stalin's youth. The primary source of our knowledge is memoirs written after he had already attained the pinnacle of power. Even an uncritical reader will notice that these memoirists are writing about the childhood and youth of a future dictator, not the early years of Ioseb Jughashvili. This aberration magnifies the tendency, common to biographies generally, toward selective exaggeration and exclusion. Depending on the situation and the writer's politics, emphasis is placed on either Ioseb's virtues and leadership qualities or his innate cruelty and psychological abnormalities. But as Ronald Grigor Suny has shown, attempts to find the future dictator in the child Ioseb Jughashvili are highly suspect.

It is commonly believed that Ioseb had a difficult childhood. Abuse and beatings by his drunkard father, as well as material deprivation, supposedly embittered the boy and made him ruthless and vindictive. But there is plenty of evidence to support a very different picture. By many measures, Stalin's childhood was ordinary or even comfortable. A number of accounts attest that his father was not only a skilled cobbler, but also that he was able to read Georgian and converse in several languages, including Russian. His mother had received some home schooling and could also read and write in Georgian. Given the low literacy rate in Georgia at the time, this would have given the family an advantage. During Ioseb's early years, Besarion Jughashvili apparently was quite successful and his family was well provided for.[3]

Later, after Besarion began to drink heavily and then abandoned his wife and child, responsibility for Ioseb's upbringing fell on his mother's shoulders. Ekaterine was a woman of strong character and a hard worker, and, starting with odd jobs, she managed to learn the craft of dressmaking. As an only child (a circumstance that would prove significant), Soso, unlike many of his peers, did not have to work and could therefore attend school. In a letter written in 1950, requesting a meeting for old times' sake, one of Stalin's childhood friends commented, "In 1894, when you graduated from the theological school, I graduated from the Gori Municipal School. You were accepted that same year into the Tbilisi Theological Seminary, but I wasn't able to continue my studies since my father had 8 children, so we were poor and we helped him."[4] Ioseb's mother, dreaming that her son would climb the social ladder to become a priest, doggedly worked to make this dream a reality and did everything she could to facilitate his education. Such strivings are hard to reconcile with the idea of a bleak, impoverished childhood.

Certainly there was discord in the family, and the drunken Besarion let loose with his fists. Soso was apparently beaten by both parents. But as Suny rightly observes, the evidence we have is insufficient either to judge whether violence within the Jughashvili family was unusual for that place and time or to assess its impact on Soso's perception of the world.[5] Stalin's childhood and adolescence seem to have been utterly typical of the environment from which he came—the world of poor, but not destitute, craftsmen and shopkeepers in a small town at the outskirts of the empire. This was a world where coarse mores coexisted with traditions of neighbor helping neighbor and periods of relative well-being alternated with hard times. Children were exposed to severity and cruelty as well as to affection and indulgence. Soso Jughashvili experienced the good and the bad—his father's harshness and his mother's limitless affection—in relatively balanced proportion. The family's financial difficulties, which came when Soso was in school, were eased by the help of friends and relatives. While at the local theological school and later at the seminary in Tiflis, Ioseb received assistance from the state and benefited from the intercession of sympathetic protectors. Despite their modest means, mother and son were fully accepted into their small community.

During an interview many years later, Stalin said, "My parents were uneducated, but they did not treat me badly by any means."[6] It is possible he was not being candid or was suppressing unpleasant childhood memories. There is little evidence regarding Stalin's feelings toward his father, who died young. To all appearances, however, he felt genuine affection for his mother. His letters to her in her later years contain lines such as the following: "Hello Mama dear! How are you getting on, how are you feeling? I haven't had any letters from you in a long time—you must be upset with me, but what can I do? I'm really very busy," and "Greetings dear mother! I'm sending you a shawl, a jacket, and medicines. Show the medicines to your doctor before taking them because a doctor has to set the dose."[7] Despite her son's meteoric rise, Keke remained in Georgia, living in a position of respect and comfort. Stalin did not attend her funeral in 1937. Throughout that year, the height of the Great Terror, he did not set foot outside of Moscow. The dedication he wrote for a memorial wreath in both Georgian and Russian still survives: "To my dear and beloved mother from her son Ioseb Jughashvili (from Stalin)."[8]

Stalin owed her a true debt of gratitude. She worked hard to protect her son from want and to enable him to get an education, and she nursed him through numerous illnesses, including smallpox, which pockmarked his face for the rest of his life. Soso also suffered a childhood mishap, exacerbated by poor medical treatment, that rendered his left arm severely disabled. The joints remained atrophied for the rest of his life, and the arm never functioned properly. Another physical defect was congenital:

two toes on his left foot were joined. It seems unlikely that these defects remained unremarked in the often heartless company of boys. Yet Soso was not an outcast. He remained on an equal footing with his peers and took part in all of their games. He had an excellent memory, always a respected quality. It does not appear that a difficult childhood sowed in Ioseb Jughashvili the cruelty that emerged in Joseph Stalin. There is also no obvious sign of what in his childhood might have turned him into a rebel.

■ THE FAILED SEMINARIAN

Ioseb's mother, whose efforts were inspired by the hope that her son would successfully overcome the social circumstances of his birth, was not the only one who noticed his intellectual abilities. When the time came to send the boy to school, Keke was able to solicit the support of well-wishers who felt strongly that the boy could profit from an education. Her aspiration that Ioseb would become a priest seemed entirely fitting. The well-wishers were the family of a priest named Khristofor Charkviani, in whose home the Jughashvilis rented a room. They helped Soso gain admission to the Gori Theological School. The Charkviani children also taught him Russian, the language of instruction. These language lessons enabled Soso to immediately enter the school's highest preparatory class— undoubtedly a significant moment in the future leader's life. Ten-year-old Soso was making an important step into the Russophone world.

He spent almost six years, from 1888 to 1894, at the Gori Theological School, a period that saw dramatic changes in the Jughashvili family. After much domestic strife, Besarion left Gori, depriving his wife and son of their means of support and imperiling Soso's continued attendance at the school. Keke was able to find help, a task undoubtedly made easier by Soso's academic success. He was a model student and was even granted a stipend. The mother took care that her son would in no way feel inferior to his classmates and always ensured that he was dressed well and appropriately for the weather. According to numerous reminiscences, Soso distinguished himself at school by his diligence and hard work. He was reputed to be a fine reader of prayers and singer in the church choir, and he got along well with the teachers. The Russian teacher, whom the children called "the gendarme" behind his back, made Soso his assistant in charge of distributing books.[9] Many decades later, in 1949, another former teacher at the school, S. V. Malinovsky, took the bold step of contacting his former pupil. "In my old age," he wrote, "I am proud that my humble efforts contributed to your education." Malinovsky requested that he be awarded a personal pension, "so that in the twilight of my days my basic needs can be met and I can die in the happy awareness that my Great Pupil did not leave me in poverty."[10] While there is evidence that this letter was placed before Stalin, the record is unclear on whether assistance was granted.

Ioseb graduated in May 1894. The certificate issued to him lists the courses he took and the grades he received. He earned a grade of "excellent" for behavior, as well as for Sacred History, Orthodox Catechism, Liturgical Exegesis and Ecclesiastical Typikon, Russian and Church Slavonic, Georgian, geography, penmanship, and liturgical chant. In Greek and arithmetic, his weakest subjects, he managed a grade of "very good." His academic success yielded a recommendation for entry into a theological seminary.[11] Despite the narrow curriculum, Soso acquired a great deal of skill and knowledge at the school in Gori and developed a passion for reading. More significant, he developed a mastery of Russian. Recollections of his time at the school paint a picture of an active child with pretentions toward leadership, pretentions undoubtedly affirmed by his standing as a top student. He seems to have had pleasant recollections of these years. Many decades later he remembered his school friends and even tried to help them. In notes dated May 1944, when he was sixty-five, Stalin wrote: "1) To my friend Petya—40,000, 2) 30,000 rubles to Grisha, 3) 30,000 rubles to Dzeradze," and "Grisha! Accept this small gift from me. . . . Yours, Soso."[12] Written in Georgian, these documents hint at bursts of nostalgia felt by an old man reflecting fondly on his adolescence.

There are vague and inconsistent accounts by memoirists claiming that Ioseb Jughashvili's rebellious behavior and break with religion dated to his days in Gori. Leon (Lev) Trotsky, one of Stalin's first biographers (and hardly an impartial one), convincingly argues that Stalin's former classmates are confusing the Gori period with events that took place later, in Tiflis.[13] The best proof of the schoolboy Soso's exemplary behavior and law-abiding attitude is the glowing assessment on his graduation certificate and the recommendation that he enroll in a seminary.

In September 1894, having successfully passed the entry examination, young Jughashvili enrolled in the Tiflis Theological Seminary. Ekaterine and her son enjoyed good fortune here as well. The seminary was more eager to have students born into the clerical estate, and others were required to pay tuition. But Ioseb's abilities, along with the intercession of friends and relatives, earned him a free room and meals in the seminary cafeteria. He was required to pay only for his courses and clothing.[14] Did the ambitious boy perceive this as a demeaning handout to a "poor relative"?

Perhaps. But it is equally possible that this grant-in-aid was viewed as a recognition of past achievements.

Stalin spent more than four and a half years in the Tiflis seminary, from the autumn of 1894 to May 1899. The move to a large city undoubtedly brought a degree of stress. However, Ioseb had not come alone but with a group of friends and acquaintances from the Gori Theological School. Furthermore, he seems to have found the course work relatively easy. He ranked eighth in his class in his first year and fifth the next year. His behavior was assessed as "excellent."[15]

Yet behind this promising façade lurked a growing dissatisfaction and insubordination. While there is no moment that stands out as marking his departure from the path of the law-abiding and well-adjusted student, we do have two well-known pieces of evidence attesting to the unbearable living conditions at the seminary. The first such testimony belongs to Stalin himself. In 1931, in an interview with German writer Emil Ludwig, he described the seminary's role in pushing him toward insurrection: "In protest against the outrageous regime and the Jesuitical methods prevalent at the seminary, I was ready to become, and actually did become, a revolutionary, a believer in Marxism as a really revolutionary teaching. . . . For instance, the spying in the hostel. At nine o'clock the bell rings for morning tea, we go to the dining-room, and when we return to our rooms we find that meantime a search has been made and all our chests have been ransacked."[16] This account is supplemented by a widely cited description by one of Stalin's classmates:

> We were brought to a four-story building and put in huge dormitory rooms with 20–30 people each. . . . Life in the theological seminary was repetitious and monotonous. We arose at seven in the morning. First, we were forced to pray, then we had tea, and after the bell we went to class. . . . Classes continued, with breaks, until two o'clock. At three we had supper. At five there was roll call, after which we were not allowed to leave the building. We felt as if we were in prison. We were again taken to vespers, and at eight we had tea, and then each class went to its own room to do assignments, and at ten it was lights out, sleep.[17]

Having only Sundays free of this regimentation probably did not much brighten the seminarians' lives, especially as the day was partially taken up by mandatory church services. It was a regime of constant surveillance, searches, denunciations, and punishments. Although the range of disciplines was somewhat broader than in Gori—in addition to scripture, church singing, Russian philology, and the Greek and Georgian languages, the curriculum included biblical and secular history and mathematics—intellectual life was constrained by dogmatism. The reading of secular literature was harshly punished and Russification was crudely enforced, insulting the national pride of Georgian seminarians. The strong undercurrent of resentment and rebellion among the students was hardly surprising. A strike had erupted the year before Ioseb enrolled. The seminarians stopped attending their classes and demanded an end to arbitrariness by the teachers and the firing of some of them. In response, the authorities closed down the institution and expelled a large number of students.

The firm suppression of unrest doubtless helps account for the lack of open protest during Ioseb's years at the seminary. Any individual or group dissent was kept underground. At first the future dictator found an outlet in romantic literary heroes exemplifying the struggle for justice, especially those from Georgian literature. One of his first models came from *The Patricide,* a novel by Alexandre Kazbegi. This was a tale of the fearless and noble avenger Koba, scourge of Russian oppressors and the Georgian aristocracy.[18] Koba became the future leader's first pseudonym, one he treasured and allowed his closest comrades to use for him throughout his life.

His fascination with romantic rebellion flavored with Georgian nationalism predictably led young Stalin to try his hand at verse. After completing his first year at the seminary, he brought a sample of his poetry to the editorial office of a Georgian newspaper, which published five poems between June and October 1895. Another poem appeared in a different newspaper the following summer. The poems, written in Georgian, extolled service to the motherland and the people. During Stalin's leadership of the Soviet Union, his poetry was translated into Russian, but these translations were not included among his collected works. He undoubtedly understood that his undistinguished and naive verse belied the image of the single-minded revolutionary:

A lark in the high clouds
Sang ever so sonorously.
And a joyous nightingale said this:
"Blossom, lovely land,
Exult, country of Georgians.
And you, Georgian,
Gladden your motherland with learning."[19]

Although such lines do nothing to soften the image of Stalin the dictator, they do attest to the pure intentions of Jughashvili the seminarian, who found inspiration in the ideas of service to the motherland and the people.

During his third year at the seminary, these vague, half-formed strivings did lead to one concrete step. Ioseb joined an illegal discussion group of seminarians and apparently assumed a leadership role within it. The books read by the group were perfectly legal but forbidden by the seminary. Entries in the journal used to keep track of the seminarians' conduct record violations by Jughashvili involving the reading of forbidden books, including novels by Victor Hugo, in late 1896 and early 1897.[20] Beginning in his third year, Ioseb's grades began to decline, and he was caught violating rules with increasing frequency.

Ioseb Jughashvili was growing increasingly radicalized. He stopped writing verse and developed an ardent interest in politics. Participating in the discussion group was no longer enough. He longed to get involved in something "real," a desire that led him to the Social Democrats, an interest in Marxism, and attendance at illegal meetings of railway workers. According to his official biography, in August 1898, while still enrolled in the seminary, Ioseb joined a Social Democratic organization and began working as a propagandist for small groups of workers. At this point, his knowledge of Marxism must have been fairly superficial, but his fascination with it was consuming. For the young seminarian, the all-encompassing nature of Marxism, almost religious in its universality, was tremendously appealing. It filled the gap in his worldview created by his disillusionment with religion. The belief that human history was governed by a set of laws and that humanity was inexorably advancing toward the higher stages of socialism endowed the revolutionary struggle with special meaning. But this fascination with Marxism hardly set young Jughashvili apart. Belief in Marxism was a veritable epidemic.

One influence on Ioseb was the older fellow revolutionaries and rebels who came to Tiflis from other regions of Georgia. The figure most often mentioned in this context is Lado Ketskhoveli. Though still a young man, he had already advanced along the path on which young Stalin was just embarking. After being expelled from the Tiflis seminary, Ketskhoveli enrolled in the Kiev Theological Seminary, where he was arrested by the authorities for possessing illegal literature. Only a general amnesty occasioned by the coronation of Tsar Nicholas II saved him from punishment. After returning to Tiflis and then moving to Baku, this committed revolutionary immersed himself in subversive work and organized an underground printing press. In 1903 he was shot by a prison guard. Legend has it that he was killed for shouting revolutionary slogans. This was the sort of man of action Ioseb looked up to.[21]

Ioseb's behavior during his final academic year at the seminary (1898–1899), when he was increasingly involved in the Social Democratic movement, clearly shows an intention to break with the past. All the indignation that had festered during his first years in Tiflis came to the surface. The seminary's conduct journal serves as a chronicle of his rebellion. In September he was caught reading excerpts from banned books to his comrades. In October he was confined to a punishment cell three times for failing to attend prayers, bad behavior during liturgy, and returning late after a school recess. Over the following months, periods of confinement alternated with reprimands for a variety of offenses.[22]

In January 1899, a serious conflict with the seminary's administration resulted in Ioseb's being prohibited from leaving the seminary for a month. Historian Aleksandr Ostrovskii attributes this punishment to an incident described in the memoirs of one of Ioseb's classmates, published in 1939.[23] According to this account, a seminary inspector searched Jughashvili's room and found forbidden books. At this point, a seminarian by the name of Kelbakiani pounced on the inspector and knocked the books out of his grasp. Helped by Jughashvili, Kelbakiani then gathered up the books and fled.[24] Among the sources that cast doubt on this account is the seminary's conduct journal for 1899, which describes Kelbakiani's infraction quite differently.[25] A search of Kelbakiani's own possessions turned up a notebook into which excerpts from prohibited literature had been copied. When the inspector refused Kelbakiani's request that the notebook be returned, the seminarian grabbed it and threw it into the toilet. The seminary rector was immediately informed of this incident and Kelbakiani was placed in a punishment cell for several hours.

According to the conduct journal, "Kelbakiani displayed strong remorse." He admitted his guilt and asked for indulgence. There is no mention of Jughashvili's involvement in this incident. All that is known for certain is that in January 1899 Jughashvili was deprived of the right to leave the seminary premises for one month, and Kelbakiani was expelled.[26] The difference in punishments may indicate that Ioseb was penalized for some other infraction or that he played only a minor role in the destruction of the notebook.

In June 1951, Kelbakiani wrote the following to his former classmate:

Comrade Soso! If you knew how impoverished I was at the present time, I am certain you would not leave me without attention. I have grown old and have no income and I am in a state of need. . . . Comrade Soso, in some way you are in my debt: you probably remember how I grabbed from the seminary inspector . . . illegal literature that was taken during a search of your drawer, for which I was expelled from the seminary. . . . I am not proud of this and am not boasting, of course. . . . Poverty has forced me to remember this. Help me, Comrade Soso.[27]

This letter was placed before Stalin. There is no record to show whether Kelbakiani was given any assistance, but his letter does shed light on the 1899 incident. Kelbakiani was undoubtedly familiar with the account published in 1939 describing the future Stalin's "heroic deed," and he generally adheres to its details. The confiscated notebook is identified as "illegal literature" and is found among Jughashvili's possessions rather than Kelbakiani's. It is, however, noteworthy that Kelbakiani unequivocally states that he himself, without help from "Comrade Soso," was the one to grab the confiscated notebook from the inspector. He is just as unequivocal on the subject of Soso's involvement in the incident and in suggesting that he, Kelbakiani, performed a favor for the future leader. Overall, it would appear that Ioseb really was involved. We can surmise, for example, that the notebook Kelbakiani destroyed belonged to Jughashvili. This may not have been reported in the conduct journal because it was not known at the time. It seems almost certain that Ioseb did not help Kelbakiani save the materials. This was among the more harmless of the legends that took shape to foster the cult of the leader.

The notebook incident aside, Jughashvili committed more than enough sins in the eyes of the seminary leadership to render him persona non grata. In May 1899 he was expelled, the formal cause being "for failing to appear at examinations for unknown reasons." One odd detail is that the certificate he was given upon expulsion, stating he had completed four years at the seminary, gives him excellent grades for behavior.[28] Stalin's biographers have long commented on the confusion surrounding the circumstances of his departure. He himself preferred to say that he was "kicked out" "for Marxist propaganda." In one interview, Ekaterine claims that she took her son out of the seminary because of his poor health.[29] There may be some truth to all these accounts—both the official formulation and the statements by Jughashvili and his mother. The seminary leadership may have been eager to rid itself of a rebel while avoiding scandal. Ioseb may have withdrawn "by mutual consent" with a commendatory certificate on the completion of four years. If so, Ekaterine and her complaints of her son's worsening health probably played a major role. In the end, Ioseb really was "kicked out," but quietly, leaving the door open for him to mend his ways.

■ UNDERGROUND, PRISON, AND EXILE

The certificate issued to Ioseb Jughashvili by the seminary would have enabled him to work in the area of religion or teach elementary school.[30] But a return to ordinary life did not interest him. In late 1899 Ioseb was hired, with the help of friends, to work at the Tiflis Meteorological Station. His job involved constant recording of instrument readings and therefore required him to live on the premises, taking care of his need for both money and housing.

Continuing to work with revolutionary groups, he soon aligned himself with the radical wing of the Tiflis Social Democratic organization, which rejected agitation through legal propaganda and instead favored fomenting strikes and demonstrations. Given the twenty-two-year-old rebel's record at the seminary and his friendship with such revolutionaries as Lado Ketskhoveli, his turn toward radicalism is hardly surprising.

The years 1900 and 1901 saw a wave of strikes in Tiflis, followed by crackdowns. Under threat of arrest, Jughashvili left the weather station and went underground. There was no turning back; he had become a professional revolutionary.

Whatever their backgrounds, Russian revolutionaries tended to have one thing in common. Their break with ordinary life and move underground took place in a moment of hatred and decisiveness: hatred for the existing order and a decision to combat it. In the Russian Empire, there was no shortage of either emotion. An authoritarian regime and social injustices created a breeding ground for rebels. The persecution to which radicals were subjected radicalized them still more. The hatred felt by Ioseb Jughashvili, aroused by the arbitrariness and obscurantism that prevailed at the seminary, was further inspired by the propaganda and actions of his more experienced comrades, those who had chosen the path of revolution before him. His decisiveness was both a feature of his character and a product of the milieu into which he was born. Anyone with social origins like his had little to lose.

In exploring the sources of Stalin's rebelliousness and ruthlessness, many historians have pointed to the atmosphere that reigned in the outlying regions of the Russian Empire. Alfred Rieber has called him a "man of the borderlands."[31] The Caucasus, a roiling cauldron of social and ethnic conflict where industrial enclaves emerged amid tribal traditions, would inevitably have played a role in shaping Stalin's character. Jörg Baberowski has written that Stalin and his comrades-in-arms "brought into the party, both at the center and edges of the empire, the culture of violence of the

Caucasian periphery, the blood feud and archaic conceptions of honor."[32] Such opinions are supported by Boris Nicolaevsky, a Social Democrat who later became a well-known historian. Before the revolution, Nicolaevsky had spent time in Transcaucasia and had even met with Jughashvili. He described the future dictator as "exceptionally vicious and vindictive" and capable of applying "the most extreme measures" in his struggle to dominate the party. Yet many of Jughashvili's opponents within the Social Democratic movement were no different. Nicolaevsky said he was told that these traits resulted from "the injection of Caucasian mores into the intraparty struggle."[33]

It is not unreasonable to take into account the mentality forged by the hardships and tragic history of the Russian borderlands. Yet the entire Russian Empire was one vast borderland: between Asia and Europe, between the promises of modernization and the deteriorating traditional ways of life, between the city and the country, between authoritarianism and democratic strivings, between the obscurantism of the regime and the bloodthirstiness of many revolutionaries. Whatever features may be particular to the Caucasus must be seen within the context of the Russian culture of extremism and violence, which merely provided an outlet for the impulse. Such a context does not, of course, relieve young Jughashvili of personal responsibility for his choices.

Revolutionaries are not all cut from the same cloth. Many throw themselves into the fight under the influence of youth, ardor, and thrill seeking. These factors were probably not what led Stalin onto this path, though they should not be discounted entirely. The future dictator could be described as a calculating revolutionary, the sort who doggedly and methodically— even cautiously—moved the revolution forward and later, when success came, had the best chance of solidifying power. He had just the right balance of decisiveness and caution, obsession and cynicism, to emerge unscathed through the revolution's countless dangers.

An overview of the activities of the Tiflis Social Democratic organization found in the files of the local gendarme administration describes Ioseb Jughashvili as "conducting himself with complete caution and constantly looking over his shoulder as he walks."[34] He managed to avoid arrest for some time, giving him a significant advantage, since many members of the Social Democratic Party were in prison, and facilitating his rise within the Tiflis party leadership. Apparently to evade arrest, he moved from Tiflis to Batum, a major center of the empire's petroleum industry. A propaganda campaign by him and his associates evidently had an effect, as Batum workers staged a spate of strikes and demonstrations. The government response was severe. On 9 March 1902, when workers stormed a prison where many of their comrades were being held, troops opened fire. At least thirteen people were killed and dozens were wounded. News of violence in Batum spread, and Jughashvili, one of the organizers of the demonstration, was arrested.

In an effort to avoid punishment, Jughashvili denied his guilt, asserting that he had been nowhere near Batum during the period leading up to the attack. In notes sent from prison, he asked his mother, friends, and relatives to give him an alibi by falsely testifying that he had arrived in Gori before mid-March.[35] One such note fell into the hands of the police. The police in Batum still could not prove that Jughashvili was directly involved in organizing the storming of the prison, but in probing his background, they brought to light his activities in Tiflis. The investigation inched along. Languishing in prison, Ioseb did what he could to improve the outcome of his case. In October and November 1902, seven and eight months after his arrest, he sent two petitions to the offices of the administrator-in-chief for the Caucasus. Citing a "worsening asphyxiating cough and the helpless situation of my aged mother, who has been abandoned by her husband for 12 years now and sees me as the only person she can count on in life," he asked to be released under police supervision. "I beseech the office of the Administrator-in-Chief not to neglect me and to respond to my request." In January 1903 Ekaterine also submitted a request to the authorities that her son be freed. Her petition, written in Russian but signed in Georgian, stated that her son, "as the breadwinner for himself and his mother, has neither the time nor the occasion to participate in conspiracies or disturbances."[36]

These entreaties proved ineffective. Ioseb remained in prison for several more months, suffering deprivation and harassment. Not until the fall of 1903, one and a half years after his arrest, was he finally sent into exile in eastern Siberia. Soon, in early 1904, he escaped from his place of banishment. Such an escape was not at all unusual. Lax security enabled many revolutionaries to flee their places of exile, although such escapes demanded careful preparation, courage, and physical endurance. Jughashvili learned from his first stint in exile and later had several opportunities to put that experience to use.

There is evidence to suggest that during the first months after his return to Transcaucasia, Jughashvili was suspected of being a double agent.[37] Social Democrats were being arrested throughout the region. Although these arrests cast a pall of suspicion over him, the lack of personnel began to facilitate his ascent within the underground movement. He rose through the ranks to the governing committee of the Transcaucasian Social Democratic organization. Other factors in his success were his active efforts in the underground and his ability to generate fiery prose. Rumors that he was collaborating with the police remained just that.

During the two years that Jughashvili spent in prison and exile, Russia's Social Democratic Party had undergone major changes. While formally a single party, in actuality it was divided between the adherents of Lenin—Bolsheviks—and the more moderate Mensheviks. Lenin advocated the creation of a militant and cohesive underground party that would serve as an instrument of revolution. It was Lenin's belief that the workers, who were to be the main force in the revolution, were not capable of developing proper revolutionary thinking on their own. They had to be taught by professional revolutionaries. Lenin's teachings were aimed at hastening revolution and speeding up "historical time." The Mensheviks felt that the party should be less rigid and accept among its ranks sympathizers as well as activists. The Mensheviks had greater respect for the workers and placed less emphasis on their own role as teachers. This approach was a natural byproduct of their core belief that the revolutionary process would move gradually and organically forward as the objective preconditions for socialism reached fruition. Jughashvili was temperamentally inclined to accept Lenin's viewpoint and to embrace his radicalism and calls to action. Furthermore, as a member of the party intelligentsia, Jughashvili welcomed the idea that professional revolutionaries must lead the workers' movement.[38] To be leaders, to show the masses the way forward—surely this was the intelligentsia's proper place within the revolution? Many of his articles were devoted to promoting Lenin's ideas.

The first Russian Revolution, in 1905, initially intensified discord between the Bolsheviks and Mensheviks but ultimately brought the two sides closer together. Both groups faced a common enemy—the government and its supporters—and both sides increasingly resorted to violence and brutality. In Transcaucasia, roiled by social and ethnic animosities, the situation was particularly dire. As usual, the government did not hesitate to use arms. In response, the revolutionaries murdered figures associated with the autocratic regime and committed arson against industrial enterprises. Ethnic pogroms fed the rush of carnage. Violence and bloodshed became commonplace. Mensheviks and Bolsheviks organized their own armed detachments and made generous use of terrorist methods.[39] Jughashvili took an active part in these events, traveling across Georgia, helping to organize strikes and demonstrations, writing leaflets and articles, and helping set up an underground printing press and militant groups. He gradually reached the forefront of the Bolshevik leadership in Transcaucasia.

In October 1905, unrest compelled the tsar to make concessions. Russia was given its first parliament, the State Duma. Political freedoms were proclaimed: freedom of conscience, free speech and assembly, and the inviolability of the person. The revolution nonetheless continued to build, and it forced maneuvering by the Social Democrats as well as the tsar. Under pressure from the ranks, the Bolsheviks and Mensheviks agreed to a reconciliation, restoring a superficial party unity. This newfound unity, however, did not advance the interests of the Bolsheviks in Transcaucasia, Jughashvili in particular, because it put the Mensheviks in charge of the region's revolutionary organizations. The election of delegates to the party's April 1906 "Unity Congress" in Stockholm put the Bolsheviks' demeaning position on full display: the future dictator was the only Transcaucasian Bolshevik delegate elected. The next congress, in London the following May, was even more humiliating. At first, only Mensheviks were elected. The Bolsheviks had to arrange by-elections so they could send at least one representative. Again, they sent Jughashvili.

Jughashvili's trips to these congresses undoubtedly expanded his sense of the world and the party, as well as his circle of contacts. There is evidence that in 1907, while traveling to London, he met with Lenin in Berlin.[40] Returning from London, he spent several days in Paris, where he stayed with fellow Georgian Grigory Chochia, a student there. He returned to Russia using the passport of a friend of Chochia's who had died. This arrangement enabled him to evade police surveillance and improved his personal safety. Forty years later, in May 1947, Chochia, then living in Leningrad, reminded Stalin of this: "In mid-1907, after you stayed with me for several days, I escorted you to the St. Lazare train station in Paris. You were so kind as to say to me, 'I will never forget your help' (you were referring to my giving you the international passport). Right now, I am greatly in need of your attention. I ask to be granted a 5–10 minute meeting with you."[41] The letter was filed away. Stalin rarely recalled his foreign travel. We do not know what he saw in Europe and how he perceived it. Did he bring any gifts to his young wife, Yekaterina Svanidze, whom he married in July 1906, or his son, Yakov, born in March 1907 (right before Ioseb left for Western Europe)? Undoubtedly, Jughashvili's mind was on the revolution.

Immediately after he returned from the West, on 13 June 1907, a group of Transcaucasian Bolsheviks staged an armed robbery of money being transported to a bank in Tiflis; the robbery has become a part of the history of the Russian revolutionary movement. At the cost of several lives, it yielded a huge sum for Bolshevik coffers: 250,000 rubles. The ringleader of this "expropriation" was Jughashvili's good friend Simon Ter-Petrosian, nicknamed Kamo. The obvious link between the two men has led some to suggest that Stalin was involved in organizing the heist and perhaps even took part in it, but there is no hard evidence.[42] Boris Nicolaevsky, who completed a thorough study of the case in the course of chronicling the Social Democratic movement, concluded that Jughashvili was informed of the activities of Kamo's group and "helped conceal them from the local party organization." But "he was in no regard a ringleader." Nicolaevsky found a document showing that Kamo was working directly with the Bolshevik center abroad, specifically an agreement between Kamo and Lenin's Bolshevik center on the details of the robbery.[43] It was Kamo, not Jughashvili, who signed this agreement.

Except for the amount stolen, the Tiflis holdup was nothing out of the ordinary. The robbery of government institutions and private individuals was widely practiced at the time, by the Bolsheviks as well as other groups. Although such actions generated income, they undermined the morals of the revolutionaries and damaged their reputation with the public. From time to time, ordinary criminals would join forces with the revolutionaries for personal gain. In fact, ideologically motivated thieves stealing to further the revolution, even if they did not take a kopeck for themselves, were sometimes hard to distinguish from the ordinary criminals. This state of affairs must have been deeply disturbing for the leaders of the Social Democratic Party. At the 1907 congress in London the Mensheviks passed a resolution prohibiting Social Democrats from conducting such robberies. This resolution did not stop Lenin and his followers. The Tiflis operation was already being planned, and they did not cancel it. That this robbery was carried out so soon after the party congress made it look particularly cynical. Controversy spread through the ranks of the Social Democrats. Not for the first time and knowing his association with Kamo, the Tiflis Mensheviks showed Jughashvili how displeased they were with him. He was forced to leave Tiflis for Baku.

In Baku, where the Mensheviks also dominated the party, Jughashvili could still rely on a stalwart group of Leninists. This major industrial center was ripe with opportunity for both agitation among the working class and combat against political opponents. Jughashvili managed to drive a wedge through the Baku organization, and the Bolsheviks took over the party leadership. But the joy of victory was overshadowed by personal tragedy. In Baku, Ioseb's wife Yekaterina died. The couple's infant son was taken in by the mother's relatives. His father had no time for him.

The unrest surrounding the 1905 revolution frightened the ruling classes and awakened the tsarist government to the need for concessions. Russia became a freer country. Serious agrarian reform was introduced that had fundamental significance for a country in which the peasantry represented an overwhelming—and explosive—majority. Historians still argue over where these reforms might ultimately have led. One thing is clear: Russia was not allowed to follow the course of reform long enough to yield results. Furthermore, alongside the reforms and concessions, the authorities began to "restore order" and more decisively and brutally combat the revolutionary underground. One victim of this post-revolutionary crackdown was Jughashvili. In March 1908 he was arrested. As before, he denied any wrongdoing, claiming that he did not belong to any revolutionary party and had spent a long time abroad.[44] These ploys did not work. After seven months in prison, he was sent into exile in Vologda Province, where he spent four months before fleeing. In the summer of 1909, he returned to Baku.

By this time, the Social Democratic organization in Baku had been infiltrated by undercover police. Failed operations and arrests aroused mutual suspicion and rising tempers among the revolutionaries. Jughashvili again came under scrutiny: new rumors emerged that he was working for the police. This idea has continued to be promoted, although most historians have never given credence to theories that he was a double agent. The opening of the archives has confirmed their skepticism. A key document used to bolster these accusations against Stalin has been definitively exposed as a forgery, produced within émigré circles after the revolution.[45]

Jughashvili spent more time in prison and exile than one would expect for a double agent. In the spring of 1910 he was again arrested and this time threatened with serious punishment. The police demanded that he be sent for five years to "the most remote reaches of Siberia." He resorted to a tried-and-true method: pleas for leniency, citing his poor health and the absence of serious evidence. In an attempt to demonstrate good intentions, he requested that he be allowed to marry a woman he had met while in exile and with whom he was living.[46] It is hard to assess what effect these "humble pleas" had, but in October 1910, instead of the five-year sentence in Siberia initially sought, Jughashvili was returned to Vologda Province to complete his previous sentence. This was a mild punishment. His term concluded in July 1911.

The year-and-a-half between his release from this term of exile and his final arrest, in February 1913, was the peak of his career in the underground. He advanced into the ranks of the Bolshevik leadership, becoming a member of the Leninist party's Central Committee in 1912. This elevation had at least two consequences. First, he now zigzagged across Russia and often spent extended periods in the two capitals, St. Petersburg and Moscow, rather than working full time in Transcaucasia. Second, he was the target of much more intense police surveillance. He engaged in underground work in Russia, assisted in the publication of Bolshevik newspapers, wrote articles, and strategized with Bolshevik representatives in the State Duma. He also became one of Lenin's closest associates. The Bolshevik leader was still in hiding outside the country and needed loyal helpers in Russia. Several times, Jughashvili traveled to meet with Lenin abroad. Detained by circumstances in Vienna for several weeks in 1913, he began work on an article addressing the party's approach to ethnic minorities. This work was of particular interest to Lenin. In lockstep with Lenin's views, Jughashvili advocated a unified Russian Social Democratic Party and argued against the fragmentation of revolutionary forces based on ethnicity.

Jughashvili exemplified this sort of inter-ethnic cooperation. He considered himself an actor on the Russian imperial—not just the Georgian—stage. Putting his youthful nationalism and Transcaucasian Social Democratic past behind him, he consciously transformed himself into Stalin. He began to use this Russian-sounding pseudonym, which symbolized his affinity with the revolutionary movement, around the time he moved into the Bolshevik party leadership.

Stalin undoubtedly deserved his standing and reputation as a prominent Bolshevik. His organizational and writing abilities, daring, decisiveness, cool head, simple tastes, adaptability, and devotion to Lenin all contributed to his elevation to the top ranks. He stuck with the party even during the crisis in the Social Democratic movement that followed the crushing of the first revolution, a crisis characterized by mass arrests of underground operators, infiltration of the organization by police agents, and a severe shortage of funds. In March 1913, an agent who had penetrated the Baku Social Democratic organization reported that "The committee is currently not undertaking any activities."[47] Meanwhile, in February, in far-off Petersburg, Stalin was arrested. He had been betrayed by fellow Bolshevik leader and Lenin favorite Roman Malinovsky, who had been working for the police for several years.[48]

FOUR YEARS IN SIBERIA

In June 1913, Ioseb Jughashvili was sentenced to a four-year term of exile in Siberia's Turukhansky Krai. From the start, this last period of exile was marked by particular hardship. Turukhansky Krai was an extremely inhospitable region. Stalin's letters during the first months were filled with pleas for help and complaints that he lacked funds and was in poor health:[49]

> It seems that I have never been in such a terrible situation. My money is gone, the intensifying cold (37 below) has brought on a suspicious cough, and I'm in a general state of ill health, have no supply of bread, sugar, meat, or kerosene (all my money has gone toward day-to-day expenses, clothing, and footwear). . . . I understand that none of you, you in particular, have time for this, but, damn it, I don't have anyone else to turn to. And I don't want . . . to croak here. This has to be taken care of today and money sent by telegraph because waiting any longer means starving, and I'm already malnourished and sick.[50]

> My hardship grows by the hour, I'm in a desperate situation, and on top of it all I've fallen ill and some suspicious cough has set in. I need milk, but . . . money, I have no money. My dear, if you get some money, send it to me immediately via telegram. I can't stand it any longer.[51]

At first there was a lingering hope of freedom. The party leadership adopted a resolution to arrange an escape for Stalin and his comrade in exile, Yakov Sverdlov. An escape would require money, but there were delays in sending it. Furthermore, the traitor Malinovsky informed the police of the escape plans. In March 1914, on orders from St. Petersburg, Stalin and Sverdlov were sent to the even more remote village of Kureika, not far from the Arctic Circle, and placed under the charge of personal wardens. Escape was almost impossible.

Stalin took this transfer as a severe blow. In late March 1914 he sent an angry letter to St. Petersburg rebuking his party comrades for their long silence and demanding to know: would there be money for an escape or not?[52] Several weeks later he changed his plans. In April he wrote to Malinovsky: "The new governor has relocated me to the far north and confiscated the money sent to me (60 r. total). We're still living, brother. . . . Someone, it turns out, has been spreading rumors that I'm not going to remain in exile for the rest of my term. Nonsense! I'm telling you and swear on the life of my dog that I will serve out my term (until 1917). At one point I thought of leaving, but now I've abandoned that idea, abandoned it for good."[53]

This letter raises questions. Was Stalin's firm assertion that he did not plan to escape intended for the eyes of the police? Or was he expressing his dissatisfaction with party comrades who had failed to help him? Perhaps he recognized the fruitlessness of any hope of escape and had made a genuine decision to remain in exile. Given that the subject of escape did not arise again, it appears that he really did reconcile himself to his fate.

Stalin's life in Kureika was shaped by events that occurred during his first months there. First, he had a falling out with Sverdlov. Upon arriving in Kureika, the two set up house together, but this arrangement did not last long. In his letters, Sverdlov only hinted at conflict with his roommate: "I'm living with the Georgian Jughashvili. . . . He's a fine fellow but too much of an individualist in practical matters. I am an adherent of some minimal order. This is a source of agitation for me at times."[54] The picture is filled in by other sources. According to the reminiscences of Anna Allilueva, the sister of Stalin's second wife, Stalin later admitted that he found various pretexts for shirking his household duties—cleaning, keeping the stove going, etc. Sverdlov wound up stuck with all the chores.[55] Khrushchev offered further information:

Stalin told the following story: "We would make dinner for ourselves. . . . The main thing we did in the way of earning a livelihood was to fish for white salmon. That didn't take any great skill. We also went hunting. I had a dog and called him Yashka. Of course for Sverdlov that wasn't pleasant; he was Yashka and the dog was Yashka, and so then Sverdlov used to wash the dishes and spoons after dinner, but I never did. I would eat and put the dishes on the dirt floor and the dog would lick everything clean. But that fellow had a passion for cleanliness."[56]

These differences over hygiene were bound to provoke discord, but there may have been other sources of conflict. The animosity that developed between Sverdlov and Stalin was so strong that they not only moved into separate houses, but also broke off contact altogether. Sverdlov wrote to his wife some time later: "After all, you know, dear one, what abominable conditions I endured in Kureika. On a personal level, the comrade I lived with there turned out to be the sort that we did not talk to one another or get together."[57]

Soon after his falling out with Sverdlov, Stalin moved into the home of the Pereprygin family—five brothers and two sisters, all orphans. Stalin, who was thirty-five, entered into an intimate relationship with the fourteen-year-old Lidiia Pereprygina. This apparently provoked an argument between Stalin and the man in charge of guarding him, which escalated into a fistfight. The local police took Stalin's side. One circumstance that may have worked in Stalin's favor was that the police chief in Turukhansky Krai was I. I. Kibirov, an ethnic Ossetian who, like Stalin, was from Georgia. It is possible that Stalin and Kibirov came to an agreement that he would be given a degree of liberty in exchange for a promise that he would not attempt to flee. Stalin not only was not charged for his transgression with a minor, but he was also given a new guard, M. A. Merzliakov, who treated him exceptionally well.[58] In 1930, when he was persecuted under the Soviet regime for having served in the tsarist police, Merzliakov turned to Stalin for help. "I am asking Com. Stalin," he wrote, "to inform our village soviet that I truly did have a friendly relationship with you while serving in Turukhansky and did not act against you." Stalin responded with a glowing recommendation: "Mikh. Merzliakov had a formal attitude toward his police duties, without the usual police zeal; he did not spy on me, did not badger me, did not pick on me, and turned a blind eye to my frequent absences."[59]

Taking advantage of this obliging attitude, Stalin managed to arrange a relatively pleasant life for himself, to the extent such a thing is possible in the Arctic. He continued to live with Lidiia Pereprygina. There were rumors —though muddled and contradictory—that the two had a child together.[60] Stalin devoted his copious free time to fishing, hunting, visiting fellow exiles in neighboring settlements, receiving guests, and taking part in local merrymaking. His financial situation stabilized enough to support his modest lifestyle. Most important is that his health improved. "I'm living as before. I feel fine. I'm completely healthy—I must have gotten used to the nature around here. And nature here is harsh: three weeks ago the temperature went to 45 below," he cheerfully reported in a letter written in late 1915.[61]

This unusual period in Stalin's life reveals some interesting aspects of his character. He was completely unfazed by the absence of creature comforts in this harsh environment. In Kureika, with a total of eight houses and sixty-seven residents, he seems to have suffered an utter absence of suitable conversation partners. Yet he endured this lack of intellectual stimulation with equanimity. Apparently he was perfectly capable of living without the revolution and felt no need to exercise his intellect. His opponents have long accused him of wasting the time spent in Turukhansky Krai. Trotsky, for example, wrote that "Any attempt to find traces of his spiritual life during this period of solitude and leisure would be in vain."[62] Indeed, Stalin's collected works feature not a single article written between early 1913 and early 1917.

Stalin's correspondence from this period, however, paints a more complicated picture. During the first year of exile, either because he still hoped to escape or simply out of habit, he did try to work. He wrote a new article on nationalities problems and sent them to a journal. He asked his comrades to send him books, journals, and newspapers. In subsequent years as well, his correspondence from exile contained references to work on articles and his need for new books.[63] But his enthusiasm was waning. In 1914, Malinovsky was exposed as a double agent. This was a crushing blow to the entire Bolshevik party, but for Stalin, who was friendly with Malinovsky and had turned to him for help, the revelation was especially painful. And there were other discouraging developments. An article that Stalin submitted to a journal was not published, his comrades failed to send him new journal issues, and he lacked the money for subscriptions. In November 1915, after two years in Turukhansky Krai, he explained his situation in a rare letter to Lenin: "My life is not great. I'm hardly doing anything. And what is there to do when you have no or almost no serious books? . . . I have lots of questions and topics in my head, but as for material—nothing. I'm itching to do something, but there's nothing to do."[64] Stalin's communication with the party leadership in emigration gradually dropped off, and he occasionally complained in letters that they had forgotten him. Indeed, Lenin's requests in 1915 to be reminded of Stalin's last name became well known: "Do you remember Koba's last name?"; "I have a big favor: find out . . . 'Koba's' last name (Iosef J. . . ?? We've forgotten)."[65]

Stalin's situation reflected the general state of affairs in the Bolshevik party. Its leadership was languishing either in forced internal exile or self-imposed exile abroad. Periods of hope, dreams, and failed attempts to activate the movement alternated with quarrels, both internally and with opponents from other parties. On both the personal and political front, the future looked gloomy for the revolutionaries. How thirty-eight-year-old Stalin imagined his future at this point is hard to know. Perhaps he tried not to think about it.

THE BULWARKS OF STALIN'S POWER

**The day and evening of 1 March 1953 at the near dacha.
Consternation among the bodyguards.**

After his guests departed in the early morning hours of 1 March, Stalin most likely went to bed. He may not have felt well.[1] He was aged and sickly. He remained in his rooms and did not, as he usually did, summon any guards or servants toward suppertime. As of early 1952, Stalin's apartment and dacha were protected by a staff of 335 security personnel.[2] Another 73 attended to his non-security needs. All told, 408 people, working in shifts at various sites, were devoted to taking care of Stalin. Stalin spent a significant portion of his time in these people's company. They walked behind him, stood guard under his windows, cooked, cleaned, and, if needed, entertained him. At the near dacha, a long corridor separated the staff quarters from the part of the house where Stalin lived. His rooms were equipped with buttons to summon staff members.

The deviation from Stalin's routine on 1 March alarmed his security team. The guards reported to their superiors that there was no "movement" within the leader's residence. Evening approached with no signs of life. The sense of alarm escalated, but if they were not summoned, nobody wanted to check on the boss. Finally, sometime after six o'clock, the guards were relieved to see a light turn on in Stalin's rooms. Everyone prepared for a call. None came. Anxiety again began to mount. The guards argued over who should go check on Stalin. Nobody volunteered.

Their hesitation was understandable. Of course, they had grown accustomed to Stalin, just as the lonely leader, for whom the hired help often served as a surrogate family, had grown accustomed to them. From time to time, Stalin and the dacha staff worked together in the garden or roasted shashlik in the fireplace. Sometimes he would come into the kitchen and lie down on the Russian brick oven to ease the pain in his back. But the distance that separated Stalin and his guards was much greater than the length of the corridor that separated their quarters from his. He was strict with his staff, and they knew better than to relax the fear they felt toward him.

The guards who protected Stalin and other members of the top leadership belonged to a special department within the Soviet security system, the Main Guard Directorate. In the early days of the regime, when the egalitarian romance of the revolution still lingered, Soviet leaders often mixed with the public. In the 1920s, Stalin's wife could still ride streetcars, and he himself walked the streets of Moscow or rode in cars with no particular precautions, though always accompanied by bodyguards. In July 1930, while vacationing in Sochi, Stalin and his wife were involved in a car crash. He was slightly injured when his head hit the windshield.[3]

Two months after the car crash, amid growing hysteria in the struggle against "enemies," the Politburo adopted a resolution "to oblige Com. Stalin to immediately desist from walking through the city on foot."[4] Stalin did not submit to this restriction. On 16 November 1931, while walking down the street, accompanied by bodyguards, from the Central Committee building to the Kremlin, he happened to run into an armed agent of an anti-Bolshevik organization who had come from abroad. The agent was so surprised that he did not have time to pull out his gun before he was arrested. A report on the incident by the Joint State Political Directorate, the OGPU (the Soviet secret police of the time), was sent to Stalin and the other members of the Politburo. Molotov made a notation on the report: "To PB members. Com. Stalin's walking around Moscow on foot must be stopped."[5] It is not known whether Stalin submitted to this demand. It is also unclear whether the encounter could have been orchestrated.

On his 1933 vacation in the south, several incidents appeared to place Stalin in danger.[6] In August, his car was hit by a truck in Sochi. The truck's driver was drunk, and Stalin was unharmed. Another incident took place on the Black Sea coast in September when a motorboat on which Stalin was riding came under rifle fire from the shore. The bullets landed in the water, and no one on the boat was injured. An investigation determined that rifles had been fired by border guards who had not been warned that a boat would be entering the protected zone.

The murder of Sergei Kirov on 1 December 1934 was a watershed moment in attitudes toward the safety of Soviet leaders.[7] Using it as an excuse, Stalin undertook a series of reprisals against former members of the party opposition, who were accused of orchestrating Kirov's murder and plotting other terrorist acts against the Soviet leadership. In 1936–1938, when terror ravaged the country, engulfing hundreds of thousands of lives, Stalin eliminated everyone suspected of disloyalty. The security apparatus was one important target of the purges, and those in charge of guarding the leaders also fell victim. In April 1937, Stalin's chief of security was arrested and swiftly executed. Of his two successors in 1937–1938, one shot himself and the other was executed. Finally, in late 1938, the uneducated but efficient Nikolai Vlasik was appointed to the post.[8] Stalin took a liking to him and kept him in the job for more than thirteen years.

Vlasik's career even survived an incident that took place in Moscow on 6 November 1942. An official car carrying Anastas Mikoyan, one of Stalin's closest associates, came under rifle fire that day as it exited the Kremlin. No one was injured, and after a brief struggle the shooter was taken into custody. It turned out that he was a soldier from a Moscow air defense unit who was likely suffering from mental health problems.[9] This incident was a terrible blow to the protection service under Vlasik's command: an unbalanced and armed soldier had been standing in plain sight at the Kremlin gates for some time, waiting for an official car to come out, without being questioned or apprehended. Vlasik was demoted, but the leader gave him a second chance. He continued to oversee Stalin's security.[10]

Vlasik seemed to enjoy Stalin's full confidence. He followed the leader everywhere, often sat down at the same table with him to eat, and was granted the right to photograph him. Under Vlasik, the Main Guard Directorate became a powerful and influential government agency. In early 1952 it comprised 14,300 people and had an enormous budget of 672 million rubles. Vlasik's directorate was responsible not only for protection, but also for the maintenance of the apartments and dachas of top-level Soviet leaders, keeping Central Committee members supplied with consumer goods, handling the transportation and lodging of foreign guests, and overseeing the construction of new government buildings. In 1951 approximately 80 million rubles of the directorate's budget went toward maintaining the dachas and apartments of the fourteen highest-ranking Soviet leaders (including expenses for protection and servants). Stalin was, of course, the most expensive of the fourteen. A total of 26.3 million rubles were spent on his apartment and dacha in 1951. This sum probably did not include such expenses as automobile transport.

Serving in the Guard Directorate was both prestigious and lucrative. In 1951 the average compensation for members of Stalin's security team (including uniforms, housing, etc.) was 5,300 rubles per month, at a time when the average monthly wage throughout the Soviet Union was 660 rubles and the average per capita income for collective farm workers was approximately 90 rubles per month.[11] In addition to material benefits, Vlasik's relationship with the leader gave him significant political influence, leading to his increasing involvement—with Stalin's encouragement—in the political intrigues that roiled around the *vozhd* (leader). Having a powerful patron and sense of impunity was intoxicating. Vlasik drank and enjoyed a promiscuous love life, and so did his subordinates.

Stalin generally tolerated such "weaknesses" as a pledge of obedience and devotion. Yet he was known to put his subordinates in their place, especially if they took too many liberties. During the summer of 1947 one of the waitresses at the near dacha informed Stalin that while he had been away, the dacha commandant and his deputy threw a party with drinking and prostitutes, for which they stole refreshments from the official supply. Furthermore, the deputy commandant and his female companions looked through papers on Stalin's desk. On Stalin's orders, the deputy commandant was arrested, interrogated at length, beaten, and shot.[12] This incident should have served as a warning to Vlasik, but it did not. Stalin continued to show a fairly relaxed attitude toward his chief bodyguard's morals. In 1950, on Vlasik's own admission, Stalin reprimanded him for "graft" and "relationships with women," yet he remained in favor.[13]

Vlasik's star waned only when the aging Stalin decided it was time for another general purge of state security. On 19 May 1952, the Politburo approved a resolution criticizing Vlasik and the entire leadership of the Ministry of State Security's Main Guard Directorate for "criminal dissipation and the uncontrolled expenditure of resources." Significant cutbacks to the directorate's personnel, functions, and budget followed. Some of its members were charged with crimes. Vlasik was expelled from the party and demoted to deputy head of a labor camp in the Urals,[14] and in December 1952 he was arrested. Running the Guard Directorate fell to the USSR minister for state security, Semen Ignatiev.[15]

The arrests, personnel cutbacks, and reorganization of the Guard Directorate undoubtedly set its members on edge. None of them, fearing for their jobs and their lives, wanted to face the consequences that could come with taking initiative. For these reasons Stalin's bodyguards were very reluctant to check on him on 1 March 1953, even though something out of the ordinary was clearly taking place.

The branches of state security, including the branch in charge of Stalin's personal safety, were one very important set of controls regulating the huge machine that historians call the Stalinist party-state. The framework that held this machine together was the Bolshevik party, bequeathed by Lenin, but repeatedly modified to fit the needs of Stalin's dictatorship. Under Stalin, the party was a rigidly centralized organization whose power rested on its unquestioned right to hire, fire, and reassign personnel. Over many years, lists of positions were compiled ("the nomenklatura"). Each position came under the purview of a particular party committee, from the *raikom* (district committee) to the TsK (the party's Central Committee). The career and fate of every official in the country depended on one of these party committees, and nobody, including the party functionaries themselves, could evade the system. Key government leaders were approved within the TsK apparat in Moscow.

The nomenklatura of TsK positions was constantly growing, a reflection of the center's pursuit of ever-greater control. In September 1952, half a year before Stalin's death, it comprised approximately 53,000 positions. Those who filled these positions were the "cream" of Soviet society, including high-level party and state officials, top military leaders, and the heads of the "creative unions" such as the Writers' Union. One step lower were officials in charge of important regional bodies: those holding nomenklatura positions within *obkoms* (oblast or provincial committees), *kraikoms* (*krai* or territorial committees), and the central committees of the Communist parties of the various republics that made up the Soviet Union. This list was also constantly growing. As of 1 July 1952 it totaled 350,000 positions.[16]

These hundreds of thousands of functionaries were the backbone of the apparat and the pillar of the dictatorship. Of course Stalin never had direct contact with the vast majority of them. Furthermore, the party-state apparat had a life of its own and was relatively free of interference from the top leadership. In the struggle to survive, prosper, and rise through the ranks, officials sought ways to get around the strict rules aimed at centralization. They could generally act as convenience dictated so long as the paper trail they left reflected adherence to the rules. Abuses of power were common. A number of historians, exaggerating the significance of these processes, have argued that the Stalinist dictatorship was unstable, and many have attempted to explain the worst features of Stalinism—mass repression especially—as arising spontaneously from below.

The documentary evidence offers no support for the idea of a "weak dictator." We do not know of a single decision of major consequence taken by anyone other than Stalin. We do not know of even a brief period when he did not exercise dictatorial control. The dictatorship developed extremely effective methods of manipulating and pressuring society and the apparat, and thus Stalin had a firm grip on power and the implementation of key decisions. Ongoing repression and purges of personnel kept society and the apparat in a state of mobilized tension. The archives have allowed historians to assess, in fairly precise numbers, the scale of the violence necessary to achieve such control. Official records show that approximately eight hundred thousand people were shot between 1930 and 1952.[17] The number who perished as a result of the regime's actions, however, was much higher, insofar as Stalin's security apparat made frequent use of fatal torture techniques and the conditions prevailing in labor camps at times made them indistinguishable from death camps. Between 1930 and 1952, some 20 million people were sentenced to incarceration in labor camps, penal colonies, or prisons. During that same period no fewer than 6 million, primarily "kulaks" and members of "repressed peoples," were subjected to "administrative exile": forced resettlement to a remote area of the USSR. On average, over the more than twenty-year span of Stalin's rule, 1 million people were shot, incarcerated, or deported to barely habitable areas of the Soviet Union every year.

Those who were shot or sent to the camps included a fair number of ordinary criminals. But the exceptional severity of laws and the criminalization of all spheres of socioeconomic and political life meant that ordinary citizens who committed minor infractions or were swept up in various political campaigns were often classified as criminals. Furthermore, in addition to the 26 million who were shot, imprisoned, or subjected to internal exile, tens of millions were forced to labor on difficult and dangerous projects, arrested, subjected to lengthy imprisonment without charges, or fired from their jobs and evicted from their homes for being relatives of "enemies of the people." Overall, the Stalinist dictatorship subjected at least 60 million people to some sort of "hard" or "soft" repression and discrimination.

To this figure we must add the victims of periodic famines or starvation, which during 1932–1933 alone took the lives of between 5 and 7 million people. The Stalinist famine was largely the result of political decisions. In its campaign to break peasant opposition to collectivization, the Stalinist government used famine as a means of "punishing" the countryside. All opportunities to relieve the situation—such as purchasing grain abroad—were rejected. Starving villages had their last stores of food expropriated.

We can conclude from this horrific summation that a significant proportion of Soviet citizens suffered some form of repression or discrimination during the Stalin period.[18] It would not be an exaggeration to say that an absolute majority were brutally suppressed by a privileged minority—except that many in that minority were also swept up in the terror.

To achieve its goals, including the implementation of mass repression and the extraction of grain from the starving countryside, the regime did not need its apparat to run with clocklike precision. The inability to achieve perfect centralization in such a vast country was compensated for by the widespread use of campaigns, which mostly followed a similar template. Campaigns were the cornerstone of Stalinist political practice. They all began with a set of goals and the assignment of specific tasks that originated with the center, usually Stalin himself. These steps were followed by the mobilization of the apparat to carry out the assigned tasks, using extraordinary methods and the total suspension of any sort of legality. As a result, a campaign took on the aura of a crisis, culminating at a point where retreat became necessary. This retreat took the form of a counter-campaign that eliminated some of those who had carried out the original campaign while solidifying its results and stabilizing the situation. This swinging pendulum led to the destruction of vast material resources and countless human lives. But within the context of the Stalinist system, the campaigns were an effective method of mobilizing a vast country toward a central goal.

Stalin himself did not need to exercise tight control over all party and government bodies in order to retain dictatorial power. It was sufficient to hold the main levers of power, the most important being control of the secret police. He understood, sooner than other Soviet leaders, that state security could be a valuable weapon in intraparty warfare. This was a key reason for his success. Once he attained control of the Soviet Union's "punitive structures," he never let it slip from his hands. He continued to use state security as an instrument of power until the day he died.

As we will see, Stalin devoted much time to the hands-on management of state security, and during certain periods—most notably during the Terror of 1937–1938—the majority of his time. He personally initiated all the main repressive campaigns, devised plans for carrying them out, and painstakingly monitored their implementation. He guided the fabrication of evidence for numerous political trials and in several instances wrote detailed scripts for how trials should play out. He had a passion for reading the cascade of arrestee interrogation protocols that came before him, and the notations he made on these documents show that he read them thoughtfully and attentively. He often wrote commentaries and issued orders for additional arrests or for the use of torture to "get to the truth." He personally sanctioned the shooting of many people. Some he knew personally; others he had never met.

In addition to the many "ordinary" functions that the chekists performed for Stalin, they also dealt with special, "delicate" matters.[19]

On 5 May 1940, on Stalin's orders, a special state security group abducted Kira Kulik-Simonich, the wife of the deputy people's commissar for defense, Marshal Grigory Kulik, as she was leaving her house.[20] She was secretly transported to prison, interrogated at length, and then quietly shot. Kulik-Simonich was the descendant of a highly placed tsarist official. Many of her relatives had been shot, and some had managed to escape abroad. She had been married before and had spent time in exile with a previous husband charged with illegal activities involving hard currency. The chekists who reported all this to Stalin embellished the story with many more transgressions, including Kulik-Simonich's affairs with foreigners. Stalin advised Kulik to divorce his wife, but when the marshal balked, Stalin ordered that Simonich be quietly done away with. When Kulik discovered his wife's disappearance, he telephoned state security chief Lavrenty Beria, who denied that his agency was involved. Kulik did not believe him and began to dig for the truth. He was summoned to the Central Committee, where he underwent a three-hour interrogation and was ordered not to "slander" state security. Furthermore, he was told, his wife was probably a spy who had fled under threat of exposure.[21] Kulik relented.

Cases like this one, where Stalin, for political reasons, felt it was not expedient to arrest and charge people openly, were no rarity. A year before Marshal Kulik's wife was murdered, in July 1939, the Soviet ambassador to China was killed along with his wife. Specially selected chekists beat their heads with hammers and then staged a car crash.[22] In early 1948, the Jewish civic leader and stage director Solomon Mikhoels, a popular and well-known figure in the USSR and the West, was similarly done away with.[23] Chekists crashed into Mikhoels with a truck and presented the incident as an accident. The evidence leaves no doubt that this murder was also carried out on Stalin's direct orders.[24] It is one of numerous acts of individual terror committed by Stalin.[25] Such targeted killings were also perpetrated overseas. The most famous is the 1940 murder of Trotsky in Mexico.

The archives contain a huge number of documents confirming that Stalin routinely used the secret police to carry out arbitrary and brutal actions based solely on his own assumptions of guilt. They leave a clear impression that Stalin personally organized acts of terror that went far beyond any reasonable sense of "official necessity." This homicidal aspect of his dictatorship obviously held special appeal for him. Immersion in a world of violence, provocation, and murder fed and intensified his pathological suspicion. Driven by fears and a certainty that he was surrounded by enemies, he felt no compunction about using violence on the grandest scale. These personal qualities were an important factor in the brutalities committed by the Soviet government from the 1920s through the 1950s.

Although Stalin relied heavily on state security, he never became beholden to it. In assigning the secret police the dirtiest work, he did not harbor illusions about the loyalty of his "sword of revolution" but instead kept his chekists in rein through periodic shake-ups and purges of their ranks. In a moment of candor, he confided to State Security Minister Ignatiev that "A chekist has only two paths—advancement or prison."[26] He remained true to this principle. From the 1930s through the 1950s, chekist organizations were subjected to waves of brutal repression. The new executioners destroyed the old, only to later wind up in the torture chamber themselves.

For many decades historians have been arguing over the antecedents and causes of Stalin's exceptional brutality. Many trace the source back to the 1917 Bolshevik Revolution, an event that, for Stalin, opened the door to power.

2 IN LENIN'S SHADOW

Historians debate the extent to which the unrest in Petrograd in late February 1917 was spontaneous. Some claim the demonstrations were organized by professional revolutionaries, but nobody can say with certainty that this was so. The revolution erupted without warning, as a result of the social destabilization caused by almost four years of war, and the tsar and his advisers did not immediately grasp the gravity of the situation. Lenin, in Switzerland, learned of the revolution by reading about it in Western newspapers. The news was also slow in reaching Stalin in Siberian exile, as the local authorities, apparently hoping the upheavals would blow over, banned their local papers from carrying reports from Petrograd.

The tsar's abdication sparked widespread jubilation. His brother, Grand Duke Mikhail, had been named Nicholas's successor, but he also relinquished the throne, thus formally ending the monarchy. Shortly thereafter, in early March 1917, a town meeting was held in Achinsk, where Stalin was exiled at the time. For some reason he was not present, but his close comrade Lev Kamenev played a major role in it. A telegram praising the grand duke's decision was sent on behalf of those gathered.[1] In 1925, when Stalin and Kamenev wound up on different sides in the struggle for power, Stalin reminded his old friend of this warm gesture toward a member of the royal family, a gesture that now looked like a serious political blunder.[2] It is unlikely, however, that Stalin felt this way in 1917. The telegram reflected the prevailing intoxication with hope and freedom. In this mood, Stalin, Kamenev, and other freed revolutionaries streamed toward Petrograd.

It took some time before Stalin and his fellow Bolsheviks found their bearings when they first were able to emerge from the underground and play a legitimate role in the new system. In the capital, they discovered divided political power. Russia's parliament, the State Duma, had formed a provisional government, composed primarily of members of liberal parties that favored the creation of a Western-style parliamentary republic. Yet at the same time, the Petrograd Soviet of Workers' and Soldiers' Deputies, a revolutionary body whose authority came from the support of rebelling workers and, most important, soldiers of the Petrograd garrison, exercised a significant share of actual power. The soviet was run by members of socialist parties: Menshevik Social Democrats and Socialist Revolutionaries (SRs). These two parties were the most influential forces within the revolutionary camp, and they had so far outmaneuvered the other parties, including the Bolsheviks. The SRs and Mensheviks were the ones setting the revolution's short- and long-term objectives. They considered the events of February a bourgeois revolution that would introduce a prolonged period of bourgeois-democratic development. They therefore believed that at the initial stage, a liberal bourgeois party should hold power and that it was for the Constituent Assembly to determine the shape of the new Russia. The attainment of socialism was a distant goal. Other, more developed capitalist countries—not Russia—would lead the way toward world socialism.

At the same time, the Russian socialists had no intention of renouncing the power that had fallen into their laps. They were not obtuse dogmatists, incapable of deviating from doctrine, but realists and pragmatists, albeit lacking in political sophistication and decisiveness. They were well aware of the dangers confronting the country. Foremost among them was civil war and the spread of a bloody rebellion that could wreak havoc and take Russia to the brink of catastrophe and collapse, not for the first time in its history. The most eloquent symbols of this danger were the millions of war-weary and embittered armed men returning from the front. In 1917, the only responsible position a politician could take was that civil war must be avoided at all costs. Maintaining civil peace was the only way to prevent massive casualties and pave the way toward a better future. The socialists leading the soviet saw it as their duty to suppress revolutionary excesses and work with the liberals and the Provisional Government. Cooperating from a position of strength, they made reasonable use of their power and placed the highest priority on maintaining peace. The official formulation of this policy of compromise was: support for the Provisional Government so long as it advanced the cause of revolution.

Many Bolsheviks, usually described as "moderate" or "rightist," endorsed essentially the same approach.[3] Kamenev was one of this faction's leaders. He and Stalin shared a bond of long-standing friendship and party collaboration. In December 1912 Stalin wrote him, "Greetings friend! I rub your nose in an Eskimo kiss. Dammit. I miss the hell out of you. I miss you—I swear on my dog! There's nobody, nobody to have a heart-to-heart talk with, devil take you."[4]

There is nothing surprising in the fact that early on, Stalin and Kamenev held similar political positions. While Lenin and many other prominent Bolsheviks remained in Switzerland, Kamenev and Stalin played an important role in leading the party in Russia. After arriving in Petrograd, they essentially took control of the Bolshevik newspaper *Pravda* and used it to promote a moderate agenda, based on the belief that the ascent of the liberal bourgeoisie to power was in accordance with the dictates of history and that socialism was a long-term prospect. The newspaper proclaimed conditional support for the Provisional Government. As members of the Petrograd soviet leadership, Kamenev and Stalin interacted closely with other socialists. The Bolsheviks were beginning negotiations to explore joining forces with the Menshevik left wing.

From the start, Kamenev and Stalin were forced to defend their stances. Lenin, dissatisfied with the political line being promoted by *Pravda*, demanded different slogans. Writing from emigration, he argued for a radical course, declaring war on the Provisional Government and advocating socialist revolution. Kamenev and Stalin worked together to parry these attacks. They heavily edited an article sent by Lenin before publishing it in *Pravda*.[5] Most likely, they truly did not understand Lenin's intentions and assumed his radicalism was simply a function of being out of touch with what was actually happening in the country.

Lenin's position, however, was based on meticulous political calculations. Kamenev's and Stalin's moderate positions opened the door to cooperation among the main socialist parties, but the cooperation never materialized. From the standpoint of the country's well-being, cooperation in a joint effort to keep radicalism at bay was the only correct course. From the standpoint of the ultimate goal of a Bolshevik takeover of sole power, it was ruinous. Taking part in a coalition, even as oppositionists, would tie the Bolsheviks' hands and deprive them of support from radical segments of the population. This was not what Lenin had in mind, and his disapproval ultimately sealed the fate of "rightist" Bolshevism.

When news of revolution in Russia reached Lenin, he was ready with a plan of action, carefully worked out in light of past political struggles. Lenin was gambling on being able to grab power before the revolutionary situation stabilized. His historical moment would be the period of revolutionary radicalization, a period he knew well based on the experience of other revolutions. Even at the early, relatively moderate stage of the revolution, Lenin advanced an extreme program for which the revolution was not quite ready. To put it another way, knowing that a tendency toward radicalization would come, he was playing a waiting game. This strategy had obvious advantages for a party whose ultimate goal was to seize power. The advancement of radical goals that many saw as reckless put the party in a class all its own. That nobody wanted to enter a coalition with it allowed it a certain freedom. A radical program also served as a means of crushing moderate forces within the party and mobilizing its more decisive elements. Finally, such a program, despite being initially rejected by the masses, would eventually gain wider acceptance as mounting despair and impatience fostered a greater acceptance of extremism.

Once he heard about the revolution, Lenin hastily prepared to leave Switzerland for Russia. Eager to enter the fray, he negotiated an agreement with the German authorities allowing him to travel to Russia across enemy territory. In so doing, he was taking a serious risk and opening himself up to accusations of collusion with the enemy or even espionage. But the ends justified the means: he needed to get to Petrograd. As soon as he stepped off the train, he publicly announced his plan of action.[6]

Lenin proclaimed that the Bolsheviks must refuse to support the Provisional Government and fight for socialist revolution and the transfer of power "into the hands of the proletariat and the poorest segments of the peasantry"—in other words, into the hands of the Bolshevik party. The fledgling democracy that had come about after the February Revolution was never given a chance to establish itself, but for Lenin, it had already outlived its usefulness. The parliamentary republic had to be replaced with a soviet republic that, under Bolshevik leadership, would introduce socialist changes. For now, Lenin mentioned just a few of the most important changes: the nationalization of land, the transformation of large estates into model farms under the control of the soviets, and the nationalization of banks or even their merger into a single national bank. In accordance with these new objectives and to clearly distinguish the Bolshevik party from other socialist parties, Lenin proposed changing its name from the Social Democratic Party to the Communist Party.

This platform met with serious opposition, both from outside the party and within. Lenin was, in essence, proposing a vaguely articulated program for the seizure of power. How would that power be used if his plan succeeded? What would socialism mean under Russian conditions? What guarantee was there that revolution in Russia would be followed by revolution in more developed countries (without which Russia would find itself isolated)? Instead of answers, these questions were met with brazen demagoguery. For now it was clear that the Leninist course was kindling civil war.

According to contemporary memoirs, during one of Lenin's speeches after his arrival in Petrograd, a party comrade who had once been close to him cried out from his seat, "That's nonsense, the ravings of a madman!"[7] Lenin's Bolshevik associates could not abide such an outcry, even if they more or less agreed with it. Yet in early April, at meetings of the leading Bolshevik organizations, Lenin's ideas were voted down by the majority. Not only did Kamenev continue to publicly oppose Lenin's ideas, but so too did Stalin.

The sharp reaction of political opponents outside the party apparently suited Lenin's purpose. He was intentionally setting up a confrontation that would distance the Bolsheviks from the country's other political forces. Within the party, however, he would have to calm the discord. It was not possible to do so by the methods Stalin would employ later. The Bolsheviks were not yet that party. The situation in the country—buffeted by the turmoil of revolution and fledgling democracy—was also different. And Lenin was a different sort of leader. He used a combination of hard-line intransigence and conciliation. A particularly important maneuver was the recruiting of "rightist" Bolsheviks, especially Stalin and Kamenev, to his side. Lenin moved cautiously, always allowing his opponents to save face. Instead of driving them into a corner, he promoted them to top party positions. In Stalin's case, this approach worked. Whatever may have been going on in Stalin's head, he quickly threw his support behind Lenin.

The endorsement that Lenin gave Stalin during Central Committee elections at the April 1917 party conference clearly reflects their close working relationship: "We have known Com. Koba for very many years. . . . He handles any responsible job well."[8] This recommendation earned Stalin a spot on the Central Committee, yielding him more votes than anyone except Zinoviev and Lenin himself.[9] Stalin saw, very directly, Lenin's huge influence within the party. After some wavering, he made a firm decision to align himself with strength.

Was Stalin merely advancing his own career, or did he actually understand and accept what Lenin stood for? Identifying the source of Stalin's initial inclination toward "moderate" Bolshevism is of fundamental importance for anyone seeking to understand the workings of his mind. Clearly, the flexibility he exhibited in March–April 1917 does not fit the image of an uncompromising, power-hungry radical. Was his apparent moderation due to Kamenev's influence? Or was he swayed by the other socialists in the

Petrograd soviet, where many of the Mensheviks were fellow Georgians? Perhaps he had not yet developed the confidence to act as an independent political figure and felt he needed someone to follow. In that case, why did he not immediately fall in line behind Lenin after receiving his letter from Switzerland? Perhaps Stalin was genuinely "moderate" in early 1917 but, like many others, changed under the force of circumstances. Historical sources offer no clear-cut answers to these questions. What we do know is that Stalin was not always a radical Bolshevik. His "moderation" and "rightism" would emerge again after Lenin's death, when the party leaders were choosing the path toward socialism, down which they would lead their vast and isolated country.

■ STALIN IN LENIN'S REVOLUTION

The escalation of Russia's February Revolution followed a typical pattern. The moderate revolutionaries who found themselves in power after the tsar's overthrow sought mainly to avoid civil war. But while these moderates vacillated, stumbled, and missed opportunities to consolidate their position, the increasingly impatient masses began looking to those who promised radical and immediate change. In this environment, Bolshevik propaganda found fertile ground. Calls for immediate withdrawal from the war, immediate expropriation of large estates and the turning over of land to the peasants, and immediate worker control of industry had broad appeal. As often happens in times of revolution, few demanded that the Bolsheviks spell out just how their program would be put into practice. The masses were inspired by a new faith. Among the Bolshevik rank and file, fewer and fewer were asking their leader the difficult question: What would come next? Lenin led the party with amazing energy, promising that socialism would somehow solve all problems. The banners of the Leninist party—"Most important—engage the enemy"; "We'll see what happens"; and "Things couldn't be any worse"—sum up the folk wisdom that guided millions to put their faith in Bolshevik promises.

Stalin was among the Bolshevik leaders who supported Lenin without demanding detailed explanations. Having cast off doubts about the suitability of socialism for a predominantly agrarian country, Stalin now proclaimed that "It is entirely possible that Russia will prove to be the country that paves the way toward socialism. . . . We must reject the obsolete notion that only Europe can show us the way. There is dogmatic Marxism and creative Marxism. I stand on the ground of the latter."[10] The ground of "creative Marxism" proved so accommodating to Stalin's political needs that he settled there permanently. In 1917, having cast aside the apprehensions of "rightist" Bolshevism, Stalin set out on Lenin's radical course toward the seizure of power and the introduction of socialism. He never wavered in this decision. The occasional inconsistencies that scholars have noted between Lenin's and Stalin's pronouncements are quite superficial and probably show only that Stalin had trouble keeping up with Lenin's frequent tactical twists and turns. Lenin himself had trouble keeping up with them.

Having set his sights on seizing power, Lenin faced a changeable and complicated situation that made it hard to choose the right moment to strike. The Bolsheviks' strategy was to maintain revolutionary momentum while awaiting the right moment to cross the line of legality. Overt action against the Provisional Government and the soviets would undoubtedly trigger a confrontation. The time for action had to be chosen carefully, but holding back also had its risks. The only way to gauge the opposing side's strength was to probe its weaknesses. Furthermore, the Bolsheviks needed to demonstrate to the radical workers and soldiers on whom they were counting that they were capable of action, not just words. Bolshevik forces had to maintain a constant state of combat readiness through "war games," one of which would turn into a real battle.

In early July 1917, armed soldiers, sailors, and workers took to the streets, marching under Bolshevik banners calling for the overthrow of the Provisional Government. Blood was spilled. The Bolsheviks did not overtly take charge of the rebels, but few were fooled. It was crystal clear to virtually everyone that they were working behind the scenes to overthrow the government. The only question—and historians continue to debate it—was the extent of their involvement in planning the demonstrations. The Provisional Government was able to crush these disturbances, but its efforts at counterstrikes proved haphazard and ineffective. The authorities launched an investigation into allegations that Lenin was a spy being financed by Germany to foment revolution. Charges that the Bolsheviks had organized the riots provided grounds for certain actions against them. The Bolshevik newspaper offices and headquarters were laid waste and shut down, and a few activists were arrested. The "moderate" Kamenev was among those arrested, while Lenin and Zinoviev remained free and went underground.

Stalin, less well known to the government, was not on the list of targeted revolutionaries. He felt so secure that he even proposed that Lenin hide out where Stalin was living at the time, in the apartment of his old friends, the Alliluevs. Stalin's friendship with the Alliluevs was long-standing and strong. In 1919 he married their daughter Nadezhda, still a teenager at the time.

Stalin accompanied Lenin and Zinoviev as they traveled from Petrograd to the suburban town of Razliv, where the two fugitives were concealed by the family of a worker, Nikolai Yemelianov, a Bolshevik sympathizer. They lived in a loft above Yemelianov's shed. Later, disguised as farm workers, they made their way to a more sparsely populated area where they took shelter in a hut. In August, Lenin moved to Finland, and from July to October Stalin did not meet with him. Nevertheless, during Stalin's dictatorship several assertions appeared claiming that he had met with Lenin not once but twice during this period. The main witness of these supposed meetings was Yemelianov.

Like many other revolutionaries, Yemelianov met a tragic fate. He and three of his sons were arrested in the 1930s. Two sons were shot, and one was released after Stalin's death. The elder Yemelianov was sent into exile in Siberia. In June 1945, apparently grasping that offering an appropriately hagiographic episode for Stalin's biography represented his best chance for leniency, he appealed to Stalin for permission to return to his village: "In 1917 you saved the life of Vladimir Ilyich Lenin by arranging for me to hide him in a hut."[11] The appeal was shown to Stalin, and soon afterward Yemelianov was permitted to return to Razliv and even to work in the Lenin Museum established there. There is no doubt that his release was decided by Stalin personally. Yemelianov's "recollection" that Stalin twice visited Lenin became part of Stalin's official biography.[12]

While Lenin was in hiding in Finland, Stalin and other Bolshevik leaders continued to strengthen the party ranks. In late July 1917 they convened the Sixth Party Congress, at which Stalin delivered speeches and generally played a prominent role. The political winds were starting to favor the Bolsheviks. Having fully recovered from the Provisional Government's ineffective efforts at suppression, they began to strengthen their position, helped by Prime Minister Aleksandr Kerensky's frequent missteps. In August, Kerensky provoked a confrontation with the commander in chief of the Russian Army, General Lavr Kornilov. With Kerensky's consent, Kornilov had sent some of his most reliable units to Petrograd to help secure the city after the unrest in July. Soon, however, Kerensky began to doubt Kornilov's loyalty to the Provisional Government. In a pivotal moment of anti-Bolshevik dysfunction, he proclaimed Kornilov to be a mutineer. This conflict distracted attention from the Bolshevik threat. When the Bolsheviks sided with Kerensky against Kornilov, they obtained the release of several of their activists from prison. Lenin remained in hiding.

In September and October, the Provisional Government's hold on power was clearly weakening, as was the influence of the Menshevik and Socialist Revolutionary soviets that supported it. The Bolsheviks, meanwhile, grew increasingly active. Lenin believed that the time to revolt and seize power had come. Again he encountered opposition within the party to his call for armed insurrection, most prominently from Kamenev and Zinoviev. Most of the other party leaders, including Stalin, supported him. Understanding that his presence would help assuage doubts about the use of force, Lenin snuck into Petrograd. The final vote on the uprising was held at a Central Committee meeting on 10 October 1917. Kamenev and Zinoviev found themselves in the minority but did not back down. The following day they wrote a letter to a wider circle of members.

They had a strong case to make. They enumerated the weaknesses of Lenin's arguments, disputing the assumption that the majority of Russians supported the Bolsheviks. They reminded their comrades of the huge difference between chanting popular slogans and putting them into effect. Furthermore, Germany was apparently prepared to reject the Bolsheviks' peace terms, and Russian soldiers were clearly in no mood for a "revolutionary war." "The soldierly masses will leave us in droves." Kamenev and Zinoviev rejected Lenin's references to imminent revolutions in the West as hypothetical. They hoped to avoid a civil war, but such avoidance required that the Bolsheviks coexist with other political forces. Now that they had majority support in many soviets, the Bolsheviks needed to gain seats within the Constituent Assembly since "only in the Soviets will the Constituent Assembly be able to find support for its revolutionary work. The Constituent Assembly plus the Soviets—this is the combined type of state institution toward which we are moving." The way events were developing, the Bolsheviks were guaranteed significant or even overwhelming influence in these legal governmental bodies. On the other hand, if they launched an insurrection and it failed, the consequences would be much worse than the aftermath of the July riots.[13]

A strategy of achieving dominance through legal and peaceful means was neither utopian nor farfetched, but it did not appeal to Lenin. It is hard to know whether he truly believed that the Bolsheviks would be crushed in a counterrevolution if they failed to act first, but it is certain that Lenin did not want his party to join a coalition or take part, even as a dominant force, in the legal political process. The armed seizure of power was the best or perhaps the only means of avoiding a coalition with Mensheviks and SRs and getting rid of the Constituent Assembly, which was due to hold elections in a few weeks. Zinoviev and Kamenev's proposal that the Bolsheviks launch a serious campaign for seats in the Constituent Assembly reflected the general recognition within the country of the importance of Russia's new parliament. Officially, the Bolsheviks also recognized it. Stalin was among the party leaders running for a seat. It is telling that on 18 October 1917, amid heated preparations to seize power, he did not forget to send the Caucasus District Electoral Commission a telegram confirming his candidacy.[14]

Clearly concealing his true thinking and offering eloquent editorializing and slogans in place of practical planning, Lenin stubbornly repeated his call to action: it was necessary and possible to seize power by force, and the time had come. What would happen after the revolution? This question seemed to worry everyone but Lenin, whose implacable obstinacy was the only real argument in favor of insurrection. For a party that was not monolithic but was strongly oriented toward its leader, a party that was tired of uncertainty and contention, Lenin's stubbornness was decisive. Most historians agree that without Lenin the October Revolution would probably never have happened.

Convinced that they were right (and not without justification, as it turned out), Zinoviev and Kamenev made a desperate move. Having been blocked from publishing in the Bolshevik press, Kamenev submitted an article to a small non-party newspaper spelling out the opposition's views. Lenin was furious and demanded that Kamenev and Zinoviev be expelled from the party. Stalin was among those opposing this measure. He responded to Lenin by using his position as editor of *Pravda* to publish a letter from Zinoviev, along with a conciliatory editorial characterizing the incident as having "run its course" and stating that "overall, we remain like-minded."[15] This is one of the few times he openly opposed Lenin on a matter of substance. What explains this mini-revolt? Was Stalin not yet free of "rightist illusions"? It is possible that while appearing to follow Lenin, in his heart he shared Kamenev's and Zinoviev's concerns. Other factors were probably at play as well, including Trotsky.

Lev (Leon) Trotsky had always played a prominent role within the Russian Social Democratic movement, but his ambitions were not limited to prominence within the party. Before the revolution, he was often at loggerheads with Lenin, and their mutual attacks often turned ugly. But as much as Lenin and Trotsky may have argued, they were also drawn to one another. Both were preoccupied with the idea of socialist revolution and fervently believed that it would soon be possible. Both were decisive and fearless of risk. Like Lenin, Trotsky learned of the revolution when he was out of the country, in the United States. He did not manage to return to Russia until May 1917, but once there he immediately entered the fray. His talents as an orator and organizer, along with his revolutionary credentials (he had been one of the leaders of the soviets during the 1905 revolution), earned him instant recognition. Upon arriving in Petrograd in 1917, Trotsky immediately understood that he and Lenin were natural allies. Their allegiance fell into place naturally, without any negotiations. Trotsky joined the Bolsheviks and Lenin immediately recognized him as a strong partner, ready to use word and deed in an unwavering battle for power. Trotsky quickly found himself at the center of events. By September he was head of the Petrograd soviet, playing a key role in plotting the insurrection.

Even as they recognized Trotsky's value to the party, Lenin's long-standing comrades could not have been happy about his meteoric ascent. To them he was an ambitious interloper. Stalin would surely have felt a certain sting of envy, if only because this rising Bolshevik star was everything he was not. During the fevered lead-up to revolution, when oratorical gifts were in demand, Trotsky could keep a crowd of thousands spellbound, while Stalin was a lackluster speaker. Trotsky was a brilliant and compelling writer, while Stalin lacked the talent for inspiring slogans or mobilizing catchphrases.

Trotsky's ascent prompted Lenin's long-term comrades-in-arms to close ranks, a realignment complicated by Kamenev's and Zinoviev's diminished standing. It was during these tumultuous months that the seeds of the anti-Trotsky alliance were sown; they would sprout shortly after Lenin's demise. Lenin must have understood the clashes taking place around him in 1917, but what he cared about most was party unity and, undoubtedly, a distribution of counterpoising power within the party leadership. He put up with the internal divisions. Kamenev and Zinoviev kept their posts, and events soon overtook intraparty strife. In the early hours of 26 October 1917, the Bolsheviks arrested members of the Provisional Government and formed their own Council (or Soviet) of People's Commissars, with Lenin as its chairman. Stalin was named people's commissar for nationalities.

After Stalin achieved power, official Soviet propaganda proclaimed him and Lenin the leaders of the revolution. His political opponents, Trotsky especially, argued that his role had actually been insignificant. The truth lies somewhere between these highly politicized interpretations. Stalin did not lead the revolution, but as a senior Bolshevik, member of the party's Central Committee, and editor of its main newspaper, he filled an important role. His choice to follow Lenin determined his place within the revolution.

What lessons did Stalin draw from his first experience in fighting to attain power? He seems to have been greatly impressed by Lenin's decisiveness, his stubborn and relentless insistence on his own program of action. Years later, when Stalin carried out his "revolution from above," one of many crises in the history of long-suffering Russia, he fully demonstrated his own talent for decisive action. Borrowing from Lenin a dogged and unscrupulous political modus operandi, he strove to seize and maintain power without worrying about what effect his actions would have on others. This principle allowed him to act with maximal ruthlessness and little constraint. Pushing his own revolution in the 1920s, Stalin, like Lenin, bet on a strategy of unrestrained radicalism.

■   **THE MILITARIZATION OF THE PARTY**
One aspect of Lenin's ruthlessness that put him in a particularly strong position was his utter lack of reluctance to provoke a civil war, which he saw as a natural element of the transition to socialism. There was no reason to expect that all of Russia, to say nothing of its allies, would compliantly accept the supremacy of radical Bolshevism. The unexpectedness of their uprising and the fatigue of the masses initially bought the Bolsheviks some time, but the situation soon changed. The illegitimacy of the new government, its crude and cynical actions, and social experiments that turned the existing order on its head inevitably met with mass resistance. The Provisional Government was toppled and replaced by a Bolshevik Council of People's Commissars. In January 1918, the Constituent Assembly disbanded. In March 1918, a humiliating and predatory separate peace with Germany was concluded. All these events paved the way toward a civil war that soon engulfed the country. Aligned against the Bolsheviks were members of the upper and middle classes ("the White movement"), persecuted socialists, and peasants angry over the confiscation of their crops. The peace with Germany also brought Russia's former allies into the Civil War. War furthermore presented opportunities for ultra-radical elements and ordinary criminals. Peasants rose up against both the Bolsheviks and the Whites, and soon innumerable groups were fighting one another. The new wave of bloodletting unleashed by the Bolsheviks grew with amazing speed and continued more or less unabated for three years, from 1918 through 1920.

In scale and loss of life, the Civil War greatly exceeded Russian casualties during World War I and the February Revolution. Of the 16 million people within the Russian Empire and Soviet Russia who demographers estimate died of wounds, hunger, or disease during 1914–1922, at least half (8 million) perished during the three years of the Civil War. Another 2 million fled the country. The horrific famine of 1921–1922, largely a by-product of the Civil War, took some 5 million lives. By comparison, "only" slightly more than 2 million Russians were killed in World War I (1914–1917).[16] These gruesome statistics set Russia apart from the other countries ravaged by World War I. War, famine, epidemics, and civil strife persisted there twice as long and took a much greater toll.

Even these awful numbers do not fully reflect the Civil War's horrors. Statistics cannot capture the pervasive misery, the numbing of human feelings, and the destruction of any sense of right and wrong. Savage murders and mass terror became commonplace. The epidemic of savagery inevitably engulfed the Bolsheviks themselves. The Civil War shaped the new state and largely determined its trajectory.

Stalin was a typical product of his time. As he did before the revolution, he continued to follow Lenin. Part of an exclusive group of influential Soviet functionaries, Stalin was a member of the government, a member of the party's Central Committee, and a member of the top leadership. He spoke with Lenin almost daily. In 1919 he was elected to the Politburo, the body that remained at the center of power in Soviet Russia and the USSR for the next seventy years, until the collapse of the Communist system. Stalin had his own area of expertise: smoothing relations between the Bolshevik center and the outlying ethnic entities that comprised the Russian Empire and then the Soviet Union. But as with all Bolshevik leaders, his "portfolio" would remain subordinate to the primary imperative of retaining power. He spent his time from 1918 to 1920 on various fronts. He was away from Moscow so often that of the fifty-one Politburo meetings held in 1919, he took part in only fourteen; in 1920 he attended thirty-three out of seventy-five.[17]

His first mission on behalf of the Soviet government came in June 1918. As hunger swept central Russia, Stalin was sent to Tsaritsyn (later Stalingrad, now Volgograd) to acquire grain from southern Russia for the country's starving center. This economic mission quickly turned into a military one. Tsaritsyn was under attack by forces hostile to the Bolsheviks. Railway lines connecting the cities of central Russia with agricultural areas were constantly being cut. Bolshevik armed forces in Tsaritsyn were organized on a model that became widespread during the early stages of the Civil War, a model that relied primarily on poorly disciplined and unprofessional partisan detachments. Aware that no successful war could be waged without a regular army, the Bolshevik leaders in Moscow—primarily Trotsky, who was in charge of the Red Army—decided to use officers from the former tsarist army and place them under the control of party commissars. This policy met with serious resistance. Newly appointed revolutionary commanders had little desire to subordinate themselves to former officers, whom they did not trust. The feeling was mutual. Indignities and mistreatment drove many officers to defect to the other side. Gradually, military necessity and pressure from Moscow forced the army to become more professional and tolerant of former officers.

Largely thanks to Stalin, Tsaritsyn became a model of revolutionary guerrilla warfare. He wielded his authority as a member of the government and Central Committee and enjoyed unimpeded control not only over the civilian government, but also over the forces of the North Caucasus Military District, headquartered in Tsaritsyn. He found a loyal and obedient helper in Kliment Voroshilov, commander of Red Army detachments retreating to Tsaritsyn from Ukraine, which had been captured by the Germans. The two men shared a mutual hostility and mistrust toward trained military professionals or "specialists." This theme often came up in Stalin's telegrams to Moscow:

Specialists are lifeless pen-pushers, completely ill-suited to civil war.[18]

If our military "specialists" (cobblers!) weren't sleeping and loafing, the [railway] line would not have been cut, and if the line is restored, it won't be because of the military men, but despite them.[19]

They, as "headquarters" workers, capable only of "drafting plans" and submitting plans for reorganization, are absolutely indifferent to operational actions, to the matter of supplies, to the control of different army commanders and generally feel like outsiders, like guests.[20]

Our new army is being built thanks to the fact that side-by-side with new soldiers, new revolutionary commanders are being born. Imposing known traitors on them [Stalin goes on to list a number of military professionals] disrupts the entire front.[21]

These comments (there are many more examples) accurately reflect Stalin's philosophy of how the Soviet military should be developed. His words were matched by actions. Stalin dismissed the experienced officers and took operational command into his own hands. His dispatches to the capital were filled with glowing reports of the results brought about by this decision. It is difficult to imagine, however, that Stalin, who had no military experience, had never served in the army, and was relying on dilettantes like himself for guidance, was able to quickly acquire the complicated skills needed to run an effective military force. Common sense and revolutionary fervor could have taken him only so far. Indeed, the Stalin-Voroshilov partisan army was not able to withstand attacks by the enemy's regular units.

In August 1918, after two months under his command, Tsaritsyn was on the verge of falling. Stalin responded to the threat of defeat with a maneuver that would later become his political signature: a hunt for "counterrevolutionary plots." A wave of arrests in Tsaritsyn swept up former tsarist officers (including those currently serving in the Red Army), former tsarist officials, businessmen, and ordinary citizens unfortunate enough to find themselves in the path of the purge. A "plot" headed by an employee of the People's Commissariat for Railroads, N. P. Alekseev, was alleged to be at the center of the counterrevolutionary movement. Alekseev was a "bourgeois specialist," a former nobleman and officer working for the Soviet government who had been sent to Tsaritsyn from Moscow on commissariat business. In short, he perfectly fit the preconceived profile of someone who would mastermind a counterrevolutionary conspiracy. The accusations leveled against the "conspirators" were boilerplate and not terribly persuasive. A case was thrown together in a matter of days, culminating in executions and an announcement in the local newspaper.

This incident might have been just another chapter in the annals of the "Red Terror" had Alekseev not been accompanied on his trip to Tsaritsyn by Konstantin Makhrovsky, a senior official from the Supreme Economic Council and a long-standing member of the Bolshevik party. In the heat of the moment, Makhrovsky was also arrested and imprisoned for several months. He was not shot, however, and eventually was released under pressure from Moscow. This left an unwanted witness eager to relate what he had observed. The indignant Makhrovsky wrote a long report chronicling how things were being done in Tsaritsyn. He made it clear that the Alekseev case had been fabricated by members of the secret police "obsessed," he wrote, "with hunting down counterrevolution." Makhrovsky's portrait of life in Tsaritsyn probably shocked some senior officials in Moscow who had been following the war from their offices:

> Here is the picture I saw: . . . N. P. Alekseev, whose face was totally covered by a mask of blood. . . . One eye was completely closed, and you

could not tell if it had been beaten out of him or was just covered by swelling. . . . They were beating Alekseev with the butt of a revolver and their fists, and, after he collapsed, they trampled him with their feet. . . .

Returning to the gallery of types, in regard to those arrested and detained by the Cheka whom I happened to see, I must make the following comment: most of them were arrested by chance, shot, and some time later notices appeared in the local paper listing those who had been shot as all sorts of criminals. . . .

Two arrestees were brought into my cell who had been held on a barge. One of them told me about the barge on the Volga holding 400 people. Using a barge as a prison started during the evacuation of Tsaritsyn. When the [anti-Bolshevik] Cossacks attacked, they put arrestees from prisons on one, and the assortment of arrestees was extremely diverse. There were 30 from a labor camp, 70 former officers, 40 members of the bourgeoisie, and the rest were arrested for a wide variety of reasons, mostly workers and peasants. The barge packed with all these people had only one latrine, and people had to stand in line for four hours and fainted. The prisoners were not given anything to eat.[22]

Makhrovsky accused not only the Cheka of abuses, but also Tsaritsyn's political leaders, including Stalin. He provided examples of people being arrested for merely arguing with Stalin.[23] Several months later, Voroshilov confirmed Stalin's leading role in organizing the terror. "These 'gentlemen,'" Voroshilov said of the former officers, "were arrested [by me] and Comrade Stalin."[24] Having developed a taste for the Tsaritsyn approach, Stalin requested that it be applied in surrounding areas. On 31 August 1918 he asked Lenin to authorize a "group of reliable people" from Tsaritsyn to "purge" the city of Voronezh of "counterrevolutionary elements." The request was granted.[25]

Stalin apparently sent his request to Lenin before he heard that the previous day, 30 August, the Bolshevik leader had been wounded by an act of terrorism attributed to the SRs. The assassination attempt opened up new prospects for Stalin and the Bolshevik party overall: the Red Terror became official policy. In early September Stalin sent a report to Moscow on behalf of the leadership of the North Caucasus District outlining plans to organize "open, mass, systematic terror against the bourgeoisie and its agents." In September and October, the Tsaritsyn Cheka, according to some sources, executed 102 people, of whom 52 were former tsarist army officers or former members of the tsarist security police.[26]

Whether the scale of the terror was due to the panic triggered by military defeat or whether it was premeditated, the threat of terror made it easier to keep the unruly Red Army in line. Furthermore, the discovery of "plots" offered convenient excuses for military failures and opportunities to demonstrate decisiveness and efficiency to the top leadership. Stalin used the threat of growing counterrevolution to demand special powers and justify his refusal to subordinate himself to the military authorities in his district.

It is not known through what channels and in what form information about the Tsaritsyn atrocities reached Moscow or how widely the Makhrovsky report and other firsthand accounts were circulated. There is evidence that the top leadership knew about Stalin's initiatives. Several months later, in March 1919, Lenin said at the Eighth Party Congress, "When Stalin was shooting people in Tsaritsyn, I thought this was a mistake; I thought that they were shooting incorrectly." (He did not, apparently, object to the executions in principle, only that they were being carried out in a disorderly manner.) Lenin even claimed he sent a telegram to Stalin asking him to be careful, although no such telegram has been discovered. Another speaker mentioned the "famous" barge in Tsaritsyn "that did so much to prevent military specialists from being assimilated."[27] Apparently, Stalin's executions were no secret, but he suffered no serious consequences as a result. The Bolshevik leaders took a relaxed attitude toward excesses committed in defense of the revolution. During the same speech to the Eighth Congress, Lenin even said that in the end the Tsaritsyners were right. Why condemn comrades over a few "holdovers of the bourgeoisie"?

While mass shootings did not much trouble Lenin, military setbacks did. As head of the Red Army, Trotsky took an implacable position toward the Tsaritsyn events. His feelings were influenced both by a strong personal dislike for Stalin and by pragmatic concerns. In his eyes, the measures taken in Tsaritsyn were a dangerous example of unconstrained action that would hinder the professionalization of the army through the institution of strict discipline and the recruitment of military professionals. He made his position clear to Lenin in a telegram dated 4 October 1918:

> I categorically insist that Stalin be recalled. Things are not going well on the Tsaritsyn front, despite an abundance of forces. Voroshilov can command a regiment, but not an army of fifty thousand soldiers. . . . Tsaritsyn must either submit [to its ranking commanders] or get out of the way. We are seeing success in all armies except the Southern one, especially in Tsaritsyn, where we have a colossal superiority of forces but total an-

archy at the top. We could get this under control in 24 hours with your firm and decisive support; in any event, this is the only way forward I see for myself.[28]

Stalin began to campaign against Trotsky. In telegrams to Lenin, he and Voroshilov accused Trotsky of making a mess of the front and behaving disrespectfully toward "prominent members of the party to please traitors from among military specialists."[29] He traveled to Moscow, hoping to talk to Lenin personally and tip the scales in his favor, but his trip was in vain. The leadership supported Trotsky's efforts to consolidate the army. In October 1918 Stalin was forced to leave Tsaritsyn. Soon thereafter, Voroshilov and other Stalin allies were also removed. From that point forward, Stalin took every opportunity to scheme against Trotsky and advance the careers of his Tsaritsyn comrades.

The experience acquired in Tsaritsyn seems to have guided Stalin throughout the remaining years of the Civil War. Although he was compelled to recognize the party policy of recruiting military professionals, Stalin apparently remained hostile toward it. He had little respect for professional military men, whom he considered politically suspect, and preferred the enthusiasm and "common sense" of true revolutionaries. In a 16 June 1919 telegram to Lenin from the Petrograd front, he wrote with slightly comical bravado and arrogance: "Naval experts assert that the capture of Krasnaya Gorka [a Petrograd fort] from the sea runs counter to naval science. I can only deplore such so-called science. The swift capture of Gorka was due to the grossest interference in the operations by me and civilians generally, even to the point of countermanding orders on land and sea and imposing our own. I consider it my duty to declare that I shall continue to act in this way in future, despite all my reverence for science."[30] Lenin, who knew that the fort had not, despite Stalin's claim, fallen from a naval attack, seems to have been amused by Stalin's swagger. He left a notation on the telegram: "??? Krasnaya Gorka was taken by *land*."[31]

Stalin's bravado stayed with him through the war's concluding stages. In the spring and summer of 1920 he was on the Southwestern Front, where the Soviet-Polish War was raging and Soviet forces were facing General Petr Wrangel, the commander of what was left of the White Army who had moved beyond his main stronghold in Crimea. At first the Polish forces dealt the Red Army crushing defeats, but the situation soon changed. The Red Army went on the offensive, made its way to Warsaw, and prepared to take it. Bolshevik leaders were euphoric. They anticipated that revolution would not only prevail in Poland, but (finally!) would also spread to other European countries. "Through Warsaw to Berlin!" was the watchword. On 13 July 1920, in response to Lenin's question about the advisability of concluding a truce with Poland, Stalin wrote: "The Polish armies are completely falling apart; the Poles have lost communication lines and management; Polish orders, instead of reaching their recipient, are increasingly falling into our hands. In a word, the Poles are experiencing a breakdown from which they won't soon recover. . . . I don't think that imperialism has ever been as weak as it is now, at the moment of Poland's defeat, and we have never been as strong as we are now, so the more resolutely we behave ourselves, the better it will be for Russia and for international revolution."[32]

Stalin's writings from this period are permeated with the hope that Red Army bayonets would coax along world revolution. On 24 July, in a telegram to Lenin that treated victory over Poland as a foregone conclusion, he proposed "raising the question of organizing an insurrection in Italy and in such still precarious states as Hungary and Czechoslovakia (Romania will have to be crushed)."[33] Stalin backed up his words with actions. On the Southwestern Front that had been entrusted to him, he was especially anxious to capture the important city of Lvov. He pressed the leaders of the First Cavalry, urging them to make a decisive charge, but in vain: Lvov evaded his grasp. The Soviet military effort was not going well in another sector of the Southwestern Front, Crimea. Units of Wrangel's army were entrenched there, and with the Red Army busy on the Polish front, Wrangel undertook successful attacks beyond the peninsula. Stalin, as one of the main officials responsible for the failures outside Lvov and in Crimea, sent reports to Moscow citing objective difficulties and blaming the inaction of the Red Army's central command. He clearly felt uncomfortable as a military commander incapable of achieving decisive success. This failure was particularly mortifying given the rapid advance on Warsaw by the Red Army that was taking place on the neighboring Western Front.

But the situation soon took another sharp turn. The invasion of Poland bogged down, the Red Army suffered heavy casualties, and the Poles ended up imposing humiliating peace terms on the Bolsheviks. Defeat on the Polish front had a number of causes, one of which can be traced directly to Stalin. It has been suggested the Red Army spread itself too thin by carrying out offensive actions in too many areas at once. For example, the First Cavalry Army, an important force, was trying to take Lvov instead of supporting the troops marching on Warsaw. Not long before the Red Army's defeat, a decision was made to move the First Cavalry Army west from Lvov, but it was never implemented. Stalin played a part in this failure. On 13 August 1920 he sent the Red Army Main Command a telegram asserting that the redeployment of the cavalry would be harmful, in that it had already begun a new offensive against Lvov. The redeployment should have been ordered earlier, he maintained, when the army was still in reserve. "I refuse to sign the order," he wrote.[34]

Stalin's refusal was probably not a major factor in the Polish debacle. In 1920, when the reasons for the Red Army's defeat were dissected, most of the blame was laid on the commanders of the Western Front in charge of the invasion of Warsaw. But Stalin's willful behavior may be why he was re-called from the front just a few days after the incident with the First Cavalry Army. He left for Moscow and never returned to military action. The laurels for victory over Wrangel that soon followed were placed on other heads.

The return to the capital was hardly triumphant. On top of his failure to achieve a decisive victory either in Lvov or against Wrangel, Stalin's refusal to carry out an order could be seen as a major factor in the Warsaw defeat. It may have been fear that he would be cast as a scapegoat, together with hurt feelings, that led him to launch a characteristic preemptive attack. On 25 August 1920, when events in Poland were clearly turning catastrophic for the Red Army, he submitted a memorandum to the Politburo calling for the creation of military reserves. On the surface, this memorandum—calling for a troop increase, expanded military production, and the formation of new units—was fully in keeping with the priorities that had dominated Bol-shevik policy throughout the Civil War. But its real importance lies in one sentence: "The latest successes of the Poles have disclosed a fundamental defect of our armies, namely, the lack of effective fighting reserves."[35] This was Stalin's attempt to place responsibility for the defeat on the shoulders of the army's main leadership. He attributed great significance to this mem-orandum and insisted on a response. On 29 August 1920 he again wrote to his Politburo colleagues: "I am drawing the attention of the Central Com-mittee to the <u>urgency</u> of the matter of the republic's military reserves that I raised . . . and which as of now (29 August) has yet to be dealt with."[36]

Trotsky ultimately provided a condescending explanation of the situ-ation and proposed creating a procurement council, on which he invited Stalin to serve. It was a clever move to invite Stalin to take on the thankless job of keeping the army of their impoverished country well supplied, and Stalin seems to have been enraged by Trotsky's response. On 30 August he sent three memoranda to the Politburo, all aimed at Trotsky. In one, he characterized Trotsky's response to his previous memorandum as a "run-around" and demanded that the Central Committee keep a closer watch over the military—in other words, over Trotsky.[37] In a second brief but categorical note, he responded to Trotsky's proposal that he join the procurement council: "I hereby state that I cannot and, consequently, will not work on Trotsky's planned procurement council."[38] To top off these hostile pronouncements, he made a risky move. He proposed creating a commission "to investigate the circumstances of our July offensive and August retreat on the Western Front."[39] Given the context of his accusations of negligence in regard to reserves, this was a clear declaration of war against Trotsky. Was Stalin aware that he was indirectly attacking Lenin as well since Lenin had been at the forefront of those urging the Polish adventure? If, in the heat of emotion, he did not immediately realize this, he certainly was informed of it soon enough.

The next day, on 1 September, a decisive showdown took place at a Politburo meeting. The main parties to the conflict—Stalin, Trotsky, and their arbitrator, Lenin—were all present. The mood was somber. Much of the meeting was spent discussing the humiliating peace with Poland. Stalin's military reserves proposal was taken up toward the end and essentially rejected. The resolution adopted recognized "Trotsky's statement that the military is taking measures in the spirit of Stalin's proposals."[40] In other words, steps were being taken and Stalin's advice on the matter was no longer required. A special council on supplying the army was chaired by Trotsky and did not include Stalin, whose refusal to serve was taken with infuriating literalness. Equally insulting was the rejection of Stalin's call for an investigation into the reasons for defeat in Poland. Lenin adamantly opposed this idea.

To the great regret of historians, no detailed stenographic record was kept of this Politburo meeting (or of many other important meetings). The only documentation is a laconic record of resolutions, a poor indicator of the passions that no doubt flared, either openly or within the hearts of the participants. Stalin resigned his military duties. His resignation was accepted, depriving him of his membership in the Military Revolutionary Council. Trotsky's authority and rights were confirmed, and he was assigned to inspect the Western Front.[41] Lenin clearly took Trotsky's side. On 20 September a Central Committee plenum adopted a decision to send Stalin "on long-term assignment to the Caucasus." He was given the job of "settling relations with highlanders" and "bringing order . . . to policy in the Caucasus and East [Soviet Asia]."[42] Perhaps this was an honorable exile, or perhaps it was a new and important assignment. In any case, several days later, at the ninth conference of the Russian Communist Party, a public confrontation took place between Stalin on one side and Lenin and Trotsky on the other. The recriminations over the Polish war that had been roiling in the Politburo erupted into public view.

At the conference, Lenin and Trotsky both spoke out against the charges Stalin had leveled against the commanders of the Western Front and, essentially, the entire Red Army command. Lenin took personal responsibility for a large share of the strategic miscalculations and rejected Stalin's call for an investigation. Trotsky made snide references to Stalin's optimistic anticipation of victory in Poland and his assurances that he would take Lvov.[43] On 23 September, a deeply offended Stalin submitted a statement to the conference's presidium. He categorically denied Trotsky's and Lenin's accusations. He reiterated his charge that the commanders of the Western Front were responsible for the defeat in Poland (a jab at Trotsky) and claimed that he, Stalin, had always advocated prudence and caution. "Comrade Lenin evidently is being merciful toward the command, but I think what is needed is mercy for the cause, not the command," he concluded caustically.[44] With the benefit of currently available documents, we can state with certainty that Stalin was lying about his past advocacy of caution. Lenin nevertheless did not challenge him, probably because Stalin's calls for decisiveness and world revolution suited his interests. Ultimately, all their fates hung on the success of their common endeavor, so they preferred to put this unpleasant chapter of defeat behind them as quickly as possible. In his call for an investigation into mistakes, Stalin looked like a dissident. Furthermore, everyone knew that he was as guilty as anyone. But as in the past, he escaped this episode generally unscathed. He left for the Caucasus, but several weeks later, in late November 1920, he returned to Moscow. Stalin's conflicts with his colleagues during these years were turning into a habit. It was not a new habit, but it was becoming more pronounced and deeply rooted. His behavior reflected the objective fact that the party was plagued by conflict spawned by principled differences and personal ambitions. This circumstance inevitably led to the formation of cliques. Stalin's was comprised of veterans of Tsaritsyn, members of the First Cavalry Army, and Transcaucasians who enjoyed Stalin's patronage and support. Other Soviet leaders were also assembling followers. The seeds of future clashes and power struggles were being sown.

The Bolsheviks' first experience running the country came in a time of war. This factor shaped both their practical approach to governing and their philosophy. Experiences acquired in Tsaritsyn and Petrograd reinforced

Stalin's intuitive mistrust of "bourgeois specialists" and his fear of conspiracies. Grain requisitions in the south and the organization of a labor army in Ukraine gave him experience using strong-arm tactics to steer the economy.[45] The Civil War accustomed the Bolsheviks to blood and ruthlessness. Atrocities lost their horror.

■ **GENERAL SECRETARY**

The Bolsheviks emerged from the Civil War as winners. But explaining to the exhausted country, or even to themselves, what they had been fighting for was no simple matter. The dream of world revolution appeared to be just that, and Lenin's idea that socialism would be immediately introduced in Russia proved catastrophically utopian, just as his opponents had warned. Attempts to abolish the market system and replace it with direct exchange under total governmental control only furthered economic collapse. Famine and devastation sparked massive anti-government protests. Huge areas were engulfed by peasant revolts. The unrest spread to cities, including such Bolshevik strongholds as Moscow and Petrograd. The rebellion by sailors of the Kronstadt garrison outside Petrograd became a symbol of the failures of the Bolshevik policy of militarized socialism. When this bastion of the 1917 revolution took up arms, "Kronstadt" became a highly fraught political watchword.

Under these circumstances, Lenin, who had a well-developed instinct for political self-preservation, allowed his steadfast principles a generous bend. In 1921–1922, Leninist socialism was replaced by the Leninist NEP (New Economic Policy). Many aspects of the Soviet economy reverted to their state before the Bolshevik revolution. The lion's share of the economy remained under state control, but certain market activities were allowed. The use of money was restored. Peasants were allowed to sell their produce after paying taxes to the state. Private small industry and trade were returned to private ownership (the entrepreneurs who ran small businesses were called "Nepmen"). Despised capitalism came to the Bolsheviks' rescue, saving their country and their hold on power. Thanks to the NEP, the USSR came back from the brink of disaster in just a few years. But before the recovery could be felt, the horrific famine of 1921–1922, a direct outcome of the Civil War, took millions of lives.

Such was the backdrop to Stalin's life during the lead-up to the death of his teacher, Lenin. The historical record does not offer evidence of any active involvement by Stalin in discussing or deciding key problems in the transition to the NEP. He followed the political course set by Lenin and was a loyal and true comrade. Lenin undoubtedly valued this loyalty. But after the Civil War, Stalin's political prominence was hardly guaranteed. Simply being a member of the Politburo assured him a certain degree of power. But in the Soviet party-political system, the degree of power a leader actually exercised was directly tied to the influence of the government agency he headed. From this standpoint, Stalin was in danger of becoming a second-tier functionary.

The conclusion of the war found Stalin running two agencies: the nationalities commissariat and the Workers' and Peasants' Inspectorate. Neither had meaningful levers of power or more than limited lobbying potential. At a closed meeting, Stalin himself characterized the nationalities commissariat as serving a purely "agitation" purpose without any "administrative rights."[46] He spent very little time at this agency. In November 1921 he submitted his resignation from it to the Politburo, but it was not accepted.[47] He did everything he could to abolish the commissariat, and in 1923 he finally succeeded. Even earlier, in 1922, he had managed to shed his duties with the Workers' and Peasants' Inspectorate. He exchanged these undesirable posts for one that was much more appealing: running the Central Committee apparat. This position moved him into the upper echelons of the leadership.

What brought about this turning point in Stalin's political career was not only his talents and energy, but also a heated battle within the Soviet leadership. The central conflict was between Lenin and Trotsky, but smaller clashes reverberated all around them. Trotsky was the only top Bolshevik who could rightfully claim to be a leader in his own right, not just a follower of Lenin. His role was more that of a partner and ally in revolution, and he behaved accordingly, earning himself a following within the party. At the end of 1920, Lenin realized that a significant portion of party functionaries, including some within the Central Committee apparat, supported Trotsky. Lenin had to respond to this challenge to his primacy. At the Tenth Party Congress in early 1921, after intense maneuvering and considerable use of his authority, Lenin made sure that his followers received a majority of votes. This outcome determined who would be chosen to run the top party organizations, and many Trotsky followers were removed from their posts. Stalin was one of Lenin's key allies in this struggle. Given Lenin's declining health, such cooperation took on new importance. Beginning in mid-1921, he was increasingly plagued by symptoms of severe cerebral arteriosclerosis. Headaches, fatigue, episodes of paralysis, and impaired speech and cognition forced him to take extended vacations.

Lenin's illness and clash with Trotsky, along with the reshuffling of party personnel, all helped Stalin play an increasingly important role in party affairs. In early 1922, this role was formalized when Stalin was appointed to the newly created post of general secretary of the Central Committee of the Russian Communist Party (of Bolsheviks)—TsK RKP(b). The job of the general secretary included overseeing the Central Committee apparat and its "leading structures"—the bureaucratic machine that carried out the will of the party. Two duties deserve particular mention: setting the agenda for Politburo meetings and deciding personnel matters. Countless mid-level functionaries now depended on Stalin for their careers.

For Stalin, the running of the party apparat was not a burden. His previous party experience and his personality made him well suited for this position. Later, even as dictator, Stalin seemed to enjoy routine bureaucratic work. Upon taking up the post of general secretary, he began to reorganize the work of the Politburo. On 31 August 1922 he announced at a Politburo meeting that certain institutions were tardy in submitting materials for consideration. A resolution was adopted to "not place any matter before the Politburo unless materials are submitted by four o'clock the previous day."[48] A few weeks later, the rule became even stricter: the deadline was pushed back to noon.[49] Through these petty decisions Stalin was gradually, and with increasing confidence, shaping how the party apparat was run.

Some interesting accounts survive of how this tendency was perceived within the apparat. Stalin's assistant, Amaiak Nazaretian, regularly corresponded with Sergo Ordzhonikidze, Stalin's old friend who was working in Transcaucasia in the early 1920s.[50] This correspondence has been preserved in Ordzhonikidze's archive. In the letters written during the summer of 1922, Nazaretian described his work under Stalin:

> Am I happy with my job? Yes and no. On one hand, I'm getting quite an education here, I know what's going on in international and Russian life, and I'm being schooled in discipline, developing precision in my job. . . . On the other, this work is purely paper pushing, painstaking, not very satisfying from a subjective standpoint; it's menial work that takes such tremendous amounts of time that you can't sneeze or squirm, especially under Koba's firm hand. Do we get along? We do. . . . You can learn a lot from him. Now that I've gotten to know him, I have extraordinary respect for him. . . . Under his stern demeanor is an attentiveness to those he works with. We're creating order in the TsK.
>
> Koba has really got me trained. . . . He's really cunning. Hard as a nut, it takes a while to understand what he's up to. . . . Despite his well-rea-

soned savagery of temperament, if I can put it that way, he is soft, he has a heart, and he knows how to appreciate people's dignity. . . . Now, the work of the TsK has really changed. What we found here was indescribably awful. Now we've shaken things up.[51]

Nazaretian felt Stalin was tremendously significant: "Ilyich has fully recovered. . . . Yesterday, Koba went to see him. He has to keep a watchful eye over Ilyich and all of Mother Russia"; "Ilyich undoubtedly has a trusty Cerberus in him, fearlessly standing guard at the gates of the TsK RKP."[52] Nazaretian's letters provide important details on how Stalin was perceived within the Bolshevik bureaucratic community. In Moscow, according to Nazaretian, an expression came into fashion: "to be going under Stalin." This referred to officials who had been summoned to Moscow from their previous posts but had not yet been assigned new jobs and were "hanging, so to speak, in the air."[53]

Such was Stalin as he appeared to his assistant early in his tenure as general secretary. Obviously, these descriptions carry an element of exaggeration, the admiration of a loyal secretary toward his boss. But the intelligent and observant Nazaretian was conveying a certain mood within the apparat. Many members of the bureaucracy began to perceive Stalin as an experienced and confident bureaucrat who held secure positions within the hierarchy. He was coolheaded, but he could be stern and unbending in standing up for his interests and opinions. At a time when the world of the Bolshevik bureaucracy was increasingly fracturing into patron-client cliques, these qualities drew him quite a few supporters.

In Nazaretian's letters, Stalin is perceived within the party as Lenin's loyal comrade, his pillar in times of political strife. And this view was largely accurate. Long years of collaboration, marred by only a few instances of discord, had created a strong bond between Lenin and Stalin. One Bolshevik left behind an eloquent memoir of a meeting between Lenin and Stalin in September 1921 in the latter's apartment. A difficult squabble among top officials in Petrograd was being settled. Lenin tried to reconcile the feuding parties while Stalin paced the room smoking his pipe. At one point, Lenin looked at Stalin and said, "That's an Asian for you—all he does is suck on his pipe!" Stalin knocked the pipe right out of his own mouth.[54] This playful manner went beyond the boundaries of the boss-subordinate relationship. For Lenin, Stalin was a comrade-in-arms with whom relations were warm enough to allow for teasing. It is difficult to imagine that he would take such liberties with Trotsky, with whom he maintained a stiff, official manner, using the polite pronoun *vy* for "you" rather than the familiar *ty*.

On 30 May 1922, an incident occurred that further attests to the close relationship between Lenin and Stalin. Lenin, who was ill and facing the prospect of paralysis, summoned Stalin to Gorki, his residence outside Moscow. He asked Stalin to procure poison so that he could have the option of taking his own life when the time came. Stalin immediately told Lenin's sister, Maria Ilinichna Ulianova, and Nikolai Bukharin, who then happened to be staying at Gorki, about this request.[55] According to Maria Ulianova's memoirs, they decided together to try to boost Lenin's spirits. Stalin went back to him and told him that the time to carry out his intention had not yet come, and the doctors were promising he would get better. Lenin, in Ulianova's account, "became noticeably more cheerful and consented, although he asked Stalin, 'Are you being deceitful?' 'When have you ever seen me be deceitful?' Stalin replied."[56]

Lenin showed his concern for Stalin in several ways. While seriously ill in Gorki in June 1922, Lenin sent a recommendation to Moscow: "Require Com. Stalin, through the Politburo, to spend one day per week, beside Sunday, entirely at his dacha outside town." The Politburo adopted the resolution.[57] In August, after Lenin's health improved, Stalin visited him regularly in Gorki. According to Maria Ulianova's memoirs, "Ilyich greeted him in a friendly manner, with jokes and laughter, and urged me to be hospitable to Stalin and bring him wine, etc."[58] Later, when he himself was in power, Stalin adopted Lenin's manner of showing concern for his subordinates.

Harmony between Lenin and Stalin lasted until the fall of 1922.

■ **QUARRELS WITH THE TEACHER**

Lenin's illness had tremendous political ramifications. The party, which was structured around a single leader, was vulnerable. The Politburo was forced to begin thinking about Lenin's successor. The "troika" of Zinoviev, Kamenev, and Stalin was growing in influence in its contest with its main opponent, Trotsky. This face-off was actually an outcome of Lenin's tactic of isolating Trotsky, but with Lenin's illness, Trotsky's isolation served to strengthen the troika, a dangerous prospect in Lenin's eyes. Hoping for a recovery from illness, Lenin attempted to shift the balance of power, and Stalin was the easiest target.

A conflict over the program for uniting the Soviet republics can be seen as the starting point of Lenin's efforts. The Civil War had created a unified state, but in the second half of 1922 it was decided to make this union official by publicly announcing the principles on which the new state would be built. For the most part, the Bolshevik leadership saw eye to eye on this issue. Nobody entertained thoughts of breaking up what had been the Russian Empire or granting real autonomy to any areas under Moscow's control. There were arguments over the form the new union would take and the degree of independence various Bolshevik entities would enjoy, but all parties to the decision were expected to submit to the discipline of a unified party.

Stalin was open about his position. He proposed that the real state of affairs and Moscow's true intentions be codified in the constitution without undue ceremony or diplomacy. He favored bringing all the major republics (Ukraine, Belarus, Georgia, Azerbaijan, and Armenia) and the smaller ethnic entities into the Russian Federation with certain rights of autonomy. Overall, this proposal was in full accord with the party line and was supported by most party officials, in both Moscow and the ethnic republics. Stalin was probably surprised when Lenin opposed his proposal and advanced his own plan to proclaim a union of "independent" Soviet republics—even though the Bolshevik leader had no intention of granting genuine independence. The motives for Lenin's position are difficult to pinpoint. Perhaps he was responding to dissatisfaction with Stalin's program among Georgian and some Ukrainian party leaders. Perhaps, with his illness receding, he simply saw this as a good opportunity to reenter the political fray.

In September 1922 Lenin began promoting his program. He criticized Stalin for being too hasty, an assessment that must have stung. Stalin resisted and made a fighting retreat, accusing Lenin of "national liberalism."[59] His feelings are easy to understand: he had been put in a humiliating position and was forced to change a stance that he had put a lot of energy into advocating. But he chose not to do serious battle with Lenin. On 28 September, an interesting exchange of notes took place between Kamenev and Stalin during a Politburo meeting:

KAMENEV: Ilyich is ready to go to war to defend independence. . . .
STALIN: I think we need to stand up to Ilyich. . . .
KAMENEV: I think so long as Vladimir Ilyich is insistent, we'd be worse off resisting.
STALIN: I don't know. Let him do as he sees fit.[60]

Stalin relented. He knew Lenin well and appreciated how powerful he still was.

In October–December 1922 a conflict surrounding the question of monopolizing foreign trade followed a similar script. At a plenum on 6 October, a majority within the Central Committee voted to somewhat loosen the monopoly. Lenin, who was away from Moscow, took a stand against the liberalization. Stalin, who supported the 6 October decision, was slow to relent and expressed reservations. Lenin undoubtedly was not pleased.

This dispute ended with a move by Lenin that Stalin must have found extremely upsetting. On the issue of monopolizing foreign trade, Lenin demonstratively brought Trotsky out of disfavor and recruited him as an ally. Lenin had often resorted to this sort of maneuver—exploiting the conflicts ever-present at the upper echelons of the party. Now, however, the circumstances were different. Lenin was seriously ill, and the jockeying for power and influence was greatly intensified. To the alarm of Stalin, Kamenev, and Zinoviev, whose influence had been growing, Lenin proposed that Trotsky continue to work with him. On 21 December 1922, immediately after a Central Committee plenum voted to uphold his opposition to liberalization, Lenin dictated a note to Trotsky, employing his wife, Nadezhda Krupskaia, as stenographer: "It seems that we've captured the position without firing a single shot, using a simple maneuver. I propose that we not stop here and continue the offensive." Lenin advised Trotsky to raise the question of foreign trade at the upcoming party congress and also to speak at the Congress of Soviets.[61] Such a move would discredit Lenin's opponents, including Stalin, before a large assembly of party functionaries.

Trotsky immediately got to work and telephoned Kamenev, who told Stalin about the call. Stalin refused to carry out Lenin's instructions to put Trotsky's speech on the schedule of the Congress of Soviets. He also called Krupskaia and reprimanded her for taking down and sending the letter to Trotsky. Apparently the reprimand was rather indelicate, or at least it seemed so to the overburdened and high-strung Krupskaia. In theory, Stalin had a legitimate grievance against Krupskaia. Just a few days previously, on 18 December, the Central Committee plenum had voted to limit contact with Lenin, who had suffered another health setback. "Personal responsibility shall be placed on Com. Stalin to isolate Vladimir Ilyich both in regard to face-to-face dealings with officials and correspondence."[62] Krupskaia had violated this directive. But Stalin had also crossed the line with his emotional outburst. The troika saw Lenin's appeal to Trotsky as dangerous and provocative.

Realizing his mistake, Stalin apologized to Krupskaia. Judging by Maria Ulianova's memoirs, he also made an attempt to reconcile with Lenin. He met with Ulianova and told her how upset he was about being estranged from him:

I couldn't sleep at all last night. . . . What does Ilyich think of me, how does he feel about me! As if I were some sort of traitor. I love him with all my heart. Find a way to tell him that.

But Lenin was implacable. Ulianova offers the following description:

Ilyich called me in to see him for something, and I told him, among other things, that his comrades send their respects. . . . "And Stalin asked me to send you his heartfelt regards and asked me to say that he truly loves you." Ilyich grinned and remained silent. "So should I send him your regards?" I asked. "You can send them," Ilyich replied rather coldly. "But Volodia," I continued. "He is, after all, very smart, Stalin." "He's not smart at all," Ilyich replied firmly, wincing.[63]

Ulianova does not say exactly when this conversation with her brother took place, but it was almost certainly in late 1922 or early 1923, when relations between Lenin and Stalin were deteriorating and threatened to rupture completely. On 24 December Lenin dictated a document to his secretary—the well-known "Letter to the Congress"—in which he expressed apprehension about divisions within the party's top leadership. Regarding Stalin, this document states, "Com. Stalin, now that he is general secretary, has concentrated immense power in his hands, and I am not sure whether he will always be capable of exercising this power with sufficient caution."[64] In another letter, dictated on 4 January, Lenin was even more categorical. He proposed removing Stalin from the post of general secretary because he was "too rude."[65]

Lenin's growing irritation was the backdrop against which the "Georgian Affair" unfolded. This episode involved a dispute between a group of Georgian Bolsheviks and the leadership of the Transcaucasian Federation, which comprised Georgia, Armenia, and Azerbaijan. The conflict was not with the entire federation leadership but with its head, Ordzhonikidze. The friendship between Stalin and Ordzhonikidze would certainly have influenced the general secretary's stance on the matter. The Georgian Bolsheviks, with variable success, were inundating Moscow with complaints about Ordzhonikidze's heavy hand. In late 1922 Ordzhonikidze gave his opponents more ammunition against him: in a fit of anger, he struck one of his adversaries. A commission headed by Feliks Dzerzhinsky was sent from Moscow to investigate.[66] Lenin took a great interest, and when the commission turned in a report favorable toward Ordzhonikidze, he was not pleased. He believed that Dzerzhinsky and Stalin were covering for Ordzhonikidze and being unfair to his beleaguered accusers.

If it had not been for the clash between an ailing Lenin and his increasingly powerful followers, the Georgian Affair would have remained a bureaucratic squabble of the sort that was commonplace within the Bolshevik party, especially early on, when their government had yet to achieve a stable footing. In Transcaucasia, infighting among competing groups continued for many years. It was Lenin who elevated this incident—artificially, one could argue—to the level of fundamental political principles since it gave him a pretext for attacking his ambitious associates. Though ill, Lenin was still prepared to fight for control of the party and was obviously looking for a way to quell the dissent that threatened to undermine his power. He saw Stalin as the symbol of that dissent.

All the evidence suggests that Lenin spent the winter of 1923 preparing to launch an attack against Stalin at the Twelfth Party Congress, scheduled for March. On 5 March 1923, having assembled the necessary materials, he again approached Trotsky with a proposal that they collaborate: "Dear Com. Trotsky! I would like to ask you to take on the defense of the Georgian Affair within the party's TsK. This matter is currently being 'pursued' by Stalin and Dzerzhinsky, and I cannot rely on their impartiality. Quite the contrary. If you agreed to defend it, I could rest assured."[67] That same day, 5 March, Lenin dictated a note addressed to Stalin in regard to an old matter —the reprimand Stalin had made against Krupskaia in December 1922. The note was curt. Lenin threatened to sever their relationship: "Dear Com. Stalin! You were so ill-mannered as to call my wife to the telephone and scold her. . . . I have no intention of so easily forgetting what has been done against me, and it goes without saying that what has been done against my wife is also done against me. I therefore ask you to weigh whether you are amenable to taking back what was said and apologize or you prefer to break off relations with me."[68]

The appearance of this letter, written two and a half months after Stalin's reprimand, has generated many hypotheses among historians. Perhaps Lenin had only just learned of Stalin's telephone call to Krupskaia. It appears more likely, however, that Lenin saw the incident as an excuse for removing Stalin from the post of general secretary, a possibility proposed by Robert Tucker.[69] All of Lenin's objections to Stalin emphasized the same point: he was too rude. Such a charge was much more persuasive and clear-cut than any of the other possible complaints he might have lodged. Rudeness toward party comrades was completely inappropriate for someone holding the post of general secretary.

The following day, 6 March, Lenin again wrote about Stalin's abrasive manner. He dictated several lines to the beleaguered Georgian Bolsheviks, instructing that copies of the note be sent to Trotsky and Kamenev. Kamenev was scheduled to travel to Georgia and was asked to deliver the note personally. "Dear Comrades!" Lenin wrote. "With all my heart I am following your case. I am outraged by Ordzhonikidze's rudeness and the connivances of Stalin and Dzerzhinsky. I am drafting a memorandum and speech for you."[70]

To the Politburo, the meaning of Lenin's actions was clear: he had declared war on Stalin. Shortly before leaving for Georgia, Kamenev wrote to Zinoviev that Lenin wanted not only reconciliation in Transcaucasia, "but also certain <u>organizational expulsions at the top</u>"—Soviet administrative jargon for firings.[71] Stalin could sense the approaching storm. On 7 March he received Lenin's ultimatum threatening to sever relations. He immediately responded with a half-hearted apology: "Although if you feel that to maintain 'relations' I have to 'take back' the words that I said . . . I can take them back, but I really can't understand what the point is, where my 'guilt' lies, and just what it is they want from me."[72] That same day Stalin sent a strictly confidential letter to Ordzhonikidze. He warned him that Lenin had sent a letter of support to Ordzhonikidze's opponents. Stalin urged caution: "Reach a compromise . . . that is natural, voluntary."[73] This letter to Ordzhonikidze clearly shows that Stalin appreciated the seriousness of the situation and was maneuvering to deprive Lenin of ammunition.

Until this decade, the authenticity of Lenin's dictated correspondence and accounts of the actions he took against Stalin have never been called into question. Recently, however, there have been attempts to demonstrate that evidence of a rupture between the two men was fabricated.[74] With no real evidence beyond an assumption of Stalin's infallibility, some revisionists have proposed that evidence of Lenin's doubts about Stalin were manufactured and placed in Lenin's archives by followers of Trotsky!

The strongest evidence of the authenticity of Lenin's dictated correspondence from this period is that nobody among Lenin's comrades-in-arms, including Stalin himself, had any doubts about it. Stalin certainly had both the cunning and wherewithal, given his control over the apparat and influence within Lenin's inner circle, to avoid falling victim to a forgery. He understood the danger of Lenin's "testament" and went to great pains to neutralize any evidence that he did not enjoy Lenin's full confidence.

There is no question that Lenin took steps against Stalin during the final weeks of his active life. The reasons are another matter. We must consider not only the intentions and motives of a masterful politician, but also the role played by his sense of imminent death. "Lenin's last struggle," as Moshe Lewin has called it, is a clear manifestation of his single-minded will toward political domination and power—his primary personality trait.[75] Illness did not break this will but, if anything, intensified it. One can only marvel at the persistence of Lenin, racked by agonizing physical and emotional suffering, as his dogged ascent to power was interrupted by forced intervals in the background. The struggle for power sustained him, energized him, and gave purpose to his battle against affliction. This was not the first time he had taken up a challenge from a comrade-in-arms, but the gravity of his illness in 1922–1923 lent any such challenge a new and urgent significance.

From the standpoint of "the technology of power," Lenin's maneuvers in late 1922 and early 1923 relied on the same sources of strength that had carried him through earlier clashes: his unquestionable authority among party functionaries and rivalries among party leaders (primarily between Trotsky and the troika). That Stalin bore the brunt of Lenin's manipulations appears to be largely a matter of chance. The positions he took in regard to the organization of the USSR and the Georgian Affair represented political miscalculations and turned out to be poorly timed. Finally, he insulted the wife of the ailing leader, exhibiting behavior unbecoming a Bolshevik. Stalin had stepped under the sword himself and so provided Lenin a perfect opportunity to reassert his political authority and subdue other Bolshevik leaders. Lenin probably had no intention of removing Stalin from the party's upper echelons. Such a move would have thrown a wrench in the mechanism he used to maintain power. Within that mechanism, Stalin was the perfect counterbalance to the ambitions of other Bolshevik leaders, as well as an irreplaceable administrator. Lenin's actions were part of a rebalancing that required a dialing back of Stalin's power.

This context is important in understanding Stalin's reactions to the disfavor being shown him by his teacher. Stalin had every reason to feel genuinely hurt. When all was said and done, his sins were no worse than those he and other Soviet leaders had committed in the past. All Bolshevik leaders contradicted and argued with Lenin, and like Stalin, they all eventually relented. Sometimes Lenin punished these transgressions by removing their perpetrators from the center of power, but he later brought them back into the fold. Lenin usually punished his subordinates out of public view to avoid wounded pride. What was different now? What was behind such a provocative and demonstrative move against a man who had served Lenin so loyally? Stalin apparently found the most convenient explanation for this lashing out, both psychologically and politically, in Lenin's illness.

As it turned out, the letter to the Georgian Bolsheviks was the last document Lenin dictated. Several days later, his health took a sharp turn for the worse. He did not speak at the party congress; the Politburo swept the Georgian Affair under the carpet and later abandoned the idea of removing Stalin as general secretary. These decisions were not charity on the part of Stalin's "friends." They were the outcome of a fierce power struggle that began during Lenin's final months and continued into 1924.

■ TRYING OUT COLLECTIVE LEADERSHIP

Although he managed to avoid the more serious dangers posed for him by the political game Lenin was playing during his final months of leadership, Stalin found himself somewhat weakened and thus more dependent on his Politburo colleagues. It is a commonly held view that the Bolshevik oligarchs who inherited power after Lenin's demise underestimated Stalin and believed him to be harmless and mediocre. This is not true. The members of the Politburo fully appreciated Lenin's concerns about Stalin and the power he held as general secretary, and they tried to limit this power. But political happenstance and, to no small degree, Stalin's skillful maneuvering undermined the plans of his rivals and enemies.

The first serious conflict that we know of within the Politburo's tightly knit opposition to Trotsky occurred during the summer of 1923. After the party congress, the successful neutralization of Lenin's attack, and the country's return to relative stability after the horrific famine, Politburo members regained enough peace of mind to take a vacation. In July 1923, while resting in the North Caucasus resort town of Kislovodsk, Grigory Zinoviev came up with a scheme to shift the balance of power within the Politburo to limit Stalin's influence. In a 30 July letter to Kamenev, who was in Moscow, he launched into a tirade against Stalin: "If the party is destined to go through a stretch (probably a very short one) of Stalin's sole power—so be it. But I, for one, have no intention of covering up this swinishness. . . . In reality, there is no troika, there is only Stalin's dictatorship. Ilyich was a thousand times right. Either a serious way out has to be found, or a long stretch of struggle is inevitable."[76]

Although the letter contained no detailed plan, it charged that Stalin was manipulating the Politburo and essentially making unilateral decisions. It is important to note the line "Ilyich was a thousand times right": Zinoviev was using Lenin's letters as ammunition against Stalin. In Kislovodsk, he discussed joint action with Bukharin, who was also upset by some of Stalin's moves, and with other prominent party figures who were vacationing in the south. No specific proposals were entrusted to paper, but Stalin was sent a "spoken letter" (Ordzhonikidze, who was leaving for Moscow, was supposed to convey a message). Because this communication was oral, we do not know in detail what was proposed. From statements made in subsequent years, it appears that the plan involved reorganizing the Central Committee secretariat. Stalin would remain a member, but Zinoviev and Trotsky would also be included. This reorganization would have created a new balance of power in Stalin's fiefdom: the Central Committee apparat.

Stalin, not surprisingly, was indignant, perhaps even furious. He responded to the grievances of his "friends" with a show of hurt feelings and accusations of their undermining unity. On 3 August 1923, immediately after meeting with Ordzhonikidze, he wrote to Zinoviev and Bukharin: "Evidently you're not hesitant to <u>make ready for</u> a break, as if it were inescapable. . . . Do as you wish—there must be some people in Russia who will see that for what it is and condemn the guilty. . . . But what fortunate people you are: you're able to dream up all sorts of fairy tales at your leisure . . . while I'm stuck here like a chained dog and turn out to be 'guilty' to boot. You can tell anyone you want. All that soft living has gone to your heads, my friends."[77]

This half-angry, half-friendly letter attests to Stalin's relatively limited options in opposing his colleagues. For their part, Zinoviev's and Bukharin's proposals signaled that they still felt they could limit Stalin's influence. They were not impressed by Stalin's expression of injury. Calmly but firmly they let him know that the matter was not settled. Soon they would be able to meet face to face in the south, where Stalin was planning to vacation in mid-August.

Stalin could not have relished this prospect. His opponents held all the cards. Their proposal to reorganize the secretariat so as to promote unity and cohesion seemed perfectly reasonable. Stalin's objections would appear to confirm Lenin's warnings that he did not want to work as part of a team. Zinoviev's accusation that Stalin was violating the principle of collective leadership also put him in an awkward position. And another idea advanced by Zinoviev and Bukharin could prove particularly dangerous— that Stalin's position on events in Germany was "incorrect."

The political crises that had shaken Germany since early 1923 had reawakened Moscow's dream of salvation through European revolution. For the Bolsheviks, who still had trouble imagining a future for the USSR if it remained the only socialist bastion, socialism in Germany would be a great relief. But they took warning from the European revolutionary movements' recent defeats. Stalin was among the Bolshevik leaders who urged restraint, while Zinoviev and Bukharin were eager to do battle, as was Trotsky, for whom world revolution remained a precondition for the victory of socialism in Russia. Realizing that his cautious approach was becoming politically dangerous and gave his rivals ammunition against him, Stalin made an effective political move. On 9 August 1923, amid frantic letter writing with Zinoviev and Bukharin, he placed a resolution before the Politburo summoning Zinoviev, Trotsky, and Bukharin back to Moscow to discuss the prospects for revolution in Germany. Naturally, all three agreed. The meeting was set for 21 August.

This change of plans gave Stalin important advantages. He deflected charges that he was not sufficiently attentive to revolutionary developments in Germany. Also, the question of reorganizing the secretariat and the collective leadership was pushed off the agenda by the more urgent German problem. Stalin had managed to disrupt Zinoviev's and Bukharin's offensive and had forced them to follow a new script. After gathering in Moscow on 21 August, the Politburo heatedly and enthusiastically discussed the impending German revolution, the assistance the USSR would provide, and the possible responses by European powers. Everyone agreed that war was imminent. Supporting his colleagues' optimism, Stalin stated: "If we really want to help the Germans, and we do want that and must help, we have to prepare for war seriously and thoroughly, since in the end it will be a matter of the existence of the Soviet Federation and of the fate of world revolution in the near future. . . . Either the revolution in Germany will collapse and they will beat us, or revolution will succeed there and everything will go well, and our situation will be assured. There is no other option."[78]

Here we see that Stalin and other Bolshevik leaders still shared the opinion that the USSR's fate was tied to the fate of world revolution, although the extent of this interdependence was not discussed in detail. What exactly did Stalin mean by "they will beat us" or "our situation will be assured"? What would this "beating" entail, and just what kind of assurance did he expect? These appear to be empty phrases, a nod to Marxist orthodoxy. When it came to tactical questions, he still sounded cautious and skeptical. He refused to support Trotsky and Zinoviev's proposal to set an exact date for the German revolution, believing it was better to make preparations and await the right moment. He also warned against hasty "leftism": "Concerning the [German Communist] leftists. They are the most dangerous people for us. A premature takeover of factories, etc., would hold great dangers for us."[79] On the question of setting an exact timetable for revolution, he wound up in the same camp as Bukharin and Aleksei Rykov.[80] The latter was the most consistent adherent of caution: "It is completely clear that everything is being bet on this one card. We are absolutely not ready. . . . We have to back off."[81]

With war supposedly looming, the reorganization of the secretariat must have seemed inconsequential. We do not know how and when this issue, which just two weeks earlier had seemed vitally important, was finally resolved—probably some agreement was reached in the corridors during breaks between meetings devoted to Germany. As a result, in September 1923 a rather pointless decision was made: Zinoviev and Trotsky were made members of the Central Committee's Organizational Bureau rather than the secretariat. This move would do nothing to solve the original problem—Stalin's excessive control over decision making, to which Zinoviev and Bukharin had so hotly objected in July and August.

An event of great political significance took place at a plenary session of the Central Committee in September. The plenum adopted a decision to place Stalin and Voroshilov on the governing bodies of the military—Trotsky's domain. Trotsky was being surrounded by his political opponents on his own turf. He stormed out of the plenum in indignation.[82]

Historians still lack information on how this highly provocative attack against Trotsky was staged. It must have emerged from behind-the-scenes collusion between (at least) Stalin, Zinoviev, and Kamenev. They may have rationalized their actions with the following logic: events in Europe were coming to a head. The role of the Red Army and the military would be crucial, as it had been during the Civil War, and the influence of the Red Army's recognized leader would grow. The military therefore had to be brought under the control of Politburo members other than Trotsky before he became too powerful. It is unclear who initiated the ejection of Trotsky from the army's leadership. What is clear is that Stalin benefited significantly from this sharp escalation in the power struggle among the party's top leadership.

Aggrieved and isolated, in October 1923 Trotsky launched a counterattack. He submitted a letter to the membership of the party's Central Committee and Central Control Commission charging that the majority of Politburo members were conducting a misguided and unsound policy. He became a magnet for dissatisfied members. A fierce struggle broke out in which Zinoviev and other Politburo members, even those who felt that Stalin was already too powerful, were forced to join forces with him. In the coming two years this polarization—the Trotsky camp versus the Stalin camp—would serve Stalin well.

Discussion of Lenin's last dictated texts, about the need to remove Stalin from the post of general secretary, was shaped by this battle. Lenin died in January 1924. In May came the next party congress. During the congress, party leaders decided to disclose Lenin's "testament." By general consensus this was done in such a way as to minimize the sting to Stalin. Lenin's final dictated words were not read at a general session of the congress but at the meetings of separate delegations.[83] This procedure made it inevitable: Stalin was reelected as general secretary. Trotsky did not speak out, but it was not his silence that helped Stalin. Trotsky's very presence was enough.

Despite his masterful handling of this situation, Stalin found himself in a vulnerable position. His virtues and shortcomings were a matter of public discussion. The very fact that such conversations could take place and that verdicts were being reached, however favorable, threatened to diminish his political authority. Rather than feeling gratitude toward those colleagues who had defended him before the congress's delegates, he seemed to respond with festering resentment. Their sympathy was demeaning; it looked too much like condescension, and their support felt like a favor that would have to be returned in kind. Stalin had no intention of paying off any political debts or allowing himself to be turned into a junior partner. Several weeks after the end of the congress he started biting the hands that fed him. In June 1924, *Pravda* published a speech by Stalin in which he found fault with some rather innocuous statements by Kamenev and Zinoviev.

This outrageous breach of the anti-Trotsky leadership's united front caused consternation among top party ranks. Historians have uncovered no documents to shed light on what prompted Stalin's public scolding of Kamenev and Zinoviev, but it appears that this incident was discussed among a close circle of party leaders during the Central Committee plenum of August 1924, and Stalin found himself outnumbered. It is hard to find another explanation for Stalin's 19 August 1924 letter of resignation, a copy of which is preserved in his archive. In this remarkable document, Stalin stated that his collaboration with Kamenev and Zinoviev in the Politburo after Lenin's retirement had yielded deplorable results, demonstrating the "impossibility of an honest and sincere political collaboration with these comrades within the framework of a single, close collegium." In light of this, he submitted his resignation from the Politburo and, accordingly, from the post of general secretary. He requested a two-month medical leave, after which he asked to be "assigned to some minor post either in Turukhansky Krai, Yakutsk Oblast, or abroad."[84]

This manipulative passive-aggressive outburst could hardly have been taken seriously. Nobody would have believed that Stalin actually intended to endure another Siberian exile, this time as a low-level paper-pusher! The full membership of the Central Committee, to whom the letter of resignation was addressed, never saw it. The matter was dealt with by a close-knit group of "friends" and allies, probably on 19 August, the day the letter appeared, or the following day. One can only assume that the establishment of an informal majority within the Central Committee took place in conjunction with the discussion of Stalin's letter. Later testimony by Zinoviev suggests that this all occurred between sessions of the Central Committee plenum, which concluded on 20 August. The majority faction, made up of the most influential anti-Trotsky members of the Central Committee, elected a *semerka*, a group of seven, to serve as its governing body. The Seven included the chairman of the Central Control Commission and all the members of the Politburo except for Trotsky and functioned as a sort of shadow Politburo.[85] Historians most often describe the establishment of this Central Committee majority faction and the Seven as an anti-Trotsky effort. This is partially true, but as Stalin's letter of resignation shows, the new unofficial body's primary task was to work behind the scenes to consolidate a majority within the Politburo and overcome internal disagreements. The Seven replaced the troika, which had not succeeded in this role.

This pivotal episode in the party's internal struggles reflects the balance of power in the Politburo during the summer of 1924. Stalin was apparently intentionally inciting conflict with Kamenev and Zinoviev, even though he could not yet be certain that other Politburo members, who were concerned with unity, would take his side. The letter of resignation was not only an obvious test of his own strength, but also a sign that he was still relatively weak. This incident was an important step toward Stalin's break with Kamenev and Zinoviev and his gradual alliance with Bukharin and Rykov. Having freed himself from the confines of the troika and now having the Seven to work with, he gained maneuverability.

Whatever personal intentions and calculations were at play in forming the anti-Trotsky coalition in 1924–1925, it gave rise to a curious system of collective leadership that has been little studied as a force shaping the system of government that developed after Lenin's death. This collective leadership involved the interaction of politically equal Soviet leaders and the relatively autonomous government agencies they headed. It featured a rather well-developed division of functions between party and governmental apparats. Government policy, shaped by compromises among the competing interests represented by these leaders and agencies, became flexible and well balanced.

The period of collective leadership was a time of productive decision making and the flourishing of the NEP. The Seven overcame the crises the NEP was designed to address and adjusted the country's economic course while avoiding measures that would have caused systemic damage. Oligarchic government lent itself to relatively moderate political and economic policies. But collective leadership began to disintegrate when the government turned to a more hard-line, radical course. As historians have long believed and as recent archival research has confirmed, the seeds of conflict that put an end to collective leadership were intentionally sown by Stalin.

■ ### THE CRUSHING OF TROTSKY AND ZINOVIEV
Ultimately, the viability of the collective leadership depended on its top leaders' willingness to adhere to the rules of their unique system of government. This system, which faced no threats beyond the personal ambitions of individual Politburo members, had marked advantages over an individual dictatorship. Whether it would survive after Lenin's demise had everything to do with the personal qualities of the three Bolshevik oligarchs: Trotsky, Zinoviev, and Stalin (in theory, these names could be given in any order—their standing was supposed to be equal). These personal qualities, however, undermined collective leadership, and intrigues among these three figures inevitably drew other highly placed Bolsheviks into the fray, destabilizing the entire collective decision-making process.

Lacking a system for resolving personal conflicts, the collective leadership resorted to rather boorish methods to isolate Trotsky and exclude him from power. In so doing, it launched a process that destroyed the last shreds of relative democracy within the Bolshevik party. In January 1925, Trotsky was removed from his post as people's commissar for military and naval affairs, ending his hold on any real power. Zinoviev proposed that he also be removed from the Politburo. This proposal made perfect sense since Trotsky had already been excluded from the Politburo's work (as well as the unofficial deliberations of the Seven). But most members of the Politburo and Central Committee did not relish such changes, which always carried unpredictable consequences, and stood firmly under the banner of "unity." Zinoviev's proposal seemed a bit bloodthirsty. The jokester Bukharin even made up an aphorism inspired by Zinoviev's anti-Trotsky zeal: "If you see that the name Othello has been replaced with 'Grigory' [Zinoviev's first name], <u>believe</u> your eyes."[86]

Stalin was well aware of these moods, and along with the rest of the Seven, he opposed Zinoviev's proposal, cunningly presenting himself as a supporter of unity and collective leadership. "We plan to take all measures that preserve the unity of the Seven come what may," he wrote to Ordzhonikidze in February 1925.[87] In actuality, the situation was coming to a head. New jabs were being exchanged between the Seven majority, on the one hand, and Zinoviev and Kamenev on the other, and Stalin's skilled hand could be seen in these intrigues. By late 1925 Zinoviev and Kamenev had formed a faction that threw down a gauntlet before Stalin, Bukharin, Rykov, and their followers.

At first the struggle for control centered on procedural matters—how and by whom the Politburo's agenda should be set, as well as how the matter of Trotsky should be handled. These seemingly innocuous questions actually expressed a heated struggle for dominance within the collective leadership, but in order for this struggle to be taken beyond the bounds of the Seven, it needed a program. One could not gain the support of party functionaries, as Zinoviev and Kamenev counted on doing, with talk of winning control of the Politburo. Zinoviev, Kamenev, and their supporters chose a more respectable theme: the struggle against the "rightist" threat of allowing the NEP—which supposedly would strengthen "capitalist elements" and prosperous peasants (kulaks)—to become entrenched. Coming from the "moderate" Kamenev and Zinoviev, who were opposing the "leftist" Trotsky, or from Lenin's widow Krupskaia (who, out of long-standing friendship, supported Zinoviev and Kamenev over Stalin), this program looked out of place, even absurd. But they had no other choice. The Politburo majority was following a "rightist" course, so in order to oppose it, they were forced to move leftward. Probably Zinoviev and Kamenev also counted on recruiting to their cause the rather sizable subset of party functionaries who were inclined against the NEP.

They miscalculated. Even those party leaders who may have felt opposed to the NEP knew on which side their bread was buttered: all power flowed downstream from the Politburo. Everything was decided by this supreme body and transmitted to the local level through the top leaders' client networks. During the Fourteenth Party Congress in December 1925, when Zinoviev and Kamenev launched a determined attack against the Politburo majority in general and Stalin in particular, they were able to count on only the Leningrad delegation, which had been handpicked by Zinoviev, the region's party boss. This backing was not enough: they suffered a crushing defeat. Furthermore, the move cost Zinoviev his Leningrad fiefdom. Immediately after the congress a large group of Central Committee members was sent to Leningrad to make sure that Stalin's protégé, Sergei Mironovich Kirov, became Leningrad's new boss. Kirov's letters indicate that this takeover did not go particularly smoothly:

> The situation is heated. There's a lot of work to be done, and even more yelling.

> Here, you get nothing without a battle. And what battles! Yesterday we were at Triangle [a reference to the party organization of the Triangle rubber factory], a collective of 2,200 people. The fighting was incredible. I haven't seen a meeting like that since the days of October, and I never even imagined that there could be such a meeting of party members. At times, it even came to fistfights in some corners of the meeting![88]

Zinoviev's loyal party followers in Leningrad and the local party apparat were dealt with ruthlessly—although by the standards of the time, "ruthless" did not extend beyond large-scale firings and transfers to remote regions of the country. This heavy-handed purge escalated the conflict between the opposition and the majority, which continued through 1926 and 1927. After a period of relative calm, in the spring of 1926 the majority found itself confronted with a newly unified opposition headed by Trotsky, Zinoviev, and Kamenev. This "marriage of convenience" (though no more so than the other alliances within the top leadership) was doomed to failure, but it made life difficult for the majority. The united opposition provided a rallying point for the dissatisfied, of whom there was no shortage. Keeping the opposition at bay demanded time, effort, and resourcefulness. Someone had to make this struggle his primary focus. By position and temperament, the best man for the job was Stalin.

The full range of intrigues perpetrated by both camps deserves a thorough study, which remains to be undertaken. Particularly worthy of attention is one basic and potent ingredient in this toxic brew: the use of state security to suppress the opposition. Gradually, with increasing frequency, the party opposition was branded the "enemy," a label the Bolsheviks had previously reserved for outsiders such as the bourgeoisie, Mensheviks, or SRs. The historical record allows us to trace the origins of this practice to

Stalin, who employed it not just in the mid-1930s, when the fight against the opposition reached its bloody apogee, but also much earlier.

On 6 June 1926, approximately seventy Moscow Bolsheviks with oppositionist sympathies gathered in a dacha community outside the capital. They chose this setting because they had been banned from holding meetings and needed to gather out of sight of the authorities. The gathering was addressed by a supporter of Zinoviev, Mikhail Lashevich, a longtime Bolshevik who had managed to keep his post as deputy head of the military commissariat. As might have been expected, an undercover agent was present at the meeting, possibly a specially infiltrated agent of the OGPU. The matter was placed in the hands of the party's investigative commission, which, try as it might, was not able to prove that the opposition's leaders had helped organize the meeting. This did not stop Stalin. In a 25 June 1926 letter to the Politburo, written while on vacation, he proposed using the "Lashevich Affair" as a pretext for destroying the Zinoviev group and expelling Zinoviev himself from the Politburo.[89] The ideological justification for this cynical move rested on the idea that the opposition was breaking the party apart. An exceptionally stormy Central Committee plenum in July 1926, during which the opposition attempted to make a decisive stand, ended in accordance with Stalin's script. The plenum passed a resolution asserting that "the opposition had decided to cross the line from legally advocating its views to creating an all-union illegal organization."[90] The next step—casting this "all-union illegal organization" as an "all-union counterrevolutionary and terrorist organization"—would take Stalin another ten years, by which time his hold on power would be firm and his opponents executed.

Stalin's plan to expel only Zinoviev from the Politburo was a diversion, an attempt to divide the opposition and demonstrate objectivity. Just months later, in October 1926, Trotsky and Kamenev were also removed. Yet the oppositionists did not lay down their arms: they used every opportunity to do battle, denouncing the Politburo majority and its policies. The mutual animosity finally reached its pinnacle when, with no other options left to them, the oppositionists resorted to an underground propaganda campaign, to which the Politburo responded with a sting operation. In September 1927 the OGPU sent an agent posing as a former officer from Wrangel's army to a printing press that, despite the official prohibition, was still publishing opposition materials. Fabricated materials were used to charge the oppositionists with belonging to a "counterrevolutionary organization" that was supposedly plotting a military coup. The OGPU carried out the arrests. This police operation was organized by Stalin. While other Politburo members were vacationing in the south, he remained in Moscow and kept the others informed.[91]

In October 1927, Zinoviev and Trotsky were removed from the Central Committee in a particularly ugly plenary session. When Trotsky attempted to address the plenum with a question, he had a book and a glass thrown at him and was forcibly pushed from the podium as shouting erupted in the hall. On 7 November, the tenth anniversary of the October Revolution, the oppositionists attempted to hold their own demonstrations in parallel with the official ones but were forcibly dispersed. These demonstrations served as an excuse for new reprisals: many opposition members were arrested and sent into exile. In December, the crushing of the opposition was officially sanctioned at the Fifteenth Party Congress. Some publicly capitulated, but Trotsky and his closest associates did not back down. Trotsky was sent to Kazakhstan and later expelled from the USSR. The majority of oppositionists, both those who had relented and those who had not, were killed during the second half of the 1930s. In 1940, on Stalin's orders, Trotsky was killed by a Soviet agent in Mexico.

The repression of the late 1920s, though relatively mild, still made a gloomy impression on the party's old guard and marked an important turning point in the party's development. As had happened during the French Revolution—whose history the Bolsheviks knew well—the Russian Revolution had begun to eat its own children. The similarities provoked a sense of dejection and unease. On 1 January 1928, soon after the opposition had been definitively crushed, Valerian Osinsky, one of the Old Bolsheviks, wrote an anxious letter to Stalin reflecting the sense that an injustice had been committed.[92]

> Dear Comrade Stalin,
>
> Yesterday I learned that V. M. Smirnov[93] is being sent somewhere in the Urals (evidently to Cherdyn District), and today, when I met Sapronov[94] on the street, I heard that he is heading for Arkhangelsk Province for the same term. Furthermore, they have to leave by Tuesday, and Smirnov only just had half his teeth removed so they can be replaced with false teeth, and now he'll have to leave for the Ural north toothless.
>
> In his day, Lenin kicked Martov[95] out of the country in comfort, first making sure that he had a warm coat and galoshes. This is because Martov was once a revolutionary. Our former party comrades who are

being sent away are deeply mistaken politically, but they are still revo-lutionaries—there's no denying this. . . . The question therefore arises: is it really necessary to drive them all up north and essentially pursue a policy of their spiritual and physical destruction. I don't think so. And I don't understand why we can't (1) send them abroad the way Lenin did with Martov or (2) settle them within the country in places with a warm climate. . . .

These sorts of banishments only create unnecessary bitterness. . . . They intensify whisperings about similarities between our current re-gime and the old police state.[96]

On 3 January Stalin sent a curt response: "Com. Osinsky! If you think about it you'll probably understand that you have no grounds, either moral or any other kind, for putting down the party or taking up the role of some sort of arbiter between the party and opposition. I'm returning your letter as insulting to the party. As for concern for Smirnov and other oppositionists, you have no grounds for doubting that the party is doing everything possi-ble and necessary in this regard."

Was Stalin's promise to do "everything necessary" for the oppositionists a kind of black humor, a hint at the coming moral and physical destruction of his opponents? There is no evidence that in 1928 Stalin was planning the purges or terror of the late 1930s. How are we to interpret the apparently genuine anger with which he responded to Osinsky? Was it merely that he was sick of talking about the opposition, worn out from years of tense strug-gle during which he had to watch every step, exercise unrelenting caution, make no false moves, hide his intentions, and conceal his actions? At the time he corresponded with Osinsky, Stalin was evidently making a critical decision that no opposition would be tolerated and no collective leader-ship was needed. Perhaps he was curt with Osinsky because he was anx-ious. Or perhaps he was confident and felt no hesitation in making it clear to Osinsky that they were no longer on the same level and "heart to heart" talks between them were no longer appropriate.

■   **THE CHOICE**
Stalin's alliance with Rykov, Bukharin, and other Politburo mem-bers, first against Trotsky and later against Zinoviev, was a tactical move in a struggle for power and influence. It is probably safe to say that the pri-mary forces driving this struggle were the personal ambitions of Lenin's heirs, their confrontational characters and outsized political ambitions,

their nasty revolutionary habit of fighting for the sake of fighting, and a propensity to see enemies at every turn. That said, in their constant skirmishes the Bolshevik leaders were also guided by certain political ideas.

The Politburo majority, including Stalin, adhered to the so-called "rightist course." This was a logical continuation of the NEP of 1921–1922. Once they saw that it would be impossible to immediately introduce a socialism free of money and markets, the Bolshevik leaders, with Lenin at their forefront, took a step backward. Keeping political power and heavy industry in the hands of the government, they allowed small industry and business owners (peasants first and foremost) relative freedom. Markets and money were rehabilitated. Nobody knew how or in what directions they should be moving. Only the general principles were clear: there would be a mixed economy combining market mechanisms, a strong state, and a monopoly on political power. There was also general agreement on the timetable: all shared Lenin's vision of the NEP as a long-term policy lasting through the 1920s.

The issue of the NEP was bound to become entangled in intraparty squabbles. Trotsky, later joined by Zinoviev and Kamenev, criticized the NEP strategy that had been devised by the Politburo majority. While not urging a total abandonment of the NEP, the oppositionists felt too many concessions had been made to the peasants and the urban bourgeoisie, and they called for greater emphasis on the development of major industries. This criticism was typical of the opposition movement in its struggle to undermine the power of those in charge and gain more for themselves: it exploited popular desires for greater equality and nostalgia for a "heroic epoch." Most important, it was short on details. Had they achieved power, the "leftist" leaders, who were fundamentally pragmatic, would most likely have shifted imperceptibly onto the "rightist" path, abandoning their radicalism under the force of the objective need to develop the economy. This assumption is supported by the past behavior of "leftist" leaders. During the Civil War, did not the ultra-revolutionary Trotsky use the tsarist officer corps as a foundation for the Red Army? Did not all the Bolshevik leaders originally support the NEP? While a member of the government, Kamenev, one of the leaders of the left opposition, always gravitated toward moderation and followed a perfectly "rightist" course. Grigory Sokolnikov, another member of the opposition, was a brilliant finance commissar under whose leadership the country stabilized its currency.[97] Often it was not principled programmatic differences that spawned conflict but ties of friendship, sore feelings, or ambition.

The consequences of this battle of political wills were devastating. The Bolshevik party endured irreparable losses of personnel. The disinclination to show mercy or compromise and the desire to decimate opponents not only took time and energy away from real problems, but it also undermined the collective leadership's will to conduct needed reforms and adjust social and economic policies. Every decision was examined under a magnifying glass, not only with an eye toward viability, but also to detect the slightest ideological vulnerabilities. Such an approach deprived the country's leadership of the flexibility and initiative it needed.

Many of the decisions made in 1926–1927, a time of fierce struggle against the opposition, were politically motivated and destructive for the economy. Measures against "capitalist elements" were primarily targeted at relatively prosperous peasants and small-scale traders. Reckless and misguided economic decisions undermined stability. Yet these measures were not catastrophic or irreversible. The NEP, like any economic strategy, demanded constant adjustments, the elimination of mistakes, and an agile response to disparities as they arose. Lacking were the political preconditions for effective decision making. And the party infighting was only making the atmosphere worse.

One sign of the unhealthy political situation was the noisy campaign waged under the banner of fighting foreign threats. In 1927, a series of international crises was used to pump up war hysteria: a note from Britain's foreign secretary, Austen Chamberlain, objecting to Soviet anti-British propaganda in February; a raid on the Soviet embassy in Beijing in April; the breaking off of diplomatic relations with Great Britain in May; the June murder of the Soviet ambassador to Poland, Petr Voikov, who had helped organize the 1918 execution of Russia's royal family; and repression against Communists in China. Calls for vigilance and military readiness spawned rumors and panic buying of manufactured goods and food supplies "in case of war." The government's fanning of martial passions was largely an attempt to counter criticism from the left, which was using foreign policy difficulties as fodder for attacks against the majority.

All of the Bolshevik leaders, both those still in power and those who had been expelled from office, took part in fanning militaristic passions. Stalin was no exception. News of Voikov's murder found Stalin vacationing in the south. In an 8 June coded telegram to Moscow he offered his take on the situation: "Received about murder of Voikov by monarchist. Sense England's hand here. They want to provoke conflict with Poland. They want to repeat Sarajevo." By comparing Voikov's murder with the event generally seen as the trigger for World War I, Stalin showed that he felt war was imminent.[98] In the coded message he urged "maximal caution" in regard to Poland but recommended conducting ruthless reprisals and purges within the USSR:

> Without delay, all prominent monarchists in our prisons or labor camps should be proclaimed hostages. We should immediately shoot five or ten monarchists and announce that with every assassination attempt, new groups of monarchists will be shot. We should give the OGPU a directive about house-to-house searches and arrests of monarchists and any sort of White Guardists throughout the entire USSR in order to completely liquidate them using all measures. Voikov's murder gives us grounds to take revolutionary measures to completely crush monarchist and White Guard cells in all parts of the USSR. The task of fortifying our own rear demands this.[99]

These statements foreshadow some of the hallmarks of Stalin's policies in the coming years. Relative prudence in foreign policy ("maximal caution") always went hand-in-hand with exceptional ruthlessness at home. The idea of "fortifying our own rear" through repression would be a cornerstone of Stalin's policy in the 1930s.

The Politburo members who had remained in Moscow adopted Stalin's recommendation. A wave of repressions swept the country. On 10 June 1927, *Pravda* reported that twenty former members of the nobility—"hostages"—had been shot. The barbaric executions of innocent people severely damaged the Soviet government's reputation. The bloodthirsty behavior of the collective leadership suggested that all the top Bolsheviks were cut from the same cloth, but this is true only up to a point. On many key issues, Politburo members were capable of independent judgment. That the members of this body did not think in lockstep offered a kernel of hope that the Bolshevik authorities could govern with a degree of rationality.

One of the last glimmers of true collective leadership could be seen in the summer of 1927. This was a time of escalating crisis, and the Politburo reached its decisions on important political matters through genuine debate. A series of short letters from Molotov to Stalin, who spent that June and July vacationing in the south, offer a window onto these debates. The main points of conflict were the nation's policies toward China and Great Britain and the question of expelling Trotsky and Zinoviev from the Central Committee. Politburo members were still conducting themselves rather independently and forming surprising (in light of subsequent events) tactical coalitions. For example, Ordzhonikidze, Voroshilov, Rykov, and Rudzutak[100] were critical of the policy toward China, where Moscow insisted, without success, on cooperation between the Kuomintang and the Communists. (Voroshilov "has reached the point of groundless name-calling toward 'your leadership over the past few years,'" Molotov complained in a letter to Stalin dated 4 July 1927.) Molotov and Bukharin, who enjoyed Stalin's support, defended the correctness of the policy.[101] Opinions were evenly split on the fates of Trotsky and Zinoviev. Kalinin,[102] Rykov, Ordzhonikidze, and Voroshilov believed that their expulsion from the Central Committee should be delayed until the party congress that fall. In telegrams from the south, Stalin unsuccessfully objected. Only after he demanded that his vote be counted in absentia and Kalinin joined those in favor of immediate expulsion did the Politburo resolve in late June to advance the timetable.[103] Nevertheless, the implementation of this decision was delayed. The opposition leaders were not expelled during the Central Committee plenum in late July–August but in October. Molotov, fresh from a contentious Politburo meeting on 4 July 1927, sent Stalin an anxious letter:

> The most unpleasant thing is the situation within the Seven.[104] In terms of questions concerning the opposition, China, and the ARK [Anglo-Russian Unity Committee], you can already see more or less distinct divisions, and over and over we're split down the middle with one deciding vote. . . . I'm increasingly wondering whether you'll need to come to Moscow earlier than scheduled. As undesirable as that might be in health terms, judge for yourself what the situation is. . . . The symptoms are bad; you can't count on stability. I haven't talked to anyone about this, but I feel the situation isn't good.[105]

How justified were Molotov's expressions of alarm? Judging from the correspondence, Stalin took these reports in stride: "I am not afraid of the situation in the group. Why—I'll explain when I come."[106] He had every reason for optimism. The clashes in the Politburo did not pose a serious threat to any of the Bolshevik oligarchs, including him. A stable balance of power was taking hold within the collective leadership. The summertime disputes Molotov described showed that the conflict within the Politburo was not among combating groups bent on crushing one another. As Stalin's follower, Molotov acted in conjunction with Bukharin. Rykov, who was close to Bukharin, was acting in coordination with Stalin's old friend Voroshilov. Kalinin, who had no strong alliances, moved from camp to camp. This sort of debate and formation of blocs was usual and helpful to the Politburo's functioning. The future of the collective leadership depended on the extent to which Bolshevik leaders were prepared to follow the rules of the oligarchy. Stalin was the weakest link in this chain.

Once the very ambitious Trotsky and Zinoviev were removed, only one power-hungry member remained in the Politburo: Stalin. The others, for a variety of reasons, were not capable of pretending to supreme power. In the pivotal post of general secretary, Stalin used the battle against the left opposition to strengthen his position. The schism within the party permitted him to play the role of preserver of Lenin's legacy and strengthened his control over the party apparat and state security. These advantages did not assure him victory, but they shifted the odds in his favor.

In December 1927, during the first plenary session of the Central Committee elected at the Fifteenth Party Congress, Stalin made a carefully calculated move: he submitted his resignation and refused to run for re-election to the post of general secretary. Now that the opposition had been crushed, he announced, it was a good time to fulfill Lenin's "testament." Earlier, he modestly explained, a "tough" man had been needed as general secretary to wage a "tough" battle against the opposition. "Now, it is no longer necessary to have tough people in such a prominent post."[107]

As Stalin had surely expected, the plenum refused to accept his resignation. This move earned him important political dividends. First, once again, it diminished the relevance of Lenin's proposal that Stalin be removed as general secretary. Second, he presented himself to top party functionaries as the driving force behind the victory over the opposition: a "tough" leader capable of "tough" measures. This toughness undoubtedly enhanced his credentials in the eyes of those who favored a "firm hand." Third, his show of loyalty, his stated readiness to retire, must have mollified those concerned about the breakdown of collective leadership and the emergence of a "gravedigger of the revolution" (as Trotsky had labeled him). Stalin had sought and found an important formal affirmation of his status. It is hard to believe that he took this risk for the sake of intraparty democracy. What came next—his famous voyage to Siberia and attacks against rightists—attests that he was acting with careful deliberation at the December plenum. This may well have been when he reached the fateful conclusion that he was destined to rule as dictator.

A WORLD OF READING AND CONTEMPLATION

Late evening of 1 March 1953. The near dacha. The mail arrives.
Only as night approached did Stalin's bodyguards, after many hours of anxious waiting, decide to enter his quarters. They were thankful to have a pretext: the mail had arrived. A bodyguard took the packet and set out for Stalin's private rooms.

We do not know the contents of this last mail delivery, but normally Stalin received a huge number of papers. Lists of items sent to him from Moscow while he was vacationing in the south give us an idea of the types of documents the *vozhd* dealt with on a regular basis. During a vacation extending from September through December 1946, he received an average of just under fifty letters, reports, and other materials per day. During his final southern vacation, August through December 1951, the average dropped to thirty-five documents—not a small number.[1] For obvious reasons, Stalin was regularly sent orders and draft orders by the highest governmental bodies—not all, but the most important ones. Reports from the foreign and military ministries and state security and intelligence bodies regularly crossed his desk. He saw summaries of the foreign press prepared by TASS, the Soviet news agency. Some of these summaries, with his notations, have been preserved in the archives. He was also brought summaries of reports by foreign correspondents in Moscow. In keeping with a habit he had developed before the war, he regularly received daily reports on the production of planes and aircraft engines. Top aviation industry officials often wrote him on specific issues. The *vozhd* had always taken a special interest in aviation, but he also received reports on the production of other military hardware. After the Korean War started in 1950, he received daily summaries of military actions and reactions to the war by the foreign press. He was also regularly informed about national stockpiles. On top of all this, the volume of correspondence between Stalin and China's leaders was growing. Finally, his mail included many letters from his top associates on various topics, requests from government agencies, and personnel proposals. Just reading all these letters and reports must have taken an enormous amount of time, and many of them required him to make decisions and compose some sort of response.

In addition to these official papers, Stalin found time to keep up with

Soviet magazines, books, and newspapers, particularly *Pravda,* which he studied attentively. The inventory of materials sent to him during his southern vacation in 1926 lists a large number of Soviet and émigré newspapers and journals, including Menshevik and White Guard publications.[2] In later years, periodicals disappeared from the list—probably not because Stalin ceased reading them but because they were delivered to him so routinely that listing them was a waste of time.

According to some memoiristic sources, Stalin claimed to read an average of four to five hundred pages a day.[3] It is difficult to imagine how he could keep up such a fantastic pace. Some days he may really have read that much or, more likely, scanned texts, focusing on the most interesting passages. In addition to the time he had to spend at his desk dealing with official papers, his workday was filled with hours-long conferences and meetings in his office. The dinners he hosted could extend for hours, as did his regular movie screenings. And he spent quite a bit of time writing. From what we know of his schedule, it appears that Stalin had little time to sit at his desk contemplating the steady stream of papers with which he was daily confronted.

He liked books. Reading played a major role in shaping his ideas. In the revolutionary milieu to which Stalin had been drawn as a youth, the value placed on intellectual pursuits and theorizing was tremendous, but these explorations were ideologically one-sided. This one-sidedness left a permanent mark on Stalin. He read "socially significant" books and studied Marx and Lenin. A literary scholar who made a thorough analysis of Stalin's writings and speeches noted the narrow scope of his erudition in literary fiction. He was well versed in literature from the Soviet period but had a poor knowledge of Russian or foreign classics.[4] Observations regarding the political and ideological blinders that limited Stalin's reading are supported by the lists of books and journals in his library, or rather those in which he made notations.[5] In total his archive holds 397 items. Of course his reading was not limited to these books, but his marginal comments and underscorings suggest that they are the ones that most captured his attention.

The lion's share of this collection is comprised of books and journals containing works by Lenin—seventy-two items in all. Stalin was an attentive student of Lenin, and some of his own works represent a recasting or popularization of Lenin's thinking. Not surprisingly, he constantly cited Lenin in his public speeches. But he also relied on Lenin's work as a sort of bible or instruction manual when dealing with affairs of state within his close circle of associates. "Whenever I was at Stalin's, either at a large or small meeting or talk," one of Stalin's commissars related, "I'd notice the following habit. If somebody made a proposal that may have been practical but a bit out of the ordinary, he'd walk up to the shelf with Lenin's books, think a moment, and pull out a little volume. Sometimes he'd say, 'Let's have a look at what Vladimir Ilyich has to say on the matter.' Sometimes he'd read something aloud; sometimes he'd just paraphrase."[6] Marx and Engels are much less evident in Stalin's articles. The archival collection of his library includes only thirteen of their works. Although Marxism was official doctrine and portraits of the bearded wise men were ubiquitous features of the Soviet landscape, Stalin occasionally allowed himself certain liberties in regard to these classics. In 1934, in memoranda to Politburo members and the ideological overseers of various party organizations, he criticized a number of Engels's works: "Only idiots can harbor any doubts that Engels was and remains our teacher. But this by no means implies we must paper over Engels's mistakes, that we must conceal them and—especially—pass them off as incontestable truths."[7]

One noteworthy portion of the collection consists of works—thirty in all—by Russian and foreign theoreticians of the Social Democratic movement, as well as prominent Bolsheviks: Aleksandr Bogdanov, Georgy Plekhanov, Bukharin, Karl Kautsky, and Trotsky, among others. Stalin also appears to have closely studied the nineteen issues of the prerevolutionary underground Bolshevik theoretical journal *Prosveshchenie* (Enlightenment) kept in his library. The rest of the items in which he made notations largely consisted of propagandistic and educational literature written while he was in power, twenty-five of which he wrote himself. Overall, the classics of Marxism-Leninism (including his own works) and works by their propagandists comprise the vast majority of the nearly four hundred books in which Stalin made notations.

Among the remaining books, one category that deserves mention is historical works, including several courses on Russian history published before the revolution. Stalin loved history and constantly used historical examples and analogies in his articles, speeches, and conversation. He arranged for new history textbooks to be written and encouraged the production of numerous historical books and films. As is well known, he felt a particular affinity for two Russian tsars: Peter the Great and Ivan the Terrible. They consolidated and enlarged Russia, built up its military might, and fought mercilessly against internal enemies. For Stalin, history was a means of legitimizing his own policies. He was not particularly interested in scholarly discussions and actual historical evidence, choosing instead to adapt the facts to his preferred narrative. Ivan the Terrible was proclaimed a stalwart defender against the forces pulling Russia apart, saving it from a second Tatar yoke. His brutal repression, as Stalin saw it, was necessary, and if anything, it did not go far enough: "It should have been done even more decisively." During the Cold War, Stalin praised Tsar Ivan for adopting "a national perspective and not allowing foreigners into his country, shielding the country from the intrusion of foreign influence." He condemned his otherwise beloved Peter the Great for taking a liberal attitude toward foreigners.[8] Even more, he molded Soviet history to justify his own policies. The falsification and rewriting of the party's history culminated in the creation of an ideological bible of the regime produced with Stalin's active participation, the *History of the All-Union Communist Party (Bolsheviks): Short Course.* Appearing in 1938, at the height of the Great Terror, this work proclaimed Stalin to be equal to Lenin as a leader of Bolshevism and the revolution. Utter fictions were inserted into many episodes of Bolshevik history; other episodes were distorted beyond recognition. The opposition leaders, who had by then been killed, were portrayed as inveterate enemies.

Military problems particularly attracted Stalin's interest. In addition to books of military regulations, he made notations in several books on the history and theory of war, such as works by the Prussian military theorist Carl von Clausewitz and the Russian theorist Aleksandr Svechin.

The few books of non-Marxist philosophy contained in the collection include Plato and a philosophical treatise by Anatole France, *The Last Pages: Dialogues under the Rose.* The small number of books on economics is dominated by Soviet works on political economics. As for literary fiction, the collection contains only a few literary journals and works by Lev Tolstoy (the novel *Resurrection*), Mikhail Saltykov-Shchedrin, Maxim Gorky, and a few Soviet writers.[9]

Of course this particular collection does not tell the whole story. We know from other sources that Stalin often read literature by contemporary Soviet authors. He offered advice on plays and screenplays and made decisions about the awarding of prizes. He had his likes and dislikes, and the latter, however talented, were often targeted for repression. Even Soviet literary lions faced ideological tongue-lashings. All were made aware of their vulnerability and utter dependence on the government's favor. Yet despite his politically slanted tastes, Stalin did have a certain ability to distinguish good writing from bad. Perhaps this is why he tolerated and even protected certain talented writers who were not helpful or were even harmful to the regime, such as Mikhail Bulgakov.[10] Still, the censors kept such writers on meager rations, just barely surviving and under constant threat of arrest. Literature and dramaturgy interested the dictator primarily as ideological tools, a means of social manipulation and brainwashing. Officially permitted writers were part of the state's vast propaganda apparatus. Amalgamated into state corporations, writers, artists, and composers were completely dependent on the state. Like state-run factories, these corporations were not very effective. They encouraged bureaucratization and mediocrity and suffocated talent. "The time is long overdue for us to focus attention on . . . the irresponsible activities of the three thousand people brought together by the Writers' Union, out of which two thousand—at least—hardly belong in literature," Maxim Gorky, Stalin's choice to lead Soviet writers, lamented in a 1936 letter.[11]

Stalin knew of Gorky's feelings (he kept this letter in his personal files), but he was hardly troubled by literary mediocrity. He lived and breathed political power, so works of art and literature were to be judged according to their ideological and propagandistic usefulness. "Simplicity" and "accessibility" were key literary virtues. He welcomed readability and straightforward political edification free of highbrow devices. The "creative intelligentsia" was called on to depict a reality that was idealized ("correct," "socialist") rather than objective. It was to bring to the masses not that which was but that which should be, while distracting them from hardships and extolling the virtue of placing the party and the state above self-interest.

The record of conversations that took place during screenings in the Kremlin movie theater offers an interesting window onto Stalin's taste.[12] He critiqued the films shown exclusively from the standpoint of political utility, which, he believed, called for the production of edifying and entertaining films "that are exciting, cheerful, and fun." "Just don't drive everyone into depression, into a labyrinth of psychology. There's no need for people to engage in pointless philosophizing," he said during one screening. He fully approved of the rollicking musical *Jolly Fellows,* the Soviet answer to Hollywood comedies. The film was not profound and politically pointed, but, as Stalin put it, it gave people "interesting and engaging relaxation." His running commentaries treated what was happening on screen as if it were real life. A few favorites were viewed over and over. *Chapaev,* about the Civil War hero of that name, for example, was viewed thirty-eight times between late 1934 and early 1936.

Stalin's taste in theater and music were equally conservative. He condemned the stage director Vsevolod Meyerhold, known for provocative experimentation, for "clownishness" and "gimcrackery."[13] The *vozhd* himself initiated a campaign against new musical forms, such as those being created by the great composer Dmitry Shostakovich.[14] Such innovations were given the derogatory term "formalism." A regular theatergoer, Stalin preferred classical drama, opera, and ballet. Countless official receptions at the Kremlin were accompanied by concerts featuring a strictly traditional repertoire.[15]

There may have been a relationship between Stalin's literary tastes and his manner of writing. It has often been noted that he was not a gifted orator, a judgment that can easily be confirmed by listening to recordings of his speeches. But his written texts are much more coherent than his impromptu speeches. As a writer, he strove for a clarity and conciseness that bordered on oversimplification. He liked to drive a point home through numerous repetitions, as if he were hammering an idea into his audience's heads. Lacking the gift (possessed by many other Bolsheviks and writers) for brilliant public speaking, Stalin simply ignored this art. His texts are dull but easily understood. He was a master of slogans and clichés. In a society where education was achieving breadth but not depth, especially in the humanities, such a public speaking style was rather effective.

As a child, Stalin used only Georgian, the language in which he composed verse and revolutionary articles in his youth. He occasionally used Georgian later in life as well. At the age of eight or nine, the future dictator began to study Russian and was able to achieve a high level of proficiency, almost to the point of making it a second native language. But until the end of his life, he spoke with a strong accent. This "accent" can also be felt in his written texts. Stalin's writing in Russian is grammatically correct and expressive, but he occasionally let slip jarring stylistic infelicities and mangled idioms. Students of Stalin's language have been able to assemble quite a few examples from his published works.[16] Such examples are also found in his day-to-day writings not intended for publication. As general secretary of the Central Committee, Stalin reviewed Politburo resolutions before they were finalized and often made changes to them. In a number of cases, the fact that he was not a native Russian speaker led to errors and ambiguities.[17]

There is scant information concerning Stalin's knowledge of other languages. He traveled abroad several times before the revolution (to

Berlin, Stockholm, London, Vienna, and Krakow), but it is unlikely that he had either the time or the need for serious study of the languages spoken in those cities. These trips were made on party business, and his time was spent mainly with party comrades. His 1913 work on the nationalities question, which made use of sources in German, was written in Vienna with the help of someone who knew that language. While in exile in Turukhansky Krai in 1913–1917, he demonstrated a desire to improve his knowledge of languages. He asked to be sent books by German authors (although it is not clear whether he was asking for the originals or translations). In February 1914 he wrote to a society in Paris that assisted Russian exiles, requesting a French-Russian dictionary and some English newspapers. A May 1914 letter that he wrote to Zinoviev urged him to send "some sort of (civic) English journal (old, new, it doesn't matter—for reading, since here there's nothing in English and I'm afraid that without practice I'll lose what English I've learned)." In November 1915 he again wrote to his comrades: "I don't suppose you could send something interesting in French or English?"[18] In 1930, while vacationing in the south, he asked his wife to send him a textbook for learning English.[19] How serious was Stalin's intention to study languages? How far did he advance? We cannot answer these questions. As far as we know, he never tried to demonstrate a knowledge of languages during any of his countless meetings with foreigners.

In the end, Stalin's self-education, political experience, and character formed a mind that was in many ways repellant but ideally suited to holding onto power. His oversimplification of reality, in which phenomena were explained in terms of a historic standoff—between classes, between capitalism and socialism—outlived his system. Whatever the sources of this simplistic worldview—his religious education, his adherence to Lenin's version of Marxism—its unidimensionality simplified the dictator's life. A model of the world based on the principle of class struggle permitted him to ignore complexity and despise his victims. It allowed the regime's most heinous crimes to be seen as a natural expression of historical laws and innocent mistakes to be seen as crimes. It allowed criminal intentions and actions to be attributed to people who intended and committed no crimes. In a relatively uneducated country, simplification was an excellent tool of social manipulation.

Stalin's theoretical model of the world was in fact tottering and unreliable. Excessively simple and ineffective, it gave rise to abundant contradictions and failures. Yet he saw any adjustments to the ideological system that might have benefited the country as threatening to the stability of his regime. So he responded to life's demands with rigid ideological and political dogmatism and agreed to limited changes only as a last resort, when crises reached a breaking point. Shielding himself from reality, he retreated—and tried to bring others with him—to the thickets of ideological scholasticism. The contents of his personal archive, which reflect what he thought was worthy of being kept close at hand, are almost completely devoid of documents that represent any sort of outside, expert perspective. Meanwhile, a huge country was engaged in the earnest study of Stalin's "expert" opinions on fields as diverse as linguistics and political economy. It followed his dictates in crushing "formalists" and "cosmopolitans." Fearing change and the pernicious influence of the West, Stalin rejected a number of scientific advances, such as genetics.[20] He believed only in what "you could touch with your hands," what he understood and felt to be politically safe.

This dogmatism and rejection of the complex posed serious impediments to the country's development. Yet even as his life came to an end, Stalin had no intention of changing the political system that had brought him power, a system that he methodically forged throughout the 1930s.

3 HIS REVOLUTION

By the end of 1928, the crushing of the "left opposition" had been transformed into Stalin's personal victory. Cohesion among the Politburo majority, which had been easy to maintain during the fight against Trotsky and Zinoviev, began to deteriorate. The growing socioeconomic crisis was paralleled by a crisis at the upper echelons of power, a volatile mix that put the system of government in peril. This political kindling was finally ignited by the state's failure to collect sufficient grain supplies in 1927, one of many signals that the NEP was not working.

The NEP model of development was doomed by a range of factors. Allowing market forces to govern the relationship between the peasants and the state violated fundamental Bolshevik doctrine. Despite the tragic experiences of War Communism, the ruling party continued to preach radical socialism and punish private economic initiative. Furthermore, Soviet agriculture was simply incapable of immediately producing the resources the government needed to support industrialization. Every camp within the ruling party—rightists, leftists, and everyone in between—was aware of the need to adjust the NEP and spur industrialization. The problem was finding how to best modify the system. The fierce battle for power severely limited the available options. The economy was once again falling victim to political conflict and the need to adhere to dogma, and no one was more guilty of putting political expediency before the needs of the economy than Stalin.

The reasons for the crisis of late 1927 were perfectly familiar to the country's leadership. Pricing policy errors and a disproportionate investment in industry, among other factors, had undermined peasant incentives to sell grain to the state and disrupted the overall economic balance. In previous years, the leaders had found successful recipes for overcoming similar crises. Such a recipe was needed again. At first the Politburo searched for solutions as a unified collective. Although they considered economic stimuli, on this occasion members decided to try intensifying pressure on the peasants through "administrative" means. This meant a campaign to expropriate grain by force, and a key component was visits by the country's leaders to grain-producing regions to inspire greater effort on the part of local officials. Molotov, who was sent to Ukraine, reported to Stalin on the first day of 1928:

> Dear Koba! I'm in my 4th day here in Ukraine—and people say I'm doing some good. I've pumped up the lazy *khokhols* [derogatory term for Ukrainians]. . . . I managed to get Ukraine's "chiefs" and "centers" to travel around to local sites and to promise to work hard. Now I'm hanging around Melitopol (a gold mine!) and also arranged a pogrom here with all the usual swearing that goes with grain collection. . . . Lots of new impressions; I'm really glad to be able to touch earth. I'll tell you all about it when I get back. Regards to all.[1]

The tone of Molotov's letter—more lighthearted than hard-line—partially reflected the relatively peaceable mood that still prevailed in the Politburo. Molotov was not yet "unmasking opportunists" or branding "kulaks" and "wreckers." He asked Stalin to give Ukraine a bonus out of its grain collections to enable the purchase of farm machinery abroad: "This is urgently needed for encouragement (plus to push production) and is expedient in all regards."

Stalin was not so jovial: he was spending his time thinking up ways to institute extreme policies. What prompted Stalin to take a sharp turn that placed him far to the left of Trotsky and Zinoviev? What drove his sudden opposition to the NEP: a belief that an ultra-leftist course was truly inevitable or self-serving political calculations? The evidence suggests a complex of motives. Some of the NEP's contradictions were indeed gradually drawing the entire top leadership leftward and leading to a restructuring of the NEP that favored more rapid industrialization. Stalin was among those who were most eager for this new direction. His political and managerial temperament inclined him toward violent measures. Furthermore, he had no expertise whatsoever when it came to dealing with the economy and probably sincerely believed it could be forced into whatever mold politics dictated. The extreme economic measures he mandated served obvious political purposes. In staking his wager on a radical course, Stalin was intentionally destroying the system of collective leadership. The battle within the Politburo that ensued permitted him to create a new majority faction that was unambiguously his to control.

[In essence, Stalin was adopting Lenin's revolutionary strategy, which called for maximally spurring leftist excesses, undercutting "moderates," and mobilizing radicals with extremist policies. To launch his revolutionary push, Lenin had had to come to Petrograd from emigration in April 1917. Stalin set out for Siberia in early 1928 with a similar purpose: to turn this distant and enormous region into a proving ground for new upheavals. The trip seems to reflect some scheming on his part. The plan had been for the Politburo's top troika—Stalin, Rykov, and Bukharin—to remain in Moscow to watch over the government, but Stalin took advantage of Ordzhonikidze's ill health to take his place on the trip to Siberia. He probably assigned Siberia to Ordzhonikidze in the first place realizing that he would not be able to go, given his poor health in late 1927. The very fact that Stalin—who did not like to travel—made such a long trip shows the seriousness of his intentions. After 1928 his official trips were few. He made some stops on the way to his southern vacations; in July 1933 he visited the White Sea–Baltic Canal; and he made one trip to the front during World War II and three to meet with Roosevelt and Churchill in Tehran, Yalta, and Potsdam. Clearly, he had his reasons for going to Siberia in 1928.

It took three days to reach Novosibirsk by train. The general secretary spent a total of three weeks in Siberia during the latter half of January and the first days of February. Most of this time was spent in meetings with the *aktiv* (local bosses and party stalwarts). Stalin extracted from them a pledge to fulfill an ambitious plan to supply the country with Siberian grain. He told the Siberian officials just how they would achieve this challenging objective, rolling out his plan to bring down the full force of the police state on the kulaks and charge them with the crime of "speculation."[2] In essence, this plan represented a return to War Communism. Many Siberian leaders objected. The change of course was so sudden that some even permitted themselves to argue with him. On 19 January the head of the Siberian branch of the agricultural bank, Sergei Zagumenny, wrote to Stalin to voice his concerns, saying he doubted the effectiveness of treating peasants like criminals for refusing to sell grain to the state. Peasants would see this as a return to the policy of mandatory sales of surplus grain to the state practiced during the early years of Soviet rule. It could make matters worse. "It seems to me that we are making too sharp a turn," he wrote. Stalin's many notations on Zagumenny's letter (underscorings and derisive comments) attest to his irritation.[3]

Stalin continued to pressure the Siberian officials and insisted that repression would be effective. At the same time, he maintained a certain restraint in his interactions. In talking about the failures of grain procurement, he stopped short of making threats and combined confident and decisive authority with displays of comradery. At a meeting in Novosibirsk, in response to a statement that he had caught *krai* officials making mistakes, Stalin answered with a conciliatory "No, I wasn't trying to catch anyone." Even the criticism leveled against Zagumenny was fairly gentle.[4] This combination of ruthlessness toward "enemies"—in this case grain-hiding kulaks—and amiability toward his party comrades is one aspect of the strategy that helped him climb to the top of the political hierarchy. It undoubtedly made a favorable impression on local party officials and was an effective way for Stalin to reassure anyone who might have doubted the changing nature of the party under his leadership.

Through pressure and persuasion, Stalin got what he wanted. Dressed in a new sheepskin coat made for him in a local workshop, he spent several weeks crisscrossing the vast expanses of Siberia. Everywhere he demanded the same thing: give us grain. As he put it in a telegram to Moscow, he "got everyone good and worked up."[5] In a subsequent telegram sent on 2 February, the eve of his return to Moscow, he triumphantly reported that "A turnaround in grain deliveries is beginning. During 26–30 January, 2.9 million poods [approximately 52,400 tons] of grain was procured, instead of the norm of 1.2 million. This is a major turning point."[6] Stalin also expressed hope that the pace of grain collection would continue to grow. In a single month, Siberia had supposedly fulfilled more than a third of its annual grain quota.

Behind these figures was escalating brutality in Siberian villages. Bands of agents empowered to use an iron fist in demanding the turnover of grain swept through the countryside. Disdaining even to pay lip service to legality, these agents followed a principle openly expressed by one of them: "What kind of bureaucratism is that? Comrade Stalin gave us our motto—press, beat, squeeze."[7] The countryside was gripped by searches and arrests. Such large quantities of grain were confiscated that peasant families were ruined. Under Stalin's influence, Siberia received more unsparing treatment than the country's other grain-producing regions, although probably not by much. Pressure from Moscow and the active involvement of highly placed emissaries subjected villages everywhere to violence and lawlessness. But the precedent for extremism set in Siberia had special significance. Coming straight from the general secretary, the order to wage war against the kulaks was seen as a universal license.

As political theater, Stalin's Siberian trip had a complex subtext. The first thing it did was change the ideological framework of the crisis. Ignoring the official line that the government had made mistakes (a point reiterated in numerous Politburo directives), Stalin shifted the emphasis onto exposing the hostile actions of kulaks and anti-Soviet forces, thus opening the door to the broad use of repressive measures. At his suggestion (his creative contribution to the 1928 grain requisitions), confiscation was not, as previously, conducted on an extraordinary basis but as part of an ongoing effort to enforce the criminal code. "Speculators" were handed over to the courts for refusing to sell grain that they themselves had planted, tended, and harvested. Such actions made a mockery of justice, but they gave extraordinary measures a legal footing and made them routine and permanent. In essence, Stalin was proposing to jettison the principles that, under the NEP, had governed interactions between the state and the countryside. Finally, Stalin's trip across Siberia confronted the government's economic apparat—and Rykov, as premier, personally—with a serious challenge. The party, embodied by Stalin, was taking charge of the country's most important political and economic problem and thus asserting its primacy.

Stalin knew that some of his colleagues would raise objections to the strong-armed measures he instigated in Siberia. He was provoking conflict with careful calculation. The Siberian trip allowed him to confront his fellow leaders from a position of strength, as an energetic leader who had succeeded by applying revolutionary methods to pressing problems. The results cast moderation in an unflattering light and made radicalism look more effective. Fissures in the Politburo started to show immediately after he returned to Moscow in February 1928. But he was apparently not quite ready for all-out war. To an outside observer it might seem that by failing to force a showdown, he was letting an exceptional opportunity slip by, but Stalin probably did not see it that way. At the time, there was no clear evidence that he would emerge victorious. This was a pivotal moment in his campaign for sole power, and he turned it into a guerrilla operation, using deceit, patience, and subversion.

■ **A SHIFT TO THE FAR LEFT**

Circumstances prevented Stalin from quickly and openly asserting primacy over his Politburo colleagues—and preventing them, in turn, from calling him to account for his recklessness. From the standpoint of his political interests, the leadership could be divided into two groups. The first consisted of potential adversaries, leaders who enjoyed a degree of independent power and influence and would oppose his rise to power. This group included Aleksei Rykov, chairman of the Council of People's Commissars (the country's premier); Nikolai Bukharin, the party's chief ideologue and editor of *Pravda;* Mikhail Tomsky, the leader of Soviet trade unions; Nikolai Uglanov, Moscow party secretary; and Mikhail Kalinin, chairman of the Supreme Soviet, the country's parliament.[8] These leaders, proponents of collective leadership and a gradual transformation of the NEP, were not happy about Stalin's ambitions or his extreme policies. The second group—only a minority of the Politburo—had close personal ties to Stalin: Vyacheslav Molotov, Central Committee secretary; Kliment Voroshilov, chief of the military commissariat; Grigory Ordzhonikidze, head of the party's Central Control Commission; and Anastas Mikoyan, head of the trade commissariat. They had looked up to Stalin and followed his lead since the revolution and Civil War. Even his friends, however, were not likely to unquestioningly support his efforts to break down the party's collective leadership and proclaim himself sole leader. In early 1928 the "Stalin faction" could be rallied and counted on only in time of war.

Waging such a war would be complicated and risky. The fevered four-year standoff with the opposition had created a deep desire for unity. The oppositionists had been castigated as schismatics who had put their personal political ambitions before the interests of the party. Any leader who openly threatened the party's newfound unity would find himself in an unpopular position. How could Stalin fight for dominance without undermining unity? There was only one solution: to surreptitiously provoke a split and then cast himself as an injured adherent of unity and his enemies as schismatics. That is the script Stalin followed.

Another concern was that the radical measures Stalin was proposing, measures close to the hearts of party leftists, had huge destructive potential. Two dangers were immediately evident. First, the peasants, knowing that their harvest would be confiscated, might simply plant less. Second, there were worrisome signals coming from the Red Army. Letters from relatives back home complaining of mistreatment were stoking anti-government sentiment in the barracks. Young peasant recruits underwent military training at bases not far from home, and emissaries streamed from the villages to the bases pleading for help.

Lacking sufficient political strength to simply sweep such realities under the rug, Stalin was forced to bide his time. Evidence from the period after his return from Siberia shows him ready for compromise. Resolutions adopted around that time, while expressing approval for the extreme measures already taken, condemned "distortions and excesses." Stalin's handling of objections to tactics used in Siberia foreshadowed the brand of political warfare he would favor in subsequent years, before he achieved complete victory. In essence, his approach was to "agree and ignore." Wishing to avoid a showdown, he put his faith in stealthy manipulation of the bureaucratic machine and a strategic reshuffling of personnel.

Everything depended on the alignment of forces within the Politburo. In 1928, with help from political intrigues, Stalin managed to weaken the Rykov-Bukharin group and strengthen unity among his friends. He also benefited from the foolish mistakes of his opponents—especially Bukharin—and likely from the use of blackmail. He may have made use of recently discovered compromising evidence against Mikhail Kalinin and Yan Rudzutak, unearthed in prerevolutionary police records in 1928 but never brought to light. A transcript of a February 1900 police interrogation has Kalinin stating: "Having been called in for interrogation as a result of a request I submitted, I wish to give frank testimony on my criminal activities." The transcript shows that Kalinin gave the police detailed information about the operations of his underground organization. Police records also showed that Rudzutak, who was sentenced to ten years' hard labor in 1909, apparently gave interrogators the names and addresses of members of his organization. The police then conducted searches and seized weapons and propagandistic literature.[9] Similar compromising materials Stalin could have used against other members of the top leadership may remain to be found.

Although there is no hard evidence to show that Stalin used these discoveries in his quest for loyal supporters, his relationship with the secret police was such that he would almost certainly have been informed about them, and his using the crude but powerful tool of blackmail would have been entirely in character. Even his friends on the Politburo understood the reasons for the split within its ranks. Stalin's pontification on the "rightist threat" did not mask his intention of achieving dominance within the Politburo. The war he was waging was starkly personal. In an attempt to reconcile the sides, Stalin's old friend and loyal follower Ordzhonikidze wrote a frank letter to Rykov amid clashes in the fall of 1928:

> Any more fighting within the party is bound to lead to unbelievably bitter upheavals. That has to be our starting point. I am absolutely convinced that we'll get over this. In terms of grain and other such issues, we can argue and decide, but it shouldn't lead to fighting.... There are no fundamental disagreements, and that's the most important thing.

... It seems that the relationship between Stalin and Bukharin has really deteriorated, but we need to do everything possible to reconcile them. It can be done.[10]

It is unlikely that Ordzhonikidze was attempting to deceive Rykov in order to help Stalin. He was merely describing the moods and views then held by the majority, including many of Stalin's supporters. The Politburo's collective leadership was still a viable and functional institution. Even as authoritarian a Bolshevik as Ordzhonikidze understood that it was better to "argue and decide" than to engage in political name calling. All Soviet leaders recognized the need to revise economic policy in favor of accelerating industrialization. Only the details were in dispute. There was no reason friction within the Politburo had to lead to a complete rupture—so long as no member of the collective leadership harbored ambitions of achieving sole power.

Attuned to the prevailing mood, Stalin paid lip service to unity while using others to undermine his opponents. In 1928 he organized rebellions within Tomsky's trade union apparat and Uglanov's Moscow party organization. By orchestrating upheavals within these organizations, Stalin managed to deprive both leaders of their "patrimonies." Furthermore, his opponents were weakened by a fatal political misstep by Bukharin, who in July 1928 secretly met with the disgraced Kamenev and gave him a candid account of conflicts roiling the Politburo. Kamenev's written account of this conversation was stolen and sent to followers of Trotsky, who, despising both Stalin and Bukharin, were only too glad to print it up on leaflets and distribute them publicly. The true story is still not entirely clear, but even if Stalin and the secret police, which was already under his control, had nothing to do with the theft of the notes, there is no doubt that he did everything he could to ensure that the leaflets were broadly disseminated.[11] Bukharin and his supporters were hopelessly compromised.

While branding Bukharin a schismatic who fraternized with the crushed opposition behind the backs of his Politburo colleagues, Stalin prepared his heavy artillery. In mid-1928, engineers from a Donetsk coal mine were subjected to a show trial based on fabricated charges—the so-called Shakhty Affair. They were charged with sabotage, and their trial was accompanied by a powerful propaganda campaign. Meanwhile, as the 1928 grain collections were again turned into a war against the kulaks, Stalin proclaimed a new theory (which he made sure was borne out): the farther socialist construction progressed, the more heated the class war would become as the enemies of socialism intensified their resistance. They would also, he warned ominously, exert influence over the party. Persistently and methodically, he introduced into party documents and propaganda the idea of "danger from the right" and from agents of hostile influence within the party. Keeping constant pressure on "the enemy," destroying him and his "rightist" allies within the party—that was how the victory of socialism and the long-awaited overcoming of difficulties and conflicts would finally be achieved. These sinister theories may have appealed to poorly educated party functionaries, but they are not consistent with what was happening in the country.

Once he had isolated the Bukharin-Rykov group, Stalin cast his final blow by blaming the two men for the "right deviation" within party ranks. In an atmosphere of political hysteria and growing radicalism, the more moderate forces within the party were compelled to remain silent. When forced to take sides, most Politburo members—each for his own reasons—chose to support Stalin. The entire Politburo became a sort of Stalin faction. One after another in 1929 and 1930, Bukharin, Tomsky, Uglanov, and Rykov were expelled from the Politburo and relegated to the status of second-tier functionaries. None survived the Terror.

Stalin's victory in the Politburo was due to political intrigues and errors by his opponents. The general secretary made good use of the vast experience building and wielding power and influence he had acquired during the years of struggle against Trotsky, Zinoviev, and Kamenev. Of no small importance was Stalin's power, as general secretary, to influence appointments. He knew how to manipulate people, how to wait for the right moment and strike with just the right amount of force to avoid scaring off potential supporters or waverers. Masking his true intentions, he presented himself as a reasonable politician and loyal member of the party community, implacable only toward enemies. In a few short years, everything would be completely different. Many who supported Stalin bitterly repented their choice once their turn for destruction came. This was Stalin's genius: to ensure that his victims developed regrets only after it was too late.

One result of the Stalin faction's victory was the approval and implementation of the Great Leap policy. Largely due to Stalin's influence, "class warfare" and "revolutionary spirit" were introduced into the economic sphere. Socioeconomic constraints were discarded as so much rubbish. No objective limits were placed on industrial plans or on capital investments in manufacturing—whatever industry needed, it would get. A tremendous wager was placed on large-scale purchases of Western equipment and even entire factories in the hope that these resources would be quickly up and running, producing an abundance of goods. The historical circumstances were propitious. With their economies languishing from the Great Depression, Western countries were more inclined to cooperate with the USSR than they might have been in times of plenty.

The ambitious five-year economic growth targets adopted in April 1929 were almost immediately rejected as too modest. Targets were increased by 50 percent, then doubled and tripled. The Five-Year Plan was changed to a Four- and even Three-Year Plan. Trying to outdo one another in this frenzy, party and economic functionaries pulled ever higher numbers out of the air. "In ten years at most," Stalin exhorted, "we must make good the distance that separates us from the advanced capitalist countries. . . . Some claim that it is hard to master technology. That is not true! There are no fortresses that Bolsheviks cannot capture."[12]

Treating the economy as a fortress to be captured plunged the country back into the War Communism of the Civil War period. Political campaigns, an enthusiastic minority, and the compulsion of the majority almost completely took the place of economic incentives and proven practices of manufacturing and labor management. A disordered financial and commercial system and skyrocketing inflation were explained away as predictable obstacles on the path toward socialism, toward the withering away of commodity-money relations and the introduction of product exchange between cities and the countryside. As foreseen by the more moderate party leaders, this mad race to industrialize left no place for the tracking of basic economic indicators. In December 1930 the new chief of Soviet industry, Grigory Ordzhonikidze, reported that even such key industrial sites as the Magnitogorsk and Kuznetsk Metallurgical Works, the Nizhny Novgorod Automotive Plant, and the Bobrikov Chemical Works were being built without finalized blueprints. In many cases, he wrote in a memorandum, "money is being spent without any budget. . . . Accounting is exceptionally weak and muddled. No one has yet been able to say how much construction of the Stalingrad Tractor Factory has cost." Stalin read this memorandum; his perfunctory notations demonstrate no desire to change the way things were being done.[13] Such an extravagant pumping up of industry needed material resources and workers. Both were taken from the countryside.

■   THE WAR ON THE PEASANTS

Stalin's costly leap forward was paid for by a sharp reduction in the entire population's standard of living, but the pain inflicted on rural pop-

ulations was particularly severe.[14] The countryside was treated like a conquered colony to be exploited rather than the country's mainstay. At first
no one doubted that in a primarily agrarian country, the peasantry would
have to foot the bill for industrialization. The only disagreements had to do
with the size of the bill and how payment would be exacted. The Bolsheviks
did not like the peasantry—they considered it a dying class—but during
the NEP, cognizant of the economic importance of agriculture, the government tried to maintain reasonable relations with the countryside, even if
that meant turning a blind eye to such politically unsavory phenomena as
the expanded use of private plots. In the late 1920s, however, the government abandoned such liberalism. The increase in capital investment in
industry—[a policy the entire collective leadership supported]—required
changing the relationship between the state and the peasantry. In late 1927
and early 1928, the still unified Politburo continued its leftward drift, mixing
repression and strong-armed tactics with the economic incentives that had
already been put in place to encourage agriculture. How well this mixed
approach might have worked will never be known since Stalin took the initiative and turned the leftward drift into a sudden leap. The radical expropriation of grain began to look very much like the confiscations carried out
under War Communism.

As Stalin's opponents had warned, these measures yielded immediate
but unsustainable results. The confiscations took away the peasants' economic incentive and led to a drop in production. Each harvest was worse
than the one before, leading the grain collectors to resort to increasingly
ruthless methods. This vicious cycle of extraordinary measures was fraught
with political crises, including mass unrest among peasants that spilled
over into the army. Those dealing with these problems on the ground
looked to Stalin, who had by then taken a leading position within the Politburo, for a way out of this cycle.

Stalin's options were limited, however, by the various ultra-leftist policies he had advocated during his political battles against the rightists. He
chose what for him personally was the simplest and safest path, however
ruinous it might be for the country. The fight against kulaks and the expropriation of peasant property were taken to their logical conclusion: lands
were confiscated and the peasants were transformed into workers in agrarian enterprises managed by the state. The method by which these changes
were achieved, labeled "collectivization," involved the large-scale forcible
movement of peasants to collective farms—kolkhozes. Nullifying the party's previous decision to make such a transition gradually, in November

1929 Stalin proclaimed that collectivization would be universal and immediate. In December came his call to destroy the kulaks as a class.

In essence, the victorious *vozhd* was intentionally provoking a new and deadly wave of revolution in the countryside. By brandishing slogans about the urgent need to crush the kulaks, he gave local stalwarts a free hand. A fevered and violent collectivization effort gripped the countryside even before the new kolkhoz project could receive serious discussion or be embodied in specific directives. In a signature Stalinist move, the party was confronted with a fait accompli. Collectivization supposedly began "from below," leaving no alternative but to support and expand the kolkhoz movement, whatever monstrous forms it might be taking. Many party careerists and radicals, sensing Stalin's strength and decisiveness, responded enthusiastically to his call. Reports of collectivization's successes poured into Moscow.

A finalized plan for collectivization was adopted in early 1930, during a special meeting of Central Committee commissions established to work out the details. Commission members—functionaries fully obedient to Stalin—at first expressed a certain hesitance. While they were in principle ready to support Stalin's push for wholesale collectivization, they urged that it take place over several years. Despite the atmosphere of class-war hysteria in the country, the commissioners tried to ease the fate of millions of kulaks, believing that while they were, of course, enemies of the entire kolkhoz system, they should not be driven into a corner. Repression should be reserved for those who actively resisted. The rest should be accepted into kolkhozes, albeit with certain restrictions. Taking this relatively moderate approach, the commission members made important organizational suggestions—for example, that instead of the total confiscation of property, peasants should be allowed to keep small plots for their own use.[15]

The proposals made by the Central Committee commissions were of great practical importance and probably the best that could be achieved given the political realities of 1930. They somewhat appeased party extremists while conceding something meaningful to the peasants. As the subsequent history of the Soviet Union has shown, allowing kolkhoz workers to keep their own personal plots saved the system, the peasants, and the entire country. In essence, the arrangement returned peasants to the status of serfs in pre-emancipation Russia, paying feudal homage to the state through their work on collective farms but able to retain some land for personal use. It allowed them to feed themselves—and much of the country— despite the poor performance of the kolkhozes.

Stalin preferred a different model: his idea was to turn the peasants into slaves of the state, fully dependent on their state jobs. He favored the total expropriation of peasant property and the incorporation of villages into a state economy where market forces would be allowed no influence. He subjected the commissions' conclusions to harsh criticism and undertook to correct their many errors.[16] By the time he was done, the collectivization plan resembled a military campaign against the traditional peasant way of life. First, Stalin drastically cut the timeline for carrying out collectivization. In several of the most important agricultural regions, the task was to be completed by the fall of 1930, and the tone of his directives made it clear to local functionaries that there was not a moment to lose. Second, he put a quick stop to all talk of integrating kulaks into kolkhozes. Such a step was categorically forbidden. Kulaks and their families were to be exiled to remote areas of the USSR, arrested, placed in camps, or shot. Finally, he put an end to all proposals that kolkhozes coexist with private peasant plots. Provisions for peasants to keep any land whatsoever were adamantly deleted from the draft directives. Ultimately, "communes"—agricultural and social utopias, the brainchild of socialist fanatics—were proclaimed to be the ideal form and goal of collectivization. In the Soviet embodiment of this ideal, peasant property became the property of the community, right down to family chickens and personal items.

These insane and inevitably bloody plans fully reflected Stalin's ideas and intentions. By pushing the pace of collectivization and annihilating the most prosperous and influential segment of the peasantry, Stalin was pursuing several goals at once. Kulak property would provide land and equipment for the collective farms, and the kolkhozes themselves would serve as conduits through which resources could be rapidly and efficiently pumped out of the countryside and into industry. One factor in Stalin's calculations was his belief (shared by many party functionaries) that a moneyless form of socialism based on the exchange of goods was right around the corner. Under forced industrialization, money would cease to be an economic regulator—good riddance, thought the party leftists.

Stalin was emboldened to wage this perilous war against the peasantry partly because he believed this population segment, despite being the country's largest, lacked the strength to pose any serious threat to the state. This assumption was only partly borne out. The peasantry really was no match for the totalitarian state, but it did offer serious resistance to collectivization and caused Stalin a good deal of trouble.

In order to fulfill Stalin's vision of a massive system of kolkhozes, the party leadership mobilized and empowered tens of thousands of people dispatched from cities, as well as local stalwarts. Spurring competition among the regions, party newspapers (*Pravda* first and foremost) voiced one demand: as quickly as possible and by whatever means necessary, drive the peasants into kolkhozes. Despite official optimism, the leadership was under no illusions that collectivization could be achieved voluntarily. One of the main instruments propelling it forward was the arrest and exile of kulaks. Fearing the fate of their repressed fellow villagers, peasants gritted their teeth and joined the despised kolkhozes.

Brandishing the threat of "dekulakization" and arrest, the authorities quickly achieved stunning collectivization results—at least on paper. While 7.5 percent of the country's peasant households belonged to kolkhozes as of 1 October 1929, by 20 February 1930 that percentage had reached 52.7.[17] Underlying this statistic was a horrific and tragic reality. People sent from the city or mobilized from the local population to carry out collectivization behaved like conquering hordes toward a defeated enemy. Anyone who refused to enter the kolkhoz was arrested and beaten. The plundering of "dekulakized" property and the raping of women were standard. Churches were closed and clergy members arrested. "Fervent" members of the Komsomol—the Communist Youth League—desecrated churches and pranced about in church vestments.

This abuse and humiliation drove the usually docile countryside to rebellion. A wave of peasant militancy swept across the country. In all of 1926–1927, the authorities identified just 63 incidents of large-scale antigovernment unrest in rural areas. In 1929 there were more than 1,300 such incidents, involving 244,000 participants. In January–February 1930 alone, there were approximately 1,500 incidents with 324,000 participants.[18] Stalin, though undoubtedly informed of the growing unrest, did not immediately respond. He was probably confident that the wave of rebellion was simply the inevitable resistance of an "obsolete class." By late February, however, he began to think again.[19] First came a report on 26 February from Kharkov, then the capital of Ukraine, containing news of unrest in the Shepetovka District, near the border with Poland. Crowds of peasants were demanding the reopening of churches and the abolition of the kolkhozes. Party activists were beaten. Other reports reaching Moscow around the same time described similar incidents in Kazakhstan, Voronezh, and even near the capital. Unrest broke out on 21 February in the Pitelinsky area of Riazan District outside Moscow. Peasants removed their livestock and family stores from kolkhozes and returned property to kulaks. Church bells were rung and delegations sent to neighboring villages to rally others to the cause. Peasants armed with stakes tried to prevent the arrests of kulaks. A policeman was killed and eight activists were wounded. OGPU agents responded with firearms, as a result of which three peasants were wounded and six killed, according to official reports.[20]

The escalating disturbances and the threat that the spring sowing could be disrupted forced the authorities to pull back. On 28 February 1930 the Politburo adopted a resolution calling on Stalin to address collectivization in the press.[21] The famous article "Dizzy with Success" was published on 2 March. It contained an optimistic assessment of the "huge strides" made in collectivization and proclaimed "the countryside's radical turn toward socialism." At the same time, Stalin condemned individual "anti-Leninist inclinations"—the spread of communes; the expropriation of all peasant property for communal use; violations of "the principle of voluntarism and accounting for local circumstances"; and the removal of church bells—placing the blame for these excesses at the feet of local officials. On 10 March, secret Central Committee directives were sent out demanding the return of some expropriated property to peasants (poultry, livestock, the lands immediately adjacent to their homes), the correction of "mistakes" made during dekulakization, and a halt to the creation of communes and the closing of churches.[22] This was a temporary retreat intended to calm the peasants and allow them to plant their crops.

Stalin's article and the Central Committee directives did little to calm tempers. Both failed to provide what was most sought: an explanation of what would be done with the kolkhozes that already existed. The peasants took this problem into their own hands. They forcibly destroyed the collective farms, took away confiscated property and seeds, and restored abolished property lines. The contradictory signals from Moscow only fanned the flames of anti-kolkhoz sentiment and provoked further disturbances by peasants, leaving local activists unsure of how to proceed. March 1930 marked the apex of the war in the countryside: there were more than 6,500 instances of mass unrest, almost half the total for the entire year. In all, approximately 3.4 million peasants took part in acts of rebellion in 1930.[23] Based on that number, it can be presumed that 1.5-2 million revolted in March. The higher figure is more likely since the political police had an incentive to underestimate participation in anti-government unrest. Some incidents were well organized; the peasants formed detachments and took over significant territory.

Uprisings were especially widespread in Ukraine, the site of almost half of the March disturbances. The authorities were particularly alarmed by rebellions in border regions. As of 16 March, fifteen out of Tulchin District's seventeen administrative areas were in a state of revolt. Representatives of the Soviet government were driven out of fifty villages and replaced with *starostas*, traditional village elders. Kolkhozes were abolished in most of the district's villages. Rebels beat members of the Communist Party and Komsomol and banished them from villages. In some places, armed rebels engaged in gun battles with OGPU punitive detachments.

For Moscow, the unrest along Ukraine's western border raised the specter of Polish intervention. On 19 March, Stalin gave Ukrainian State Political Directorate (GPU) chief Vsevolod Balitsky a dressing down, demanding that he stop "making speeches and act more decisively." The wounded Balitsky replied that he was personally traveling to "the sectors under threat" and was not just overseeing the fight "from a train car."[24] But he did carry out Stalin's orders. Ordzhonikidze, who traveled to Ukraine for an inspection, wrote that the disorders in border areas were being put down with "armed forces using machine guns and in some places cannons. There are 100 killed and shot and a few hundred wounded."[25]

Having very little weaponry, the peasants could not withstand well-armed OGPU detachments and mobilized Communists. Their isolated attempts to join forces—by sending messengers and delegations to neighboring villages or sounding the alarm using church bells—were ineffective. The uprisings remained fractured and uncoordinated. Such weaknesses made the task of mobile punitive detachments easier and permitted them to control large areas at once. Mass arrests of the uprisings' ringleaders, kulaks, and the rural intelligentsia, along with the demonstrative brutality of government forces, undermined the resistance. Furthermore, the peasants' behavior was much more civilized than the government's. They generally did not kill their tormentors but merely drove them out of their villages. As a result, the government forces suffered few casualties, partly due to false promises. Another important factor in the diminishing disturbances was the spring sowing. The peasants had little time for rebellion when there were crops to be planted. The fall harvest—on which life itself depended—would not come unless they dropped what they were doing and headed to the fields. By the time the 1930 harvest came, ruthless collectivization had resumed, and the majority of peasants had been forced into kolkhozes.

Collectivization was the cornerstone of Stalin's dictatorship, and all the other features of the Stalinist system can be seen as deriving from it. Wholesale violence against the country's largest class required a large apparatus of oppression, complete with a system of camps and places of exile. Beyond making it clear that terror was the primary instrument of government, collectivization completely and almost instantly severed countless traditional social connections, accelerated the atomization of society, and made ideological manipulation much easier. The rampant and merciless pumping of material and human resources out of the countryside enabled the pursuit of insanely ambitious economic goals.

Forced collectivization and ineffective industrialization dealt the country a blow from which it never fully recovered. In 1930–1932, hundreds of thousands of "wreckers" and "kulaks" were shot or imprisoned in camps, and more than 2 million kulaks and their family members were sent into exile.[26] Many of those exiled were just as doomed as those who were shot. Kulak families were sent to live in barracks not suitable for habitation and sometimes simply dropped off in open fields. Terrible living conditions, backbreaking labor, and hunger brought on mass fatalities, especially among children.[27]

The situation for peasants who were not arrested or exiled was hardly better. The Soviet village, ravaged by collectivization, was seriously degraded. Agricultural production plummeted, and the livestock sector was hit hard. Between 1928 and 1933 the number of horses dropped from 32 million to 17 million, heads of cattle fell from 60 million to 33 million and pigs from 22 million to 10 million.[28] Despite such declining productivity, the state pumped an ever-growing share of its yield out of the countryside. And yet throughout the Soviet period, the kolkhozes were unable to adequately feed the country. Most Soviet citizens survived on meager rations. Many periods were marked by famine. One of the worst was the famine of 1931–1933, the predictable result of Stalin's Great Leap.

■   FAMINE

When the time arrived to announce the results of the First Five-Year Plan, Stalin had to be creative. Exercising the privilege of power, he did not cite a single actual figure but simply proclaimed that the emperor was indeed wearing clothes. The Five-Year Plan, he said, had been fulfilled ahead of schedule![29] Of course the investment of vast resources and tons of equipment purchased from the West did yield results. Many modern factories were built, and industrial production did increase significantly. But there was no miracle. The unachievable five-year targets were, predictably, not achieved. The actual production figures were not even close: 6.2 million metric tons of cast iron in 1932 instead of the desired 17 million; 21.4

million tons of petroleum instead of 45 million; 48,900 tractors instead of 170,000; 23,900 automobiles instead of 200,000.[30] The state of consumer goods manufacturing was particularly lamentable.

But the main problem with the First Five-Year Plan was that it established a ruinously inefficient approach to industrialization. Vast sums and resources were poured into undertaking construction that was never completed; into equipment for which no use was ever found, purchased from abroad out of Soviet gold reserves; into wasteful redesigns, the inevitable result of excessive haste; and into goods so poorly produced as to be unusable. The task of arriving at an approximation of these losses rests with historians. Much better known are the statistics from another tragic result of the Great Leap—the toll taken by the Great Famine.

This famine, which reached its peak over the winter of 1932–1933, took the lives of between 5 million and 7 million people.[31] Millions more were permanently disabled. In a time of peace and relatively normal weather, agriculturally rich regions were ruined and desolated. Although the famine was a complex phenomenon, posterity has every right to call it the Stalin Famine. The Stalinist policy of the Great Leap was its primary cause; moreover, it was Stalin's decisions in 1932 and 1933 that, instead of easing the tragedy, made it worse.

The famine was the inevitable result of industrialization and collectivization. From a productivity standpoint, the kolkhozes were a poor substitute for the destroyed farms of those who had been branded "kulaks." The only advantage of the kolkhozes was that they gave the state a convenient means of channeling resources out of the countryside. The exceptional exploitation of peasants had two effects: agricultural workers were physically weakened by hunger, and they were deprived of any incentive to work, leading to despondency and apathy. They knew in advance that everything they grew would be taken by the state, dooming them, at best, to semi-starvation. Several years of this policy led to a gradual decline in output. In 1932 the crops did not grow well and were also poorly harvested.

The state's interests and those of the peasants were diametrically opposed. The state was extremely aggressive in taking from the countryside as many resources as possible. The peasants, like famine victims all over the world, used "the weapons of the weak."[32] They sabotaged the fulfillment of their obligations to the state and tried to stash away stores to feed themselves. Stalin was well aware of the hostility of the forcibly collectivized countryside, but he placed the blame fully on the peasants' shoulders. They had declared war, he proclaimed, against the Soviet government.

The looming crisis was obvious to everyone, including Stalin, long before the famine entered its most critical phase. There were obvious steps that, if they did not prevent the famine altogether, could at least have diminished its impact. The first would have been to establish set norms for grain deliveries to the state—in other words, a move from a system of confiscation to a system of taxes. This step would have given the peasants an incentive to boost production. Stalin, however, rejected this approach.[33] He preferred to take as much as possible from the countryside without any constraints. Another step to alleviate the famine might have been to reduce grain exports or even buy grain abroad. Such purchases were made on a limited basis during the spring of 1932, so they were in principle possible.[34] But Stalin refused to make further purchases. Any concessions that hinted at the misguidedness of the Great Leap were contrary to his nature and politically dangerous to his dictatorship. To alleviate the pressure on the peasants there would have to be a reduction in the pace of industrial growth. Reluctantly, Stalin did agree to such a reduction in 1933, but his slowness to take action cost millions of lives.

⌈By the autumn of 1932, critical delays, stubbornness, and cruelty had led Stalin himself into a dead end. No good options remained. The harvest produced by the devastated countryside in 1932 was even worse than the poor harvest of 1931. Meanwhile, industrialization continued apace, and the Soviet Union's foreign debt for purchases of equipment and raw materials reached new heights. Given these circumstances, there was only a little room to maneuver. The government could mobilize all available resources, or dip into reserves, or appeal for international aid, as the Bolsheviks had done during the famine of 1921–1922.[35] These measures came with economic and political costs, but they were possible. Stalin probably did not even consider them. Instead, the state intensified pressure on the countryside.⌋

Documents discovered in recent years paint a horrific picture. All food supplies were taken away from the starving peasants—not only grain, but also vegetables, meat, and dairy products. Teams of marauders, made up of local officials and activists from the cities, hunted down hidden supplies— so-called *yamas* (holes in the ground), where peasants, in accordance with age-old tradition, kept grain as a sort of insurance against famine. Hungry peasants were tortured to reveal these *yamas* and other food stores, their families' only safeguard against death. They were beaten, forced out into sub-freezing temperatures without clothing, arrested, or exiled to Siberia. Attempts by peasants dying of hunger to flee to better-off regions were ruthlessly suppressed. Refugees were forced to return to their villages, doomed to slowly perish, or be arrested. By mid-1933 some 2.5 million people were in labor camps, prisons, or exile.[36] Many of them fared better than those who starved to death "in freedom."

At its peak in late 1932 and early 1933, the famine afflicted an area populated by more than 70 million people: Ukraine, the North Caucasus, Kazakhstan, and some Russian provinces. This does not mean that the remaining Soviet population of 160 million was eating normally. Many in regions not officially in a state of famine lived on the edge of starvation. The entire country was hit by epidemics, primarily typhus. Millions suffered serious illnesses, were left disabled, or died several years after the famine from the damage it had inflicted on their bodies. And no statistics can measure the moral degradation it caused. Secret OGPU and party summaries (svodkas), especially during the early months of 1933, are filled with accounts of widespread cannibalism. Mothers murdered their children, and deranged activists robbed and tormented the population.

While the entire country suffered from famine and mass repression, Ukraine and the North Caucasus were the most affected.[37] It was in these two important regions of the USSR where the policy of punishing grain requisitions and terror were most brutally applied. Two interrelated reasons explain Stalin's focus on these areas. The first could be described as economic. Ukraine and the North Caucasus supplied as much as half of all grain collected by the state. But in 1932–1933 they turned over 40 percent less than the previous year. While this decline was partially compensated by Russian grain-producing areas, which despite going hungry had significantly overfulfilled their plans, they could not completely make up the shortfall. In 1932 the state collected almost 20 percent less grain than in 1931.[38] These figures partially explain the demands Stalin placed on Ukraine and the North Caucasus. He wanted "his" grain and was infuriated that they were not providing it.

Second, Stalin saw the crisis of 1932 as the continuation of the war against the peasantry and as a means of consolidating the results of collectivization, and he had a point. In a letter to the Soviet writer Mikhail Sholokhov on 6 May 1933, he wrote: "The esteemed grain growers were in essence waging a 'quiet' war against Soviet power. A war by starvation."[39] He undoubtedly considered the peasantry of Ukraine and the North Caucasus to be at the forefront of this peasant army battling the Soviet government. These regions had always been hotbeds of anti-Soviet sentiment, and Ukraine had been at the forefront of the anti-kolkhoz movement in 1930.

Repeated incidents of unrest flared up in both Ukraine and the North Caucasus in 1931–1932. A further cause for concern was Ukraine's border with Poland. Stalin feared that Poland, in its hostility toward the USSR, could exploit the Ukrainian crisis.[40] Overall, as Hiroaki Kuromiya points out, Stalin was suspicious of all peasants, but "Ukrainian peasants were doubly suspect both for being peasants and for being Ukrainian."[41]

By proclaiming grain collection to be a war, Stalin was untying his own hands and the hands of those carrying out his orders. The ideological basis for this war was the Stalinist myth that "food difficulties" resulted from acts of sabotage by "enemies" and "kulaks." Any suggestion of a link between the crisis and government policy was categorically rejected. By blaming all food shortages on "enemies" and on the peasants themselves while also promoting the idea that the scale of the famine was being maliciously exaggerated, Stalin relieved himself and the central government of any obligation to help the hungry. A statement by the general secretary in February 1933 at a congress of kolkhoz shock workers shows the depth of his cynicism: "One of our achievements is that the vast masses of the poor peasants, who formerly lived in semi-starvation, have now, in the collective farms, become middle peasants, have attained material security. . . . It is an achievement such as has never been known in the world before, such as no other state in the world has yet made."[42] This statement came at a time when thousands were dying every day.

Stalin could not deceive everyone. In May 1933, as the famine raged, he met with Colonel Raymond Robins, an American progressive who sympathized with Soviet Russia. Robins was famous for his meetings with Lenin as a member of the Red Cross mission to Russia in 1917–18. Counting on Robins's help in strengthening relations with the United States, Stalin was friendly toward the American and adopted a tone of sincerity and candor. He knew that Robins was well informed about Soviet realities and did not dare deny that his country was afflicted by famine. In response to a direct question about the poor harvest of 1932, Stalin, after some lengthy equivocation, did admit that "some peasants are currently starving." The reasons he gave for the famine exhibited impressive inventiveness and imagination. Parasitically inclined peasants, he argued, who had joined the kolkhozes late and were not earning anything through them, were the ones starving. Independent peasant farmers who did not work on their own plots but lived by stealing grain from kolkhozes were also "going terribly hungry." They supposedly were left with nothing to eat after the introduction of harsh penalties for theft.[43] To top off these lies, Stalin assured Robins that the state was helping the victims of famine, even though the kolkhoz members themselves were against such aid: "The *kolkhozniks* are really mad at us—you shouldn't help idlers, let them die. That's how they are."[44] Robins was probably not convinced, but as a true diplomat, he did not press Stalin.

While it is difficult to know how much Stalin believed of his own explanations, his conversations with Robins tell us something about his thinking. First, he apparently knew about the famine and recognized it as an actual fact, not a fiction made up by "enemies." Second, he does not appear to put much store in his own accounts of underhanded plotting by enemies and wreckers. He does not mention this "problem" once in his talks with Robins, which may suggest an awareness of the true causes of the famine and its ties to collectivization. It is doubtful, however, that he ever admitted any mistakes, even to his closest associates. Only mythic explanations of reality served his purpose. Claims about enemies, sabotage by peasants, or mistakes by local bosses permitted him to deflect guilt and doom millions without wavering.

Stalin's comments do not reveal exactly what he knew about the famine. What did he have in mind when he admitted to Robins that some peasants were "going terribly hungry"? Did he see in his mind's eye images of walking skeletons; desperate people foraging through buried animal remains; mothers, mad from hunger, murdering their own children? Probably not. He only encountered ordinary people at orchestrated events, and Moscow, which he regularly saw from his car window, was the relatively well-fed façade of Soviet power. OGPU reports that have recently come to light offer a detailed description of the famine, of cannibalism, and spreading anti-Soviet sentiments among the populace.[45] But we do not know whether Stalin read these reports. One compelling document we do know he read is Mikhail Sholokhov's letter of 4 April 1933.[46] In horrific detail, the appalled writer described what was taking place near his home in Veshenskaya, in the Northern Caucasus:

> I saw things that I will remember until I die. . . . During the night—with a fierce wind, with freezing temperatures, when even the dogs hide from the cold—families thrown out of their homes [for failure to fulfill their grain quotas] set up bonfires in the lanes and sat near the flames. They wrapped the children in rags and placed them on ground that had been thawed by the fire. The unceasing crying of children filled the lanes. . . . At the Bazkovsky kolkhoz they expelled a woman with a baby. She spent the night wandering through the village and asking that she and

the baby be allowed inside to get warm. No one let her in [there were severe penalties for aiding "saboteurs"]. By morning the child had frozen to death in the mother's arms.

Sholokhov's letter describes how suspected hoarders were coerced into handing over their grain: mass beatings, the staging of mock executions, branding with hot irons, and hanging by the neck to induce partial asphyxiation during interrogations, among other methods. The writer did not attempt to whitewash the fact that the criminal abuses being perpetrated in the Veshensky District were part of a purposeful campaign by the regional authorities—not "deviations" by local zealots. But for obvious reasons, he did not press this point.

Stalin took the news in stride. He ordered that the Veshensky District be given additional grain assistance and that an investigation be conducted into the abuses Sholokhov described. Overall, however, he supported the local authorities. In a response to Sholokhov he accused the writer of taking a one-sided view and of covering his eyes to sabotage by peasants. The local leadership, some of whom were at first condemned to harsh punishment for abuses, were ultimately acquitted. On Stalin's orders they were simply removed from their posts and given reprimands. They were not even expelled from the party.[47] Stalin had no intention of retreating from his war against the peasants, however many innocent lives were taken in the process.

■ THE "MODERATE"

The victory over the peasants had all the hallmarks of defeat. Despite the campaign's extreme ruthlessness, the grain procurement plan was not fulfilled. And the 20 percent decline in grain collections between the meager harvest of 1931 and the disastrous one of 1932, bad as this was, paled in comparison to the decimation of the livestock sector. If ruthless measures could not squeeze food out of the countryside, what should be done next? Continuing a policy of confiscation—*prodrazverstka*—would only kill off the population. Furthermore, the policy of forced industrialization was proving untenable. The mad surge of capital investment in heavy industry had reached its limit. Trotsky's call to make 1933 "a year of capital repair" resonated with Stalin's opponents, who called on him to reduce the pace of growth.[48]

Even the relentless terror machine was beginning to falter. By 1933 the large network of camps and prisons could not handle the growing flood of arrestees. The government took urgent steps to create remote settlements capable of accommodating 2 million internal deportees, but this program failed because of a lack of resources. In the end, only about 270,000 people were sent into internal exile.[49] The seemingly limitless capacity for destroying and isolating "enemies" apparently had its limits. And while the execution, arrest, and deportation of vast numbers helped the government maintain control, even Stalin could see that these tactics were doing as much to undermine the smooth running of the system as to bolster it.

All this dysfunction weakened the USSR at a time of escalating international tension. One of the first signs of looming war was Japan's occupation of Manchuria in late 1931. "The Japanese are certainly (certainly!) preparing for war against the USSR, and we have to be ready (we must!) for anything," Stalin wrote to Ordzhonikidze in June 1932.[50] An urgent buildup of military forces was begun in the Soviet Far East. But trouble was also brewing in Europe. In January 1933, while the Soviet Union was in the throes of famine, the Nazis came to power in Germany. The Bolsheviks' European strategy, which was centered on building relations with Weimar Germany, had to be immediately revamped. Faced with growing threats from east and west, Stalin was forced to seek alliances with Western democracies. On 19 December 1933 the Politburo adopted a top secret resolution concerning the USSR's possible entry into the League of Nations and conclusion of a regional mutual defense pact against Germany with a number of Western countries, including France and Poland.[51] Stalin understood that this new foreign policy would not be possible unless he sent clear signals that the Stalinist USSR was a "normal" country and not simply a convenient enemy of fascism. The Soviet regime would need to improve its reputation. Soviet leaders did not have to exchange their military service jackets for tailcoats, but they at least needed to button up.

Stalin had led the Bolsheviks into a dead end. The resources that had made the First Five-Year Plan possible had been used up. Too late for countless victims of his policies, he agreed to measures that could and should have been taken years before.

First among them were some minor but critical concessions to the peasantry. Although the Stalinist state continued to rely primarily on compulsion in the countryside, there were important changes. Essentially recognizing the tremendous harm done by limitless confiscations, in January 1933 the government introduced set quotas for grain deliveries (a food tax or *prodnalog,* in official Soviet parlance). The peasants were promised that predictable quotas would be set for the amount of produce to be taken and that they would have the right to sell the surplus. The resolution mandating this change was never put into practice, but it was a milestone in the transition from the Stalin-era War Communism of the First Five-Year Plan to the Stalin-era NEP of the Second. It was within the framework of this transition that other, more practical and effective, decisions were adopted.

Stalin grudgingly allowed peasants to have small private plots that they were allowed to cultivate for their own benefit, a concession of great importance to the survival of the countryside and the country overall. At the first congress of "kolkhoznik-udarniks" (collective farm shock workers) in February 1933, he promised that the state would help each kolkhoz household acquire a cow over the coming two years.[52] Laws guaranteeing ownership of farm plots were gradually put into place. This expansion of private agriculture was critically important, paving the way toward a new compromise between the state and the peasants. The peasants, who earned almost nothing working on collective farms, would now be able to make ends meet by farming their private plots. Despite being subject to exorbitant taxes, these plots were exceptionally productive. Although private agriculture took up a miniscule amount of land compared with the kolkhozes, official statistics from 1937 show that it provided 38 percent of the country's vegetables and potatoes and 68 percent of its meat and dairy products.[53] When yet another famine hit after the poor harvest of 1936, it was private agriculture that helped the country survive, once again underscoring how flawed the original collectivization plan had been. If the mad rush toward total collectivization had been adjusted to allow private plots, peasants (and Soviet agriculture) would not have been utterly ruined overnight.

Also long overdue and unavoidable were changes to industrial policy. The first limited signs that the state was being compelled to pull back from the destructive policy of forced industrialization and repression against those running the Soviet economy came in 1931–1932. During the Central Committee plenum of January 1933, Stalin provided a new set of slogans to go with the new policies. While proclaiming new class battles ahead, he nevertheless promised that the pace of industrial construction during the Second Five-Year Plan would be significantly reduced. Unlike many other slogans, this one did not prove empty. Alongside reduced growth for capital investment in industry, in 1934–1936 various experiments and reforms were introduced aimed at enhancing enterprises' economic independence and reviving financial incentives for labor. By this time, the idea of an economy based on the exchange of goods had been definitively rejected as "leftist," "money" and "commerce" were no longer dirty words, and the need to strengthen the ruble was a hot topic. That Stalin was reorienting the economic signposts became apparent in his remarks during a discussion on abolishing the ration system at the November 1934 plenum:

> Why are we abolishing the ration system? First and foremost it is because we want to strengthen the cash economy. . . . The cash economy is one of the few bourgeois economic apparatuses that we, socialists, must make full use of. . . . It is very flexible; we need it. . . . To expand commercial exchange, to expand Soviet commerce, to strengthen the cash economy— these are the main reasons we are undertaking this reform. . . . Money will start to circulate, money will come into fashion, which hasn't been the case for some time; the cash economy will be strengthened.[54]

Underlying this liberalization was a recognition of the importance of personal interests and material incentives. The sermons on asceticism, calls for sacrifice, and hostility toward high salaries that had characterized the First Five-Year Plan were replaced by a focus on "culture and a prosperous life." Instead of the mythic images of a future of abundant socialism that had been promoted with the First Five-Year Plan, the Soviet people, especially the urban population, were now offered the prospect of tangible creature comforts: a private room, furniture, clothing, a tolerable diet, and expanded leisure. The possibility of an improved standard of living was being deliberately used to motivate the workforce.

The improved quality of life after the successful harvest of 1933 was, of course, remarkable only in contrast with the previous years' mass famine. The full store shelves seen in major cities came as some rural areas continued to starve. But compared to 1932–1933, these pockets of hunger were "nothing," just as the ongoing arrests and deportations could be seen as "nothing" compared with previous years. For a while, state terror continued at a low and predictable pace. The pullback began with a special directive Stalin signed in May 1933 calling for the release of some of those arrested for "minor crimes" from overcrowded prisons and prohibiting the secret police from conducting mass arrests and deportations.[55]

Stalin continued to demonstrate adherence to "socialist legality." It was on his instigation that in February 1934 the Politburo voted to abolish the odious OGPU and place the political police under the newly formed People's Commissariat for Internal Affairs (NKVD), blending it with the more innocuous branches of law enforcement and public safety. On paper, people's rights in the regular judicial system were expanded, and the power of extrajudicial bodies—the instruments of mass terror—was reduced.[56] The handling of certain legal matters in which Stalin clearly had a hand was especially significant. Within the Soviet political system, it was these signals from the *vozhd* that showed the way forward for government officials.

One of the first such signals had to do with the conviction of Aleksei Seliavkin. During the witch hunt of the early 1930s Seliavkin, a senior heavy-industry official and decorated Civil War veteran, had been sentenced to ten years for selling classified military documents. In a petition sent from labor camp, Seliavkin stated that his interrogators had dictated a false confession and forced him to sign it under threat of being shot.[57] This petition came at an opportune time. Stalin (without whose consent Seliavkin would never have been arrested in the first place) now signaled leniency. Not surprisingly, an investigation showed that the secret police had fabricated the evidence. On 5 June 1934 the Politburo annulled Seliavkin's sentence and demanded "attention to serious deficiencies in the handling of the case by OGPU investigators."[58]

The annulment of Seliavkin's sentence was just the start. In September 1934 Stalin ordered the Politburo to establish a commission to investigate several other cases that had been brought against "wreckers" and "spies." He called on the commission to free the innocent, purge the OGPU of perpetrators of certain "investigative techniques," and punish them "without favoritism." "In my opinion," he wrote, "this is a serious matter and it has to be pursued to the end." Surviving documents show that this commission actually took its work seriously, assembling evidence of secret police abuses. There was no shortage of cases.[59]

Then came the murder of Leningrad party boss Sergei Kirov. The commission never completed its task.

Had it not been for Kirov's murder, would there have been a serious effort to put an end to secret police abuses? The evidence suggests otherwise. Although there were fewer arrests in 1934, the victims of repression still numbered in the hundreds of thousands. Stalin himself sent contradictory signals. In September 1934, at the height of the campaign for "socialist legality," the Politburo sanctioned the execution of a group of employees of the Stalin Metallurgical Factory in Siberia who were accused of spying for Japan. It was Stalin who instigated the roundup, writing: "Everyone caught spying for Japan should be shot."[60] There were other examples. The foundation of Stalin's system of oppression was never dismantled. The "moderation" of 1934 was nothing more than a temporary adjustment in the level of terror.

Although this moderation was inconsistent and limited, it did imply recognition that the Great Leap policy had been misguided. In theory, this forced change-of-course might have cast an unfavorable light on Stalin and prompted dissatisfaction with him. Such apparently logical inferences have inspired historians to posit the existence of plots and intrigues against Stalin among the party ranks. One focus of these theories is Sergei Kirov, a close Stalin associate and the Leningrad party boss. The confusion surrounding the circumstances of Kirov's murder and the crackdown that followed it have led some to conclude that Kirov was actually behind the new political moderation, making him someone an anti-Stalin movement might rally around. This speculation, of which there has been a great deal, is based solely on the memoirs of people with only a second- or third-hand knowledge of the central facts in the matter.[61]

Setting aside the many discrepancies in these "eyewitness" accounts, we are left with the following picture. During the Seventeenth Party Congress a number of senior party officials (various names are mentioned) discussed the possibility of removing Stalin as general secretary and replacing him with Kirov. Kirov rejected this proposal, but Stalin got wind of the plans. According to some accounts, Kirov himself told Stalin what others were plotting. During Central Committee elections at the congress, many delegates supposedly voted against Stalin. On learning about this, Stalin allegedly ordered the removal of any ballots where his name was crossed out. Ten months later, he organized Kirov's murder in order to remove a dangerous rival. These contradictory accounts have never inspired much confidence, and now that the archives have been opened, they appear even less convincing. A number of painstaking searches have failed to turn up even circumstantial evidence of a plot against Stalin.

The details of Kirov's party career offer scant evidence that he enjoyed an independent political position and much to suggest that he did not. Like other Politburo members in the 1930s, Kirov was a Stalin man. His initiatives were confined to the needs of Leningrad—requests for such items as new capital investment and resources or for the opening of new stores. He rarely came to Moscow to attend Politburo meetings or participated in voting on Politburo resolutions or the polling of its members. Not only was Kirov not a reformer, but the available documents do not even show that he took any serious part in developing or implementing high-level political decisions. He was Stalin's faithful comrade-in-arms and remained so to the end. Within the party he was never regarded as a political leader on a par with Stalin, and he did not promote any political programs that differed from Stalin's.[62] His death had an incomparably greater effect on the country's development than his life. As often happens, it was his death that turned Kirov into a legend.

■ **THE MURDER**

Kirov was killed on 1 December 1934 in Leningrad's Bolshevik headquarters in the Smolny Institute, a neoclassical building that formerly housed Russia's first educational institution for girls. In the seven decades between the 1918 attempt on Lenin's life and the end of the Soviet regime, this was the only successful assassination attempt against a senior Soviet official. But that is not what has drawn the attention of historians. The shots fired in the Smolny Institute were followed by a new intensification of repression that is often treated as a step toward the Great Terror of 1937–1938 and the ultimate consolidation of Stalin's dictatorship. The obvious political benefit that Stalin derived from Kirov's murder has led historians to suspect he had a hand in bringing it about. Such suspicions even became part of official propaganda during Khrushchev's de-Stalinization effort and Gorbachev's perestroika. Although it is rarely helpful when politicians involve themselves in the interpretation of past events, this case may be an exception. The numerous commissions established by Khrushchev and Gorbachev compiled and studied a great body of evidence, which gives us a rather full picture of what occurred in Leningrad on 1 December 1934 and during the murder's aftermath.[63]

On the evening of 1 December, a meeting of party stalwarts was scheduled to take place in Leningrad's Tauride Palace. Kirov was to give a speech on the outcome of the Central Committee plenum that had taken place in Moscow the previous day. The topic at hand was the upcoming abolition of the ration system, a change that would affect virtually the entire population of the country. An announcement of the meeting had already been published in newspapers, and Kirov spent the entire day preparing his speech. At approximately four o'clock he summoned a car and headed to his Smolny office. Using the building's main entrance, he climbed to the third floor, where his office and the offices of the oblast committee were located. He walked down the third floor's main corridor to a smaller corridor to the left that led to his office. It was the job of his bodyguard, Mikhail Borisov, to keep watch over the party boss inside the building. Borisov followed Kirov at a slight distance. When Kirov turned into the small corridor leading to his office, Borisov continued down the main corridor. Kirov remained out of his sight for some moments.

Leonid Nikolaev, a party member and former employee of the Leningrad

Oblast Committee, was preparing to shoot Kirov that evening at the Tauride Palace. To gain entry he needed an invitation card, and he had come to Smolny to get one, counting on help from acquaintances who worked there. Because he had a party membership card, he had no trouble entering the building. While wandering its corridors, Nikolaev unexpectedly saw Kirov walking toward him. Nikolaev turned away and let Kirov pass. Since there was nobody between him and his target, Nikolaev decided to carry out his plan immediately. He followed Kirov into the corridor leading to his office, ran up to him, and shot him in the back of the head. Nikolaev then attempted to shoot himself in the temple but was prevented from doing so. Borisov and several Smolny staff members had come running at the sound of gunfire and saw Kirov lying bloody on the floor. It was all over in an instant.

Doctors and the heads of the Leningrad NKVD were summoned to Smolny. Stalin was telephoned at his Kremlin office. As soon as he was told of Kirov's death, the general secretary convened a series of meetings. Early the following morning, on 2 December, he arrived in Leningrad on a special train. That same day he joined other members of the team from Moscow in interrogating Nikolaev. Stalin could hardly have failed to notice that Nikolaev was not a typical ideologically motivated terrorist.

In December 1934 Leonid Vasilyevich Nikolaev was 30 years old. He had been born into a working-class family in St. Petersburg and lost his father at an early age. His family struggled with poverty, and rickets prevented Leonid from walking until the age of eleven. The record of his recruitment for military training provides a detailed description of his physical features at age twenty: long arms that extended to the knees, an elongated torso, and a height of approximately five feet. Nikolaev was often ill and had a quarrelsome disposition, but his early professional life was nevertheless fairly successful. Since his social origins were of the "correct" sort, he was able to get a job working for the Komsomol and join the party, steps that opened the door to other advantageous positions, including working for the Leningrad Oblast Committee in the same building where he later killed Kirov. But being prone to conflict, he could not hold any job for long. He was unemployed during the months leading up to the murder and spent his time filing grievances with various institutions and plotting revenge. The numerous diaries, letters, and other writings that were confiscated after his arrest show him to have been mentally unstable. His letters of grievance recounted various perceived injustices, demanded a job and a resort voucher, adopted a threatening tone, and assumed the pose of a hero whose name would go down in history alongside the great revolutionaries of the past.

Another factor contributing to Nikolaev's state of mind was his relationship with his wife, Milda Draule, whom he met when they both worked for the Komsomol. Draule, age thirty-three in 1934, appears to have been an attractive woman whose career, unlike Nikolaev's, was advancing successfully. In 1930, long-standing connections led to a secretarial job at the Leningrad Oblast Committee offices. There were rumors before Kirov's death that Draule was having an affair with him, and speculation about an affair has persisted ever since.[64] There is reason to believe that Kirov's childless marriage was an unhappy one. His wife, four years his senior, was often ill and spent months at a time away from home in sanatoriums or rest homes. Although there is no hard evidence to prove that Kirov and Draule were intimate, the possibility has to be recognized. Even if Nikolaev did not believe the rumors, one can only assume that they fostered animosity toward Kirov.

Such was the man brought before Stalin at Smolny on 2 December. The *vozhd* was undoubtedly briefed on Nikolaev's less than sterling work and party history and may even have been discreetly informed of the rumors about Kirov and Draule. Nikolaev's appearance tended to support the idea that the shooting was the act of an embittered loner of questionable mental competence. He was brought before the Moscow commission shortly after a severe hysterical fit brought on by the murder and his own failed suicide attempt. Molotov, who was with Stalin, remembered Nikolaev as follows: "Mousey. . . . Short and skinny. . . . I think something must have made him angry . . . and he looked like something had offended him."[65]

What Molotov remembers is probably what Stalin saw too, but treating Nikolaev as an unstable loner did not suit his purposes. Even before he left for Leningrad, an official account of Kirov's murder had been crafted. The following day, Soviet newspapers reported that Kirov had died "at the treacherous hand of an enemy of the working class." This interpretation was entirely predictable. At who else's hand could a Politburo member perish? Something as mundane as murder by a jealous husband was unthinkable. Only a devious enemy of the people would fit the part. Any other interpretation cast not only Kirov but also the entire regime in an unfavorable light, making it look incapable of protecting its leaders from deranged loners. The agreed-upon narrative fit Stalin's extreme suspiciousness and hunger for power.

Before returning to Moscow on the evening of 3 December, Stalin ordered that a case be fabricated to show that Nikolaev belonged to an organization comprised of former oppositionists, followers of Zinoviev, who had wielded power in Leningrad in the 1920s as head of city government. This task was assigned to Moscow-based NKVD investigators and Stalin's political commissars—Nikolai Yezhov and Aleksandr Kosarev, who remained behind in Leningrad. Two years later, at the February–March 1937 plenum, Yezhov said the following about the task assigned him: "Com. Stalin . . . called me and Kosarev and said, 'Look for murderers among the Zinovievites.'"[66] This assignment would, of course, require creativity and law breaking. Not only had Nikolaev never belonged to any oppositionist group, but the NKVD had also never turned up the slightest evidence of oppositionist sympathies. The only way to link Nikolaev and the Zinovievites was to manufacture evidence, so under Stalin's watchful eye, this is what the chekists did. During the investigation, Stalin was sent approximately 260 arrestee interrogation protocols and many reports. He met with senior members of the NKVD, the procuracy, and the Supreme Court's military collegium to discuss the investigation and trial. The historical record shows that he personally orchestrated the court sessions and assembled the groups of defendants in the Kirov case.[67]

In accordance with Stalin's orders, a series of trials was held in late 1934 and early 1935. Dozens of former oppositionists, whom investigators claimed had links to Nikolaev, were sentenced to be shot or imprisoned.[68] Political and moral responsibility for Kirov's murder was placed on the shoulders of the former opposition leaders Zinoviev and Kamenev, who were also put on trial. The evidence on which they were convicted was blatantly fabricated. Stalin was settling scores with his old political rivals and charging them with crimes they had not committed.

Stalin's exploitation of Kirov's murder has prompted a great deal of suspicion over the years. Many have accused Stalin of organizing the shooting itself. The first serious attempts to look into such accusations were undertaken during the Khrushchev thaw and continued with small interruptions into the early 1990s. These investigations have turned up some circumstantial evidence of Stalin's involvement but no proof. At this point, it is unlikely any will be found.

Until the early 1990s, most theories about a plot by Stalin against Kirov adhered to the same basic storyline. Displeased by Kirov's growing popularity, Stalin decided to deal with the situation and then use the murder as a pretext for mass repression. With this goal, the general secretary either directly or implicitly assigned Genrikh Yagoda, then NKVD chief, to handle the matter.[69] Yagoda sent a trusted protégé, Ivan Zaporozhets, to serve as deputy in the Leningrad branch of the NKVD, where he could lay the groundwork for this supposed "act of terrorism." Nikolaev was chosen to carry out the deed and was armed and taken under Zaporozhets's wing. When he was arrested by NKVD agents after trying to carry out the assassination before 1 December, Zaporozhets arranged to have him released. After Kirov's murder, those involved in the conspiracy killed the bodyguard, Mikhail Borisov, because he knew too much. On 2 December he was killed in a staged accident while being taken to Stalin by truck for questioning. Such is the basic narrative proposed by those suspecting Stalin of complicity in Kirov's death.

This narrative does not stand up to careful examination. First of all, it is unclear why Stalin would enter into a conspiracy so fraught with risk, given that Kirov was a faithful client rather than a political rival. The evidence is also not convincing. To start with, the argument that Nikolaev would not have been able to get a firearm without help is flawed. The restrictions on gun ownership that were introduced later in the decade (partly in response to the Kirov murder) did not yet exist. Nikolaev acquired his revolver in 1918, when the country was awash in firearms, and had legal possession of it for sixteen years.[70] Such ownership was nothing out of the ordinary, especially for a party member.

As for Nikolaev's multiple detentions by the NKVD before 1 December and his "miraculous" release, records show only one such incident, not the several that some authors claim. On 15 October 1934, Nikolaev was detained by NKVD agents near Kirov's home but released shortly thereafter after his documents were checked. According to Nikolaev's own testimony, on that day he ran into Kirov and several companions and followed them to Kirov's house but did not work up the nerve to speak to Kirov. "Back then I was not thinking about committing murder," Nikolaev stated during his 2 December interrogation. After the murder, this incident, which was recorded in the NKVD incident log, was specially investigated. The NKVD agents who freed Nikolaev had a simple and convincing explanation: he had produced his party membership card and also an old identification card showing that he had worked at Smolny. His desire to approach Kirov to ask about the possibility of a job was "natural and did not arouse suspicion."[71]

A cornerstone of the theories that Kirov's murder was part of a plot is the death of the bodyguard, Borisov. During the second half of 1933, Kirov's security team had grown to fifteen people, each with his own job. Borisov was charged with meeting Kirov at the entrance to Smolny, accompanying him to his office, waiting in the reception area while Kirov worked, and accompanying him out of the building when he left. One other member of the team—an NKVD agent like Borisov—was N. M. Dureiko, who watched over

Kirov as he moved around the third floor of Smolny.[72] When the shot was fired, Dureiko was walking toward Kirov in the small corridor leading to his office. It could be argued that Dureiko was just as culpable in not preventing the murder as Borisov. Nevertheless, those promoting the idea of a plot have never taken an interest in Dureiko. If the plotters felt they had to do away with Borisov, why did they leave Dureiko alive?

Much importance has been assigned to the fact that Borisov did not follow Kirov when he turned toward his office, thus allowing Nikolaev to carry out his assassination, but Borisov's behavior is not as sinister as the conspiracy theorists have made it out to be. If we put ourselves in the shoes of this fifty-three-year-old bodyguard who had been protecting Kirov since he had arrived in Leningrad in 1926, his behavior seems entirely normal. All those years, day in and day out, he had to stick close to a man who, by many accounts, was not easy to guard. Kirov was reportedly annoyed when his bodyguards remained too close, and at times he even escaped from them. With his long experience working for Kirov, Borisov was surely sensitive to his boss's moods and tried not to irritate him. On 1 December in Smolny he kept his usual distance. Furthermore, as he walked down the corridor, Kirov stopped several times to have short conversations. Discretion demanded that Borisov step aside at such times. There was nothing unusual about this behavior.

On 2 December, the Moscow commission decided to question Borisov. He was escorted to Smolny by two other NKVD agents. Because no cars were available (not surprising given how many officials had suddenly descended on Leningrad from Moscow), Borisov was brought in a truck that turned out to be in disrepair. The driver lost control of the vehicle and crashed into a building. Borisov's head hit a wall of the building, and he died in the hospital without ever regaining consciousness. This is the sequence of events established by investigations and expert assessments conducted at various times, and there is no evidence to the contrary.[73] Proponents of a plot reject the idea that the vehicle crashed by accident and claim that Borisov was murdered.

The idea that Stalin was behind Kirov's murder has all the hallmarks of a conspiracy theory. Such theories tend to rest on the idea that if an event benefits some sinister person, he must have brought it about. They tend to deny the possibility of random occurrences and ignore the fact that chance events happen all the time. The idea that Stalin conspired to kill Kirov has received far too much attention. Even if he did have a hand in Kirov's death, this possibility hardly changes our understanding of him or his era. In the annals of the dictator's crimes, Kirov's murder would have been one of the least heinous.

■ REHEARSAL FOR THE GREAT TERROR

According to Stalin's relative Maria Svanidze, he was extremely upset by Kirov's murder. "He became pale and haggard, and there was a hidden suffering in his eyes." "I feel so alone," he reportedly confided to his brother-in-law, Pavel Alliluev.[74] There is no reason to doubt these accounts. Tyrants often combine exceptional cruelty and complete indifference to the deaths of millions with extreme sentimentality toward those near to them. In Stalin, Kirov's murder brought out both extremes. The way he used his friend's death as a pretext for a new campaign of terror is beyond cynical. Oppositionists falsely accused of plotting Nikolaev's crime were not the only ones swept up in the Kirov tributary of what would become the raging river of the Great Terror. Many thousands of Leningraders (so-called "formers"—former members of the nobility and clergy and former tsarist officials and military officers, among others) were sent into exile and to camps. The party was purged and articles of the penal code providing for the arrest of anyone suspected of "counterrevolutionary activities" were put to energetic use.

For a long time it was believed that this campaign marked the beginning of the wave of repression that came crashing down on the country during the second half of the 1930s. But a closer look at the sequence of events suggests a slightly different picture. In 1935 and 1936, terror coexisted with remnants of "moderate" policies. On 31 January 1935, at the very height of the "Kirov repression," the Politburo, on Stalin's instigation, adopted a decision to pass a new Soviet constitution.[75] A central feature of this document was the granting of voting rights to numerous groups previously unenfranchised as "alien elements." Now elections were to be direct and ballots secret rather than open, as they had been. These changes suggested the adoption of a more democratic constitutional model to replace the "revolutionary" one that excluded people with suspect class credentials. In a memorandum accompanying the draft Politburo resolution on the new constitution, Stalin wrote:

> In my opinion, this matter of a constitution for the Union of SSRs is a lot more complicated that it might seem at first glance. First of all, the electoral system has to be changed not only in the sense of making voting more direct. It also has to be changed in the sense of replacing open vot-

ing with closed (secret) voting. We can and must see this matter through to the end and not stop halfway. The situation and alignment of forces in our country is such that we can only benefit politically from this. I am not even talking about the fact that the need for such a reform is dictated by the interests of the international revolutionary movement since such a reform will definitely serve as a mighty weapon in the fight against international fascism.[76]

This memorandum suggests that even after Kirov's murder, Stalin counted on exploiting the advantages of the "moderate" course in both domestic and international affairs. International considerations were probably the main force driving his interest in liberalization. The growing threat from Germany and Japan was bringing the USSR closer to the Western democracies. In May 1935 the Soviet Union signed a treaty of mutual assistance with France and Czechoslovakia. The Seventh World Congress of the Comintern, held that summer, allowed for cooperation with socialist governments and endorsed the idea of an inclusive popular front against fascism. Hoping for leftward movement by the West European countries and a growth in pro-Soviet sentiments, Stalin saw a need to enhance the image of the "motherland of socialism" as a prosperous and democratic country.

The promise to restore the voting rights of those labeled socially alien was the centerpiece of a policy of reconciliation. In Stalin's mind, in addition to the vast numbers he considered true enemies in the country, there were also many more or less innocent victims of the bitter class struggle. Young people in particular had to be brought over to the regime's side. Continuing to discriminate based on family background threatened to expand the ranks of the government's potential opponents. An important signal in the reconciliation campaign was a piece of political theater Stalin performed at a meeting of combine operators in early December 1935. When a Bashkir kolkhoznik by the name of A. Tilba proclaimed from the podium, "I may be the son of a kulak, but I will fight honorably for the cause of workers and peasants and for the building of socialism," Stalin interjected a phrase that became famous: "The son does not answer for the father."[77] In fact, sons and daughters did answer for their fathers, and fathers for their children, but "alien elements" now had a better prospect of making their way in Soviet society. The promise of equal voting rights was accompanied by other liberalizing campaigns. For example, hundreds of thousands of people convicted of nonpolitical crimes were released from prison or rehabilitated.

A degree of social stability was needed to secure and promote the positive economic trends that began to appear in late 1933 and continued into 1934. The miserable experience of previous crises had taught Stalin the economic price to be paid for each new campaign of repression. In 1935 he made the most significant concession to the peasantry since the beginning of collectivization: the right to farm private plots was enshrined in law and somewhat expanded. This step enabled an improvement in the country's food situation. Similar improvements could be seen in industrial sectors in 1935–1936. In November 1935 Stalin invented a new slogan: "Life has become better, life has become more cheerful!" That year, the ration system began to be phased out, and certain limitations on salary increases were abolished. Financial incentives boosted productivity. These were good years for the Soviet economy.

One might think that the fruits of moderation would have inspired Stalin to try more of it. They did not, and a new wave of terror became increasingly evident. Historians are still trying to understand his motives for expanding repression at a time of social stability and an improving economy. Did Stalin truly believe that the country was threatened by terrorist conspiracies? Did he actually fear for his life? There is a fair amount of evidence to the contrary. Stalin commanded the NKVD to find proof that former oppositionists had gone underground and formed terrorist organizations, but try as it might, the NKVD was unable to do so. The cases that were brought did not have the ring of truth, and Stalin must have understood that they were fabricated. In any event, he did not make any changes in his daily life that would indicate a concern for his own safety. He adhered to his daily work schedule, traveled south for vacations, and occasionally went out among the people to demonstrate his solidarity.

On the evening of 22 April 1935, some of Stalin's relatives and fellow Politburo members gathered at his Kremlin apartment. Stalin was with his children. His daughter Svetlana asked permission to take a ride on the metro, which had recently opened. Stalin, in a good mood, decided to organize an excursion. Since no preparations had been made for this outing, he and his companions were surrounded by crowds of passengers at each station. Maria Svanidze wrote in her diary: "There was an unimaginable commotion and people rushed to greet the *vozhds,* cried 'Hurray,' and ran after us. We were all separated, and I came close to being crushed against a column. . . . It was a good thing that by then the police and bodyguards had arrived." Stalin's fourteen-year-old son Vasily "was the most agitated of all." But Stalin "was cheerful and asked the construction supervisor, who appeared out of nowhere, endless questions." At the next station Stalin again went onto the platform, but his relatives, including his daughter Svetlana, stayed in the metro car, "frightened by the unrestrained delight of the crowd, which in its excitement toppled a cast-iron lamppost not far from the *vozhds* at one station." After visiting the metro, Stalin went to his dacha. Vasily, traumatized by the crowds, "threw himself onto his bed and cried hysterically" as soon as he returned home. The adult relatives took sedatives.[78]

Would a man living in serious fear of attack venture—let alone relish— such an excursion? The intensification of repression that came in late 1934 was prompted by more complex calculations. Kirov's murder provided an ideal pretext for action of the sort any dictatorship relies on to promote its central task: solidifying the power of the dictator. Admittedly, by late 1934, Stalin was already a dictator, but dictatorships, like any unstable system of government, depend on the constant crushing of threats. During this period, Stalin faced two such threats, which at first glance appear unrelated. The first was the remnant of the system of "collective leadership" within the Politburo, and the second was the survival of a significant number of former oppositionists. These threats belonged to what might be called Bolshevik tradition. They hung over Stalin like a sword of Damocles, reminders that there were alternatives to sole dictatorship. His fellow Politburo members enjoyed significant administrative, if not political, independence. They ran the various branches of government and had a host of clients from within the party and state apparats. The bonds of institutional and clan loyalties, along with the vestiges of collective leadership and intraparty democracy, were the last impediments to sole and unquestioned power.

In a speech given in early 1937, Stalin divided senior officials into several categories. He labeled one "the generals of the party" (the three or four thousand most senior officials) and another "the party's officers" (thirty to forty thousand mid-level officials).[79] Until the mid-1930s, the party's old guard had held a place of honor within these two groups, but Stalin had reason to distrust these respected figures. Whatever they might say from the podium, however earnestly they swore allegiance to him, he knew: these party elders well remembered that Lenin's testament at one point almost brought Stalin's political career to an end, and he had held onto power only through the support of Zinoviev and Kamenev; that in the late 1920s Stalin had managed to defeat the Rykov-Bukharin group only with the support of the Central Committee; and that party policy in the 1930s had brought about catastrophic failures. By 1937, party functionaries had every reason to regard Stalin as "first among equals," but not so long ago he had been one among many jockeying for position. Stalin knew that the old guard had the clearest memory of that time.

Over long years of collaboration, the Old Bolsheviks had established close relationships with each other. Stalin periodically shuffled the deck, but it was hard to disrupt the networks of personal loyalty that had formed around officials at various levels. Leaders took "their people" with them from job to job. The people in these networks had divided loyalties: they served the dictator, but they also had their own patrons within the Politburo or other high-level bodies. Of course all of these groups lacked formal cohesion and political power. No one has yet found evidence of a serious effort by them to oppose Stalin. At most, they expressed their dissatisfaction privately. But like any dictator, Stalin assumed the worst. He anticipated being stabbed in the back the moment the domestic or international situation worsened. Replacing the old guard with absolutely devoted younger stalwarts was a critical aspect of his program to solidify his position. The growing threat of war provoked the *vozhd*'s anxiety and desire to secure his power in case the unexpected happened. "The conqueror's peace of mind requires the death of the conquered." This phrase, attributed to Genghis Khan, was underlined in one of the books in Stalin's library.[80]

The conquered—the repentant and humiliated former oppositionists— were indeed a worrisome subgroup within the community of Old Bolsheviks. Although the secret police kept a close watch over them, the former oppositionists were still party members in good standing. Many held posts within the government and even the party apparat, or they had senior positions in major economic enterprises. Most Old Bolsheviks remembered the role the oppositionists had played during the glory days of the revolution. Kirov's murder and the fabricated case alleging that followers of Zinoviev and Kamenev were involved in a terrorist plot changed everything. The former opposition was transformed overnight from comrades who had once committed political indiscretions into "enemies" and "terrorists."

The former oppositionists were not the only ones affected by this sudden transformation. Among the old guard it was hard to find anyone who was not in some way tied to them. A significant proportion of Soviet generals had served under Trotsky, who had founded the Red Army and led it for many years. Many up-and-coming functionaries had "erred" in their youth. In the 1920s, either because they were not yet sure which way the winds were blowing or were simply following their hearts, many had at some point supported the opposition. Others developed friendships with future members of the opposition during their years underground and during the revolution or when they fought side by side during the Civil War. Some had recently collaborated with repentant oppositionists. In short, in striking a blow against the former oppositionists, Stalin launched a huge shake-up in the party ranks. It allowed him both to take care of political opponents who might have been lurking in the shadows and to purge the apparat overall, including getting rid of some of his Politburo comrades.

Between 1935 and early 1937, the persecution of former oppositionists was accompanied by shake-ups at the highest echelons of power. The Kirov murder strengthened the position of three enterprising young men: Nikolai Yezhov, Andrei Zhdanov, and Nikita Khrushchev. Yezhov's promotion was especially significant. It was on his shoulders that Stalin placed direct responsibility for conducting the purge. After acquitting himself well in fabricating cases during the Kirov Affair, Yezhov was entrusted with a new assignment—the Kremlin Affair. In early 1935 a group of support staff working in government offices located in the Kremlin—maids, librarians, and members of the Kremlin commandant's staff—were arrested and accused of plotting against Stalin. Among those arrested were several relatives of Lev Kamenev, who was charged with hatching the plot.[81] The arrestees came under the authority of Stalin's old friend Avel Yenukidze, who oversaw the running of all Kremlin facilities, and he was accused of abetting the plot.[82] Stalin took a great interest in the Kremlin Affair. The archives show that he regularly received and read arrestee interrogation protocols, made notations on them, and gave specific instructions to the NKVD.[83]

Although Yenukidze was not a member of the Politburo, he was an intimate part of the system of collective leadership insofar as he was close friends with many top officials, including Stalin himself. Stalin in essence used Yenukidze to test the durability of the collective leadership system. This was the dictator's first significant strike against his inner circle. The test was successful. The Politburo offered only weak resistance, and Yenukidze was fired, arrested, and shot. For a while Stalin trod carefully, taking the operation one step at a time, but gradually the cleansing of the top nomenklatura picked up steam. A turning point was the first Moscow show trial of former opposition leaders in August 1936. After being extensively tortured, the defendants, who included Kamenev, Zinoviev, and other prominent party figures, were proclaimed terrorists and spies and then shot.

The August trial took the hunt for enemies to a new level of hysteria. Stalin appointed Yezhov to take over the NKVD, and under the *vozhd*'s guidance, he began preparing new trials and intensified the purge of the party and state apparats. In January 1937 a second show trial was held, this time of former oppositionists who held senior positions overseeing the economy and industrial enterprises. They were charged with wrecking and espionage. Stalin's close associates, compromised by ties with supposed enemies, gave in. Only Ordzhonikidze would not allow his underlings in the heavy-industry sector to be arrested, sparking a conflict with Stalin that ended with Ordzhonikidze's suicide.[84] This desperate act shows how helpless the Politburo members felt before Stalin, whose control of the secret police made him an indomitable force. The *vozhd*'s long-standing comrades-in-arms, to say nothing of middle-level functionaries, were a fractured force. They fell all over one another in an effort to ingratiate themselves with Stalin, each hoping to save his own skin.

Such was the state of affairs when the already thinned ranks of the nomenklatura convened for the February–March Central Committee plenum of 1937. During the plenum, Stalin ordered that repression be continued, and Yezhov made a speech calling for a case to be brought against the leaders of the "right deviation," Nikolai Bukharin and Aleksei Rykov (their fellow "rightist," Mikhail Tomsky, had already killed himself in August 1936). The plenum of course approved Yezhov's proposal. Bukharin and Rykov were arrested, and in March 1938 they were convicted to be shot at the third Moscow show trial. Like the other trials, this one was followed by a wave of spurious convictions across the country.

The repression that roiled the party and state apparats came down with particular force on the "power structures," the NKVD and the army—organizations that Stalin thought posed the greatest threat to his dictatorship. Once Yezhov took over the NKVD, he destroyed his predecessor, Yagoda, and many of his associates. In June 1937, after being tortured, a large number of senior military officers, including the deputy people's commissar for defense, Mikhail Tukhachevsky, were given death sentences based on trumped-up charges of belonging to an "anti-Soviet Trotskyite military organization."[85] Soon afterward, a wave of arrests swept through the entire army. Scholarly investigation of recently opened archives can now set decades-long debate to rest: the Tukhachevsky Affair and the entire anti-military campaign was based on evidence fabricated by the NKVD under Stalin's direct supervision. The charges brought against the military leaders had absolutely no basis in fact.[86]

At first, repression was primarily targeted at key members of the government, party, state security services, and military and had little effect on ordinary citizens. If the terror had been limited to the party-state nomenklatura, one might agree with those who have argued that Stalin's main goal was to destroy the party's old guard and install a new generation of functionaries blindly devoted to him. He did undeniably pursue this goal. But in the second half of 1937, the terror was brought to bear on a much larger swath of the Soviet population, and this expansion is what made it "the Great Terror." In terms of their scale and the number of victims, these later operations greatly overshadowed those primarily targeted at officials. After shooting a significant fraction of the nomenklatura, Stalin brought his terror to its logical conclusion. Having solidified power at the top, he undertook to purge the country of a suspected fifth column. The threat of a major war exacerbated Stalin's paranoia. Hundreds of thousands of innocent people paid the price.

TREPIDATION IN THE INNER CIRCLE

**The initial arrival of the four at the near dacha,
early morning hours of 2 March 1953.**

The bodyguard entered Stalin's apartments with the packet of mail and
started looking for him. After walking through several rooms, he finally
found the *vozhd* in the small dining room. The sight must have been
extremely disturbing. Stalin was lying helpless on the floor, which was
wet beneath him.[1] This last point is important not for reasons of schaden-
freude or as an evocative detail but because it affected subsequent events.
It appeared to the bodyguard that Stalin was unable to speak, but he did
make a small hand gesture, beckoning him to approach. The bodyguard
summoned his colleagues, who helped him lift Stalin onto the couch.
They then rushed to telephone their immediate superior, State Security
Minister Semen Ignatiev. According to the bodyguards' later accounts,
Ignatiev refused to make any decisions and told them to call members of
the top leadership: Beria and Malenkov.

Ignatiev's reaction was perfectly understandable. He was behaving just
as the bodyguards had done several hours earlier, when they were afraid
to enter Stalin's rooms uninvited. Ignatiev did not want to take responsibility for a decision to summon doctors to the *vozhd*. This was a ticklish
matter for a man who, just two years earlier, had been plucked from the
relatively cozy position of Central Committee department head and
assigned to hunt for enemies of the people as minister of state security.
He must have rued the day Stalin picked him for this job, which carried
a high price for failure. From then on he lived in fear. Upon hearing that
Stalin had suffered some sort of stroke, his only desire was to hand decision-making responsibility to somebody else.

Having failed to get any guidance from their boss, the bodyguards
managed to find Malenkov, who then informed the other members of the
ruling Five: Beria, Khrushchev, and Bulganin. This made sense. Without
a clear understanding of Stalin's condition, Malenkov did not want to go
to the dacha by himself or be the only one to sanction the summoning of
doctors. Any decisions should be made collectively. The four men agreed
to meet at the dacha to assess the situation and give each other cover for
whatever actions were taken.

Both Khrushchev's memoirs and the bodyguards' accounts describe the top leadership's extreme caution after arriving at the dacha in the middle of the night. They were afraid of doing anything that might provoke Stalin's wrath if he recovered. According to Khrushchev, at first they did not even enter Stalin's apartments, choosing instead to interrogate the bodyguards. What they heard made them even more nervous. That Stalin was incapacitated and had apparently urinated on himself put the leaders in a difficult position. They knew he would not want anyone to see him in such a state. What if this was just a passing episode? Stalin would not look fondly on anyone who had witnessed his humiliating helplessness. As Khrushchev describes it, once they learned from the bodyguards that Stalin "now seemed to be sleeping, we thought that since he was in such poor shape, it would be awkward for us to appear at his side and make our presence officially known. So we went back to our homes."[2]

Khrushchev's memoirs apparently do not tell the whole story. According to the bodyguards, before leaving, the four designated Malenkov and Beria to enter Stalin's rooms and personally assess his condition. Such an assessment required two men for obvious reasons. If all four went, they would make unnecessary noise and risk rousing the *vozhd*. And none of them wanted to go in by himself. Khrushchev and Bulganin thus waited in the bodyguards' quarters while Beria and Malenkov snuck stealthily in to look at Stalin, terrified of waking him. The bodyguards recalled one slapstick detail: Malenkov's new shoes made a squeaking noise, so he took them off and carried them under his arm. As the two men approached, they could hear Stalin lightly snoring. After emerging, Beria berated the bodyguards for raising a fuss over nothing. Stalin was just sleeping. The bodyguards defended their actions, explaining that matters had been much worse a few hours earlier.[3] Dismissing the bodyguards' concerns, the four men returned to Moscow.

Some historians and commentators have detected conspiratorial overtones in this episode and blame Stalin's death on the decision not to call for medical help. This interpretation is doubtful. First, according to the doctors who performed the autopsy, Stalin's stroke was the result of atherosclerosis that had been developing for years.[4] Quick intervention would not have saved him. On the other hand, his fellow leaders could not have known this. They did not understand the implications of providing or withholding medical care, and their failure to summon doctors could have contained some malicious intent. Many Soviet leaders, in their hearts, surely did not wish their abusive leader long life. Nevertheless, less sinister explanations must also be considered. Stalin's associates were simply afraid of intervening. They were not used to taking the initiative, and they knew Stalin's suspicious and capricious nature all too well. During those days in early March, everyone involved—the bodyguards, Ignatiev, and the other members of the Five—behaved exactly as Stalin had trained them to behave. They tiptoed nervously forward, always looking over their shoulders and trying to shift as much responsibility as possible onto each other.

For many years, even Stalin's closest associates and friends, people with whom he had shared long years of struggle, had lived under the constant threat of destruction. A dictator can only be sure of his power if those around him are at his mercy. After destroying the former opposition leaders, in 1937–1938 Stalin proceeded to have a significant portion of the Politburo shot. The close relatives of some of his surviving associates were also arrested or killed. The brother of Politburo member Lazar Kaganovich committed suicide, and Kalinin's wife wound up in a camp.[5] This suppression of potential oligarchs continued after the war. The Leningrad Affair did away with Nikolai Voznesensky and Aleksei Kuznetsov, two members of the younger generation who had risen to prominence under Stalin.[6] Molotov's wife was arrested around the same time. In the final months of his life, Stalin lashed out at Molotov and Mikoyan, essentially removing them from power. His death would provide the only guarantee against new purges.

At some point in their careers, virtually everyone in the top Soviet leadership had to endure a ritual of humiliation and repentance followed by renewed oaths of allegiance to the *vozhd*. Stalin would cast his comrades into disfavor only to later bring them back into the fold. He was generous with rebukes and liked to orchestrate verbal floggings in the press and at various meetings. And when he lost his temper, it was a horrifying sight to behold. Minister of Foreign Trade Mikhail Menshikov told of one instance when he incurred Stalin's wrath during a meeting by failing to properly hear his question. "He gave me a furious look," Menshikov recalled, "and launched a fat pencil at me as hard as he could, hurling it along the length of the table in my direction. For a moment everyone froze and waited to see what would happen next."[7] After Stalin's death, Ignatiev complained about having been subjected to constant dressings-down: "Comrade Stalin reprimanded me using fouler language than I'd ever heard in my life and called me an idiot."[8] When the writer Konstantin Simonov attended the Central Committee plenum in October 1952, he was struck by the furious, "almost ferocious" and "unrestrained," tone of Stalin's speech denouncing Molotov and Mikoyan.[9] Stalin's temper and unpredictability, especially during his final years, were made worse by his declining health.

Top Soviet officials lived a golden-cage existence. While they exercised life-and-death power over their subordinates, they were at the constant mercy of their ultimate boss. Their security, transportation, incoming and outgoing correspondence, special telephone lines, dachas, and apartments—all were handled by state security, which was entirely under the dictator's control. Such control meant that Stalin knew everything about how and with whom these officials spent their time. As if that were not enough, he apparently asked the secret police to install listening devices to spy on certain Politburo members.[10]

Despite the oppression of the collective leadership, periodic manifestations of oligarchy inevitably threatened Stalin's sole power. Though very much under his thumb, his fellow leaders did enjoy a certain administrative autonomy as the heads of major government institutions, and they independently made many decisions of consequence for the running of the country. Furthermore, their authority expanded as Stalin's physical frailty diminished his involvement in day-to-day decision making. Stalin was aware of this threat. Konstantin Simonov recorded a typical comment by the *vozhd* about his comrades, as reported by an eyewitness:

> Even when differences remain, they will come to some agreement on paper and present the issue to me in that form. . . . The managers understand that I cannot know everything; all they want from me is a stamp with my signature. Yes, I cannot know everything, so I pay attention to differences, to objections, and I try to make sense of why they come up, where the real problem lies. The managers do their best to conceal these from me; they go along with the votes but they conceal the differences, all so that they can get a stamp with my signature. What they want out of me is my stamp.[11]

Stalin's method for penetrating the defenses of this mutual protection society could best be described as scattershot. The dictator's underlings never knew what question might suddenly interest him. They never knew whether Stalin would react to a particular decision and, if so, how or when. The constant threat of a random attack allowed him to keep the apparat and his close associates in a state of tension that helped to compensate for his lack of total control over them. The *vozhd*'s effort to maximize his power over his subordinates was helped by the number of channels through which he received information. The government and party bureaucracies, the courts, and state security all kept an eye on one another and constantly tried to prove their vigilance and effectiveness by denouncing one another to Stalin, zealously exposing others' warts while concealing their own.

Repression, the constant threat of punishment, and Stalin's temper and whims made the life of top Soviet officials almost as difficult as that of the powerless man or woman on the street. His "comrades" lived and worked under constant stress. One long-term Soviet diplomat left the following remembrance of the country's minister of foreign affairs, Andrei Vyshinsky, one of Stalin's most devoted and successful associates: "Vyshinsky was terrified of Stalin. Every Thursday he would go and report to him, and well beforehand, in anticipation of this encounter, his mood would sour. The closer it came to Thursday, the gloomier and more irritable he got. . . . But by Friday, when it was all behind him, he allowed himself to relax for a day or two. Experienced people knew that this was when it was best to report to him on the most complicated matters or approach him with requests of a personal nature."[12]

Stalin was a merciless boss. He expected total dedication from his subordinates and favored a military management style: orders had to be carried out unquestioningly and at any cost—no excuses. In addition to the constant danger of arrest and the excessive workload, the lives of Stalin's close associates were made difficult by his nocturnality. To accommodate the *vozhd*, the apparat worked both at night, when Stalin was awake, and during the day, when the rest of the country was up. The stresses of working for Stalin apparently made some stronger. A number of his closest associates lived many years. Molotov and Kaganovich, for example, nearly reached the century mark. But not everyone had the iron constitution and adaptability needed to survive the demands Stalin placed on his subordinates. A Central Committee document written in 1947 admitted that "An analysis of the health of the party and government's leading cadres has shown that many individuals, even among the relatively young, suffer from diseases of the heart and the circulatory and nervous systems sufficiently serious to impact their ability to work. One cause of these diseases is stressful work not only during the day, but also during the night, and often even on holidays."[13] As long as Stalin was alive, nothing could be done about this problem, but soon after his death a resolution was adopted requiring regular government offices to remain closed at night, and the bureaucracy began to run in a more normal way.

Stalin kept himself at the center of the huge machine used to manipulate officials. He initiated and guided repression, orchestrated all major reassignments, and was constantly reshuffling people so that nobody grew too comfortable in a particular job. Like any dictator, he strove to instill a sense of fear, adoration, and instinctive devotion in his underlings. Vyacheslav Molotov, a diehard follower of the dictator, described Lazar Kaganovich as a "two hundred percent Stalinist."[14] These were the sorts of people Stalin tried to cultivate.

A key element of the process by which the Soviet government—including its very top leadership—was "Stalinized" was the mass purges of the 1930s. In a matter of months, the purges destroyed the party's old guard and replaced it with fresh faces, unburdened by excessive knowledge of the past or ideas about how the country might be run differently. "New stock" replaced officials who had earned their places in the Soviet government during the revolution. By 1940, after the Terror had receded, 57 percent of party secretaries in the regions of Russia and on the central committees of the Soviet Union's ethnic republics were under the age of thirty-five.[15] Many ministers, generals, directors of major enterprises, and leaders of cultural unions were between thirty and forty.

Stalin gave these upstarts tremendous power, allowing them to preside over their own little dictatorships. The fates, even the lives, of millions were in their hands. The distribution of significant resources and the functioning of gigantic enterprises depended on them. They formed their own caste, which lived by its own laws and enjoyed its own privileged world. The members of this caste did not know hunger or material want. They were not affected by the catastrophic shortage of housing or the backwardness of the health care system. They lived in spacious apartments and dachas, protected by guards. Their cars sped past overcrowded public buses and trolleys. Whoever did their shopping did not have to line up for hours outside empty stores. Their salaries and tax-free supplemental pay (known as "envelopes") exceeded by orders of magnitude the meager pay of ordinary citizens. The fees paid to Soviet writers privileged to belong to the nomenklatura reached the hundreds of thousands of rubles, in some cases generating annual incomes of up to a million rubles, many thousands of times what a Soviet peasant survived on.[16] Dazzled by the sense of belonging to an all-powerful government corporation and by their own importance, they were utterly free of compassion, self-reflection, or understanding of the "other."

Stalin was the gatekeeper for the world of the nomenklatura. Entry could be gained only with his favor and support. For those fortunate enough to survive, the horrible fates of their predecessors and the continuing repression only intensified their gratitude toward the dictator. Stalin was twice the age of many members of this new generation of officials. Many of them knew little of the party's revolutionary period or of former leaders who were now labeled enemies. For them, Stalin was the ultimate authority, the leader of the revolution, the victorious generalissimo, and a theoretician on a par with the founders of Marxism.

Stalin strove variously to feed this image. He cultivated an inferiority complex in his close associates: "You are blind like little kittens. Without me the imperialists would strangle you."[17] Gradually he acquired the exclusive right to advance any initiative of significance, leaving the operational details to his comrades. His speeches, conversations, and letters were like lectures that he laced with contrived profundities. He liked to assign meaning to events and show off his vast knowledge and deep understanding of problems. The self-confident tone of his pontificating often belied the flimsiness and artificiality of his reasoning. But who would dare challenge him? For most functionaries, who tended to lack sophistication, Stalin's utterances had an almost sacred quality. However, it was not just his monopoly on theoretical pronouncements that made the *vozhd* the voice of authority. He was well read and had a good memory, as well as a knack for pithy aphorisms. He would spend time preparing for his meetings, and it enabled him to show an impressive knowledge of detail. Such knowledge left a deep impression on many who witnessed these performances.

The primary reason that every utterance by Stalin carried such weight was that these were the words of an enormously powerful dictator who inspired both horror and adoration. To promote this image, he adopted the manner of a judge and master of destinies. During conferences he did not fraternize with other attendees but strolled around, pipe in hand. Before the spellbound gazes of onlookers, he reasoned out loud as if mulling weighty decisions. Stalin never publicly spoke of himself as a great man. It was enough that official propaganda shouted his greatness to the point of absurdity. Aware that brilliance stands out nicely against a façade of modesty, Stalin presented himself as a mere disciple of Lenin and servant of the party and the people. Every opportunity was taken to highlight this "humility." He feigned impatience or even embarrassment when greeted with the inevitable standing ovation. He peppered his speeches with self-deprecation and folksy humor. He helped certain visitors to his dacha with their coats. After arriving at a reception arranged by Mao Zedong during the Chinese leader's January 1950 visit to Moscow, Stalin greeted the cloakroom attendant but turned down his services. "Thank you, but this is something even I seem to be able to manage." After removing his coat, he hung it on a hanger himself.[18] This affected modesty did not prevent Stalin from asserting his own worth when warranted. In 1947 he personally edited his official biography, inserting the following: "Masterfully performing the job of *vozhd* of the party and people and enjoying the full support of the Soviet people, Stalin nevertheless did not allow even a shadow of self-importance, conceit, or self-admiration into anything he did." Thirteen million copies of this biography were printed.[19]

Stalin must have believed that if he was going to hold on to power, he had to be considered infallible. On occasion he recognized that mistakes were made, but they could never be his. Misguided decisions and actions were attributed to "the government," officials, or—most often—the plotting of enemies. The idea that he might bear personal responsibility for the country's afflictions was rejected out of hand. He was, however, willing to take credit for its achievements. Boundless power inevitably gave him, as it does any dictator, a belief that he was endowed with remarkable prescience. But unlike the mystically inclined Hitler, who believed he was following a higher calling, Stalin's belief in his infallibility probably had more to do with his untrusting nature and anxieties. He was sure that the only person he could count on was himself. Around him swarmed enemies and traitors. At times, this political paranoia was the cause of unfathomable tragedy. Such was the case in 1937–1938.

4 TERROR AND IMPENDING WAR

Throughout 1937, the wave of repressions against members of the nomen-klatura and former oppositionists continued to grow. In August, this wave turned into a tsunami when the ranks of the repressed were expanded from a few tens of thousands of officials to hundreds of thousands of ordinary Soviet citizens. It was at this point that the repression of 1937–1938 earned the name given it by Robert Conquest: "the Great Terror."[1]

After the archives were opened, we learned that the Great Terror was actually a series of operations approved by the Politburo and aimed at different groups. The most far-ranging of these operations—the one against "anti-Soviet elements"—was carried out in fulfillment of NKVD Order No. 00447, approved by the Politburo on 30 July 1937 and planned for August through December. Each region and republic was assigned specific numerical targets for executions and imprisonments in camps. The quotas for the destruction of human lives were very much like those for the production of grain or metal. During the first stage, approximately two hundred thousand people were to be sent to the camps and more than seventy thousand were to be shot. Yet Order No. 00447 allowed for flexibility: local officials had the right to ask Moscow to increase the permitted number of arrests and executions. It was clear to everyone involved that this right was actually a duty. After expeditiously reaching initial targets, local authorities sent Moscow new "increased obligations," which were almost always approved. With Moscow's encouragement, the initial plan for destroying "enemies" was fulfilled several times over.

The first "anti-Soviet elements" affected by the operation were the ku-laks, who, according to Order No. 00447, had continued their "anti-Soviet subversive activities" after returning from camps and exile. Order No. 00447 placed so much emphasis on kulaks that it has often been called "the kulak order." This is a misnomer, however, since it provided for the arrest and execution of many other population groups: former members of parties that opposed the Bolsheviks, former members of the White Guard, surviving tsarist officials, "enemies" who had completed their sentences and been released, and political prisoners still in the camps. Toward the end of the list came common criminals.

This list of targets suggests that the operation's purpose was the extermination or imprisonment of anyone the Stalinist leadership considered a current or potential threat. This goal was even more clear-cut in the "nationalities" operations that were conducted alongside the "anti-Soviet elements" operation. The "nationalities" operations were also planned in Moscow and governed by special NKVD orders approved by the Politburo. They had a catastrophic impact on the Soviet Union's ethnic Poles, Germans, Romanians, Latvians, Estonians, Finns, Greeks, Afghans, Iranians, Chinese, Bulgarians, and Macedonians. The Soviet leadership viewed all these groups as ripe for recruitment by hostile foreign powers. A special operation was also conducted against Soviet employees of the Chinese Eastern Railway, who had returned to the USSR from Harbin after the railway was sold to Japan in 1935.

The two campaigns, the "anti-Soviet elements" and the "nationalities" operations, comprised the Great Terror. It was a highly centralized effort begun in the summer of 1937 and concluded in November 1938. Based on the most recent knowledge, approximately 1.6 million people were arrested, and 700,000 of them were shot.[2] An unknown number perished in NKVD torture chambers. Over the roughly year-and-a-half duration of the Great Terror, approximately 1,500 "enemies" were killed every day. None of Stalin's other crimes against the Soviet population matched the Great Terror in either scale or savagery, and human history offers few episodes that compare.

These figures explain why the Great Terror has come to symbolize Stalin's dictatorship and personal cruelty. That Stalin himself was the inspiration behind the Terror has never been disputed by serious scholars, and further evidence of his involvement was found after the opening of the archives, which revealed how closely Moscow directed the operations. Having put to rest any lingering doubts that Stalin was the instigator and organizer of the Great Terror, historians have now turned to the task of reconstructing his plans and calculations during these bloody months. Scholars have debated Stalin's motives for years. The horrific nature of his deeds has led some to think he might have been insane. Clinical proof of such a possibility is undoubtedly beyond reach at this point, but we do have extensive evidence of Stalin's mental state during this period. For the first time in many years he did not take his usual summer vacation in the south, remaining in Moscow to oversee the roundup. More telling are the many notations and instructions he left on interrogation protocols and the vast body of correspondence between him and the NKVD during this period.

> Com. Yezhov: Very important. You have to go through the Udmurt, Mari, Chuvash, and Mordov republics; go through them with a broom.[3]

> Beat Unshlikht for not naming the Polish agents for each region.[4]

> Comrade Yezhov: Very good! Keep on digging and cleaning out this Polish spy filth.[5]

> You don't need to "check," you need to arrest.[6]

> Valter (a German). Beat Valter.[7]

One important source for understanding the fury Stalin unleashed in 1937–1938 is the complete transcripts of his speeches and remarks from this period; these have recently become available. Unusually convoluted and incoherent, they are filled with references to conspiracies and omnipresent enemies. In remarks to a meeting of the defense commissar's council on 2 June 1937, Stalin asserted, "Every party member, honest non-member, and citizen of the USSR has not only the right but also the duty to report any failings that he notices. Even if only 5 percent are true, it will still be worthwhile."[8] In another example, the top-performing workers in the metallurgical and coal industries, while being honored with a special reception at the Kremlin on 29 October 1937, were told by Stalin that he was not certain he could trust even them: "I'm not even sure that everyone present, I truly apologize to you, is for the people. I'm not sure whether even among you, I again apologize, there might be people who are working for the Soviet government but at the same time have set themselves up with some intelligence agency in the West—Japanese, German, or Polish—for insurance." These words, which must surely have surprised those present, were expunged from the official record of the reception.[9]

These examples, of which there are many, are consistent with a statement made by the commissar for foreign trade, Arkady Rozengolts, and contained in his NKVD case file. Rozengolts, who knew Stalin well, described him as "suspicious to the point of insanity" and felt that by 1937 he had changed. In the past, Rozengolts noted, whenever he had reported to Stalin, the *vozhd* had calmly signed whatever papers needed his signature. Now he would fall into "a fit, a mad fit of rage."[10] This rage was undoubtedly an important factor in the huge scope and brutality of the Great Terror. By the same token, Stalin's agitated state does not fully explain the decisions he made throughout this period. Pivotal questions remain unanswered. With whom was Stalin so furious, and why did this fury emerge specifically then?

To understand the nature of Stalin and his regime it is important to keep in mind that the Soviet Union was born out of war. The country came into being as a result of World War I, established itself through victory in the Civil War—a victory that involved overcoming foreign intervention—and was perpetually preparing for the next war. Having come to power solely through war, Bolshevik leaders always believed their power could be taken away by the coordinated efforts of a foreign enemy and domestic counter-revolutionary forces. War readiness, for them, had two aspects: a strong military economy and a secure homeland. The latter required destroying internal enemies.

The gradual move toward terror during the second half of the 1930s co-incided with growing international tensions and a growing threat of war. In addition to Japanese aggression along the Soviet Union's Far Eastern borders, events in Europe were increasingly alarming: Hitler had come to power, and Poland, which lay between the USSR and Germany, seemed in Stalin's eyes to favor relations with Germany over the USSR. Western pow-ers were pursuing a policy of appeasement toward the Nazis, and the Rhine-land had been remilitarized in 1936. Another factor influencing Stalin's for-eign policy was the civil war in Spain, which convinced him that England and France were incapable of standing up to Germany. He had little faith in the Western democracies in any case. A policy of non-intervention no longer made sense for the Soviet leadership, and it decided to enter the war in support of Spain's Republicans, who were fighting Hitler's ally, General Francisco Franco. Stalin, observing the situation in Spain, became further convinced of the need to purge the homeland in the interests of military readiness. The Spanish Civil War was bringing to the fore a familiar assort-ment of ills, including anarchy, guerrilla warfare, sabotage, a drifting and ambiguous line dividing the front from the rear, and all manner of treach-ery. This was the war that gave us the concept of the fifth column. In Octo-ber 1936, at a critical moment when four columns of Francoist forces were approaching Madrid, the Nationalist general Emilio Mola claimed to have a "fifth column" within the Republican-held city that would rise up and help his forces take it. This term quickly became embedded in the Soviet leaders' political lexicon.

War in Spain and repression in the USSR escalated in parallel. When the conflict broke out in Spain, on 18 July 1936, the Stalinist leaders initially reacted with caution. But catastrophic defeats suffered by the Republican army led them to intervene. On 29 September 1936, the Politburo adopted a plan of action.[11] (It may be significant that this decision coincided with Yezhov's appointment as head of the NKVD.) The Spanish defeats were taking place alongside setbacks in Europe and the Far East. On 25 October 1936, Italy signed a treaty with Germany, followed on 25 November by the Anti-Comintern Pact between Germany and Japan. All of these developments seemed to heighten the danger of war.

Newly available archives confirm that Stalin was heavily involved in Spanish affairs. The evidence clearly shows that he believed Republican defeats were caused by saboteurs in the ranks. He demanded that the internal enemy be dealt with decisively. On 9 February 1937 Soviet representatives in Valencia and Madrid were sent a telegram asserting that a series of failures at the front had been directly caused by treachery at headquarters: "Make use of these facts, discuss them, observing caution, with the best of the Republican commanders . . . so that they may demand . . . an immediate investigation of the surrender of Malaga, a purge of Franco agents and saboteurs from army headquarters. . . . If these demands by front-line commanders do not produce immediately the necessary results, put it . . . that our advisers may find it impossible to continue working under such conditions."[12] A few days later, he repeated these demands: "We tell you what our firmly established opinion is: that the General Staff and other headquarters must be purged thoroughly of their complement of old specialists who are unable to understand the conditions of civil war and, in addition, are politically unreliable. . . . Headquarters must be reinforced with fresh people, staunch and full of fighting spirit. . . . Without this radical measure the Republicans will unquestionably lose the war. This is our belief."[13]

At the same time that Stalin was dispatching telegrams to Spain, the notorious February–March 1937 Central Committee plenum, which signaled an intensification of repression, was taking place in Moscow. Stalin, reading a draft of the speech Molotov planned to make to the plenum, made some comments in the margins. He underlined the parts where Molotov talked about Trotsky ordering his followers in the USSR "to save their strength for the most important moment—for the start of war—and at that moment to strike with total decisiveness at the most sensitive points in our economy."[14] Near the words "those incapable of fighting the bourgeoisie, who prefer to cast their lot with the bourgeoisie rather than the working class, have abandoned [the party]," Stalin made a notation: "This is good. It would be worse if they abandoned us in time of war."[15] The theme of the special danger posed by wreckers and spies in wartime ran through the speeches delivered at the plenum, including Stalin's: "Winning a battle in time of war takes several corps of Red Army soldiers. But reversing that victory at the front requires just a few spies somewhere in army headquarters or even division headquarters, able to steal the battle plans and give them to the enemy. To build a major railway bridge would take thousands of people. But to blow it up, just a few people would be enough. There are dozens, hundreds of such examples."[16]

Stalin took an active hand in preparing an article for the 4 May 1937 issue of *Pravda,* titled "Certain Insidious Recruitment Techniques Used by Foreign Intelligence." This lengthy piece, taking up the bottom halves of three pages, was an important element of the Great Terror's ideological underpinning. It was reprinted in various publications, actively used in propaganda, and discussed at party study groups. We can see from the initial draft, which Stalin filed in his personal archive, that he modified its headline, which originally read "Certain Methods and Techniques Used by Foreign Intelligence," to give it a more sinister tone.

This article, unlike others that Stalin helped produce, was not at all theoretical. It described specific (most likely fictitious) instances in which Soviet citizens, especially those sent overseas on state business, had been recruited by foreign intelligence agencies. These examples made the article credible and persuasive. Stalin contributed almost an entire page of text describing an instance in which a Soviet official working in Japan met regularly with an "aristocratic lady" in a restaurant. During one such meeting, a Japanese man in a military uniform appeared, claimed to be the woman's husband, and made a scene. Another Japanese man appeared and offered to help resolve the matter, but only after the Soviet citizen agreed in writing to keep him informed of what was happening in the USSR. This "helpful intermediary" turned out to be an agent of Japanese intelligence, and the Soviet citizen became a spy.[17]

In the months that followed, Stalin's suspicions were translated into massive police operations. During the spring and summer of 1937, the urgent call to expose spies and forestall potential treason became the basis for a case against a counterrevolutionary organization within the Red Army. On 2 June 1937, Stalin explained the goal of the plot to members of the defense commissar's Military Council: "They wanted to turn the USSR into another Spain."[18] Reports of treachery and anarchy in Spain were an important component of the propaganda campaign to "intensify vigilance" and fight against "enemies" within the USSR. In June and July 1937, when the government was preparing to launch large-scale operations against domestic anti-Soviet elements, Soviet newspapers were filled with articles about arrests of German spies in Madrid and of Trotskyites in Barcelona and the fall of the Basque capital Bilbao brought about by a treacherous commander in the Basque army. Also during that summer, the Spanish Republican government created a special state security agency to counteract espionage and combat the "fifth column"—the Servicio de Investigacion Militar (SIM), which sent tentacles into all parts of Republican Spain and brutally suppressed any opposition. The methods used by this new structure prompted sharp criticism even by sympathetic leftists in Western countries. Intensified repression in the Soviet Union was being mirrored in Spain (including by Soviet agents operating there).[19] The Spanish Republican police and the Soviet secret police each worked to crush their own "fifth columns."

In July the situation in the Far East became even more tense after Japan invaded China. Two important events occurred on 21 August 1937. First, the USSR and China, both with eyes on Japan, signed a non-aggression pact. Second, a resolution was adopted by the Council of People's Commissars and the Central Committee to "Expel the Korean Population from Border Regions of the Far Eastern Territory." In the fall of 1937 a massive operation was undertaken to arrest and deport Koreans from this vast region. More than 170,000 people were expelled. The expressed goal was to "prevent the penetration of Japanese espionage into the Far Eastern Territory."[20]

The idea that the country had to be purged of a potential fifth column, a recurring theme throughout the 1930s in the USSR, was an article of faith among Stalin's close associates. Even many decades later, they referred to it:

> Nineteen thirty-seven was necessary. If you consider that after the revolution we were slashing left and right, and we were victorious, but enemies of different sorts remained, and in the face of the impending danger of fascist aggression they might unite. We owe the fact that we did not have a fifth column during the war to '37.[21]

> This was a struggle against a fifth column of Hitlerite fascism that had come to power in Germany and was preparing war against the country of the Soviets.[22]

There is little doubt that Stalin encouraged these ideas among his fellow Politburo members. From their narrow perspective, he had a logical and convincing argument. The Soviet government had many internal enemies who might be keeping a low profile at the moment but were ready to leap into action as soon as the USSR was challenged by a foreign power. The relatively independent old party nomenklatura, which still had ties to the military and the NKVD, might seek to take charge. Former oppositionists were surely eager to take revenge after long years of humiliation and persecution. The kulaks and the perpetually starving peasants might band together with former members of the nobility, White Guard, and the clergy to follow the example of the Bolsheviks in 1917 and turn war with a foreign enemy into a civil war against a despised regime. Then there were the Soviet Union's many ethnic minorities with ties to neighboring countries—Germans and Poles especially—who Stalin suspected would collaborate with an enemy based on ties of blood. The way to eliminate these dangers was to destroy as many potential enemies and collaborationists as possible. Such was the logic of Stalin's fearful and ruthless mind as the threat of war grew. In the fevered imaginations of his inner circle, such a fifth column loomed orders of magnitude larger than it could possibly have been in reality. Phantom threats overshadowed the very real dangers confronting the Soviet Union.

■ WAS IT ALL YEZHOV'S FAULT?

Stalin claimed to have had no part in his own atrocities. He told the renowned Soviet aeronautical engineer Aleksandr Yakovlev that it was all Yezhov's fault: "Yezhov was a beast! A degenerate. You'd call him at the commissariat, and they'd tell you, 'He went to the Central Committee.' You'd call the Central Committee, and they'd tell you, 'He went to his office.' You'd send someone to his house, and it turns out that he's lying on his bed dead drunk. Many innocent lives were lost. That's why we shot him."[23]

The winding down of the Great Terror in late 1938 and early 1939 was accompanied by a campaign to deflect suspicion away from its true perpetrators. This effort was helped by Yezhov's removal and the very public unmasking of "slanderers" who had submitted denunciations against honest people—supposedly a major cause of the repression. Even today some are willing to argue Stalin's innocence, proposing pseudo-scholarly theories that the Great Terror erupted spontaneously on the initiative of local officials. Of course, once Moscow issued its orders, the momentum generated was bound to look elemental. In the bureaucratic language of the Stalin era, the behavior of zealous officials was labeled *peregiby* (excesses). But it was not excesses that determined the scale and ferocity of the Terror. The documentary evidence shows that large-scale operations rarely deviated from Stalin's orders.

After Moscow's arrest and execution quotas were received by the NKVD headquarters of each oblast (province) and *krai* (a territory similar to a province but containing semi-autonomous administrative units), the regional NKVD chief would gather the heads of local (municipal and district) NKVD offices for a meeting, at which the regional quota would be parceled out among the administrative entities (districts, towns, villages, settlements). The first source used in compiling a list of enemies was the card files that the political police kept on various suspected "anti-Soviet elements," as well as any other compromising materials that came to hand. After a victim was arrested, an investigation was conducted to expose his or her "counterrevolutionary ties" or uncover the existence of "counterrevolutionary organizations."[24] The necessary "evidence" was obtained using a variety of methods, most often torture, which was officially sanctioned by the country's top leadership. The forms of torture were brutal and sometimes caused an arrestee's death. One major goal of interrogation was to obtain testimony implicating others, thus generating a second wave of arrestees, who in turn provided more names. These police operations could, in theory, continue indefinitely, or until the potential pool of victims had been thoroughly drained. Such operations did not continue only because Stalin had full control of the state security system and party apparat and could close the spigot whenever he wanted. Every decision to sentence a presumed enemy to a labor camp or to be shot was approved in Moscow.

At first it was assumed that these large-scale operations would conclude at the end of 1937. Gradually, the date was moved back to November 1938. On 17 January 1938, Stalin sent NKVD chief Yezhov new orders:

> The SR [Socialist Revolutionary Party] line (both left and right) has not been fully uncovered. . . . It is important to keep in mind that there are still many SRs in our army and outside the army. Can the NKVD account for the ("former") SRs in the army? I would like to see a report promptly. Can the NKVD account for "former" SRs outside the army (in civil institutions)? I also would like a report in two–three weeks. . . . What has been done to expose and arrest all Iranians in Baku and Azerbaijan? For your information, at one time the SRs were very strong in Saratov, Tambov, and the Ukraine, in the army (officers), in Tashkent and Central Asia in general, and at the Baku electrical power stations, where they became entrenched and sabotaged the oil industry. We must act more swiftly and intelligently.[25]

This document is one of many pieces of evidence that Stalin played the decisive role in organizing the Great Terror and that Yezhov was following his orders. Archival records clearly show Stalin to be the initiator of all key decisions having to do with purges of party and government institutions and the mass operations that swept up ordinary citizens. He not only ordered the arrest and execution of hundreds of thousands of people, but he also took a strong interest in the details. He sent telegrams about the need to make particular arrests, threatened dire consequences for insufficient vigilance, and signed lists of members of the nomenklatura to be executed and imprisoned. In many cases he personally decided whether someone would be shot or sent to a labor camp.[26] Overseeing the large-scale operations to wipe out enemies took up a significant portion of the dictator's time in 1937–1938. Over a twenty-month period from January 1937 to August 1938, he received fifteen thousand *spetssoobshchenii* (special communications) reporting on arrests and the conduct of various secret police operations or requesting approval for a particular act of repression, usually accompanied by interrogation protocols (transcripts). On a typical day, he received twenty-five documents from Yezhov, some running to many pages.[27] Furthermore, the record of visitors to Stalin's office shows that during 1937 and 1938, Yezhov visited him almost 290 times and spent a total of 850 hours with him. The only person who visited more often was Molotov.[28]

Yezhov was a capable and motivated pupil. He organized the trials of former oppositionists and conducted day-to-day oversight of the giant machine of repression. He personally participated in interrogations and issued orders to apply torture. To please Stalin, who always demanded greater efforts in the fight against enemies and constantly pointed to new threats, Yezhov encouraged his subordinates to exceed the Politburo's targets for mass arrests and executions and to fabricate new conspiracies. To encourage them, the NKVD and Yezhov personally were lavished with praise throughout 1937 and most of 1938. Yezhov was given every conceivable award and title and simultaneously held several key party and government posts. Cities, factories, and kolkhozes were named after him.

Despite these signs that Stalin was pleased with his people's commissar for internal affairs, there is evidence that the *vozhd* was maintaining a certain distance, even as Yezhov and his organization were lavished with praise for their excellent work in exposing enemies. Inevitably, Stalin eventually brought the mass extermination to a halt and blamed the "excesses" and "violations of law" on Yezhov and his subordinates. Stalin laid the groundwork for Yezhov's removal gradually and systematically. In August 1938, he appointed Lavrenty Beria, first party secretary for Georgia, to serve as Yezhov's deputy. On the surface, nothing had changed. Yezhov still seemed to enjoy power and favor. But now, by his side was a man he would never have chosen. Several months later Yezhov even alluded to Beria's appointment in a letter to Stalin, describing it as showing "an element of mistrust toward me" and admitting that he saw "[Beria's] appointment as preparation for my being relieved."[29] He was right. Unable to cope with the stress of the situation, he descended into alcoholism and lost control of both the NKVD and himself.

Two months after Beria's appointment, Stalin took further steps toward Yezhov's removal. On 8 October 1938 the Politburo established a commission to draft a resolution concerning the NKVD. Yezhov's subordinates began to be arrested. Beria's henchmen set to work beating testimony against Yezhov out of them, just as Yezhov's henchmen had done when he was building a case against his precedessor, Genrikh Yagoda. On 17 November the Politburo adopted a transparently hypocritical and mendacious resolution remarking on NKVD successes in destroying "enemies of the people and foreign intelligence agencies' espionage-sabotage networks" but also condemning "shortcomings and perversions" in the NKVD's work.[30] While repeatedly demanding an intensified struggle against enemies, Stalin had never questioned the mission of mass terror that he himself had conceived and promoted. Yezhov and the NKVD now stood accused of doing what Stalin had ordered them to do. If Yezhov had been allowed to make a serious case for himself, he would have had no trouble doing so. But as he knew better than anyone, that was not how the Stalinist system worked. All he could do was hope and repent.

Having done his job, the faithful Yezhov was no longer needed. He was arrested and shot as the head of a (nonexistent) counterrevolutionary organization within the NKVD. Stalin apparently did not feel the need to goad excessive public outrage, and Yezhov's downfall was arranged without fanfare. The cautious tidiness with which he was removed shows that Stalin was reluctant to draw public attention to the activities of the NKVD and the mechanics of the Great Terror. Yezhov was Stalin's senior scapegoat. He paid the ultimate price so that his *vozhd* could remain above suspicion. For the Soviet people, the Terror became the "Yezhovshchina"—a term using a Russian suffix suggesting some rampant evil.

The final stage of the Great Terror—its unwinding, which Stalin carefully controlled—mainly targeted Yezhov's top lieutenants at the NKVD. A miniscule number of ordinary citizens swept up by the large-scale operations—primarily those who had fallen into NKVD clutches during the second half of 1938—were released. The machinery of terror remained in place with only minor adjustments, and ruthless repression continued until Stalin's death. The *vozhd* never stopped believing that enemies were all around or demanding that they be unmasked, arrested, and tortured. But he never again resorted to repression on the scale seen during 1937–1938.

Stalin must have been aware of the Terror's devastating consequences, yet he never, either in public or even within his inner circle, questioned its necessity. But the consequences could not have escaped his attention. A huge number of those responsible for running the Soviet economy had been arrested. Workplace discipline suffered, and engineers were afraid to propose any changes or innovations that might later subject them to un-scrupulous accusations of "wrecking." The Terror led to a sizable decline in the rate of growth in industrial production.[31] The military too suffered from a shrinking pool of experienced and competent commanders and a decline in discipline and responsibility. The Red Army was so heavily affected by repression that the Soviet leadership was forced to return many previously arrested or discharged commanders to service, at least those the NKVD had not yet had time to execute.[32]

The Great Terror of 1937–1938 put huge stresses on Soviet society and caused widespread misery. Millions of people were directly affected. Many who escaped being shot, confined to labor camps, or subjected to internal deportation lost their jobs or were evicted from their apartments or even towns for the sole crime of having ties to "enemies of the people." Such abuses and upheavals could not be forgiven and passively accepted. Al-though fear was a fairly effective means of keeping the population from expressing its displeasure, grievances were lodged. In 1937–1938, these grievances mainly took the form of the millions of complaints that came pouring into government and party offices. In January 1937 alone, 13,000 complaints were filed with the procuracy, and in February–March 1938 the number reached 120,000.[33] It has not yet been established how many letters and petitions were sent to Stalin himself during the Great Terror or how many actually reached his desk. The records are either inaccessible or were not preserved. We can only assume that Stalin's office was inundated with such petitions. The *vozhd* could not have been entirely shielded from his subjects' desperation, grief, and disillusionment.

What was Stalin's reaction to the suffering of his fellow citizens? The his-torical record gives no clear answer to this question, but there is no evi-dence that he felt the slightest remorse or pity. Nevertheless, he could not entirely ignore political realities. Although he still despised imaginary ene-mies and feared imaginary conspiracies, he never repeated his experiment in large-scale terror. After 1938, repression continued on a smaller scale and in a more routine manner.

■ THE SEARCH FOR ALLIES

The Great Terror damaged the Soviet Union's international reputation. Stalin undoubtedly understood that people in the West, especially on the left, were shocked to learn that prominent revolutionaries were being put to death. In an effort to minimize the impact on public opinion, the campaign of repression was paralleled by an energetic propaganda campaign. Accounts of the Moscow trials—at which Lenin's comrades-in-arms and other Old Bolsheviks admitted plotting terrorist acts against Stalin and háving ties with foreign intelligence agencies—were translated into European languages and widely circulated. Prominent Western intellectuals and cultural figures were invited to Moscow. The German writer Lion Feuchtwanger met personally with Stalin and then wrote a book casting the Soviet Union in a favorable light. Caught between the hammer of Nazism and the anvil of Stalinism, many were ready to delude themselves as to the regime's true nature. The West's political decision makers, however, had every reason not only to distrust Stalin, but also to see the hysteria over supposed enemies as evidence of weakness. The purge of Red Army commanders and the execution of well-known Soviet marshals in particular made the regime appear unstable. The West clearly saw the Terror in very different terms than Stalin. Obsessed with the idea of a fifth column, Stalin simply failed to understand that his moves to arrest and shoot so many of his own citizens looked more like weakness and instability than strength.

To some extent the Western observers were right. Signs of the Terror's devastating impact on Soviet military might soon became apparent. In June 1938, the NKVD general in charge of the Far East, Genrikh Liushkov, crossed the Soviet border into Manchuria and offered his services to the Japanese. This was of course a traitorous act, but Liushkov was pushed in that direction by Stalin. After faithfully serving the regime and spilling rivers of other people's blood, he realized it would soon be his own turn to bleed. When a summons came to report to Moscow, Liushkov decided that his best option was to defect. Given his years as a top NKVD official in Moscow, his experience working face-to-face with Stalin, and his role as secret police chief of the militarily critical Far Eastern region, he had a great deal to offer. He was well informed about military readiness in the Far East and the makeup and placement of Soviet troops—and he shared all this information with the enemy. Stalin further undermined military preparedness in the Far East by ordering another wave of arrests within the army. Meanwhile, in July and August 1938, the Red Army clashed with Japanese forces near Lake Khasan, an area near the borders with Korea and China. Stalin closely monitored this conflict and demanded decisive action. In a conversation with the commander of the Far Eastern front, Marshal Vasily Bliukher (who had expressed his reluctance to use aviation), Stalin issued the following order: "I don't understand your fear that bombing might hurt the Korean population or your fear that aviation won't be able to fulfill its mission because of fog. Who forbade you to hurt the Korean population in time of war with Japan? Why would you care about Koreans when the Japanese are striking at lots of our people? What do a few clouds matter to Bolshevik aviation when it wants to truly defend the honor of its Motherland?"[34]

While the Battle of Lake Khasan ended favorably for the Soviet side, the clash exposed significant shortcomings in the combat readiness of Red Army troops and command structures. As usual, Stalin assumed that the army's poor performance was the result of treachery. Marshal Bliukher was arrested and died in prison after being brutally tortured.

Repression and the perception of Soviet weakness were not the primary causes of Stalin's deteriorating relations with the West. The mass arrests just added to Western leaders' list of reasons for mistrusting him. A warming of relations with France in the mid-1930s did not last, despite the threat posed to both countries by the rapid rise of Nazism. In the Spanish Civil War, the Soviet Union and Western democracies found themselves in frequent disagreement. Underlying this tendency toward poor relations, despite their common collective security concerns, was the fundamental incompatibility of Stalinism with "bourgeois" democracy. During the second half of the 1930s Western leaders preferred to appease Hitler rather than form an alliance with Stalin, a trend that reached its climax with the Munich Agreement. On 30 September 1938, the leaders of Great Britain and France, Neville Chamberlain and Édouard Daladier, signed an agreement with Hitler and Mussolini handing over Czechoslovakia's Sudetenland, an area primarily populated by German speakers, to Germany. Czechoslovakia was forced to accept this devastating pact. The Soviet Union was simply ignored, even though it and France had signed mutual assistance agreements with Czechoslovakia. Stalin was shut out of European great power politics.

Stalin undoubtedly took such marginalization as a personal insult. Munich only intensified his fear that the democracies and fascists were conspiring against the USSR and planning to channel Nazi aggression east-ward. He could not respond from a position of strength. In addition to expressing his outrage, in late September Stalin ordered a Red Army troop buildup along the USSR's western border, a purely demonstrative move that is unlikely to have worried the Germans. In any event, just days later, in mid-October, the Politburo decided to disband the reserve units that had been mobilized in response to the events in Czechoslovakia. A total of 330,000 troops, 27,500 horses, and 5,000 vehicles and tractors were re-leased from active duty.[35]

In practical terms, Stalin could do little about the Munich Agreement beyond trying to drive a wedge between the Western democracies and Hit-ler. To this end, he made a series of statements condemning Great Britain and France, while opening the door to improved bilateral relations with Germany. The most significant overture to Germany came during a speech at the Eighteenth Party Congress in March 1939, in which Stalin warned the English and French that he had no intention of "pulling the chestnuts out of the fire" for them (a line that earned this address the nickname "the chest-nut speech" in the West) and accused them of attempting to provoke con-flict between the USSR and Germany. He told Germany that the Western powers had not succeeded in "enraging the Soviet Union against Germany, poisoning the atmosphere, and provoking conflict with Germany on no apparent grounds."[36] These pronouncements took on special significance several days later when Europe's fragile peace was broken. Hitler, confident that no one would stop him, seized the entire territory of Czechoslovakia. Even the most optimistic observers now realized that Munich had made world war all but inevitable. As a third party to the growing conflict, Stalin and the Soviet Union were in a position to choose sides.

The spring and summer of 1939 were a time of urgent diplomatic ma-neuvering and negotiation. Understanding the nature of these efforts and the actual intentions of the parties involved was difficult enough for their direct participants, to say nothing of historians today. Nobody trusted anybody, and all were trying to outsmart their adversaries and partners alike. Such confusion was surely true of the talks between the Soviet Union and the Western powers of England and France. Progress was painfully slow, despite the efforts of Soviet foreign affairs commissar Maksim Lit-vinov, who staked his reputation on building cohesion among anti-Hitler forces.[37] In early May 1939, Stalin relieved Litvinov of his duties and put Molotov in charge of foreign affairs. This change was undoubtedly in-tended as a gesture of friendship toward Germany, but it also radically reshaped foreign policy decision making. The new arrangement allowed Stalin to take full control of foreign affairs, not only in terms of their guiding principles (as he had always done), but also their day-to-day operations. Molotov, with whom Stalin was in almost constant conversation, was a more convenient foreign-policy right hand than Litvinov, who rarely visited Stalin's office. Such practical details were important to the *vozhd*. At the top tier of Soviet power, government was adapted to Stalin's habits and rhythms, and the choice of Molotov to oversee foreign affairs at this critical time is a prime example of this adaptation.

What was uppermost in Stalin's mind during this period—putting pressure on his Western partners or exploring the possibility of an alliance with the Nazis? It is tempting to assume that he had decided to align himself with Hitler long before the fateful events of 1939. Arguments in favor of this view include the general idea of an affinity between totalitarian regimes and Stalin's mistrust of the changeable Western democracies, which seemed inclined to retreat in the face of brute force. But the foundation for a Nazi-Soviet alliance was actually flimsy. The available evidence offering insights into Stalin's thinking is open to interpretation. On one hand, Mikoyan reported that Stalin spoke approvingly of Hitler's 1934 purges.[38] We also know that the Soviet leader initiated overtures aimed at establishing direct contact with Hitler.[39] Most damning of all was the result: an impressive demonstration of Soviet-German "friendship" in the fall of 1939. But on the other hand, there is convincing evidence that Stalin had little faith in Hitler as a potential ally. If he trusted the German leader, there likely would not have been a powerful anti-Nazi propaganda campaign waged in the USSR or mass repression against Soviet Germans—both of which were carried out over the strong objections of the Nazi government. Stalin's attitude toward the Germans seemed to alternate between approval and annoyance. Responding to a September 1938 NKVD memorandum about the destruction of a cemetery dating to World War I for German soldiers and officers in Leningrad Oblast, rather than replying with his usual laconic "in favor," Stalin wrote, "Correct (tear it down and fill it in)."[40] The German interpreter present at negotiations with Foreign Minister Joachim von Ribbentrop in Moscow also offers some insight into the Soviet leader's mindset. Stalin apparently rejected a draft of an upbeat press communiqué with the words: "Don't you think that we should give more consideration to public opinion in both our countries? We've been slinging mud at one another for years now."[41]

Whatever Stalin's true inclinations were, it was Hitler who took the initiative in bringing about a Soviet-German non-aggression pact. As soon as the German chancellor decided that his invasion of Poland, scheduled for 1 September, would require Soviet cooperation, he took steps to promote a rapprochement between the two countries. On 21 August Stalin received a personal correspondence from Hitler hinting rather transparently at his plans for Poland and expressing the urgent desire to conclude a non-aggression pact within a few days. Hitler asked that Stalin receive von Ribbentrop in Moscow the very next day or at least on 23 August. On 21 August Molotov handed Stalin's response to the German ambassador in Moscow. Von Ribbentrop could come to Moscow on the later date.[42]

Stalin and Molotov were both there to receive the German foreign minister. The meeting was cordial, even amicable. Each side got what it wanted. In addition to the non-aggression pact, Stalin insisted that a secret protocol be drawn up stipulating that Germany and the Soviet Union would divide up Eastern Europe. The eastern portion of Poland, which then included the western parts of both Ukraine and Belarus; Latvia; Estonia; and Finland were recognized as belonging within the Soviet sphere. Germany also supported Soviet pretensions to Bessarabia. Western Poland and Lithuania would go to Germany. Subsequent negotiations gave Lithuania to the Soviets. The protocol wound up being a sort of Brest-Litovsk in reverse. Hitler needed a worry-free border with the USSR, and he would pay for it with territorial concessions.

Stalin kept the threads of the Soviet-German negotiations in his own hands. The only other person involved was Molotov. What history calls the Molotov-Ribbentrop Pact was actually an agreement between Stalin and Hitler. Stalin took total responsibility for the "friendship" with Germany and doubtless had very specific motives for entering into the risky alliance. The nature of these motives is one of the most important questions facing his biographers.

First, there were the political and moral aspects of the problem. Stalin, no doubt, was fully aware of the agreements' political and moral undesirability. We can infer this from the persistence with which the Soviet Union denied that a secret protocol existed. When copies came to light, Soviet leaders proclaimed them to be forgeries. Stalin understood that the sudden switch from hatred toward the Nazis to friendship would be ideologically disorienting, both within the USSR and in the world Communist movement. This problem was secondary, however, and could be dealt with using the boilerplate explanation: the pact was in the ultimate interests of socialism. Within the USSR, skeptics could be dealt with in the usual manner. The moral issue actually took on greater weight later, after Germany's defeat, when the international community condemned Nazism as an absolute evil.

In 1939, even the most democratic of Western politicians took a flexible approach to dealing with the Nazis—anything to avoid war. Great Britain and France could hardly be proud of these policies, and it would be naive to expect Stalin to sympathize with their approach. Nobody was refusing to deal with Hitler out of principle; it was a matter of what agreements were achievable and acceptable. In terms of political pragmatism, Stalin was no worse than the Western parties to the Munich Agreement. In signing the Munich pact, Great Britain and France not only shielded themselves from Hitler's aggression—or so they thought—but also placed a number of small countries, not just the Sudetenland, in peril. Stalin took his self-interest a step further and joined in the division of Eastern Europe. He was sure that Munich had pushed Hitler's aggression eastward, so it only made sense for him to set the Führer's mind at rest about the East and attempt to turn him back toward the West. From the Soviet perspective, Stalin was only trying to get back what was rightfully Russia's. Redressing a historical injustice by restoring parts of the Russian Empire that had been taken by force when the country was weakened by war and revolution must have been a part of the Soviet dictator's thinking. This motive drew sympathy not only within the USSR, but among some foreigners as well.

It is difficult to say how prominently emotional and moral consider-ations figured in Stalin's thinking. Surely they were far outweighed by the immediate risk of war. There is a broad spectrum of opinion on the geo-strategic reasons for the agreement with Germany. At one end are those who point to the speech Stalin allegedly gave to the Politburo on 19 August 1939, just before the pact was signed. One version of this speech, published in France in late 1939, caused a sensation as a supposed exposé of Stalin's expectations of what war would mean for the USSR. The French publica-tion quotes him giving the following justification for the pact with Hitler: "We are absolutely convinced that if we conclude an agreement to ally with France and Great Britain, Germany would be forced to give up on Poland and seek a modus vivendi with the Western powers. War would be averted and the subsequent course of events would prove dangerous for us."[43]

This alleged speech made it seem as if Stalin believed war was needed to weaken the West, expand the USSR's boundaries, and help spread commu-nism in Europe. These supposed remarks compromised Stalin in Hitler's eyes and made the French Communist Party look like an agent of hostile forces. Publication of this "top secret" document clearly served somebody's interest.

Most historians have never assigned much significance to this forgery. Neither the Politburo archive nor Stalin's own files contain even circumstantial evidence of such a speech—or even that the Politburo met on 19 August. This is not surprising. Based on what is known about Stalin's dictatorship in the late 1930s, it is hard to believe he would speak so openly to his Politburo comrades, for whose opinions—and even existence—he felt no need whatsoever. The "transcript of Stalin's speech," like many other well-known forgeries, promotes a particular viewpoint in regard to Stalin and his actions. According to this extreme view, Stalin concluded a pact with Hitler because he wanted war in Europe as a means of carrying out his plans.

The views reflected in the forgery differ sharply from statements by Stalin for which we do have a reliable source. Georgy Dimitrov, the head of the Comintern at the time, recorded in his diary the following remarks by Stalin, made at a meeting on 7 September: "We would rather have reached agreement with the so-called democratic countries, so we conducted negotiations. But the English and French wanted to use us as field hands and without paying us anything! We, of course, would not go work as field hands, especially if we weren't getting paid."[44] Nobody should feel compelled to take Stalin's words at face value. But the possibility that he was driven toward his pact with Hitler by his country's isolation and a sense that he was undervalued by his Western allies deserves serious consideration.

The diversity of opinions concerning Stalin's motives in August 1939 reflects the complexity of events and abundance of international intrigues during the lead-up to World War II. In recent times, however, pieces of historical evidence have become available that clarify the situation. The negotiations among the Soviet Union, England, and France were fraught with problems, and both the Soviet and the Western sides were to blame for their lack of progress. Stalin saw in the Western nations' obstinacy further confirmation of their intent to appease Hitler at the expense of the USSR. Most likely, he thought war between Germany and Poland was inevitable however the other powers were aligned, and he was probably right. It was difficult to predict how such a war would affect his country. The Nazis would be right on Soviet borders. Hitler was prepared to pay a fair price for a pact that would grant Soviet blessing to this arrangement. For Stalin, the pact offered nearly risk-free expansion of Soviet territory and a chance to create a buffer between his country and the war about to be unleashed on Europe.

Then there were the Japanese. In the spring of 1939, clashes were already erupting between Soviet and Japanese troops in Mongolia. The first engagements did not end well for the Red Army, but by the time of the von Ribbentrop negotiations, the Soviet side was achieving significant victories. These strengthened Stalin's position in his dialogue with Germany. The signing of the pact was a diplomatic blow to Japan. At least for the near term, it could not count on its German ally in its confrontation with the USSR. There is no serious argument against assuming that Stalin was guided by all these considerations.

In August 1939, Stalin had every reason to consider himself ascendant. He had concluded an agreement with the world's strongest military power and averted a war with it, at least for the time being and possibly for a long time to come. He had won back much of the territory lost by Russia two decades earlier. He could anticipate reaping third-party benefits as the warring European countries created a new balance of power on the continent. The pact with Germany and secret protocol were morally distasteful and they diminished the Soviet Union's reputation with progressives around the world, but these were relatively minor concerns. Was Stalin looking into the distant future and plotting the creation of a Communist empire extending over a large part of Europe? Such a prospect must have been hard to envision in 1939. Did he conclude the pact in order to provoke war in Europe? Given Nazi aggression, such a provocation seems hardly necessary. It is another matter that we will never know how the war would have played out had Stalin not signed the agreement with Hitler and continued to try to make common cause with England and France.

We will also never know how the Molotov-Ribbentrop pact and secret protocol would look today had Stalin used these documents simply to restrain Germany and expand the Soviet sphere of influence. In that case, posterity would have seen the Soviet-German understanding as an unsavory but understandable and pragmatic maneuver by a savvy politician. But Stalin was the iron-fisted ruler of a totalitarian system. He used the agreement not simply to keep the Nazis out of the small countries along the USSR's border, but also to assimilate new territories. And assimilation, in Stalin's world, meant aggression and the brutal purging of society.

■ AS WAR RAGED

Germany invaded Poland on 1 September 1939. Poland's allies, Great Britain and France, responded with a declaration of war, and World War II was under way. The Nazis swept through Poland almost unopposed. The British and French forces that came to Poland's defense assembled too slowly and seemed in no great hurry to fight. The Red Army's entry into Poland, and the line dividing this country between Germany and the USSR, had been determined during the von Ribbentrop negotiations in Moscow the previous month, but Stalin was also in no hurry to begin military actions. The Soviet invasion began only on 17 September, after the outcome of Germany's Polish campaign was fully evident. Clearly, Stalin preferred to wait until the risk of an invasion was minimal and Soviet aggression would not look like it had been coordinated with Germany's. The Red Army primarily occupied the parts of western Ukraine and western Belarus that Poland had seized in 1921. The official propaganda claimed that Soviet actions were being taken on behalf of the Ukrainian and Belarusian peoples and described the invasion as an act of "liberation." This interpretation suited Western politicians, who still hoped to win Stalin to their side.

The reality bore little resemblance to the image promoted by Soviet propaganda. The Soviet absorption of western Ukraine and western Belarus was not a joyous reunion of divided nations. For the first year and a half of their sovietization, the new territories underwent the same violent social engineering that the USSR had been experiencing for decades. The goal was to force them into the Soviet mold: do away with the capitalist economic system, inculcate a new ideology, and destroy any real or imagined hotbeds of dissent against the regime. The traditional methods were used. "Suspicious" people were shot, sent to labor camps, or exiled to the Soviet interior; private property was expropriated; and farming was brought into the kolkhoz system. The Stalinist regime was trying to eliminate, in just months, any potential for anti-Soviet collaboration. An important component of this bloody effort was the notorious Katyn massacre. On 5 March 1940 the Politburo adopted a decision to put to death many thousands of Poles held in prisoner-of-war camps or regular prisons in the western provinces of Ukraine and Belarus. The victims were largely members of the Polish elite: military and police officers, former government officials, landowners, industrialists, and members of the Polish intelligentsia. A total of 21,857 people were shot in April and May 1940.[45] In exterminating these people, Stalin was clearly attempting to head off any movement to restore the prewar Polish leadership.

Stalin proceeded more cautiously and gradually in the Baltic states, which the Molotov-Ribbentrop pact had recognized as falling into the Soviet sphere of influence. Immediately after the partition of Poland and the settlement of various issues with Germany, in late September and October 1939 the Soviet leadership forced Estonia, Latvia, and Lithuania to permit

Soviet military bases on their territory, including in the Baltic Sea ports. Molotov and Stalin personally took on the task of intimidating their Baltic neighbors during negotiations at the Kremlin. These meetings were tense. When the representatives of the Baltic governments insisted on preserving their sovereignty and neutrality, Molotov threatened them with war and refused to make the slightest concession. Stalin applied a softer touch and offered a few insignificant compromises, reducing, for example, the number of troops to be stationed in the Baltic countries. The intransigence of the Baltic representatives evidently irritated him, but he kept his temper. According to the Latvian foreign minister, Stalin wrote, doodled, strolled around the room, and picked up books and newspapers while others were speaking. At critical points he interrupted and went off on tangents, expounding at length on abstruse ethnographic or historical topics.[46]

The Soviet side obviously had the advantage. Red Army units were already positioned along the Baltic nations' borders. Germany—the only possible counterweight to the Soviet Union—was acting in concert with the USSR. Stalin, nevertheless, did not hurry to overwhelm his victims, instead taking what he wanted a little at a time. Until Soviet troops entered Latvia, Lithuania, and Estonia, Stalin applied a tactic he shared with Comintern head Dimitrov: "It's not good to rush ahead! . . . Slogans should be advanced that suit the particular stage of the war. . . . We think we've found in mutual assistance pacts (Estonia, Latvia, Lithuania) a form that permits us to bring a number of countries into the Soviet Union's orbit of influence. But for this, we need to hold back—to strictly respect their internal regimes and independence. We won't try to sovietize them. The time will come when they'll do it themselves!"[47]

The prediction Stalin makes in the last sentence of this explanation betrays his ultimate goal: to sovietize and absorb the countries and territories added to his country's sphere of influence under the Molotov-Ribbentrop pact. From a historical standpoint, he could justify this goal as the reconstitution of the Russian Empire. As military strategy, it surely made sense to establish strong control over areas through which an attack might come. But the future—the who, what, when, and where of the impending war— was shrouded in uncertainty, and Stalin was forced to wait. For now, he preferred to play a balancing game and went out of his way to avoid unnecessarily irritating either Great Britain and France or, especially, the Führer. There were many small signs of Stalin's caution during this period. We see it, for example, in his reaction to a report from Belarus on a speech given to the republic's parliament by army group commander Vasily Chuikov. Intoxicated by his easy victory in Poland, Chuikov told his audience in this speech, which went out over the radio, "If the party says the word, we'll march to that tune—first Warsaw, then Berlin!" Furious, Stalin wrote Chuikov's boss, Voroshilov: "Com. Voroshilov. Chuikov is evidently at least a fool, if not an enemy element. I say he should be given a spanking. At the very least."[48] While Chuikov apparently survived, many other Soviet citizens who expressed anti-Nazi sentiments were not so lucky. Between August 1939 and the beginning of war between Germany and the USSR, expressions of anti-Hitlerism were treated as a crime in the Soviet Union.

Stalin's stealthy approach to expansion was bound to hit a stumbling block eventually, and that stumbling block was Finland. In October 1939, having won the concessions he wanted from Latvia, Lithuania, and Estonia, the Soviet dictator turned his attention to his Nordic neighbor, which the Nazis had recognized as part of the Soviet sphere of influence. Finland was presented with much harsher demands than the Baltic countries. In addition to the placement of Soviet military bases in Finland, the USSR demanded a large portion of Finnish territory near Leningrad in exchange for land in less populated border regions. On the surface, these demands appeared perfectly reasonable. The USSR wanted to be able to defend Leningrad—the country's second capital and a major center of defense production—and its approaches from the Baltic Sea. But Finland, a former province of the Russian Empire that had received its independence in 1917, suspected the USSR of imperial ambitions. The Finns remembered the horrors of the 1918 civil war, which had largely been provoked by their Communist neighbor. They also noted the recent example of Czechoslovakia, which had given up the Sudetenland only to be entirely taken over by Hitler. Finland categorically refused the Soviet demands. Stalin decided to use force.

The Red Army invaded Finland in late November, having every reason to believe that its campaign would be short and successful. Finland was a tiny country with no more than 4 million inhabitants—forty times smaller than the Soviet population. The territory, economic resources, and military might of the two countries were not comparable. The 26 tanks with which Finland began the war would have to fend off 1,500 Soviet ones. Furthermore, the USSR would be able to throw significant additional troops and resources into the battle, and it did so as the conflict—known as the Winter War—unexpectedly continued. Staking success on overwhelming force, Stalin decided to make Finland the site of his first experiment applying a different takeover model from the one used in the Baltic states. The Red

Army brought with it the "people's government of Finland," consisting of Communists hand-picked in Moscow. This was the government that would be installed to rule a defeated Finland.

But the people's government of Finland never took office. The Finns showed the Red Army fierce and capable resistance. As the war dragged on, a strongly anti-Soviet mood spread throughout the rest of the world. The USSR was expelled from the League of Nations, and France and England prepared to intervene on the Finnish side. Stalin decided not to tempt fate. Despite a series of victories made possible by a major buildup of forces, in March 1940 he signed a peace treaty with Finland. Plans to sovietize the USSR's northern neighbor were set aside. The Finns wound up losing a significant portion of their territory and economy, but they maintained their independence. The Red Army lost approximately 130,000 troops, either killed in combat, dying from wounds or disease, or missing in action. More than 200,000 were wounded or frostbitten. The Finnish losses were significantly lower: 23,000 killed or missing in action and 44,000 wounded.[49] The war, a major symbolic defeat for the USSR and Stalin personally, exposed weaknesses in every component of the Soviet military machine. Historians have proposed that it was this conflict that prompted Hitler to push forward his timetable for invading the Soviet Union.

Soviet failure in Finland contrasted ominously with Hitler's triumphant advance. Soon after the Winter War, in April–June 1940, Germany occupied a number of West European countries, forcing France to capitulate in just weeks. British troops were evacuated from the continent, and Italy entered the war on Germany's side. France's quick and inglorious fall radically changed the situation in the world. Khrushchev later described how upset and worried Stalin was about the French defeat, lamenting the country's inability to put up a fight.[50] Even if Khrushchev's account is tainted by hindsight, there is no reason to doubt Stalin's general sense of alarm. The Soviet leader had lost his former maneuvering room between the warring sides. A strategy that had looked rock solid had suddenly turned to dust. Now there would be no easy way out through a mutually convenient treaty. A huge threat hung over the Soviet Union. The nation that had been its sole if unreliable ally began to look like a mortally dangerous enemy.

Stalin reacted feverishly. As Germany solidified its control over Western Europe in the summer of 1940, Latvia, Lithuania, and Estonia were incorporated into the USSR, as were Bessarabia and part of Bukovina, both of which had been taken from Romania. A top priority for the Stalinist leadership was the rapid sovietization of these new possessions. A large-scale expropriation of private property was accompanied by a massive purge of the population. Repression now fell on the newly integrated western regions. As usual, in addition to the arrest and execution of "unreliable" citizens, many were exiled to remote areas of the Soviet interior. In four relocation campaigns in 1940 and the first half of 1941, some 370,000 people were moved from western Ukraine, western Belarus, the Baltic states, and Bessarabia into the Soviet interior. This was a huge number given the small populations of these regions.[51]

Busy as he was dealing with hundreds of thousands of "suspect" people in the newly sovietized areas, Stalin did not forget about faraway enemies. In August 1940 Lev Trotsky was killed in Mexico on his orders. An NKVD agent who had penetrated Trotsky's inner circle killed the former opposition leader with an ice pick. Stalin had long stalked his most implacable, energetic, and eloquent foe. Was he driven by a personal thirst for revenge or concern that Trotskyites within the USSR might rally in time of war? Most likely both factors played a role.

Having subdued the territories stipulated for Soviet control under his agreements with Hitler, Stalin faced the question: What now? On one hand, the success of the German war machine made friendship with Hitler more important than ever. On the other, the growing threat that Nazi aggression posed to the USSR made such friendship increasingly dangerous. Soviet and German interests were clashing in Finland, where Germany, having occupied Norway, was making inroads as a result of the outcome of the Winter War. The two powers were also clashing in the Balkans due to Hitler's desperate need for Romanian oil. Stalin also hoped to gain a share of Romania and Bulgaria and achieve a long-standing Russian imperial goal: control over the Turkish Straits.

For Stalin, the signing of the Tripartite Pact among Germany, Italy, and Japan on 27 September 1940 was bad news. The three aggressor countries were agreeing to help each other divide up the rest of the world. Germany and Italy were recognized as dominant in Europe, and Japan in Asia. In theory, this agreement was aimed at Great Britain and the United States. But Stalin had every reason to worry.

Believing it necessary at this stage to avoid exacerbating tensions with the Soviet Union, in November 1940 Hitler made a conciliatory gesture by inviting Molotov to Berlin. During negotiations with Hitler and von Ribbentrop, the Soviet foreign minister insisted that his country's interests be recognized in Finland, the Balkans, and the Turkish Straits. Hitler was equally firm, especially when it came to Soviet claims in Finland and Romania. While avoiding making specific promises, Hitler suggested that the USSR become a fourth partner in the Tripartite Pact, take part in dividing up the British Empire, and determine exact Soviet spheres of influence through further negotiations.[52] Both sides apparently were probing to see what such an arrangement might offer. Was this four-way alliance ever a real possibility? On one hand, we know that while these negotiations were going on, Hitler was already hatching plans to invade the USSR. We also know that Stalin was entirely aware of the threat posed by Germany. On the other hand, in August 1939, when the Molotov-Ribbentrop Pact was being concluded, the Soviet Union and Germany were just as fundamentally hostile toward one another. Everything had changed in an instant once Stalin and Hitler found a point of common interest.

On 25 November 1940, shortly after his return from Berlin, Molotov gave the German ambassador in Moscow the Soviet conditions for a four-way pact. Here, Stalin was again resorting to the tactic that had yielded success in August 1939. In exchange for the support of his partners (and with an understanding that significant amounts of Soviet raw materials would be supplied to Germany), he issued four specific demands. First, German troops must pull out of Finland. In exchange he would guarantee that Finland would remain friendly toward Germany and supply it with timber and nickel, a point on which Hitler had particularly insisted during his talks with Molotov. Second, Stalin laid claim to Soviet influence in Bulgaria, including the conclusion of a mutual assistance treaty and the establishment of Soviet military bases near the Turkish Straits. Third, the three partners must recognize the Soviet Union's right to expand southward through Iran and Turkey to the Persian Gulf. Fourth, Japan must give up claims to coal and oil concessions in North Sakhalin in exchange for "fair compensation."[53] This program, which closely mirrored the aspirations of the Russian Empire, probably included everything Stalin wanted, and he was undoubtedly prepared to bargain. The submission of these conditions to Berlin indicated, presumably, his readiness to cast his lot with the aggressor countries.

It has been asserted, however, that Stalin never seriously considered Hitler's proposal to form a four-way pact and that the demands sent to Berlin on 25 November were a delaying tactic, intentionally designed to be unacceptable to Germany. The most significant evidence cited by proponents of this view is an account of a Politburo meeting on 14 November 1940, during which Molotov supposedly reported on his negotiations in Berlin. The account has Stalin stating that Hitler could not be trusted and that the time had come to prepare for war against Germany. But there is no record of any such Politburo meeting or of Stalin making this remark. The only source of this information is Yakov Chadaev, chief of administration for the Sovnarkom (Sovet Narodnykh Kommissarov; the Council of People's Commissars —the Soviet cabinet), who claimed to have been present and to have taken notes at the meeting.[54]

There are several reasons to doubt Chadaev's account. First, Molotov could not have been in Moscow on 14 November since that is the day he boarded the train home from Berlin. Furthermore, it is hard to understand why Stalin would have wanted to hold such a meeting, especially one including people who were not Politburo members.[55] Most other major foreign policy decisions during the prewar years (including the Nazi-Soviet Pact of 1939) were not voted on by the Politburo. Stalin kept his foreign policy cards close to the vest, at most consulting with Molotov. The talks exploring joining the Tripartite Pact were a closely held state secret.

Another piece of evidence casting doubt on the meeting is the log of visitors to Stalin's office, which shows no activity between 6 and 14 November. It is nearly certain, therefore, that Stalin spent these days at his dacha.[56] Finally, there is no evidence of any Politburo meetings in November, and even if there had been, Chadaev is unlikely to have been allowed to attend, to say nothing of his taking notes. As chief of administration for the Sovnarkom, he gained easy access to Stalin only after the *vozhd* became chairman of that body in May 1941. The fact remains that on 25 November 1940, Stalin responded quickly and substantively to Hitler's proposal for an enhanced alliance. Berlin did not react to Stalin's conditions, despite being prodded by Moscow. Soon after Molotov left Berlin, Hungary, Romania, and Slovakia— three countries entirely dependent on Hitler's will—joined the pact, followed in March 1941 by Bulgaria, which Stalin had so insistently claimed for his sphere of influence. In April Germany took over Greece and Yugoslavia.

In December 1940, Hitler approved plans to invade the USSR in May 1941. The only allies Stalin had left were his own people. The *vozhd* spent the final months before Hitler marched into the Soviet Union consolidating his power and making extraordinary efforts to bolster the country's military strength.

■   **THE CONSOLIDATION OF SUPREME POWER**

One important result of the Great Terror was the dramatic shift in the balance of power within the Politburo. Remnants of collective leadership survived into the mid-1930s, but by late 1937 the Politburo was entirely

Stalin's mother, Ekaterine (Keke) Jughashvili.
Russian State Archive of Social and Political History.

Stalin as a pupil at the Gori Theological School in the early 1890s.
Russian State Archive of Social and Political History.

Stalin as a young revolutionary, early 1900s.
Russian State Archive of Social and Political History.

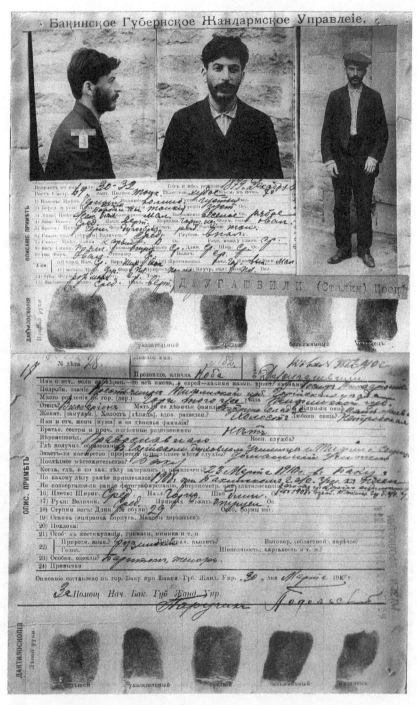

From party archives, a 1910 arrest record for Stalin from the files of the tsarist
political police in Baku. Russian State Archive of Social and Political History.

Stalin at the Tsaritsyn front in 1918. Russian State Archive of Social and Political History.

Lenin and Stalin at Gorki, Lenin's residence outside Moscow, in 1922, a few months before Lenin's death prompted a fierce power struggle. Russian State Archive of Social and Political History.

Stalin with Rykov (left) and Bukharin (right), December 1927. Rykov and Bukharin were shot in 1938. Russian State Archive of Social and Political History.

The *vozhd* with his faithful comrades in 1934. Left to right: Kirov, Kaganovich, Ordzhonikidze, Stalin, and Mikoyan. Kirov was shot later that year by the husband of a staff member, and Ordzhonikidze committed suicide in 1937. Russian State Archive of Social and Political History.

Stalin with his wife, Nadezhda Allilueva, Voroshilov, and Voroshilov's wife Yekaterina relaxing in the south in 1932 (with a bodyguard to the right) a few months before Nadezhda's suicide. Russian State Archive of Social and Political History.

On vacation in 1933. Stalin's daughter Svetlana sits on the lap of then Georgian party boss Lavrenty Beria. Russian State Archive of Social and Political History.

The loving father: Stalin with Svetlana, 1933.
Russian State Archive of Social and Political History.

A visit in the south, 1933. Left to right: chief of the Red Army General Staff Aleksandr Yegorov; Defense Commissar Kliment Voroshilov; Stalin; Soviet military leader Mikhail Tukhachevsky; Abkhaz leader Nestor Lakoba. Lakoba died in 1936 under mysterious circumstances and was soon proclaimed an "enemy of the people." Tukhachevsky was shot in 1937 and Yegorov in 1938. Russian State Archive of Social and Political History.

The near dacha, where Stalin lived (starting after his wife's suicide) and died. Russian State Archive of Social and Political History

A rare family gathering in the mid-1930s. Left to right: Stalin's son Vasily, Leningrad party boss Andrei Zhdanov, daughter Svetlana, Stalin, and Stalin's son (by his first wife) Yakov, who was killed in a Nazi POW camp. Russian State Archive of Social and Political History.

Stalin inspects new military hardware at the Kremlin, September 1943. Russian State Archive of Social and Political History.

The Allies: Churchill, Roosevelt, and Stalin in Crimea, February 1945.
Russian State Archive of Social and Political History.

Generalissimo Stalin immediately after the war.
Russian State Archive of Social and Political History.

Stalin and his comrades at a celebration in January 1947. Left to right: Beria, Kaganovich, Malenkov, Molotov, Kuznetsov, Stalin, Kosygin, Voznesensky, Voroshilov, and Shkiriatov. Two years later Kuznetsov and Voznesensky were arrested and shot. Russian State Archive of Social and Political History.

Stalin at a party congress in 1952, four months before his death.
Unflattering photographs like this one were not published. Russian State
Archive of Social and Political History.

Millions of copies of Stalin's works were published in all languages. After his death they provided tons of recycled paper pulp. Russian State Archive of Social and Political History.

subject to Stalin's will. The Terror brought his power to new heights. He was now a full-fledged dictator in whose hands rested the lives not only of ordinary citizens, but also those of his most esteemed fellow leaders. Five Politburo members (Stanislav Kosior, Vlas Chubar, Robert Eikhe, Pavel Postyshev, and Yan Rudzutak) were shot, and one (Grigory Petrovsky) was expelled from the upper echelons and survived only because Stalin chose to show him clemency. Another name on the list of Stalin's high-ranking victims was Grigory Ordzhonikidze, driven to suicide by Stalin's ruthlessness. But even the top leaders who held onto their posts found themselves in an impotent and demeaning position, forced to carefully walk the line between power and death and unable to protect their most valued subordinates or even close friends and relatives. The names of top leaders inevitably came up in the countless confessions the NKVD extracted under torture. It was up to Stalin to decide what denunciations and incriminations should be taken seriously. Anyone could suddenly be labeled an enemy.

As Stalin's longtime comrades disappeared from the top leadership, younger faces took their place. As noted, these replacements were an important element of his consolidation of power. Lacking the revolutionary credentials of the older generation, these young leaders owed their standing directly to Stalin and were entirely dependent on him. In March 1939 Andrei Zhdanov and Nikita Khrushchev, members of this second generation, were granted full membership in the Politburo. At the same time, a member of the third generation, Lavrenty Beria, was made a candidate member. In February 1941 three other members of the third generation were added: Nikolai Voznesensky, Georgy Malenkov, and Aleksandr Shcherbakov.[57] These appointments did not simply represent the normal advance of competent leaders up the career ladder. Stalin made a point of placing young officials in important posts, often as counterweights to his older, more deserving colleagues.

Changes to the composition of the Politburo were just one manifestation of processes taking place under the surface that ultimately destroyed the formal aspects of the collective leadership and substituted new unofficial or quasi-official institutions adapted to the administrative and political needs of Stalin's dictatorship and lifestyle. The deterioration of the Politburo's meaningful role was brought to its logical conclusion when it essentially ceased to function as a formal institution. During the years of the Great Terror, it was replaced by a narrower group within the leadership, always chaired by Stalin. In early 1938 the "Secret Five" took shape, consisting of Stalin, Molotov, Voroshilov, Mikoyan, and Kaganovich. This group, though not an official body, largely took the place of the Politburo. The only vote that mattered was Stalin's. In addition to his deliberations during meetings of the Five, Stalin settled many questions with individual members of the leadership. These ad hoc decision-making mechanisms bore little resemblance to constitutional structures or procedures and depended purely on the will of the *vozhd*. The meetings, following Stalin's habits and nocturnal lifestyle, took the most varied forms. Matters of state could be decided day or night, in Stalin's Kremlin office or at his dacha, in the movie theater or during long hours at the dinner table.

The next level of the pyramid of power consisted of governmental bodies to which Stalin delegated particular authority while retaining overall control. This system first took shape within the party's Central Committee apparat, which had the mission of promulgating ideology and selecting and assigning senior party and state officials. These key areas were overseen personally by Stalin's protégés, Zhdanov and Malenkov, who could make relatively trivial decisions on their own but had to bring more consequential ones to Stalin for approval. In January 1941, Stalin explained the Central Committee's new modus operandi: "It's been four or five months since we in the Central Committee have convened the Politburo. All questions are prepared by Zhdanov, Malenkov, and others in separate meetings with comrades who have the necessary expertise, and the job of governing is only going more smoothly as a result."[58]

On the government side, accommodating the commissariats, departments, and committees of the Sovnarkom to the dictator's needs was more difficult. The Sovnarkom oversaw the entire Soviet economy, which was then laboring under the strain of urgent preparations for war. Stalin sought to make the bureaucracy into something he could steer at will, but the sluggishness and unmanageability of its agencies sent him into fits of irritation and temper. His frustration led to numerous attempts to reorganize how the system was managed by the country's top leadership. Finally, in March 1941, a new governmental body was created: the Bureau of the USSR Sovnarkom, consisting of Sovnarkom chairman Molotov and his deputies. This bureau was created as a governing group within the Sovnarkom, much like the leading group within the Politburo.

As part of the political intrigue around the reorganization, the relatively young Nikolai Voznesensky became first deputy to the government's chairman, Molotov. His appointment to such an important post, over the heads of more senior members of the Politburo such as Mikoyan and Kaganovich, heightened tensions within Stalin's inner circle. Even in memoirs written decades later, Mikoyan could not hide his hurt feelings: "But what struck us most of all about the composition of the Bureau leadership was that Voznesensky became first deputy chairman of the Sovnarkom. . . . Stalin's motives in this whole leapfrog were still not clear. And Voznesensky, being naive, was very pleased with his appointment."[59] In giving this important job to Voznesensky, Stalin may have been intentionally pitting him against Molotov, hinting that the Sovnarkom chairman was not able to handle all his duties and needed a younger and more energetic deputy. In any event, the entire government reorganization came with a chorus of reprimands and accusations directed against Molotov's Sovnarkom leadership. This was a clear sign that Stalin had something up his sleeve.

His plans became evident a month after the Sovnarkom Bureau was established. On 28 April 1941 Stalin sent a memorandum to Bureau members explaining that it had been created for the purpose of straightening out government operations and bringing an end to "chaos" within the economic leadership, which continued to decide "important questions related to the building of the economy through so-called 'polling.'" As an example of the inappropriate use of polling (having members of a committee vote on a circulated document individually rather than meeting to discuss it in person), Stalin pointed to a draft resolution concerning the construction of an oil pipeline in the Sakhalin area. Molotov had signed the document, he wrote indignantly, even though it had not been discussed by the Sovnarkom Bureau. After labeling this practice "paper-pushing and scribbling," he issued an ultimatum: "I think 'management' of this sort can't go on. I propose discussing this question in the Central Committee's Politburo. And for now, I feel compelled to say that I refuse to participate in voting through polling on any draft resolution whatsoever concerning economic questions of any consequence whatsoever if I don't see the signatures of the Sovnarkom Bureau indicating that the draft has been discussed and approved by the Bureau of the USSR Sovnarkom."[60]

This outburst must have taken Molotov by surprise. Polling was standard practice in Soviet decision making. As recently as January 1941, Stalin himself had criticized the Sovnarkom for "parliamentarianism," by which he meant that its members were having too many meetings. As everyone involved surely noticed, Stalin offered only one example of "incorrect" polling—and not a particularly compelling one, as the question of the Sakhalin pipeline probably did not require detailed discussion at a bureau meeting. The charges leveled in the April memorandum sounded frivolous, and Molotov and the other Politburo members must have realized that they were a pretext. The discussion of Stalin's memorandum led to a Politburo decision, dated 4 May 1941. It read in part as follows:

I. In the interests of full coordination between Soviet and party organizations and the unconditional assurance of unity in their work as leaders, as well as to further enhance the authority of Soviet bodies given the current tense international situation, which demands every possible effort by Soviet agencies in the defense of the country, the Politburo unanimously resolves:

1. To appoint Com. I. V. Stalin Chairman of the Council of People's Commissars [Sovnarkom] of the USSR.

2. To appoint Com. V. M. Molotov Deputy Chairman of the USSR Sovnarkom and to place him in charge of the foreign policy of the USSR, leaving him in the post of People's Commissar for Foreign Affairs.

3. Inasmuch as Com. Stalin, who, on the insistence of the Central Committee's Politburo, retains the position of first secretary of the TsK VKP(b) [Central Committee of the All-Union Communist Party (Bolsheviks)], will not be able to allot sufficient time to work in the TsK Secretariat, to appoint Com. A. A. Zhdanov Com. Stalin's deputy in the TsK Secretariat, relieving him of his duties overseeing the TsK VKP(b) Directorate for Propaganda and Agitation.[61]

No documents or memoirs have been located that shed light on the discussions leading up to this resolution, but some clues are offered by its wording, which equates the reorganizations with a return to the Leninist revolutionary model of leadership. The leader of the party and the country, it states, should head the government, especially at a time of looming war. If Stalin had fully bought into the logic that it was important to adhere to the original Soviet model, he would have had to renounce the post of Central Committee secretary since Lenin was the founder and leader of the party but did not hold that post. But he chose to take both the top party and government posts for himself.

At last the dictatorial system of government was complete. At the top of the hierarchy stood the dictator himself. With the title of general secretary of the party added to that of chairman of the government, the supreme power he had been exercising for some time was made official. The Politburo's leading group—a subset of its membership hand-picked by Stalin—would serve as his consultative body. One step down the hierarchy were two governing bodies: the secretariat of the party's Central Committee, headed by

Zhdanov, and the Sovnarkom Bureau, headed by Voznesensky. These two bodies served as the dictator's arms. They took care of the routine running of the country and brought consequential matters to Stalin for approval.

This reorganization was undoubtedly motivated by more than a desire for efficiency. Stalin's decision to give himself, the leader of the party, the added title of chairman of the government told the country and the world that at a time of international instability, the Soviet Union had consolidated its leadership. Again, Stalin's personality—his hunger to possess not only real power, but also all of its accouterments and his tendency to regard even his closest comrades with suspicion—also has to be taken into consideration. The latter quality was surely a factor in his decision to accelerate the advance of the younger generation and put Zhdanov and Malenkov in charge of the Central Committee apparat. Voznesensky—not Molotov, the logical choice—was appointed to serve as Stalin's first deputy in his role as government chairman. Beria, another member of the new generation, oversaw the network of security agencies. Stalin's old comrades, even those who remained at the upper echelons of power, suffered significantly diminished standing as they made way for their younger colleagues.

Molotov was a particular target of Stalin's displeasure. After long years of devoted service and exceptional closeness with the *vozhd,* Molotov was deprived of the Sovnarkom chairmanship and was not even appointed Stalin's first deputy. Stalin took every opportunity to demonstrate his disdain for Molotov. One of the last recorded manifestations of his irritation toward his longtime comrade occurred not long before the outbreak of war. In May 1941, at a meeting of the newly constituted Sovnarkom Bureau, Stalin took Molotov to task. Yakov Chadaev, the Sovnarkom's chief of administration, who was taking minutes at the meeting, recalls:

> Stalin did not conceal his disapproval of Molotov. He very impatiently listened to Molotov's rather prolix responses to comments from members of the Bureau. . . . It seemed as if Stalin was attacking Molotov as an adversary and that he was doing so from a position of strength. . . . Molotov's breathing began to quicken, and at times he would let out a deep sigh. He fidgeted on his stool and murmured something to himself. By the end he could take it no longer:
>
> "Easier said than done," Molotov pronounced in a low but cutting voice. Stalin picked up [Molotov's] words.
>
> "It has long been well-known," said Stalin, "that the person who is afraid of criticism is a coward."

Molotov winced, but kept quiet—the other members of the Politburo sat silently, burying their noses in the papers. . . . At this meeting I was again convinced of the power and greatness of Stalin. Stalin's companions feared him like the devil. They would agree with him on practically anything.[62]

What was behind this abusive treatment of a faithful colleague? Perhaps Stalin was taking out his frustrations over the state of Soviet foreign relations. Or perhaps, in the lead-up to war, he was making an example of his old comrade to keep the rest of the leadership in line. In any event, the result was a further centralization of power and a top leadership afraid to voice dissent. Critical questions of war and peace, concerning the fates of millions, rested solely in the dictator's hands.

■   A PREEMPTIVE STRIKE?

On 5 May 1941, the day after his appointment as chairman of the government, Stalin went to meet with members of the Soviet military at a traditional Kremlin reception for graduates of military academies. At a similar event six years earlier, on 4 May 1935, Stalin had come out with the slogan, "Cadres solve everything!" This time the watchword the *vozhd* shared with his military guests was classified and did not appear in the press. In May 1941, just six weeks before the outbreak of war with Germany, he called for a switch from a defensive to an offensive posture enabled by a powerful Red Army.[63]

While these remarks have attracted the particular interest of scholars, it is important to note that he had made similar comments in the past. In October 1938, for example, he told a gathering the following:

> Bolsheviks are not just pacifists who long for peace and reach for arms only if they're attacked. That's not true. There will be times when Bolsheviks are the invaders; if the war is just, if the situation is right, and if the conditions are favorable, they will go on the offensive themselves. They are by no means against invading, against any war. The fact that we're now shouting about defense—that's a veil, a veil. All countries mask their true selves: "If you live with wolves, you have to howl like a wolf." [Laughter.] It would be stupid to spill your guts and lay them on the table.[64]

In April 1940, when speaking to the military council in the aftermath of the Winter War, Stalin continued to address this topic. He spent a long time explaining to the officers that "an army that has been cultivated not for attacking but for passive defense" cannot be called modern.[65]

Obviously when Stalin made these statements, in 1938 and early 1940, he had no intention of invading Germany. But as certain historians and commentators have pointed out, by 1941 the situation was very different. The German Army massed along the Soviet border and ready to pounce on the USSR might very well have convinced Stalin of the advisability of a preventive strike. A variety of arguments and pieces of evidence (albeit circumstantial) have been used to defend this viewpoint.[66] For a biographer of Stalin, this question is far from secondary. Are we seeing, in 1941, a "different Stalin"—not the cautious incrementalist who could be drawn into a fight only when he felt himself in a position of strength but a daring leader who believed the Red Army was prepared to challenge the Wehrmacht? Such an assumption is in fundamental conflict with the traditional view of the prewar Stalin, which is based on the reminiscences of Soviet marshals and evidence of his vacillating inconsistency in the months leading up to the war. Convincing evidence that Stalin was firmly resolved to go on the offensive has yet to surface. There is no serious basis for revising the traditional view that Stalin was fatally indecisive and even befuddled in the face of the growing Nazi threat.

It is, however, true that during 1940 and 1941 Stalin worked hard to strengthen the Red Army and prepare the country for the upheaval of war. In 1940, for the fourth year in a row, he did not take a vacation in the south. His primary concern was the army and the munitions industry. The accelerated buildup of heavy industry and its defense branches had been a priority since the late 1920s. The Stalinist approach to industrialization made this buildup especially costly, but in the end, the sacrifice of millions of ruined peasants and Gulag slaves and the expenditure of the vast country's significant resources did have a military and economic effect. By the time war with Germany broke out, the Soviet Union had more than twenty-five thousand tanks and eighteen thousand fighter planes, three to four times more than Germany.[67] Such figures have inspired proponents of the theory of a "preventive war" to claim that the USSR was ready to take on Germany. But statistics often lie. In the Soviet case, the true story was often one of poor quality weaponry and padded figures, made worse by a shortage of well-trained military personnel. In any event, Stalin and the military leadership did not believe all this military hardware was sufficient. Having a military threat right at their doorstep demanded special measures. Ominous rumors of the might of the German Army and the quality of its weaponry were reaching the USSR from vanquished Europe. During the prewar period, the Soviet Union made a desperate attempt to increase output and modernize at the same time. By 1940, military production was two and a half times what it had been in 1937.[68] This was an extraordinary increase. Special emphasis was placed on the production of new types of weapons, modern tanks and planes especially. Key to this modernization effort were purchases of military hardware from Germany, enabled under the Nazi-Soviet Pact.

Despite the energy put into this buildup, progress was slow. There are well-known examples from the tank and aviation industry. Of the 25,000 tanks in the Soviet arsenal as of June 1941, only 1,500 were of modern design, and only a quarter of Soviet military aircraft was new.[69] This is not to say that the remaining tanks and planes were useless. It does, however, show that the job of modernizing the Soviet military was far from complete. The leadership knew this.

Stalin had a much better understanding of the problems plaguing the Soviet military economy than do today's proponents of the preventive war theory, who focus exclusively on munitions-industry production statistics. The army and munitions industry were part of a huge socioeconomic machine with myriad interdependent parts. There was a limit to how much could be spent on the military buildup, especially as the prewar years coincided with yet another slowdown in the Soviet economy, associated with an imbalance between investment and resources. Such crucial resources as metal and electricity were in short supply, and the diversion of so much investment toward military production meant cutting the already scant resources put toward meeting the basic needs of Soviet citizens. Prices and taxes were rising, most of the population was getting by on a meager ration, and in some rural areas there were signs of famine. In late 1939 a ban was placed on the sale of flour and bread in the countryside. Hungry peasants rushed to cities and towns to buy these items, which were in short supply there too. The leadership in Moscow was inundated with desperate pleas for help. In February 1940, a woman wrote from the Urals, "Joseph Vissarionovich, something really terrifying has begun. . . . I've so wasted away I don't know what will become of me." Someone in Stalingrad wrote to the Central Committee that "We don't have time to sleep anymore. At two in the morning people begin lining up for bread, and by five or six there are already 600–700–1,000 people standing outside the stores. . . . You might be interested to know what they're feeding workers in the cafeterias. What they used to give to swine they now give to us."[70]

The country's top leadership was fully aware of the situation. The Politburo made repeated attempts to address the shortages, giving priority to major cities and industrial enterprises. The food crisis exacerbated the problems of employee turnover and absenteeism that had always plagued the Soviet economy. As the country mobilized for war, harsh measures were introduced to combat these problems. On 26 June 1940, as France was succumbing to the Nazis, the USSR enacted a new law lengthening the workday and work week and making it a crime to be late or to leave one's place of employment without permission. Soviet peasants had lost their freedom of movement long ago. Now factory and office workers lost theirs. In the year between the enactment of this law and the start of war, it was used to convict more than three million people.[71] Of them 480,000 served prison terms up to four months.[72] The rest, though not imprisoned, were forced to perform compulsory labor for up to six months. The convicted were often allowed to remain at their jobs, but a significant share of their meager pay was deducted, condemning them and their families to hunger.

Such extreme laws and the declining standard of living took a toll on Soviet society, whose suffering only increased Stalin's deeply ingrained fear of a fifth column. Whereas the purges of the prewar years had been targeted primarily at the western areas recently annexed by the USSR, Stalin now began to worry, and with reason, that people throughout Soviet society could prove disloyal to him in time of war. Too many had suffered at the hand of the government; too many had starved or eked out a meager existence. The propagandistic claims of monolithic unity at both the front and the rear were intended for the people, for foreign enemies, and for gullible posterity. Stalin was not among the gullible.

Soviet propaganda described the Red Army as the people's own flesh and blood, and it was. Within the Red Army, the unique features and contradictions of the Stalinist system were manifested in concentrated form. Between January 1939 and June 1941 the Soviet armed forces more than doubled in size. This rapid increase came with the same fundamental problem that plagued Stalinist "leaps forward" in general, especially the rapid industrialization of the early 1930s. Ambitious attempts to calculate exactly what equipment—even what entire factories—had to be purchased from the West failed miserably. Young, untrained Soviet workers produced defective products, damaging factory equipment in the process. Stalin's understanding of the complex interdependence between technical and social progress was expressed in the updating of the slogan "Cadres solve everything!" to "Technology solves everything!" The rapidly growing Red

Army needed not only to be armed but also trained. It is difficult to say which was the harder task.

Between 1937 and 1940, the Soviet officer corps grew more than two and a half times. As a result, a sizable proportion of commanders lacked the requisite knowledge and experience. During the war Stalin reproached one of his generals for the quality of army officers: "You in the military in your time ruined the army by sending all sorts of junk into academies and administration."[73] As usual, he was blaming others for problems that were primarily his fault. It was on his initiative that in the 1930s, tens of thousands of commanders, men who would have been capable of serving their country with distinction, were fired, sent to the camps, or shot for political reasons. But the damage to the Red Army was not measured only in numbers. Until the outbreak of war (and to a lesser extent even during it), repression had distorted the decision-making process, including promotions, making it possible for time-serving incompetents, skilled primarily in expressions of loyalty, to make successful careers. It also discouraged a commander's most important quality—a willingness to take the initiative—and instead encouraged excessive caution. As was well known from anti-wrecking campaigns, repression subverted the authority of those in charge and undermined discipline. The problems of rule breaking and drunkenness that had always plagued the Red Army were magnified.

The Soviet leadership could see that there was trouble within the army. The clearest signal was the Winter War with Finland. The unexpected foiling of the Red Army by an incomparably weaker enemy dealt the Soviet military's reputation a stunning blow that could not have come at a worse time. After the peace treaty was signed, Stalin conducted a review to determine what had gone wrong. Countless deficiencies in the arming and training of soldiers were discovered, along with problems in the command system. Stalin removed his old friend Kliment Voroshilov from the post of people's commissar for defense and replaced much of the military's leadership. These changes brought little improvement. In April 1941, approximately one year after the shake-up, the Politburo looked into accidents in military aviation. It turned out that even in peacetime, an average of two to three planes was lost in accidents every day. Furious, Stalin placed all the blame on the air force leadership.[74] On the very eve of war, a new wave of arrests roiled the military command.

Stalin did not allow his focus on the Red Army to distract him from keeping an eye on his adversary's forces. The ruthless efficiency of the Wehrmacht was extremely alarming. Delegations of Soviet weapons experts who visited German munitions plants under a Soviet-German cooperation agreement returned home with glowing reports. Delegation members were unable to hide how impressed they were and wrote of the huge successes of the German weapons industry. In keeping with the Russian saying "Fear has big eyes," Soviet intelligence and the military and economic leadership constantly exaggerated the enemy's strength. In 1940 the new people's commissar for airplane production, Aleksei Shakhurin, reported to Stalin that Germany's aviation industry had twice the capacity of its Soviet counterpart. The reports Stalin received from his intelligence agencies significantly exaggerated both the potential of German industry and the size of its armed forces.[75] As a result of these overestimates, the enemy looked much more imposing that it actually was.

The sources of Stalin's prewar anxiety are a huge subject that cannot be fully addressed within the scope of this book. Clearly, he had good reason to fear war with Germany. One way he may have reacted to this fear was with a desire (which many believe he felt) to delay the start of war in order to give the Soviet Union time to strengthen its military capabilities and hope that international events would take a favorable turn. He certainly had reason to hope that war would be delayed. One of the most convincing reasons was the idea that Hitler would not be so foolhardy as to mire his forces on two fronts by engaging the Soviet Union while he had Great Britain and the increasingly active United States threatening his rear. Stalin was not alone in this line of reasoning. Hitler, fully aware of how much sense this theory made, took care to exploit it. Secure in the knowledge that he was preserving the element of surprise, he did indeed take the risky plunge of engaging enemies on two fronts—largely because his enemies saw such a move as an impossibility. Nazi propaganda spread disinformation to perpetuate this mistaken idea. Stalin wound up the victim of his belief in Hitler's instinct for self-preservation.

A few peripheral factors strengthened Stalin's faith that Hitler would not hurry to attack the USSR. For one, Soviet-German economic cooperation was thriving. Soviet exports were feeding Germany's appetite for raw materials. Goods imported into Germany from three different countries traveled across Soviet territory, so war with the USSR would undermine some of Germany's important economic ties. The intelligence reports reaching Stalin's desk were contradictory. His predisposition to believe Hitler would not attack soon influenced his intelligence agencies, who preferred to tell Stalin what he wanted to hear. Such a cause-and-effect sequence is hardly unique in world history.[76]

Stalin's reaction to a 17 June 1941 intelligence report claiming that an attack was imminent is well known. Just days before the actual invasion, he wrote to the state security commissar, "You can send your 'source' from German aviation headquarters back to his f**king mother. This is disinformation, not a 'source.'"[77] Even if Stalin may have been correct in this case, clearly reactions like this frightened intelligence officials and discouraged them from speaking up, rendering them much less effective. It was safer to say what Stalin wanted to hear or be silent, and those in charge of the country's security and military readiness increasingly opted for safety. Stalin got what he wanted. He alone had the right to an opinion. Everyone waited to see what the dictator had to say, hoping he knew what he was doing. Unfortunately, he did not.

PATICNT NUMBER 1

The summoning of the doctors to the near dacha
on the morning of 2 March 1953.

Beria, Khrushchev, Bulganin, and Malenkov returned to their homes, leaving Stalin on the couch without medical attention. Perhaps out of fear, or perhaps out of unspoken ambivalence toward his recovery, Stalin's comrades rejected the idea that they were facing a medical emergency. After Malenkov and Beria checked on the *vozhd* and found him sleeping, they proceeded to dismiss what the bodyguards had told them about his symptoms. Had he really had some sort of fit? The bodyguards were not doctors. Their imaginations could have been playing tricks on them. His colleagues probably also remembered that Stalin had recently accused his own doctors of being murderers. Who would take responsibility for calling a doctor (or summoning a murderer, as the *vozhd* might see it) unless he were absolutely sure one was needed? A simple need for emergency medical care was transformed into a multidimensional political problem.

Stalin's bodyguards spent the remainder of the night in a state of anxiety. No doubt worried that they could be held accountable if Stalin died, they again asked for guidance from above and reported that things did not seem right with the boss. This time the four comrades decided to send a team of doctors to the dacha. Before doing so, however, they convened the Bureau of the Central Committee Presidium[1] so that the summoning of medical luminaries would look like a collective decision by the party leadership. Should Stalin recover, his anger would fall on everyone at once. On the morning of 2 March the doctors arrived at Stalin's bedside.

The renowned Soviet cardiologist Aleksandr Miasnikov, one of the medical experts summoned to attend Stalin, gives a detailed description of the visit in his memoirs. "The diagnosis," he wrote, "was clear to us, thank God: hemorrhage in the left cerebral hemisphere of the brain caused by hypertonia and atherosclerosis."[2] The doctors gave Stalin generous doses of various stimulants but without any real hope of preventing death. From a medical perspective, his condition was no mystery. An autopsy confirmed the initial diagnosis, revealing a large cerebral hemorrhage and severe damage to the cerebral arteries due to atherosclerosis.[3]

Stalin had been a sickly old man. He would have turned seventy-five later that year.

In totalitarian regimes, too much depends on the personality of the dictator. From the time he came to power, Stalin's health was a topic of worldwide interest. During his lifetime there was periodic speculation in the Western press that he was ill or even near death. People in the Soviet Union whispered similar rumors. Scholars and commentators looked to Stalin's physical and mental health as possible keys to understanding his personality and the brutality of his dictatorship. For a long time speculation surrounding Stalin's health was based on unfounded assumptions. Only recently have we gained access to Stalin's surviving medical records and testimony by the doctors who monitored his health and examined him after his death.

The only one of the Jughashvilis' three children to live to adulthood, the future dictator suffered a variety of ills growing up. At an early age, Ioseb came down with smallpox, which left his face permanently pockmarked. He also had a bout of malaria.[4] Then, through some sort of accident, the details of which have never been clear (some say he was hit by a horse-drawn carriage), he severely injured his left arm. The injury caused his arm to atrophy, giving him problems for the rest of his life. In 1898 Ioseb wrote to the rector of the Tiflis Theological Seminary asking to be excused from a reexamination "due to a disease of the chest that has long plagued me and that grew more severe during examinations."[5] He sought to be released from police custody in October and November 1902 because of his "predisposition toward pulmonary consumption" and worsening cough.[6] Apparently his juvenile tuberculosis eventually abated, and he did not show signs of the disease later in life.

As a professional revolutionary, Stalin had to endure many hardships: prison, exile, and an unsettled existence even in times of freedom. During one term of exile he became ill with typhus.[7] His most difficult trial was his final exile in Turukhansky Krai, which lasted three years. He had difficulty adapting to the harsh climate, austere living conditions, isolation from "the world at large," and forced idleness, and in letters to friends he complained of a "suspicious cough" brought on by "intensifying cold (37 below)" and a "general state of ill health."[8] Overall, however, the tsarist government was immeasurably kinder to convicts than the Stalinist dictatorship. Had young Stalin had to endure so many imprisonments and exiles in the sort of Gulag system he went on to create, he most likely would not have survived.

The revolution and Civil War not only put millions in their graves, but also deeply affected the Bolshevik party and undermined the health of its leaders. In March 1921 Stalin underwent an appendectomy.[9] On 23 April 1921, out of concern for their health, the Politburo voted to grant Stalin, Kamenev, Rykov, and Trotsky extended vacations.[10] In late May, Stalin left for the North Caucasus and did not return to Moscow until 8 August, almost two and a half months later. In 1922 he skipped his vacation, but in July the Politburo compelled him to spend three days a week out of town.[11] Once the Civil War ended, spending time in the fresh air of Moscow's leafy suburban dacha communities became an established lifestyle for the top Bolshevik leadership. Stalin and his family commandeered the country home of a former petroleum industrialist. Later, after the death of his wife, the *vozhd* built himself a new dacha, more convenient to Moscow. This famous country home (the "near" dacha in Volynskoe) was Stalin's main residence for nearly two decades and will forever be associated with him. It was here that he died.

At the dacha, Stalin would spend time with his immediate family and other relatives or get together with his comrades. In addition to the festive dinners with lots of alcohol (described above), Stalin's dacha lifestyle also included games, such as billiards or *gorodki* (a Russian game similar to skittles), although the dictator himself was not a big lover of physical activity. "He preferred stretching out on a deckchair with a book and his documents or the newspapers. And he could sit at the table with his guests by the hour," his daughter Svetlana recalled.[12] This penchant for immobility only increased with age.

Another significant part of Stalin's life were his vacations in resort areas of southern Russia. He spent time in the south every year from 1923 to 1936 and from 1945 to 1951.[13] These trips were working vacations. A constant stream of documents was forwarded to him, and he kept up an active correspondence with his comrades back in Moscow, a practice that generated invaluable records for historians. But there was also time for rest and relaxation. While in the south Stalin treated his numerous diseases: rheumatoid arthritis, bouts of tonsillitis, long-lasting intestinal disturbances, and neurasthenia.[14] His ailments were also eased by therapeutic baths. "I am getting better. The Matsesta waters (near Sochi) are good for curing sclerosis, reviving the nerves, dilating the heart, and curing sciatica, gout, and rheumatism," he reported to Molotov on 1 August 1925.[15]

But Stalin was not a conscientious patient. His chronic ailments were exacerbated by his lifestyle and bad habits: smoking, drinking, rich foods, and overwork. Like most people, Stalin alternated between taking care of his body and inflicting damage. In May 1926 he left for a vacation in the Caucasus. After a brief stop in Sochi he set out with Mikoyan to travel through Georgia, where he visited his native Gori before going to stay with Ordzhonikidze in Tiflis. Letters from the head of Stalin's Sochi-based security team, M. Gorbachev, suggest that this was a boisterous trip. While "under the influence," as Gorbachev put it, on a whim, Stalin suddenly summoned him from Sochi to Tiflis but then forgot he had done so. When Gorbachev showed up, Stalin was surprised to see him. When it became clear what had happened, everyone "had a good laugh." Gorbachev was forced to hurry back to Sochi, covering the vast distance at breakneck speed.[16] Continuing his spree, Stalin spent a long time driving around the Caucasus and wound up returning to Sochi in bad shape. "I returned to Sochi today, 15 June," he reported to Molotov and Bukharin. "In Tiflis I came down with a stomachache (I got food poisoning from some fish) and am now having a hard time recovering."[17] Gorbachev wrote to Stalin's assistant, Ivan Tovstukha, "Overall, the boss wound up paying quite a price for this trip across the Caucasus in terms of his health. Mikoyan and Sergo [Ordzhonikidze] turned him topsy-turvy."[18] Stalin called for a doctor, went on a diet, and began to take the waters on a regular basis.[19] The doctor who treated him in Sochi, I. A. Valedinsky, recalled that his patient complained of pain in his arm and leg muscles. When his doctors forbade him to drink, Stalin asked, "But what about cognac?" Valedinsky replied that "on Saturday you can let loose, on Sunday you should rest, and on Monday you can go to work with a clear head." "Stalin liked this response, and the next time he arranged a '*subbotnik*' [a word usually used for mandatory 'volunteer' work on Saturdays], it was very memorable for me," Valedinsky wrote, although he did not explain what made this particular gathering so unforgettable.[20]

References to his poor health are scattered throughout Stalin's later correspondence as well. While on vacation in July 1927, he wrote to Molotov: "I'm sick and lying in bed so I'll be brief."[21] According to Valedinsky, that year he also complained of pain in his arm and leg muscles. Therapeutic baths were followed by the usual *subbotnik*. Stalin invited his doctors to dine with him "and was so generous with the cognac," Valedinsky wrote afterward, "that I did not make it home until the following day, on Sunday."[22] In 1928, before taking a curative bath in Sochi, Stalin again complained of pain in his arms and legs. The rheumatoid arthritis in his left arm was progressing.[23] During a vacation in August 1929 Stalin wrote to Molotov that "I am beginning to recuperate in Sochi after my illness in Nalchik."[24] In 1930, while undergoing treatment in Sochi, he fell ill with tonsillitis. His teeth also hurt. In September 1930 he wrote to his wife that the dentist had "sharpened" eight of his teeth in one go, so he "was not feeling very well."[25] In 1931 he again took therapeutic baths. "I spent about 10 days in Tsqaltubo. I took 20 baths. The water there was marvelous, truly valuable," he wrote to Yenukidze.[26] That September he wrote to his wife that he was vacationing in Sochi with Kirov. "I went one time (just once!) to the seaside. I went bathing. It was very good! I think I'll go again."[27] Apparently he used the Russian word for "bathing" because he could not swim.

The vacation Stalin took in 1932 was one of his longest. The log of visitors to his Kremlin office shows that he did not receive anyone there between 29 May and 27 August—almost three months. The apparent reason for such a long break was poor health. The following spring the foreign press was still speculating that Stalin was seriously ill. On 3 April, *Pravda* took the unprecedented step of publishing a response by Stalin to a query by the Associated Press: "This is not the first time that false rumors that I am ill have circulated in the bourgeois press. Obviously, there are people in whose interest it is that I should fall seriously ill and for a long time, if not worse. Perhaps it is not very tactful of me, but unfortunately I have no information to gratify these gentlemen. Sad though it may be, the fact is that I am in perfect health."[28] Behind this characteristically mocking response was genuine irritation. Stalin's symptoms were serious, and rest and relaxation in the beneficial climate of southern Russia apparently did not alleviate them. "It seems I won't be getting better anytime soon," Stalin wrote to Kaganovich from the south in June 1932. "A general weakness and real sense of fatigue are only now becoming evident. Just when I think I'm beginning to get better, it turns out that I've got a long way to go. I'm not having rheumatic symptoms (they disappeared somewhere), but the overall weakness isn't going away."[29] Soon, however, he felt well enough to make a 230-mile trip across the Black Sea by motor boat.[30]

Regular trips to the south inspired Stalin to build new vacation homes there. These construction projects began in 1930 and continued for the rest of his life. "We've built a marvelous little house here," he wrote of his new dacha outside Sochi in August 1933. A month later he wrote of another residence: "Today I visited the new dacha near Gagry. It's turned out (they just finished building it) to be a splendid dacha."[31]

In 1933 Stalin was away from his Kremlin office from 17 August to 4

November. On 18 August he left Moscow to travel south with Voroshilov. The trip—by train, boat, and automobile—took seven days, during which they visited several regions of the country. Stalin spent the remainder of his vacation traveling (including by sea), entertaining guests, and, inevitably, working. This vacation was apparently among the more enjoyable. The situation in the country had somewhat stabilized after the devastating famine, putting the Soviet leadership in a good mood. Moreover, Stalin enjoyed relatively good health. "Koba felt great the entire time," Voroshilov wrote to Yenukidze. His only health problem was some tooth pain.[32]

Stalin's vacation the following year was less successful. In 1934 he caught influenza and returned to Moscow having lost weight.[33] Kirov, who accompanied Stalin that summer, also did not enjoy himself. "As fate would have it, I wound up in Sochi," Kirov wrote, "which I'm not happy about—the heat here isn't tropical; it's hellish. . . . I really regret that I came to Sochi."[34] Things did not go well in 1935 either: Stalin again caught influenza and injured his finger when the head of his security team accidentally slammed a car door on it. Stopping in Tiflis toward the end of this vacation to visit his mother, he came down with a stomach ailment.[35] In 1936, Stalin's letters to his comrades-in-arms back in Moscow during August through October are brief, harsh, and often ill humored. They contain no personal information, just orders. They are largely devoted to the topic of "enemies of the people," especially arrangements for the first Moscow show trial against Zinoviev and Kamenev.

Nineteen thirty-seven had a gloomy start both for the country, which was succumbing to another round of repression, and for Stalin, who began the year with a bout of tonsillitis. (By 5 January he had sufficiently recovered to enjoy dinner with his comrades and doctors, followed by dancing to phonograph records.)[36] Despite his continued poor health, for the first time in many years he did not leave Moscow on vacation. The decision to stay was undoubtedly due to his intimate involvement in the purging of Soviet society. He also stayed in Moscow the following few summers. After the winding down of the Great Terror, the impending war prevented him from relaxing down south. In 1939, for example, he spent August embroiled in difficult negotiations with Western powers and then the Nazis, resulting in the pact with Hitler. He had recently turned sixty, and his health had not improved. In records dated February 1940, Valedinsky mentions another episode of tonsillitis and a bad cold.[37]

The outbreak of war in the summer of 1941 pushed the already hard-working leader to his limits. Unlike many Soviet citizens, of course, he was not going hungry or enduring long days of backbreaking labor, but the additional workload and responsibilities put a greater strain on his health. In September 1944 discussions with the United States ambassador to Moscow, Averell Harriman (who was attempting to arrange for the Soviet leader to meet with Roosevelt and Churchill), Stalin explained that he would not be able to leave the country because of "increasingly frequent illnesses." According to one account of these talks, "In the past Com. Stalin would have the flu for one or two days, but now it was lasting for one and a half or two weeks. He was showing his age."[38] In his categorical refusal to travel by plane, Stalin may have been overdramatizing his health problems, but not by much. A number of memoirs describe Stalin's frail health during the war years. Whenever the situation at the front permitted it, the dictator retreated to his dacha and worked from there.

In October 1945, shortly after the surrender of Japan, Stalin took his first southern vacation in several years.[39] Toward the end of his life these trips were shifted to later in the year, usually commencing in August or September and ending in December. Apparently he preferred to enjoy the peak of summer at his dacha outside Moscow and to head south when the weather up north turned cold. His vacations also grew longer. In 1946–1949 they extended to three or three and a half months, and in 1950 and 1951 he spent four and a half months out of town.[40] While at his southern residences, Stalin engaged in more or less the same activities as in Moscow. He spent time working on the day's mail and writing to his comrades. He also received visitors, although fewer than in Moscow. As in Moscow, however, he enjoyed presiding over festive gatherings at the dinner table and playing billiards. But some activities were specific to his vacation lifestyle. During his visits to Russia's resort towns, he took therapeutic baths, went for walks, and traveled. In 1947 he expressed a desire to travel by car from Moscow to Crimea, although the poor quality of the roads allowed him to get only as far as Kursk, where he boarded a train. Long car trips were evidently bad for his rheumatism. A number of memoirs report that he nevertheless preferred the less comfortable jump seats to the cushioned back seat.[41] He seldom stayed in one place very long when visiting the south, moving among his continuously growing collection of dachas.[42] Sometimes he would invite his daughter and son to join him, occasioning a sort of family reunion that, for a number of reasons, was not possible in Moscow.

After the war, these visits to the south alternated with long periods when Stalin barely left his Moscow dacha. Visits to his Kremlin office became increasingly rare, primarily due to his deteriorating health.

He continued to suffer from stomach pain and intestinal disturbances, accompanied by fever, throat problems, colds, and influenza. His atherosclerosis was progressing.[43] Despite scattered attempts to do so, he was by now simply incapable of changing his sedentary lifestyle. The copious fare served at his frequent late-night dinner gatherings was surely not good for him. According to Milovan Djilas, who visited Stalin's dacha several times in the 1940s, "The selection of food and drink was huge, with an emphasis on meat dishes and hard liquor."[44] The leader of the Hungarian Communist Party, Matyas Rakosi, recalled the following:

> The atmosphere at these dinners was free and easy; people told jokes—often even dirty ones—to the raucous laughter of everyone present. Once they tried to get me drunk, but wine doesn't affect me, which earned me recognition and a bit of surprise from those in attendance. Our last dinner together was in the fall of 1952. When Stalin left the room at three in the morning, I commented to the Politburo members, "Stalin is already 73; aren't such dinners, stretching so late into the night, bad for him?" His comrades assured me that Stalin knew his limits.[45]

Stalin brought up his age and the importance of cultivating a new generation of leaders with increasing frequency.[46] Deep down, however, he must have hoped for the best. In November 1949, when the Albanian leader Enver Hoxha expressed the wish that Stalin would live to one hundred, the Soviet leader joked: "That's not enough. Back home in Georgia we have old people still alive at 145."[47] As Stalin's daughter Svetlana attested, "In later years he wanted to continue in good health and live longer."[48]

In 1952, Stalin did not travel south. Even though he remained in Moscow, he visited his Kremlin office only fifty times, an average of less than once a week. On 21 December 1952, for his seventy-third birthday, his daughter Svetlana made her final visit to her father's dacha. "I was worried at how badly he looked," she recalled. "He must have felt his illness coming on. Maybe he was aware of some hypertension, for he'd suddenly given up smoking and was very pleased with himself. . . . He'd been smoking for fifty or sixty years."[49] By this time his atherosclerosis was well advanced. The autopsy performed two and a half months later showed that damage to the arteries had greatly impeded blood flow to the brain.[50]

To what extent was Stalin's death hastened by a lack of professional care? It is widely believed that he did not see any doctors during the final months of his life due to arrests at government hospitals in connection with the Doctors' Plot (see chapter 6 below). Svetlana Allilueva writes:

He was probably aware of an increase in his blood pressure, but he hadn't any doctor to take care of him. Vinogradov [a renowned doctor who had treated Stalin], the only one he trusted, had been arrested and he wouldn't let any other doctor near him.

Somewhere or other he got hold of some quack remedies, and he'd take some pills or pour a few drops of iodine into a glass of water. Moreover, he himself did a thing no doctor would ever have allowed: Two months after I last saw him and just twenty-four hours before his stroke he went to the bathhouse near the dacha and took a steam bath, as he'd been accustomed to doing ever since Siberia.[51]

Allilueva's testimony has to be taken with a grain of salt. She rarely saw her father and knew little about his life. Her reminiscences offer a subjective view of events. No archival documents have been found to clarify whether Stalin was under the care of doctors during the final months of his life. Nothing has been written about the quality of his health care at that time. Perhaps no treatment in the world would have helped.

We are equally in the dark about another complex question: the effect Stalin's ailments had on his decisions and actions. Without solid evidence, speculation on this subject remains just that. What we do know is that Miasnikov, one of the doctors summoned to his deathbed, believed that the extensive damage to Stalin's cerebral arteries uncovered during his post mortem must have affected his character and behavior:

I believe that Stalin's cruelty and suspiciousness, his fear of enemies and loss of the ability to assess people and events, his extreme obstinacy —all this was the result, to a certain extent, of atherosclerosis of the arteries in his brain (or rather, atherosclerosis exacerbated these traits). Basically, the state was being governed by a sick man. . . . Sclerosis of the blood vessels in the brain developed slowly, over the course of many years. Areas of cerebral softening that had originated much earlier were discovered in Stalin.[52]

These observations by a distinguished doctor are entirely consistent with the testimony of Stalin's associates. Even the most devoted among them, Vyacheslav Molotov, admitted, "In my opinion, Stalin was not quite in possession of his faculties during his final years."[53] A historian, as well, would have no trouble coming up with "oddities" and inappropriate responses in Stalin's political behavior. But historians are not doctors. While keeping their subjects' possible ailments in mind, they try not to dwell on them.

5 STALIN AT WAR

The 22 June 1941 surprise attack came with plenty of warning. The previous evening Moscow's military leadership received a report: a sergeant in the German army had crossed the border with the news that an invasion would begin the following morning.[1] Stalin was immediately informed, and the military leaders and Politburo gathered in his office to decide how to respond. People's Commissar for Defense Semen Timoshenko and Army Chief of Staff Georgy Zhukov, according to the latter's memoirs, asked for a directive allowing them to bring troops to a state of combat readiness.[2] Stalin was doubtful: "Could it be that the German generals sent us this defector to provoke a clash?" After hearing out his military chiefs, he concluded, "It would be premature to issue such an order. The matter might still be resolved peacefully. We should issue a brief order indicating that an invasion could start with provocative actions by German units. To avoid complicating matters, forces in border districts should not give in to any provocations."[3] The order reached troops shortly after midnight.

Stalin and the Politburo continued to discuss the alarming news until they finally parted ways, exhausted, around three o'clock in the morning. It was not long before Zhukov telephoned Stalin to report that German troops had launched an invasion. After briefly trying to refuse the general's demand that the *vozhd* be summoned to the phone, his chief bodyguard finally went to wake him:

> After about three minutes, I. V. Stalin came to the phone.
>
> I informed him of the situation and asked for permission to commence an armed response. I. V. Stalin was silent. All I heard was his heavy breathing.
>
> "Did you understand what I said?"
>
> Again silence.
>
> "Will there be orders?" I persisted.[4]

Zhukov's memoirs seem to suggest that Stalin withheld permission to respond to the attack and simply ordered Zhukov and Timoshenko to the Kremlin. But in 1956 Zhukov offered an important detail about this conversation that was never included in his memoirs. During the telephone call, he said, Stalin issued an order to the troops: "This is a provocation by the German military. Do not open fire to avoid unleashing wider action."[5] There is no reason to disbelieve this account.

According to Zhukov, he and Timoshenko arrived at Stalin's office at 4:30 a.m. to find the Politburo already there. This timing contradicts the log of visitors to Stalin's office, which states that Timoshenko and Zhukov's first visit on 22 June occurred at 5:45.[6] A simple explanation could be that the 4:30 meeting took place not in Stalin's office but in his Kremlin apartment. In any event, after being updated by his military chiefs, Stalin again expressed doubts: "Couldn't this just be a provocation by German generals? . . . Hitler surely doesn't know about this." He sent Molotov to meet with Germany's ambassador, Friedrich von der Schulenburg.[7] As Zhukov describes it, he and Timoshenko asked Stalin to order a counterstrike, but Stalin told them to wait until Molotov returned.

The idea that the attacks were a conspiracy by German generals and were unknown to Hitler fit perfectly with Stalin's thinking. Further evidence that the Soviet leaders harbored serious illusions about Hitler can be found in Molotov's behavior during his meeting with Schulenburg, which began at 5:30 that morning. Obeying instructions sent by his government, Schulenburg, clearly upset, read Molotov the following brief notification: "In view of the intolerable threat to Germany's eastern border posed by the massive concentration and readying of all the armed forces of the Red Army, the German government feels compelled to take military countermeasures." Molotov's reaction suggests that he did not understand what was actually happening. He began to dispute that Soviet forces were concentrated along the border and concluded with the almost desperate question: "Why did Germany sign a non-aggression pact only to break it so easily?"[8] He tried to convince Schulenburg that the USSR was innocent in this matter and that it was Germany that was being treacherous, although he must have understood that even if the German ambassador believed him, nothing could be done. Schulenberg was just the messenger.

This meeting took place right in the Kremlin, so by 5:45 Molotov was already back in Stalin's office, along with Beria, Lev Mekhlis, Timoshenko, and Zhukov.[9] As Zhukov describes it, upon hearing from Molotov that Germany had declared war, Stalin "silently dropped into his chair and became immersed in thought. A long and painful pause ensued." Stalin agreed to issue a directive ordering the destruction of the invading enemy and added, "So long as our troops, with the exception of aviation, do not violate the German border anywhere for now."[10] This order was issued to the troops at 7:15 a.m., almost four hours after the invasion began.[11] It showed that the top leadership still did not understand what was happening. Stalin did not sign the order. It went out over the signatures of Timoshenko, Malenkov, and Zhukov.

In the hours that followed, Stalin conferred with his fellow leaders on several questions. Among the most pressing was how Soviet citizens would be informed that their country was at war. It was not just a matter of an official statement but of how the war was to be presented, what political slogans would be put into play, and what objectives were to be pursued. Stalin's comrades felt strongly that he should be the one to speak to the country, but he refused. The job fell to Molotov. Of course Stalin understood the political drawbacks of this decision, but he simply did not know what to say. The situation was fraught with uncertainty. Molotov's speech announced that the country was at war, emphasized that Germany was the aggressor, and expressed confidence that the Soviet Union would prevail. He ended with the words, "Our cause is just. The enemy will be crushed. Victory will be ours." Throughout this horrific war, these watchwords were emblazoned on posters and banners and repeated over the airwaves.

The archives contain a version of the speech written and edited in Molotov's hand.[12] The speech he actually delivered was somewhat different from this initial draft and added references to Stalin. It started with the introductory statement, "The Soviet government and its head, Comrade Stalin, have asked me to make the following announcement." A paragraph was added toward the end calling on the people to "rally their ranks" around the party, the government, and "our great leader Comrade Stalin." These references to Stalin were undoubtedly designed to preclude any doubts and rumors that might have arisen from his silence.

Molotov's speech exposes a central political concern worrying Stalin during the war's early hours. The brief remarks repeatedly emphasized the idea that the German aggression was completely unprovoked and that the USSR had meticulously adhered to the non-aggression pact. As the speech put it, "The German government was not once given grounds for complaining to the USSR that it was not fulfilling the agreement." Molotov emphasized that Germany "is the invading side" and even called the German fascists "traitors." Implicit in this word choice is the idea that there was an understanding between the two countries that could be betrayed.

The English historian John Erickson has suggested that Molotov's speech exposed a sense of unease and even humiliation on the part of the Soviet leadership.[13] It was as if Molotov were taking the German explanation for the invasion at face value and defending the Soviet Union against charges of aggressive intent. Was this insistence on Soviet adherence to the pact intended for Hitler in the faint hope that the invasion had indeed been launched by rogue generals? Or was the idea of Soviet blamelessness meant to influence public opinion in the West, in whose eyes it was suddenly important to seem a victim, rather than a partner, of Nazism? Or was the speech meant purely for the domestic audience in an effort to fan indignation toward a treacherous enemy?

Five minutes after noon, Molotov left Stalin for twenty minutes, during which his voice was broadcast over the radio while Soviet officials streamed in and out of Stalin's office. A general army mobilization was announced. The situation remained ambiguous. Stalin decided to send high-ranking emissaries to the front: Zhukov, Shaposhnikov, and Kulik.[14] The use of plenipotentiaries to represent him remained Stalin's preferred method of overseeing the war throughout its duration.

At 9:15 p.m., another directive went out to Soviet forces, again over the signatures of Timoshenko, Malenkov, and Zhukov.[15] The results of the first day of fighting were sugarcoated. While recognizing that the German forces had achieved "minor successes" in a number of areas, the directive claimed that in most border sectors "attacks were repelled with heavy enemy casualties." Having painted this optimistic picture, the directive went on to spell out the goal: deal a counterblow and destroy the enemy. In his memoirs, Zhukov noted his disapproval of the directive's wording and his feeling that it did not reflect the true state of affairs.[16]

In truth, Stalin did not have accurate information about the first day of combat. Communication with frontline forces had broken down, and commanders at all levels were afraid to deliver bad news. Stalin himself had a hand in creating a distorted picture. On 23 June the first Red Army Main Command's combat overview was published in newspapers. The *vozhd* labored over the wording of this summary himself. "After fierce battles," the overview read, "the enemy was beaten back and suffered great losses." Supposedly there were only two points at which the Germans were able to penetrate the border by 10–15 kilometers.[17] In reality, the first day of fighting was catastrophic. According to official Soviet sources, on 22 June the Red Army lost 1,200 airplanes, many of which were destroyed while still sitting on airfields. German figures record more than 1,800 Soviet airplanes lost, of which approximately 1,500 were destroyed on the ground. In one day the Germans advanced 60–80 kilometers into the Baltic states, 40–60 kilometers into Belarus, and 10–20 kilometers into Ukraine.[18]

Despite lacking accurate information and his understandable desire to hope for the best, Stalin must have realized the seriousness of the situation. According to eyewitnesses, he was stunned by the outbreak of war. As Zhukov describes it, "During the first day he was not able to really take himself in hand and get a firm grip on events. The shock to I. V. Stalin caused by the enemy invasion was so strong that his voice even became softer and his instructions on organizing the military effort were not always appropriate to the situation."[19] Chadaev later recalled, "Early on the morning of 22 June I caught sight of Stalin in the corridor. He had arrived at work after a brief sleep. He looked tired, worn out, and sad. His pockmarked face was sunken. You could see he was depressed."[20]

Stalin's indecisiveness during the war's first hours and his refusal to make a radio address on 22 June clearly show that he was not himself. His indecisiveness continued the following day, when it came time to set up a command headquarters. He refused to formally take charge of General Command Headquarters, and Defense Commissar Timoshenko took over that responsibility. Officially, Stalin's membership in the Command Headquarters was on a par with those of Molotov, Voroshilov, Semen Budenny,[21] Zhukov, and Admiral Nikolai Kuznetsov.[22] A number of other Politburo members and military leaders were given the status of advisers to Command Headquarters.[23] This system was extremely inefficient. Though officially in charge of the war effort, Timoshenko in fact had little authority among his colleagues. According to Kuznetsov, the members of Command Headquarters and the top leaders "had no intention of subordinating themselves to the people's commissar for defense. They demanded reports and information from him, and even made him account for his actions."[24] Timoshenko was certainly not able to go over Stalin's head. The chain of command became long and tangled, and the system whereby decisions were made and implemented was highly disorganized.

Stalin's prewar strategy had failed. He had not managed to avoid war, and furthermore, it had gotten off to a worse start than anyone might have imagined. In addition to the military catastrophe, he had suffered a devastating blow to his self-esteem. Nobody could openly criticize him for his miscalculations, but he must have known that not only his colleagues in the leadership but also tens of millions of Soviet citizens were reproaching him in their thoughts.

■ THE STATE DEFENSE COMMITTEE

Stalin's actions during the war's first days were frenetic, confused, and reactive. Even though he did not grasp the situation and was not qualified to manage armies, he tried to do something simply because it was impossible to do nothing. He tried desperately (and incompetently) to strike back at the Germans. Many, if not most, of these efforts only made matters worse.

Stalin clearly understood the dangers facing his country. There is convincing evidence that during the war's very first days he tried to barter away Western portions of the USSR in exchange for a truce. Beria was assigned to arrange a meeting between his representative and the Bulgarian ambassador, whose country was allied with the Nazis. The Bulgarian ambassador was asked to determine what conditions might be acceptable for a peace with Berlin. What lands was Germany claiming?[25] Just how this initiative ended is unknown. Probably the Bulgarian ambassador was reluctant to act as an intermediary. But the attempt itself speaks volumes. Whether Stalin was truly prepared to give up Soviet lands or was just hoping to break the momentum of Germany's offensive, he clearly felt less than confident about the Red Army's defensive capabilities.

This negotiation attempt was not the only sign of Stalin's pessimism. In parallel with a general mobilization and the preparation of new defensive lines in the interior, he ordered a massive evacuation campaign during the war's earliest days. Not only were people and material resources moved away from the front line, but a secret evacuation of the capital got under way, even though the Germans were nowhere near. On 27 June the Politburo approved an order to urgently (within three days) remove from Moscow the government's precious metal and gem reserves, the Soviet Diamond Fund, and valuables held in the Kremlin armory. On 28 June it was decided that currency held in Moscow's Gosbank and Gosznak depositories should be immediately relocated, and on 29 June, that the commissariat apparats and other top government offices should be moved to the rear. On 2 July the Politburo resolved to move Lenin's sarcophagus from his tomb in Red Square to Siberia, and on 5 July, to move government and Central Committee archives.[26]

An official summoned to Stalin's office on 26 June later recalled the following: "Stalin did not look his usual self. He didn't just look tired. He had the appearance of someone who had endured a profoundly upsetting experience. Until I met with him, I had a feeling based on various pieces of circumstantial evidence that we were taking a heavy beating along the borders. Maybe defeat was looming. After I saw Stalin, I understood that the worst had already happened."[27] The next few days brought no relief. Stalin was increasingly aware of the futility of his orders and how difficult it was to manage the army.

Just a week after the war began, alarming news reached Moscow about the grave situation along the Western Front and that Minsk, the capital of Belarus, had already fallen into enemy hands. Communication with the troops had largely broken down. A tense pause settled in at the Kremlin. On 29 June, for the first time since the war began, no meetings were scheduled in Stalin's Kremlin office. According to Mikoyan, that evening Molotov, Malenkov, Beria, and he gathered at Stalin's, probably at his Kremlin apartment or his dacha. Stalin telephoned Timoshenko, but the defense commissar did not seem to know anything.[28] The military leaders were not in control of the situation. Alarmed, Stalin, in violation of long-standing practice, proposed to the Politburo members that they all go to the defense commissariat.[29] Here, finding further confirmation that the catastrophe had become gigantic, he showered the generals with rebukes and accusations. Unable to withstand the tension, Zhukov, head of Command Headquarters, broke into tears and ran to a neighboring room. Molotov went to comfort him. This scene evidently had a sobering effect on Stalin. He understood that putting pressure on his military leadership would not help. According to Mikoyan, as he and Molotov were leaving the commissariat, Stalin said, "Lenin left us a great legacy. We, his heirs, have pissed it all away."[30] Crude language was not unusual for Stalin, but in this case it revealed an extreme state of inner turmoil. After leaving the commissariat, Stalin apparently went to his dacha.

The following day, 30 June, Stalin did not show up at his Kremlin office or anywhere else in Moscow. Given the growing crisis, this withdrawal from his duties was truly reckless. The huge machine of government had been specially designed so that it could not run without him; inevitably, it started to break down. Something had to be done, and Molotov took the initiative. He was the most senior member of the informal hierarchy within the Politburo. According to various eyewitnesses, after losing track of Stalin, Molotov began calling him at the dacha.[31] When he was unable to get a response—or, more likely, after bearing the brunt of Stalin's dark mood—he concluded that Stalin was truly struggling. According to Mikoyan, Molotov said that "Stalin is so exhausted that he doesn't care about anything; he's lost all initiative and is in a bad way."[32] This account was indirectly confirmed many years later by Molotov himself in interviews conducted by the writer Feliks Chuev: "He didn't show himself for two or three days; he was at the dacha. He was certainly suffering and a little depressed."[33] Molotov's memory seems to have failed him on certain details: Stalin did not seclude himself at the dacha for even two full days, let alone three, but given the catastrophic circumstances, even a brief absence by the country's leader must have seemed an eternity.

Alarmed, Molotov called a meeting with Beria, Malenkov, and Voroshilov. There was no talk of officially removing Stalin from power or even taking over his duties. Instead the group tried to figure out how to lure Stalin out of his dacha and make him do his job. This was a delicate task. One simply did not show up at Stalin's dacha without an invitation, and under the circumstances they could only imagine how he might react to an unsanctioned visit. Furthermore, it would not be easy explaining their reason for coming to see him. Nobody wanted to be the one to tell Stalin that his breakdown was placing the entire country in jeopardy. But these men were not neophytes when it came to political maneuvering, and they devised a brilliant plan. They decided to go together (certainly nobody wanted to go alone!) and present Stalin with a proposal for creating a supreme authority to oversee the war effort: the State Defense Committee, to be headed by Stalin himself. In addition, the committee would include the four men who had come up with the plan. Molotov would serve as first deputy to the committee chairman.

The creation of the State Defense Committee solved multiple problems at once. Now Stalin's fellow leaders could visit him at his dacha without implicitly reproaching him for not showing up at the Kremlin. That the committee would be headed by Stalin demonstrated his continued leadership and the Politburo's firm support, while the fact that it was a small committee of his most faithful comrades allowed them to privately help him make decisions as he recovered his mental balance. Finally, the four men together interacting with Stalin at this delicate time helped protect each of them from the full force of Stalin's outbursts.

Once Molotov, Malenkov, Voroshilov, and Beria had agreed on the idea of the committee, Mikoyan and Voznesensky were called to Molotov's office. They were two members of the leadership group that the four men had decided not to include in the committee, but it was important that they also come to the dacha as a demonstration of unity.

Mikoyan left behind an account of what happened when the delegation arrived at Stalin's dacha late in the day on 30 June. The *vozhd* was sitting in an easy chair in the small dining room. He looked at his unexpected visitors inquisitively and asked why they had come. As Mikoyan describes it, "He looked calm, but somehow strange." After hearing Beria, the chosen spokesman for the delegation, present the proposal to create a State Defense Committee, Stalin raised only one objection: he wanted Mikoyan and Voznesensky included as well. Beria was ready with the argument against expanding the membership: someone had to lead the Council of People's Commissars. Stalin relented.[34]

Mikoyan's memoirs were edited by his son Sergo, who took a number of liberties with his father's original text, which is preserved in the archives.[35] In editing his father's account of this incident, Sergo clearly tried to create the impression that Stalin was frightened by his comrades' visit, inserting embellishments such as "Upon seeing us, he [Stalin] seemed to cower in his chair" and "I [Mikoyan] had no doubt: he had decided that we were there to arrest him."[36]

Was Stalin really frightened? How should we interpret this meeting? Unquestionably, it was an exceptional moment in the history of his dictatorship. However deferential their demeanor, Stalin's associates had violated his supreme authority in at least five ways. (1) They had come unbidden to the dacha, (2) having worked out an enormously important initiative behind his back, and (3) they urged that their proposal be adopted in the form they had agreed on among themselves. (4) They had formalized Molotov's role as second-in-command in the government despite the fact that he was out of favor with the *vozhd*, and (5) they had decided to exclude Voznesensky from the committee, even though just that May, when Stalin had taken over the chairmanship of the Council of People's Commissars, he had chosen Voznesensky over Molotov to serve as his first deputy. In essence, Stalin's closest colleagues were letting him know that in the face of an existential threat, the post-Terror leadership had to be consolidated and that he had better abandon any thought of further shake-ups at the top. This was a unique episode; in his time in power, Stalin saw nothing like it before or after. It signaled a temporary change in the nature of the dictatorship and the emergence of a wartime political compromise, a rebalancing of power within the Politburo somewhere between the flexibility Stalin had demonstrated in the early 1930s, when he was first consolidating his dictatorship, and the tyranny he was exercising when the war broke out. This arrangement endured almost until the war's end.

The day after the meeting at the dacha, the establishment of the State Defense Committee was announced in newspapers. The fact that the committee's membership was limited to Stalin, Molotov, Beria, Voroshilov, and

Malenkov did not mean that the rest of the Politburo's top leadership had lost its influence. Mikoyan and Voznesensky had important jobs keeping the economy running. Zhdanov was focused on the defense of Leningrad. Given the critical nature of wartime supply and evacuation, Kaganovich's responsibilities as railway commissar were pivotal. In February 1942, Mikoyan, Voznesensky, and Kaganovich also joined the committee.[37]

The establishment of the State Defense Committee was the first in a series of organizational changes that eventually placed supreme leadership in the Soviet war effort in Stalin's hands. On 10 July General Command Headquarters, which had been headed by Defense Commissar Timoshenko, was replaced with a Supreme Command Headquarters, headed by Stalin. On 19 July the Politburo passed a resolution making Stalin people's commissar for defense and, on 8 August, supreme commander.[38] The customary order was restored. Stalin was once again the sole leader of both the people and the army, decisive and confident of victory. An important milestone in "Stalin's return" was his famous radio address on 3 July.

Whereas Molotov had gone to the Central Telegraph Building, next door to the Kremlin, to make his nationally broadcast speech of 22 June, Stalin demanded that radio facilities be set up in the Kremlin itself. The telegraph service's already overwhelmed technical staff had no choice but to comply. Cables were extended to the Council of People's Commissars building. Stalin read his address sitting at a little table with microphones and a bottle of Borzhomi mineral water.[39] From the very start it was clear that the address would not conform to his usual style. "Comrades! Citizens! Brothers and sisters! Fighters of our army and navy! It is to you, my friends, that I speak!"[40] The speech, different from any other in his career, was long talked about and remembered. Glued to their radios or studying his words in the newspaper, people sought an answer to the most pressing questions: What did the future hold? When would the war be over? Stalin offered little cause for comfort. While greatly exaggerating German losses ("The enemy's best divisions and the best units of its aviation have been smashed"), he was forced to acknowledge that "This is a matter of . . . the life and death of the Soviet state, the life and death of the peoples of the USSR." Ominously, he called on the people to recognize "the full depth of danger that threatens our country," to organize a partisan struggle in German-occupied territories, to create militia detachments, and to remove or destroy all material resources from territories under threat from the enemy. He used two difficult-to-translate words in characterizing the war: *vsenarodny* (of all the peoples) and *otechestvenny* (domestic or "of the fatherland," but often translated as "patriotic" in the context of World War II). Anyone listening could draw only one conclusion: the war would be long and hard.

The people and especially the army deserved some explanation for what had gone wrong. They deserved scapegoats, and the search did not take long. The breakdown of Soviet defenses was attributed to missteps under the leadership of General Dmitry Pavlov, commander of the Western Front. He and many of his subordinates were tried and shot. The orders, signed by Stalin, were widely circulated within the army.[41]

■   **THE BLUNDERER IN CHIEF**

According to Soviet General Staff statistics, between the start of the war and 1 January 1942, 4.5 million members of the Red Army and Navy were killed, wounded, or captured. Of this total, 2.3 million were listed as missing in action or taken prisoner.[42] These estimates were probably low. Nevertheless, they show that much of the army that was thrust into battle on 22 June 1941, including a large number of newly formed units, was completely wiped out. The causes of this catastrophe need further study. Clearly they included insufficient war readiness, the massive casualties resulting from the enemy's use of surprise, and the military and organizational advantages of the Wehrmacht. Despite countless examples of heroism and steadfastness, the Red Army was demoralized. Another important factor was incompetence on the part of the military and political leadership.

Lacking a firm grasp of the situation, Moscow was often too slow in its decision making, and many of its decisions were bad. The links in the chain of command, the General Staff especially, were not fully functional, and it took a long time to establish reliable communication with the forces in the field. "Even the Chinese and Persian armies," Stalin scolded his subordinates, "understand the importance of communication when it comes to managing an army. Are we really worse than the Persians and the Chinese? How can you manage units without communications? . . . We can't stand for this absurdity, this disgrace, any longer."[43] During the early stages of the war, Stalin spent a great deal of time in a special room set up next to his Kremlin office conducting conferences via telegraph. This was a cumbersome means of communication, the main beneficiaries of which are the historians who today have access to tapes of the conversations. The army and the rear were largely managed using plenipotentiary "helpers." These plenipotentiaries gathered information for Stalin and, with varying degrees of success, helped him deal with the never-ending bottlenecks plaguing transport, industry, and the overall war effort. This system, apparently unavoidable during this time of defeat and disorganization, was extremely inefficient.

Stalin, who had no experience commanding a modern army, did the best he could, relying largely on common sense rather than military science. On 27 August 1941 he sent the Leningrad leadership the following advice on organizing the city's defenses: "Position a KV tank an average of every kilometer, in some places every 2 kilometers and in some every 500 meters, depending on the terrain. Behind these tanks or between them position other less powerful tanks and armored vehicles. Behind this line of tanks, in back of it, place heavier artillery. Infantry divisions will be immediately behind the tanks, using the tanks not only as a strike force, but also as a shield."[44] To achieve this plan, Stalin was prepared to allocate 100–120 KV tanks, the newest and best heavy tanks in the Soviet arsenal, a mighty force in the right hands.

Stalin's involvement in tactical actions, sometimes even at the platoon level, shows just how disorganized the military command was.[45] The first months of the war offered many painful lessons in the futility of uncoordinated counterattacks. Poorly planned, they often led to huge losses and achieved little. The Red Army's leaders had scant knowledge of how to thwart an enemy advance or minimize casualties through the use of tactical retreats to positions prepared in advance. Stalin insisted on holding every inch of ground, no matter the cost. Retreat was not allowed until it was too late. The result was the encirclement of Soviet armies and their gradual destruction, one unit at a time.

Seeing battlefield failures left and right often heightened Stalin's tendency to suspect treachery. Playing up to his suspicions, on 19 August 1941 Georgy Zhukov, then commanding the Reserve Front, sent Stalin the following report: "I believe that the enemy knows our entire defensive system very well, all the operational-strategic alignments of our forces, and knows what capabilities we have at hand. It seems that the enemy has its own people among our very senior officials with immediate knowledge of the overall situation."[46] Ten days later, Stalin himself wrote to Molotov, who was then in Leningrad: "Does it seem to you that someone is intentionally paving the way for the Germans?"[47] This paranoia most likely had no serious consequences. Stalin, well aware of how dangerous it would be to start a witch hunt among Soviet generals in the midst of war, limited himself to accusations of cowardice. Few generals were arrested. More often they were deprived of their command or demoted and reassigned.

Intangibles such as patriotic readiness for self-sacrifice and determination to defend the motherland could partly compensate for a shortage of weaponry, battlefield experience, and tactical skill. Heroism and self-sacrifice by Soviet soldiers existed side by side with the demoralization brought on by the overwhelming force of the German assault, and Stalin received abundant evidence of both.[48] He believed in the importance of intangibles and attributed the failures of the Red Army to panic, the wholesale surrender of Soviet units, mass desertions, and the absence of a firm command. With shrinking faith in the army's ability to consolidate its own ranks, when it came time to ensure that his commanders absorbed his own ideas about leadership and discipline, he resorted to tried-and-true methods. In July 1941 he resurrected the institution of the military commissar, loyal and eagle-eyed party representatives who would be assigned to work side by side with every commander at every level.[49] The commissars were given vast powers, to be exercised largely through "special" (secret police) departments within the army. According to official statistics, between the outbreak of war and 10 October 1941, 10,201 members of the Red Army were shot, 3,321 of them in front of their units.[50] Even these numbers hardly tell the full story of repression at and around the front lines.

To ensure that the troops fought as hard as they could, Stalin made it not only shameful but also illegal to be taken prisoner. The provisions making capture by the enemy a crime were contained in the notorious Order No. 270, issued by Supreme Command Headquarters on 16 August 1941. Judging by its style, the order was mostly (if not solely) written by Stalin. It required that those taken prisoner be killed "by any means, either from the ground or from the air." The families of commanders who joined the ranks of "malicious deserters" were to be arrested. Families of soldiers who allowed themselves to be taken prisoner were deprived of their government pensions. The order was read out loud in every unit of the army.[51] Treating capture as treasonous doomed former Soviet prisoners of war to discrimination long after the war concluded.

Using a combination of threats and promises of reinforcements, Stalin tried to instill in his military the will to be unyielding. On 11 July 1941, when the Germans had reached the outskirts of Kiev, Stalin sent Ukrainian party secretary Khrushchev a telegram that read: "I warn you that if you take even one step toward pulling your troops back to the left bank of the Dnieper and fail to defend the fortified districts on the right bank of the Dnieper, you will all face brutal retribution as cowards and deserters."[52] On 16 July he signed a State Defense Committee order to defend Smolensk to the last. Any thought of surrendering the city was "criminal, bordering on outright treason against the Motherland."[53] Throughout the Battle of Smolensk, which lasted until September, the surrounded Red Army put up a dogged fight, delaying the German advance across the Central Front to Moscow. Hitler's decision to move a sizable portion of his forces from the Central Front to Ukraine and Leningrad also helped slow the Nazi advance toward the capital. Throughout July and August Stalin continued to hope that Soviet forces would hold the line. Beyond it stood their three major capitals: Leningrad to the north, Moscow in the center, and Kiev to the south. Time was working against the Germans. Fall was coming, with its slushy roads, and the first frosts would not be far behind.

Demonstrating that the Red Army could put up a good fight was important for Stalin's negotiations with his Western allies, Great Britain and the United States. Right after the German invasion, the leaders of these countries expressed full support for the Soviet people in their fight against the Nazis. Then began the complicated process of working out relations and holding talks about what form support would take. President Roosevelt sent his adviser, Harry Hopkins, to Moscow to obtain firsthand information. Stalin gave Hopkins an exceptionally warm welcome and tried to demonstrate decisiveness and confidence of victory. When their talks were interrupted by an air raid, the Soviet leader brought Hopkins in his own car to the bomb shelter at metro station Kirovskaia, where they were met by bodyguards and Internal Affairs Commissar Beria. One Soviet official left a description of the scene:

> [Beria] took Stalin by the arm and tried to bring him down below, making some remark about danger. Stalin responded curtly and rudely, which is how he always spoke when he was irritated: "Get away from me, coward!" . . . Stalin stood in the middle of the dark courtyard and looked into the black sky at the German plane in the searchlight's cross beams. Hopkins stood next to him, also watching. Then something happened that did not happen very often during night raids. The German Junker started to fall uncontrollably from the sky—it must have been hit. And just then the anti-aircraft artillery hit a second plane. Stalin said, and the interpreter told Hopkins:
> "That's what will happen to everyone who comes to us with a sword. And anyone who comes in the name of the good will be welcomed as a dear guest."
> He took the American by the arm and led him below.[54]

In such demonstrations of steadfastness, together with the fierce fight put up by the Red Army, the Western allies saw something for which they were ardently hoping: Hitler's blitzkrieg was being impeded. They could and should help the Russians. On 29 September through 1 October 1941, a conference of the three powers—the USSR, Great Britain, and the United States—was held in Moscow. Britain's minister of supply, Lord Beaverbrook, led the British delegation, and Averell Harriman, the U.S. ambassador to the USSR, acted as President Roosevelt's personal representative. On the Soviet side, negotiations were conducted by Stalin and Molotov. The Moscow Conference concluded with important specific agreements on assisting the Soviet war effort. The scope of assistance gradually grew. Western tanks and planes supplied through Lend-Lease made a significant contribution along the Soviet-German front. By war's end, the Red Army was mostly driving American-made trucks. Lend-Lease also played a crucial role in supplying communications equipment, locomotives, railcars, and food to the Soviet Union. "If not for Lend-Lease, victory would have been greatly hindered," Stalin told Roosevelt during their meeting in Crimea in February 1945.[55]

The USSR's new allies were clearly worried about the grim situation along the Soviet-German front. Not long before the Moscow Conference, disaster had struck the Southwestern Front, where a ferocious battle was being waged over Kiev. According to Zhukov, in late July he had informed Stalin of the difficult situation and proposed abandoning Kiev and focusing on fortifying the eastern bank of the Dnieper to prevent the Germans from breaking through the Southwestern Front's right flank. Stalin responded with a gruff refusal, removed Zhukov as chief of the General Staff, and sent him to the Western Front.[56] The situation in Ukraine continued to deteriorate. In early August the Sixth and Twelfth Armies—approximately 130,000 men—found themselves completely encircled by the Germans outside Uman.[57] On 8 August, after an advance by German troops, Stalin summoned the commander of the Southwestern Front, General Mikhail Kirponos, to confer with him via telegraph. He began the meeting in his usual manipulative manner, attributing to Kirponos intentions he had not openly expressed but that might be expected. "We have received information that the front has decided to surrender Kiev to the enemy with a light heart supposedly due to a shortage of units capable of holding Kiev. Is that true?" Kirponos assured Stalin: "You have been misinformed. The Front's Military Council and I are taking every measure to prevent Kiev from surrendering under any circumstances."[58] Stalin ordered him to stand firm and promised help in a few weeks.

It was obvious that the Soviet armies in the vicinity of Kiev were in danger of being encircled. In early September, the Southwestern Command, with the support of the General Staff in Moscow, proposed that forces be urgently pulled back. Stalin categorically refused. "Just the mention of the harsh necessity of relinquishing Kiev was enough to throw Stalin into a rage and cause him to momentarily lose his composure," Aleksandr Vasilevsky wrote in his memoirs.[59] On 14-15 September, the Germans closed the ring, encircling some 452,700 Soviet troops east of Kiev,[60] the worst defeat of the war thus far. On 20 September, Kirponos and the rest of the Southwestern Command were killed in combat. The opportunity to surrender Kiev but preserve the army had been lost. The destruction of this huge force further strengthened the Germans' strategic advantage.

Historians of every stripe, even those favorably disposed toward Stalin, place most of the blame for this catastrophe on his shoulders. Zhukov claims that Stalin implicitly acknowledged his own guilt. When putting Zhukov in charge of the Leningrad Front in September 1941, Stalin brought up the general's warning about the threat to the Southwestern Front and said, "Your report to me back then was accurate, but I did not understand it quite correctly."[61]

Defeat in Ukraine heightened the danger to Leningrad. By 8 September the city was completely surrounded. The following day the Germans launched a new offensive that took the front line to its doorstep. On 11 September Zhukov replaced Voroshilov as commander of the Leningrad Front.[62] As Zhukov later told the writer Konstantin Simonov, Stalin considered the fall of Leningrad inevitable.[63] On 13 September the *vozhd* received the commissar of the navy, Nikolai Kuznetsov, in his Kremlin office, where they discussed scuttling the ships docked in Leningrad if the city was taken. That very day Stalin approved a plan to destroy the fleet.[64] Over the next two weeks, fighting in the Leningrad suburbs became particularly brutal. As the Germans fiercely battled toward the city, Soviet soldiers, in a show of mass heroism, fought tooth and nail to repel their attacks. By the end of September the advance came to a halt. The Leningrad Blockade, one of the most horrific chapters in World War II—and one of the most astounding testaments to the fortitude of the Soviet people—began. Over the course of the blockade, hundreds of thousands of civilians died of hunger or German shelling.

■ **INSIDE BESIEGED MOSCOW**

Hitler's hopes of taking Moscow before winter were revived by the destruction of a huge Soviet force in Ukraine, and he reassigned a sizable part of the German Army to the Moscow offensive. On 7 October most of the Red Army's Western and Reserve Fronts were encircled in the vicinity of Vyazma, and on 9 October the Bryansk Front was also surrounded. The road to Moscow had been cleared. The fighter pilot Aleksandr Golovanov describes how he was summoned to Stalin's office around this time. He found the *vozhd* alone, sitting silently in his chair with some untouched food before him.

> I had never seen Stalin like this. The silence was oppressive.
>
> "A great misfortune, a great sorrow has befallen us," I finally heard Stalin's quiet but distinct voice say. "The German has broken through our defenses outside Vyazma...."
>
> After a pause, either asking me or talking to himself, Stalin said just as quietly:
>
> "What are we going to do? What are we going to do?!..."
>
> He then raised his head and looked at me. Never before or after have I seen a human face express such horrible emotional anguish. We had met and spoken just two days before, but in those two days he had grown extremely haggard.[65]

According to Zhukov, Stalin was suffering from influenza at the time, but staying in bed was not an option. He continued to work, overseeing defensive preparations and the redeployment of all possible reserves to the outskirts of Moscow. As part of this effort, Zhukov was called from the Leningrad Front and put in command of the defense of Moscow. On 8 October Stalin signed a State Defense Committee order to prepare to destroy 1,119 plants and factories in the city and oblast of Moscow.[66] On 14 October the Germans captured Rzhev and Kalinin. They were just kilometers from Moscow.

As Mikoyan described it, at nine in the morning on 15 October, members of the top Soviet leadership gathered (Mikoyan mentions Molotov, Malenkov, Voznesensky, Shcherbakov, and Kaganovich). Stalin informed the group that the Germans might soon breach Moscow's defenses and proposed evacuating foreign diplomatic missions and government offices. According to Mikoyan, Stalin did not want Moscow to be surrendered, even if that meant fighting within the city until reserves capable of expelling the Germans arrived. He himself would remain in the capital as long as possible. At the conclusion of discussions, Stalin signed a State Defense Committee order dated 15 October,[67] stating that "Com. Stalin will be evacuated tomorrow or later, depending on the circumstances."[68] Provisions were made. According to Aleksandr Vasilevsky, who was among a small group of General Staff members who remained with Stalin, planes were readied for a last-minute evacuation.[69]

The decision to evacuate Moscow prompted a brief and frantic effort to destroy or pack up files, followed by a mass exodus, primarily by party and government officials, of which there was no shortage in the capital. Even after the evacuation, "utter chaos reigned" in the Central Committee building: "The locks on many desks and the desks themselves were forced open, and forms and every sort of correspondence were scattered all over the place, including classified papers. . . . Top secret documents that had been brought to the boiler room to be burned were left in piles, unburned."[70] In the confusion, many officials abandoned the offices and enterprises with which they had been entrusted in order to save themselves, their families, and their property. A line of official vehicles snaked out of the city. There were many cases of theft of government property and valuables. According to official statistics, on 16 and 17 October more than a thousand of Moscow's Communist Party members destroyed their membership documents.[71] The flight of government and party officials in combination with rampant rumors provoked a general panic that grew into unrest. According to documentary evidence and eyewitness accounts, this unrest lasted for several days and fell into three main categories. First was the looting of stores and warehouses, especially those stocked with liquor, often accompanied by orgies of drunkenness. Second were attacks, often involving theft, on cars leaving Moscow filled with evacuees and their property. Third were spontaneous protests at factories and plants, including defense production facilities, by workers who had not been paid their promised wages and were upset by rumors that their places of employment were about to be destroyed. Feeling betrayed and abandoned, in many cases workers prevented the removal of equipment and demanded that the factories be cleared of the explosives that had been put in place to destroy them.[72]

Most of the top leadership did not leave Moscow on 15 October, as initially planned, and on the following day Stalin summoned a number of his associates to his apartment. Aviation industry commissar Aleksei Shakhurin, who was the first to arrive, describes this meeting in his memoirs. The Kremlin, he writes, looked deserted. The anteroom into Stalin's apartment was open, and he found the *vozhd* smoking and silently pacing the dining room. There were signs of evacuation preparations, such as empty bookshelves. Stalin was wearing his usual jacket and pants, which were tucked into boots whose creases were riddled with holes. Noticing Shakhurin's surprise on seeing such boots, Stalin explained that his other footwear had already been removed. Soon Molotov, Malenkov, Shcherbakov, and the others arrived. Stalin did not invite anyone to sit down. Pacing back and forth he asked everyone who arrived the same question: "How are things in Moscow?" Shakhurin reported that at one factory not all the workers had received their pay, that the streetcars and metro were not running, that bakeries and other stores were closed, and that instances of looting had been observed. Stalin responded with the following orders: fly in money using airplanes and fix the situation with public transportation and stores. He tried to calm himself and his comrades: "Well, it's not too bad. I thought it would be worse."[73] Over the next few days the situation in Moscow really did stabilize, largely because the mass detention and arrest of "suspicious elements" began after a state of siege was declared on 20 October.[74]

Stalin's comment that he had expected worse disorder in Moscow is consistent with his way of thinking. He was undoubtedly worried about the possibility of disturbances. The danger that conflict with a foreign enemy could be used to start a civil war—a formula used by the Bolsheviks in 1917—greatly affected Stalin's political decision making in the late 1930s. The catastrophic start of the war could only have revived such fears. Yet anti-government and defeatist tendencies did not reach a critical level in the Soviet rear, in large part because of the secret police system put in place before the war. After 22 June 1941 this system was not relaxed; it became, if anything, more ruthless. Nevertheless it would be wrong to attribute political stability solely to repression. A blend of patriotism, growing hatred of the Nazis, a sense of duty, and a tradition of subservience led people to unite in the name of victory. The few large-scale disturbances about which historians have learned more from recently opened archives were mainly caused by the government's panicked actions and a sense of defenselessness on the part of the population.

While Moscow offers some of the most dramatic examples of unrest, there were others. One well-documented case is the disorder that broke out in Ivanovo Oblast, northeast of Moscow. As the Germans approached, plans were being made to evacuate local textile mills. Rumors spread that the mills would be blown up, that food supplies were being trucked out, and that party and government officials were fleeing the area. Textile workers, fearing that they would be left to starvation and slaughter, erupted in spontaneous uprisings on 18–20 October. They tried to prevent the removal of equipment and beat some plant managers and party activists. Cries could be heard from the crowds: "They'll take our equipment and leave us without work"; "All the big shots have fled the city and we've been left on our own"; "Makes no difference to us if we work for Hitler or Stalin."[75] A combination of persuasion and arrests eventually restored calm. Furthermore, the situation at the front was improving, and it was no longer necessary to evacuate Ivanovo's textile plants.

By late October, Soviet troops had halted the enemy advance in the Central Direction. In addition to determined fighting by the Red Army, which suffered huge losses, the exhaustion of German troops and the mud and slush of autumn helped bog down the invasion. Urgent measures were now needed to prevent renewed Wehrmacht attacks on Moscow. Stalin was very involved in improving the capital's defenses, forming new fighting units, and overseeing the production of military hardware, especially tanks and aircraft. In many cases he turned his Kremlin office into a sort of master control center for dealing with logistical questions and overseeing cooperation among enterprises.

He also remained personally involved in the minute planning of combat operations. As in previous months, he closely followed the situation at the front, demanded thorough accounts of operations, and issued detailed orders in a broad array of areas. He was clearly eager to go on the offensive, whether or not the time or resources were available, in the hope that unexpected attacks would put pressure on an enemy that had spread itself thin across a huge front. His commanders did not always agree. In November Zhukov, now commanding the Western Front, objected to one such plan. Stalin demanded that counterstrikes immediately be launched in the areas of Volokolamsk and Serpukhov to disrupt German preparations for offensive action. Zhukov tried to explain that he simply lacked the forces to prepare both a defense and an attack. Stalin brought the argument to a close: "Consider the question of a counterstrike to be settled. Submit your plan this evening." He then immediately called a member of the Western Front's military council, Bulganin, and threatened: "You and Zhukov have gotten pretty full of yourselves. But even you can be called to account!"[76] The hastily organized offensives achieved little. Zhukov, who was trying to maintain a reserve force capable of dealing with a new German offensive, was probably right.

Stalin was much more effective in the area of propaganda. Taking advantage of the relative tranquility at the front in early November, he ordered that the usual celebration be held to honor the anniversary of the October Revolution. He understood that carrying on with this annual event in the besieged capital would have a tremendous propaganda impact. On the eve of the anniversary, 6 November, a huge celebratory gathering was held at the Maiakovskaia metro station. A train parked at the station was set up with a cloakroom and tables of food for party and military leaders. Speeches in honor of the revolution's anniversary were followed by a concert, but the centerpiece of the event was Stalin's address to the country, only his second public appearance since the war had begun. Clearly he was expected to provide some sort of explanation for the German forces' ability to take so much Soviet territory and to offer some idea of what lay ahead. When would the war end? This was the question on the mind of every Soviet citizen. The *vozhd* admitted that the danger hanging over the country "has not only not receded but has intensified." Overall, however, he was optimistic. Citing huge (and fictitious) German casualty statistics, he pronounced that Germany's human reserves "are already drying up," while the Soviet Union's reserves were "only now being fully deployed."[77]

The following day, the anniversary itself was marked with a military parade through Red Square. This was a risky undertaking since a few days earlier, on 29 October, German planes had dropped a large bomb right on the Kremlin. A total of 146 people were injured and 41 were killed.[78] The Luftwaffe could certainly strike again. In anticipation of this possibility, a parallel parade was held in Kuibyshev (today's Samara), the city chosen as the reserve capital should Moscow fall. In case of an attack during the Moscow parade, radio coverage of the celebration would switch to Kuibyshev. No such attack took place.[79]

Stalin addressed the parading troops with a short speech delivered from atop Lenin's Mausoleum. He recalled the glorious victories of prerevolutionary commanders and of the Bolsheviks during the Civil War. Speaking of the coming German defeat, he was so bold as to speculate on the timing: "In just a few months, just a half year, perhaps a year, Hitler's Germany will collapse under the weight of its own crimes."[80] This assurance seems to reflect his understanding of the military situation, and it soon led him to demand an offensive on all fronts.

The celebrations in Moscow—especially Stalin's speeches—were part of a major propaganda campaign through every possible medium. The military parade on Red Square was captured on film, but for some reason Stalin's speech was not. It was decided to stage the speech in an improvised studio. A mockup of Lenin's tomb was built in one of the halls of the Great Kremlin Palace, and Stalin repeated his speech for the cameras on 15 November.[81] In December, movie theaters began showing *The Parade of Our Troops on Moscow's Red Square on 7 November 1941,* including the reenactment of Stalin's speech. Over seven days, beginning December 4, two hundred thousand viewers watched the film in Moscow alone. Hundreds of copies were sent to towns across the country.[82]

On the same day Stalin reenacted his speech for the cameras, after lengthy preparations the still overwhelming forces of the Wehrmacht launched a new attempt to take Moscow. The advance covered significant ground and in some areas managed to reach the boundaries of the Soviet capital. Nevertheless, the Red Army, bolstered by a constant stream of reinforcements, was able to prevail. Just when the Germans had used up their last reserves and had come to a halt, the Red Army, almost without pause, launched a surprise counteroffensive. By January 1942 the enemy had been driven back 100–250 kilometers from Moscow. Finally there was true cause for celebration.

■ THE DEFEATS OF 1942

The offensive by Soviet troops outside Moscow, together with successes on other fronts, inspired hope throughout the entire anti-Nazi world but also exposed the Red Army's weakness and the enduring advantage of the Wehrmacht. Soviet troops demonstrated a strong will to fight but could not achieve some important objectives the Soviet leadership placed before them. Meanwhile, the Germans dug in and prepared their own counteroffensive.

On 10 January 1942, Red Army units received a letter critiquing past operations and looking ahead to upcoming ones. The tone and style of the letter suggest that much of it was written by Stalin. It was generally critical of the way in which German defenses had been breached during the December counteroffensive. The widely dispersed actions by the Red Army, which was stretched thin along the entire front, were characterized as incorrect. "The offensive can achieve the necessary effect," it read, "only if we create a force capable of overwhelming the enemy in one sector of the front." A second major failing was the poor use of artillery. "We often throw the infantry into an offensive against the enemy's defensive line without artillery, without any artillery support, and then complain that the infantry is not advancing against a well-defended and dug-in enemy. . . . This is an offense, not an offensive—an offense against the Motherland, against the troops forced to endure senseless casualties."[83] The Supreme Command demanded regular artillery support for attacking units, not just during the preparatory stages of an offensive. Here too the main emphasis was on concentrating artillery where the thrust of the attack would be focused.

These were sensible and important observations on the perils of frontal attacks, which entail large casualties, and the need to concentrate forces and maneuver skillfully. But in planning the winter campaign of 1942, Stalin ignored his own warnings and insisted on attacking on all fronts at once. He wanted the swift, victorious conclusion to the war that he had promised during his 7 November 1941 address. This idea was also expressed in secret documents. Stalin's basic assumption, apparently based on the intelligence reports he was receiving, was that Germany had used up its reserves. In his 6 November 1941 speech he claimed that the Germans had lost 4.5 million men during four months of war, and the subsequent reports he received tended to support these fantastic numbers. For example, German casualties as of 1 March 1942 were estimated at 6.5 million.[84] These figures, five or six times higher than the actual ones, were probably the result of the usual Soviet system of distortion, in which the *vozhd* was told what he wanted to hear.

The plan for the summer campaign, approved in March 1942, provided for a shift to strategic defense and a buildup of reserves for the next offensive. Stalin wound up issuing orders that conflicted with this decision and led to the staging of offensive operations in multiple sectors. "After reviewing the plan of action adopted for the summer of 1942, I must say that its weakest aspect is the decision to conduct defensive and offensive actions at the same time," Marshal Vasilevsky wrote several decades later.[85] This opinion also prevails in scholarly literature on the subject.

During the summer of 1942, offensives were planned for Crimea, the Central Direction, and around Kharkov and Leningrad. Stalin was heavily involved in the planning of these operations. In matters of staffing, where he was, as usual, worried about selecting leaders capable of acting decisively, his personnel choices again reveal his shortcomings as supreme commander. He sent Lev Mekhlis, the head of the Red Army's Main Political Directorate, to represent Moscow in Crimea. Mekhlis, who had served as Stalin's secretary, was fanatically loyal to the *vozhd*, energetic, decisive, and ruthless, but he was completely ignorant of military science.

Voroshilov was assigned to the Volkhovsky Front, outside Leningrad, despite having been earlier dismissed from the Leningrad Front for incompetence. His special relationship with the *vozhd* allowed him to turn down this assignment, infuriating Stalin. On 1 April 1942 the Politburo adopted a decision, dictated by Stalin, subjecting Voroshilov to savage criticism. The disclosure of his reason for turning down this command was obviously meant to embarrass him. The former defense commissar was quoted as saying that "The Volkhovsky Front is a difficult front" and that he did not want to fail at the job. The Politburo resolved to "(1) Recognize that Com. Voroshilov did not prove himself in the work assigned him at the front. (2) Send Com. Voroshilov to perform military work away from the front lines."[86] This was an empty gesture: Voroshilov was not banished from Stalin's inner circle. Nevertheless, the resolution, which became known to a wide circle of top officials, may have been a warning to others.

The Southwestern Command was not a particular source of Stalin's complaints. Aware of his inclinations, the front commander, Timoshenko, and military council member, Khrushchev, proposed an offensive to retake Kharkov. After confronting objections from the General Staff, Stalin decided to maneuver. He approved the Ukrainian operation but pronounced it an internal matter for the front's commanders. This decision did not change anything, but it relieved Stalin of some responsibility for how it turned out.

The poorly conceived plans for the offensive led to more heavy losses and damaged the overall strategic situation. The first disturbing sign was defeat in Crimea. The German counteroffensive, launched on 8 May 1942, crushed Soviet troops in twelve days and sealed the fate of the Crimean city of Sevastopol, which had been under siege for eight months. Large-scale heroism was not enough to prevent catastrophe. The city fell in July after the Germans brought in significant forces from other fronts. According to the Sovnarkom's chief of administration, Chadaev, Mekhlis tried to make his excuses to Stalin in person, waiting outside the *vozhd*'s office. Chadaev described what happened when Stalin appeared in the doorway: "Mekhlis jumped up from his seat: 'Hello, Comrade Stalin! Permit me to report.' Stalin paused for a moment, looked Mekhlis up and down, and with a voice filled with emotion pronounced: 'Damn you!' He then headed straight into his office and slammed the door. Mekhlis slowly lowered his arms to his sides and turned toward the window in distress."[87]

The following day, 4 June 1942, Stalin signed a Supreme Command directive to the military councils of all fronts and armies on the reasons for defeat in Crimea. The style of the directive, which pointed out that the Crimean forces had been crushed despite having a significant numerical advantage, suggested he had a hand in composing it. The commanders in Crimea, including Mekhlis, were accused of incompetence and inability, removed from their positions, and stripped of their rank.[88] Nevertheless, Mekhlis did not fall out of favor with Stalin and continued to be given important posts. Zhukov later speculated that Stalin was relatively lenient in punishing those who had directed the Crimean catastrophe "because he was aware of his own personal responsibility for it."[89]

The effort to retake the eastern Ukrainian city of Kharkov was also planned with Stalin's full support. The attack began on 12 May and at first seemed to promise success. A few days in, however, everything changed. The Germans, who were thought to be focused on capturing Moscow, were in fact planning a decisive offensive in the south. Timoshenko's poorly conceived plans for Kharkov only made their task easier. Despite warnings that the huge Soviet force now risked encirclement, Stalin refused to halt the attack on Kharkov in order to deal with this threat. By the time he decided to suspend the offensive, it was too late.[90] According to General Staff statistics, 277,000 Red Army troops were lost—killed, wounded, or captured—in the Second Battle of Kharkov.[91] The Germans had again been handed a strategic advantage. Hitler's forces were now able to move quickly toward the Caucasus and the Volga.

Stalin placed the blame for this defeat squarely at the feet of his commanders, although they were not castigated as harshly as those involved in the Crimean debacle.[92] A few months later, on 24 September 1942, Georgy Malenkov, who had been sent to represent Headquarters at the Stalingrad Front (constituted primarily from the forces of the Southwestern Front), wrote to Stalin: "While we're on the subject of Timoshenko. . . . Now that I've been able to see how he's been working here, I can say that Timoshenko looks like a good-for-nothing, indifferent to the fate of the Soviet government and the fate of our motherland."[93] Given Malenkov's usual caution, we can assume that he was expressing an opinion with which he knew the *vozhd* would agree. As with Mekhlis, however, Stalin kept Timoshenko within his inner circle but used him for less critical assignments.

Accusing generals of mistakes and a lack of decisiveness was a leitmotif of Stalin's directives throughout 1942. The generals themselves took a different view. Marshal Konstantin Rokossovsky, for example, wrote in his memoirs that the defeats during the summer of 1942 stemmed from the fact that Headquarters kept repeating the mistakes of the early stages of the war. Commands from the top "did not correspond to the situation" and "only played into the hands of the enemy." Instead of gradually pulling troops back to lines prepared in advance (in the summer of 1942, the River Don), Headquarters kept demanding counterattacks. Troops hurriedly moved toward the Germans "with no time to concentrate, on the fly, went into battle disorganized against an enemy that under these circumstances enjoyed a huge numerical and qualitative advantage. . . . This was all done in a manner that had nothing to do with the military science we were taught in the colleges and academies, during war games and maneuvers, and it went against all the experience we acquired during the two previous wars."[94]

Refusing to recognize any fault on the part of the Supreme Command, Stalin continued to attribute failure solely to the cowardice, treachery, or, at best, incompetence of his subordinates. The ultimate expression of this logic was the notorious Order No. 227, issued on 28 July 1942, just when the German advance in the south seemed unstoppable. Stalin, who undoubtedly wrote the order himself, was exceptionally harsh: "Panic-mongers and cowards must be exterminated on the spot." Commanders "who retreat from battle positions without an order from above [are] traitors against the Motherland." He demanded that commanders be put on trial, starting with army commanders who sanctioned unauthorized retreat. The order provided for the creation of penalty battalions and companies, the ranks of which would be filled by people arrested for violating the Stalinist code of conduct, to be used as cannon fodder at the start of attacks. Anti-retreat units became a regular part of the army and were tasked with "shooting on the spot panic-mongers and cowards in the case of panic and disorderly retreat by division units."[95] These units were not disbanded until October 1944.

The fight against "panic-mongers," "cowards," and "saboteurs" was a centerpiece of Stalin's military policy during the summer of 1942, and fear and panic were indeed a problem. Given the hardships of battle and the long string of defeats, troop morale was inevitably low. But as during the Terror, Stalin's tendency to see saboteurs and wreckers as the root of all failures had no basis in reality. The mental state of Soviet soldiers in the face of the well-organized might of the German Army was just one of many threads in the tangled web of reasons for Red Army retreats. Often orders were disobeyed because they were poorly conceived or simply not realizable. Draconian measures at the front did not guarantee victory. A few weeks after Order No. 227 was issued, the Germans reached the outskirts of Stalingrad.

Beside cowardice and treason, another explanation for Soviet defeats that featured prominently in Stalin's mind was that Hitler was not distracted by a second front in Western Europe. Within the top leadership, the Nazi leader's ability to concentrate his forces on the Soviet front due to inaction by the Allies was a frequent source of anger and frustration. After heavy pressure from Stalin, during a visit by Molotov to Great Britain and the United States in May and June of 1942, Churchill and especially Roosevelt expressed their intention to open up a second front that autumn.

These vague promises began to look increasingly chimerical as the situation worsened on all fronts. To soften the blow of his failure to open a European front, Churchill went to see Stalin in Moscow.[96] On 12 August 1942 the two men had their first face-to-face meeting. Stalin found himself in a weakened position due to the numerous defeats suffered by the Soviet side. Meanwhile, the Allies' losses in North Africa and the Mediterranean gave them an excuse for delaying a French landing.

Stalin did not hide his irritation at Churchill's explanation. The atmosphere during the first hours of negotiations was extremely tense. The Soviet leader, abandoning diplomacy, disparaged the Allies' wavering and advised them not to fear the Germans. Churchill was just as blunt. He reminded Stalin that Great Britain had been battling the Nazis for a full year, an unmistakable reference to the fact that Britain was already at war with Hitler while Stalin was helping him carve up Poland. With these reproaches out of the way, the allies, who greatly needed one another, settled down to serious discussion. Having given a great deal of thought to his negotiation strategy, Churchill delivered his good news: a landing of American and British forces was planned for the northern coast of French Africa that fall. Stalin took this opportunity for conciliation. He praised the new plan, and subsequent talks went more smoothly. Stalin made the friendly gesture of inviting Churchill to his Kremlin apartment for his last night in Moscow, 15 August, where the evening passed convivially.

The conclusions to be drawn from Churchill's visit were clear. The USSR would be able to count on its allies mostly for material assistance. Stalin told Churchill that his country particularly needed trucks and aluminum. For now, the Germans could continue fighting on the Eastern Front without worrying about a serious challenge from the West, and the Red Army would continue to suffer defeat and failure. In the south the Germans had entered Stalingrad, had captured the important Don and Kuban agricultural regions, and were drawing near to the petroleum deposits of the North Caucasus and Transcaucasia. According to official Soviet statistics, from January through October 1942 alone, 5.5 million Red Army soldiers had been killed, wounded, or captured.[97] Gradually, however, the formation of new armies and the heroism of the defenders of Stalingrad and the Caucasus allowed the front to stabilize. Hitler's shortage of manpower, as he simultaneously pursued several difficult objectives, also helped shift the momentum. In the ruins of Stalingrad, Soviet troops fought German divisions in pitched battle. By all appearances, this was a replay of late 1941. The battered German armies could advance no farther. Having inflicted huge losses, the

Red Army now had an opportunity to seize the initiative. The question was how and when to strike back.

■ STALINGRAD AND KURSK

The counterstrike came outside Stalingrad. This famous Soviet victory was the culmination of heroic efforts and huge sacrifices by the entire country. It showed that Stalin, too, had finally learned from past defeats. The well-prepared Soviet offensive outside Stalin's namesake city began on 19 November 1942. A few days later, Germany's 330,000-man force in Stalingrad, led by General (soon to be Field Marshal) Friedrich Paulus, was surrounded. After thwarting German attempts to break through the encirclement, on 2 February 1943 Soviet forces finally compelled the enemy to capitulate. The protracted battle cost the Germans hundreds of thousands of soldiers and officers. More than 90,000 were taken prisoner, including Paulus himself. The victory marked a major turning point in the war.

Despite this impressive triumph, Stalin continued to act with caution. In planning the new campaign, the Soviet Supreme Command tried not to spread its forces too thinly. The main counterstrike was focused on the Southwestern Direction, where the enemy had already suffered huge losses and was largely disorganized. Hoping to repeat the success of Stalingrad, in January 1943 Stalin ordered the encirclement of the German forces retreating from the North Caucasus. Elsewhere, counteroffensives in the Voronezh and Kharkov Directions made promising beginnings. And on 18 January 1943, at the northern end of the vast Soviet-German Front, the Leningrad Blockade was finally broken and the city again became accessible to Central Russia via land. The liberation of the country's long-suffering historic capital had enormous symbolic and emotional significance.

Amid the rejoicing, Stalin's comrades were eager to crown him with victor's laurels. On 19 January 1943, during a visit to the Voronezh Front, the chief of the General Staff, Vasilevsky, joined the front's leaders in addressing a coded message to Molotov, Beria, and Malenkov. They proposed that following the "unparalleled successes of our troops at the front," Stalin deserved the title "generalissimo of the Soviet Union." The telegram described Stalin as the "organizer of our victories, a genius and great commander." The members of the top leadership, who may very well have inspired this initiative in the first place, greeted the proposal with enthusiasm. On 23 January Molotov, Beria, Malenkov, and Mikoyan signed a motion to that effect and placed it before the Politburo. Nevertheless, it wound up being filed away.[98] Stalin must have felt that his elevation to the rank of generalissimo was premature. Despite hopeful signs, many hard battles lay ahead. Hundreds of thousands of Soviet families were still receiving the dreaded notifications that a loved one had been killed in action. Stalin eventually got the title of generalissimo, but later, after final victory in 1945. For now he settled for the gold-embroidered shoulder boards of a marshal. The resolution elevating him to that rank was published on 7 March 1943. Before Stalin, in January and February respectively, Zhukov and Vasilevsky were also given this honor.

The rank of marshal was more than sufficient for now. Events at the front soon showed that the Red Army was not safe from further defeats. Significant victories came in the form of the liberation of the North Caucasus and Stavropol and Krasnodar Krais. On the other hand, the Red Army could not carry out its plan to encircle German units in these areas. The enemy managed to maintain its numbers and retreat to the Donets Basin, the lower reaches of the Kuban, and the Taman Peninsula. Soviet forces were successful during early 1943 along the Voronezh, Bryansk, and Southwestern Fronts. Voronezh was liberated in January, and Kursk, Belgorod, and Kharkov in February. But soon the momentum shifted back to the Germans. One reason for this shift was some bad decisions by the Soviet Supreme Command. The Soviet armies were attacking along a broad front, but the enemy, which had stealthily concentrated its forces at strategic points, counterattacked. In March it again occupied Kharkov and Belgorod. The Red Army achieved only modest results in its Western Direction offensive, and its efforts in February and March along the Northwestern Front were not effective.

In April through June 1943, a strategic lull set in as the two sides prepared their summer campaigns. As the Soviet military leaders' memoirs make clear, nobody doubted that the Germans would strike first at the Kursk salient. By attacking the flanks, the Wehrmacht could encircle and destroy the large number of Soviet forces within the salient and recapture the strategic initiative. The Germans knew that unless they could eliminate the Kursk salient, they would face serious danger. Yet there was some question as to whether the Germans would attack at all. Deciding against an anticipatory offensive, Stalin agreed to meet the enemy from a well-prepared defensive posture, in the hope that it would allow the Red Army to crush the German forces and transition to an offensive posture from a much stronger position.

The decision to focus on defense shows that Stalin was learning from past mistakes. Whereas earlier he had preferred large-scale lightning attacks before the enemy had time to regroup, he now understood the need to wait, plan, and prepare. Restraint was not easy for him. Twice in May, intelligence suggested that the Germans were about to strike. Soviet forces were put on high alert, but each time proved to be a false alarm. According to General Vasilevsky, in both cases Stalin favored a preemptive attack. "It took quite an effort by us, by Zhukov, me, and Antonov,[99] to convince him not to do that," Vasilevsky wrote.[100] June came, and the Germans still did not attack. Stalin was uneasy and again began pondering a first strike. This time, too, he listened to his generals, who convinced him that it would be advantageous to wait out the enemy.

The generals were right. The Battle of Kursk began on 5 July 1943 and continued until 23 August. Huge forces, a total of 4 million troops, were arrayed on both sides. This was a major tank battle, and the Soviet side had twice as many as the Germans. The Nazi leaders still hoped that superior organization and up-to-date weaponry—especially the Tiger and Panther tanks—could earn them another victory. It might have turned out that way had they not also faced superior numbers and a more mature and better-prepared force. After wearing down the enemy through a week of fierce fighting from a defensive posture, the Red Army struck back.

At the height of the counteroffensive, in early August 1943, Stalin visited the front for the first and last time. During the early morning hours of 2 August he boarded a special train disguised to look like a freight carrier that stopped close to his dacha. The part of the front closest to Moscow, the Rzhev-Vyazma salient, the site of preparations for an offensive operation, was chosen for the visit. After arriving at the closest train station, Stalin and his entourage continued by automobile. He spent 3 and 4 August visiting the command posts of each front and meeting with the leaders planning offensives. Here he learned that Soviet troops had retaken Orel and Belgorod. Stalin telephoned Moscow and ordered an artillery salute in honor of this victory. The visitors returned to the train for dinner, and on the evening of 5 August it left for Moscow. Stalin returned to his Kremlin office.[101]

Stalin did not like to travel even in peacetime and left Moscow only for vacations. Officially, he was inspecting preparations for the Smolensk offensive operation. In fact, there was no military necessity for this, and his visit did nothing to prevent the operation's failure. The real reason for the trip lay in what we now call "optics." The leader of a country at war has to show solidarity with his army and a willingness to share in its hardships. During the first stage of the war, when Moscow itself was on the front line and Stalin's presence in the besieged capital was of tremendous political significance, solidarity could be demonstrated by his staying in place. Stalin must have understood that even after the tide of war began to turn, such demonstrations were important to sustain his reputation as an involved and compassionate leader.

Stalin managed to transform his sole visit to the front lines into a matter of routine. During the summer of 1943 he conducted a heated correspondence with Roosevelt and Churchill. In response to the Allies' refusal to open a second front in northern France in 1943, Stalin refused to participate in summits and grew dilatory in his correspondence. His explanation was that he was too busy rallying the troops. In early August he wrote to his coalition partners: "I have just returned from the front. . . . I have had to make more frequent visits to the troops than usual." "I have been compelled to personally spend more time in various sectors of the front and put the interests of the front before all else."[102]

After returning from the Western Front, Stalin again had to turn his attention to developments in the south, where the Kursk offensive was still raging. The Battle of Kursk put an end to any chance for a German victory, but most of the Nazi forces escaped encirclement and withdrew to prepared defensive lines. Building on Soviet successes, the Supreme Command organized offensives in Ukraine, Crimea, and the Central Direction. The German forces switched to a defensive posture, launching only intermittent counterattacks. The most important developments were taking place at the southern end of the Soviet-German Front. In September the Red Army managed to capture the German bridgehead on the right bank of the Dnieper. At the same time, Hitler's forces were pushed out of the economically important Donets Basin and, to the south, Novorossiisk and the Taman Peninsula. In the predawn hours of 6 November the Red Army liberated the Ukrainian capital of Kiev. By the autumn of 1943, Hitler's forces had been rendered incapable of large-scale offensives. The Red Army advanced six hundred kilometers to the south and three hundred to the west, but these impressive victories came at the expense of heavy losses inflicted by a still capable enemy. Furthermore, many of the objectives assigned by Headquarters were not met. Soviet forces had made little progress in the Western and Northwestern Directions. The attempt to liberate Crimea had failed, and fierce counterattacks by the Wehrmacht made it impossible to build on the ousting of the Nazis from eastern Ukraine. The Germans were managing to evade a decisive blow. The successful approach used in Stalingrad, of encircling and liquidating enemy army groups, could not be repeated. The bloody war would not end any time soon.

British and American forces also made progress in 1943. Large deployments of German troops were defeated in North Africa and Sicily, and the southern portion of the Italian peninsula was occupied, bringing down Mussolini's regime and taking Italy out of the war. The Allies were also achieving success against Japan, and Germany's submarine fleet suffered significant losses in the Atlantic, making shipments of supplies and troops from the United States less dangerous. Allied bombing of Germany was causing increasing devastation. The British and Americans no longer worried that the Soviet Union would collapse under the weight of war, and such a realization relieved some of the pressure for major sacrifices by the Western allies. Moreover, the idea of an advance through the Balkans was beginning to look like a viable alternative to the opening of a second front in northern France. Churchill favored the Balkan approach, but Roosevelt, based on American interests, maintained his previous commitment to a landing on the French coast.

For Stalin, the opening of a second front remained a top priority in relations with his allies. While he of course wanted to relieve the suffering of his battered and exhausted country, he also saw such an opening as a matter of political prestige and a sign of his standing within the Big Three. Not surprisingly, on hearing in June 1943 that Churchill and Roosevelt were planning to postpone the opening of a front in northern France until the next year, his response was icy. "I must inform you," he wrote his partners on 24 June, "that this is a matter not just of disappointing the Soviet government but of preserving its trust in its allies, trust that has been put to serious tests."[103] In August, the Soviet ambassador, who enjoyed good relations with the British establishment, was pointedly recalled from London. But the allies could not afford total alienation, and none wanted to go anywhere near the point of breaking off relations. This was evident in the decision that soon followed, after contentious negotiation, to hold the first face-to-face meeting of the Big Three. In November 1943 the allies gathered in Tehran, the site proposed by Stalin. This concession by Roosevelt and Churchill at least took some of the sting out of their decision to delay an invasion.

This trip, Stalin's first outside the Soviet Union since coming to power, did not take him far from the Soviet border. After traveling to Baku by train, he took a short flight to the Iranian capital. As far as we know, this was Stalin's first and last flight in an airplane, and he appears to have been anxious about it. According to the memoirs of General Sergei Shtemenko, who accompanied Stalin on the trip, a problem developed at the airport in Baku. Stalin refused to fly in a plane piloted by a high-ranking member of Soviet aviation, General Golovanov (mentioned above), and preferred to be flown by a less eminent pilot. "General-colonels rarely fly airplanes; we'd be better off flying with a colonel," he is quoted as saying.[104] Golovanov categorically denies this account, but he does say that while still in Moscow, Stalin wanted to discuss plans for the flight in detail. Among his instructions, he ordered Golovanov to check the reliability of the pilot.[105] Stalin apparently had a difficult time during the flight. While meeting with UK Ambassador Archibald Kerr and U.S. Ambassador Harriman in September 1944, he told them that his ears hurt for two weeks afterward.[106]

The Tehran Conference got under way on 28 November 1943. This was Stalin's third meeting with Churchill and his first with Roosevelt. Face-to-face contact with Roosevelt was particularly important. Stalin knew that the American and British leaders did not see eye to eye on everything, and one point of difference was the opening of a second front in northern France. Roosevelt and Stalin, each for his own reason, both advocated this second front. Stalin had two powerful cards in his pocket: the Red Army's victories and a promise to take up arms against Japan after Hitler's defeat. Beside a desire for good long-term relations with the USSR and its help against Japan, Roosevelt was also motivated by his reluctance to have Red Army troops moving deep into Western Europe. The result was a promise in Tehran that the United States and Great Britain would open a second front in the north of France in May 1944. Discussions also covered future Soviet efforts against Japan, the creation of a postwar international security system, the borders of a postwar Poland, and other issues. Stalin had every reason to come away pleased.

■ **VICTORY AND VENGEANCE**

The Allied successes in 1943 left no doubt that Germany would ultimately lose the war, but when? How many lives would be sacrificed before that happened? Having learned a bitter lesson, Stalin no longer tried to assign a timetable to the fall of the Reich. The Germans put up a desperate fight. Holed up in defensive positions, they launched only occasional counterattacks. Meanwhile, the Red Army pushed forward, sometimes quickening the pace, sometimes slowing it. Both sides endured heavy casualties.

During the first five months of 1944 the Red Army achieved impressive victories at both ends of the huge Soviet-German Front, in Ukraine and outside Leningrad. Its forces, fighting fiercely, advanced hundreds of kilometers, in places even going beyond the Soviet border into Romania. But in the center of the Eastern Front, the Germans were unassailable. For the

Red Army, the campaign of the summer of 1944 was dedicated to destroying the enemy forces at the front's center. The well and stealthily prepared operation in Belarus was one of the most significant of the entire war. It led to the destruction of a huge Wehrmacht force.

Celebrating his triumph, Stalin ordered up an impressive propaganda spectacle. For several hours, beginning on the morning of 17 July, a column of more than fifty-seven thousand German prisoners of war, with generals and officers at the head of the line, was paraded through central Moscow. That evening they were loaded onto trains and sent to camps. Crowds of Muscovites lined the streets to observe this extraordinary event. "As the column of prisoners of war passed by," Beria reported to Stalin, "the population behaved in an organized manner." He described for the *vozhd* the shouts that could be heard: "Numerous enthusiastic exclamations and salutes in honor of the Red Army and our Supreme Commander-in-Chief," as well as "anti-fascist cries of 'Death to Hitler,' 'Death to fascism,' 'Let the scoundrels die,'" etc. After the columns had passed, crews of water trucks were brought in to pointedly wash the streets clean.[107] On 16 August a similar spectacle took place in Kiev.[108]

This demeaning procession of German prisoners symbolized the impending collapse of Nazism. On 6 June 1944, British, American, and other Allied troops landed on the beaches of Normandy. Overwhelmed by the Red Army in 1944, Germany's allies Romania and Finland laid down their arms. Red Army troops liberated all Soviet territory, expelled Hitler's forces from a significant portion of Eastern Europe and the Balkans, and moved toward the borders of Germany itself.

These decisive victories were primarily the result of the Soviet Union's military and economic superiority, attained through the entire country's sacrifices and exertion. By June 1944 the Soviet armed forces exceeded 11 million people. Red Army assets included field forces numbering 6.6 million, approximately 100,000 mortars and artillery, 8,000 tanks and self-propelled artillery, and 13,000 combat aircraft. In terms of personnel, the ratio of forces along the Soviet-German Front was 1.5:1 in favor of the Red Army; for mortars and artillery, 1.7:1; and for combat aircraft, 4.2:1. The two sides were approximately equally matched in tanks.[109] Furthermore, the Soviet side had significant reserves, while the capacity of the Reich and its allies was shrinking by the day. The Red Army and its commanders, led by Stalin, were growing increasingly confident, bolstered by the wealth of their resources and the experience acquired through years of catastrophe and, finally, victory.

For Stalin, managing the army and continuing to increase its might remained a high priority. Furthermore, liberated areas of the country lay in ruins and desperately needed to be rebuilt. The Nazis had exterminated millions of Soviet civilians, especially Jews. Many towns and villages were completely depopulated.[110] A 1 July 1944 letter to Stalin from the head of Belarus offers a glimpse of the state of territories that had been under German occupation: "There are 800 people left in Vitebsk; before the war there were 211,000. . . . Zhlobin has been completely destroyed. There is a small number of wooden buildings and the frames of three stone ones. There is no population in the city."[111]

In addition to repairing physical destruction, the liberation of Soviet territories confronted the leadership with new political problems. For varying durations—from a few weeks to three years—tens of millions of people had lived under Nazi occupation. Many had either been forced to collaborate or had done so out of conviction. Many others had fled to serve with pro-Soviet partisans or had done what they could to help them. Most had simply tried to survive in the new order. Stalin felt no responsibility for the suffering of Soviet citizens who, in Soviet bureaucratic language, "resided in occupied territory." Like soldiers taken prisoner by the Germans, anyone who lived in captured territory was classified as "suspicious." As part of their reintegration into the USSR, liberated areas had to be cleansed of the taint of occupation, and the means of accomplishing this was mass repression. The crime being prosecuted now was abetting the enemy. Stalin was adamant: no mercy could be shown. On 28 December 1943, Beria submitted a memorandum to him about the discovery in Ukraine of so-called "Volksdeutsche"—people with German roots. This population, Beria claimed, were privileged supporters of the Nazis during the occupation. Stalin gave the order: "Arrest them all and keep them in a special camp under special observation and use them for work."[112]

As the war wound down, a new principle shaped Stalinist repression: collective responsibility for collaboration with the occupiers. This principle was expressed in the wholesale internal deportation of a number of Soviet ethnic groups. During late 1943 and the first half of 1944, several peoples were forcibly relocated: Kalmyks, certain North Caucasian ethnic groups (Chechens, Ingush, Karachai, Balkars), and Crimean Tatars, as well as all the Bulgarians, Greeks, and Armenians living in Crimea. Stalin's decision to exile these groups was partially motivated by real evidence of collaboration and noncompliance with government mobilization efforts during the war, mainly evasion of recruitment into the army.[113] But the principle of collective responsibility and punishment had a broader significance. Even before the war, the government had had difficulty integrating many of these peoples into Soviet society. The war only confirmed that this task had never been completed. Moving them to remote areas of the USSR, in Stalin's mind, was a way of solving this problem once and for all. But the job had to be done right. Entire peoples, bound by common ancestry and heritage, had to be relocated. If anyone was left behind to keep the ancestral hearth burning, many others would try to escape exile and return home. In the case of Crimean Tatars, Stalin was probably also worried about their proximity to Turkey, which he regarded as a potentially hostile force. As the ethnic deportations continued in mid-1944, the border regions of Georgia were also targeted. They were purged of Turks, Kurds, and a few other ethnic minorities viewed by the Soviet authorities as fertile ground for Turkish influence and espionage. These expulsions were essentially a continuation of Stalin's long-standing prewar policy of preventative ethnic purging. But the war drove the sweeping nature of the deportations and the decisiveness with which they were carried out. Much of the inhumanity of war stems from the inhuman acts it is used to justify.

The ethnic deportations of 1943–1944 swept up more than a million people. Such a massive endeavor required large numbers of troops and state security personnel. Stalin had the final word in deciding the fates of entire peoples. He was kept constantly informed on the progress of the deportations, and these reports are now available to historians in what is known as "Stalin's special file" among NKVD materials.[114] Because of the number of deportees involved (approximately one-half million), the relocation of Chechens and Ingush was particularly complicated and difficult. Beria went personally to the North Caucasus to oversee the effort. On 17 February 1944 he wired Stalin to report that the preliminary stage of the operation had been completed.[115] His telegram made it clear that what the Soviet leadership feared most was "incidents"—resistance by the deportees. For this reason, the authorities relied on the element of surprise. Troops assembled under the pretext of training exercises arrested the most active members of the community as a precaution. Stalin, who followed the operation closely, apparently advised Beria not to rely solely on the "chekist and troop operations" but to also try to undermine solidarity among the deportees. In a 22 February telegram, Beria reported to Stalin that he had carried out his "instructions." He had summoned top Chechen and Ingush officials and demanded that they help assure that the deportation was carried out without "excesses." To promote calm, Beria informed Stalin, he solicited the help of religious leaders and other local authorities. In exchange, these officials and elders were promised certain privileges in their place of exile, including increased rations and the right to bring property with them. "I believe that the operation to evict the Chechens and Ingush will be carried out successfully," he reported.[116] The following day, 23 February, he proudly described the beginning of the operation, adding: "There were six attempts to resist by individuals that were suppressed through arrest or use of arms."[117] Stalin could rest assured that the task was in good hands.

Like many of Stalin's political tools, reprisals against real and imagined collaborators were a double-edged sword. After the exceptional violence of war, attempts to instill a desire for vengeance against collaborators weakened the army's morale and spawned brutality and abuses. Many incidents served to illustrate the danger of spontaneous eruptions when millions of young men are thrown into a brutal war. Heroism and self-sacrifice coexisted alongside the basest human behaviors and duty, compassion, and decency alongside criminality and rancor. All sorts of people were in the army, including criminals who had been released from the camps early to fight. Documents from 1944 show that Stalin was repeatedly informed of crimes against civilians by soldiers in liberated areas. In late July, Beria wrote him about the arrest of a group of soldiers and junior officers in a tank repair unit in Moldavia after they had gone on a drunken rampage of robbery and rape against the local population.[118] A similar report from Beria in late September informed Stalin of a rape by members of the Red Army in Crimea. This report also recounted instances of robbery and armed encounters with the local police.[119] Summaries of crimes committed by members of the military in September, October, and December also contained descriptions of robberies, rapes, and even murders, both far from the front and close to the fighting.[120] All were committed against Soviet citizens on Soviet territory.

The situation was much worse when the army entered foreign territory, especially Germany. Feelings of vengeance toward Germans, carefully cultivated by Soviet military propaganda, were not the only reasons for a host of crimes—robbery, murder, and rape—by Soviet soldiers and officers against German civilians. Atrocities by the Nazis within the Soviet Union, the exceptional brutality of the war, the ignorance and criminal pasts of some members of the Red Army, and the weakening of discipline under combat conditions all contributed to, but did not excuse, the firestorm of violence.[121] Stalin was informed of his army's behavior. On 17 March 1945, Beria sent him and Molotov a report on the rapes of German women and their subsequent suicides in eastern Prussia.[122] With the opening of archives from this period, the number of known incidents of this sort will only grow. The history of a dispute with the Yugoslav leadership offers evidence of Stalin's attitude toward such behavior by his military. In late 1944, when the Red Army reached Yugoslav territory and liberated the country together with Yugoslav units, alarming accounts of crimes by members of the Soviet armed forces began to appear. According to the prominent Yugoslav Communist politician and writer Milovan Djilas, there were more than a hundred cases where women were raped and murdered and more than a thousand robberies. The Yugoslav leadership appealed to the Red Army command but was curtly rebuffed. The Yugoslavs were accused of slander. When the matter reached Stalin, he supported his military men and made crude political accusations against the Yugoslavs. Later, when he decided that the conflict needed to be quelled, he had a conciliatory discussion with Djilas during a dinner at his dacha in April 1945:

> Imagine a man who has fought his way from Stalingrad to Belgrade—thousands of kilometers across his desolated land, seeing the death of his comrades and the people closest to him! Can such a man really react normally? And what's so terrible if he misbehaves with a woman a bit after such horrors? You imagined the Red Army to be ideal. It isn't ideal and wouldn't be ideal even without a certain percentage of criminal elements—we opened up the prisons and took everyone into the army. . . . You have to understand war. And the Red Army isn't ideal. The important thing was for it to beat the Germans—and it's beating them well. Everything else is secondary.[123]

If this was Stalin's attitude toward crimes committed on the territory of an allied state, where the government was controlled by Communists loyal to Moscow, it is hardly surprising that he had no desire to take serious measures to prevent abuses in Germany. Stalin's calculations were obvious. All he cared about was the army's military success. If it could be rewarded for its efforts at the expense of the enemy's civilian population, that was fine with him. Nor was he especially worried about reproaches by his Western allies. Remarks made to him by President Roosevelt on 4 February 1945, before the Yalta Conference got under way, probably did not evade his attention: "Roosevelt states that now that he has seen the senseless destruction perpetrated by the Germans in Crimea, he would like to destroy twice as many Germans as have been destroyed so far. We definitely have to destroy 50,000 German-Prussian officers. He, Roosevelt, remembers how

Marshal Stalin proposed a toast in Tehran to the annihilation of 50,000 German-Prussian officers. This was a very good toast."[124]

At some point, however, Stalin had to make a choice. "Misbehaving with women," which he considered a reward for military success, was clearly turning into a problem. Crimes perpetrated by the Soviet military were beginning to serve Nazi propaganda purposes and were feeding German opposition to the Red Army that was not being expressed against the Western Allies. On the eve of a decisive battle for Berlin, Stalin sent the army a clear political signal. On 14 April 1945, *Pravda* published a scathing critique of a work by the well-known Soviet writer and commentator Ilya Erenburg, hailed for his many furious calls for the killing of Germans. Suddenly these calls, which had been perfectly in harmony with Soviet propaganda, were deemed inappropriate. *Pravda* explained at length that there is no such thing as a united Germany, that not all Germans behave the same, and that many of them—more and more with time—were turning away from Nazism and even fighting it. Judging by the article's style, it had been touched by Stalin's pen, and certain fragments were probably its product.

Political posturing and even the introduction of punishment for crimes by Soviet soldiers improved the situation only slightly. Violence toward civilians within the Soviet zone of occupation continued even after the fighting ended. In the summer of 1945, alarmed by the scale of violence, the supreme commander of the occupying Soviet force, Marshal Zhukov, issued orders demanding an end to "plunder, violence, and abuses in regard to the local population." After these demands had little effect, in early September Zhukov issued a more radical order. Remarking that the "criminality of military service members has significantly grown," he ordered that soldiers be confined to their barracks and obliged officers to move in with their subordinates to maintain order. Stalin, on learning of this order, demanded that it be rescinded. One argument against it was that "If this order falls in the hands of the leaders of foreign armies, they will not fail to label the Red Army an army of looters." In place of Zhukov's strict measures, Stalin proposed more vigorous political work, with the troops bringing guilty officers before so-called officer honor courts. The excesses in Germany continued.[125]

■   **TWEAKING THE MILITARY DICTATORSHIP**

On 31 July 1943, Stalin signed a directive addressed to the commanders of the Southern Front that stated, among other things, the following: "I believe it is shameful for Front commanders to allow, through negligence and poor organization, our four infantry regiments to be surrounded by enemy forces. In the third year of war one would think you would have learned how to correctly lead troops."[126] This comment reflects how Stalin felt about his two-year experience at the helm of a country at war. His commanders, he believed, were long overdue in mastering skills that had been lacking or poorly developed when the war first broke out. Probably the supreme commander did not feel this assessment fully applied to himself, but his behavior suggests that he knew there were shortcomings in his leadership during the early stages of the war and he was making an effort to correct them. In style and substance, the military "reforms" he put in place reflected his preferred approach to any problem. Whether he was industrializing a backward country or waging war, his experiments in leadership had many innocent victims.

One reason for the Germans' early success against Soviet defenses was the low level of competence up and down the Soviet chain of command. Lacking trust in his generals (sometimes with good reason), Stalin managed using the techniques with which he was most familiar: strong-armed police measures that instilled fear. Commanders were forced to work under the watchful eye of political commissars and NKVD "special departments." Disorganization and panic were addressed through executions in front of the ranks, penalty battalions, and anti-retreat units. Stalin's parallel army of discipline-keepers rushed from crisis to crisis, both at the front and in the rear. As defensive lines collapsed, the enemy advanced, and Stalin lost faith in his commanders, he developed an array of strategies that wound up depriving commanders of flexibility and often increased Red Army casualties.

These heavy-handed and repressive measures probably do not indicate a conscious choice so much as Stalin's desperation. As strong as his tendency toward violence was, he was certainly aware of the danger inherent in applying it to his own military during a war. He must have grasped that sending troops into battle with guns at their backs was not the ideal way to instill a fighting spirit. He also must have known that on the battlefield it was particularly important to have a single decision maker able to exercise judgment without a political commissar looking over his shoulder. The catastrophes of 1941–1942 clearly showed that unsophisticated and rushed maneuvers combined with pressure from political commissars were not the road to success. Fundamental changes were needed in the way the war was being managed. But when could he introduce these changes? Obviously not while the Red Army was fighting with desperate intensity to hold back the German advance. An opportunity may have presented itself in early 1942, after the Red Army's first victories. But Stalin's impatience and his wager on a quick victory only led to further defeat. The lull that set in during the fall of 1942 was used for other purposes, as can be seen in the careful preparations to encircle the Germans in Stalingrad. On the eve of that victory, Stalin finally turned his attention to introducing fundamental changes.

On 9 October 1942, the Politburo passed a resolution to establish full *edinonachalie*—an ideological buzzword used during forced industrialization to signify a single responsible decision maker—and abolish the institution of the military commissar within the Red Army.[127] Former commissars would now become deputy commanders. A directive signed by Stalin that same day granted officers additional privileges and assigned orderlies to the commanders of all army units, all the way down to the platoon level. The duties of these orderlies included "serving the personal everyday needs of commanding officers and carrying out their assignments."[128] In January 1943, shoulder boards, which in 1917 had been abolished as a symbol of the tsarist army, were introduced to Red Army uniforms. The title of marshal was given to some senior commanders. The introduction of *edinonachalie,* along with privileges, medals, and promotions, was intended to empower the Red Army's senior officers. The realities of war forced Stalin to show more trust in his military.

After the war's chaotic first stage, there was a change in Stalin's interactions with top military command structures, especially the General Staff. "I have to admit," Vasilevsky later stated, "that at the beginning of the war the General Staff was thrown into a state of disarray and, strictly speaking, you could not say that it was operating normally. . . . At the beginning of the war Stalin disbanded the General Staff."[129] This disarray meant that a great many decisions were made by Stalin alone, without input from the General Staff. As Vasilevsky described it, things began to change only in September 1942.[130] By fall 1943 a regular schedule was established for consultation between Stalin and the General Staff. At the start of his workday, around ten or eleven in the morning, he heard by telephone the General Staff's first report on the situation at the fronts. Around four or five in the afternoon he heard a report on how things had gone during the first half of the day. Close to midnight, the heads of the General Staff came to him personally with a summary of the day's events. During these meetings, which took place either at Stalin's Kremlin office or his dacha, the group would study the situation at the fronts on maps, and directives were adopted to be sent to the field. Other decisions were made as well. Politburo members often took part in these meetings, as did the heads of various military or civilian bodies. In some cases, the heads of the General Staff visited Stalin several times in a day.[131] The regularity of these meetings led to better management of the war.

In addition, Stalin had many meetings with other military and civilian leaders. Front commanders were not usually expected to report in person on their assessments and plans, but they were often summoned to Moscow for brief face-to-face meetings. Although Stalin always had the last word, many of these meetings featured a genuine discussion of problems and even debates over large and small questions. A number of memoirs report that as the situation at the fronts improved, meetings grew more business-like, and the atmosphere became more relaxed and informal. Stalin paced the room as he listened to reports. By remaining on his feet, he lessened the hierarchical divide between him and his military subordinates, who also stood. The *vozhd* smoked a great deal, but others could also smoke without asking permission. Boxes of *papirosas* (filterless Russian cigarettes) lay on the table. Members of the top Soviet leadership sat around the table and kept silent until Stalin asked them a question.[132] Less inclined to dictate his own terms or interfere in operational decisions, Stalin became noticeably more respectful toward the military leaders as the war continued.

> During the second phase of the war, Stalin was not inclined to be hasty in making decisions and usually listened to reports, including upsetting ones, without any sign of irritability, without interrupting, just smoking, pacing, sitting down from time to time, and listening.[133]

> Less and less often he imposed his own solutions to individual questions on Front commanders—attack this way and not that way. Earlier he would impose his way, tell them in what direction and in which specific sector it would be more advantageous to attack or to concentrate forces. . . . By the end of the war there wasn't a hint of this.[134]

Stalin's new demeanor was largely a result of his growth as a military leader. As the war progressed, he acquired a huge store of both negative and positive experience. "After the Battle of Stalingrad and especially Kursk," Marshal Vasilevsky wrote, "he rose to the height of strategic leadership. Now Stalin was thinking in terms of modern warfare and grasped all the issues involved in preparing and conducting operations." This view of Stalin's new sophistication was shared by many of the military leaders who worked with him during the war.[135]

Stalin's focus on the day-to-day details of operations at the fronts allowed him little time to deal with other matters, particularly the economy. Many spheres of socioeconomic life were removed from the dictator's harsh control as the lines of division among government institutions underwent a spontaneous wartime revision. Under the military dictatorship, at the top of the pyramid was, as always, Stalin, who made decisions either solely or during meetings held either in his Kremlin office or at his dacha. The participants in these meetings included military leaders and the *vozhd*'s closest comrades. The meetings did not fit into any of the orderly categories of government. Depending on their content, decisions made at these meetings, or solely by Stalin, were drawn up and circulated to those charged with carrying them out in the name of one of the top governmental bodies—the Politburo, the Council of People's Commissars, the State Defense Committee, or the Supreme Command. Meanwhile, many questions having to do with the day-to-day running of the country, including the wartime economy, were being decided without Stalin's direct involvement. Molotov, for example, was in charge of the SNK (the Council of People's Commissars) and regularly presided over the decision-making bodies that basically oversaw all aspects of government not directly tied to military operations.[136] In December 1942 a new body was established to oversee the work by industry and the transportation sector to meet the needs of the front: the State Defense Committee's Operational Bureau.[137] Led at first by Molotov, as the war wound down, it was taken over by Beria.[138] Members of the Politburo and the State Defense Committee also served on these critical managerial bodies, where they had the authority to resolve important issues quickly. Not all of the resolutions produced by these bodies went to Stalin for approval.

In addition to their duties serving on these top government bodies, each of Stalin's associates had his own individual "portfolio." As the war persisted, this system of putting members of the leadership in charge of particular areas became embedded. For example, in February 1942, the following purviews were assigned to members of the State Defense Committee: Molotov was placed in charge of the production of tanks, Malenkov of aviation, Beria of armaments, Voznesensky of ammunition, and Mikoyan of supplying the army with food and uniforms.[139] These portfolios could change over time. Whatever assignments were given to these top leaders, under the pressures of war and by sheer necessity they operated with significant administrative latitude. What mattered were results. If they met their production targets, they were successful. This system worked, and Stalin had neither the time nor the desire to change it.

The increased autonomy enjoyed by Stalin's associates inevitably spilled over into the political sphere and affected their interactions with the *vozhd*. As Mikoyan attests, "During the war there was a certain solidarity among our leadership. . . . Stalin, who understood that during this difficult time an all-out effort was required, fostered an atmosphere of trust, and every member of the Politburo carried a tremendous load."[140] This understanding, of course, did not mean that Stalin's dictatorial dominance over the Politburo was replaced by oligarchic rule. Stalin set the rules of collective leadership. As the situation stabilized at the front and victory over the enemy approached, there were signs that he intended to do away with the slight liberalizations that circumstances had forced upon him. For Mikoyan, the first such sign was a slap on the wrist he received from the *vozhd*. On 17 September 1944 he sent Stalin a draft resolution on advancing grain to a number of oblasts.[141] Although the proposal was rather moderate and did not give the oblasts everything they were asking for, Stalin made a display of his anger, writing onto Mikoyan's resolution: "I vote against. Mikoyan is behaving in an anti-state manner and is being led around by the oblast committees and is corrupting them. He has completely corrupted Andreev.[142] The procurement commissariat should be taken away from Mikoyan and given to Malenkov, for example."[143] The Politburo did so the following day.[144]

Another sign of coming changes at the top was a shake-up within the military leadership undertaken by Stalin in late 1944. In November the Politburo appointed Nikolai Bulganin to serve as Stalin's deputy at the defense commissariat and made him a member of the State Defense Committee.[145] Bulganin was also given important powers in interacting with the army.[146] His expertise lay in civilian affairs, but during the war he served on the councils of a number of fronts, thus acquiring some military experience and even the rank of general. His assignment to the defense commissariat, and the broad powers he was given, could only mean that Stalin was creating a new counterweight to the military, in particular to the deputy defense commissar and deputy supreme commander, Marshal Zhukov. Evidence can be seen in the demonstrative dressing-down given to Zhukov just two weeks after Bulganin's appointment. In December 1944 Stalin accused Zhukov of exceeding his authority in approving artillery field manuals and issued him a reprimand. The order criticizing Zhukov was circulated to all top military leaders.[147]

As painful as this lashing out must have been for Stalin's subordinates, his attacks did little to roil the upper echelons of power or change his relative moderation in dealing with the members of the Politburo or the military leadership. Lower down the hierarchy, however, there was no sense of liberalization. The war lent a certain legitimacy to Stalin's brutality, especially given the extreme ruthlessness of the enemy. The intensity of state violence during the war years was comparable to that of the Terror. In addition to the general hardships of war, the front suffered (as noted) from executions, anti-retreat units, and penalty battalions, while members of the civilian population suffered arrest, execution, mass deportations, mobilization, and the mass starvation that resulted from forced grain requisitions by the state and the collapse of agriculture in some of the Soviet Union's most productive areas. While the context of these hardships differed from those experienced in the late 1930s, to those enduring them they must have felt very much the same. As they mounted, just as he had done toward the conclusion of the Terror, Stalin made certain concessions to the populace that cost him little but brought certain tactical advantages.

The best known concession was a reconciliation with religious institutions and the faithful, most important the country's Orthodox majority. This departure from the anti-religious campaigns of the 1920s and 1930s, from the destruction of churches and the mass executions of clergy members and believers, in favor of the opening of cathedrals and relative freedom of religion, was part of an overall adjustment in official ideology. Russian patriotism was being encouraged before the war, and a revival of images of the heroic past, many placed on a par with the legacy of Bolshevism and the revolution, became more pronounced during the war years.[148] Under Stalin's orders, portraits of the great eighteenth- and nineteenth-century generals Aleksandr Suvorov and Mikhail Kutuzov were placed alongside the photograph of Lenin that hung in his office. To medals based on the symbolism of the revolution were added those commemorating Suvorov, Kutuzov, Prince Aleksandr Nevsky, and Admiral Pavel Nakhimov. At the front, those who had fought in World War I were allowed to wear their tsarist medals along with their Soviet ones.

The new attitude toward religion received a stunning stamp of approval in September 1943, when a previously unimaginable meeting between Stalin and the leaders of the Russian Orthodox Church was publicly announced. Three metropolitans were brought to Stalin's Kremlin office during the night of 4–5 September. They talked with the unusually amiable *vozhd* for one hour and twenty minutes.[149] After an eighteen-year prohibition, they were granted permission to appoint a patriarch for the Russian Orthodox Church and were even offered the option of using airplanes to bring bishops to Moscow so as to accelerate the selection. Stalin consented to the opening of courses in theology to prepare priests and even proposed organizing theological seminaries and academies. He also supported requests to open new churches and free arrested priests, and he proposed that church leaders improve priests' material well-being by setting up special food stores and assigning them cars. He gave the future patriarch the gift of a three-story house with a garden in the center of Moscow, formerly the home of the German ambassador, including all its furnishings. After discussing a few more items, Stalin escorted the metropolitans to the door of his office.[150] The next day, the meeting with church leaders and the upcoming election of a new patriarch were reported in newspapers.

Historians have made a rather thorough study of the reasons for Stalin's about-face on religion. Of course the former seminary graduate with the unfinished theological education had no intention of returning to the bosom of the church or asking forgiveness for his sins. Needing to strengthen relations with his allies, he had to respond to the concerns of Western public opinion and influential church circles about the plight of believers in the USSR. Furthermore, the liberation of occupied Soviet territories raised the practical question of what to do about the many churches the Germans had built there. The usual Bolshevik approach of shutting them down was impossible. He needed a reconciliation with the church. Religion had to be put under tight control but not destroyed. Far from the bottom of the list of reasons for this change was Stalin's awareness of the role religion played in uniting the country, in earning the emotional support of the masses, who had endured terrible trials. Soviet values, force-fed into the minds of millions, could not satisfy the spiritual needs of a huge and ancient people. The goal of achieving a universal vision of the path forward turned out to be unattainable. Stalin's grasp of this reality brought him one step closer to victory.

■   **THE STAGES OF VICTORY: CRIMEA,
BERLIN, POTSDAM, MANCHURIA**

The entry of the huge Red Army into Germany was a long-awaited and joyous occasion for the Soviet people and the *vozhd*. The enemy would be finished off in its own den. The time for retribution had come. Such natural and inevitable feelings inspired heroism and self-sacrifice during the war's final battles, when every Soviet soldier could taste victory and was eager for the final assault. Stalin had every reason to be proud of his army.

One of the Red Army's most successful operations came in January and February 1945. Taking just three weeks to advance five hundred kilometers from the Vistula to the Oder, the Soviet forces shattered critical Nazi lines of defense. Bridgeheads were created for an offensive against Berlin itself, but several months of bloody battles still lay ahead. The German forces defending their country put up a stubborn resistance and even launched counteroffensives, forcing the Red Army to take heavy casualties. Knowing this, Stalin did not hurry to enter Berlin in February. It would take several weeks to eliminate the threat of German counterattacks against the exposed flanks of the advancing Soviet fronts and to bring in reinforcements. Hard-earned experience had taught him prudence.

The victories of early 1945 had put the Soviet side in a favorable position to negotiate with the Allies on the postwar future. Negotiations first became a practical necessity in late 1944, when the Red Army was advancing through the Balkans and the Western Allies entered France and Italy. In October 1944, Churchill again flew to Moscow to meet with Stalin. The British prime minister raised the question of spheres of influence in Europe, the Balkans in particular. Stalin is unlikely to have been put off by this political cynicism. He agreed that "England should have the right to a decisive voice in Greece,"[151] and he was also willing to apportion a Western "share" of influence in Romania, Hungary, Bulgaria, and Yugoslavia. The presence of the Red Army in these countries (unlike in Greece) had brought them under Soviet control. For Stalin, this control was decisive. The question of Poland, high on the list of diplomatic issues Churchill brought to Moscow, was much more contentious. By the time of Churchill's visit in late 1944, the USSR had broken off relations with the official Polish government, which had spent the war in exile in Britain, and was promoting a Communist alternative. Britain and the United States did what they could to prevent this outcome. On 1 August 1944, as the Red Army approached, the Polish government in exile organized an uprising in Warsaw with the goal of seizing power in the capital before the arrival of Soviet forces and the pro-Soviet government they were bringing with them. The Red Army, for a variety of reasons, stopped its advance, and the Nazis drowned the uprising in blood. This tragic episode became a source of sharp division between Stalin and his allies, who charged him with intentionally holding back aid to the uprising. This charge was largely just, but Stalin, guided by his own reality, had no intention of relenting. The London Poles had not launched the uprising to help him, so why should he help them?

Burdened by different problems but still united by their common foe, the Big Three met outside the Crimean resort city of Yalta in February 1945. This stunningly beautiful corner of the Soviet Union had only recently been liberated from Nazi occupation and lay in ruins. Sparing no effort or expense, in record time the Soviet authorities created a haven amid the destruction, including residences for the three leaders and their large retinues. Particular attention was paid to security. Camouflage covering was set up to protect against enemy air raids and sturdy shelters were built. Crimea, recently roiled by mass arrests and deportations, was subjected to yet another round of purges. "Suspicious elements" were rounded up and taken into custody. A whole army of security personnel was brought to the area. Stalin alone was protected by a force of one hundred operatives and five hundred NKVD troops, plus his usual bodyguards.[152]

With victory around the corner, the Yalta Conference would have to address a wide range of urgent questions on which the fate of the world hung. At stake were the future of Germany, a redrawing of the map of Europe, and the worldwide balance of power. Generally speaking, the participants' goals were simple. Although their motives and priorities differed, each of the parties wanted to leave Yalta with as many items on his diplomatic wish list as he could. But as long as the war continued, the Allies had to depend on one another and adjust their aspirations to military and political realities. They compromised on many issues. The zones of occupation in Germany were settled. The guiding principles on which a united nations organization would be founded were outlined. The idea was discussed of the Soviet Union annexing new territories at Poland's expense (western Ukraine and Belarus), for which Poland would be compensated with German lands to its west. In exchange for a promise to enter into the war with Japan, Stalin extracted an agreement from the Allies that Soviet borders would be shifted outward to encompass new territory in the Far East and that the country's interests in northern China would be recognized.

But as the contours of a new world took shape, so did the battle lines of the Cold War. It was not possible to reach a real compromise in regard to Poland. Stalin was determined to put this country under the control of his handpicked government, even if that involved making a few concessions on paper. Another contentious issue was the question of reparations from Germany, a point of particular interest for Stalin.

Perhaps even more indicative of the gulf dividing the Allies was the attitude of Soviet state security personnel in Crimea. The hordes of Westerners who descended on Soviet territory were treated as an enemy penetration. The ships used to bring the Allies' supplies for the conference were surrounded by round-the-clock patrols. Their crews, when given shore leave, were kept under tight NKVD control. "The entire agent apparatus has been instructed and directed to uncover the nature of ties between foreigners and the port's military personnel and civilians. Female agents who will come into close contact with foreigners have been given particularly careful instructions," read one report to the NKVD leadership.[153] One can only imagine what these instructions were.

With every passing week, Stalin's mistrust of the Western Allies grew, strongly influencing Soviet military plans. Wehrmacht units clearly preferred to surrender in the West, while in the East they fought to the bitter end. Stalin had every reason to fear the possibility, if not of a separate peace, at least that the Allies might make certain separate agreements with the Germans. During the final months of the war, everyone understood what the advances of Allied armies meant for postwar Europe's political landscape. Negotiations in March 1945 in Bern between U.S. intelligence agents and representatives of the Nazis to discuss Germany's capitulation in Italy only heightened Stalin's suspicion.

Had it not unfolded amid other conflicts between the Soviet leadership and the Western Allies, especially in regard to Poland, the Bern incident might not have provoked open confrontation. After lengthy wrangling, on 3 April 1945 Stalin sent Roosevelt a sharply worded letter in which he questioned whether it would be possible to "preserve and strengthen trust between our countries." Now that the archives have been opened, we can see that this letter, unlike many others that went out over his signature, was written entirely by Stalin himself and that he revised it to achieve a sterner tone.[154] Despite the growing friction, Roosevelt, who was committed to cooperating with Stalin, responded with restraint. A letter received by Stalin on 13 April 1945 sought to assure him that "minor misunderstandings of this character should not arise in the future."[155] This letter was one of Roosevelt's final political acts and is part of his testament in regard to relations with the Soviet Union. By the time Stalin received it, Roosevelt was already dead. Stalin appears to have been genuinely saddened by this loss. Nevertheless, he was soon distracted by new and urgent matters.

Worried about his fellow Allies' rapid advance, Stalin decided to speed up the Soviet takeover of the German capital as much as possible. The attack on Berlin began on 16 April 1945, one month earlier than the date Stalin had given his allies.[156] Despite the Soviet forces' overwhelming advantage in manpower and hardware, this key battle was not easy. Out of more than 2 million soldiers of the Red Army and Polish Second Army who took part in the Berlin operation, more than 360,000 were killed, wounded, or went missing in action.[157] German units put up a determined fight in defense of their capital.

The politically motivated decision to push forward the operation created great hurdles for the Red Army. Although delaying the offensive slightly would have made little difference to its outcome, Stalin required the front commanders to rush the advance of their forces at any cost. This accelerated pace, given the need to break through well-defended enemy positions, meant heavier casualties. The record speed of the operation and the concentration of a huge force directed against Berlin necessitated constant adjustments to the overall plan and field directives. According to the head of the General Staff's Main Operational Directorate, General Sergei Shtemenko, Supreme Command Headquarters was in a state of turmoil throughout the Berlin operation. The General Staff leadership was summoned to Command Headquarters several times a day, sometimes at odd hours; many instructions were drafted under extreme time pressure; and the lightning speed of events made organized operations difficult.[158] But no matter how hurriedly things were done at Headquarters, some historians believe that Stalin could not possibly "react to the changing situation in time."[159] It is unclear whether this lag in the flow of information to and from Headquarters had any real consequences. The performance of the Soviet Supreme Command and Stalin in the Berlin operation has received little scholarly scrutiny.

But no matter how many obstacles were thrown in the Red Army's path, they were not enough to save the Nazis. On 25 April, Soviet units coming from one direction met U.S. forces coming from the other on the Elbe River. The victors' absolute numerical superiority and high morale sealed the fate of the Third Reich. Early in the morning on 1 May, Stalin learned through an urgent telephone message from Marshal Zhukov that Hitler had committed suicide in his Berlin bunker the day before.[160] On 2 May, the Berlin garrison capitulated. During the night of 8–9 May, the final surrender was formulated and signed by Germany. On 24 June, Moscow held a long-awaited and impressive victory parade. Then, on 27 June, Stalin was awarded the title of generalissimo.

Now the leader of a major world power, in July 1945 Stalin set out for a vanquished Berlin for yet another Big Three conference. No firsthand accounts of Stalin's last trip outside the Soviet Union have been preserved. What did he see through the windows of his train? With whom did he meet or spend time during this journey? Undoubtedly he knew the upcoming meeting with his fellow leaders would not be an easy one. With victory, the disagreements among the Allies had only grown more contentious. The Soviet dictator would have his first meeting with the new American president,

Harry Truman, among whose advisers advocates of a hard line toward the USSR were gaining ascendancy. The Western Allies were displeased by the sovietization of Romania and Bulgaria, to say nothing of unresolved arguments about the Polish government. Stalin did not trust the Americans and British. This mistrust was fanned when Truman privately informed him of American atom bomb tests. The principles of German demilitarization, de-Nazification, and democratization were unanimously approved, but the Allies argued bitterly about everything else. The search for compromises and mutual concessions was spurred by fears that the war-weary world could be plunged into a new confrontation, by Soviet hopes for economic cooperation with the West, and by Western hopes that the USSR would enter the war against Japan. In the end, Stalin managed to finalize an agreement allowing Poland to expand its territory at the expense of Germany and the Soviet Union to incorporate the Konigsberg area. He did not, however, get his way on reparations or on the creation of Soviet bases on the Turkish Straits and the Mediterranean.

Having achieved what he could in Europe, Stalin turned his attention to acquiring Japanese lands and gaining footholds in northern China. In Yalta he had agreed to join the war against Japan two or three months after Germany surrendered. Knowing how eager the United States was for Soviet help, he had been able to extract very advantageous terms. The "status quo" was preserved in the Mongolian People's Republic, keeping it under de facto Soviet control. The USSR regained the southern portion of Sakhalin, which Russia had lost in the Russo-Japanese War of 1905, and a commercial port and military base in northern China, along with the railroad line leading to it. Of fundamental significance to the USSR was the Allies' agreement to recognize Soviet sovereignty over the strategically important Kuril Islands.

These agreements all remained in force up to the Berlin Conference, but now, for the first time in history, the nuclear factor came into play. The fact that the Americans had an atom bomb gave them much greater leverage. For one thing, fear of this powerful new technology could lead Japan to surrender even before the Soviet Union entered the war. Stalin preferred not to take the risk. He applied the same strategy in the Far East that he had used in Europe, where actual military possession of territory was more meaningful than agreements at the bargaining table. After the United States used its atom bombs against Japan, Stalin ordered the Red Army to launch an urgent offensive, giving his forces a deadline of 9 August 1945 to turn the Yalta concessions into a reality on the ground. The Soviet numerical advantage coupled with high morale and a seasoned fighting force brought about a quick victory. Even after Japan's capitulation, Soviet forces continued to advance until all territories granted to the USSR at Yalta had been occupied. Then Stalin tried to take a little extra. In the Far East this meant pretentions to jointly occupy Japan proper and share in governing the country using a model similar to the one being applied in Germany. This effort was probably more a test of the new American president's will than an actual demand, but it was accompanied by military preparations. After being decisively rebuffed by the Americans, Stalin quickly backed off, but not without some resentment. Disputes over Japan remained an irritant in Soviet-American relations for months. Japan itself did not recognize the Soviet capture of the Kuril Islands as legitimate.

For the millions of Soviet people who survived the horrors of war, the disputes and ambitions of politicians were peripheral. The country, finally at peace, could look to the future with hope.

FAMILY

2 March 1953 at the near dacha. The arrival of the daughter.
Once the seriousness of Stalin's condition became clear, his children, Svetlana and Vasily, were called to the dacha. This was largely a symbolic gesture. Over time, Stalin's family had come to play less and less of a role in his life.

Stalin met his first wife when he was still a young revolutionary adventurer. Returning to Tiflis in 1905 after escaping from his first exile and traveling through Transcaucasia, he moved in with the Svanidze family. There were five members of this family: Aleksandr Svanidze, who was involved in the revolutionary movement, and his sisters—Sashiko, Kato (Yekaterina), and Masho—as well as Sashiko's husband, whom Stalin had known in the seminary. Sashiko and Kato were well-known dressmakers in the city who had nothing to do with the revolutionary movement. So when he brought Iosif Jughashvili into the household, Aleksandr tried to keep this outsider as far away as possible from his sisters.[1] Nevertheless, an infatuation developed between Iosif and Yekaterina, who were both young and attractive. Kato's sisters could not have been happy about her involvement with an impoverished seminary dropout. Some light is shed on this period by a letter sent to Stalin forty years later, in 1946. An acquaintance of Stalin and the Svanidze family from his Tiflis days asked for help and rather artlessly implied that Stalin owed him a favor. First, Stalin had used the letter writer's room for assignations with Yekaterina. Second, when Stalin proposed to Kato and "the relatives were opposed," "I told her, if you like him, don't listen to anybody, and she heeded my advice."[2]

The Svanidze family was basically presented with a fait accompli, and in July 1906 the couple was married.[3] This new family member inevitably entangled the Svanidzes in his world. Soon after the wedding, Yekaterina was arrested as an accomplice of revolutionaries. The matter was resolved thanks to her sister Sashiko, who used her ties to wives of police officers. Yekaterina spent about two months under arrest, but instead of being held in a jail cell, she was kept in a local police chief's apartment—apparently at the request of the chief's wife, who was a client of the dressmakers.[4] One important argument for closing Yekaterina's case was that she was pregnant. In March 1907 the future dictator's first child, Yakov, was born.

Family life and revolution did not mix. Iosif moved his wife and son with him to Baku, where Yekaterina fell seriously ill. In November 1907 she died. This was a heavy blow to Iosif. Unable to take adequate care of his son, he left Yakov with his wife's family.

There were other women in Stalin's life. Evidence survives of a relationship with Stefaniia Petrovskaia, a young revolutionary from the landowning class, that began in 1909, when both were exiled to Solvychegodsk in Vologda Province. After serving out her term, Petrovskaia followed Iosif to Baku. When he was arrested in June 1910, the future dictator even asked the police for permission to "enter into lawful wedlock" with her. The permission was granted, but the wedding never took place. In September 1910 Jughashvili, still a bachelor, was again sent into exile.[5] During this second exile in Solvychegodsk he registered his place of residence (in the home of M. P. Kuzakova) together with fellow exile Serafima Khoroshenina, suggesting that the two were intimate. Soon, however, Khoroshenina was transferred out of Solvychegodsk.[6] According to rumors now being promoted by some journalists, Stalin then began a relationship with his landlady, Kuzakova, resulting in the birth of a son. There is no hard evidence of this relationship. After finishing his term of exile a few months after the supposed affair with Kuzakova, Jughashvili spent some time living in Vologda. Here he became acquainted with an eighteen-year-old schoolgirl named Pelageia Onufrieva, the fiancée of one of his fellow exiles, Petr Chizhikov. The future dictator flirted openly with the girl and gave her a book with the inscription, "To clever, nasty Polya from the oddball Iosif." When Pelageia left Vologda, Jughashvili sent her facetious cards, such as: "I claim a kiss from you conveyed via Petka [Chizhikov]. I kiss you back, and I don't just kiss you, but passionately (simple kissing isn't worth it). Iosif."[7] In his personal files, Stalin kept a photograph of Chizhikov and Onufrieva dating to his time in Vologda: a serious, pretty, round-faced girl in glasses and a serious young man with regular features and a moustache and beard.

The jocular cards, presents, and photograph attest to the thirty-three-year-old Jughashvili's interest in the young woman but do not prove that he was romantically involved with her. We have only a few vague hints. Around the same time that Stalin left Vologda, in 1912, Chizhikov went to visit his parents in Ukraine, where he fell ill and died suddenly, without marrying Pelageia, as he may or may not have intended. Onufrieva suffered the sort of misfortune that befell many of her compatriots. After Chizhikov's death she married, and as her erstwhile gallant admirer presided over the country, her husband was arrested. It is not known whether she ever tried to appeal to Stalin for help. She died in 1955, having lived her entire life in Vologda.[8]

The evidence that Iosif Jughashvili had an affair with the even younger Lidiia Pereprygina during his last Turukhansky exile is more solid, although rumors that they had a son together have not been proved. In any case, Stalin never recognized Pereprygina's son or any other illegitimate children attributed to him.

Returning to St. Petersburg after the February 1917 revolution, Stalin was ready to turn a new page. The Alliluev household provided a place of warmth after the upheavals of life underground. The attraction this family held for him is understandable. Stalin had known them since his years in Tiflis and had corresponded with them during his final exile in Kureika. The head of the family, Sergei Alliluev, was a longtime party member who had been arrested many times. The family's two sons and two daughters were often left without adult supervision and led rather freewheeling lifestyles. Iosif was particularly fond of the youngest, the sixteen-year-old schoolgirl Nadezhda, who reciprocated his feelings despite the twenty-three-year difference in their ages. To a young woman from a revolutionary family, he must have seemed like the ideal man: a tried-and-true revolutionary, brave and mysterious but also personable. In 1919 Stalin and Nadezhda tied the knot. As to the nature of their relationship before marriage, we can only guess.

Nadezhda, a party member beginning in 1918, was a model Bolshevik wife. She worked in Lenin's secretariat (Lenin knew the Alliluevs and even lived in their apartment in 1917). In 1921 the Stalins had their first child, Vasily. Nadezhda had a hard time keeping up with childrearing, work, and party activism and apparently neglected the last. In late 1921 she was expelled from the party as "ballast with no interest in the life of the party whatsoever." Only through the intercession of top party officials, including Lenin, was her membership restored, although she had to spend a year earning her way back in as a candidate member. Such were the times. Nadezhda herself probably believed in the ideals of equality and party democracy and was not offended by her treatment. In her request to be readmitted she promised to "prepare herself for party work."[9]

In addition to the birth of Vasily, Nadezhda's life was complicated by the introduction of Stalin's first son, Yakov, into the family. Letters to her mother-in-law, Ekaterine Jughashvili, in 1922 and 1923 included cautious complaints: "Yasha is going to school, fooling around, and smoking, and does not listen to me"; "Yasha is also healthy, but he's not putting much effort into his schoolwork."[10] Yakov, fifteen in 1922, was just six years younger than his stepmother. A few years later, in 1926, Nadezhda wrote of Yakov to a female friend: "I have already lost all hope that he will ever come to his senses. He has absolutely no interests and no goal."[11] The boy was also not getting along with his father. Conflict over his intention to marry ended tragically: when he failed to get his father's consent, he tried to commit suicide. On 9 April 1928 Stalin wrote to Nadezhda: "Tell Yasha from me that he has behaved like a hooligan and a blackmailer with whom I have nothing in common and with whom I can have nothing further to do. Let him live wherever he wants and with whomever he wants."[12] For a while Stalin's relationship with his eldest son was in a state of suspension, but on the eve of the war, when Yakov was studying at the Artillery Academy, Stalin was apparently pleased with him. On 5 May 1941, Yakov was present at a large Kremlin reception in honor of military academy graduates. In his remarks to the gathering, Stalin joked that "I have an acquaintance who studied at the Artillery Academy. I looked over his notes and found that a great deal of time is being spent studying cannons that were decommissioned in 1916."[13] This was an obvious reference to Yakov's notes, a sign that the two were spending time together.

In early 1926 Nadezhda gave birth to a daughter, Svetlana. In sharing the good news with Ordzhonikidze's wife, Zinaida, who was vacationing in the south, Nadezhda wrote, "In short, we now have a complete family."[14] But with Stalin immersed in his official duties and embroiled in a battle for power, this was no usual family. No doubt he loved his wife and children, but for the most part he loved them from a distance. They spent brief stretches of time together at the dacha outside Moscow and while on vacation in the south. Nadezhda, as if emulating her husband, was always busy with work, party activism, and her studies. In a letter to a friend a month before Svetlana's birth, she wrote, "I very much regret that I've again fettered myself with new family responsibilities," obviously referring to the impending arrival of her second child. "In our time it's not very easy since there are such an awful lot of new prejudices, and if you're not working, then of course you're a *'baba'* [peasant woman, used derogatively for women in general]. . . . You just have to have an area of expertise that enables you to escape being someone's errand girl, as usually happens in 'secretarial' work, and do everything that has to do with your area of expertise."[15] Young and energetic, Nadezhda sincerely and energetically strove to adhere to the new model of the "Soviet woman." This was not easy. Her surviving letters show that to the end of her life her writing was riddled with syntactic errors. In an effort to make up for the shortcomings of her education, she became an assiduous student. In 1929 she enrolled in the Industrial Academy, hoping to receive, in keeping with the ethos of the times, an advanced technical education. Her children were largely handed over to nursemaids, governesses, and tutors. A housekeeper and cook took care of the Stalin Kremlin household. An important part in Vasily and Svetlana's lives was played by relatives, as well as their peers among the children of other Soviet leaders who lived in the Kremlin. Together they formed a boisterous band that spent time together at suburban dachas and each other's Kremlin apartments.

This manner of family life had its advantages and logic. The infrequency of time spent together could perhaps make "the heart grow fonder" and actually strengthen family ties. But the few surviving letters between Stalin and Nadezhda, written during vacations between 1929 and 1931, attest to both love and tension in their relationship. "I send you a big kiss, like the kiss you gave me when we parted," Nadezhda wrote to her husband. She said she missed him and asked doting questions about his health and treatments. Stalin responded in kind. He tenderly called her Tatka and Tatochka ("Write about everything, my Tatochka") and even resorted to baby talk. As a loving father, he was always asking about the children: "How are things with Vaska, with Setanka [his nickname for Svetlana]?" "Have Setanka write me something. And Vaska too." He sent lemons and peaches home to his family. But this sweetness and consideration could suddenly be darkened by jealousy and irritation. In September 1930, after spending part of her husband's vacation with him and then returning to Moscow, Nadezhda wrote him a letter filled with reproach: "This summer I didn't feel that delaying my departure would make you happy; quite the opposite. Last summer I could really sense that, but not this time. Of course, there was no point staying with such a mood." A few weeks later she wrote: "For some reason I'm not hearing anything from you. . . . Probably you're distracted by your quail-hunting trips. . . . I heard from an interesting young woman that you looked great, . . . that you were marvelously cheerful and you wouldn't let anyone sit still. . . . I'm glad to hear it." Stalin made a halfhearted effort to dispute her implications: "As for your assumption that I did not consider it desirable for you to stay in Sochi, your reproaches . . . are unfair"; "You're hinting at some trips. I'm telling you that I have not traveled anywhere (anywhere at all!) and I have no intention of traveling."[16]

Nadezhda's jealousy was not without grounds. Stalin could be a flagrant philanderer, and his wife was quick to take offense. Many who observed the relationship firsthand commented on Nadezhda's frail mental health. Mental illness apparently ran in the family, afflicting her mother and at least one of her siblings. It is probably here, at the intersection of Stalin's unfaithfulness and Allilueva's mental illness, that the roots of the tragedy should be sought.

On 8 November 1932, the anniversary of the October Revolution that brought them all to power, Stalin and Allilueva joined other top Soviet leaders and their wives for a celebratory dinner at the Kremlin. The details of what took place at this dinner are unknown. Perhaps Stalin drank too much and started openly flirting with some of the wives.[17] Perhaps Nadezhda was simply in a bad mood or Stalin said something hurtful to her. Or perhaps she was the one who provoked an argument. Whatever the cause, there was an argument, and Nadezhda returned to their Kremlin apartment alone. Sometime during that night she took her own life, using a small pistol that had been a gift from her brother Pavel.

Some have speculated that Allilueva was upset about her husband's policies and felt ardent sympathy for their victims, including those dying from the devastating famine then taking millions of lives. Their daughter, Svetlana, wrote of a suicide note left by her mother that contained, among its grievances, political accusations, although she had no firsthand knowledge of this note and was citing other people's descriptions of it. There is absolutely no hard evidence that Nadezhda objected to her husband's policies. None of her surviving letters mentions the horrific events taking place in the country: violent collectivization, the internal deportations of hundreds of thousands of peasants, and the arrests of countless suspected "enemies." Her letters give the impression that she, like the rest of the Bolshevik elite, was completely isolated from the suffering of tens of millions outside the Kremlin walls. On 10 July 1932, during the famine, when peasant mothers were watching their children starve to death, Nadezhda wrote a note to Stalin's assistant Aleksandr Poskrebyshev complaining that she was not receiving her usual supply of new works of fiction from overseas and asked that the head of the OGPU, Yagoda, do something to fix the problem.[18] Admittedly, we do not know for sure whether Nadezhda ever said anything against her husband's repressive policies in the months before her death, in part because the usual correspondence between Stalin and his wife while he was away on vacation is missing for 1932. Perhaps these letters were destroyed, or perhaps Nadezhda was with her husband during his entire vacation. No evidence has been found to explain the absence of such letters.

His wife's suicide was apparently a great blow to Stalin. Grief over the loss and pity for his children were combined with anger. Nadezhda had betrayed and humiliated him, cast a cloud over his reputation, and made his personal life a subject of sordid conjecture that endures to this day. "She did a very bad thing. . . ; she maimed me for the rest of my life," he told relatives some two and a half years later.[19]

Out of habit, Stalin's family led its customary life for a few years after Allilueva's death. Almost every member of the household maintained his or her role within the family routine. Seeking relief from painful memories, Stalin moved to a new apartment in the Kremlin and began construction of the near dacha. The children remained under the care of governesses and nursemaids in Moscow and at the old dacha. Stalin, Vasily, and Svetlana were surrounded by the same relatives, especially the families of Pavel and Anna Alliluev (Nadezhda's brother and sister) and Aleksandr Svanidze (the brother of Stalin's first wife). This was a complicated and often unsavory world. The relatives schemed to outshine one another in Stalin's eyes. Apparently Pavel Alliluev's wife even had a brief affair with the dictator.[20] Stalin appears to have enjoyed the competition among his relatives.

After Nadezhda's death, Stalin tried to spend more time with his children. While they were having dinner together in the Kremlin apartment, he asked them how things were going in school, and he sometimes came to the dacha to pick them up and take them to the theater. On occasion, he brought them with him when he vacationed in the south. He was especially fond of Svetlana, who was a promising student and very attached to her father. He began to play a little game with his daughter, calling her *khoziaika* (which could be translated as "housekeeper" or "the boss") while he played the role of the *sekretarishka* (little secretary) who followed her orders: "Setanka-Housekeeper's wretched Secretary, the poor peasant J. Stalin." Svetlana would write out orders for her father: "I order you to let me go to Zubalovo tomorrow"; "I order you to take me to the theater with you"; "I order you to let me go to the movies. Ask them to show *Chapaev* and an American comedy." Stalin responded with facetious pomposity.[21] Other members of Stalin's inner circle were appointed Svetlana's *sekretarishkas,* playing along with the *vozhd.* "Svetlana the housekeeper will be in Moscow on 27 August. She is demanding permission to leave early for Moscow so that she can check on her secretaries," Stalin wrote to Kaganovich from the south on 19 August 1935. Kaganovich replied on 31 August:

"Today I reported to our boss Svetlana on our work, she seemed to deem it satisfactory."[22] Until the war began, father and daughter exchanged affectionate letters. "I give you a big hug, my little sparrow," he wrote to her, as he had once written to his wife.[23]

Stalin's relationship with his sons was much more fraught. For many years he avoided Yakov and his family, and Vasily gave him a great deal of trouble.[24] The boy understood very early that he was the son of a powerful man. He preferred soccer to studying and often behaved defiantly toward those around him. "Vasily thinks he's an adult and insists on getting what he wants, which is often foolish," the commandant of the Zubalovo dacha reported to Stalin in 1935, when Vasily was fourteen. The situation only grew worse with time. Unable to tolerate the outrageous behavior of his imperious student, in 1938 one of Vasily's teachers complained to the boy's father, telling Stalin that Vasily was getting special treatment from the school administration and that he sometimes used threats of suicide to get his way. Stalin thanked the teacher for his honesty and described his son in extremely negative terms: "Vasily is a spoiled youth of average ability, a little savage (a real Scythian!) who is not always truthful, loves to blackmail weak authority figures, is often rude, and has a weak, or rather, unfocused will. He has been spoiled by 'kith and kin,' all the while emphasizing that he is 'the son of Stalin.'" He asked the teacher to be firmer and promised that he would "take him by the scruff of the neck" from time to time. As was often the case, the letter was all for show, and the matter was ultimately resolved in typical Stalin manner. A purge of the school was conducted and the directors were fired, along with the teacher who had dared complain to Stalin. Vasily was sent to study at an aviation school in Crimea, where the special treatment continued. He was met at the train station with great fanfare by the school's leadership, quartered away from the other cadets in a hotel, and fed special meals in the officers' mess. Once, obviously pulling a prank, Vasily ordered some special dish. Since the local cook did not know how to make it, someone was sent to a nearby town to find out. Vasily rode all over Crimea in a car and also on a motorcycle. His education was overseen by senior military officials in Moscow. In 1940 he graduated with the rank of lieutenant. He liked to fly, but his character showed no sign of improvement. The system created by the father did irreversible harm to the son.

Vasily's departure for Crimea came just as the old Stalin-Alliluev-Svanidze extended family ceased to exist. During the Great Terror, Stalin began to annihilate his own relatives. Between late 1937 and late 1939,

Aleksandr Svanidze, his wife, and the husband of Anna Allilueva were arrested and then shot. In late 1938, apparently unable to endure the stress, Pavel Alliluev also died. Stalin had nothing further to do with those relatives who remained at liberty. The war further diminished the family. During its first days, Yakov, who, unlike Vasily, received no special protection, was taken prisoner by the Germans. Stalin ordered the arrest of Yakov's wife but later freed her. Some accounts maintain that Stalin was offered Yakov in exchange for certain German generals (Paulus is most often named) but that he refused. There is no documentary evidence of this claim, and the story lacks credibility since it is hard to understand what would motivate Hitler's leadership to pursue such an exchange. When the war ended, Stalin was given testimony by Yakov's fellow prisoners.[25] After Germany was defeated, Yakov's 1941 interrogation protocol was seized, and testimony was obtained from the guards and commandant of the camp where he died.[26] All this evidence shows that Yakov comported himself honorably as a prisoner. He was shot by a sentry while attempting to leave the prison grounds in 1943. Perhaps this news improved Stalin's opinion of his son, and it may explain why, during his final years, the *vozhd* took an interest in his young granddaughter, Yakov's daughter.

Vasily and Svetlana were disappointments for Stalin during the war. Vasily, who was stationed near Moscow, would host drunken parties at the Zubalovo dacha. At one such gathering, in late 1942, sixteen-year-old Svetlana met the thirty-eight-year-old Soviet filmmaker Aleksei Kapler, who had gained prominence as the screenwriter of popular films about Lenin and the revolution. The two began an affair that ended several months later when Stalin ordered Kapler's arrest. Apparently he was furious over Svetlana's relationship with Kapler, whom she has described as her first love, and considered it all the more inappropriate in wartime. According to Svetlana, his reaction forever destroyed the closeness between them:

> I'd never seen my father look that way before. . . . He was choking with anger and was nearly speechless. . . . "Your Kapler is a British spy. He's under arrest!" . . .
>
> "But I love him!" I protested at last, having found my tongue again.
>
> "Love!" screamed my father, with a hatred of the very word. And for the first time in my life he slapped me across the face, twice. "Just look, nurse, how low she's sunk!" He could no longer restrain himself. "Such a war going on, and she's busy the whole time---------!" Unable to find any other expression, he used the coarse peasant word.[27]

The next blow came from Vasily. By early 1943 he held the rank of colonel and had been placed in charge of an air regiment. That April he and a group of his subordinates decided to do some fishing. The fish were stunned using explosives. One shell exploded on land, killing one of the regiment's officers and wounding Vasily with shrapnel. He, of course, was treated at the Kremlin hospital in Moscow. Stalin was enraged. Apparently this escapade was one transgression too many, or so one might conclude from an order issued by People's Commissar for Defense I. V. Stalin on 26 May 1943:

(1) Immediately remove V. I. Stalin from his position as commander of an air regiment and do not give him any other command posts in the future until I permit it.
(2) Inform the regiment and former regimental commander Colonel Stalin that he is being removed from his post for drunkenness and debauchery and for spoiling and corrupting the regiment.[28]

Being long accustomed to his father's empty threats, Vasily was not terribly worried by this reproach. Indeed, he was soon given new, more senior posts, and by war's end he was a twenty-four-year-old general. Stalin's son could get away with almost anything. Around the same time Svetlana, now a university student, married a former schoolmate. She soon gave birth to a son, named Iosif after his grandfather. Nevertheless, Stalin refused to meet with his son-in-law, who was Jewish and had not fought in the war. Perhaps he consented to the marriage only to avoid the acrimony that came with the Kapler affair.

Once Germany was defeated and wartime pressures receded, Stalin did not return to his family—or rather did not allow his family back into his life. He had grown accustomed to solitude and his nocturnal lifestyle, and he rarely made time for his children. Apparently he never developed grandfatherly feelings. By now he was in his declining years, weary, in poor health, and obsessed with thoughts of treachery and the hunt for enemies. The final blow dealt against his family was the arrest of Pavel Alliluev's wife and Nadezhda's sister Anna. They were released only after his death.

Stalin's children, admittedly, were hardly a comfort in his old age. Vasily sank rapidly into alcoholism and dissipation, and by his thirtieth birthday he was already an old man, plagued with a number of chronic diseases. Thanks to his father's indulgence, he nevertheless held increasingly senior army posts and squandered government funds with impunity.

The younger Stalin greedily chased the good life: he built and repeatedly renovated his suburban estate, spent lavishly on an elaborate hunting lodge, and established sports teams, luring top athletes with huge salaries and apartments. He had goods shipped in from Germany via airplane, ran through a series of lovers and wives, and drank heavily in the company of sycophantic hangers-on. Toward the end of Stalin's life, after yet another scandalous episode, the father removed the son from the key post of air commander for the Moscow Military District. Vasily was sent to study at a military academy, thereby removing any remaining constraints on his drinking. Meanwhile, Svetlana divorced the husband her father did not like and married one he did—Yuri Zhdanov, son of Stalin's late comrade. This marriage, however, was not happy and did not last long.

After his death, Stalin's children suffered deeply symbolic fates. Vasily, after drunkenly insulting his father's successors, was put in prison and died in exile at the age of forty. Svetlana married an Indian Communist. When she was given permission to travel to India for his funeral, she took the opportunity to defect and move to the United States, where she died in 2011. While in emigration, Svetlana published a memoir of life in the Stalin family, *Twenty Letters to a Friend,* which was both nostalgic and embellished. She placed the blame for her father's pathological cruelty on the scheming and insinuations of Lavrenty Beria. In the end, her attitude toward the system her father created was most eloquently expressed by her defection to the country that he considered socialism's most fearsome enemy.

6 THE GENERALISSIMO

Victory elevated Stalin to unprecedented heights. The exultant show of military might that paraded across Red Square in June 1945 was an important symbol of his new power, now more secure than ever and legitimized with the title of generalissimo. But Stalin was a seasoned enough politician to know that victory, which had transformed the Red Army into one of the most formidable forces on the planet, was just the first step on the long and difficult postwar path toward regaining and holding the country's status as a world power. The Soviet Union was a weakened nation. The extent of suffering and devastation that had befallen it is almost unimaginable. Contemporary demographers speak of 27 million lives lost, and many of those lives were young—the country's future. Thousands of towns and villages lay in ruins, and many people were forced to improvise some form of shelter. Several million wounded veterans needed government support. The demobilization of an army of 11 million and the transition to a peacetime economy also demanded significant resources. The postwar famine—a tragic testament to the devastation wreaked on collectivized agriculture and to the weakness of the Stalinist distribution system—peaked in 1946–1947. As many as 1.5 million people died of hunger or disease. Many millions were afflicted by dystrophy and other serious illnesses causing permanent disability. As usual, cannibalism raised its ugly head during the famine years. To all these hardships were added desperate guerrilla wars in western Ukraine and the Baltic states, territories that had been absorbed into the Soviet Union on the eve of the war and given a taste of Stalinist terror.

There was also a whole new set of international challenges. Relations with the Allies had cooled considerably. Stalin's Soviet Union and the Western democracies, brought together in a marriage of convenience by Nazi aggression, had little in common. Negotiations to resolve the postwar repartition of the world opened up new areas of contention, but the Soviet Union was too weak to put up a decisive fight. It was unnerved by the United States' nuclear monopoly and devoted huge resources to ending it.

A particular danger facing the Stalinist regime was the incongruity between the symbolic triumph of victory for Soviet society and the hard realities of daily life. The war had taken millions of Soviet citizens beyond the country's borders to Europe, an experience that many found shocking. The victors saw that the slaves of capitalism enjoyed a standard of living immeasurably better than theirs. They now knew that for years official Soviet propaganda had been pulling the wool over their eyes. Tens of millions of peasants, many of whom had fought in the war, dreamed of dismantling the kolkhoz system and believed that their sacrifices at the front had earned them this reward. A threatening gulf was opening up between the Soviet people's postwar expectations and their reality. As they struggled to overcome extreme daily hardships, mourned the dead, and listened to stories from returning soldiers, people's conversations inevitably drifted toward ideas and topics that were taboo: the price of war and victory, the questionable privileges enjoyed by party and government officials, and the causes of hunger and deprivation. The system's usual response to such "incorrect" thinking was arrest and prosecution for "anti-Soviet propaganda." But would that response work in the new, postwar USSR?

Apparently Stalin was not sure how to address these challenges. In the immediate aftermath of victory, he sent mixed messages to the country, including hints at a coming liberalization. Take, for example, the remarks made at a reception honoring Red Army commanders on 24 May 1945:

> Our government made more than a few mistakes; there were moments of desperation in 1941–1942, when our army was on the retreat, abandoning our native villages and cities. . . . Another people might have told its government: you have not met our expectations; go away; we will put another government in your place that will sign a truce with Germany and ensure us peace. But the Russian people did not choose to do that since they believed in the correctness of their government's policies and chose to make sacrifices in order to secure the destruction of Germany. And this trust the Russian people placed in the Soviet government proved to be the decisive force that secured a historic victory against an enemy of humanity—against fascism. Thanks to the Russian people for this trust![1]

This hint of penitence was an effective gesture by a confident, popular, and triumphant leader. But soon Stalin began to sense that such statements could be perilous. They opened the door to discussion of critical questions about the past war, and echoes of these discussions were starting to reach him. In November 1945, he was told about a letter from a propagandist in the Buriat-Mongol republic who was being asked during lectures just what Stalin meant when he mentioned mistakes by the Soviet government: "I, of course, was not able to answer this question. . . . I earnestly ask you, Com. Stalin, for your explanation as to what should be the answer to this question."[2] More to the point was a letter from N. M. Khmelkov from the village of Maly Uzen in Saratov Oblast that asked, "How could we allow it to happen that when the war broke out the German Army was better armed than our army?" Khmelkov recalled prewar promises that the Red Army would soon be fighting "on the territory from which the enemy comes" and concluded by asking Stalin a central question, the validity of which Stalinists reject to this day: "Victors are not judged. But a victorious people is obliged to figure out whether victory was achieved with the least possible expenditure of effort and resources and with the fewest possible casualties, and if it was not, then why: were we given too little time to prepare for war, were the cogs in a complex machine operating poorly . . . and failing its more complicated parts?"[3] Stalin instructed that Khmelkov's letter be filed away.[4] He had no intention of responding to such questions or "figuring out" what mistakes the government might have made. To forestall undesirable discussion of the price of victory, the performance of the military leadership, and hopes for postwar liberalization, he launched a series of ideological counterattacks.

The first of these was a reappraisal of the toll taken by the war and the reasons for defeat. In an obvious attempt to downplay the nation's losses, in March 1946 Stalin officially stated that "as a result of the German invasion, the Soviet Union irretrievably lost approximately 7 million in fighting with the Germans and because of the German occupation and the driving of Soviet people into German hard labor."[5] This was a strange number to pick, and it was far from accurate, but it is possible to see how Stalin might have arrived at it. According to General Staff estimates, approximately 7 million Red Army soldiers were killed in the war or died of wounds and disease.[6] He must have known that he was distorting the truth when he included the victims of occupation and those taken to work in Nazi labor camps in this figure. Soviet war losses no longer looked quite so terrible, and the matter was put to rest for many years.

While it may have been easy enough to hide the true number of Soviet war dead, the Red Army's catastrophic retreat was another matter. How had the Germans been able to advance all the way to the Volga? At best, discussion of this ignominious episode could be suppressed. The horrible defeats suffered during the war's first eighteen months cast a shameful light on the regime and on Stalin himself, diminishing his stature as the architect of victory. Soviet propaganda had a few stock arguments to explain those early defeats: the might of Hitler's war machine, which enslaved Europe; the fact that the Red Army had not finished rearming; and the Nazis' perfidious surprise attack. Apparently Stalin felt these arguments were not enough. Cautiously and gradually, he tried to introduce another idea into the propaganda arsenal, one that exonerated him as supreme commander: that the Red Army's retreat was a calculated move designed to wear down the enemy. There was a well-known historical precedent that made this argument understandable and familiar: Kutuzov's 1812 strategy of allowing Napoleon's army to enter deep into Russian territory, even relinquishing Moscow, before counterattacking, a strategy that is credited with preserving the army and saving the country.

An opportunity to promote this new way of explaining the retreat came in the form of a letter Stalin received in early 1946 from Ye. A. Razin, a military academy instructor. Razin was writing the *vozhd* with general questions about doctrine, but Stalin responded in a letter by offering specific and far-reaching guidelines for understanding Soviet military history. He underscored two central ideas. First, Lenin was not "an expert in the military sciences" during the Civil War years or at any other time. Thus Stalin was the only Soviet leader who qualified as a true commander in chief. The second idea offered a more favorable interpretation of the early, catastrophic stage of the war. "A retreat, under certain disadvantageous conditions," Stalin wrote, "is just as legitimate a form of combat as an offensive." He noted the need to take a closer look at the counteroffensive "after an enemy's successful offensive, [when] the defender gathers strength, switches to a counteroffensive, and hands the enemy a decisive defeat." Bolstering this idea with historical parallels, Stalin cited the example of the ancient Parthians, who "lured" Roman forces deep inside their country and then "struck with a counteroffensive and annihilated them." He also offered the example of Kutuzov's counteroffensive against the French, calling him a "brilliant" commander.[7]

Of course, Stalin did not draw a direct line between these historical precedents and the events of 1941–1942, but the implication was obvious. The defeats of the war's first stage were transformed into a manageable phase of preparation for a counteroffensive, a "legitimate form of combat," and not a catastrophe caused by egregious blunders at the top or a broken chain of command. Aware of the questionable validity of this recontextualization, Stalin did not widely disseminate his letter at first. It was written in late February 1946 but not published until a year later.

The letter to Razin contained another thought that preoccupied Stalin in the first months after the war: the need to avoid "kowtowing to the West," including showing "unwarranted respect" for the "military authorities of Germany." The first expression of this sentiment is found in a letter written by Stalin during the autumn of 1945 to his comrades in Moscow while he was vacationing in the south. Denouncing unnamed "senior officials" who were "thrown into fits of childlike glee" by praise from foreign leaders, he wrote, "I consider such inclinations to be dangerous since they develop in us kowtowing to foreign figures. A ruthless fight must be waged against obsequiousness toward foreigners."[8]

These loosely formulated ideas were Stalin's response to the "contamination" of Soviet society by the ideological influence of the Western allies and to the danger of an inferiority complex on the part of the impoverished victors. Over time, the "fight against kowtowing" took the form of specific campaigns and institutions. In August 1946 a Central Committee resolution was published on "The Magazines *Zvezda* and *Leningrad*" in support of an irate speech to Leningrad writers delivered by Central Committee secretary Andrei Zhdanov. The targets of his ire were the satirist Mikhail Zoshchenko and the poet Anna Akhmatova. The former's writings, according to Zhdanov, were poisoned by the "venom of a brutish hostility to the Soviet system." Akhmatova was labeled a "whore and a nun, in whom licentiousness is combined with prayer."[9] Discussion of the resolution was made mandatory at party meetings across the country—in regional party organizations, factories, and kolkhozes—and marked the beginning of a severe scolding given to the creative intelligentsia.

A leitmotif of the attack on writers was the unmasking of "kowtowing to the contemporary bourgeois culture of the West"—a formulation that clearly came from Stalin's own pen. Indeed, archival documents show that Stalin was behind Zhdanov's vitriol and that he read and edited his speech.[10] The archives further reveal that Stalin was the driving force behind other actions designed to promote ideological lockstep, such as the well-known case of the married scientists Nina Kliueva and Grigory Roskin, who were developing a cancer drug in Moscow. In 1947 they were groundlessly accused of passing secret information to the Americans. The couple was accused of "kowtowing and servility to anything foreign."[11]

These shrill ideological clichés were variations on the canonical themes of Leninism and Stalinism: the USSR, since it was building the most advanced social system, would always and in all respects surpass the rest of the world; the capitalist powers, sensing their inevitable demise, would be ready at any moment to unleash war against the birthplace of socialism. The recent war and the gradual move toward a new "cold" war served to confirm this thinking.

Many years of research, especially since the archives of the former USSR and other countries of the socialist bloc have opened up, have provided a wealth of information on the origins of the Cold War. Nevertheless, scholars may never reach agreement about its real causes, which side should take the larger share of blame, and the true motives and calculations of the opposing powers. The Cold War was more a gradual evolution than an event with a clear beginning. The world leaders involved in this process were not simply looking out for their countries' fundamental interests, but were also reacting to specific, often unexpected situations with decisions that were often illogical. Stalin was no exception.

The intensifying conflict between the World War II Allies was fed by the utter incompatibility of their systems, their competing desires to expand their spheres of influence, mutual grievances dating to the prewar years, and a shared need for a foreign enemy. Specific issues tended to exacerbate the general suspicion and animosity. America's nuclear monopoly and its reluctance to let the Russians take part in the occupation of Japan were among the many frustrations Stalin felt in dealing with the United States. In a meeting with Averell Harriman at the Soviet leader's southern dacha in October 1945, Stalin angrily wondered out loud whether the United States "needs not an ally but a satellite in Japan? I must say that the Soviet Union is not suited to that role. . . . It would be more honorable for the USSR to leave Japan entirely rather than remain there like a piece of furniture."[12] For his part, Stalin angered Western leaders, already fundamentally opposed to Soviet communism, with his thinly veiled desire to sovietize Eastern Europe using the Red Army and local Communists.

It is hard to imagine what mutual concessions might have prevented a breakdown in relations between two such different systems. Such a breakdown could only be delayed by tactical calculations and political factors, including the illusion on the part of Western public opinion that an enduring alliance was actually feasible (Soviet public opinion had little say in the matter). Relations also remained civil so long as Stalin harbored hope for Western concessions, particularly in the areas of economic aid and reparations from Germany. The devastation and famine afflicting the USSR after the war made the need for assistance particularly pressing. That Eastern Europe—now within the Soviet sphere of influence—not only suffered its own famine and devastation but was also home to significant anti-Communist sentiment also forced him to act with circumspection.

Stalin was restrained in his personal relations with Western leaders. He preferred to let Molotov take hard-line stances during diplomatic negotiations, while he himself would periodically step in and make demonstrative concessions that allowed the Western side to save face or prevented it from breaking off talks. As during the war, Stalin tried to play the Americans and British against one another. In April 1946, after Churchill's "Iron Curtain" speech in Fulton, Missouri, Stalin met with the U.S. ambassador in Moscow. After accepting the gifts of a safety razor and transistor radio, Stalin offered a "friendly" warning: In pursuing their own interests, "Churchill and his friends" might try to push the United States away from the USSR.[13]

Such face-to-face diplomacy was no match for the powerful forces at play. Truman responded to Soviet attempts to gain footholds in Iran, Turkey, and Greece with a plan to help rebuild Europe, the centerpiece of which became known as the Marshall Plan. Stalin responded by turning down the aid offered under the plan (as did other East European states, under Soviet pressure) and by creating an international Communist organization, the Cominform. During the Cominform's first conference, Zhdanov echoed Stalin's idea that the world was being divided into "two camps."[14] Efforts to sustain the wartime alliance gave way to the traditional call to stand up to "international imperialism."

On the domestic side, the return to prewar political thinking and practices occurred even earlier. Stalin's conservative inclinations played no small role. Given the array of complex problems facing him, as he approached his seventieth birthday, he neither took an interest in reforms or experiments nor saw any reason to change his country's long-range goals for economic development. He offered a number of production targets in a speech to an election meeting on 9 February 1946: 500 million tons of coal, 60 million tons of steel, 50 million tons of cast iron, 60 million tons of petroleum. Considering the actual figures for 1946—only 13.3 million tons of steel and 9.9 million tons of cast iron were produced, along with 163.8 million tons of coal and 21.7 million tons of petroleum—such targets were obviously wildly ambitious. Furthermore, as the economic historian Eugene Zaleski has noted, a program like Stalin's, purely focused on output targets, reflected a simplistic understanding of economic development.[15]

Stalin showed his preference for tried and true methods during the famine of 1946–1947, when, as in 1932, draconian laws were enacted against the pilfering of state property. Two 4 June 1947 decrees provided for sentences ranging from five to twenty-five years in a camp for theft. Between 1947 and 1952, more than 2 million people were convicted of this charge. Many if not most were simply ordinary people who committed minor crimes in the face of great material deprivation. Parents who stole a loaf of bread for their hungry children were sentenced to many years in a camp. Mass repression was not limited to the prosecution of theft. Arrests for political crimes continued, and harsh laws were also put in place to combat violations of workplace discipline. Approximately 7 million such sentences, an average of 1 million per year, were handed down between 1946 and 1952.[16] In Stalin's last years, the Gulag grew into a sprawling network that played a central role in the life of the country. On 1 January 1953, more than 2.5 million people were being held in camps, penal colonies, and prisons. "Special settlements" in remote regions held another 2.8 million.[17] Some 3 percent of the population was either incarcerated or under internal exile.[18]

Mass repression, in the form of large-scale arrests, executions, and internal exile, was now largely focused on the newly absorbed parts of the Soviet Union, where fierce guerrilla campaigns raged. Stalin received regular reports on the pacification of mutinous areas.[19] For the years 1944–1952, according to incomplete official statistics, approximately a half million people were killed, arrested, or forcibly exiled from Lithuania, Latvia, and Estonia, along with an equal number in the western provinces of Ukraine.[20] For these small republics and provinces, whose populations totaled just a few million, these were astounding numbers. The Stalinist system had neither changed nor grown less repressive.

■   KEEPING THE LEADERS IN THEIR PLACE

An important aspect of Stalin's postwar consolidation of power was a return to routine shake-ups at the upper echelons of government and the preemptive humiliation of his devoted and obedient comrades. The stable leadership that had governed the country during the war was probably perceived by Stalin as a compromise necessitated by circumstances. Now that they had performed their tasks, he no longer needed influential marshals and members of the State Defense Committee. And as his physical state declined, his tendency toward suspicion grew.

On 9 October 1945 the Politburo adopted a resolution granting Stalin a vacation so that he could "rest for a month and a half."[21] This was his first trip to the south in nine years, and he may have left reluctantly. The foreign press was full of speculation. On 11 October he received a set of TASS news synopses regarding talk in the West about his poor health and the jockeying for position among potential successors. According to the summary, the *Chicago Tribune's* London correspondent, citing diplomatic sources, wrote about a bitter behind-the-scenes power struggle between Zhukov and Molotov, both vying to replace Stalin. Zhukov was supposedly supported by the army and Molotov by the party apparat.[22] A week later, the TASS synopsis included a statement by the Soviet ambassador in France: "Over the past ten months we have been asked fifteen times to confirm reports of Stalin's death." An article about Molotov in a Norwegian newspaper stated that "For public opinion in the U.S.A., England, and other freedom-loving peoples, Molotov represents a new, strong Soviet Union that demands the status of an equal among the world's great powers."[23] Stalin was not mentioned. The article spoke only of his successors.

These foreign press reports reflected the Western view of the postwar configuration of power. The long and horrific war was receding into history, as were the leaders who had achieved victory. Roosevelt was dead. The defeat of the Conservative Party in Great Britain had sent Churchill into retirement. Stalin was aging and rumored to be ill. For the Western observer, these were all elements of the same coherent picture. Stalin, of course, did not share this view. Any hint that the Soviet leader might be replaced only heightened his indignation and suspicion, the brunt of which was borne by his closest comrades—primarily Molotov, as he was first on the list of possible successors. Attacks against Molotov were also a convenient pretext for another shake-up. The ruling Five throughout the war had consisted of Stalin, Molotov, Beria, Malenkov, and Mikoyan. This grouping had been in place uncomfortably long.

Stalin's growing irritation with Molotov was on full display during the September 1945 meeting of the Council of Foreign Ministers in London, convened to discuss the new postwar order and peace terms with the vanquished countries.[24] At the outset, Molotov took a liberty in regard to a procedural question. Yielding to a request by the Western Allies, he agreed that in addition to the Soviet Union, United States, and Great Britain, France and China would also be allowed to take part in the drafting of treaties. Under previous agreements, France and China were to be involved in designing terms only with Italy and Japan respectively. Molotov did not see a problem with this change, and strictly speaking there was none. France and China would only offer input on the treaties; they were not given any vote on their approval. Agreeing to this arrangement made perfect sense. Hoping for a productive meeting, Molotov did not want to waste time by provoking conflict over secondary questions.

His concession would likely have gone unremarked had the negotiations not reached a seemingly insuperable stalemate. Stalin demanded that the Soviet Union be given a real role in deciding the fate of Japan. The Western side would not even place that question on the agenda. Stalin demanded that one of Italy's colonies in North Africa be placed under Soviet trustee-ship, thus giving his country a solid foothold on the Mediterranean. The Western side refused. The sides also reached an impasse over Romania and Bulgaria. Considering these countries "satellites" (Stalin actually used the cognate in a telegram he sent to Molotov during the meeting), the Soviet authorities had already installed pro-Communist governments there.[25] The United States and Great Britain refused to recognize these governments or sign any accords with them. Stalin decided to increase pressure on his partners, even when it looked as if talks might break down. The question about France and China, whose participation was supported by the United States and Great Britain, offered a convenient pretext. On 21 September Stalin reprimanded Molotov for his procedural concession, and Molotov repented: "I admit that I committed a grave oversight. I will take immediate measures."[26] The following day he withdrew his agreement. The Western Allies were enraged. On the surface it looked as if this simple procedural question had brought the talks to a standstill.

This incident vividly illustrates Stalin's manipulative personality. While cultivating the image of a moderate and predictable politician in the eyes of his fellow Allies, he forced his comrades to do his dirty work. He was in-censed when Molotov revealed that the withdrawal of consent for France's and China's participation came on his orders. For a long time afterward he reminded Molotov of this and similar instances, accusing him of trying to present himself as a reasonable alternative to the inflexibility of "the Soviet government and Stalin."[27]

These potshots at Molotov were a sign that a more serious attack was on the way. An essential role was played in this drama by the TASS summa-ries of the foreign press, which Stalin pored over during his vacation. Molo-tov's troubles began with a 1 December 1945 news item by a correspondent for Britain's *Daily Herald*, reporting rumors that Stalin might be stepping down as chairman of the Council of People's Commissars and that Molo-tov might resume that post. The TASS summary quoted the correspondent as saying that the political leadership of the Soviet Union was currently in

Molotov's hands, with general directives from the Politburo.[28] For Molotov, nothing could have been more damaging, especially when Stalin was out of Moscow for the first time in years. Furious, on 2 December Stalin telephoned Molotov to demand that more stringent censorship be exercised over the dispatches sent out by foreign correspondents. Molotov gave the foreign affairs commissariat's press office the appropriate orders.[29] The next day, however, there was a bureaucratic snafu. The TASS summary for 3 December included a *New York Times* piece that had been published on 1 December, before Stalin's order to tighten control. The *Times* item, like the *Daily Herald* article, hinted at discord among the Soviet leadership and a weakening of Stalin's position.[30] Stalin read the TASS account of the *Times* article on 5 December. Apparently that same day he read a 3 December Reuters report that mentioned a relaxing of censorship in regard to foreign correspondents in the USSR. The press agency claimed that after Western journalists collectively had complained to the Soviet authorities, Molotov had said to an American at a 7 November reception, "I know that you correspondents want to get rid of Russian censorship. What would you say if I agreed to this on condition of reciprocity?" A few days later, according to Reuters, the Western press corps actually did see signs of relaxed control.[31]

These reports gave Stalin more than enough ammunition to charge Molotov with scheming against him. On 5 December the *vozhd* sent Molotov, Beria, Mikoyan, and Malenkov a telegram demanding that the matter be investigated.[32] The following day the four sent Stalin a detailed response. The *New York Times* article had a simple explanation. It had gone through censorship on 30 November, three days before Stalin asked Molotov to tighten control. The explanation for the Reuters report was just as persuasive. Molotov really had ordered a relaxation of censorship in November since the censors "often unnecessarily marked out individual words and expressions in the telegrams sent by foreign correspondents." As for the conversation at the 7 November reception, Molotov claimed that "words were attributed to him that he did not say."[33]

After receiving this response, Stalin went into a rage, either genuine or feigned. That same day, 6 December, he sent a sharply worded telegram to Moscow. Ignoring all the reasonable arguments offered by the four, he stated that Molotov bore the blame for the appearance of "libels against the Soviet government" in the foreign press. Furthermore, Molotov's liberal attitude toward foreign correspondents represented an intentional effort to change "the course of our policies." After accusing Malenkov, Beria, and Mikoyan of connivance, Stalin directed extremely harsh words at Molotov.

"I am convinced that Molotov does not care about the interests of our state and the prestige of our government," he wrote, "so long as he gains popularity within certain foreign circles. I can no longer consider such a comrade to be my first deputy." To add insult to injury, Stalin sent his telegram only to Malenkov, Beria, and Mikoyan, asking them to summon Molotov and read him its contents but not give him a copy. The reason he gave was extremely insulting to Molotov: "I did not send [the telegram] to Molotov since I have doubts about some of those close to him."[34]

This telegram contained the strongest accusations Stalin had ever made against a member of his inner circle (unless, of course, we include the Politburo members whom he had executed). The four men were undoubtedly frightened. On 7 December Beria, Malenkov, and Mikoyan sent Stalin a coded telegram in which they reported on the firm approach they had taken in dealing with their associate. "We summoned Molotov to us and read him the telegram in full. After pausing to think, Molotov said that he had made a lot of mistakes but felt that mistrust toward him was unjust, and then he began to cry."[35] There is no way to know whether they were describing this confrontation accurately. This was a drama played out for one spectator who was not even in the theater. What mattered was not the drama itself but the account of how the confrontation was handled, which had to be designed to satisfy Stalin. Molotov played along. That same day he sent Stalin his own telegram: "Your coded telegram was filled with deep mistrust toward me as a Bolshevik and a man, which I take as the most serious party warning for all my work going forward, wherever that might be. I will try through my deeds to earn your trust, in which every honest Bolshevik sees not simply personal trust, but the trust of the party, which is dearer to me than my life."[36] Judging by the correspondence that followed, Stalin felt that he had achieved the desired effect. He clearly knew that Molotov's "crimes" had no significance, and his underling had never disobeyed any direct instruction. Molotov had simply used his own discretion on occasions when Stalin's long-distance guidance was intermittent and vague.

The Molotov scandal was dropped quickly because its true purpose lay elsewhere: Stalin wanted to make changes to the top leadership. He began this reorganization as soon as he returned to Moscow. On 29 December 1945 he brought his old comrade Andrei Zhdanov into the inner circle. The Five were now Six. In October 1946, Nikolai Voznesensky was also admitted to the group, meaning that the country was now governed by the Seven.[37]

The return of the "Leningraders"—Zhdanov and Voznesensky—into Stalin's inner circle provoked competition within the Politburo. Malenkov and

Beria, who had pushed the Leningraders aside during the war, were now forced to concede power to them. In May 1946 Stalin removed Malenkov from the post of Central Committee secretary, accusing him of covering up irregularities in the aviation industry, which had been his portfolio during the war. Malenkov's responsibilities overseeing the Central Committee apparat were handed over to Zhdanov. Around the same time, a blow was struck against Beria. Stalin forced Beria's protégé, Minister for State Security Vsevolod Merkulov, to resign his post in disgrace.[38] A dangerous development was that Stalin appointed the former head of military counterintelligence, Viktor Abakumov, with whom Beria did not get along, to take Merkulov's place.[39] According to the rules of Stalinist shake-ups, the new minister was expected to uncover misconduct or—better yet—crimes by his predecessor. Abakumov was well suited to this role. Both Merkulov and Beria were clearly in danger. As Merkulov attested after Stalin's death, "The story of my departure from the Ministry of State Security gave Beria a number of unpleasant moments. Beria himself told me that because of me he was in trouble with Comrade Stalin."[40]

Beria's and Malenkov's ordeals were relatively painless. Both remained within the top leadership. Presumably they were just being shown who was boss and reminded that they were dispensable. Stalin clearly had no intention of dismantling the system of supreme power that had taken shape. He just wanted to create new counterpoises, new centers of competition.

Stalin was just as calculating in dealing with the military leadership. By the war's end, the status of the Soviet Union's marshals and generals was understandably sky-high. For Stalin, who cherished his own reputation as a commander, their popularity was politically undesirable: the victory could be the work of only one genius. Stalin was also concerned about possible conspiracies. The generals, intoxicated by thoughts of their own brilliance, made matters worse. State security, which was always in competition with the military, reported to Stalin on conversations at celebratory dinners where generals lavished one another with praise and made disparaging comments about their *vozhd*. Stalin's natural response was repression. Inevitably his first target was Zhukov, the most famous and influential of the wartime military leaders. Zhukov's life now hung by a thread. Stalin ordered the arrest of a number of generals close to Zhukov and had a case opened against Zhukov himself. A month later, after Malenkov's demotion and Merkulov's firing, Zhukov and other military leaders received a dressing down. A 9 June 1946 order, issued by the minister for the armed forces of the USSR and signed by Stalin, described the wartime commander's transgressions as follows: "Marshal Zhukov, having lost all modesty and carried away by a sense of personal ambition, felt that his services had not been sufficiently valued and took credit in conversations with subordinates for designing and carrying out all of the Great Patriotic War's major operations, including those operations with which he had nothing to do."[41] This condemnation was obviously motivated by Stalin's jealousy and anger at a lack of proper deference from this national hero and other military leaders and his desire to cut them down to size. But he was not prepared to go so far as to physically annihilate Zhukov, who was too symbolic a figure and too closely associated with him. Public discrediting and demotion would suffice. The order relegated Zhukov to a secondary post commanding a military district. Given the fate of some of Stalin's other close associates over the years, such a command might even be considered a reward. Zhukov had lost a great deal but not everything. Toward the end of his life, Stalin agreed to readmit Zhukov to the Central Committee, a sign that he was finally back in the *vozhd*'s good graces.

By late 1946 these reshufflings had evened out the balance of power among Stalin's associates. The firings, demotions, and public humiliations more or less restored the structure of top government that had existed before the war. Stalin could now leave his associates in relative peace as he dealt with the country's pressing economic problems.

■   CURRENCY REFORM AS A REFLECTION OF THE SYSTEM

Militarization, physical devastation, famine, an inefficient ration system, crippled agriculture, a degraded social infrastructure, and a reliance on compulsion in mobilizing the labor force—such were the features of the postwar Soviet economy. War's toll was, of course, reflected in the sorry state of the budget. The government had financed the war's huge costs primarily by printing money. The predictable result was spiraling inflation. Something had to be done about the excess currency circulating through the economy. To reduce the amount of money in circulation, the Soviet leadership ordered new rubles printed and old rubles devalued.

In his memoirs, the wartime finance commissar, Arseny Zverev, states that by late 1943 he had already discussed such measures with Stalin.[42] Evidence that the finance commissariat was planning for currency reform so early can also be found in the archives. Toward the end of 1943 it was decided that the reform would be introduced after the war by reducing the buying power of the ruble through increased prices, exchanging old rubles for new ones, and abolishing the ration system.[43] This is largely the program that went into effect a few years later.

Now that the war was over, the problem of stabilizing the country's finances and doing away with rationing took on tremendous political importance. Doing away with ration cards even more quickly than in capitalist countries would demonstrate the advantages of socialism. The reform measures were planned for 1946, but the famine forced a delay. Throughout that year, Finance Commissar Zverev sent Stalin several memoranda on the upcoming reforms. Judging by Stalin's notations on these documents, he took a great interest in the topic.[44] As preparations reached their final phase, Zverev had frequent face-to-face meetings with the *vozhd*. According to the log of visitors to Stalin's office, during the period leading up to the reform's introduction on 14 December 1947, Zverev was there thirteen times.[45]

Finally, on 13 December 1947, the Politburo voted to approve the main documents instituting the currency reform and abolishing ration cards. It was stipulated that the measures would be announced over the radio at six o'clock in the evening on 14 December and in newspapers the following day. Overnight, between 14 and 15 December, the population was deprived of a significant portion of its savings. For every ten rubles people had in their possession, they would now receive one. There was a more complex system to deal with bank deposits. Accounts with under three thousand rubles were not affected, but those with three to ten thousand rubles would be compensated at a rate of two new rubles for every three old ones. Deposits over ten thousand rubles were compensated at a rate of one to two.

The Politburo was fully aware that the reform would not be popular. A large part of its resolution, which was intended for publication, was devoted to a detailed explanation of the move's necessity, utility, and fairness. Keenly in tune with widespread prejudices, the text asserted that the reform would hit hardest at "speculative elements who have amassed large stores of money." This assertion was false: the most well-off Soviet citizens were in the best position to convert their cash into other forms of wealth. Nevertheless, the idea that the currency reform was a means of confiscating ill-gotten gains proved extremely popular. As usual, the resolution did not neglect to mention the financial hardships faced by the toiling masses in capitalist countries. Its wording suggests that Stalin played an active role in drafting it. Among the revisions made in his handwriting is the added promise that this would be the Soviet people's "final sacrifice."[46]

Major reforms are always fraught with difficulty. The new rubles began to be printed in 1946 for introduction at the end of 1947, but at first a high percentage proved defective. To maintain secrecy, the new money was not delivered to Gosbank branches, of which there were many, but to specially set up storage facilities evenly distributed around the country. The new rubles were transported in special, heavily guarded train cars. Finally, when it came time to exchange rubles, in addition to regular Gosbank branches, 46,000 exchange points were set up, for which 170,000 workers were hired.[47]

No amount of secrecy, of course, could hide such a major operation from public view. Rumors began to spread and became more persistent after salaries and pensions for the second half of November were paid ahead of schedule. Overall, however, the public did not know what the reform would look like. Spurred by contradictory rumors, people scrambled to save their nest eggs. At first the panic affected purchases of durable goods and valuables. On 29 November 1947, Internal Affairs Minister Sergei Kruglov reported to Stalin that customers were flooding stores to buy manufactured goods and crowding into banks to withdraw their savings. Store shelves were emptied, and even items for which there had previously been no demand disappeared. Stores sold out of furniture suites going for tens of thousands of rubles—huge sums, given that the average annual salary for laborers or office workers was approximately 7,000 rubles. One suite costing 101,000 rubles that had languished on the showroom floor for years now had four competing buyers. Customers bought furs, fabrics, watches, jewelry, pianos, and rugs.[48] On 30 November Kruglov reported that hundreds of people had lined up outside Moscow's department stores before opening. People from neighboring oblasts flooded into the city. Huge lines of up to five hundred people formed outside savings banks. After two days of this buying frenzy, the authorities decided to take action. Kruglov informed Stalin that most stores had been closed under the pretext of renovation or taking inventory. The stores that remained open removed valuable items such as gold jewelry from sale. And some were forced to shut their doors because they had nothing left to sell.[49]

Kruglov's report of 2 December was not much different. Now that consumer goods were in short supply, people had started to buy up whatever they could find, including musical instruments and phonographs. One store that had been selling six pianos a year sold all eleven it had in stock over two days—30 November and 1 December. The shortage of manufactured goods led to a run on non-perishable food items such as smoked sausage, canned goods, candies, tea, and sugar. This hoarding prompted an order to remove these items from sale. Restaurants did a brisk business, and "drunken individuals would take wads of cash out of their pockets and cry: 'Look at all this paper.'" Other regions reported similar spending sprees.[50] If Stalin read such reports—and there is every reason to believe he did—he was given an eye-opening lesson on the lives and economic logic of ordinary Soviet citizens.

It is interesting that the authorities refrained from heavy-handed measures to halt the frenzy. Beginning in early December there was a noticeable increase in small savings bank deposits, an obvious effort to spread savings over multiple small accounts that would counteract the reform's intention of removing rubles from circulation.[51] Even then, no steps were taken. Stalin could see how unpopular the reform was and did not want to further inflame sentiment against it.

By 15 December it was all over, and the straightforward operation of exchanging old rubles for new and revaluing deposits began. During the eight-day period from 16 to 23 December 1947, Stalin received visitors in his office five times. Each time, Zverev was among them. His visits on 16 and 17 December—the reform's first days—both lasted two hours. Each time, a significant fraction of the Politburo was also present.[52] On 3 January 1948 Zverev sent Stalin a report on the reform's results. It was filled with statistics that must have been encouraging to the government but disheartening to the rest of the population. Before the reform, on 1 December 1947, there were 59 billion rubles in circulation. As a result of the spending spree and ruble exchange, there were now only 4 billion. Deposits in savings accounts had been reduced from 18.6 billion old rubles to 15 billion new ones.[53] The percentage by which prices decreased following the abolition of ration cards was modest in comparison with the number of rubles that had been taken out of people's pockets. The price of bread went down by 20 percent and meat by only 12 percent. Some prices even increased. Woolen fabrics, for example, went up by 27 percent, while clothing in general rose by 11 percent. Overall, the index of state retail prices after the reform went down to 83 percent of what it had been beforehand.[54] Having exchanged ten old rubles for one new one, a consumer's purchasing power was now reduced by a factor of eight. The lion's share of the population's savings had been confiscated.

To some extent the "shop window effect" that followed—the presence of more goods in stores, even if few could afford them—should have softened the blow. But in Stalin's USSR, the shop windows were still not very impressive. Poor output in both the agricultural and consumer goods sectors and the general sluggishness of the state-run economy meant that even relatively weak post-reform demand could not be satisfied. As usual, special measures were taken only in major urban centers, Moscow and Leningrad first and foremost. Generous supplies of food and manufactured goods had been warehoused there in advance. But even in these cities, there were limits placed on purchases: bread—two kilograms per customer; meat and meat products—one kilogram; sausage—half a kilogram; milk—one liter; footwear—one pair; socks—two pairs; soap—one bar; matches—two boxes, etc.[55] In the capitals and in some other major cities, the end of rationing led to supply problems. A few weeks later, Moscow began to receive complaints about empty store shelves, limits on purchases despite the supposed end of rationing, and special shops set up for officials only. One letter from Belgorod read: "Today is the sixth day in a row that my wife stood in line for bread from 2 in the morning to 10, but, alas, all six days she came home without bread." Facing long lines, high prices, and empty stores, people looked back on the days of ration cards with nostalgia.[56]

Not all population segments suffered equally. People in major cities, especially those receiving high salaries or otherwise affluent, were not greatly affected by the reform. Before the devaluation it had been relatively simple for them to convert their old rubles into goods. After the reform they took advantage of the relative availability of goods and the drop in prices in urban *rynoks* (food markets where peasants could charge a market price for the goods produced on their private plots). But the price drop hit the peasants hard. Deprived of their savings, uncompensated for their labor on kolkhozes, and forced to carry a heavy tax burden, they were desperate for cash. The reduction in state prices, however modest, pushed down food prices in the *rynoks*, further depressing their income. Once again, the country's rural majority was the main victim of Stalin's policies.

Although the government promoted the reform as a tool in combating the illegitimate acquisition of wealth, in fact it had the opposite effect. Corrupt officials and those operating in the shadow economy managed to convert their cash into luxury goods, which they resold at a profit after the devaluation. In Moscow's Tushino District, for example, two store directors (both members of the Communist Party) embarked on a large-scale money-making scheme. Using their own money, they bought up suits, fabrics, hundreds of pairs of shoes, and other items. These goods were stashed away until after the reform, when they were gradually sold at *rynoks* through a network of sellers, as well as through the directors' stores. The following figures give an idea of how typical such operations were: during the last two weeks of December 1947, approximately 3,000 people working in the retail sector were arrested, of whom 1,100 were store directors and approximately 900 were party members. Such arrests continued at the same rate through January and February.[57] And this was only the tip of the iceberg.

Another common practice spurred by the devaluation was the backdating of savings account deposits made after the terms of the reform were announced. Many large accounts were broken into smaller ones under the three-thousand-ruble limit. The true scale of such malfeasance is unknown, but records show that this subterfuge was practiced in all regions of the country by a significant proportion of officials. According to incomplete data for March 1948, in just twenty-six oblasts, *krais,* and republics, more than two thousand officials, including senior party and law enforcement officials, were prosecuted for violating the currency reform law.[58] Party secretaries and the heads of state security and internal affairs branches were found guilty of such operations. Cases were also uncovered where top regional officials tried to subvert justice. Central Committee records show multiple cases where "certain regional party bodies have dragged out investigations of cases associated with violating the currency law, and in some cases they have even taken under their protection 'major' party and government officials, shifting the full burden of guilt on secondary individuals."[59] Another case file stated that "a significant proportion of senior party and government officials have essentially escaped punishment."[60]

Researchers have yet to find evidence of Stalin's reaction to this malfeasance. The absence of major shake-ups in the wake of the monetary reforms suggests that he maintained a fairly condescending attitude toward this blatant corruption. This stance was nothing new. Stalin consistently demonstrated tolerance for the moral failings of his faithful underlings. He cared about political loyalty and administrative competence.

While the currency reform cast a spotlight on many of the Stalinist system's flaws, it also had a positive impact on the country's economic development. Ambitious reconstruction plans for 1948 were surpassed. Having taken so much money out of people's pockets, the government could print more without risking inflation, a move that was a great help in making up budgetary shortfalls. The relative financial stability achieved in early 1949 enabled wholesale pricing reform in heavy industry, which in turn created the preconditions for industrial development. Economic indicators for 1948 suggested that the most damaging consequences of the war had been overcome and that the main objectives of postwar recovery had been met. The end of the devastating famine of 1946–1947 was especially important. In

1948 the gross grain yield came close to prewar levels, and the production of potatoes (a staple of the Soviet diet) broke all prewar records. In the words of Donald Filtzer, the Soviet Union had entered a period of "attenuated recovery." Nevertheless, Stalin-style industrialization was able to meet only the most basic needs of the population.[61]

■   ### CONSOLIDATING THE SOVIET SPACE

While this economic recovery was under way in the USSR, neighboring countries were still roiled by political instability. In early 1948 the liberal democratic government of Czechoslovakia was overthrown in a coup, making Czechoslovakia the last East European country to join the Communist bloc. Establishing Communist control of these countries was, however, just the first step. They had to adopt the Stalinist model of internal development, pledge to be loyal satellites of the USSR, and unquestioningly submit to Stalin as the supreme leader of the bloc. A number of obstacles stood in the way. Despite repression, the presence of the Red Army, the suppression of educated segments of society, and the expansion of state control of the economy, for some time the newly Communist countries retained a degree of socioeconomic, cultural, and political diversity. Furthermore, the majority of East Europeans opposed the Communists, and power struggles within the Communist parties prevented the emergence of the kinds of dictatorial leaders needed to implement Stalinist socialism. Worse, a number of East European leaders showed signs of unacceptable "liberalism," preferring a more flexible model of socialism over the Soviet model.[62]

One "bad example" for any wavering Communists was Yugoslavia's Josip Broz Tito. In the spring of 1948 he became embroiled in a conflict with the Soviet Union that quickly escalated. Stalin was confronted with a worthy adversary. Tito was a born dictator who, unlike some other Communist leaders, had not simply been placed in power by Moscow but had earned it fighting the Nazis. His hand was further strengthened by the absence of Soviet troops in Yugoslavia. Tito pretended to political independence and aspired to be a leader of the Communist bloc, and he translated these pretensions into actions. In short, he ignored one of the key principles of Stalinization: total submission to Moscow.

Stalin's hope that severe public accusations would drive a wedge through the Yugoslav leadership and spark mutiny against Tito was disappointed. Tito made quick work of the Kremlin's Yugoslav clients and emerged from the showdown stronger. This defeat was a painful blow for Stalin. For the first time since the struggle with Trotsky, he was being opposed by a major leader within the Communist movement. And unlike Trotsky, Tito had real power and forces capable of protecting him from the ice picks of Stalin's professional killers. Tito's insubordination was not simply a blow to Stalin's self-respect, but also a dangerous precedent and a crack in the monolithic Soviet bloc. Others might follow Tito's lead.

The dangers of Titoism intensified confrontations with the West. The first serious standoff in Germany between the USSR and its former allies also came in 1948. The Soviet blockade of the Western sectors of Berlin was met with determined resistance. The system used to supply the Western zone by air—the Berlin Airlift—not only demonstrated the effectiveness of the Western bloc, but also promoted its consolidation. In April 1949 the agreement that established NATO was signed. The following month Stalin was forced to lift the blockade, and that autumn, Germany was formally divided into two separate states.

These foreign policy setbacks ignited Stalin's suspicions and insecurity and strengthened his resolve to force Stalinization in the East European Communist bloc. Moscow intensified its interference in the internal affairs of its satellites, and demands for accelerated sovietization became more implacable and impatient. Using his familiar methods of purges and fabricated political charges, Stalin initiated and oversaw a campaign against "enemies" within the leaderships of the socialist countries. In late 1948 he succeeded in getting rid of Poland's unyielding leader, Wladyslaw Gomulka. In Hungary, advisers from Moscow helped orchestrate a case alleging a far-reaching espionage organization, supposedly led by the country's former minister for internal affairs, Laszlo Rajk. In September 1949 Rajk was convicted and given the death sentence. In December, after a lengthy process of fabricated charges (again with the help of Soviet security advisers), the former secretary of the Bulgarian central committee, Traicho Kostov, was put to death. Stalin kept a close watch over all these cases and sanctioned both the falsification of evidence and the death sentences. Rajk's and Kostov's trials prompted arrests in other Communist countries.[63] These tactics brought about a concentration of power in the hands of dictators entirely dependent on Stalin and ready to implement any policy he liked.

While overseeing the Stalinization of the Communist bloc, the Soviet dictator still found time to consolidate his power at home—or rather to preempt any possibility that it could be undermined. Setting an example for his satellites, Stalin launched yet another wave of domestic purges. The themes and victims depended to some extent on random developments. One such development was the death of Stalin's close comrade Andrei Zhdanov in August 1948. Zhdanov's duties as Stalin's deputy for party affairs and as head of the Central Committee apparat were taken over by Georgy Malenkov, a shift that upset the balance of power within Stalin's inner circle. Having lost their patron, the Leningrad group, most prominently represented by Gosplan chairman Voznesensky and Central Committee secretary Kuznetsov, found itself weakened, and the group's rivals, Beria and Malenkov, were now stronger. Such shifts prompted a new bout of behind-the-scenes struggle. The combination of these intrigues, international tensions, and Stalin's political calculations spawned the Leningrad Affair, the last purge to roil the upper echelons of power in the USSR. Before it was over blood had been spilled.[64]

Through the efforts of Malenkov and Beria, who probably did not expect their actions to be as damaging as they proved to be, Stalin received compromising materials against the Leningraders. The infractions these materials exposed were relatively minor. In one instance a decision was made to hold a major trade fair in Leningrad without consulting all of the proper authorities. In another, Voznesensky's agency, Gosplan, made certain errors in putting together plans and misplaced some documents—common occurrences in the highly bureaucratic Soviet system. There were also several instances when regional leaders, mostly Leningraders, attempted to use Voznesensky and Kuznetsov for patronage, but such attempts too were nothing out of the ordinary. They were all the sort of typical rule-bending that Stalin could simply ignore or use as ammunition. He chose to do the latter.

During a Politburo meeting presided over by Stalin in February 1949, Kuznetsov, Voznesensky, and other functionaries close to them were charged with attempting to turn the Leningrad party organization into their own fiefdom. Particularly ominous was a resolution comparing their actions to those of Zinoviev in the 1920s, "when he attempted to turn the Leningrad organization into a power base for his anti-Leninist faction."[65] In the months that followed, charges against the beleaguered Leningraders snowballed. They were accused of enemy activity and even espionage. In September 1950, after months of interrogations and torture, Voznesensky, Kuznetsov, and a number of other leaders were sentenced to death in a closed Leningrad courtroom. Several hundred others were given death sentences, imprisoned, or exiled. The purge also affected other regions of the country, where natives of Leningrad held senior posts or had sought support from highly placed Leningraders in Moscow.

The way the Leningrad Affair unfolded suggests that Stalin was using it to pursue multiple goals. It may have been part of his ongoing pattern of intimidation to consolidate power. The accusations of patronage and the large-scale dismantling of networks of officials who made their careers in Leningrad were typical of the preemptive strikes Stalin liked to launch against informal networks within the nomenklatura.[66] He may also have viewed the Leningrad Affair as part of a larger shake-up at the upper echelons. In any event, the fabrication of evidence against the Leningraders at first unfolded in synchrony with Stalin's attacks against his old comrades Molotov and Mikoyan. These assaults seem all the more likely to be connected as Molotov had maintained close professional ties with Voznesensky and was on friendly terms with him. Furthermore, while the Leningrad Affair was in full swing, Mikoyan's son was preparing to marry Kuznetsov's daughter and, rather surprisingly, proceeded with this plan.

Whatever the reasons for Stalin's displeasure, Molotov and Mikoyan were its most natural targets. They were his oldest and most distinguished comrades, symbols of the collective leadership that might have been, and the presumptive heirs of the aging *vozhd*. The task of bolstering his personal power—Stalin's prime obsession—required him, he felt, to periodically discredit his most influential associates in order to weaken their influence.

For several years the actions Stalin took against Molotov in late 1945 were known only within the narrow circle of the Politburo. Molotov continued to perform key governmental functions: he chaired a number of Council of Ministers commissions, headed the Ministry of Foreign Affairs, and had a voice on a wide array of questions. This status began to change in 1948. On various pretexts, Stalin used reprimands and limitations on his authority to diminish Molotov's standing. The main means of pressure was the fabrication of evidence against Molotov's ethnically Jewish wife, Polina Zhemchuzhina, showing her to be involved with "anti-Soviet" Jewish organizations. Stalin demanded that Molotov divorce her. "Stalin," Molotov later recalled, "came up to me at the Central Committee: 'You have to divorce your wife!' And she said to me, 'If it's necessary for the party, then we'll get divorced.' In late 1948 we divorced."[67]

On 29 December 1948, "evidence" compiled by state security in the Zhemchuzhina case was brought before the Politburo. She was expelled from the party, a move that meant that arrest was imminent. Molotov abstained from voting, an action that put him in direct conflict with Stalin.[68] On 20 January 1949 Molotov sent the *vozhd* a formulaic expression of remorse:

> During Central Committee voting on a proposal to expel P. S. Zhemchuzhina from the party I abstained, which I admit to be politically mistaken. I hereby state that having thought over this question, I vote in favor of the Central Committee decision, which corresponds to the interests of the party and the state and teaches a correct understanding of the meaning of Communist Party membership. Furthermore, I admit my grievous guilt in that I did not duly restrain Zhemchuzhina, someone close to me, from false steps and ties with anti-Soviet Jewish nationalists, such as Mikhoels.[69]

In March 1949, Molotov was dismissed from the post of foreign minister, and Mikoyan was relieved of his duties as minister for foreign trade. These dismissals did not mean that the two men were cast out of the government. Both remained members of the Politburo and deputy chairmen of the government, and in these capacities they fulfilled important administrative functions. But their political authority was damaged, an outcome that undoubtedly was Stalin's true objective.

The use of Zhemchuzhina's origins in formulating the charges against her reflected a policy of state anti-Semitism that Stalin launched as confrontation with the West intensified. In early 1948 he ordered state security to destroy the prominent Jewish intellectual and theatrical director Solomon Mikhoels. Later that year he ordered the dissolution of the Soviet Jewish Anti-Fascist Committee, which had been founded during the war to mobilize international support for the USSR. The authorities had begun to view the committee as a nest of spies with ties to foreign intelligence agencies. Over the next few years, the Jewish Anti-Fascist Committee Affair gradually engulfed more victims, until it ended with a closed trial held from May through July 1952. All the defendants but one were shot.[70] In 1949, the arrests of Jewish public figures were supplemented with a wide-ranging campaign against "cosmopolitanism." Many Soviet Jews were arrested, fired from their jobs, and made targets of discrimination and contempt.

Newly available documents confirm what most historians have long believed: such campaigns could not have been conducted without Stalin's support and involvement. This fact raises legitimate questions about the motives behind Stalin's anti-Semitism. It is tempting to assume that in the final years of Stalin's life he merely became more open about a Judophobia he had always held as a predictable aspect of his general misanthropy. The evidence, however, suggests that his postwar anti-Semitism was primarily a product of domestic and foreign policy calculations. A complex set of historical factors lay behind his turn toward anti-Semitism as a political tool.

Foremost among these factors was the evident growth in anti-Semitism in the USSR. In no small part because of Nazi propaganda, anti-Semitic feelings and beliefs had spread among certain segments of Soviet society. During the war, even highly placed Soviet functionaries did not hesitate to lace their reports with anti-Semitic comments. In January 1944 the deputy commander of Soviet air forces, General Grigory Vorozheikin, wrote to Stalin and other Soviet leaders about the problem of having too many members of the military working in comfortable jobs at headquarters or in commissaries. Regarding those manning the commissaries that sold items to the troops—*voentorgs*—he wrote, "At the fronts they're called not 'voentorgs' but 'abramtorgs.' . . . All of these 'abramtorgs' should be sent to fight."[71] Among the letters Stalin placed in his personal archive during the postwar years we find some expressing anti-Semitic feelings and others complaining about the spread of anti-Semitism. One writer, who accused Jews of shirking physical labor, offered a proposal on how to "reeducate" them: "Separating Jews, as a worthy nation, into a separate republic . . . and making them work on a justly organized basis would be widely approved by all the other peoples of the Soviet Union."[72] Stalin undoubtedly was aware of the prevalence of such feelings and took them into consideration.

Like any totalitarian regime, the Stalinist dictatorship needed to keep society mobilized. This goal was achieved both by provoking anxiety about external threats and by using domestic groups as scapegoats, thereby channeling dissatisfaction away from the country's leaders. The spread of anti-Semitism shows that Jews were the most convenient target for social stigmatization. In the immediate aftermath of the war, however, Stalin was not able to exploit popular anti-Semitism. The complicated games being played in the international arena and the fact that there were advantages still to be derived from his alliance with the West forced him to be circumspect. The ideological campaigns of the first postwar years, designed to combat the rather amorphous idea of "kowtowing to the West," were intended as "ideological education" for the intelligentsia and probably had little resonance among the general population.

The situation changed as tensions spiked with the West, as embodied by the United States with its strong Jewish community. As relations with the new Jewish state of Israel broke down and Israel became allied with the United States, Soviet Jews became more suitable targets. As Yuri Slezkine put it, "The Jews as a Soviet nationality were now an ethnic diaspora potentially loyal to a hostile foreign state."[73] The new ideological paradigm that took shape in 1948–1949 brought Stalin's campaign against kowtowing into line with his exploitation of anti-Semitism. The two coalesced in the campaign against "cosmopolitans," appropriately understood by the Soviet masses as targeting Soviet Jews and their foreign patrons. A 1949 letter selected to be shown to Stalin captures the essence of this campaign: "Just as the entire German people bear responsibility for Hitler's aggression, so too the Jewish people must bear responsibility for the actions of the bourgeois cosmopolitans."[74] State anti-Semitism was transformed into a tool of social manipulation.

Stalin's personal prejudice undoubtedly played an important role in this new twist in the political line. There are many signs that during the final years of his life, he viewed Jews as a "counterrevolutionary" nation, much as he had viewed Poles, Germans, and the peoples of the North Caucasus before and during the war. The repression of the 1930s, the Stalinist regime's failure to protect its citizens from the Holocaust, and postwar anti-Semitism had all dampened the revolutionary fervor many Soviet Jews felt during and after the revolution. Now, Stalin assumed, Jews had turned their gaze westward, toward the United States, and were prepared to serve the West with the enthusiasm they had once shown for the revolution. "Any Jew-nationalist is an agent of American intelligence," Stalin told a meeting of the party's top leadership in late 1952. "Jew-nationalists believe that their nation was saved by the U.S.A. (there you can become rich, a bourgeois, etc.). They feel they have an obligation to the Americans."[75] These suspicions were only intensified by the Jewish wives of some of his closest associates and by his own daughter's Jewish husband. Stalin's political anti-Semitism, taking deep root during his final years, became a key factor in both domestic and foreign policy.

■ MEETING WITH MAO

The setbacks Stalin faced in Europe were partly compensated by the advance of communism in Asia. On 1 October 1949, a Communist victory in the protracted Chinese civil war resulted in the proclamation of the People's Republic of China (PRC) under the leadership of Mao Zedong. The Soviet leadership immediately established diplomatic relations with the new government and severed all ties with the defeated Kuomintang.

The Communist victory in China no doubt strengthened the Soviet Union's position in the Cold War, but it brought with it a new set of problems associated with the building of Sino-Soviet relations. Despite its dependence on the USSR, Communist China was too imposing a force to remain just another satellite. Stalin had reason to suspect that Mao might confront him with the same assertive intractability he had encountered in Yugoslavia. Considering China's size and its importance within the Third World, such recalcitrance could have much more serious consequences. A major source of friction was economic problems. The need to provide aid to a war-torn friendly power was a heavy burden for the financially strained Soviet Union.

Even before the Chinese Communists had come to power, Stalin had retained personal control over contacts with them. Through Soviet military intelligence he had set up radio communication with Mao, whose army was based in northeastern China. This line of communication was maintained through special Soviet emissaries, who also served as Mao's physicians. Although Mao and Stalin kept up a continuous written correspondence, this was not enough for the Chinese revolutionary leader, who repeatedly expressed a desire to visit the Soviet Union. Probably he saw such a visit in symbolic as well as practical terms: he needed to confirm his status as the leader of the Chinese people and a partner (albeit junior) of Stalin. But Stalin kept finding ways to forestall a visit. At first he felt it inadvisable to demonstrate close ties with the Chinese Communists when they were not the country's official government. The situation in China was extremely fluid, and a Communist victory seemed far from certain.

After several postponements by Moscow, Mao began to lose patience. On 4 July 1948 he informed Stalin that he intended to set out for Harbin and fly from there to Moscow. Ten days later he received the following response: "In view of the commenced grain harvest work, the leading comrades will leave for the provinces in August, where they will remain until November. Therefore the party's Central Committee is asking Com. Mao Zedong to time his visit to Moscow for the end of November so as to have an opportunity to see all the leading comrades."[76] Mao had no choice but to comply, but he made his annoyance plain. Stalin's excuse sounded ridiculous, and the Chinese leader did not try to pretend otherwise. The Soviet communications officer attached to Mao even felt compelled to inform Stalin of Mao's reaction:

I have known Mao Zedong for more than 6 years and could tell that his smile and the words "hao, hao—good, good," spoken as he was listening to the translation, did not mean that he was happy with the telegram.

... He was sure that he would be going immediately. Probably the trip became necessary for him. He waited for a reply with great eagerness. ... Mao Zedong's suitcases were being packed, and even leather shoes were bought (like everybody here, he wears cloth slippers), and a thick wool coat was tailored. ... So now he is outwardly calm, polite and attentive, courteous in a purely Chinese manner. But it is hard to see his true soul.

This visit was becoming a serious headache. From August through December 1948, as the Communists achieved a string of decisive victories, Mao continued to insist on coming. In a telegram dated 28 September 1948 he wrote, "On a series of questions it is necessary to report personally to the Central Committee and to the *glavny khoziain* [the boss or chief]." In early January 1949 he again expressed his desire to come to Moscow to report to the "*glavny khoziain.*" Stalin stood firm. In January 1949 the Soviet side again canceled a scheduled visit. Anastas Mikoyan was sent to the Chinese instead. As Mikoyan later recalled, in discussing this matter Stalin had justified the refusal to receive Mao by saying that it would "be interpreted in the West as a visit to Moscow to receive instructions. ... This would lead to a loss of prestige for the Chinese Communist Party and would be used by the imperialists and the Chiang Kai-shek clique against the Chinese Communists."[77] This explanation fit nicely with Stalin's policy of caution and demonstrative neutrality.

During Mikoyan's visit in February 1949, the Communist march to victory entered a decisive phase. Negotiations were begun on the terms of military and economic assistance from the USSR and what to do about treaties between the Soviets and the Kuomintang. A friendship and cooperation treaty, along with associated accords, had been signed with the Chiang Kai-shek government in August 1945. These documents stemmed from agreements reached with the Allies in Yalta: in exchange for Stalin's promise to enter the war against Japan, the United States and Britain had agreed to give to the USSR lands that the Russian Empire had lost in the 1905 Russo-Japanese War. The Kuomintang government had recognized the independence of the Outer Mongolian Soviet satellite, the People's Republic of Mongolia; the Soviet Union's rights to build a military base in Port Arthur; and its long-term lease of the port of Dalny. The Chinese-Changchun Railway, which connected Port Arthur and Dalny with the USSR proper, had been brought under Soviet administration. There was lingering dissatisfaction over these forced concessions in China. With time, the Soviet presence inside the country began to look increasingly like a politically dangerous anachronism. Both Moscow and the Chinese Communist leadership understood this. Mutual concessions were expected; it was only a question of degree.

After the Chinese Communists finally achieved victory, Stalin no longer had grounds to avoid Mao's visit. Furthermore, given the new situation, a face-to-face meeting would be extremely helpful in resolving key questions regarding the Sino-Soviet relationship. Mao left Beijing on 6 December 1949. After a ten-day trip he arrived at Moscow's Yaroslavl Station on 16 December, exactly at noon. Mao's interpreter recalled that the station clock struck twelve just as they pulled up, making the arrival all the more dramatic.[78] A famous photograph capturing the meeting on the station platform shows the head of the honor guard in the front row with his saber drawn, Bulganin in his marshal's uniform, Molotov, and Mao. The Chinese Communist leader, tall and stout next to the slight Molotov and Bulganin, looked imposing in his large fur collar and high fur hat. Later that evening Stalin received Mao in his Kremlin office.

Did the Soviet and Chinese leaders like each other? They certainly had much in common. Both were born in remote provinces to families that were poor but not destitute. Both despised their fathers and loved their mothers. Despite material deprivations, each had obtained an education, joined the revolutionary underground in his youth, and overcome his modest social origins. Each had received much of his education through independent, unguided reading and showed a penchant for abstract, philosophical topics and radical ideas. Both wrote verse and enjoyed literature idealizing rebels and brigands with forceful personalities, physical strength, and indomitable will. Neither had a talent for languages, knew a single foreign language, or even spoke his dominant language very well. Stalin's accent was strongly Georgian, Mao's Xiang (Hunanese).[79] Both were ruthless and decisive. Mao fully shared Stalin's views on attaining sole dictatorial powers and governing and largely borrowed the Soviet leader's methods, carrying out purges, liquidating former comrades, embracing forced rapid industrialization, and presiding over a great famine. The characterization of Mao prepared for the Soviet leadership in 1949 by the doctor and radio communications specialist A. Ya. Orlov describes the Chinese leader as "Unhurried, even slow. . . . He moves steadily toward any goal he sets, but not always following a straight path, often with detours. . . . Is a natural performer. Is able to hide his feelings and can play whatever role is needed."[80] This description greatly resembled Stalin. In December 1949, when Stalin was celebrating his seventieth birthday, Mao was about to turn fifty-six. Understandably,

Mao looked up to Stalin. Among the Chinese leadership, the Soviet leader was referred to as "the old man."[81]

Mao showed his respect for Stalin during the 16 December meeting. He made no demands and did not insist on anything, instead asking for advice and listening to it attentively. Stalin approved of this form of interaction. On hearing Mao's unwelcome but not unexpected question about the fate of the 1945 Sino-Soviet agreement, he launched into a lengthy explanation. The Soviet side wanted to "formally" preserve the existing agreement, he stressed, but was prepared to make certain changes that would be advantageous to China. Spelling out the political drawbacks of scrapping the agreement altogether, Stalin explained that it had been part of the Yalta agreements with the United States and Great Britain. Annulling it would "give America and England the legal grounds to raise questions about modifying also the treaty's provisions concerning the Kurile Islands and South Sakhalin." It is unclear whether Mao immediately understood how spurious this argument was; he certainly grasped it later. In any event, he took an understanding tone, and the conversation moved on to pleasanter subjects. Stalin agreed to requests for aid. The talks ended on a high note. Stalin even paid Mao the compliment of proposing to collect and publish his works in Russian.[82]

Despite the atmosphere of goodwill and warmth, the meeting must have left Mao with mixed feelings. Of course the Chinese leader was given many promises and generous displays of respect. In the end, however, Stalin had refused to give him an item near the top of his wish list: an accord that would supersede the 1945 agreement. Politically, such an accord was a high priority for Mao. As subsequent events would show, he decided to bide his time.

The following days were a bustle of activity not conducive to the discussion of weighty matters. A number of foreign guests arrived for Stalin's seventieth birthday. On 21 December a grand celebration was held at the Bolshoi Theater. Mao was seated in the first row of the presidium with Stalin and was the first foreign guest to give a speech. "When Mao Zedong stepped up to the podium," the Hungarian Communist Party leader Matyas Rakosi later recalled, "an ovation erupted the likes of which the Bolshoi Theater had probably never seen. I could see that this exultation and such a reception had an effect on Mao Zedong."[83]

Despite this show of respect, when the fanfare subsided Mao found himself in an unenviable position. Stalin's refusal to sign a new treaty left a major purpose of his visit unfulfilled. Most historians view the events that unfolded over the rest of his stay in Moscow as a subtle war of nerves. Stalin was clearly showing Mao who was boss. Mao, in response, applied his own form of pressure. After Stalin's death he claimed to have insisted on his demands, but he was probably exaggerating. In fact, claiming illness (he was indeed in a poor physical state), he demonstratively went into seclusion, refusing to take part in various events on his schedule and announcing that he had decided to return to China a month earlier than planned.[84] This tactic was to bear fruit.

Scholars have offered a variety of explanations for Stalin's change of position, but probably he had been prepared to strike a deal from the start. Skilled negotiator that he was, Stalin began the talks with a refusal because he was wary that China's strongly nationalistic new leaders might make excessive demands. This was an effective ruse. Mao apparently sensed what Stalin was up to and proved himself a worthy sparring partner. After Stalin agreed to continue negotiations, Mao began to drag his feet. Negotiations were to begin after the arrival of a group of Chinese leaders, but Mao instructed them to take their time. At first they delayed their departure from China, and then they chose a slow means of transportation to the Soviet capital—train.

It was not until 22 January 1950 that talks resumed among Stalin, Mao, and Mao's associates in Stalin's office. Stalin and Mao both reaffirmed their intention of concluding new agreements and gave instructions on drafting them. After some tough negotiating, on 14 February the Treaty of Friendship, Alliance, and Mutual Assistance was signed in the Kremlin by the USSR and the PRC, along with a number of ancillary treaties. The Soviet side lost almost all of the huge advantages it had gained through the Yalta compromises and the 1945 Sino-Soviet treaty. Under the 1945 agreement, the Chinese-Changchun Railway and Port Arthur were given to the Soviet Union for thirty years, but under the 1950 agreement they were to be returned to China by the end of 1952. China was to take back property leased by the USSR in the port of Dalny almost immediately. As a result, the Soviet Union lost its ice-free port on the Pacific and material resources of significant value. Some authors have described these agreements as "generosity unprecedented in international treaties."[85] The new Chinese leaders did, however, pay a price. They renounced all claims to Outer Mongolia and also signed a secret protocol banning citizens of third-party countries from being given concessions or conducting business in Manchuria and Xinjiang, thereby allowing the USSR to retain exclusive privileges in these border zones.

It seemed at the time that the USSR, while relinquishing many tactical advantages, was gaining a critical global edge. The country with the planet's largest population now belonged to the Soviet bloc. China had become the gravitational center and a source of real assistance for the many movements throughout Asia opposing Western influence in the region. The idea that the USSR was surrounded by capitalist countries—an enduring theme of Soviet propaganda—had been turned on its head. One could now talk about socialist encirclement of the Western world.

Immediately after signing the treaties, Stalin again showed his respect for the new Chinese leaders by attending a reception held by the Chinese embassy at the Metropol Hotel that same day, 14 February. According to Stalin's interpreter, Nikolai Fedorenko, the choice of where to hold the reception was a source of disagreement between Stalin and Mao. The Soviet leader proposed the Kremlin, but Mao preferred, as a matter of prestige, to hold it elsewhere. "The Kremlin," he explained, "is a place for state receptions by the Soviet government. Our country, a sovereign state, finds this unsuitable." Stalin responded that he could not attend such a reception: "I never attend receptions at restaurants or foreign embassies. Never." Mao insisted. After a conspicuous pause, throughout which Mao kept his intent gaze on the Soviet leader, Stalin relented: "Fine, Comrade Mao Zedong, I'll come if you want me to so much."[86] A standard invitation in the name of the Chinese ambassador to the USSR, handwritten, arrived requesting the presence of Generalissimo Stalin and his wife (the invitation of whom may have reflected diplomatic protocol but more likely showed that the Chinese knew nothing about Stalin's personal life). The attire: dress uniforms with medals.[87]

Stalin's appearance was the highlight of the reception. He was late, and as Fedorenko describes it, an aura of anticipation hung over the banquet hall as everyone whispered the same question: Would he show up? He was greeted, Fedorenko wrote, "with loud applause and noisy exclamations of delight." Stalin stopped, paused, and then headed toward Mao. A round of toasts began. "Everyone who spoke, and not only they, kept their eyes on the two figures standing side by side and occasionally engaging one another in conversation." After lengthy and tiresome toasts and ovations, Stalin made a gesture. Once the room settled into silence, he pronounced a toast to Mao and the success of the People's Republic of China. All drained their glasses in synchrony. "There was another burst of applause, enthusiastic exclamations, and general rejoicing."[88]

On 16 February Stalin hosted a farewell luncheon in honor of the Chinese. The following day the delegation set off for Beijing by train. The heyday of "Sino-Soviet friendship" had begun. With the support of the USSR, China repaired its economy and built hundreds of new factories in its most important sectors. The Korean War, which began shortly after Mao Zedong's visit, strengthened the bond between the two regimes, especially its military component. Beneath the surface, however, was the tension that had already manifested itself during Mao's visit. Proclamations of common ideological objectives and unity against a common enemy could not hide differences rooted in diverging national interests. The coming to power of the Chinese Communists was just the beginning of a complicated relationship in which both states pretended to the role of leadership of the international Communist movement. The principles Stalin established to guide his relationship with his vast neighbor to the east would work only so long as the Chinese leadership felt dependent on Soviet aid and support. Like much else that Stalin left to his heirs, these principles would not be viable for long.

■   **THE THREAT OF WORLD WAR III**

The Communist victory in China coincided with another important development. In late August 1949, having devoted tremendous resources to developing a nuclear capability, the Soviet Union conducted its first test of an atom bomb.[89] With the success of this test, the Stalinist system showed that it was ready to do whatever it took to achieve high-priority military objectives. Lavrenty Beria was put in charge of the atom bomb project, a telling choice given his reputation for ruthlessness and decisiveness. He must have known that failure at this high-priority task could have brought his career—even his life—to a sudden end. Later, after Stalin's death, he recalled that he left for the test site in Kazakhstan "in a dejected mood."[90] Soon, however, he was able to breathe a sigh of relief.

Possession of an atom bomb, despite its tremendous significance for the Soviet Union's stature as a military power, is unlikely to have gone to Stalin's head. He probably took sober account of both the relatively limited options for using such a weapon and the real balance of power in the world. The Western powers had shown decisiveness in opposing the Soviet bloc and building up their already impressive military potential. Stalin could not rely on force alone. In the realm of foreign policy (much more than domestic policy), he exercised caution and pragmatism. Over several years the situation in Korea, the site of the first "hot" war between the Western and Communist blocs, offered examples of Stalin's approach.

After the defeat of Japan in 1945, Korea was partitioned along the 38th parallel. North of the parallel, the Japanese surrendered to Soviet troops, and in the south, to the United States. As in Europe, a pro-Soviet government was established in the Soviet-occupied zone and a pro-Western one in the U.S.-occupied zone. The starting point for this process was the installation of puppet regimes by each side. The Americans put in power a seventy-year-old professor named Syngman Rhee, who had spent thirty-three years in exile in the United States, where he received his education. In the North, Moscow installed a thirty-three-year-old Red Army officer, Kim Il Sung.

Several years after the capitulation of Japan, Korea was far from calm. Small military clashes and saber rattling were a part of everyday life. Both sides were coming to the conclusion that the only path to reuniting Korea was through war—a war kept at bay only by the presence of American and Soviet troops. Fearing a direct confrontation, Stalin and the American leaders preferred to tread with caution. Stalin's approach was summed up in instructions he gave to Soviet representatives in North Korea in May 1947: "We should not meddle too deeply in Korean affairs."[91] In late 1948 Soviet troops left the country, and the United States began to withdraw its contingent the following summer.

The North Korean leaders saw the American departure as opening the door to military action, but in the fall of 1949 Stalin was still rejecting their insistent requests to sanction an armed offensive against the South. In early 1950, with the victory of Mao Zedong in China and the return home of North Korean units that had fought alongside the Chinese Communists, the situation began to change. Kim Il Sung hoped that the Chinese might offer the Korean Communists reciprocal assistance. He intensified pressure on Moscow, hinting at the possibility of a reorientation toward China.[92] Stalin was confronted with a convoluted web of arguments for and against war that historians are still trying to sort out today.

The principles of realpolitik that often guided Stalin in the international arena called for caution. Continuing the policy of a divided Korea while strengthening the Communist North as a force to counteract the Americans seemed like the best option. Kim Il Sung's demands, or rather insistent requests, to reunify the country by force were easy for him to continue to turn down. The China factor aside, the North Korean leaders were still Stalin's puppets. Only the USSR could give the North Koreans arms and other vital resources needed for the government to survive. The Chinese themselves relied on Soviet assistance.

Tilting the scales in the other direction was the great-power urge for expansion, the natural tendency to fill a void and capture territory that was not clearly spoken for. Many scholars believe that Stalin may have been emboldened by a statement the Americans made in January 1950 about the sphere of the United States' national interests that included no mention of Korea. It sounded like an admission of American weakness after defeat in China. Optimistic assurances by Kim Il Sung and a wager on a pro-Communist uprising in the South's rear offered the prospect of a blitzkrieg that would confront the United States with a fait accompli and leave no time for effective intervention. Also heavily weighing the scales on this side were the pretentions of the USSR, and Stalin personally, to the role of leader of the revolutionary movement in the Third World. Finally, Stalin may have wanted to compensate for setbacks in Europe.

Whatever his thinking was, in early 1950 Stalin decided in favor of action and signaled Kim Il Sung that he could begin preparing an invasion. In April Kim came to Moscow to meet with Stalin and discuss the details.[93] Together they outlined a plan and timeline for the war, and with the help of the USSR, the North Koreans began urgent preparations. By the time combat began, they had acquired a huge advantage over the South. On 25 June 1950, Kim Il Sung's troops began their offensive. Like many other attempts at blitzkrieg, this one met with defeat. The rapid response by the United States, which Stalin had worried about but chosen to discount, dramatically changed the situation. The American leadership saw the aggression in Korea as the start of a broad Soviet offensive that would ultimately include Europe.[94] Having decided to intervene, the Americans quickly outmaneuvered the Soviet bloc diplomatically. A session of the UN Security Council, convened the very day military operations began, condemned the North as the aggressor (Yugoslavia abstained and the Soviet ambassador was absent).[95] Soon afterward, American troops landed in South Korea and were quickly joined by forces from fifteen other states, a fact that was of greater political than military significance.

Despite some initial successes by the North, this start to the war dampened Kim Il Sung's confidence. Stalin demanded that the war go on and encouraged the North Koreans with advice and new deliveries of military hardware. "In our opinion the attack absolutely must continue and the sooner South Korea is liberated the less chance there is for intervention," Stalin wrote the Soviet ambassador in Pyongyang on 1 July 1950.[96] But the wager on a victorious conclusion to the war before serious American forces could reach the peninsula failed. After capturing almost all of South Korea by September, the North Koreans were not able to fully expel its government. The Americans launched a powerful counterstrike. Under the UN flag, coalition forces advanced rapidly and by the end of October had captured most of North Korea and taken Pyongyang. The time had come for the Soviet side to play its final card: the Chinese "volunteers."

Now began the confusing and still little-studied negotiations between Stalin and the Chinese leadership. At one point it appeared they had ended in failure. On 13 October Stalin sent the following directive to Kim Il Sung: "We feel that continuing resistance is pointless. The Chinese comrades are refusing to take part militarily. Under these circumstances you must prepare to evacuate completely to China and/or the USSR. It is of the utmost importance to withdraw all troops and military hardware. Draw up a detailed plan of action and follow it rigorously. The potential for fighting the enemy in the future must be preserved."[97]

The Soviet ambassador urgently met with the North Korean leaders and read them Stalin's telegram. As the ambassador reported, "Kim Il Sung stated that it was very hard for them [to accept Stalin's recommendation], but since there is such advice they will fulfill it."[98] How serious was Stalin's directive? Was he truly prepared to lose North Korea? Apparently he was. If the Chinese refused to send troops, Stalin had no other option since he categorically rejected the idea of bringing in Soviet troops. It is also possible, however, that Stalin believed the decision to evacuate forces might lead the Chinese to think twice. The American advance was more threatening to China than to the USSR. Furthermore, having announced his intention to withdraw, Stalin continued to try to engage the Chinese. He made concessions on the question of arms deliveries and offered more specific promises to deploy Soviet air cover. These efforts bore fruit. Mao agreed to enter the war. "The old man writes to us that we must step up," is how he described Stalin's demands to his comrades.[99]

Battered by the Chinese, the South Koreans and their allies withdrew from North Korea. In early 1951 they lost Seoul for the second time. Then came a counterstrike from the South. It was beginning to look like neither side could achieve a decisive victory. The Soviet Union tried to stay in the shadows, although Stalin did keep his promise to provide covert air support for Kim Il Sung's and Mao Zedong's forces. The main victims of this great-power standoff were the Korean people. Millions of lives were lost, and the Koreans were forced to live as a divided nation. Those in the North endured one of history's most brutal dictatorships, a regime that largely followed the Stalinist model.

The Korean War heightened international tensions and spurred the arms race. While the development of military industries had always been an unquestioned priority for the Soviet leadership, during the final years of Stalin's life the buildup moved to a new level. In January 1951 a meeting was held between the Soviet leadership and top officials from the Eastern bloc. Archival documents relating to this meeting remain classified. The only reason historians know it even took place is that it is mentioned in various memoirs. The most detailed description of what happened there is given in the memoirs of Hungarian Communist Party leader Matyas Rakosi. According to his account, the Soviet side was represented by Stalin and several members of the Politburo and military. The East European countries sent their first party secretaries and defense ministers (only the Polish party secretary was absent). Sergei Shtemenko, chief of the General Staff of the armed forces of the USSR, gave a speech about the growing threat from NATO and the need to counterbalance it with a military buildup by the socialist countries. The Soviet leadership assigned the satellite countries the task of greatly increasing the size of their armies within three years and creating a military-industrial foundation to support this enhanced military might. Shtemenko provided specific numerical targets.

Rakosi states that Shtemenko's numbers provoked debate. He quotes the Polish defense minister, Konstantin Rokossovsky, as saying that the army the Poles were being asked to assemble by 1953 was already being planned but would not be attainable until 1956. Other representatives also questioned their countries' abilities to manage such a rapid buildup. The Soviets, however, were adamant. Stalin answered Rokossovsky that the timetable set forth by the Poles could remain in place only if Rokossovsky could guarantee no new wars before 1956. Absent such a guarantee, it was better to adopt Shtemenko's proposal.[100]

We do not know what plans were on the drawing board for the Soviet military or to what extent they were realized. There is nevertheless sufficient evidence to conclude that Stalin was aiming for a serious military buildup. According to official figures, the army, which had been reduced to 2.9 million soldiers by 1949, had reached 5.8 million by 1953.[101] Investment in the military and naval ministries, as well as production of military arms and hardware, grew by 60 percent in 1951 and 40 percent in 1952. As a comparison, government investment in the non-military sectors of the Soviet economy grew by 6 percent in 1951 and 7 percent in 1952.[102]

Development of nuclear weaponry and delivery systems remained the highest-priority and most expensive military program. In addition to the nuclear project, significant resources were dedicated to rocket technology, jet-propelled aviation, and an air defense system for Moscow.[103] During the final months of his life, Stalin showed his determination to outpace his rivals in the arms race. In February 1953 he approved major programs in aviation and naval ship construction. The first provided for the creation of 106 bomber divisions by the end of 1955, up from 32 as of 1953. In order to outfit new divisions, the plan was to build 10,300 planes during 1953–1955 and increase the air and naval forces by 290,000 people. The second program allocated huge resources to the construction of heavy and medium cruisers before 1959. Soviet military bases were established in the Far Eastern regions of Kamchatka and Chukotka, close to the maritime boundary with the United States.[104]

Did this buildup mean that Stalin was planning to launch a preemptive strike and unleash a new world war? There is no evidence to support this line of speculation. It is important to note that the massive arms buildup programs were planned to take place over several years. Historians of Soviet foreign policy also note Stalin's caution and pragmatism in the international arena. During the postwar years he behaved toward the West approximately as he had toward Nazi Germany before the war. He preferred behind-the-scenes maneuvering over direct confrontation. This approach had been on display in the Korean War. While encouraging its continuation, Stalin had consistently avoided direct conflict with the Americans. He had intentionally dragged out the signing of an armistice, seeing the war as a way to let others get their hands dirty weakening the United States. In a private conversation with the Chinese leader Zhou Enlai a few months before his death, Stalin frankly and cynically explained: "This war is causing the Americans a lot of headaches. The North Koreans have lost nothing, except for the casualties they took during this war. . . . You have to have self-control, patience. Of course you have to understand the Koreans— they've taken a lot of casualties, but you have to explain to them that this is something big. You have to have patience, you have to have great self-control."[105]

It took Stalin's death to free the Koreans from the obligation of taking casualties to further another country's interests. His heirs pursued a policy of relaxing international tensions and reducing the burden of the arms race. By July 1953 a decision was made to conclude a truce in Korea. Stalin's death brought an end to the USSR's ruinous military buildup, including the creation of armadas of bombers. The country could not endure the strains of the arms race and demanded the reforms that Stalin had refused to give it.

■ THE INVETERATE CONSERVATIVE

Military spending was not the only reason for a ballooning government budget during Stalin's final years. There is copious evidence of the *vozhd*'s passion for large-scale, expensive projects toward the end of his life. These projects were often cast by official propaganda as "the Stalinist building of communism." They included huge hydroelectric power plants, canals, and rail lines into the nation's inaccessible polar reaches. To strengthen communication with newly acquired Far Eastern territories, a ferry crossing and a 13.6-kilometer underwater tunnel to the island of Sakhalin were planned, along with a rail line connecting the tunnel with the country's train network. As was usually the case with Stalinism, behind the appealing propagandistic façade lurked an unsavory reality: communism was largely being built on the backs of prisoners.[106]

Exorbitant spending on infrastructure once again plunged the Soviet economy into financial crisis. The chaotic proliferation of projects led to losses on uncompleted construction, which later had to be finished at far greater cost than initially projected. In 1951 and 1952 this extravagance reached its limit. Construction projects fell behind schedule and the launch of new ones was delayed. The picture was completed by stagnation in agriculture and consumer spending—the sectors that funded heavy industry. Undaunted, Stalin devised a plan for a new surge of capital investment in 1953.[107] At the end of his life he stubbornly repeated the mistakes of the First Five-Year Plan's forced industrialization.

As far as can be determined from available documents, this unfolding crisis was not seriously discussed at the upper echelons of power. Until the very end Stalin demanded the expansion of heavy industry and military buildup at any cost. As in the past, he agreed to limited concessions and policy adjustments only when problems grew so severe that his hand was forced. Clearly unwilling to acknowledge the systemic crisis, he reluctantly addressed only its most obvious manifestations.

As often happened, the first signs of approaching calamity came from the most disadvantaged sector of the Soviet economy: agriculture. The Soviet countryside bore the brunt of unbalanced economic policies and of the new obligations and taxes that supported growing government expenditures. Under the inefficient kolkhoz system, agriculture was stagnant and incapable of feeding the country. The livestock situation was particularly bad. Even official Soviet statistics showed that there were no more head of cattle in the country in early 1953 than there had been in 1939, and that number was one-third less what it had been in 1928. The number of pigs in

1953 was the same as in 1928.[108] The numerous complaints sent to Moscow from across the country painted a desperate picture. Some of these cries for help reached Stalin.

Among the letters received in October and November 1952 and selected to be shown to Stalin were a few complaints from various parts of the USSR about the hardships suffered on collective farms.[109] A veterinarian from the Orekhovo-Zuevo District of Moscow Oblast, N. I. Kholodov, called for incentives for work by kolkhozniks, who were essentially forced to labor for no pay. Kholodov wrote:

> According to our press, we have tremendous achievements in agriculture. . . . Let us take a look at how matters stand in reality. The rye was poorly harvested, poorly because there is colossal waste in the harvesting process. . . . The potatoes have been harvested somehow, but what kind of a harvest is this? They were dug up by workers mobilized from plants and factories who were drawing 50% of their salaries for this period, and they do not try to gather all the potatoes because they do not have an interest in this; they try to finish up as quickly as possible and gather only what is on top. . . .
>
> Now let us look at animal husbandry. Even talking about it is embarrassing: annual yield of milk from year to year does not exceed 1,200–1,400 liters per forage-fed cow. This is ridiculous—it's what you get from your average goat.[110]

Alongside these tales of dysfunction in the countryside, Stalin's mail in late 1952 contained eloquent accounts of empty store shelves in cities. In early November the *vozhd* took notice of a letter from V. F. Deikina, the party secretary for a railway station in Riazan Oblast. She wrote:

> It is now October, and here we have to wait in line for black bread, and sometimes you can't get any at all, and workers are saying so many unpleasant words and they don't believe what's written [in newspapers] and say that we're being deceived. . . . I'll stick to the facts since there's not enough paper to describe it all and send it in a letter.
>
> 1. You have to stand in line for black bread.
> 2. You can't get white bread at all.
> 3. There's neither butter nor vegetable oil.
> 4. There's no meat in the stores.
> 5. There's no sausage.
> 6. There are no groats of any kind.

7. There's no macaroni or other flour products.
8. There's no sugar.
9. There are no potatoes in the stores.
10. There is no milk or other dairy products.
11. There is no form of animal fat (lard, etc.). . . .

I'm not a slanderer and I'm not being spiteful; I'm writing the bitter truth, but that's the way it is. . . . The local leadership gets everything illegally, under the table, so to speak; their underlings deliver everything to their apartments. For them the people can do as they please; that's not their concern. . . . I am asking for a commission to be sent to bring the guilty to justice, to teach the right people how to plan for needs. Otherwise, those with full bellies don't believe the hungry.[111]

Despite its critical tone, this letter was entirely politically "correct." Deikina was trying to combat the deficiencies and abuses of local officials who did not know how to properly "plan for needs." The letter did not delve into the causes of the lack of food in the country. This was the sort of letter Stalin could like. Averky Aristov, recently appointed as the Central Committee secretary in charge of local party organizations, was sent to investigate. On 17 November 1952 Stalin held a meeting of Central Committee secretaries in his office. As Aristov recounted several years later, Stalin asked him to deliver his findings. Aristov reported that for a long time there had been shortages of bread, cooking oil, and other food items in Riazan Oblast. Stalin grew furious and ordered that the oblast party secretary be removed from his post. Aristov and others present tried to intercede on behalf of the officials from Riazan. Things were no different, they explained, in many other regions, including Ukraine, the country's "bread basket."[112]

Following the meeting, Riazan Oblast was allocated food from government supplies. Such measures, of course, did not solve the problem. The country's leadership was again faced with the task of salvaging the agricultural sector. Under the pressure of circumstances, Stalin agreed to review proposals to raise the price paid by the state for livestock produced by kolkhozes. At stake was the fundamental question of whether peasants deserved to be compensated for their labor. The exceptionally low "purchase price" paid to kolkhozniks barely masked the fact that everything they produced for the state was basically being confiscated. Growing food was tremendously unprofitable, and those who grew it had no incentive to produce more.

In December 1952 a commission headed by Nikita Khrushchev was established to draft a resolution raising livestock purchase prices.[113] After working for several weeks, the commission wound up provoking Stalin's displeasure. The *vozhd* was highly suspicious of attempts to change the existing system for pumping resources out of the countryside. To the dismay of his comrades, who had agreed on an increase in livestock prices, Stalin proposed significantly increasing taxes on the peasantry. Anastas Mikoyan later recalled Stalin's reasoning: "What is a peasant? He'll turn over his extra hen and that's an end to it."[114] Khrushchev and his politically seasoned colleagues on the commission chose the safest course of action. They bided their time. The Soviet leaders would shield themselves from Stalin's anger while they waited for his death. When it finally came, the overdue agricultural reforms were put in place immediately and on a larger scale than initially planned. Stalin's heirs raised procurement prices and lowered taxes on peasants. Although the deep-rooted flaws in the kolkhoz system were preserved, these measures had a positive effect. For the first time in many decades the peasants were given relief, and some improvement in agricultural production was achieved.

Reducing the financial burden on the countryside inevitably came with a reduction in extravagant spending on major infrastructure projects. Just a few days after Stalin's death, on 10 March 1953, the chairman of Gosplan presented the new head of the Soviet government, Georgy Malenkov, a report on major construction projects that were "behind schedule for completion."[115] The report stated that it was being presented at Malenkov's request. Members of the top leadership were apparently losing no time in implementing the changes they had been constrained from making while the *vozhd* was alive. They quickly halted many of Stalin's ambitious projects, including the construction of canals, hydroelectrical systems, and rail lines through difficult terrain. Investment in the military was also reduced.[116] The funds thus freed up could now be put toward dealing with the severe crises in agriculture and social welfare. The Stalinist industrialization system, enabled by the population's low living standard and by the exploitation of the countryside as if it were an internal colony, could now be gradually dismantled.

These decisions were adopted and realized with unprecedented speed in the months following Stalin's death. The new leaders' decisiveness clearly shows that it was specifically Stalin who was the main obstacle to transformation for long years. Until the very end, the dictator's personal political and economic modus operandi remained extraordinarily conservative and protective. His death opened the door to innovations that were long overdue.

■ THE DEATH THROES OF THE DICTATORSHIP

At the end of his life, Stalin was at the pinnacle of his power. His authority was unassailable and not under threat from any source. But he did not feel that way. Like other dictators, he never stopped fighting for power and never quite trusted his subjects. The methods he used in his never-ending battle for power were universal and simple. They included the elimination of any potential threat from within his inner circle, unrelenting oversight of the secret police, the encouragement of competition and mutual control among the various components of government, and the mobilization of society against perceived enemies both internal and external.

After destroying the Leningraders, Stalin began adjusting the balance of power within the Politburo, creating counterweights to the growing influence of Malenkov and Beria. In 1949 he brought Ukrainian party chief Khrushchev to Moscow and made him a Central Committee secretary and head of Moscow's party organization. Soon afterward he began to actively promote Bulganin, who had faithfully served him as defense minister. In April 1950, on Stalin's suggestion, Bulganin was appointed first deputy chairman of the Council of Ministers. For a while this promotion gave Bulganin privileged access to the *vozhd*. Soon, however, Stalin became disenchanted with his protégé and stripped him of his authority. This happened without particular acrimony. Bulganin remained a member of the top leadership. A period of relative equilibrium among key Politburo members set in, but it was just the calm before the storm.

An important factor in Stalin's last battle for power was his declining health. Lightening his workload by relinquishing certain duties or gradually handing over power to subordinates was out of the question. Instead, the weakening *vozhd* consolidated his dictatorship with enviable energy, compensating for reduced vigor with combativeness. Fierce blows were leveled against the most vulnerable points in the hierarchy of power. The first involved yet another wave of arrests at the Ministry of State Security, over which Stalin never ceased to keep tight control. In July 1951, based on the usual assortment of trumped-up charges and incriminating denunciations, Stalin ordered the arrest of state security minister Viktor Abakumov, who quite recently had been a favorite. The party functionary Semen Ignatiev was appointed in his place. Abakumov's arrest predictably opened the door to a large-scale purge of the ministry.

Having terrified the chekists, Stalin left for a vacation of more than four months. While in the south, he continued to keep a close eye on state security. The inventory of materials sent to Stalin between 11 August and 21

December 1951 includes more than 160 Ministry of State Security memoranda and reports. He also received an indeterminable number of coded telegrams from the ministry, as well as Politburo and Council of Ministers resolutions having to do with state security.[117] In October Stalin summoned Ignatiev to the south and ordered him to "kick all the Jews out" of the ministry. When Ignatiev naively asked, "Where to?" Stalin explained to the inexperienced minister: "I'm not saying you should throw them out onto the street. Lock them up and let them stay in prison."[118] Ignatiev turned out to be a quick learner. Mortally terrified, he obediently launched a series of arrests and fabricated cases having to do with a "Zionist plot" within his ministry. For Stalin, extending his campaign of state anti-Semitism to state security was a perfectly logical step. Jews, members of a suspect nation and potential henchmen of world imperialism, could not be allowed to work in the regime's most sacred realm. The next targets were just as logical. Immediately after state security, Stalin initiated purges against highly placed functionaries in several branches of the party-state apparat.

The next round of repression was also orchestrated from his dacha in the south. In September 1951 he received a visit from Georgia's minister for state security, Nikolai Rukhadze. As Rukhadze testified under interrogation after his arrest, Stalin made some general comments at the dinner table about the dominance of Mingrelians (Megrels) in Georgia; he noted that Beria was a Mingrelian and was giving patronage to this group.[119] This comment was the first hint at the target of the next campaign: Georgian officials and their patron. Soon after Rukhadze's visit, the head of Stalin's security team, Nikolai Vlasik, reported to the *vozhd* that people were complaining about having to pay bribes to enter Georgian colleges and universities. That this information fit perfectly with Stalin's new focus is hardly surprising. Vlasik, who had spent a good portion of his life by Stalin's side, had developed a keen sense of his moods and a talent for telling him what he wanted to hear. He could tell that Stalin was thirsting for blood and sought out the compromising materials that would help satisfy his boss's craving. Rukhadze was assigned to look into Vlasik's allegations.

On 29 October 1951, Rukhadze reported to Stalin that the bribery charges mostly could not be confirmed.[120] This made no difference. Stalin had decided on a purge in Georgia, and it was only a matter of time before he invented a pretext for it. On 3 November he telephoned Rukhadze and asked him for information about patronage by Georgia's second party secretary, Mikhail Baramiia, the former procurator of the city of Sukhumi, who had been accused of taking bribes. Rukhadze did as he was told, preparing a document suggesting that Baramiia had protected Mingrelian officials guilty of crimes.[121] The case was handled expeditiously. With Stalin's active involvement, sweeping repression was unleashed in Georgia. Many of the republic's leaders, including Baramiia, were arrested. More than eleven thousand people were deported to remote areas of the Soviet Union.[122]

The Mingrelian and Leningrad Affairs largely followed the same template. Both started with accusations of abuse of power and political protectionism (shefstvo), quickly followed by the arrest and torture of disgraced officials, leading to fabricated evidence of "anti-Soviet" and "espionage" organizations. As in Leningrad, here too Stalin targeted a specific clan of Soviet officials with ties to influential members of the country's leadership—in this case Beria.[123] Whether to make a mockery of him or simply teach him a lesson in humility, Stalin assigned Beria to hold a plenum of Georgia's Central Committee in 1952, at which he was forced to expose his former clients and feign shock and anger at their behavior. Undoubtedly Beria saw the purge in Georgia as a personal threat. Immediately after Stalin's death he managed to put a stop to the Mingrelian Affair and had its targets freed and returned to senior positions.[124]

Beria weathered the storm. Like many before him, however, he emerged with a renewed sense of the fragility of his political and physical existence. Stalin apparently had his sights on more important targets. The first shot was fired after the Nineteenth Party Congress, which convened in October 1952 after a thirteen-year break. Instead of giving the keynote speech, Stalin limited his appearance at the congress to a brief closing statement. It was as if he was saving his diminishing strength for the main event: the plenum of the newly elected Central Committee, which immediately followed the congress. The plenum would determine the makeup of the party's top governing bodies, most important the Politburo. The election was expected to be a mere formality. Members of the Central Committee usually voted for the candidates proposed from on high without wasting their breath on discussion. But in this case Stalin caught everyone by surprise and introduced some surprising changes.

His main innovation was the abolition of the Politburo and the creation of two new bodies. The first, which formally replaced the Politburo, was called the Presidium of the Central Committee of the Communist Party of the Soviet Union.[125] Whereas the Politburo had included nine members with full voting rights and two candidate members, the new Presidium was much larger, comprising twenty-five full members and eleven candidate members. The expansion would add younger and relatively unknown party leaders, giving Stalin an even freer hand in regard to his older comrades. The political essence of the reorganization was summed up, probably correctly, by Anastas Mikoyan: "Since the makeup of the Presidium was so broad, if needed, the disappearance of Presidium members out of favor with Stalin would not be so noticeable. If between congresses five or six people disappeared out of twenty-five, that would look like an insignificant change. If, on the other hand, five or six people out of nine Politburo members disappeared, that would be more noticeable."[126]

This was exactly the sort of apprehension Stalin needed to keep the will of the old guard and potential heirs in check. Not satisfied with the threat implicit in the expanded Central Committee Presidium, Stalin continued his psychological warfare. His next proposal—the creation of a nine-member bureau to serve as the Presidium leadership—was just as unexpected. In principle, the Presidium Bureau made sense. The unwieldy Presidium would hardly be capable of efficient decision making. But Stalin, as he had often done, could of course create a narrow leadership group without formal approval by the Central Committee plenum. The true purpose of this toying with democracy became immediately clear once he disclosed his proposed candidates for the bureau. It turned out that he did not feel it was possible for him to nominate two of his oldest associates—Molotov and Mikoyan—for membership. To add insult to injury, he topped off this announcement by giving the two a public tongue-lashing.

These two men—Molotov in particular—were seen within the party and among the people as the *vozhd*'s natural heirs. This perception is specifically why Stalin chose to publicly discredit them by making it known that he did not consider them worthy leaders of the party and the country. Just what charges he brought against Molotov and Mikoyan we do not know, as there is no verbatim transcript of the plenum. Judging by the contradictory recollections of those who took part, Stalin concocted an amalgam of political smears, bending facts and quasi-facts to his purpose. He brought up Molotov's supposed concessions to foreign correspondents and his mistakes at the 1945 foreign ministers' conference and claimed that Molotov, with Mikoyan's support, had proposed raising the procurement prices for grain in order to incentivize work by the peasants. These misdeeds were painted with the brush of "rightist opportunism." Stalin may even have mentioned Molotov's wife and his pro-Jewish sympathies.[127] In the end, the content of the criticism mattered little. The main point was obvious: nobody was worthy of succeeding Stalin. The only hope was that he would live on for many years. Molotov and Mikoyan came to the podium to express their devotion to Stalin. This too only underscored his greatness. Stalin's manner signaled to the gathering that Molotov's and Mikoyan's justifications were not worth listening to. Before Mikoyan could finish what he was saying, according to one eyewitness, Stalin gave a dismissive wave of the hand. "The hall immediately began to react very emotionally, and people started to yell: 'Enough of your self-justification!' . . . 'Stop trying to fool the Central Committee!' Mikoyan wanted to say something else, but the hall interrupted him and he sat back down."[128] This demonstration of devotion to the *vozhd* and disdain for apostates brought the plenum to a fitting end.

Despite being anathematized, Molotov and Mikoyan formally held onto most of their official powers—and, most important, their lives—but neither they nor any other member of Stalin's inner circle could feel truly safe. There was also alarming news coming from the country's socialist neighbors. In November 1952, shortly after the conclusion of the Nineteenth Party Congress, the Czechoslovak party leader Rudolf Slansky was put on trial along with other senior party officials. The defendants were found guilty and executed. Recent research has shown that Stalin exercised close personal control over the Slansky trial.[129] Slansky was a Jew, and his trial served as a prelude to Stalin's next act of intimidation: the Doctors' Plot.

The affair that has come to be known as the Doctors' Plot, to which Stalin devoted a significant portion of his final months, unfolded within a general campaign of state anti-Semitism. The foundation of the case was information "dug up" by state security about murderous doctors, mostly Jewish, working in government health care facilities serving the Soviet leadership. Accusations against "wrecker doctors" who supposedly killed or plotted to kill Soviet leaders was a leitmotif of the political trials of the 1930s. Toward the end of his life Stalin returned to this theme, possibly because of anxiety about his own mortality or perhaps because he saw in the fabrication of a case against Kremlin doctors a way of putting pressure on their patients. Over many months, Stalin obsessively presided over the fabrication of evidence against Jewish doctors and their supposed patrons within the Ministry of State Security. His eagerness to lash out at this group led him to spew foul threats at Ignatiev, calling state security agents obese "hippopotamuses" and promising to drive them "like sheep" and "give it to them in the mug."[130]

During October and November 1952, when the curtain had closed on the first act of the drama taking place at the upper reaches of government, Stalin approved the arrest of a number of doctors, including Petr Yegorov, head of the body that oversaw Kremlin health services; Vladimir Vinogradov, Stalin's personal physician; and two professors, Miron Vovsi and Vladimir

Vasilenko. Stalin met with the heads of state security and instructed them to use torture on the arrestees.[131] On 15 November 1952, Ignatiev reported to him that these instructions had been carried out: "Means of physical coercion were used on Yegorov, Vinogradov, and Vasilenko and interrogation was intensified, especially in regard to foreign intelligence. . . . Two workers capable of carrying out special assignments (using physical punishment) in regard to particularly important and particularly dangerous criminals were selected and already used in this case."[132]

Stalin soon put the "confessions" extracted through these brutal techniques to use. On 1 December 1952, during a meeting of the Central Committee Presidium, questions tied to "wrecking within the field of medicine" and "information on the state of the USSR Ministry of State Security" were placed before the gathering. In keeping with his initial idea of collusion between "wrecker doctors" and state security "conspirators," the main targets of Stalin's attack were "Jewish nationalists" and chekists. At a subsequent Central Committee Presidium meeting on 4 December, a resolution titled "On the Situation in the Ministry of State Security" was adopted, calling for "active offensive actions" in intelligence work and intensified party control over the ministry. It defended the use of extreme methods in the fight against "enemies" with the idea that "Many chekists hide behind . . . rotten and harmful reasoning that the use of diversion and terror against class enemies is supposedly incompatible with Marxism-Leninism. These good-for-nothing chekists have descended from positions of revolutionary Marxism-Leninism to positions of bourgeois liberalism and pacifism."[133] Stalin summed up this position more succinctly in a closed-door meeting: "Communists who take a dim view of intelligence and the work of the cheka, who are afraid of getting their hands dirty, should be thrown down a well head first."[134]

At some point Stalin decided that the Doctors' Plot should be turned into a major campaign. In early January and with his active involvement, two press items were prepared: a TASS report about the arrest of a group of "wrecker doctors" and a lead article for *Pravda* on the same subject. The public was told of the discovery of "a terrorist group made up of doctors whose goal, using wrecking treatments, was to shorten the lives of the Soviet Union's prominent figures." These alleged crimes were being committed on orders from an international Jewish bourgeois-nationalist organization and U.S. and British intelligence services.[135] The Soviet people were urged to exercise vigilance toward enemies receiving support from the imperialist world.

The publication of these items, on 13 January 1953, launched a large-scale ideological campaign designed to inflame anti-Semitism and bring "vigilance" to a fevered pitch. There were widespread rumors of possible pogroms and the internal resettlement of Soviet Jews. In the decades that followed, these rumors evolved into assumptions that Stalin might have been planning show trials against the doctors and the removal of Jews from the European USSR to the Far East, as had been done to Caucasian peoples during the war. Recently opened archives, despite thorough searches, have revealed no direct or indirect evidence to support either assumption. Given that either show trials or a roundup of an entire ethnic group would have required tremendous logistical effort, the absence of any trace of evidence is persuasive.[136]

And even the maniacal Stalin, who by now was truly ill, saw no need for a resettlement program or large-scale arrests. The Doctors' Plot campaign was entirely sufficient to his purpose. Remaining within the realm of ideas rather than actions, it manipulated the public mood and fostered a psychology of war-readiness in the absence of any looming war, thereby distracting people from their daily hardships. The arrests of prominent doctors also forced Stalin's comrades to live in a state of anxiety as they tried to guess what testimony would be beaten out of their physicians in the bowels of the Lubyanka. Like other similar acts of demonstrative violence, the Doctors' Plot had a foreign-policy aspect. Some historians believe that Stalin viewed this new campaign of anti-Semitism as a means of putting pressure on his Western opponents, the United States in particular. He was using the implicit threat of anti-Semitic pogroms to extract concessions from Western leaders, who knew no other way to influence him.[137]

Historians can debate whether calculation or mania played the greater role in Stalin's final campaigns. In either case, his actions attest to a relentless striving to hold onto power until he reached the ultimate impediment: death. The final leg of the journey toward this impediment began on Saturday evening, 28 February 1953, when he invited his four currently closest comrades—Malenkov, Beria, Khrushchev, and Bulganin—to his dacha for the last dinner gathering of his life. The following day his bodyguards found him paralyzed, and the agonizing over whether or not to summon members of the highly suspect medical profession began.

THE DICTATORSHIP COLLAPSES

A conference in the Kremlin, 2–5 March 1953, and the death of Stalin.
The arrival of the doctors on the morning of 2 March 1953 fundamentally
changed the situation. The very fact that they had been summoned to Stalin's dacha meant that the seriousness of his condition was officially recognized. The doctors confirmed the worst: a stroke had brought the *vozhd* to
death's door. For the first time in many decades, and completely unexpectedly, the USSR was faced with a transfer of power at the highest level.

Like Lenin, Stalin had not anointed a successor or created a legal
mechanism for the orderly transfer of power. Instead he did everything
he could to hinder the emergence of a successor and to instill a sense of
political unworthiness in his associates. By concentrating high-level decision making in his own hands, he ensured that the other members of the
Politburo were poorly informed and had little authority even over those
areas for which they were immediately responsible. Driven by a thirst for
power, political self-centeredness, and senile emotional instability, the
Soviet dictator seemed to display an "Après moi le déluge" attitude toward
the post-Stalinist future.

Thus one can only marvel at the ease with which Stalin's heirs got
through the critical period of the interregnum. There were a number of
reasons why they could do so. One was that even during Stalin's lifetime
his comrades had developed a certain independence and the ability
to work with one another. Each oversaw a particular component of the
party-state apparat. It was not unusual for them to meet without Stalin
to work on specific practical matters of government. One set of administrative entities that met quite regularly were the various executive and
administrative bodies that came under the Council of Ministers. Officially,
Stalin headed these bodies, but he never took part in their day-to-day
work. Furthermore, during his lengthy southern vacations the Politburo
grew accustomed to deliberating without him. Also, the members of the
leadership were united by their common terror of the dictator. Although
there was competition to get closer to him, Stalin's comrades were careful
not to provoke his fury, and they worked to maintain equilibrium within
the leadership group. The Leningrad Affair had shown that no one was
safe. There was an elaborate interplay among the instinct for self-preser-

vation, institutional interests, and the need to fend off threats against the system. Dealing as they did with the day-to-day challenge of keeping the country afloat, Stalin's colleagues were keenly aware of the urgent need for change to which he seemed willfully blind. This awareness led to an informal effort to conceive solutions, whose realization was blocked only by Stalin. Gradually and inexorably, under the shadow of dictatorship, the oligarchic system took embryonic form. It was only a matter of days from the first news of Stalin's fatal illness that the oligarchy emerged as a force.

At 10:40 on the morning of 2 March, an official meeting of the Central Committee Presidium Bureau was convened. It was the first time in many years that a meeting took place in Stalin's Kremlin office without him. In addition to all the members of the Bureau (except for Stalin), the attendees were Molotov, Mikoyan, Nikolai Shvernik (the chairman of the Supreme Soviet), Matvei Shkiriatov (chairman of the Party Control Commission), I. I. Kuperin (head of the Kremlin's health administration), and the neuropathologist R. A. Tkachev. For twenty minutes the group considered one matter: "The finding of the council of physicians concerning the cerebral hemorrhage of Comrade I. V. Stalin that took place on 2 March and the resulting severe state of his health."[1] The Bureau approved the doctors' diagnosis and established a schedule for members of the leadership to keep watch by the *vozhd*'s bedside. The presence of Molotov and Mikoyan, despite their being out of favor with Stalin and formally expelled from the Bureau, is of central importance. Their inclusion was an act of defiance against the *vozhd* and an effort to restore the old collective leadership, as well as a natural and sensible step aimed at maintaining unity in a time of crisis. The Soviet leaders, certain that Stalin would not recover, were undertaking to change the system of supreme power that he had established.

At 8:25 that evening, the same assemblage of newly fledged oligarchs again convened in Stalin's office to consider an official medical update: "On the state of health of Comrade I. V. Stalin as of the evening of 2 March."[2] With every passing hour it became clearer: Stalin had not long to live. The doctor Aleksandr Miasnikov later recalled: "On the morning of the third the council of physicians had to submit an answer to Malenkov's question about the prognosis. The only answer we could give was a negative one: death was inevitable. Malenkov gave us to understand that he expected such a finding, but then stated that he hoped that medical measures could extend his life for a sufficient time, even if they could not save it. We understood that he was referring to the need to allow time to organize a new government and, at the same time, prepare public opinion."[3]

Records indicate that on the morning of 3 March the Soviet leaders were already assuming that Stalin would not recover and planning accordingly. At noon another meeting was held, this time without any doctors, at which a resolution was adopted to report Stalin's illness in the press and to convene a Central Committee plenum.[4] The decision to convene a plenum signaled preparations to transfer power, even while the exact configuration of the new leadership remained an open question. Malenkov and Beria took upon themselves the task of formulating specific proposals. They had plenty of time to do so. The members of the Presidium kept vigil at Stalin's dacha, two at a time. Malenkov and Beria were teamed for this duty, as were Khrushchev and Bulganin. The shifts lasted many hours, and there was time for far-ranging discussion.

The fourth of March marked a turning point. That day's newspapers contained the first official announcement of Stalin's illness. With no hope for a recovery, the only option was to accustom the country and world to the news. The same day, Beria and Malenkov prepared proposals for reorganizing the upper echelons of power that were later discussed by the leadership group, including Molotov and Mikoyan. The 4 March document containing these proposals was confiscated from the safe of Malenkov's assistant in 1956.[5] For now we do not know what the initial draft contained, but we know that it outlined the main decisions that were officially adopted the following day.[6]

Stalin's heirs completely dismantled the governmental structure he had put together during his final months of life. The expanded Central Committee Presidium created on Stalin's orders in October 1952 was abolished with the stroke of a pen. The Central Committee's Presidium Bureau was proclaimed to have a new membership: Molotov and Mikoyan were added, and the young protégés whom Stalin had made part of the expanded Presidium were expelled from its ranks. In essence this upset meant a return, under a new name, to the collective leadership that had once existed as the Politburo. Stalin's title of chairman of the Council of Ministers was given to Malenkov. This title did not mean, however, that Malenkov was recognized as Stalin's heir or that he possessed Stalin's powers. The new system was designed to include numerous counterpoises that would protect against the appearance of a new tyrant. Malenkov, unlike Stalin, did not simultaneously hold the post of Central Committee secretary; that post was given to Khrushchev. The men designated as Malenkov's first deputies—Beria, Molotov, Bulganin, and Kaganovich —were in no way his juniors within the nomenklatura system. This reshuffling created a balance and satisfied the interests of all the members of the top leadership. Later, none of the participants in the reorganization recalled any controversy or rancor.

This new arrangement was formally approved by the oligarchs at a joint meeting of the Central Committee plenum, the Council of Ministers, and the Supreme Soviet Presidium on 5 March 1953. Soviet dignitaries gathered in a hall of the Grand Kremlin Palace. One participant, the writer Konstantin Simonov, left the following description of the ceremony's atmosphere:

> I arrived long before the appointed time, about forty minutes early, but more than half of the participants had already gathered in the hall, and ten minutes later everyone was there. Maybe two or three people arrived less than a half hour before the start. There were several hundred people there, almost all acquainted with one another . . . sitting in total silence and waiting for the start. We were sitting side by side, shoulder to shoulder; we saw one another, but nobody said a word to anyone else. . . . Until the very start it was so quiet in the hall that if I had not sat in that silence for forty minutes myself, I would never have believed that three hundred people sitting so tightly packed could keep quiet like that.[7]

Finally the members of the presidium that was about to be voted into existence appeared. The entire event lasted forty minutes, from 8:00 to 8:40 p.m. The resolutions that the top leadership had already agreed on were, as usual, obediently approved. The Stalin factor was dealt with simply and elegantly. He was deprived of the top posts of chairman of the government and secretary of the Central Committee and then formally included in the Central Committee Presidium. From now on, whatever his physical fate, Stalin's political future and his comrades' liberation from his tyrannical powers were faits accomplis. As Simonov remarked, "There was a sense that right there, in the Presidium, people were freed from something that had been weighing them down, that had bound them."[8]

Stalin endured this formal deprivation of power for only one hour. At 9:50 p.m. he died. His death was agonizing, as if in confirmation of the folk wisdom that only the righteous are granted an easy death. His daughter Svetlana, who spent her father's final days by his side, recalled:

> The death agony was horrible. He literally choked to death as we watched. At what seemed like the very last moment he suddenly

opened his eyes and cast a glance over everyone in the room. It was a terrible glance, insane or perhaps angry and full of the fear of death and the unfamiliar faces of the doctors bent over him. The glance swept over everyone in a second. Then something incomprehensible and awesome happened that to this day I can't forget and don't understand. He suddenly lifted his left hand as though he were pointing to something above and bringing down a curse on us all. The gesture was incomprehensible and full of menace, and no one could say to whom or at what it might be directed. The next moment, after a final effort, the spirit wrenched itself free of the flesh.[9]

Stalin's comrades did not linger at his bedside. A half-hour later, at 10:25 p.m., they were already back in his Kremlin office, several kilometers away.[10] All the main matters of state had been resolved. What remained were the funeral arrangements. The new leaders created a commission to handle these arrangements and appointed Khrushchev to head it. They also adopted a decision to place the sarcophagus with Stalin's embalmed body in Lenin's mausoleum. State security and the propaganda apparat were given their orders. The editor-in-chief of *Pravda,* Dmitry Shepilov, spent ten minutes at this meeting. One deeply symbolic detail impressed him the most: "The chair Stalin had occupied as chairman for thirty years was empty; nobody sat in it."[11]

For a while, the Soviet leaders were genuinely equal and united in their determination to prevent the emergence of another tyrant. After what they had endured under Stalin, they were ready to do away with the system of terror, even if that entailed some undesirable political consequences. By 3 April 1953, after the appropriate preparations, the Central Committee Presidium resolved to "fully rehabilitate and release from custody the doctors and members of their families arrested in association with the so-called Case of the Wrecker-Doctors." Thirty-seven people were freed. The state security officers who "particularly applied themselves in the fabrication of this provocational case" were to be brought to justice.[12] The next day this resolution was announced in the newspapers, occasioning a variety of responses and a certain consternation among the *vozhd*'s most ardent supporters. Other political cases in which the collective leadership had a personal interest were quietly subjected to a quick review. Molotov's wife was released from prison. Kaganovich's brother, who had taken his own life on the eve of the war after charges of wrecking, was pronounced innocent. The Mingrelian Affair, which had cast a shadow on Beria's reputation, was also reviewed. Many other prominent victims of political repression were set free or posthumously rehabilitated. After taking care of their own, Stalin's heirs began to grant relative freedom to the rest of the country. They were driven in this direction not only by conscience, but also by the growing crisis that had already been apparent under Stalin. The death of the man who had been unwilling to entertain any talk of change opened the door to reforms to be implemented with amazing speed and decisiveness.

Two pillars of the dictatorship—state security and the Gulag—were significantly reformed. One symbol of this reform was a Ministry of Internal Affairs order, dated 4 April 1953, banning the use of torture against arrestees. The order recognized the problem of "arrests of innocent Soviet citizens" and "the widespread use of various means of torture: the brutal beating of arrestees; the round-the-clock use of handcuffs behind the back, in isolated cases for several months; long-term sleep deprivation; and locking up unclothed arrestees in cold punishment cells, etc." Threatening harsh punishment of anyone who violated the order, the ministry's leadership demanded that torture chambers be closed in prisons and that the implements of torture be destroyed.[13] When the order was read out loud to all state security operatives, it must have made quite an impression. These reforms continued into the spring and summer of 1953, bringing major changes to the camp system. A mass amnesty announced for those convicted of non-political crimes cut the inmate population in half. Many factories and construction projects that were still using a prisoner work force and being overseen by the ministry were shut down or transferred to the economic ministries.[14] A large-scale effort to rehabilitate the victims of Stalinist terror lay in the near future.

Significant changes to economic policy were made within weeks. Unwieldy construction projects were scaled down, and the rush to "build communism" and expand Soviet military capabilities that was putting such a strain on the economy was brought to a halt. The resources thus freed up were directed toward alleviating the crisis in agriculture and meeting the needs of ordinary citizens. The prices paid for agricultural products were raised, and the tax burden on peasants was reduced. A marked improvement in output, especially in the area of livestock, came with amazing speed.[15] Soon there would be ambitious programs to ease the plight of ordinary citizens, including a massive effort to expand housing.

Domestic reforms were accompanied by a moderation of foreign policy. On 19 March 1953 the Council of Ministers passed a resolution calling for "an end to the war in Korea as soon as possible."[16] After tense negotiations, an armistice treaty was signed on 27 July 1953. Moscow gave its blessing to a liberalization of Communist regimes in Eastern Europe. On 2 June 1953 a Council of Ministers directive spelled out Soviet objections to the policies of the East German government and called for measures to improve the republic's political situation.[17]

In short, Stalin's "ungrateful" heirs had little trouble eliminating many of the excesses for which the *vozhd* bore sole responsibility. Their reforms fundamentally changed the Soviet regime. It was no longer "Stalinist"; it was less brutal and more predictable and flexible. Dictatorship, as a form of government in the Soviet Union, had been dealt a blow from which it never recovered. Internal struggles at the upper reaches of government would more than once lead to power changing hands, but never again would a Soviet leader wield the sole power exercised by Stalin.

THE FUNERAL

The *Vozhd*, the System, and the People

For three days beginning on 6 March 1953, the Soviet Union said its ceremonial farewells to Joseph Stalin. His coffin was put on display in the very center of Moscow, in the House of Unions' Hall of Columns, the traditional site for public mourning of Soviet leaders that had earlier served as the House of Receptions for Moscow's nobility. At four o'clock on the afternoon of the sixth, the public was let in to pay its final respects. The viewing of the body was poorly organized, and the provisions made for the crush of people who headed toward the House of Unions were not conducive to public safety. Those trying to get one last look at the dictator streamed into narrow streets filled with police and trucks meant to serve as barriers. In the chaos and panic many suffered disabling injuries or were crushed to death. The files of investigations into these events have yet to be made accessible to historians. In remarks made to a small gathering in 1962, Khrushchev said that 109 people in the crowd died that day.[1]

No information about this addition to the long series of Soviet tragedies appeared in newspapers, which were filled with grandiloquent expressions of sorrow and grief for the late *vozhd*. People's true feelings came out in a flood of letters, as eyewitnesses to the tragedy registered their complaints with various government offices:

> This is not the first time that during the movement of a large crowd the police were transformed into a helpless organization, or rather into violators of order. How distressing it was when—in front of a crowd of hundreds and foreigners darting about with their cameras—they began to retrieve the injured and crushed and send them off in ambulances. A simply shocking scene.[2]

> For five hours people were herded all over Moscow, and none of the police knew where the line was! The police were running into columns made up of many thousands of people, with their cars causing casualties, cries, and groans. Hundreds of thousands of people were walking around the blocked-off streets leading to the Hall of Columns and could not find the way in! . . . Only a wrecker could announce that access would begin at four but announce the route at nine.[3]

In many ways these letters captured the essence of the Stalin era, both in their lexicon—with references to foreigners "darting about with their cameras" and "wreckers"—and in the events they describe: the police turning into violators of public order. Relying on brute force, the dictatorship had attained its goals at the expense of countless victims. The boundary between rational order and destructive chaos was blurred. Those charged with maintaining order wound up wreaking havoc.

Perhaps the tragedy in Moscow forced Stalin's heirs to ponder the police state's shortcomings, but for now they had no option but to rely on the institutions and methods bequeathed to them. Stalin's funeral, set for 9 March, was prepared much as the viewing in state had been, but possibly with a bit more care. The top priority was security, ensured by 22,600 secret police agents, policemen, and soldiers. Thirty-five hundred vehicles were commissioned to block streets.[4] The government approved a minute-by-minute schedule of funeral events: the carrying of the coffin from the House of Unions, its placement in front of the Lenin Mausoleum in Red Square, a mourning gathering for the public, the carrying of the coffin into the mausoleum. Several hours before the ceremony, six thousand soldiers and fifteen thousand members of a "delegation of workers" were brought to Red Square.[5] This time everything went according to plan.

Although incompetent officials bear much responsibility for the casualties in Moscow, another cause of the tragedy was the sheer number of people wanting to catch one last glimpse of the *vozhd*. What drove them? Was it love, curiosity, mass psychosis, or a rare opportunity for a spontaneous display of emotion? Apparently all these elements were present, along with many others. The few available documents that shed light on the public mood reveal a complex range of responses to the *vozhd*'s illness and death. On 5 March 1953, State Security Minister Ignatiev presented the Soviet leadership with a report on soldiers' reactions to the news that Stalin was ill. The document described a certain pattern in the reaction of the "faithful." One common thread was sympathy toward Stalin the man, who, according to Soviet propaganda, was the embodiment of goodness and benevolence: "My family takes this news as a terrible sorrow befalling our country"; "He worked very hard, and that took a toll on his health." "Positive" responses often involved expressions of concern over the future of the country and the responder's own future. Two points long emphasized by Soviet propaganda played a part in such positive responses: Stalin was irreplaceable and war was looming: "It's kind of scary. Who will take his place after his death?"; "Maybe this will speed up the onset of a

Third World War." The chekists also reported on "negative" and "hostile" statements: "Serves him right"; "That's just fine"; "Stalin won't hang on for long, and that's even better. You'll see that everything will immediately change."[6] All such letters led to arrests or at least an investigation.

March 1953 saw a surge in arrests and convictions of people charged with "anti-Soviet agitation" for expressing satisfaction with Stalin's death or otherwise denigrating him. A forty-four-year-old Muscovite named S. M. Telenkov, who worked at a scientific institute, drunkenly proclaimed in a commuter train, "What a fine day it is today; today we buried Stalin. There'll be one less scoundrel around and now we can get back to living." R. S. Rybalko, a twenty-eight-year-old working-class woman from Rostov Oblast, was convicted of using profanity in regard to Stalin. Ya. I. Peit, who had been forcibly resettled in Kazakhstan, was sentenced for destroying and stomping on a portrait of Stalin after an official mourning ceremony. Upon hearing of Stalin's death, P. K. Karpets, a thirty-two-year-old railroad worker from the Ukrainian city of Rovno, swore and exclaimed, "Smell that? The corpse is already stinking." Ye. G. Gridneva, a forty-eight-year-old female railroad worker from Transcaucasia, was not able to contain herself and commented to a coworker, "A dog dies a dog's death. It's good that he died. There won't be any kolkhozes and life will be a little easier."[7]

The expressions of anti-Stalin sentiment that came to secret police attention were just the tip of the iceberg. Most people had been trained to keep their opinions to themselves. The ubiquity of informants and the habit of fear kept free expression to a minimum, to say nothing of more demonstrative forms of protest. The choice was simple: either accept—or pretend to accept—official values or find yourself in a camp or face to face with an executioner. This circumstance diminishes the value of such normally candid sources as diaries. One must assume that even in the privacy of their own homes, Soviet citizens exercised self-censorship and used their diaries more as potential alibis than vehicles for frankness. Newspaper reports on mass demonstrations, summaries prepared by state security on the public mood, and letters written to the authorities by ordinary citizens provide only part of the picture. Furthermore, many of these documents are still hidden in closed archives. Historians attempting to fathom the public mood during the Stalin era still face major obstacles.

The 190 million people living in Stalin's Soviet Union on the eve of his death constituted an exceptionally complex community that bore little resemblance to the "New Man" featured on the covers of Soviet magazines.[8] Many factors worked to give cohesion to Soviet society and promote support for the regime, and the motives for this support could vary from sincere enthusiasm to reconciliation with the inevitable to ordinary submission in the face of overwhelming power. The huge scale of violence and terror made fear and compulsion the backbone of the Stalinist system, albeit hidden behind a façade of enthusiasm. At the same time, loyalty and belief in the system and the man were not always feigned. The perpetual fear that was the primary instrument for unifying the people and suppressing independent thought was used alongside "positive" mechanisms of social manipulation. Both the carrot and the stick were applied to keep Soviet society moving in the desired direction.

One by-product of the regime's policies was the creation of a large privileged class of officials. Those holding all but the most junior government or party posts enjoyed many benefits, including high social status and significant material perquisites. After the mass purges of the second half of the 1930s, the ranks of the Soviet nomenklatura stabilized. Repression against officials during the postwar period was more the exception than the rule. Furthermore, there is evidence that on the eve of Stalin's death, officials and their relatives were essentially immune from prosecution. The requirement that any arrest or prosecution of a party member be approved by the leadership of party committees led to a bifurcation of the judicial system. In many cases members of the nomenklatura and their relatives avoided prosecution for administrative or criminal offenses that would bring severe punishment to an ordinary citizen.[9]

Another category—"the country's best people"—approached the status of officials within the huge party-state apparat. These "best people" could be found in every social segment and professional group, including workers, peasants, writers, artists, and scientists. The best known examples were the so-called Stakhanovites, real or imagined shock workers at the forefront of production who were held up for admiration as "beacons" of the Soviet spirit. Enjoying a stature somewhere between ordinary citizens and officials, the Stakhanovites quickly assimilated the latter's value system, although in theory they kept working away as before. They served as spokespeople, lobbying for the interests of enterprises and regions and enjoying significant material privileges. A typical representative of this category of beneficiary of the Stalinist system was the eponymous miner Aleksei Stakhanov, who earned celebrity and Stalin's favor through his record-breaking productivity. He quickly developed a taste for the nomenklatura lifestyle and bombarded Stalin with requests:

Joseph Vissarionovich! Give me a nice car and I will justify your trust. Soon the Stakhanovite movement will be ten years old, and I'm going to Donbas and will again show people how to work. I keep asking and they keep giving me some broken down war trophy clunker, but if just once I got something nice, I'd stop asking. . . . Also, about the apartment. . . . I can't get anywhere with my requests to fix it up. The walls are dirty, the furniture is frayed and broken . . . , while other people get their walls papered with silk twice a month and get all sorts of furniture. This isn't correct, so I'm asking for a renovation and new furniture so I won't be ashamed to invite people to my apartment.[10]

Another consequence of the channeling of benefits to the upper crust of Soviet society was the policy of disproportionately allotting resources to cities, especially major ones. Forced industrialization and militarization widened the gulf in living standards and social status between the rural majority and urban minority.[11] Many urbanites, especially in the capitals and major industrial centers, belonged to a relatively privileged and well-remunerated class. During years of famine they may have been hungry, but since they received a government ration, they were not dying of starvation like the peasantry. They had internal passports, unlike the peasants, and relative freedom of movement. Urban populations also enjoyed better health care and a well-developed cultural and educational infrastructure. In the stores of Moscow and Leningrad, where most food and consumer goods were sent, shoppers could find what they needed and even had a degree of choice.[12] The relative accessibility of educational institutions and high-paying jobs gave urbanites much better economic prospects. The monetary reform, which reduced prices in state stores while increasing taxes on peasant production, disproportionately favored the residents of capitals and industrial centers. These measures forced peasants to sell the products of their private plots at lower prices in urban markets. The consequences of these policies apparently escaped Stalin's awareness. Mikoyan, whose duties placed him in charge of certain commercial matters, offers the following account:

I told him [Stalin] that we could not lower the prices on meat and butter, on white bread, first of all because they were in short supply and second because it would affect the procurement prices, which would have a negative effect on the production of these products, and when these goods are in short supply and with this reduction in prices there would be huge lines, which would lead to profiteering; after all, workers cannot go to the store during the day, so the profiteers would buy up all the goods. . . . But Stalin insisted, saying that this was necessary in the interests of the intelligentsia.[13]

Mikoyan here nicely sums up the predictable effect of the politically motivated price reduction: shortages, lines, and a shadow market. But these were of little concern to Stalin. His focus was on the regime's bulwark, the privileged segment of society in major cities. The government's preferential distribution of resources made even the average urbanite many times better off than the rural population. One symptom of this inequality was the number of young rural women streaming into cities to work as housekeepers for urban families for no more than bread and shelter. Clearly, the urban minority and the rural majority had starkly divergent perceptions of reality. It was the urbanite viewpoint that found voice in memoirs and diaries and has disproportionately influenced contemporary understandings of day-to-day life under Stalin.

Another factor that led Soviet society to tolerate and even support the dictatorship was war. Memories of the horrors of the world and civil wars, the victory over the Nazis (paid for with 27 million lives), and the fear of a third world war all had a huge impact on perceptions—and not only in the Soviet Union. Stalin enjoyed the image of a savior who had delivered the world from a terrible evil. For decades afterward, the 1945 victory lent legitimacy to the Stalinist regime and those of his successors.[14]

The list of historical circumstances that enabled the Stalinist system to endure could be continued, but even in conjunction with an ever-vigilant apparatus of repression they could not completely hide the contradictions inherent in Soviet society or suppress widespread dissatisfaction. From the moment they came to power as a radical revolutionary party, the Bolsheviks relied on a strategy of dividing society and suppressing the fraction that, for reasons of class origin or societal role, was considered hostile to socialism. This strategy included killing off the members of the hostile groups.[15] The Stalinist revolution devoted tremendous resources to purging society of these "elements." Furthermore, along with the nobility, bourgeoisie, tsarist officers and officials, and anyone else proclaimed persona non grata after 1917, the largest segment of the population was stigmatized: the peasantry. During collectivization, many peasants were branded kulaks and shot, exiled, or driven out of their native villages. Millions of people from every sector were persecuted on a variety of pretexts and put into the camp system or simply killed. Aware that these measures had earned the dictatorship true enemies, Stalin intensified his preemptive purges, most notably during the Great Terror of 1937–1938. Repression begat repression. By the end of his rule a significant proportion, if not the majority, of Soviet citizens had at one time or another been arrested, imprisoned in a camp, forcibly relocated, or subjected to some softer form of mistreatment.

The regime's victims did not necessarily turn into conscious opponents. Terror often had the opposite effect. Intimidation made people more governable and submissive and forced them to demonstrate their loyalty. But it would be wrong to assume that submission was the only possible reaction. The historical record attests to the existence of widespread anti-government feelings or even active forms of resistance. For understandable reasons resistance was most common when the dictatorship was first being consolidated—most notably peasant revolts during collectivization in 1930 and its aftermath.[16] The Terror and the stabilization of the system sharply curtailed opportunities for overt action, especially on a large scale. But it is important to note that access to secret police archives, which would reflect the true state of affairs in the late Stalin era, is extremely limited. We may learn that our image of the 1940s generation as silent and submissive is misinformed.

A root cause of widespread dissatisfaction was the Soviet Union's low standard of living.[17] Agriculture, its productivity severely undermined by collectivization, lurched between crisis and stagnation. Almost every year, the Stalinist government acknowledged that famine or "food difficulties" affected either a large swath of the country, as in 1931–1933 and 1946–1947, or some particular regions. Even in the best years the average diet was meager. Most people lived primarily on grains and potatoes. Budgetary studies conducted on the eve of Stalin's death, during the relatively prosperous year 1952, established the following daily nutritional intake in worker and peasant families: the average Soviet citizen consumed approximately 500 grams of flour products (primarily bread), a small amount of cereals, 400–600 grams of potato, and approximately 200–400 grams of milk or milk products. These items accounted for the bulk of the typical diet. Anything else, especially meat, was a special occasion. The figure for per capita consumption of meat and meat products averaged 40–70 grams per day and 15–20 grams of fat (animal or plant oils, margarine, or fatback). A few teaspoons of sugar and a bit of fish completed the picture. Average citizens could permit themselves an average of one egg every six days. These rations are approximately equal to the dietary norm for prison camps.[18] The figures were produced by the Central Statistical Directorate, which was under constant political pressure and probably painted an overly rosy picture. Averages could be inflated, for example, by selecting workers at the high end of the pay spectrum or peasants from relatively prosperous kolkhozes in the study. Also, the budgetary studies did not factor in the often poor quality of the food. A resident of Chernigov Oblast wrote to Stalin in November 1952, "Now they are baking black bread, and even that is of poor quality. It is impossible to eat such bread, especially for people in poor health."[19]

The supply of manufactured goods was just as bad. Prices of factory-made items were traditionally kept exceptionally high. People had to settle for simple, relatively cheap products, but few could afford even these. For example, in 1952 only one out of every four peasants could afford leather footwear.[20] Some lacked even the simplest footwear and clothing. As one resident of a village in Tambov Oblast wrote to Stalin in December 1952, "In our kolkhoz the kolkhozniks have one article of winter clothing for 3–4 family members, and children in 60 percent of the population cannot go to school since they don't have the clothing."[21]

For the majority of the population the housing situation was no better. Under Stalin, housing was the chronically underfunded stepchild that received whatever resources were left after priority items had been taken care of. For years the housing shortage grew continually worse—and then came the devastation of war. As of the beginning of 1953 there was an average of 4.5 square meters of residential housing per urban resident.[22] When temporary residents and those without official registration were taken into account, this ratio grew even worse. The quality of housing was also low. Only 46 percent of state-owned residential space came equipped with running water, 41 percent with sewage hookups, 26 percent with central heating, 3 percent with hot water, and 13 percent with a bathtub.[23] Even these figures reflected the higher standards found in major cities, chiefly the two capitals. A striking indicator of the housing crisis was the prevalence of urban "barracks"—flimsy temporary communal housing without plumbing—and the increasing number of people registering such barracks as their residences. In 1945 approximately 2.8 million people lived in urban barracks, but by 1952 the number had grown to 3.8 million. More than 337,000 people in Moscow lived in barracks.[24]

Another source of hardship for the Soviet people was the exceptionally difficult working conditions in industry and agriculture. The poorly developed system of material incentives led to widespread coercion in the workplace. The use of slave labor was of course most blatant within the Gulag system, but supposedly free industrial and agricultural workers also often toiled under compulsion. The workforce for certain industries, especially the most poorly paid and dangerous, was assembled by pressing young people into service through compulsory mobilization. Evasion was punishable by a term in a labor camp. Beginning in 1940, emergency labor laws were used to bind workers to their places of employment. Peasants, who were essentially not paid for their work in kolkhozes, were prosecuted for failure to fulfill their work quotas. Between 1940 and 1952 approximately 17 million people were convicted of tardiness, leaving their place of employment without permission, or evading mobilization.[25] This huge number, which fails to capture the extent of violations of workplace discipline, belies the propagandists' exultation of Soviet workers' selfless enthusiasm.

Between the two extremes of devotion and opposition to the regime, the vast majority made empty shows of loyalty but were largely indifferent to politics. Only marginally influenced by propaganda and trying their best to evade the grip of repression, most took comfort in tradition and ritual. Despite state repression of priests and active church members, especially in the 1930s, most Soviet citizens held onto their faith. During the census of January 1937, 57 percent of respondents over the age of sixteen identified themselves as religious—more than 55 million people. Surely many others hid their faith out of fear of persecution.[26]

In the area of inter-ethnic relations, Stalin left a problematic legacy. The relative liberalism of the early Bolshevik regime, which built what historian Terry Martin calls an "affirmative action empire," came to an end in the early 1930s.[27] Under Stalin, nationalities policy grew increasingly brutal. Mass arrests and executions based on nationality, the internal exile of entire peoples, and the effort to use russification to create a single Soviet nationality laid a minefield under the country's future.[28] Explosions started to go off while Stalin was still alive, when guerrilla wars roiled western Ukraine and the Baltic states. Although a degree of inter-ethnic unity was actually achieved, behind the propaganda façade extolling the "friendship of peoples" seethed many inter-ethnic conflicts.[29] The "Russian question" that grew out of the contradictory position of the Russian majority—simultaneously the bulwark of the Soviet empire and one of its chief victims—promoted instability and ultimately destroyed the Soviet Union, an interpretation advanced by Geoffrey Hosking.[30]

What did Stalin know about the real life of "his" people? The Albanian

Communist leader Enver Hoxha visited Moscow in 1947 and later recalled Stalin saying, "To govern, you have to know the masses, and in order to know them, you have to walk among them."[31] Stalin could hardly claim to adhere to his own wisdom. After his famous visit to Siberia in 1928, most of which was spent meeting with functionaries, he almost never walked "among the masses." Official meetings with representatives of the workers were carefully orchestrated propaganda spectacles. During better days, Stalin would occasionally indulge his taste for theatrics and suddenly appear in public. But even these spontaneous meetings inevitably took on the aura of "Christ appearing to the people." In September 1935, accompanied by several Soviet leaders, he toured the outskirts of Sochi and encountered small groups of vacationers. On Stalin's initiative a spontaneous "fraternization" was allowed. One vacationer left a striking account of the event:

> Comrade Stalin . . . stopped us with the following words: "Why are you leaving comrades? Why are you so proud that you shun our company? Come here. Where are you from?" We walked up to him. . . . "Well, let's get acquainted," Comrade Stalin said, and he introduced us to each of his companions in turn and introduced himself as well. "This is Comrade Kalinin, this is the wife of Comrade Molotov . . . and this is I, Stalin," he said, shaking everyone's hand. "Now we'll all have our pictures taken together," and Comrade Stalin invited us to stand next to him. . . . While the photographers were working, Comrade Stalin kept making fun of them: he said they were "mortal enemies" and were always trying to interfere with one another. He asked that they photograph not only him but "all the people." . . . Then Comrade Stalin began to invite the woman selling apples from a kiosk . . . and a salesman from the food stand to come have their pictures taken. It took a long time before the disconcerted saleswoman could be persuaded to leave her store. Comrade Stalin told her that "it's not good to be so proud" and told the photographers not to take the picture until she came. "The saleswoman," Stalin proclaimed, "should become the most respected woman in our country." Finally she came and the photo shoot continued. An empty bus drove up, and Comrade Stalin invited the driver and conductor to have their pictures taken.[32]

Obviously such "walks among the people" did little to enhance Stalin's understanding of them, and even these mostly stopped after the 1930s. The *vozhd* never took an interest in seeing the conditions in which the

Soviet people were living, what they bought and where, what sort of health care or education they received. His knowledge of "the masses" came mostly from what he read in his office. So far we know of two main sources from which he gleaned knowledge of daily life: summary reports from state security about the public mood and letters and complaints from ordinary citizens. A steady stream of such letters arrived in government offices, including some addressed to him personally.

As far as can be determined from archival studies, state security summaries were a major source of information for the Soviet leadership in the 1920s and 1930s. These reports contained rather candid assessments of the situation in the country, albeit from a chekist perspective, which saw almost all crises and difficulties as the work of enemies. There were a number of types of reports, some providing an overview of sociopolitical processes, others devoted to matters of economics or politics. One problematic aspect of these reports was their length. The leaders for whom they were prepared had to spend hours poring over them. In recent years historians have published a number of informational state security summaries dating to the prewar period.[33] These publications, however, are based on copies found in state security archives—not in Stalin's personal archive. We do not currently know the extent to which, or in what form, they are contained in the Politburo archive, which is part of the Archive of the President of the Russian Federation. Historians therefore cannot be sure to what extent the leadership in general or Stalin in particular read these secret police summaries. There is evidence to suggest that they were mostly unaware of these reports' contents.

We know more about Stalin's familiarity with letters from Soviet citizens. It would not be an exaggeration to say that most of the country sent complaints, requests, and petitions on a wide array of topics to all sorts of government offices. Such letter writing was an extremely common practice and was even encouraged by the authorities. Within the highly centralized system, letters to the government were one of the few ways of solving everyday problems. The government was virtually the only employer. It also had authority over the allocation or construction of housing. Government stores supplied (or were supposed to supply) all basic needs. Government hospitals were the only places to obtain treatment for serious illnesses. The government determined the rather narrow category of people eligible for pensions or benefits and the size of the payments. Given the flaws of the Soviet judicial system, citizens turned to bureaucrats to resolve conflicts and disputes. Abuses by officials within the huge bureaucratic apparat occasioned countless grievances. Arrests, forcible relocations, imprisonments in camps, or death sentences against tens of millions of people generated millions of complaints and pleas for relief. Arrestees themselves wrote, as did their relatives, and even unrelated people sometimes worked up the courage to intercede on behalf of an acquaintance or colleague. This pursuit of justice was encouraged by the state since it created the illusion of impartial leadership.

Another practice that was encouraged was denouncing abuses or "enemy activity." Stalin made it no secret that he held denouncers and informers in high regard. All denunciations, including anonymous ones, were investigated. The government's attitude is eloquently illustrated by the fact that even prisoners who were deprived of all other rights had the right to submit denunciations. In February 1936 the NKVD chief signed an order calling for the installation of boxes in all camps, prisons, and penal colonies into which inmates could insert statements addressed to him personally or the head of the Gulag directorate. "The boxes shall be sealed with the seal of the Directorate of Camps," the order read, "and only the head of the camp or his deputy (in camps) and the head of the Department of Detention Centers or his deputy (in prisons and penal colonies) shall open them." All correspondence was to be sent to the NKVD chief personally and "under no circumstance concealed." Inmates were to be informed of "the purpose of these boxes."[34]

Taking advantage of the regime's eagerness to uncover enemies and the almost total impunity enjoyed by slanderers, many Soviet citizens used denunciations to game the system. Informers used the government to attain their own mercenary objectives—to settle scores, get rid of annoying neighbors sharing the same communal apartment, or eliminate those competing for the same job. For the hapless multitudes at the bottom of the societal hierarchy, denunciations were the only means of taking revenge against powerful officials. The state implicitly encouraged people to use this disgraceful means of fighting for their rights.

In addition to complaints and denunciations, the archives abound with "helpful" letters. Some offered ideas for reorganizing government agencies or for various socioeconomic innovations; some offered ideas for renaming cities or creating new holidays or ceremonies; others sought to correct "errors" in the press. Writing such letters was one of the few outlets for activism available to ordinary citizens. These letters may have contained an element of self-promotion as their authors tried to draw the top leadership's attention to themselves.

As the supreme authority, Stalin, of course, was all these correspondents' prime addressee. It is hard to know the precise number of letters addressed to him personally, but it apparently exceeded several hundred thousand per year.[35] Obviously not all of them reached his desk; he was shown a selected sample. The nature of this sample is of interest from a number of perspectives. Primarily, it shows how well informed Stalin was about people's lives and tells us what he expressed an interest in seeing. No doubt the apparat was given criteria for selecting the letters he would be shown.

Handling letters addressed to Stalin was a complicated bureaucratic process. Within the Central Committee's Special Sector, which served as Stalin's personal secretariat, was a division dedicated to processing his mail. After the war this division was called the Special Sector's "Fifth Section." In early 1950 it had a staff of twenty.[36] They received and logged letters addressed to Stalin and immediately forwarded a significant portion of them to various agencies for review. The heads of the Special Sector, especially Stalin's personal assistant, Aleksandr Poskrebyshev, were shown the most important and interesting letters.[37] Poskrebyshev further filtered them, leaving just a few of the most interesting for his boss. As a result of this tiered system, Stalin saw just a tiny percentage of the hundreds of thousands of letters sent to him, and over time this number shrank. In early 1946 Stalin saw about ten letters per month, but by 1952 he was shown just one or two.[38]

This small sample revealed little about real life in the Soviet Union. Most of the letters reaching Stalin's desk belonged to one of three categories: queries on matters of theory, letters from old acquaintances, and a large number of letters of support. On extremely rare occasions he might be shown correspondence that tiptoed around some unsavory aspect of Soviet reality. Overall, the letters he saw reflected the *vozhd*'s growing desire to live in the past or savor hopes for the future. Pressing matters of real consequence likely to provoke negative emotions were avoided.

As ignorant of the life of the people as the *vozhd* was, the people knew even less what kind of a man he was. Partly due to his personality and partly out of calculation, Stalin, unlike many other dictators, rarely spoke before large audiences. He preferred to express himself in writing. The aggressive propaganda of Stalin's articles, interviews, and theoretical works created the impression that the invisible *vozhd* was ever-present and all-knowing. His cryptic sententiousness gave him a certain charisma.

Tight control over the alchemy of official "Staliniana" has created false and doubly majestic images of Stalin and his accomplishments.[39] These images outlive the man himself and have an appeal even in contemporary Russia. The collapse of the Soviet Union, the stresses of the transitional period, corruption, poverty, and glaring social inequality all feed the longing for a social utopia. A significant portion of Russian society seeks recipes for the present by looking to the Stalinist past. Popular images of the greatness of the Stalinist empire—of equality and the fight against corruption, of the joy and purity of this distant life undone by "enemies"— are exploited by unscrupulous commentators and politicians. How great is the danger that a blend of historical ignorance, bitterness, and social discontent will provide fertile ground for pro-Stalinist lies and distortions to take root?

Could it really be that Russia in the twenty-first century is in danger of repeating the mistakes of the twentieth?

ΠΟΤΕS

Preface

1. Adam. B. Ulam, *Stalin: The Man and His Era* (New York, 1973); Robert C. Tucker: *Stalin as Revolutionary, 1879–1929: A Study in History and Personality* (New York, 1973), and *Stalin in Power: The Revolution from Above, 1928–1941* (New York, 1990).

2. Robert Service, *Stalin: A Biography* (London, 2004); Hiroaki Kuromiya, *Stalin: Profiles in Power* (New York, 2005); Sarah Davies and James Harris, eds., *Stalin: A New History* (New York, 2005); Miklos Kun, *Stalin: An Unknown Portrait* (Budapest and New York, 2003); Ronald Grigor Suny, *Stalin and the Russian Revolutionary Movement: From Koba to Commissar* (forthcoming from Oxford University Press). Concerning Stalin the dictator and his relations with the rest of the Soviet leadership, see Oleg V. Khlevniuk, *Master of the House: Stalin and His Inner Circle* (New Haven and London, 2008), and Yoram Gorlizki and Oleg Khlevniuk, *Cold Peace: Stalin and the Soviet Ruling Circle, 1945–1953* (New York, 2004). Some works have attempted to peer into Stalin's inner world: A. J. Rieber, "Stalin, Man of the Borderlands," *American Historical Review* 106, no. 4 (2001): 1651–1691; Erik van Ree, *The Political Thought of Joseph Stalin: A Study in Twentieth-Century Revolutionary Patriotism* (London and New York, 2002); B. S. Ilizarov, *Tainaia zhizn' Stalina* (Moscow, 2002); Donald Rayfield, *Stalin and His Hangmen: The Tyrant and Those Who Killed for Him* (New York, 2005). Many works on the Terror and the Gulag have added to our understanding of Stalin's personal role in organizing mass repression: Jonathan Brent and Vladimir Naumov, *Stalin's Last Crime: The Plot against the Jewish Doctors, 1948–1953* (New York, 2003); V. N. Khaustov and L. Samuel'son, *Stalin, NKVD i repressii. 1936–1938* (Moscow, 2009); Jörg Baberowski, *Verbrannte Erde: Stalins Herrschaft der Gewalt* (Munich, 2012). Despite copious literature on World War II, Stalin's role as supreme commander in chief has yet to be adequately investigated. An analogous lacuna exists in regard to the Cold War and Stalin's handling of foreign policy.

3. Dmitri Volkogonov, *Stalin: Triumph and Tragedy* (New York, 1991); Edvard Radzinsky, *Stalin: The First In-Depth Biography Based on Explosive New Documents from Russia's Secret Archives* (New York, 1997); Simon Sebag Montefiore: *Stalin: The Court of the Red Tsar* (London, 2003), and *Young Stalin* (London, 2007).

4. Collections of letters have been published as part of the Annals of Communism Series: Lars T. Lih, Oleg V. Naumov, and Oleg Khlevniuk, eds., *Stalin's Letters to Molotov, 1925–1936* (New Haven, 1995), and R. W. Davies et al., eds., *The Stalin-Kaganovich Correspondence, 1931–1936* (New Haven and London, 2003).

5. A. A. Chernobaev, ed., *Na prieme u Stalina. Tetradi (zhurnaly) zapisei lits, priniatykh I. V. Stalinym (1924–1953 gg.)* (Moscow, 2008).

6. S. V. Deviatov et al., *Moskovskii Kreml' v gody Velikoi Otechestvennoi Voiny* (Moscow, 2010), pp. 113–114.

7. RGASPI, f. 558, op. 1–11. (An *opis'* [op.] is the equivalent of a drawer in a filing cabinet.) Opis' 11 comprises Stalin's personal archive, brought to RGASPI from the Presidential Archive of the Russian Federation (the former Politburo Archive).

8. "Thematic" folders *(tematicheskie papki)* are subject-specific folders of documents that were submitted to the Politburo and Stalin; they comprise the main historical component of the Presidential Archive.

9. Sergei Khrushchev, ed.: *Memoirs of Nikita Khrushchev,* vol. 1: *Commissar* (University Park, PA, 2004); *Memoirs of Nikita Khrushchev,* vol. 2: *Reformer* (University Park, PA, 2006); and *Memoirs of Nikita Khrushchev,* vol. 3: *Statesman* (University Park, PA, 2007); A. I. Mikoian, *Tak bylo. Razmyshleniia o minuvshem* (Moscow, 1999); Anastas Ivanovich Mikoyan, *The Memoirs of Anastas Mikoyan* (Madison, CT, 1988).

10. In a splendid review published soon after Mikoyan's memoirs came out in Russian, Michael Ellman convincingly argued that Mikoyan's text had been altered (Michael Ellman, "The Road from Il'ich to Il'ich," *Slavic Review* 60, no. 1 [2001]: 141). In a response, Mikoyan's son Sergo categorically stated, "I did not 'correct' my father's stories" (*Slavic Review,* 60, no. 4 [2001]: 917). This vague formulation came with an important subtext. Sergo Mikoyan was not saying that he did not alter the dictated manuscript, leaving open the possibility that he did supplement the initial transcript of his father's dictation with subsequent accounts by the elder Mikoyan that were not "correct." Clearly, any such additions should have been made explicit or, better yet, placed in a footnote.

11. See, for example, Sergo Beria, *Beria, My Father: Inside Stalin's Kremlin* (London, 2001).

12. E. Yu. Zubkova, "O 'detskoi' literature i drugikh problemakh nashei istoricheskoi pamiati," in *Istoricheskie issledovaniia v Rossii. Tendentsii poslednikh let,* ed. G. A. Bordiugov (Moscow, 1996), pp. 155–178.

The Seats of Stalin's Power

1. Georgy Maksimilianovich Malenkov (1902–1988) was a party bureaucrat who worked for many years in the Central Committee apparat. In the late 1930s, he was elevated by Stalin to the highest echelons of power, buoyed by the waves of mass repression. During the dictator's last years, Malenkov served as his deputy within the government and the Central Committee Secretariat. After Stalin's death he was appointed chairman of the Soviet government, an appointment that seemed to label him as Stalin's unofficial heir. However, Malenkov lost out to Khrushchev in the battle for supreme power and was forced into humiliatingly low-level posts before spending his remaining years in retirement. Other unsuccessful rivals for power had the relative democratization of the USSR to thank for their fates. Under Stalin, disgraced politicians generally paid with their lives.

Lavrenty Pavlovich Beria (1899–1953) began his career in state security. In the early 1930s, Stalin put Beria in charge of Georgia and in 1938 brought him to Moscow and appointed him people's commissar for internal affairs (head of the NKVD, the main agency of state security); as such, he was assigned to purge the ranks of the secret police and wind down the Great Terror. In subsequent years,

Beria became one of Stalin's closest associates. He was his deputy within the government and oversaw the Soviet nuclear project, as well as other important divisions of the Soviet system, including the Gulag. After Stalin's death, Beria brought all "punitive organs" under his own control. This move alarmed the other Soviet leaders. They closed ranks and had Beria arrested, accused of countless crimes, and shot. Legends circulated that Beria had had special influence over Stalin and that many of the crimes of the Stalinist regime were his handiwork. In fact, Beria was just one of the men who implemented Stalin's orders and did not play a notably independent role in carrying out the mass repression. See Amy Knight, *Beria: Stalin's First Lieutenant* (Princeton, NJ, 1993).

Nikita Sergeevich Khrushchev (1894–1971) came to Moscow from Ukraine to study at the Industrial Academy, where he got to know Stalin's wife, Nadezhda Allilueva. This acquaintance provided the first impetus to his career, and he began to advance through the ranks of the Moscow party committee. In the late 1930s, new opportunities for advancement came as other officials succumbed to the mass repression. He was appointed party secretary for Ukraine, one of the most important Soviet republics. After the war, Stalin placed him in charge of the party organization in Moscow. In the wake of Stalin's death, Khrushchev became head of the Central Committee apparat. This post enabled him to outmaneuver Stalin's other political heirs and become the new Soviet leader. However, Khrushchev was not Stalin. His democratic reforms (the Khrushchev Thaw), his condemnation of Stalin's Cult of Personality, and his advocacy of freedom for Gulag prisoners, along with numerous tactical blunders, led to a plot against him. In late 1964, he was deprived of his post by purely legal means, but not of his life. He lived out his days as a pensioner. While in retirement, he dictated his well-known memoirs. See William Taubman, *Khrushchev: The Man and His Era* (New York, 2003).

Nikolai Aleksandrovich Bulganin (1895–1975) was among those who rose through the ranks to fill the vacancies created in the Soviet apparat by the Great Terror. Stalin began to promote Bulganin at the end of the war. As a counterweight to career military men, the civil servant Bulganin was placed in senior posts in the defense commissariat and eventually appointed defense minister. Contemporary accounts portray Bulganin as an expressionless functionary who simply followed orders. After Stalin's death, Bulganin chaired the Council of Ministers, succeeding the disgraced Malenkov. However, he picked the losing side during Khrushchev's rise to power and was sent into retirement.

2. Vyacheslav Mikhailovich Molotov (1890–1986) was one of Stalin's closest comrades-in-arms, their relationship dating back to prerevolutionary times. From then on, Molotov served as Stalin's faithful supporter and played a key role during Stalin's struggle for supreme power. In return, Molotov was appointed to top government posts. In 1930–1941, he chaired the Soviet government (the Council of People's Commissars). When Stalin himself took over this post in 1941, Molotov was made his deputy. For many years Molotov was in charge of foreign affairs. Within the country and the party, he was seen as Stalin's heir. For this reason, toward the end of his life, Stalin began to clamp down on Molotov and, in late 1952, eventually expelled him from the ruling circle. Nevertheless, Molotov remained

loyal to Stalin even after his death. This loyalty was one source of tension between Molotov and Khrushchev, who encouraged criticism of the Cult of Personality. Molotov lost out to Khrushchev during the decisive clash of 1957. He held a succession of minor posts before being forced into retirement. See Derek Watson, *Molotov and Soviet Government: Sovnarkom, 1930–41* (Basingstoke, UK, 1996).

Anastas Ivanovich Mikoyan (1895–1978) was one of the revolutionary and party activists from Transcaucasia who, thanks to Stalin, wound up making a brilliant career in Moscow. For several decades, Mikoyan was in charge of Soviet trade and the food and consumer-goods industry. In late 1952, Mikoyan fell into disgrace, together with Molotov. After Stalin's death, he restored his position and gave his allegiance to Khrushchev. He played an important role in resolving the 1962 Cuban Missile Crisis. After Khrushchev's removal, Mikoyan's career went into decline. Nevertheless, he is considered a model Soviet political survivor, renowned for his adaptability.

Kliment Yefremovich Voroshilov (1881–1969) was one of Stalin's closest friends during the 1918–1920 Civil War. In the mid-1920s, Stalin placed him in charge of the Red Army, a post for which Voroshilov was clearly not well suited. Shortly before the 1941 German invasion, Stalin was forced to replace him. During World War II, Voroshilov formally remained among the country's top leadership; however, he held secondary posts. After Stalin's death, Voroshilov was appointed to the figurehead post of president of the USSR. He supported Molotov and the other Soviet leaders who opposed Khrushchev in 1957 and soon thereafter went into retirement.

3. Yoram Gorlizki, "Ordinary Stalinism: The Council of Ministers and the Soviet Neo-patrimonial State, 1946–1953," *Journal of Modern History* 74, no. 4 (2002): 699–736.
4. Interview with Admiral I. S. Isakov in K. Simonov, *Glazami cheloveka moego pokoleniia* (Moscow, 1989), p. 433.
5. A. A. Chernobaev, ed., *Na prieme u Stalina. Tetradi (zhurnaly) zapisei lits, priniatykh I. V. Stalinym (1924–1953 gg.)* (Moscow, 2008), p. 7.
6. V. Bogomolova et al., comps., *Moskovskii Kreml' tsitadel' Rossii* (Moscow, 2009), pp. 310–313.
7. After Shumiatsky's arrest in 1938, these records were given to Stalin and placed in his personal archive. They have been published in K. M. Anderson et al., comps., *Kremlevskii kinoteatr. 1928–1953* (Moscow, 2005), pp. 919–1053.
8. Nadezhda Sergeevna Allilueva (1901–1932) grew up in the family of a proletarian revolutionary with whom Stalin had long been acquainted. She and Stalin were married in 1919. Allilueva worked in Lenin's secretariat and in the editorial offices of a Moscow journal before enrolling in the Moscow Industrial Academy. Further details can be found in the section on Stalin's family preceding chapter 6 below.
9. This and subsequent information about Stalin's dacha comes from *1953 god. Mezhdu proshlym i budushchim* (exhibition catalogue) (Moscow, 2003), and S. V. Deviatov, A. Shefov, and Iu. Iur'ev, *Blizhniaia dacha Stalina. Opyt istoricheskogo putevoditelia* (Moscow, 2011).
10. Svetlana Alliluyeva, *Twenty Letters to a Friend,* trans. Priscilla Johnson McMillian (New York, 1967), p. 21.
11. Deviatov, Shefov, and Iur'ev, *Blizhniaia dacha Stalina,* p. 287. Lozgachev has pro-

vided information relating to the postwar years, but there is evidence suggesting that Stalin took an active interest in the productivity of the dacha lands in earlier years as well.

12. Lazar Kaganovich mentions the existence of such a notebook in F. I. Chuev, *Kaganovich. Shepilov* (Moscow, 2001), p. 137.

13. Letter to Lazar Kaganovich, 24 September 1931. Cited in R. W. Davies, et al., eds., *The Stalin-Kaganovich Correspondence, 1931–36* (New Haven and London, 2003), p. 98.

14. In Sergei Khrushchev, ed., *Memoirs of Nikita Khrushchev,* vol. 2: *Reformer* (University Park, PA, 2006), p. 117.

15. In Sergei Khrushchev, ed., *Memoirs of Nikita Khrushchev,* vol. 1: *Commissar* (University Park, PA, 2004), p. 290.

16. M. Dzhilas [Milovan Djilas], *Litso totalitarizma* (Moscow, 1992), p. 108.

17. From an account by Hungarian leader Mátyás Rákosi (*Istoricheskii arkhiv,* no. 3 [1997]: 117).

18. *1953 god. Mezhdu proshlym i budushchim,* p. 75.

19. Andrei Aleksandrovich Zhdanov (1896–1948) joined the Bolshevik party before the revolution and afterward held various provincial party posts. In 1934 Stalin brought him to Moscow and made him a Central Committee secretary. After Kirov's murder, Zhdanov replaced him as Leningrad party boss. Until his death he remained one of Stalin's closest comrades-in-arms and enjoyed good relations with the leader. Zhdanov's son was briefly married to Stalin's daughter.

20. In Khrushchev, *Memoirs of Nikita Khrushchev,* vol. 1, pp. 102–103.

21. In Khrushchev, *Memoirs of Nikita Khrushchev,* vol. 2, p. 68.

22. Ibid., p. 117.

23. Ibid., pp. 146–147.

24. Dmitri Volkogonov, *Stalin: Triumph and Tragedy* (New York, 1991), p. 571.

25. This idea is developed in Erik van Ree, *The Political Thought of Joseph Stalin: A Study in Twentieth-Century Revolutionary Patriotism* (London and New York, 2002).

26. Cited in G. Dmitrov, *Dnevnik* (Sophia, 1997), p. 128.

27. Cited in V. M. Berezhkov, *Riadom so Stalinym* (Moscow, 1999), p. 371. Berezhkov was Stalin's interpreter.

Chapter 1. Before the Revolution

1. L. M. Spirin, "Kogda rodilsia Stalin: Popravki k ofitsial'noi biografii," *Izvestiia,* 25 June 1990; *Izvestiia TsK KPSS,* no. 11 (1990): 132–134.

2. A. Ostrovskii, *Kto stoial za spinoi Stalina?* (Moscow, 2002), pp. 88–89. Ostrovskii's book was the first biography to focus on Stalin's youth and was based on newly discovered documents from Moscow and Georgian archives. Other works appeared later: Miklos Kun, *Stalin: An Unknown Portrait* (Budapest and New York, 2003); Simon Sebag Montefiore, *Young Stalin* (London, 2007); Ronald Grigor Suny, *Stalin and the Russian Revolutionary Movement: From Koba to Commissar* (forthcoming from Oxford University Press). My account of Stalin's early life draws on these books to varying degrees.

3. Ostrovskii, *Kto stoial za spinoi Stalina?*, pp. 86–88, 93, 99.
4. RGASPI, f. 558, op. 11, d. 878, l. 73. Unless otherwise noted, translations are by Nora Favorov.
5. R. G. Suny, "Beyond Psychohistory: The Young Stalin in Georgia," *Slavic Review* 46, no. 1 (1991): 52.
6. Stalin, *Works,* vol. 13, p. 115. Interview with the German author Emil Ludwig, 13 December 1931.
7. Cited in Iu. G. Murin, comp., *Iosif Stalin v ob"iatiiakh sem'i. Iz lichnogo arkhiva* (Moscow, 1993), pp. 6–19.
8. RGASPI, f. 558, op. 11, d. 1549, l. 83.
9. Ostrovskii, *Kto stoial za spinoi Stalina?*, pp. 96–97, 102–104.
10. RGASPI, f. 558, op. 11, d. 876, l. 12.
11. RGASPI, f. 558, op. 4, d. 4, l. 1; d. 5, l. 1.
12. Cited in Dmitri Volkogonov, *Stalin: Triumph and Tragedy* (New York, 1991), pp. 7–8.
13. L. D. Trotsky, *Stalin,* (Benson, VT, 1985), vol. 1, pp. 32–33.

    Lev Davidovich Trotsky (1879–1940) was, for a while, perceived both within the fledgling Soviet state and internationally as second only to Lenin in leading the Bolshevik revolution. The peak of his glory came during the Civil War, in which he led the Red Army to victory. After the war, Trotsky took an active part in the struggle for power and influence that erupted among the Soviet leaders. In 1928, after losing this struggle, Trotsky was sent into exile. He remained politically active in emigration and worked to expose his political nemesis, Stalin, on whose orders he was killed in 1940 in Mexico by a Soviet agent.
14. Ostrovskii, *Kto stoial za spinoi Stalina?*, pp. 108–111.
15. Ibid., pp. 124–125.
16. Stalin, *Works,* vol. 13, pp. 115–116. Interview with the German author Emil Ludwig, 13 December 1931.
17. Cited in V. Kaminskii and I. Vereshchagin, "Detstvo i iunost' vozhdia: Dokumenty, zapiski, rasskazy," *Molodaia gvardiia,* no. 12 (1939): 65.
18. Robert C. Tucker, *Stalin as Revolutionary, 1879–1929: A Study in History and Personality* (New York, 1973), pp. 80–82.
19. RGASPI, f. 558, op. 4, d. 600, ll. 1–7; f. 71; op. 10, d. 266, ll. 7–11.
20. RGASPI, f. 558, op. 4, d. 32, ll. 1–2.
21. Suny, *Stalin and the Russian Revolutionary Movement,* ch. 3.
22. RGASPI, f. 558, op. 4, d. 53, ll. 1–15; Ostrovskii, *Kto stoial za spinoi Stalina?*, p. 148.
23. Ostrovskii, *Kto stoial za spinoi Stalina?*, p. 149.
24. Kaminskii and Vereshchagin, "Detstvo i iunost' vozhdia," pp. 84–85.
25. RGASPI, f. 558, op. 4, d. 53, l. 13.
26. Ibid., op. 4, d. 60, ll. 1–3.
27. Ibid., op. 11, d. 879, l. 45.
28. Ibid., op. 4, d. 65, ll. 1–4.
29. Trotsky, *Stalin,* vol. 1, p. 44.
30. Ostrovskii, *Kto stoial za spinoi Stalina?*, pp. 154–155.
31. A. J. Rieber, "Stalin, Man of the Borderlands," *American Historical Review* 106, no.

5 (2001): 1651-1691; Alfred J. Rieber, "Stalin as Georgian: The Formative Years," in *Stalin: A New History*, ed. Sarah Davies and James Harris (Cambridge, 2005), pp. 18-44.

32. I. Baberovski [J. Baberowski], *Vrag est' vezde. Stalinizm na Kavkaze* (Moscow, 2010), p. 15.

33. Documents from Boris Nicolaevsky's archive published by Iu. G. Fel'shtinskii and G. I. Cherniavskii in *Voprosy istorii*, no. 14 (2012): 16.

34. RGASPI, f. 558, op. 4, d. 72, l. 9.

35. Ostrovskii, *Kto stoial za spinoi Stalina?*, pp. 188-189.

36. RGASPI, f. 558, op. 4, d. 619, ll. 175-177.

37. Ostrovskii, *Kto stoial za spinoi Stalina?*, pp. 212-218.

38. Erik van Ree, "The Stalinist Self: The Case of Ioseb Jughashvili (1898-1907)," *Kritika* 11, no. 2 (2010): 265-266; Suny, *Stalin and the Russian Revolutionary Movement*, ch. 4.

39. Erik van Ree, "Reluctant Terrorists? Transcaucasian Social-Democracy, 1901-1909," *Europe-Asia Studies* 40, no. 1 (2008); Suny, *Stalin and the Russian Revolutionary Movement*, ch. 9.

40. Ostrovskii, *Kto stoial za spinoi Stalina?*, p. 254.

41. RGASPI, f. 558, op. 11, d. 896, l. 115.

42. For more details on the heist, see Montefiore, *Young Stalin*. See also Suny, *Stalin and the Russian Revolutionary Movement*, ch. 11. Miklos Kun has uncovered some evidence that Stalin assisted in the preparations for Kamo's operation (*Stalin*, pp. 77-79).

43. Documents from Boris Nicolaevsky's archive published by Iu. G. Fel'shtinskii and G. I. Cherniavskii in *Voprosy istorii*, no. 7 (2010): 34, and no. 9 (2010): 11.

44. Ostrovskii, *Kto stoial za spinoi Stalina?*, p. 292.

45. Z. I. Peregudova, *Politicheskii sysk Rossii (1880-1917 gg.)* (Moscow, 2000), pp. 242-274.

46. Ostrovskii, *Kto stoial za spinoi Stalina?*, pp. 329-330.

47. Cited in Peregudova, *Politicheskii sysk Rossii*, p. 246.

48. Roman Vatslavovich Malinovsky (1876-1918) was a metalworker, labor union activist, and member of the Bolshevik party who enjoyed Lenin's special patronage. In 1912 he was elected to the State Duma and in 1913 became chairman of the Duma's Bolshevik faction. Meanwhile, he served many years as a police double agent. Under threat of exposure, he fled Russia in 1914. In 1918 he returned to Soviet Russia hoping to be pardoned. Instead, he was shot.

49. These letters were opened by the police and therefore survive in police archives. Copies of them are also in the Stalin Collection (Ostrovskii, *Kto stoial za spinoi Stalina?*, pp. 396-398; RGASPI, f. 558, op. 11, d. 1288, ll. 12-14, 18, 28, 32-35).

50. Letter to Roman Malinovsky in late November 1913.

51. Letter to T. A. Slavotinskaia, dated 20 November 1913.

52. RGASPI, f. 558, op. 1, d. 52, l. 1; Ostrovskii, *Kto stoial za spinoi Stalina?*, pp. 402-403.

53. RGASPI, f. 558, op. 1, d. 5394, ll. 2-3; A. V. Kvashonkin et al., comps., *Bol'shevistskoe rukovodstvo. Perepiska. 1912-1927* (Moscow, 1996), p. 19.

54. Ia. M. Sverdlov, *Izbrannye proizvedeniia*, (Moscow, 1957), vol. 1, p. 227.

55. A. S. Allilueva, *Vospominaniia* (Moscow, 1946), p. 115.

56. In Sergei Khrushchev, ed., *Memoirs of Nikita Khrushchev*, vol. 2: Reformer (University Park, PA, 2006), p. 132. Translation slightly edited.

57. Sverdlov, *Izbrannye proizvedeniia*, vol. 1, p. 280.

58. RGASPI, f. 558, op. 11, d. 1288, ll. 15–16; B. S. Ilizarov, *Tainaia zhizn' Stalina* (Moscow, 2002), pp. 289, 291, 294–297; Ostrovskii, *Kto stoial za spinoi Stalina?*, p. 393.

59. RGASPI, f. 558, op. 11, d. 773, ll. 79–82; Ilizarov, *Tainaia zhizn' Stalina*, pp. 297–298.

60. In any event, Stalin soon ceased to have anything to do with Pereprygina. After he left exile she married and was later widowed with eight children (Ilizarov, *Tainaia zhizn' Stalina*, p. 310).

61. Letter to O. Ye. Allilueva dated 25 November 1915. RGASPI, f. 558, op. 1, d. 55, l. 2; Kvashonkin et al., *Bol'shevistskoe rukovodstvo*, p. 21.

62. Trotsky, *Stalin*, vol. 1, pp. 248–249.

63. Kvashonkin et al., *Bol'shevistskoe rukovodstvo*, pp. 17–20; Ostrovskii, *Kto stoial za spinoi Stalina?*, pp. 397–401, 412–413, 415.

64. RGASPI, f. 558, op. 1, d. 54, l. 1.

65. V. I. Lenin, *Polnoe sobranie sochinenii*, vol. 49 (Moscow, 1970), pp. 101, 161.

The Bulwarks of Stalin's Power

1. There is a tradition that views Stalin's final illness and death as the result of a poisoning organized by Beria. One of the most recent attempts to assess the medical evidence for this view can be found in Jonathan Brent and Vladimir Naumov, *Stalin's Last Crime: The Plot against the Jewish Doctors, 1948–1953* (New York, 2003).

   The basic events of Stalin's last days can be retraced by drawing on multiple sources. In addition to the well-known reminiscences of Khrushchev, who was among the leaders that kept watch over the dying Stalin (Sergei Khrushchev, ed., *Memoirs of Nikita Khrushchev*, vol. 1: *Commissar* [University Park, PA, 2004], pp. 147–149), new sources have appeared, including accounts by Stalin's bodyguards recorded by Dmitri Volkogonov and Edvard Radzinsky (Dmitri Volkogonov, *Stalin: Triumph and Tragedy* [New York, 1991], pp. 571–572; Edvard Radzinsky, *Stalin: The First In-Depth Biography Based on Explosive New Documents from Russia's Secret Archives* [New York, 1997], pp. 566–572). Here I make use of all three publications.

2. Here and below, on the topic of the Main Guard Directorate, see RGASPI, f. 17, op. 166, d. 858, ll. 2–20. It is unclear from the documents in question whether this information applies to all of Stalin's dachas or only to the one in Volynskoe. In any case, the guards and servants were primarily concentrated at the Volynskoe dacha, where Stalin lived.

3. S. V. Deviatov et al., *Garazh osobogo naznacheniia. 1921–2011* (Moscow, 2011), pp. 162–163.

4. RGASPI, f. 17, op. 162, d. 9, l. 54; V. N. Khaustov et al., comps., *Lubianka. Stalin i VChK-GPU-OGPU-NKVD. Ianvar' 1922–dekabr' 1936* (Moscow, 2003), pp. 255–256.

5. According to a report by senior officials of the Joint State Political Directorate (OGPU) to Stalin, the agent was prevented from making an attempt on Stalin's

life by an undercover OGPU agent who had infiltrated the organization and was accompanying the foreign agent. Under interrogation, the foreign agent stated that during an initial attempt he was simply unable to grab his revolver, which was hidden deep under his clothing. The rather large security detail accompanying Stalin prevented him from making a second attempt. ("Zapiska OGPU Stalinu. 18 noiabria 1931 g.," *Istochnik,* no. 3 [1996]: 161–162; Khaustov et al., *Lubianka. Stalin i VChK-GPU-OGPU-NKVD,* p. 286.)

6. *Gosudarstvennaia okhrana Rossii. 1881–2006* (exhibition catalogue) (Moscow, 2006), pp. 47–49.

7. Sergei Mironovich Kirov (1886–1934) was a Russian revolutionary and Civil War figure. In 1921–1926 he served as party chief in Azerbaijan. His career benefited from his years as one of Stalin's clients in Transcaucasia and the personal friendship that developed between the two. In 1926, after the crushing of the opposition, Kirov was appointed to replace Zinoviev as head of the Leningrad party organization, a position that led to his elevation to candidate member of the Politburo. On 1 December 1934 he was killed by a lone gunman. It was long believed that Kirov's murder was arranged by Stalin, but most historians have since rejected this possibility.

8. Nikolai Sidorovich Vlasik (1896–1967) was born into a peasant family in Belarus, received an elementary-school education, and later supported himself as an unskilled laborer. He fought in the tsarist army during World War I and later joined the Red Army. In 1919 he went to work for state security, where he rose through the ranks. The numerous vacancies created by the mass arrests of 1937–1938 accelerated Vlasik's career. In 1952 he was arrested, and two years after Stalin's death he was sentenced to ten years in exile. He was pardoned in 1956.

9. After a lengthy investigation, the soldier was shot in 1950.

10. S. V. Deviatov et al., *Moskovskii Kreml' v gody Velikoi Otechestvennoi Voiny* (Moscow, 2010), pp. 161, 164–167.

11. Figures are for 1950. E. Iu. Zubkova et al., comps., *Sovetskaia zhizn'. 1945–1953* (Moscow, 2003), p. 501; V. P. Popov, *Rossiiskaia derevnia posle voiny [iiun' 1945–mart 1953]* (Moscow, 1993), p. 146.

12. N. V. Petrov, *Pervyi predsedatel' KGB Ivan Serov* (Moscow, 2005), pp. 87–89.

13. From Vlasik's testimony at his 1955 trial; V. M. Loginov, *Teni Stalina. General Vlasik i ego soratniki* (Moscow, 2000), p. 152.

14. RGASPI, f. 17, op. 166, d. 858, ll. 2–8.

15. Semen Denisovich Ignatiev (1904–1983) was born into a peasant family and began his career in the Komsomol (Communist Youth League). After studying at the Industrial Academy in 1935, he landed a job in the Central Committee apparat. For many years he headed various regional party organizations. In 1950 he was placed in charge of the Central Committee department that handled party personnel matters, an important post. In 1951, after a wave of arrests within the leadership of the USSR Ministry of State Security, Stalin appointed Ignatiev to head this institution. Under Stalin's orders, Ignatiev falsified a number of political cases. After Stalin's death this action almost cost him his career or even his life, but Khrushchev's support saved him. Ignatiev was sent to work in the provinces and, in 1960, into retirement.

16. Russian State Archive of Contemporary History (RGANI), f. 5, op. 29, d. 3, l. 2; d. 16, ll. 94, 108.

17. On the sources of the statistics offered here, see O. Khlevniuk, *Stalin u vlasti. Prioritety i rezul'taty politiki diktatury. Istoriia stalinizma: Itogi i problemy izucheniia* (Moscow, 2011), pp. 63–65.

18. In early 1937 the total population of the USSR was 162 million, and in early 1953 it reached 188 million. The adult population was, of course, much lower, totaling in 1937, for example, approximately 100 million.

19. Soviet security services have gone through numerous reorganizations and renamings. By tradition, they continued to be called by their initial acronym—ChK (*chrezvychainaia komissiia*, or extraordinary commission). This is the origin of the term "cheka" or "chekist." Stalin himself often used this designation.

20. Grigory Ivanovich Kulik (1890–1950) fought alongside Stalin during the Civil War. With Stalin's patronage, he enjoyed a successful military career and in 1940 was elevated to marshal. During the war with Germany, like many other Civil War-era commanders, he did not acquit himself particularly well. In 1942 he was tried and stripped of his rank and given a series of junior command positions. Stalin's lack of trust in Kulik was reciprocated. In 1947 he was arrested along with several other generals who had criticized Stalin in frank discussions with one another. In 1950 he was shot.

21. May 1940 letter from the chairman of the Party Control Commission, Andrei Andreev, to Stalin in regard to the Kulik case; K. A. Stoliarov, *Palachi i zhertvy* (Moscow, 1998), pp. 272–276. RGASPI, f. 73, op. 2, d. 17, ll. 128–148.

22. Stoliarov, *Palachi i zhertvy,* pp. 267–271.

23. Solomon Mikhailovich Mikhoels (1890–1948) was a stage director, actor, and leader of the Jewish community. During World War II, he headed the Soviet Jewish Anti-Fascist Committee, which mobilized strong support for the Soviet Union in the West. The fact that he was awarded the Stalin Prize (the highest honor granted to cultural figures) immediately after the war testifies to the importance of his services. Nevertheless, soon thereafter Mikhoels became one of the first victims of Stalin's changing foreign policy priorities and the launching of an anti-Semitic campaign in the USSR.

24. G. V. Kostyrchenko, *Tainaia Politika Stalina. Vlast' i antisemitizm* (Moscow, 2001), pp. 388–392.

25. N. V. Petrov, *Palachi* (Moscow, 2011), pp. 66–68.

26. Ignatiev related this statement during testimony given on 27 March 1953, after Stalin's death (ibid., p. 307).

Chapter 2. In Lenin's Shadow

1. Lev Borisovich Kamenev (1883–1936), the son of an engineer, studied law at Moscow University before being expelled for revolutionary activities. He was one of Lenin's closest associates. Kamenev first met Stalin when they were both engaged in revolutionary work in Transcaucasia. After the 1917 revolution, Kamenev held a number of senior posts within the Soviet government and was among those contending for power after Lenin's death. He became an opposition leader in the

1920s. Once Stalin solidified his victory over the opposition, he dealt brutally with his old friend. In late 1934, Kamenev and his fellow oppositionists were arrested on fabricated charges that they had been involved in Kirov's murder. In August 1936, Kamenev was convicted of espionage and terrorism in the first of a series of major show trials and put to death.

2. Lars T. Lih, Oleg V. Naumov, and Oleg Khlevniuk, eds., *Stalin's Letters to Molotov, 1925–1936* (New Haven, 1995), pp. 101–103, 131–132.

3. There is a vast body of literature on Bolshevik activities during the Russian revolutionary period, including the following: E. N. Burdzhalov, *Russia's Second Revolution: The February 1917 Uprising in Petrograd,* trans. and ed. D. J. Raleigh (Bloomington and Indianapolis, 1967); Alexander Rabinowitch, *The Bolsheviks Come to Power* (Chicago and London, 2004); Richard Pipes, *The Russian Revolution* (New York, 1990). For Stalin's role in the revolution, see Robert M. Slusser, *Stalin in October: The Man Who Missed the Revolution* (Baltimore and London, 1987), and Ronald Grigor Suny, *Stalin and the Russian Revolutionary Movement: From Koba to Commissar* (Oxford University Press, forthcoming), chs. 18 and 19.

4. Cited in A. V. Kvashonkin et al., comps., *Bol'shevistskoe rukovodstvo. Perepiska. 1912–1927* (Moscow, 1996), p. 16.

5. V. I. Lenin, *Polnoe sobranie sochinenii,* vol. 31 (Moscow, 1969), pp. 11–22, 504.

6. Ibid., pp. 103–112.

7. Cited in N. N. Sukhanov, *Zapiski o revoliutsii,* vol. 2, bk. 3 (Moscow, 1991), p. 16.

8. Cited in *Sed'maia (Aprel'skaia) Vserossiiskaia konferntsiia RSDPR (bol'shevikov). Petrogradskaia obshchegorodskaia konferentsiia RSDPR (bol'shevikov). Protokoly* (Moscow, 1958), p. 323.

9. Grigory Yevseevich Zinoviev (1883–1936) was one of Lenin's closest comrades-in-arms. After the revolution, he headed the Leningrad party organization and the Comintern. Failing to take over leadership of the party after Lenin's death, he became an opposition leader and suffered persecution as the opposition was routed. In 1934, Zinoviev, along with Kamenev, was arrested based on fabricated evidence of complicity in Kirov's murder. In August 1936, he and Kamenev were convicted at the first Moscow show trial and shot.

10. Speech by Stalin, 3 August 1917, at the Russian Social Democratic Workers' Party (RSDRP) Sixth Party Congress; *Shestoi s"ezd Rossiiskoi sotsial-demokraticheskoi rabochei partii (bol'shevikov). Avgust 1917 g. Protokoly* (Moscow, 1958), p. 250.

11. RGASPI, f. 558, op. 11, d. 890, l. 8.

12. For a detailed investigation of these events, including evidence based on recently discovered documents, see V. T. Loginov, *Neizvestnyi Lenin* (Moscow, 2010), pp. 261–264.

13. Statements by Zinoviev and Kamenev on 11 October 1917; *Protokoly Tsentral'nogo Komiteta RSDRP(b). Avgust 1917–fevral' 1918* (Moscow, 1958), pp. 87–92.

14. RGASPI, f. 558, op. 1, d. 66, l. 1.

15. *Protokoly Tsentral'nogo Komiteta RSDRP(b). Avgust 1917–fevral' 1918,* p. 115.

16. R. W. Davies, Mark Harrison, and S. G. Wheatcroft, eds., *The Economic Transformation of the Soviet Union, 1913–1945* (Cambridge, 1994), pp. 62–64.

17. Protocols of Politburo meetings; RGASPI, f. 17, op. 3, dd. 1–125.

18. Letter from Stalin to Lenin and Trotsky, 22 June 1918; RGASPI, f. 558, op. 1, d. 5403, l. 1; Kvashonkin et al., *Bol'shevistskoe rukovodstvo,* p. 40.

19. Letter from Stalin to Lenin, 7 July 1918; RGASPI, f. 558, op. 1, d. 248, l. 1; I. V. Stalin, *Works,* vol. 4 (Moscow, 1954), pp. 120–121.

20. Telegram from Stalin to Trotsky and Lenin, 11 July 1918; RGASPI, f. 558, op. 1, d. 1812, ll. 1–2; Kvashonkin et al., *Bol'shevistskoe rukovodstvo,* p. 42.

21. Letter from Stalin to Lenin, 3 October 1918; RGASPI, f. 558, op. 1, d. 5410, l. 1; Kvashonkin et al., *Bol'shevistskoe rukovodstvo,* p. 52.

22. RGASPI, f. 558, op. 1, d. 5718, ll. 177, 178, 191, 195, 197.

23. Ibid., ll. 196–198.

24. Speech by Voroshilov at the Eighth Party Congress in March 1919; *Izvestiia TsK KPSS,* no. 11 (1989): 160.

25. Letter from Stalin to Lenin, 31 August 1918; RGASPI, f. 558, op. 1, d. 5408, l. 4; Kvashonkin et al., *Bol'shevistskoe rukovodstvo,* p. 46.

26. I. S. Rat'kovskii, *Krasnyi terror i deiatel'nost' VChK v 1918 godu* (St. Petersburg, 2006), pp. 151, 170.

27. *Izvestiia TsK KPSS,* no. 11 (1989): 157, 168.

28. Cited in Kvashonkin et al., *Bol'shevistskoe rukovodstvo,* p. 54.

29. Ibid., pp. 52–53.

30. I. V. Stalin, *Works,* vol. 4 (Moscow, 1947), p. 271.

31. V. I. Lenin, *Polnoe sobranie sochinenii,* vol. 50 (Moscow, 1970), p. 389.

32. RGASPI, f. 558, op. 1, d. 1815, ll. 2–4; Kvashonkin et al., *Bol'shevistskoe rukovodstvo,* pp. 142–143.

33. RGASPI, f. 558. op. 1, d. 5521, l. 2. Kvashonkin et al., *Bol'shevistskoe rukovodstvo,* p. 148.

34. RGASPI, f. 558, op. 1, d. 4137, l. 1; d. 1943, l. 1; Kvashonkin et al., *Bol'shevistskoe rukovodstvo,* p. 155.

35. RGASPI, f. 558, op. 1, d. 1961, ll. 1–2; Stalin, *Works,* vol. 4, p. 358.

36. RGASPI, f. 558, op. 1, d. 4681, l. 1.

37. RGASPI, f. 558, op. 1, d. 4458, ll. 1–3; Stalin, *Works,* vol. 4, pp. 360–362.

38. RGASPI, f. 558, op. 11, d. 126, l. 4.

39. Ibid., op. 1, d. 5213, l. 1; Kvashonkin et al., *Bol'shevistskoe rukovodstvo,* p. 156.

40. RGASPI, f. 17, op. 3, d. 106, l. 5.

41. Ibid., ll. 3, 4.

42. *Izvestiia TsK KPSS,* no. 3 (1991): 167.

43. *Deviataia konferentsiia RKP(b). Protokoly* (Moscow, 1972), pp. 60–61, 76–77; Iu. N. Amiantov et al., comps., *V. I. Lenin. Neizvestnye dokumenty. 1891–1922* (Moscow, 1999), pp. 382, 390.

44. RGASPI, f. 558, op. 1, d. 5541, ll. 1–2; Kvashonkin et al., *Bol'shevistskoe rukovodstvo,* pp. 160–161.

45. Stalin's involvement in organizing the so-called Ukrainian Labor Army during the winter and spring of 1920 was an attempt to militarize labor by using the army as a labor force, primarily in the coal mines of Ukraine.

46. Meeting of a section of the Twelfth RKP(b) Congress on the nationalities question, 25 April 1923; *Izvestiia TsK KPSS,* no. 4 (1991): 170. For a detailed account of Stalin's

work in the People's Commissariat for Nationalities, see Jeremy Smith, "Stalin as Commissar of Nationalities," in *Stalin: A New History*, ed. Sarah Davies and James Harris (New York, 2005), pp. 45–62, and V. Denningkhaus [Victor Dönninghaus], *V teni "bol'shogo brata." Zapadnye natsional'nye men'shinstva v SSSR. 1917–1938 gg.* (Moscow, 2011), pp. 84–91.

47. RGASPI, f. 17, op. 3, d. 234, l. 2.

48. Ibid., d. 310, l. 2.

49. Politburo resolution, 19 October 1922; RGASPI, f. 17, op. 3, d. 318, l. 4.

50. Grigory Konstantinovich Ordzhonikidze (1886–1937) was one of Stalin's closest friends and comrades-in-arms. In the 1920s he was a top party leader in Transcaucasia before being transferred to Moscow to take up the important post of chairman of the Party Control Commission. In this capacity he helped in Stalin's climb to power. In the 1930s Ordzhonikidze was put in charge of Soviet heavy industry. He tried to oppose Stalin's repression of key personnel, leading to conflict between the two men. In February 1937 Ordzhonikidze committed suicide. How he died became widely known only after Stalin's death. See Oleg V. Khlevniuk, *In Stalin's Shadow: The Career of "Sergo" Ordzhonikidze* (New York, 1995).

51. Letters from Nazaretian to Ordzhonikidze, 14 June and after 9 August 1922; RGASPI, f. 85, op. 1c, d. 13, ll. 6, 10; Kvashonkin et al., *Bol'shevistskoe rukovodstvo*, pp. 256, 257, 262, 263.

52. Letters from Nazaretian to Ordzhonikidze, 12 July and after 9 August 1922; RGASPI, f. 85, op. 1c, d. 13, ll. 7, 10; Kvashonkin et al., *Bol'shevistskoe rukovodstvo*, pp. 259, 263.

53. Letter from Nazaretian to Ordzhonikidze after 9 August 1922; RGASPI, f. 85, op. 1c, d. 13, l. 10. Kvashonkin et al., *Bol'shevistskoe rukovodstvo*, p. 263.

54. Reminiscence by N. A. Uglanov, written in January 1925, at a time when Stalin had not yet established his sole power; *Izvestiia TsK KPSS*, no. 4 (1989): 196.

55. Nikolai Ivanovich Bukharin (1888–1938) was a Bolshevik leader and theoretician. He took Stalin's side in the confrontation with Trotsky, Zinoviev, and Kamenev, but after Stalin was victorious over these oppositionists, Bukharin himself became Stalin's victim. Bukharin advocated a more moderate course and a gradual transition out of the NEP. Stalin labeled Bukharin and his supporters as "right deviationists." The expulsion of the rightists from the party's leadership helped Stalin solidify his dictatorship. Bukharin was arrested in 1937 and shot the following year. (See Stephen F. Cohen, *Bukharin and the Bolshevik Revolution: A Political Biography, 1888–1938* [New York, 1973]; Paul R. Gregory, *Politics, Murder, and Love in Stalin's Kremlin: The Story of Nikolai Bukharin and Anna Larina* [Stanford, CA, 2010]).

56. Cited in *Izvestiia TsK KPSS*, no. 12 (1989): 198. For another version of Ulianova's reminiscence, see *Izvestiia TsK KPSS*, no. 3 (1991): 188.

57. *Izvestiia TsK KPSS*, no. 4 (1989); RGASPI, f. 17, op. 3, d. 303, l. 5.

58. Cited in *Izvestiia TsK KPSS*, no. 12 (1989): 198. Maria Ulianova's memoirs were found among her papers after her death. They were obviously not intended for publication. Their candor and confessional nature add to their credibility as a source.

59. *Izvestiia TsK KPSS*, no. 9 (1989): 191–216.

60. Ibid., p. 209.

61. Ibid., no. 12 (1989): 191.

62. Ibid., pp. 189, 191.

63. Cited in ibid., pp. 198–199.

64. V. I. Lenin, *Polnoe sobranie sochinenii,* vol. 45 (Moscow, 1970), p. 345.

65. Ibid., p. 346.

66. Feliks Edmundovich Dzerzhinsky (1877–1926) was active in the revolutionary movement in Russia and spent many years in exile, prison, and labor camps. After the revolution he headed the Emergency Commission or Cheka, the Bolsheviks' notorious state security organization. In the 1920s, while still head of the political police, he also ran the commissariats of transport and industry. He was still active at the time of his death from heart failure.

67. V. I. Lenin, *Polnoe sobranie sochinenii,* vol. 54 (Moscow, 1975), p. 329.

68. Ibid., pp. 329–330.

69. Robert C. Tucker, *Stalin as Revolutionary, 1879–1929: A Study in History and Personality* (New York, 1973), p. 277.

70. V. I. Lenin, *Polnoe sobranie sochinenii,* vol. 54, p. 330.

71. *Izvestiia TsK KPSS,* no. 9 (1990): 151; emphasis by Kamenev.

72. Ibid., no. 12 (1989): 193.

73. Ibid., no. 9 (1990): 151–152.

74. V. A. Sakharov, *Politicheskoe zaveshchanie Lenina: Real'nosti istorii i mify politiki* (Moscow, 2003). See also a critical discussion of this book in *Otechestvennaia istoriia,* no. 2 (2005): 162–174.

75. Moshe Lewin, *Lenin's Last Struggle* (New York, 1968).

76. Cited in V. P. Vilkova, comp., *RKP(b). Vnutripartiinaia bor'ba v dvadtsatye gody. Dokumenty i materialy. 1923* (Moscow, 2004), p. 129; emphasis by Zinoviev.

77. Ibid., pp. 135–136; emphasis by Stalin.

78. Transcript of a discussion of the international situation at the 21 August 1923 Politburo meeting. *Istochnik,* no. 5 (1995): 118, 124.

79. Ibid., p. 126.

80. Aleksei Ivanovich Rykov (1881–1938) was a well-known Bolshevik who served as the Soviet premier after Lenin's death. An economic moderate, he joined forces with Stalin in opposing Trotsky, Zinoviev, and Kamenev. Together with Bukharin, Rykov was accused of "right deviation" and removed from the leadership. He was arrested in 1937 and put to death in 1938.

81. Ibid.

82. Vilkova, *RKP(b). Vnutripartiinaia bor'ba,* pp. 147–151.

83. *Trinadtsatyi s"ezd PKP(b). Stenograficheskii otchet* (Moscow, 1963), pp. xxi–xxii.

84. RGASPI, f. 558, op. 11, d. 126, l. 68.

85. V. Nadtocheev, "'Triumvirat' ili 'semerka'?" in *Trudnye voprosy istorii, ed.* V. V. Zhuravlev (Moscow, 1991), pp. 68–70.

86. *Izvestiia TsK KPSS,* no. 8 (1991): 182.

87. RGASPI, f. 558, op. 11, d. 777, ll. 27–28.

88. Letters from Kirov to Ordzhonikidze dated 10 and 16 January 1926. Kvashonkin et al., *Bol'shevistskoe rukovodstvo,* pp. 315, 318.

89. Lih, Naumov, and Khlevniuk, *Stalin's Letters to Molotov,* pp. 115–116.

90. A. G. Egorov, ed., *KPSS v rezoliutsiiakh i resheniiakh s"ezdov, konferentsii i plenumov TsK,* vol. 4 (Moscow, 1984), pp. 49–50.

91. See, for example, Stalin's letter to Rykov, Voroshilov, and Molotov dated 20 September 1927; RGASPI, f. 558, op. 11, d. 797, ll. 84–85.

92. Valerian Valerianovich Osinsky (1887–1938) was an Old Bolshevik who took part in various opposition movements and was a follower of Trotsky at one point. Soon after the departure mentioned in the letter to Stalin, Osinsky was removed as head of the Central Statistical Directorate. Nevertheless, in later years he held various senior economic posts. He was shot during the Terror.

93. Vladimir Mikhailovich Smirnov (1887–1937) was a long-standing party member and an active participant in the revolution and Civil War who became involved in the opposition in the 1920s. In 1928 he was exiled to the Ural region for three years, a term ultimately extended to 1935, at which point he was again arrested. He was shot in 1937.

94. Timofei Vladimirovich Sapronov (1887–1937) was a long-standing party member and a Moscow Bolshevik leader. After the revolution he held senior government posts. In the 1920s he joined the opposition. In 1928 he was exiled to the Arkhangelsk region for three years. The term of his exile was extended to 1935, as was Smirnov's. In 1935 he was again arrested, and in 1937 he was shot.

95. Yuly Osipovich Martov (1873–1923) was a leader of the Social Democratic movement in Russia. He collaborated with Lenin during the early stages of his revolutionary career, but in 1903 the two men broke off relations, and later Martov headed the Menshevik party. He participated in the revolutionary movement in Russia but condemned the 1917 Bolshevik overthrow of the Provisional Government. He later tried to work with the Bolsheviks and democratize the Bolshevik dictatorship. In 1920 he was sent abroad and later died of tuberculosis.

96. Osinsky's letter and Stalin's following response are in RGASPI, f. 558, op. 11, d. 780, ll. 12–14; *Istochnik,* no. 6 (1994): 88.

97. Grigory Yakovlevich Sokolnikov (1888–1939), a long-standing party member, escaped abroad after being exiled to Siberia. After the revolution he became a member of the top leadership. His greatest success was the monetary reforms he introduced during the 1920s, which provided Soviet Russia with a stable currency. Sokolnikov was subjected to persecution due to his involvement with the opposition. In 1927 he announced his break with the opposition and for some time held various senior government posts. He was shot during the Stalinist Terror.

98. During his speech to the Fifteenth Party Congress in December 1927, Stalin again spoke of an intervention being prepared against the USSR and drew an analogy with the shooting in Sarajevo (I. V. Stalin, *Works,* vol. 10 [Moscow, 1949], pp. 281, 288).

99. RGASPI, f. 558, op. 11, d. 71, ll. 2–40b.

100. Yan Ernestovich Rudzutak (1887–1938) was a long-standing Bolshevik who spent years in tsarist prisons. After the revolution he held senior party and government posts before being shot during the Stalinist Terror.

101. RGASPI, f. 558, op. 11, d. 767, ll. 35–39, 45–48, 56–60.

102. Mikhail Ivanovich Kalinin (1875–1946) was a long-standing Bolshevik who shortly

after the revolution was appointed chairman of the Soviet parliament and held the largely figurehead post of president of the USSR until his death. One of the more moderate members of the Bolshevik leadership, he nevertheless submitted to power. After some wavering, he threw his support behind Stalin. Kalinin's wife was arrested in the 1930s and released shortly before her husband's death.

103. RGASPI, f. 558, op. 11, d. 767, ll. 35–39, 45–48; d. 71. ll. 11, 13–14.
104. Molotov uses this term since not only Politburo members took part in voting, but also the chairman of the Party Control Commission, Ordzhonikidze, whose post excluded him from Politburo membership.
105. RGASPI, f. 558, op. 11, d. 767, ll. 56–60.
106. Cited in Lih, Naumov, and Khlevniuk, *Stalin's Letters to Molotov,* p. 139.
107. RGASPI, f. 558, op. 11, d. 1110, l. 181.

A World of Reading and Contemplation

1. RGASPI, f. 558, op. 11, d. 105, ll. 20–126; d. 117, ll. 1–173.
2. Ibid., op. 11, d. 70, ll. 85–114.
3. B. S. Ilizarov, *Tainaia zhizn' Stalina* (Moscow, 2002), p. 143.
4. M. Ia. Vaiskopf, *Pisatel' Stalin* (Moscow, 2000), pp. 17–22.
5. RGASPI, f. 558, op. 3, dd. 1–392. There exists a legal document *(akt)* instructing that all of Stalin's books with notations be placed in his archive. Books from Stalin's Kremlin and dacha libraries that did not contain any handwritten markings were placed in the library of the Institute of Marxism-Leninism or other research libraries. Whether or not the libraries Stalin left behind at the time of his death were properly catalogued and preserved is an open question. Some books, including those with notations, have disappeared. However, the books that were preserved in the Stalin archival collection appear to be a representative sample.
6. Former Soviet transport commissar I. V. Kovalev, in an interview with G. A. Kumanev. Cited in *Novaia i noveishaia istoriia,* no. 3 (2005): 165.
7. Cited in R. W. Davies et al., eds., *The Stalin-Kaganovich Correspondence, 1931–1936* (New Haven and London, 2003), p. 381.
8. Cited in A. Artizov and O. Naumov, comps., *Vlast' i khudozhestvennaia intelligentsiia* (Moscow, 1999), pp. 499, 583, 613. Memorandum from Stalin concerning the script of the film *Ivan the Terrible,* 13 September 1943; speech by Stalin at a meeting of the Orgburo, 9 August 1946; conversation between Stalin and the creators of the film *Ivan the Terrible,* 26 February 1947: see Maureen Perrie, *The Cult of Ivan the Terrible in Stalin's Russia* (Basingstoke and New York, 2001).
9. B. S. Ilizarov claims to have found a copy of Fedor Dostoevsky's *The Brothers Karamazov* with notations by Stalin in a library (Ilizarov, *Tainaia zhizn' Stalina,* p. 411).
10. Mikhail Afanasyevich Bulgakov (1891–1940) was a novelist and playwright. Some of his early plays were staged in the 1920s but were harshly criticized for ideological flaws. Gradually, Bulgakov's works were banned and he was deprived of his livelihood. Stalin, who liked Bulgakov's works, gave the writer some support. Bulgakov was given some work, although most of his writing remained prohibited. His best known work, *The Master and Margarita,* was published many years after Stalin's death.

11. Letter from Gorky to the head of the Communist youth organization, 14 April 1936. Cited in L. V. Maksimenkov, comp., *Bol'shaia tsenzura. Pisateli i zhurnalisty v Strane Sovetov. 1917–1956* (Moscow, 2005), p. 413.

12. As mentioned above, in 1934–1936 the head of the Soviet film industry, Boris Shumiatsky, took notes at several dozen film screenings hosted by Stalin for other top Soviet leaders. K. M. Anderson et al., comps., *Kremlevskii kinoteatr. 1928–1953* (Moscow, 2005), pp. 919–1053. The quotes in this paragraph are from this volume.

13. Letter from Stalin to members of the Russian Association of Proletarian Writers, 28 February 1929. Cited in Artizov and Naumov, *Vlast' i khudozhestvennaia intelligentsiia,* p. 110.

Vsevolod Emilyevich Meyerhold (1874–1940) was a theatrical director and producer and an adherent of revolutionary theatrical experimentation. Meyerhold's works fell out of favor after the proclamation of the Stalinist doctrine of socialist realism. In 1939 Meyerhold was arrested, and he was shot the following year.

14. Dmitry Dmitryevich Shostakovich (1906–1975) is considered one of the twentieth century's leading composers. On Stalin's instructions, he was branded a "formalist" and persecuted in 1936 and 1948. To come to terms with the authorities, Shostakovich was periodically compelled to create "correct," ideologically acceptable works.

15. V. A. Nevezhin, *Zastol'ia Iosifa Stalina. Bol'shie kremlevskie priemy 1930-kh–1970-kh gg.* (Moscow, 2011), pp. 282–308.

16. Stalin's mangling of idioms is difficult to convey in translation. For examples, see Vaiskopf, *Pisatel' Stalin,* p. 23.

17. For an example, see RGASPI, f. 17, op. 163, d. 471, l. 16; d. 494, l. 14.

18. Cited in A. Ostrovskii, *Kto stoial za spinoi Stalina?* (Moscow, 2002), pp. 399, 400–401, 409, 413.

19. Iu. G. Murin, comp., *Iosif Stalin v ob"iatiiakh sem'i. Iz lichnogo arkhiva* (Moscow, 1993), pp. 30–31.

20. Ethan Pollock, *Stalin and the Soviet Science Wars* (Princeton, 2006).

Chapter 3. His Revolution

1. RGASPI, f. 558, op. 11, d. 767, l. 76.

2. Minutes from an 18 January 1928 meeting of the Siberia Krai party leadership attended by Stalin; *Izvestiia TsK KPSS,* no. 5 (1991): 196–199.

3. Ibid., pp. 199–201.

4. Stalin's speech at a 20 January 1928 closed meeting of the party leadership of Siberia Krai; RGASPI, f. 558, op. 11, d. 118, ll. 23–34; *Izvestiia TsK KPSS,* no. 6 (1991): 203–212.

5. RGASPI, f. 558, op. 11, d. 119, l. 84.

6. Ibid., l. 106; *Izvestiia TsK KPSS,* no. 7 (1991): 178.

7. Cited in I. I. Ikonnikova and A. P. Ugrovatov, "Stalinskaia repetitsiia nastupleniia na krest'ianstvo," *Voprosy istorii KPSS,* no. 1 (1991): 76.

8. Mikhail Pavlovich Tomsky (1880–1936) was a long-standing member of the Bolshevik party and a Soviet trade union leader after the revolution. In 1922 he took charge of the All-Union Council of Trade Unions and joined the country's top

leadership. After Stalin defeated the rightists, Tomsky was relegated to low-level positions. In 1936, under threat of arrest, he took his own life.

Nikolai Aleksandrovich Uglanov (1886-1937) was a long-standing member of the Bolshevik party who held senior posts in Moscow and the provinces after the revolution. In 1924 he was appointed head of Moscow's party organization, a position that assured him a place at the upper echelons of power. In 1928 he was removed from his post through Stalin's intrigues, given a low-level position, and subjected to persecution. He was arrested and shot during the Terror.

9. RGASPI, f. 85. These recent additions to the *fond* have not yet been assigned an *opis'*: d. 2, ll. 1–11, 28–30.

10. Cited in A. V. Kvashonkin et al., comps., *Bol'shevistskoe rukovodstvo. Perepiska. 1912–1927* (Moscow, 1996), p. 58.

11. New documents pertaining to the conversation between Bukharin and Kamenev and the circumstances under which it came to light have been published. See V. P. Danilov and O. V. Khlevniuk et al., eds., *Kak lomali NEP. Stenogrammy plenumov TsK VKP(b). 1928–1929 gg.*, vol. 4 (Moscow, 2000), pp. 558–567, 685–699.

12. Speech delivered at the First All-Union Conference of Leading Personnel of Socialist Industry, 4 February 1931. I. V. Stalin, *Works*, vol. 13 (Moscow, 1954), p. 43. The translation has been slightly revised.

13. RGASPI, f. 558, op. 11, d. 145, ll. 43–54.

14. I borrow the term "war on the peasants" from Andrea Graziosi, *The Great Soviet Peasant War: Bolsheviks and Peasants, 1917–1933* (Cambridge, MA, 1996).

15. V. P. Danilov et al., eds., *Tragediia sovetskoi derevni. Kollektivizatsiia i raskulachivanie. 1927–1939*, vol. 2 (Moscow, 2000), pp. 35–78.

16. Ibid., pp. 75–76, 85–86.

17. Ibid., p. 11.

18. Ibid., pp. 703, 789. See also Lynne Viola, *Peasant Rebels under Stalin: Collectivization and the Culture of Peasant Resistance* (New York and Oxford, 1996).

19. In the 1960s V. P. Danilov had an opportunity to acquaint himself with the relevant Politburo archive documents, which have still not been made generally available to historians; Danilov et al., *Tragediia sovetskoi derevni*, vol. 2, p. 833.

20. Ibid., pp. 279, 324. Lynne Viola et al., eds., *Riazanskaia derevniia v 1929–1930 gg. Khronika golovokruzheniia* (Moscow, 1998).

21. Danilov et al., *Tragediia sovetskoi derevni*, vol. 2, p. 270.

22. Ibid., pp. 303–305.

23. Ibid., p. 804. According to OGPU figures for 1930, 2.5 million people took part in the 10,000 disturbances (out of 13,800) for which an estimate was made. Assuming an average of 245 people per disturbance, we arrive at a figure of 3.4 million people for all 13,800 incidents. It should be borne in mind, however, that the OGPU data were probably not complete.

24. Cited in V. Vasil'ev and L. Viola, *Kollektivizatsiia i krest'ianskoe soprotivlenie na Ukraine* (Vinnitsa, 1997), pp. 213–219, 221.

25. RGASPI, f. 85, op. 1c, d. 125, l. 2; Vasil'ev and Viola, *Kollektivizatsiia i krest'ianskoe soprotivlenie*, p. 233.

26. V. N. Zemskov, *Spetsposelentsy v SSSR. 1930–1960* (Moscow, 2003), pp. 16, 20.

27. Lynne Viola, *The Unknown Gulag: The Lost World of Stalin's Special Settlements* (New York, 2007).

28. R. W. Davies, Mark Harrison, and S. G. Wheatcroft, eds., *The Economic Transformation of the Soviet Union, 1913-1945* (Cambridge, 1994), p. 289.

29. Speech to a Central Committee plenum, 7 January 1933. Stalin, *Works,* vol. 13, pp. 161-217.

30. O. Latsis, "Problema tempov v sotsialisticheskom stroitel'stve," *Kommunist,* no. 18 (1987): 83.

31. R. W. Davies and Stephen G. Wheatcroft, *The Years of Hunger: Soviet Agriculture, 1931-1933* (Basingstoke, 2004), pp. 412-415.

32. James C. Scott, *Weapons of the Weak: Everyday Forms of Peasant Resistance* (New Haven, 1985).

33. On proposals submitted to Stalin in 1932 to introduce fixed grain procurement norms, see N. A. Ivnitskii, *Kollektivizatsiia i raskulachivanie (nachalo 30-kh godov)* (Moscow, 1994), p. 191.

34. Politburo resolution, 29 April 1932; RGASPI, f. 17, op. 162, d. 12, l. 115.

35. Judging by reports from the head of the Procurement Committee to Stalin, as of 1 July 1933—i.e., before the deliveries of grain from the 1933 harvest—Soviet grain reserves, including all grain cultures, totaled approximately 1.4 million metric tons, including more than 1 million tons of grains for human consumption (APRF [Archive of the President of the Russian Federation], f. 3, op. 40, d. 27, ll. 123, 133). Davies and Wheatcroft found these figures in the archives of the Procurement Committee (*The Years of Hunger,* p. 229). It is known that peasant households in Russia annually consumed an average of 262 kilograms of grain per capita. That figure suggests that these reserves would have been sufficient to provide normal rations for approximately 4 million people for an entire year or even more people at below-standard rations. Even more striking is the quantity of grain exported during the famine. Although the government was forced to cut back, grain exports still totaled 1.8 million tons in 1932 and 223,000 tons during the first half of 1933 (Danilov et al., *Tragediia sovetskoi derevni,* vol. 3, pp. 33-34; Davies and Wheatcroft, *The Years of Hunger,* p. 440).

36. Oleg V. Khlevniuk, *The History of the Gulag from Collectivization to the Great Terror* (New Haven and London, 2004), p. 62; Zemskov, *Spetsposelentsy v SSSR,* p. 20.

37. While formally part of the Russian Federation, the North Caucasus was geographically, economically, and ethnically (due to a significant Ukrainian population) tied to Ukraine.

38. Davies and Wheatcroft, *The Years of Hunger,* pp. 448-449, 470.

39. Cited in Iu. Murin, comp., *Pisatel' i vozhd'. Perepiska M. A. Sholokhova s I. V. Stalinym. 1931-1950 gody* (Moscow, 1997), p. 68.

    Mikhail Aleksandrovich Sholokhov (1905-1984) has been called a classic writer of Soviet literature and enjoyed Stalin's particular patronage. Despite his success, Sholokhov continued to live in his native village in the Don region of Russia, a location that exposed him to the realities of collectivization and the Terror. On several occasions Sholokhov appealed directly to Stalin for help.

40. R. W. Davies et al., eds., *The Stalin-Kaganovich Correspondence, 1931–1936* (New Haven, 2003), pp. 179–181.
41. Hiroaki Kuromiya, *Stalin: Profiles in Power* (New York, 2005), pp. 111–112. Historians continue to argue about the anti-Ukrainian nature of the famine and whether it represents a case of genocide. See, for example, Andrea Graziosi, *Stalinism, Collectivization and the Great Famine* (Cambridge, MA, 2009).
42. Stalin, *Works,* vol. 13, pp. 253–254.
43. Stalin was referring to a law enacted 7 August 1932 that provided for draconian penalties, including execution, for stealing kolkhoz property.
44. RGASPI, f. 558, op. 11, d. 799, ll. 24–25, 30–31. A transcript of these discussions was first published in 1951: I. V. Stalin, *Sochineniia,* vol. 13 (Moscow, 1951), pp. 260–273. The published version of the text was redacted and the discussion of the state of the countryside cited here was cut.
45. Danilov et al., *Tragediia sovetskoi derevni,* vol. 3, pp. 527–528, 661–665.
46. Cited in Murin, *Pisatel' i vozhd',* pp. 28–58.
47. Ibid., pp. 68, 145–147.
48. Within the party, many people knew of Trotsky's speeches. They were even quoted at the January 1933 Central Committee plenum, albeit labeled as "slanderous" (RGASPI, f. 17, op. 2, d. 514. vyp. 1, l. 55).
49. Khlevniuk, *History of the Gulag,* pp. 56, 57–58, 68.
50. RGASPI, f. 558, op. 11, d. 779, l. 47.
51. RGASPI, f. 17, op. 162, d. 15, ll. 154–155; G. M. Adibekov et al., eds., *Politbiuro TsK RKP(b)-VKP(b) i Evropa. Resheniia 'osoboi papki'* (Moscow, 2001), pp. 305–306.
52. Stalin, *Sochineniia,* vol. 13, p. 252.
53. Davies, Harrison, and Wheatcroft, *The Economic Transformation of the Soviet Union,* p. 127.
54. RGASPI., f. 17, op. 2, d. 530. ll. 78–98.
55. Khlevniuk. *History of the Gulag,* p. 63.
56. Peter H. Solomon, Jr., *Soviet Criminal Justice under Stalin* (New York, 1996), pp. 153–195.
57. APRF, f. 3, op. 58, d. 71, ll. 11–31.
58. RGASPI, f. 17, op. 162, d. 16, ll. 88–89. Subsequently, Aleksei Seliavkin fared relatively well. He survived the repression of 1937–1938 and fought in World War II, earning the rank of colonel. He even managed to publish his memoirs in the early 1980s (A. I. Seliavkin, *V trekh voinakh na bronevikakh i tankakh* [Kharkov, 1981]), a testament to the position of respect he held in Soviet society.
59. Khlevniuk, *History of the Gulag,* pp. 121–123.
60. RGASPI, f. 17, op. 162, d. 17, l. 31; V. N. Khaustov et al., comps., *Lubianka. Stalin i VChK-GPU-OGPU-NKVD. Ianvar' 1922–dekabr' 1936* (Moscow, 2003), p. 566; V. N. Khaustov and L. Samuel'son, *Stalin, NKVD i repressii. 1936–1938* (Moscow, 2009), p. 70.
61. A major part in promoting such accounts was played by the works of Roy Medvedev. See, for example, Roy Medvedev, *Let History Judge: The Origin and Consequences of Stalinism* (New York, 1972).
62. For more details, see Oleg V. Khlevniuk, *Master of the House: Stalin and His Inner Circle* (New Haven and London, 2008), pp. 108–116.

63. An examination of the most important evidence is offered in Matthew E. Lenoe, *The Kirov Murder and Soviet History* (New Haven and London, 2010). My discussion of this event relies heavily on this highly professional and detailed study and on A. Kirilina, *Neizvestnyi Kirov* (St. Petersburg and Moscow, 2001).
64. One of the most recent publications on this subject is based on documents from the archives of the RF Federal Protection Service, the agency responsible for protecting senior officials. See S. Deviatov et al., "Gibel' Kirova. Fakty i versii," *Rodina*, no. 3 (2005): 64.
65. Cited in F. Chuev, *Sto sorok besed s Molotovym* (Moscow, 1991), p. 310.
66. Cited in *Voprosy istorii*, no. 2 (1995): 16–17.

    Nikolai Ivanovich Yezhov (1895–1940) played a central role in carrying out Stalin's plans for the mass purges and repression in 1935–1938. Yezhov initially oversaw this campaign in his capacity as the Central Committee secretary charged with monitoring the NKVD. In late 1936 he was placed directly in charge of the organization. Under Stalin's guidance, Yezhov conducted the large-scale repressive operations of 1937–1938 that constituted the core of the Great Terror. After carrying out the duties that had been placed on his shoulders, Yezhov was arrested and shot.

    Aleksandr Vasilyevich Kosarev (1903–1939) was head of the Komsomol, the Soviet youth organization. He was arrested in 1938 and shot in 1939.
67. A. N. Artizov et al., comps., *Reabilitatsiia: Kak eto bylo*, vol. 2 (Moscow, 2003), pp. 546, 548–549, and vol. 3 (Moscow, 2004), pp. 491–492.
68. Nikolaev's relatives also met tragic fates. Almost all of them—his mother, two sisters, his younger sister's husband, his brother's wife, and, in addition to Milda Draule herself, her sister, her sister's husband, and even Nikolaev's neighbor— were shot or perished in prison (Kirilina, *Neizvestnyi Kirov*, p. 367).
69. Genrikh Grigoryevich Yagoda (1891–1938) served as deputy chairman of the OGPU beginning in 1923 and as people's commissar for internal affairs (NKVD chief) from 1934 to 1936. He was arrested in 1937 and shot in 1938.
70. Artizov et al., *Reabilitatsiia*, vol. 3, pp. 466–467. Nikolaev officially registered his revolver in 1924 and 1930.
71. Ibid., pp. 490, 499.
72. Ibid., p. 493.
73. Kirilina, *Neizvestnyi Kirov*, pp. 344–347; Artizov et al., *Reabilitatsiia*, vol. 3, pp. 494–498.
74. Cited in Iu. G. Murin, comp., *Iosif Stalin v ob"iatiiakh sem'i. Iz lichnogo arkhiva* (Moscow, 1993), p. 168.
75. RGASPI, f. 17, op. 163, d. 1052, l. 152.
76. Ibid., ll. 152, 153. For the complete text of Stalin's memorandum, see ibid., f. 71, op. 10, d. 130, ll. 13–15.
77. Cited in *Pravda*, 2 December 1935.
78. From the diary of Maria Svanidze; cited in Murin, *Iosif Stalin v ob"iatiiakh sem'i*, pp. 173–175.
79. Speech at the March 1937 Central Committee plenum; cited in *Voprosy istorii*, no. 3 (1995): 14.

80. D. A. Volkogonov, *Triumf i tragediia,* vol. 2, pt. 2 (Moscow, 1989), p. 249.

81. *Izvestiia TsK KPSS,* no. 7 (1989): 86–93.

82. Avel Safronovich Yenukidze (1877–1937) was a long-standing member of the Bolshevik party who became friends with Stalin when they were both working in the revolutionary underground in Transcaucasia. After the revolution Yenukidze held a senior post in the Soviet parliament. Among his duties was accommodating the material needs of the top Soviet leadership. In that post he developed a reputation as someone who enjoyed a lavish lifestyle, and it probably contributed to his fall from favor. In 1935 he was removed from his senior post based on fabricated charges and in 1937 he was shot.

83. Khaustov et al., *Lubianka. Stalin i VChK-GPU-OGPU-NKVD,* pp. 599, 601–612, 618–619, 626–637, 638–650, 663–669.

84. An account of the relationship between these two men is offered in Oleg V. Khlevniuk, *In Stalin's Shadow: The Career of "Sergo" Ordzhonikidze* (New York, 1995).

85. Mikhail Nikolaevich Tukhachevsky (1893–1937) was a Bolshevik hero of the Civil War who had held senior posts in the Red Army before being appointed deputy to the people's commissar for defense, Kliment Voroshilov, with whom he had numerous run-ins. Stalin and many other Soviet military leaders were suspicious of Tukhachevsky as a potential conspirator because of his long years serving under Trotsky. Tukhachevsky and many of his fellow military leaders were shot based on fabricated political charges.

86. Khaustov and Samuel'son, *Stalin, NKVD i represii,* pp. 106–121.

Trepidation in the Inner Circle

1. On this point the bodyguards' accounts are fully consistent with Khrushchev's. See Sergei Khrushchev, ed., *Memoirs of Nikita Khrushchev,* vol. 2: *Reformer* (University Park, PA, 2006), p. 147; Edvard Radzinsky, *Stalin: The First In-Depth Biography Based on Explosive New Documents from Russia's Secret Archives* (New York, 1997), p. 573.

2. Khrushchev, *Memoirs of Nikita Khrushchev,* vol. 2, p. 147.

3. Radzinsky, *Stalin,* p. 573.

4. A. L. Miasnikov, *Ia lechil Stalina* (Moscow, 2011), pp. 302, 304–305.

5. Lazar Moiseevich Kaganovich (1893–1991) was one of Stalin's closest associates in the 1930s. Beginning in 1931 he essentially acted as Stalin's deputy in party matters. Before the war his political influence was somewhat diminished, and he was sent to work in economic posts, but because of his boundless devotion to Stalin, he continued to be a part of the inner circle. In 1957 he opposed Khrushchev's ascent and was forced into retirement. He lived to be almost one hundred and remained a confirmed Stalinist until his death. See E. A. Rees, *Iron Lazar: A Political Biography of Lazar Kaganovich* (London and New York, 2012).

6. Nikolai Alekseevich Voznesensky (1903–1950) was a member of the post-revolutionary generation of Stalinist functionaries. He joined the party after the Civil War, studied at Moscow's Institute of the Red Professoriat, and went on to hold several government posts. Voznesensky's career benefited from his time working directly under Andrei Zhdanov in Leningrad. When Zhdanov was promoted to the

top leadership, he took his clients with him. Voznesensky also benefited from all the job openings created by mass repression. In 1938 he was appointed to head the State Planning Commission, and in 1941 he became Stalin's first deputy chairman at the Council of People's Commissars. After the war he became a member of the country's top leadership, but after Zhdanov's death in 1948 he, along with Zhdanov's other protégés, began to lose influence. In 1949 Stalin arranged the series of fabricated cases that constituted the Leningrad Affair. Voznesensky was arrested and shot.

Aleksei Aleksandrovich Kuznetsov (1905-1950) also rose to prominence under Zhdanov's patronage. He held many party posts in Leningrad and was transferred to Moscow after the war. There he became a Central Committee secretary and was placed in charge of CC personnel matters. He was arrested and shot in association with the Leningrad Affair.

7. M. A. Men'shikov, *S vintovkoi i vo frake* (Moscow, 1996), p. 138.
8. Note from Ignatiev to Beria dated 27 March 1953; cited in N. V. Petrov, *Palachi* (Moscow, 2011), p. 299.
9. K. M. Simonov, *Glazami cheloveka moego pokoleniia* (Moscow, 1989), pp. 341-343.
10. Pavel Sudoplatov claims that in 1950 Stalin ordered that listening devices be installed to spy on Molotov and Mikoyan (Pavel Sudoplatov et al., *Special Tasks: The Memoirs of an Unwanted Witness—A Soviet Spymaster* [New York, 1994], p. 332). Even if Sudoplatov is mistaken about the time and target of this eavesdropping, the very mention of such orders by Stalin reflects an actual phenomenon recalled by this highly placed security official.
11. Simonov, *Glazami cheloveka moego pokoleniia*, pp. 160-161. Quoted from Yoram Gorlizki and Oleg Khlevniuk, *Cold Peace: Stalin and the Soviet Ruling Circle, 1945-1953* (New York, 2004), p. 83.
12. Interview with V. G. Trukhanovsky in *Novaia i noveishaia istoriia*, no. 6 (1994): 78-79.
13. Cited in O. V. Khlevniuk et al., comps., *Politbiuro TsK VKP(b) i Sovet Ministrov SSSR. 1945-1953* (Moscow, 2002), p. 399. See also Yoram Gorlizki, "Ordinary Stalinism: The Council of Ministers and the Soviet Neopatrimonial State, 1946-1953," *Journal of Modern History* 74, no. 4 (2002): 723-725.
14. Cited in Khlevniuk et al., *Politbiuro TsK VKP(b) i Sovet Ministrov SSSR*, p. 409.
15. O. V. Khlevniuk et al., comps., *Regional'naia politika Khrushcheva. TsK VKP(b) i mestnye partinye komitety. 1953-1964* (Moscow, 2009), p. 161.
16. In early 1951 Soviet ministers were paid a monthly salary of twenty thousand rubles, and their deputies received ten thousand (RGANI, f. 5, op. 25, d. 279, l. 17). Other senior officials in Moscow and around the country received salaries totaling several thousand rubles, as well as significant perquisites. L. V. Maksimenkov, comp., *Bol'shaia tsenzura. Pisateli i zhurnalisty v Strane Sovetov. 1917-1956* (Moscow, 2005), p. 627, describes fees totaling in the millions of rubles paid to writers. For comparison, the average per capita income of a peasant household in 1950 was less than one hundred rubles per month (V. P. Popov, *Rossiiskaia derevnia posle voiny [iiun' 1945-mart 1953]* [Moscow, 1993], p. 146). Meanwhile, many top officials were not subject to taxes, while the tax burden on the population at large was constantly growing.

17. Cited in Khrushchev, *Memoirs of Nikita Khrushchev,* vol. 2, p. 89.
18. N. Fedorenko, "Nochnye besedy," *Pravda,* 23 October 1988, p. 4.
19. *Izvestiia TsK KPSS,* no. 9 (1990): 113, 118.

Chapter 4. Terror and Impending War

1. Robert Conquest, *The Great Terror: Stalin's Purges of the 1930s* (New York, 1968). The orders and other documents associated with the large-scale operations of 1937–1938 have been published in English translation (see Oleg V. Khlevniuk, *The History of the Gulag from Collectivization to the Great Terror* [New Haven and London, 2004], pp. 140–165). By now there is a vast literature outlining the mechanism by which the Terror was carried out. Among general works on the subject available in English are J. Arch Getty and Oleg V. Naumov, eds., *The Road to Terror: Stalin and the Self-Destruction of the Bolsheviks, 1932–1939,* updated and abridged edition (New Haven, 2010); David R. Shearer, *Policing Stalin's Socialism: Repression and Social Order in the Soviet Union, 1924–1953* (New Haven and London, 2009); Paul Hagenloh, *Stalin's Police: Public Order and Mass Repression in the USSR, 1926–1941* (Washington, D.C. and Baltimore, 2009).
2. State Archive of the Russian Federation (GARF), f. R-9401, op. 1, d. 4157, ll. 201–205. These figures have appeared in numerous publications. See, for example, Khlevniuk, *History of the Gulag,* pp. 165–170, 289–290.
3. Note written by Stalin on a telegram from the NKVD chief for Sverdlovsk Oblast; dated 10 September 1937; cited in V. N. Khaustov et al., comps., *Lubianka. Stalin i Glavnoe upravlenie gosbezopasnosti NKVD. 1937–1938* (Moscow, 2004), pp. 348–351.
4. Instructions to Yezhov (most likely), dated 13 September 1937; ibid., p. 352.
5. Note written by Stalin on a progress report from Yezhov concerning the "operation to liquidate Polish espionage cadres"; dated 14 September 1937; ibid., pp. 352–359.
6. Stalin's instructions written in response to an NKVD summary of testimony by arrestees; dated 30 April 1938; ibid., pp. 527–537.
7. Stalin's instructions written in response to an NKVD report on a "terrorist group" within the rubber industry; dated 2 September 1938; ibid., pp. 546–547.
8. Cited in N. S. Tarkhova et al., comps., *Voennyi sovet pri narodnom komissare oborony SSSR. 1–4 iiunia 1937 g.* (Moscow, 2008), p. 137.
9. Cited in V. A. Nevezhin, comp., *Zastol'nye rechi Stalina. Dokumenty i materialy* (Moscow, 2003), pp. 132–135.
10. Rozengolts was arrested on 7 October 1937; V. N. Khaustov and L. Samuel'son, *Stalin, NKVD i repressii. 1936–1938* (Moscow, 2009), pp. 138–139.
11. RGASPI, f. 17, op. 162, d. 20, l. 87.
12. APRF, f. 3, op. 65, d. 223, l. 90; Oleg Khlevniuk, "The Reasons for the 'Great Terror': The Foreign-Political Aspect," in *Russia in the Age of Wars 1914–1945, ed.* Silvio Pons and Andrea Romano (Milan, 2000), pp. 165–166.
13. APRF, f. 3, op. 65, d. 223, l. 142.
14. RGASPI, f. 558, op. 11, d. 772, l. 14.
15. Ibid., l. 88.
16. "Stenogramma zasedanii fevral'sko-martovskogo plenuma 1937 g.," *Voprosy istorii,* no. 3 (1995): 13–14.

17. RGASPI, f. 558, op. 11, d. 203, ll. 62, 77–78.
18. Cited in Tarkhova et al., *Voennyi sovet pri narodnom komissare oborony SSSR*, p. 133.
19. Edward Hallet Carr, *The Comintern and the Spanish Civil War* (London and Basingstoke, 1984), p. 44.
20. RGASPI, f. 17, op. 162, d. 21, l. 157; N. F. Bugai, "Vyselenie sovetskikh koreitsev s Dal'nego Vostoka," *Voprosy istorii*, no. 5 (1994): 144.
21. F. Chuev, *Sto sorok besed s Molotovym* (Moscow, 1991), pp. 390, 391, 416.
22. L. M. Kaganovich, *Pamiatnye zapiski* (Moscow, 1996), pp. 549, 558.
23. Cited in A. S. Iakovlev, *Tsel' zhizni* (Moscow, 1987), p. 212.
24. The discovery of "counterrevolutionary groups" (rather than lone enemies) was one of the primary goals of the process of extracting confessions from arrestees.
25. Cited in Khlevniuk, *History of the Gulag*, p. 163.
26. A detailed study of Stalin's role in organizing the Terror has been done using a vast body of archival documents. See Khaustov and Samuel'son, *Stalin, NKVD i repressii.*
27. These calculations were made based on the clerical numbering of Yezhov's reports published in Khaustov et al., *Lubianka. Stalin i Glavnoe upravlenie gosbezopasnosti NKVD.* I am grateful to N. V. Petrov, who pointed out the possibility of using this source.
28. Oleg V. Khlevniuk. *Master of the House: Stalin and His Inner Circle* (New Haven and London, 2008), p. 270.
29. RGASPI, f. 671, op. 1, d. 265, l. 22.
30. *Istoricheskii arkhiv*, no. 1 (1992): 125–128.
31. Official figures for industrial growth gave 28.7 percent for 1936, 11.2 percent for 1937, and 11.8 percent for 1938. Economists have calculated that using modern methods, these figures would correspond to 10.4, 2.3, and 1.1 percent growth respectively. See R. W. Davies, Mark Harrison, and S. G. Wheatcroft, eds., *The Economic Transformation of the Soviet Union, 1913–1945* (Cambridge, 1994), pp. 302–303.
32. During 1937–1938 a total of thirty-five thousand commanders were discharged from the Red Army (not including the air force and navy). Many of them were arrested. As of early 1940, approximately eleven thousand of them had been returned to the army, so approximately twenty-four thousand were lost. A sense of the scale of this attenuation can be gained by comparing these figures to the number of graduates of military colleges and academies during the three-year period of 1935–1937: slightly more than twenty-seven thousand (*Izvestiia TsK KPSS*, no. 1 [1990]: 186–189). It goes without saying that the officers who had been discharged, arrested, and then returned to duty suffered serious emotional trauma that affected their performance. Furthermore, the fear that they too could be arrested surely also had an effect on those who were not.
33. GARF, R-8131, op. 37, d. 112, l. 16.
34. Cited in A. I. Kartunova, "1938-i. Poslednii god zhizni i deiatel'nosti marshala V. K. Bliukhera," *Novaia i noveishaia istoriia*, no. 1 (2004): 175.
35. RGASPI, f. 17, op. 162, d. 24, l. 17.
36. Stenographic record of the Eighteenth Party Congress; *XVIII s"ezd Vsesoiuznoi Kommunisticheskoi Partii (b). 10–21 marta 1939 g.* (Moscow, 1939), pp. 12–15.

37. Maksim Maksimovich Litvinov (1876–1951), who joined what would become the Bolshevik party long before the revolution, served the cause of Soviet foreign affairs in one capacity or another most of his adult life. After years as deputy commissar and then commissar, he fell into disgrace in the late 1930s. During the war, Stalin decided to take advantage of the ties Litvinov had developed in the West and the reputation he enjoyed there and appointed him Soviet ambassador to the United States. Toward the war's end Litvinov was dismissed for the final time, but he was never arrested and was allowed to live out his life.

38. A. I. Mikoian, *Tak bylo. Razmyshleniia o minuvshem* (Moscow, 1999), p. 534.

39. S. Z. Sluch, "Stalin i Gitler, 1933–1941: Raschety i proschety Kremlia," *Otechestvennaia istoriia,* no. 1 (2005): 98–119.

40. RGASPI, f. 17, op. 166, d. 592, l. 107.

41. Cited in G. Ia. Rudoi, comp., *Otkroveniia i priznaniia. Natsistskaia verkhushka o voine "tret'ego reikha" protiv SSSR* (Moscow, 1996), p. 65.

42. V. G. Komplektov et al., eds., *Dokumenty vneshnei politiki SSSR. 1939,* vol. 22 (Moscow, 1992), vol. 1, p. 624; vol. 2, p. 585. This correspondence was also preserved in Stalin's personal archive: RGASPI, f. 558, op. 11, d. 296, ll. 1–3.

43. Cited in S. Z. Sluch, "Rech' Stalina, kotoroi ne bylo," *Otechestvennaia istoriia,* no. 1 (2004): 114. In this article Sluch provides a detailed history of this alleged speech and persuasively argues that it was a fake.

44. Cited in G. M. Adibekov et al., eds., *Politbiuro TsK RKP(b) VKP(b) i Komintern. 1919–1943. Dokumenty* (Moscow, 2004), pp. 780–781.

45. Anna M. Cienciala, Natalia S. Lebedeva, and Wojciech Materski, eds., *Katyn: A Crime without Punishment* (New Haven and London, 2007).

46. Alfred Bilmanis, comp., *Latvian-Russian Relations: Documents* (Washington, D.C., 1944), pp. 196–197.

47. Cited in L. E. Reshin et al., comps., *1941 god,* vol. 2 (Moscow, 1998), pp. 595–596.

48. Notation by Stalin on a coded message from Belarusian Central Committee secretary Ponomarenko to Stalin; dated 13 November 1939; RGASPI, f. 558, op. 11, d. 66, l. 13.

49. O. A. Rzheshevskii and O. Vekhviliainen, eds., *Zimniaia voina 1939–1940* (Moscow, 1999), vol. 1, pp. 324–325.

50. Sergei Khrushchev, ed., *Memoirs of Nikita Khrushchev,* vol. 1: *Commissar* (University Park, PA, 2004), p. 266.

51. Khlevniuk, *History of the Gulag,* p. 236.

52. Soviet transcripts of Molotov's conversations with Hitler and von Ribbentrop on 13 November 1940 have been published in G. E. Mamedov et al., eds., *Dokumenty vneshnei politiki* (Moscow, 1998), vol. 23, bk. 2, pt. 1, pp. 63–78.

53. Ibid., pp. 135–137.

54. G. A. Kumanev, *Riadom so Stalinym* (Smolensk, 2001), pp. 463–470.

55. According to Chadaev in ibid., the chairman of Gosplan, Nikolai Voznesensky, was also at the meeting. At the time, Voznesensky was not yet a Politburo member.

56. A. A. Chernobaev, ed., *Na prieme u Stalina. Tetradi (zhurnaly) zapisei lits, priniatykh I. V. Stalinym (1924–1953 gg.)* (Moscow, 2008), pp. 317–318.

57. Aleksandr Sergeevich Shcherbakov (1901–1945) was a member of the post-revolu-

tionary generation that Stalin placed in charge of propaganda within the Central Committee apparat. In 1938 he was made first secretary of Moscow's party organization as well as a Central Committee secretary. Shcherbakov died at an early age.

58. Remarks by Stalin at a meeting on 17 January 1941 as recorded by V. A. Malyshev in his diary; cited in *Istochnik*, no. 5 (1997): 114.

59. Mikoian, *Tak bylo*, p. 346.

60. RGASPI, f. 558, op. 11, d. 769, ll. 176–176ob.

61. *Istoricheskii arkhiv*, no. 5 (1994): 222.

62. Cited in Yoram Gorlizki and Oleg Khlevniuk, "Stalin and His Circle," in *The Cambridge History of Russia*, ed. Ronald Grigor Suny, vol. 3 (Cambridge, 2006), p. 248.

63. Stalin actually spoke at this reception several times, but for simplicity's sake, I will treat these remarks as a single speech. The stenographic record of Stalin's remarks has not been preserved, but several witnesses describe him as saying essentially the same thing. See Nevezhin, *Zastol'nye rechi Stalina*, pp. 273–296.

64. Speech by Stalin at a meeting of Moscow and Leningrad propagandists; *Istoricheskii arkhiv*, no. 5 (1994): 13.

65. E. N. Kul'kov and O. A. Rzheshevskii, eds., *Zimniaia voina 1939–1940* (Moscow, 1999), vol. 2, pp. 281–282.

66. Debate around this topic has become particularly active over the past twenty years. Overall, the numerous arguments in favor of the idea that Stalin was planning a preventive strike—some of which appear to be politically motivated—do not seem to warrant serious attention, but this theory has generated a number of works presenting interesting evidence and arguments. I make use of statistical data offered in a study by Mikhail Meltiukhov, although I am not convinced by his overall argument. See M. Mel'tiukhov, *Upushchennyi shans Stalina. Sovetskii Soiuz i bor'ba za Evropu. 1939–1941* (Moscow, 2002).

67. Ibid., pp. 360, 392–393.

68. Davies, Harrison, and Wheatcroft, *The Economic Transformation of the Soviet Union*, p. 321.

69. Mel'tiukhov, *Upushennyi shans Stalina*, pp. 392, 393.

70. Cited in E. A. Osokina, *Za fasadom "stalinskogo izobiliia"* (Moscow, 2008), pp. 272–277.

71. *Voenno-istoricheskii zhurnal*, no. 1 (1991): 17.

72. In September 1940, the government permitted such convicts to be sent to the Gulag to serve their prison terms, a violation of its own law (GARF, f. R-5446, op. 57, d. 79, l. 31). These prisoners suffered a terrible fate, and they were not always released after serving the short terms handed down by the courts.

73. From a 15 April 1942 conversation between Stalin and General Nikolai Biriukov, one of the heads of the Main Mechanized Directorate; N. Biriukov, *Tanki-frontu. Zapiski sovetskogo generala* (Smolensk, 2005), pp. 143–144.

74. Reshin et al., *1941 god*, pp. 54–55.

75. Mel'tiukov, *Upushchennyi shans Stalina*, p. 246; M. Iu. Mukhin, *Aviapromyshlennost' SSSR v 1921–1941 godakh* (Moscow, 2006), pp. 154–155, 291–299.

76. David Murphy, who has made a careful study of all available Soviet intelligence reports on the eve of the war, gives Soviet espionage rather high marks. However, he

notes an effort on the part of the leaders of Soviet intelligence to adapt their findings to Stalin's preconceptions. In this regard, Murphy draws historical parallels: the reluctance of the conservative government of Great Britain in the 1930s to properly assess the Nazi threat and the myopic focus of U.S. intelligence on hunting down weapons of mass destruction in Iraq, while earlier administrations missed clues of an impending terrorist attack on U.S. soil. See David E. Murphy, *What Stalin Knew: The Enigma of Barbarossa* (New Haven and London, 2005), pp. xviii–xix.

77. Cited in Reshin et al., *1941 god,* pp. 382–383.

Patient Number 1

1. Sergei Khrushchev, ed., *Memoirs of Nikita Khrushchev,* vol. 2: *Reformer* (University Park, PA, 2006), p. 148.
2. A. L. Miasnikov, *Ia lechil Stalina* (Moscow, 2011), pp. 294–295.
3. Ibid., p. 302.
4. B. S. Ilizarov, *Tainaia zhizn' Stalina* (Moscow, 2002), p. 110.
5. RGASPI, f. 558, op. 1, d. 4327, l. 1.
6. Ibid., op. 4, d. 619, ll. 172, 173.
7. Ilizarov, *Tainaia zhizn' Stalina,* p. 110.
8. Letter from Stalin to Malinovsky, November 1913; cited in A. Ostrovskii, *Kto stoial za spinoi Stalina?* (Moscow, 2002), pp. 397–398.
9. Ilizarov, *Tainaia zhizn' Stalina,* p. 110.
10. RGASPI, f. 17, op. 3, d. 154, l. 2.
11. Ibid., d. 303, l. 5.
12. Svetlana Alliluyeva, *Twenty Letters to a Friend* trans. Priscilla Johnson McMillan (New York, 1967), p. 33.
13. No information has been found about Stalin's travels in the south in 1924, although an August 1924 Politburo decision granted him a two-month vacation; RGASPI, f. 17, op. 3, d. 459, l. 2.
14. Ilizarov, *Tainaia zhizn' Stalin,* pp. 112–113, 118–119.
15. Cited in Lars T. Lih, Oleg V. Naumov, and Oleg Khlevniuk, eds., *Stalin's Letters to Molotov, 1925–1936* (New Haven, 1995), p. 91.
16. RGASPI, f. 558, op. 11, d. 69, ll. 53–54.
17. Cited in Lih, Naumov, and Khlevniuk, *Stalin's Letters to Molotov,* p. 113.
18. RGASPI, f. 558, op. 11, d. 69, l. 670b.
19. Ibid., l. 68.
20. From Valedinsky's memoirs; cited in *Istochnik,* no. 2 (1998): 68.
21. Cited in Lih, Naumov, and Khlevniuk, *Stalin's Letters to Molotov,* p. 138.
22. Cited in *Istochnik,* no. 2 (1998): 69.
23. Ibid., p. 69; Ilizarov, *Tainaia zhizn' Stalin,* pp. 112–113.
24. Cited in Lih, Naumov, and Khlevniuk, *Stalin's Letters to Molotov,* p. 175.
25. Iu. G. Murin, comp., *Iosif Stalin v ob"iatiiakh sem'i. Iz lichnogo arkhiva* (Moscow, 1993), p. 32.
26. RGASPI, f. 558, op. 11, d. 728, l. 29.
27. Cited in Murin, *Iosif Stalin v ob"iatiiakh sem'i,* p. 37.
28. I. V. Stalin, *Works,* vol. 13 (Moscow, 1954), p. 136. Translation slightly revised.

29. Cited in O. V. Khlevniuk et al., comps., *Stalin i Kaganovich. Perepiska. 1931–1936* (Moscow, 2001), p. 180.
30. S. V. Deviatov et al., *Garazh osobogo naznacheniia. 1921–2011* (Moscow, 2011), p. 157.
31. Letters from Stalin to Yenukidze, dated 16 August and 13 September 1933; RGASPI, f. 558, op. 11, d. 728, ll. 38, 40.
32. Letter dated 7 September 1933; cited in A. V. Kvashonkin et al., comps., *Bol'shevistskoe rukovodstvo. Perepiska. 1912–1927* (Moscow, 1996), p. 254.
33. From the diary of Maria Svanidze; cited in Murin, *Iosif Stalin v ob"iatiiakh sem'i*, p. 158.
34. Letter to A. I. Ugarov, dated 16 August 1934; cited in A. Kirilina, *Neizvestnyi Kirov* (St. Petersburg and Moscow, 2001), p. 141.
35. From the diary of Maria Svanidze; cited in Murin, *Iosif Stalin v ob"iatiiakh sem'i*, p. 183.
36. From the memoirs of Dr. Valedinsky; cited in *Istochnik,* no. 2 (1998): 70.
37. Ibid., p. 70.
38. RGASPI, f. 558, op. 11, d. 377, l. 60.
39. Stalin left Moscow on 9 October 1945 and returned 17 December; O. V. Khlevniuk et al., comps., *Politbiuro TsK VKP(b) i Sovet Ministrov SSSR. 1945–1953* (Moscow, 2002), p. 398.
40. Ibid.
41. Deviatov et al., *Garazh osobogo naznacheniia,* p. 201.
42. Descriptions of Stalin's lifestyle at his southern dachas can be found in the memoirs of the Georgian party boss Akaky Mgeladze, a young protégé of Stalin who enjoyed his particular favor; A. I. Mgeladze, *Stalin. Kakim ia ego znal,* (n.p., 2001).
43. Stalin's medical records; RGASPI, f. 558, op. 11, d. 1483, ll. 1–101; Ilizarov, *Tainaia zhizn' Stalina,* pp. 126, 129.
44. M. Dzhilas [Milovan Djilas], *Litso totalitarizma* (Moscow, 1992), p. 60.
45. Cited in *Istoricheskii arkhiv,* no. 3 (1997): 117.
46. Mgeladze, *Stalin,* p. 125.
47. Cited in E. Khodzha [Enver Hoxha], *So Stalinym. Vospominaniia* (Tirana, 1984), p. 137.
48. Alliluyeva, *Twenty Letters,* p. 22.
49. Ibid., pp. 206–207.
50. Miasnikov, *Ia lechil Stalina,* p. 302.
51. Alliluyeva, *Twenty Letters,* p. 207.
52. Miasnikov, *Ia lechil Stalina,* pp. 304–305.
53. Transcript of a conversation in March 1978 published in F. Chuev, *Sto sorok besed s Molotovym* (Moscow, 1991), p. 324.

Chapter 5. Stalin at War

1. The following descriptions of meetings in Stalin's office on 21 and 22 June 1941 are based on G. K. Zhukov, *Vospominaniia i razmyshleniia* (Moscow, 2002), vol. 1, pp. 260–269; A. I. Mikoian, *Tak bylo. Razmyshleniia o minuvshem* (Moscow, 1999), p. 388; and A. A. Chernobaev, ed., *Na prieme u Stalina. Tetradi (zhurnaly) zapisei lits, priniatykh I. V. Stalinym (1924–1953 gg.)* (Moscow, 2008), pp. 337–338.
2. Semen Konstantinovich Timoshenko (1895–1970) was a commander of the First

Cavalry Army during the Civil War, in which capacity he worked closely with Stalin. He went on to make a successful military career and, after the debacle in Finland, replaced Voroshilov as defense commissar and was elevated to marshal. However, during the war with Germany, Timoshenko did not prove to be particularly able and was forced into the background. After the war and until his retirement in 1960 he was given secondary posts commanding various military districts.

Georgy Konstantinovich Zhukov (1896–1974) made a military career after serving with the Red Army during the Civil War. He advanced rapidly through the ranks during the late 1930s, when purges among the officer corps created opportunities. Zhukov proved an able commander during military conflicts with Japan in 1939. Before the war with Germany he was appointed chief of the General Staff. The war proved to be his finest hour. He rose to be one of the Soviet Union's leading marshals and served as deputy to the commander in chief (Stalin). When it was over, Zhukov fell into disfavor but enjoyed a brief return to prominence after Stalin's death, serving as defense minister from 1955 to 1957. Khrushchev, however, was wary of the ambitious marshal and forced him into retirement. After Khrushchev was expelled as Soviet leader, Zhukov was allowed to publish his memoirs (the first edition of which came out in 1969). Although they were heavily censored, they remain an important source for historians of the Great Patriotic War (as the war with Germany is known in Russia). Recent editions of his memoirs restore materials excised by the censors, but we will never know to what extent Zhukov self-censored his original manuscript.

3. Zhukov, *Vospominaniia i razmyshleniia,* vol. 1, p. 260.

4. Ibid, p. 264

5. Cited in a speech written by Zhukov in May 1956 to be given at a Central Committee plenum that was to be devoted to the Cult of Personality but never took place; cited in *Istochnik,* no. 2 (1995): 147.

6. Chernobaev, *Na prieme u Stalina,* p. 337.

7. Cited in Zhukov, *Vospominaniia i razmyshleniia,* vol. 1, p. 265.

8. Cited in L. E. Reshin et al., comps., *1941 god* (Moscow, 1998), vol. 2, p. 432.

9. Chernobaev, *Na prieme u Stalina,* p. 337.

Lev Zakharovich Mekhlis (1889–1953) was one of Stalin's assistants in the 1920s, after which he held a number of senior posts and enjoyed Stalin's wholehearted trust. After war with Germany broke out, Stalin put Mekhlis in charge of the political offices within the Red Army that were supposed to exercise political control over commanders. Mekhlis's bungling at the front infuriated Stalin but did not undermine his trust in his faithful helper. Mekhlis went on to hold a number of senior posts on various fronts. After the war, he was put in charge of the Ministry of State Control. Poor health forced him into retirement. He died several weeks before Stalin and was buried at the foot of the Kremlin walls, alongside other Soviet leaders and heroes.

10. Cited in Zhukov, *Vospominaniia i razmyshleniia,* vol. 1, p. 265.

11. Reshin et al., *1941 god,* p. 431.

12. For versions of Molotov's speech, see *Istoricheskii arkhiv,* no. 2 (1995): 34–39.

13. John Erickson, *The Road to Stalingrad* (London, 2003), p. 177.

14. Boris Mikhailovich Shaposhnikov (1882–1945) was one of the few Red Army officers to retain Stalin's trust even as he reached a position of seniority. On the eve of the war with Germany and during its initial phase Shaposhnikov was head of the army's General Staff and deputy defense commissar, but he had to resign due to illness. He died a few weeks before the fall of Berlin.

15. Reshin et al., *1941 god*, pp. 439–440.

16. Zhukov, *Vospominaniia i razmyshleniia*, vol. 1, p. 268.

17. *Rodina*, no. 4 (2005): 4.

18. M. I. Mel'tiukhov, *Upushchennyi shans Stalina. Sovetskii Soiuz i bor'ba za Evropu. 1939–1941* (Moscow, 2002), p. 413.

19. Zhukov, *Vospominaniia i razmyshleniia*, vol. 1, p. 340.

20. Memoirs of Chadaev published in *Otechestvennaia istoriia*, no. 2 (2005): 7.

21. Semen Mikhailovich Budenny (1883–1973) commanded the First Cavalry Army during the Civil War and was a supporter of Stalin during this period. He went on to become a marshal and held top military posts, including first deputy people's commissar of defense.

22. Admiral Nikolai Gerasimovich Kuznetsov (1902–1974) was head of the naval commissariat and commander in chief of the navy from 1939 to 1946. After the war he fell into disfavor and was demoted, but in 1951–1953 he was again placed in charge of the naval ministry. He lost command of the navy for good in 1955 after the loss of a battleship.

23. RGASPI, f. 17, op. 162, d. 36, l. 22; *Izvestiia TsK KPSS,* no. 6 (1990): 196–197.

24. N. G. Kuznetsov, *Nakanune* (Moscow, 1989), p. 327.

25. N. V. Petrov, *Palachi* (Moscow, 2011), p. 85–93.

26. *Otechestvennye arkhivy*, no. 2 (1995): 29–32; *Izvestiia TsK KPSS,* no. 6 (1990): 208–209, 212–214.

27. Interview by Georgy Kumanev of I. V. Kovalev, who was serving as deputy commissar for state control when the war broke out and was in charge of rail transport. *Novaia i noveishaia istoriia*, no. 3 (2005): 149–150.

28. Reshin et al., *1941 god*, p. 497; F. Chuev, *Sto sorok besed s Molotovym* (Moscow, 1991), p. 52.

29. In his memoirs Zhukov states that Stalin came to the defense commissariat twice (*Vospominaniia i razmyshleniia*, vol. 1, p. 287); however, there are no other sources to corroborate this assertion.

30. Mikoyan's recollections are reported in Reshin et al., *1941 god*, pp. 497–498.

31. Letter to the Soviet leadership from Lavrenty Beria after his arrest in 1953; published in *Istochnik*, no. 4 (1994): 7; recollections of Anastas Mikoyan published in Reshin et al., *1941 god*, pp. 498–499.

32. Cited in Reshin et al., *1941 god*, p. 498.

33. Cited in Chuev, *Sto sorok besed s Molotovym*, p. 330.

34. Recollections of Anastas Mikoyan published in Reshin et al., *1941 god*, pp. 498–499.

35. The original text is among Mikoyan's personal papers, which are held by RGASPI.

36. Mikoian, *Tak bylo*, p. 391.

37. Iu. A. Gor'kov, *Gosudarstvennyi Komitet Oborony postanovliaet (1941–1945)* (Moscow, 2002), pp. 30–31.

38. *Izvestiia TsK KPSS*, no. 7 (1990): 208, and no. 8 (1990): 208; RGASPI, f. 17, op. 163, d. 1319, l. 93.

39. Interview of Ivan Peresypkin, wartime communications commissar, by Georgy Kumanev; *Otechestvennaia istoriia*, no. 3 (2003): 65.

40. The speech is cited in *Pravda*, 3 July 1941.

41. Order by People's Commissar for Defense Stalin, 28 June 1941. In V. A. Zolotarev, ed., *Russkii arkhiv. Velikaia Otechestvennaia. Prikazy narodnogo komissara oborony SSSR. 22 iunia 1941 g.–1942 g.*, vol. 13 (2–2) (Moscow, 1997), pp. 37–38.

42. G. F. Krivosheev et al., *Velikaia Otechestvennaia bez grifa sekretnosti. Kniga poter'* (Moscow, 2009), pp. 60–61.

43. Conversations between Stalin and commanders in the Western Direction, 26 July 1941; cited in V. A. Zolotarev, ed., *Russkii arkhiv. Velikaia Otechestvennaia. Stavka VGK. 1941 g.*, vol. 16 (5–1) (Moscow, 1996), pp. 92–93.

44. RGASPI, f. 17, op. 167, d. 60, l. 49.

45. D. A. Volkogonov, *Triumf i tragediia*, vol. 2, pt. 1 (Moscow, 1989), p. 167.

46. Cited in Zolotarev, *Russkii arkhiv. Velikaia Otechestvennaia. Stavka VGK. 1941 g.*, vol. 16 (5–1), p. 361.

47. RGASPI, f. 558, op. 11, d. 492, l. 35; *Izvestiia TsK KPSS*, no. 9 (1990): 213.

48. V. N. Khaustov et al., comps., *Lubianka. Stalin i NKVD-NKGB-GUKR "Smersh." 1939–1946* (Moscow, 2006), pp. 317–318.

49. For the texts of these decisions with changes entered by Stalin, see *Vestnik arkhiva Preszidenta Rossiiskoi Federatsii. Voina. 1941–1945* (Moscow, 2010), pp. 37–40.

50. Khaustov et al., *Lubianka. Stalin i NKVD-NKGB-GUKR "Smersh,"* pp. 317–318.

51. Reshin et al., *1941 god*, pp. 476–479.

52. Cited in *Izvestiia TsK KPSS*, no. 7 (1990): 209.

53. *Istoricheskii arkhiv*, no. 1 (1993): 45–46.

54. Interview of I. V. Kovalev by Georgy Kumanev published in *Novaia i noveishaia istoriia*, no. 3 (2005): 160–161.

55. RGASPI, f. 558, op. 11, d. 235, l. 123.

56. Zhukov, *Vospominaniia i razmyshleniia*, vol. 1, pp. 350–353.

57. Krivosheev et al., *Velikaia Otechestvennaia bez grifa sekretnosti*, p. 84.

58. Cited in Zolotarev, *Russkii arkhiv. Velikaia Otechestvennaia. Stavka VGK. 1941 g.*, vol. 16 (5–1), pp. 108–109; *Izvestiia TsK KPSS*, no. 9 (1990): 199–200.

59. A. M. Vasilevskii, *Delo vsei zhizni* (Moscow, 1978), p. 132.

   Aleksandr Mikhailovich Vasilevsky (1895–1977) was a renowned Soviet marshal and leading figure in the Great Patriotic War who served as deputy chief and then chief of the General Staff and commanded Soviet troops in the Far East during the war with Japan. After the war he served as minister of defense.

60. Krivosheev et al., *Velikaia Otechestvennaia bez grifa sekretnosti*, p. 85.

61. Interview with Zhukov published in K. Simonov, *Glazami cheloveka moego pokoleniia* (Moscow, 1989), p. 361.

62. Zolotarev, *Russkii arkhiv. Velikaia Otechestvennaia. Stavka VGK. 1941 g.*, vol. 16 (5–1), pp. 175.

63. Simonov, *Glazami cheloveka moego pokoleniia*, pp. 361–363.

64. *Voenno-istoricheskii zhurnal*, no. 1 (1992): 77, and nos. 6–7 (1992): 17; Zolotarev,

Russkii arkhiv. Velikaia Otechestvennaia. Stavka VGK. 1941 g., vol. 16 (5-1), pp. 378-379.

65. A. E. Golovanov, *Dal'niaia bombardirovochnaia . . .* (Moscow, 2004), p. 78.

66. *Izvestiia TsK KPSS,* no. 12 (1990): 210-211.

67. Mikoian, *Tak bylo,* p. 417. Mikoyan writes that this was on 16 October, but he definitely refers to the discussion of the order to evacuate Moscow that was actually adopted on 15 October. This meeting evidently took place in Stalin's apartment.

68. *Izvestiia TsK KPSS,* no. 12 (1990): 217.

69. Interview with Aleksandr Vasilevsky in Simonov, *Glazami cheloveka moego pokoleniia,* p. 446.

70. NKVD report dated 21 October 1941; published in *Istochnik,* no. 5 (1995): 152.

71. M. M. Gorinov et al., comps., *Moskva voennaia. 1941-1945. Memuary i arkhivnye dokumenty* (Moscow, 1995), p. 550; *Izvestiia TsK KPSS,* no. 1 (1991): 217.

72. Gorinov et al., *Moskva voennaia,* pp. 111, 116-119; Mikoian, *Tak bylo,* pp. 419-420.

73. A. I. Shakhurin, *Kryl'ia pobedy* (Moscow, 1990), pp. 156-157.

74. *Izvestiia TsK KPSS,* no. 1 (1991): 215-216, and no. 4 (1991): 210-214; *Istoricheskii arkhiv,* no. 3 (1997): 92.

75. S. V. Tochenov, "Volneniia i zabastovki na tekstil'nykh predpriiatiiakh Ivanovskoi oblast osen'iu 1941 goda," *Otechestvennaia istoriia,* no. 3 (2004): pp. 42-47; *Istoricheskii arkhiv,* no. 2 (1994): 111-136.

76. Cited in G. K. Zhukov, *Vospominaniia i razmyshleniia* (Moscow, 2002), vol. 2, pp. 26-27.

77. Cited in *Pravda,* 7 November 1941.

78. S. V. Deviatov et al., *Moskovskii Kreml' v gody Velikoi Otechestvennoi Voiny* (Moscow, 2010), p. 87.

79. Ibid., pp. 57-61, 64.

80. *Pravda,* 8 November 1941.

81. Deviatov et al., *Moskovskii Kreml',* p. 61.

82. K. M. Anderson et al., comps., *Kremlevskii kinoteatr. 1928-1953* (Moscow, 2005), p. 639.

83. Cited in V. A. Zolotarev, ed., *Russkii arkhiv. Velikaia Otechestvennaia. Stavka VGK. 1942 g.*, vol. 16 (5-2) (Moscow, 1996), pp. 33-35.

84. R. V. Mazurkevich, "Plany i real'nost'," *Voenno-istoricheskii zhurnal,* no. 2 (1992): 24-25.

85. Vasilevskii, *Delo vsei zhizni,* p. 189.

86. Cited in *Istochnik,* no. 5 (1995): 41.

87. GARF (not yet catalogued). From the memoirs of Yakov Chadaev.

88. Zolotarev, *Russkii arkhiv. Velikaia Otechestvennaia. Stavka VGK. 1942 g.*, vol. 16 (5-2), pp. 236-239.

89. Interview with Georgy Zhukov in Simonov, *Glazami cheloveka moego pokoleniia,* p. 366.

90. Vasilevskii, *Delo vsei zhizni,* pp. 195-196.

91. Krivosheev et al., *Velikaia Otechestvennaia bez grifa sekretnosti,* p. 179.

92. Zolotarev, *Russkii arkhiv. Velikaia Otechestvennaia. Stavka VGK. 1942 g.*, vol. 16 (5-2), pp. 263-264.

93. After reading this letter, Stalin placed it in his personal archive. RGASPI, f. 558, op. 11, d. 762, ll. 6-8.

94. K. K. Rokossovskii, *Soldatskii dolg* (Moscow, 2013), p. 211.

    Konstantin Konstantinovich Rokossovsky (1896-1968) was a much-acclaimed marshal of the Great Patriotic War. He was arrested during the purges and spent 1937-1940 in prison. During the war he was placed in charge of armies and fronts. In 1949-1956 he served as Poland's minister of defense before holding senior posts in the Soviet ministry. His rather candid memoirs, *Soldatskii dolg* (A soldier's duty), were published in 1968 with major excisions. An uncensored edition came out in 1997.

95. Cited in Zolotarev, *Russkii arkhiv. Velikaia Otechestvennaia. Stavka VGK. 1942 g.,* vol. 16 (5-2), pp. 276-279.

96. O. A. Rzheshevskii, *Stalin i Cherchill'. Vstrechi. Besedy. Diskussii* (Moscow, 2004), pp. 348-383.

97. Krivosheev et al., *Velikaia Otechestvennaia bez grifa sekretnosti,* pp. 60-61.

98. *Rodina,* no. 4 (2005): 65.

99. Aleksei Innokentievich Antonov (1896-1962) was a senior Soviet military officer who served as deputy head of the General Staff during the war years and often reported directly to Stalin.

100. Vasilevskii, *Delo vsei zhizni,* pp. 311.

101. A. Eremenko, *Gody vozmezdiia* (Moscow, 1986), pp. 36, 38; Dmitri Volkogonov, *Stalin: Triumph and Tragedy* (New York, 1991), p. 481; Deviatov et al., *Moskovskii Kreml',* pp. 184, 186.

102. *Perepiska Predsedatelia Soveta Ministrov SSSR s prezidentami SShA i prem'er-ministrami Velikobritanii vo vremia Velikoi Otechestvennoi Voiny 1941–1945 gg.* (Moscow, 1957). Stalin's letter to Churchill is dated 9 August 1943 (vol. 1, pp. 141-142). Stalin's letter to Roosevelt is dated 8 August 1943 (vol. 2, p. 77).

103. Stalin's letter to Churchill, 24 June 1943, which he sent that same day to Roosevelt for his information; *Perepiska,* vol. 2, pp. 72-75.

104. Cited in S. M. Shtemenko, *General'nyi shtab v gody voiny* (Moscow, 1989), p. 148.

105. Golovanov, *Dal'niaia bombardirovochnaia,* pp. 351-356.

106. RGASPI, f. 558, op. 11, d. 377, l. 61.

107. Cited in Gorinov et al., *Moskva voennaia,* pp. 694-695; *Istochnik,* no. 2 (1995): 138-139.

108. *Istoricheskii arkhiv,* no. 1 (1997): 66-68.

109. V. A. Zolotarev, ed., *Russkii arkhiv, Velikaia Otechestvennaia. Stavka VGK. 1944–1945,* vol. 16 (5-4) (Moscow, 1999), p. 12.

110. For an examination of the populations affected by mass killings in the geographic region between Germany and the Soviet Union by both Stalin and Hitler, see Timothy Snyder, *Bloodlands: Europe between Hitler and Stalin* (New York, 2010).

111. *Vestnik arkhiva Preszidenta Rossiiskoi Federatsii. Voina. 1941–1945,* pp. 346-348.

112. Khaustov et al., *Lubianka. Stalin i NKVD-NKGB-GUKR "Smersh,"* p. 405.

113. Alexander Statiev, "The Nature of Anti-Soviet Armed Resistance, 1942-1944: The North Caucasus, the Kalmyk Autonomous Republic, and Crimea," *Kritika: Explorations in Russian and Eurasian History* 6, no. 2 (Spring 2005): 285-318.

114. V. A. Kozlov and S. V. Mironenko, eds., "*Osobaia papka" Stalina. Iz materialov Sekretariata NKVD-MVD SSSR. 1944–1953* (Moscow, 1994).

115. GARF, f. R-9401, op. 2, d. 64, l. 167.

116. Ibid., l. 166.

117. Ibid., l. 165

118. Ibid., d. 66, ll. 9–10, 40–46.

119. Ibid., ll. 334–340.

120. Ibid., d. 67, ll. 319–324; d. 68, ll. 268–273.

121. N. M. Naimark, *Russians in Germany: A History of the Soviet Zone of Occupation, 1945–1949* (Cambridge, MA, 1995).

122. Khaustov et al., *Lubianka. Stalin i NKVD-NKGB-GUKR "Smersh,"* pp. 502–504.

123. Cited in M. Dzhilas [Milovan Djilas], *Litso totalitarizma* (Moscow, 1992), p. 82.

124. Transcript of conversations between Stalin and Roosevelt; RGASPI, f. 558, op. 11, d. 235, l. 8.

125. N. V. Petrov, *Po stsenariiu Stalina: Rol' organov NKVD-MGB SSSR v sovetizatsii stran Tsentral'noi i Vostochnoi Evropy. 1945–1953* (Moscow, 2011), pp. 44–52.

126. Cited in V. A. Zolotarev, *Russkii arkhiv. Velikaia Otechestvennaia. Stavka VGK. 1943 g.*, vol. 16 (5–3) (Moscow, 1996), p. 185.

127. RGASPI, f. 17, op. 3, d. 1045, l. 55.

128. Zolotarev, *Russkii arkhiv. Velikaia Otechestvennaia. Stavka VGK. 1942*, vol. 16 (5–2), p. 420.

129. Interview with Aleksandr Vasilevsky in Simonov, *Glazami cheloveka moego pokoleniia*, p. 446.

130. Vasilevskii, *Delo vsei zhizni*, pp. 496–497.

131. Shtemenko, *General'nyi shtab v gody voiny*, pp. 102–104. V. A. Zolotarev, ed., *Russkii arkhiv, Velikaia Otechestvennaia. General'nyi shtab v gody Velikoi Otechestvennoi voiny. 1941*, vol. 23 (12–1) (Moscow, 1997), pp. 11–12.

132. From a 2 April 1965 memorandum from Marshal Konev to the Central Committee Presidium; Shtemenko, *General'nyi shtab v gody voiny*, pp. 104, 192; I. S. Konev, *Zapiski komanduiushchego frontom* (Moscow, 2000), p. 498.

133. Interview with Zhukov in Simonov, *Glazami cheloveka moego pokoleniia*, p. 377.

134. Konev, *Zapiski komanduiushchego frontom*, p. 498.

135. Vasilevskii, *Delo vsei zhizni*, p. 497.

136. The SNK Bureau's Commission on Current Issues existed from June 1941 to December 1942. The SNK Bureau met in regular session from December 1942 through August 1945. Background on the establishment of these bodies can be found in RGASPI, f. 17, op. 163, d. 1326, l. 233; d. 1350, l. 40; d. 1356, ll. 120–121; d. 1406, l. 27.

137. Ibid., d. 1356, ll. 120–121.

138. Ibid., d. 1406, l. 27.

139. State Defense Committee resolution dated 4 February 1942; RGASPI, f. 644, op. 2, d. 36, ll. 32–35.

140. Mikoian, *Tak bylo*, p. 465.

141. APRF, f. 3, op. 52, d. 251, l. 93.

142. In December 1943, Andrei Andreev, a Central Committee secretary and Politburo member, was appointed people's commissar for agriculture.

143. APRF, f. 3, op. 52, d. 251, l. 93; Mikoian, *Tak bylo,* p. 466.

144. RGASPI, f. 17, op. 163, d. 1420, l. 136.

145. Bulganin was made a member of the State Defense Committee in place of Voro-shilov, with whose performance Stalin was displeased. Ibid., op. 3, d. 1051, l. 44, 46.

146. V. A. Zolotarev, ed., *Russkii arkhiv. Prikazy narodnogo komissara oborony SSSR. 1943–1945 gg.,* vol. 13 (2–3) (Moscow, 1997), p. 332.

147. Ibid., p. 337–338.

148. David Brandenberger, *National Bolshevism: Stalinist Mass Culture and Forma-tion of Modern Russian National Identity, 1931–1956* (Cambridge, MA, and Lon-don, 2002).

149. Chernobaev, *Na prieme u Stalina,* p. 417.

150. From notes taken by the head of the Council on the Affairs of the Russian Ortho-dox Church, G. G. Karpov, on the meeting between Stalin and the church leaders. GARF, f. R-6991, op. 1, d. 1, ll. 1–10; M. I. Odintsov, *Russkie patriarkhi XX veka* (Mos-cow, 1994), pp. 283–291.

151. Rzheshevskii, *Stalin i Cherchill',* p. 420; Michael Ellman, "Churchill on Stalin: A Note," *Europe-Asia Studies* 58, no. 6 (September, 2006): 969–970.

152. GARF, f. R-9401, op. 2, d. 94, ll. 15–27. *Istoricheskii arkhiv,* no. 5 (1993): 123–128.

153. Cited in D. Omel'chuk and S. Iurchenko, "Krymskaia konferentsiia: Neizvestnye stranitsy," *Svododnaia mysl,* no. 2 (2001): 122–123.

154. *Perepiska,* vol. 2, pp. 204, 205; V. Pechatnov, *Stalin, Ruzvel't, Trumen: SSSR i SShA v 1940-kh gg.* (Moscow, 2006), pp. 305–306.

155. *Perepiska,* vol. 2, pp. 211, 212; Commission for the Publication of Diplomatic Doc-uments under the Ministry of Foreign Affairs of the U.S.S.R., comp., *Correspon-dence between Stalin, Roosevelt, Truman, Churchill and Atlee during World War II* (Honolulu, 2001), p. 214.

156. Secret telegram from Joseph Stalin to Dwight D. Eisenhower on the eve of the Battle of Berlin; *Novaia i noveishaia istoriia,* no. 3 (2000): 180–181.

157. Krivosheev et al., *Velikaia Otechestvennaia bez grifa sekretnosti,* p. 171.

158. Shtemenko, *General'nyi shtab v gody voiny,* p. 265.

159. V. A. Zolotarev and G. N. Sevast'ianov, eds., *Velikaia Otechestvennaia Voina. 1941–1945. Voenno-istoricheskie ocherki,* vol. 3 (Moscow, 1999), p. 279.

160. *Rodina,* no. 4 (2005): 99.

Family

1. A. Ostrovskii, *Kto stoial za spinoi Stalina?* (Moscow, 2002), pp. 235–236.

2. This letter was included in a summary of incoming correspondence prepared for Stalin and then sent to Bulganin, evidently so he could look into granting the requests for assistance; RGASPI, f. 558, op. 11, d. 895, l. 59.

3. Ostrovskii, *Kto stoial za spinoi Stalina?,* p. 249.

4. Ibid., pp. 251–252.

5. Ibid., pp. 308–309, 329, 332–334.

6. Ibid., pp. 340–341.

7. Cited in ibid., pp. 349, 357.

8. *Izvestiia TsK KPSS,* no. 10 (1989): 190.
9. *Izvestiia TsK KPSS,* no. 8 (1991): 150.
10. Cited in Iu. G. Murin, comp., *Iosif Stalin v ob"iatiiakh sem'i. Iz lichnogo arkhiva* (Moscow, 1993), pp. 7–8.
11. Ibid., p. 154.
12. Ibid., p. 22.
13. Cited in V. A. Nevezhin, *Zastol'ia Iosifa Stalina. Bol'shie kremlevskie priemy 1930-kh–1970-kh gg.* (Moscow, 2011), p. 279.
14. "Pis'ma N. S. Alliluevoi Z. G. Ordzhonikidze," *Svobodnaia mysl',* no. 5 (1993): 74.
15. Letter from Nadezhda Allilueva to Maria Svanidze, 11 January 1926; cited in Murin, *Iosif Stalin v ob"iatiiakh sem'i,* p. 154.
16. Ibid., pp. 22–40.
17. Simon Sebag Montefiore explores possible scenarios of what took place that evening in the prologue to his book *Stalin: The Court of the Red Tsar* (London, 2003).
18. RGASPI, f. 558, op. 11, d. 786, ll. 123–124.
19. According to the diary of Maria Svanidze; cited in Murin, *Iosif Stalin v ob"iatiiakh sem'i,* p. 177.
20. Ibid., pp. 157–158.
21. Svetlana Alliluyeva, *Twenty Letters to a Friend,* trans. Priscilla Johnson McMillan (New York, 1967), pp. 151–152.
22. Cited in R. W. Davies et al., eds., *The Stalin-Kaganovich Correspondence, 1931–1936* (New Haven, 2003), pp. 297, 304.
23. Alliluyeva, *Twenty Letters,* p. 151.
24. The discussion of Vasily's relationship with Stalin is based on Murin, *Iosif Stalin v ob"iatiiakh sem'i,* pp. 54–65, 68–69.
25. GARF, f. R-9401, op. 2, d. 93, ll. 276–278; V. N. Khaustov et al., comps., *Lubianka. Stalin i NKVD-NKGB-GUKR "Smersh." 1939–1946* (Moscow, 2006), pp. 493–494; Murin, *Iosif Stalin v ob"iatiiakh sem'i,* pp. 92–93.
26. Murin, *Iosif Stalin v ob"iatiiakh sem'i,* pp. 69–89, 96–100.
27. Alliluyeva, *Twenty Letters,* p. 180.
28. Cited in Murin, *Iosif Stalin v ob"iatiiakh sem'i,* pp. 91–92.

Chapter 6. The Generalissimo

1. Cited in *Pravda,* 25 May 1945.
2. Letter from G. Tsydenov, 23 October 1945; RGASPI, f. 558, op. 11, d. 865, l. 6.
3. Letter dated 16 February 1946; RGASPI, f. 558, op. 11, d. 867, ll. 14–15; E. Iu. Zubkova et al., comps., *Sovetskaia zhizn'. 1945–1953* (Moscow, 2003), pp. 612–613.
4. The summary of incoming correspondence that included quotes from this letter features a notation by Poskrebyshev: "Archive." It could only have been made on Stalin's instructions since a number of other letters from the summary were sent to be taken care of by the appropriate official; RGASPI, f. 558, op. 11, d. 867, ll. 1–2.
5. *Pravda,* 14 March 1946.
6. G. F. Krivosheev et al., *Velikaia Otechestvennaia bez grifa sekretnosti. Kniga poter'* (Moscow, 2009), p. 42. Without citing a source, Dmitri Volkogonov states that in January 1946 Stalin was given a figure of 15 million dead, including 7.5 million soldiers

killed, dying of wounds, or missing in action; Dmitri Volkogonov, *Stalin: Triumph and Tragedy* (New York, 1991), p. 505. It has not been possible to verify this information.

7. For the original of Stalin's letter, edited in his own hand, see RGASPI, f. 558, op. 11, d. 794, ll. 85-89. The letter was published in the magazine *Bol'shevik* in 1947 (no. 3, pp. 6-8).

8. From a coded telegram from Stalin to Molotov, Beria, Malenkov, and Mikoyan dated 10 November 1945; cited in L. V. Maksimenkov, comp., *Bol'shaia tsenzura. Pisateli i zhurnalisty v Strane Sovetov. 1917-1956* (Moscow, 2005), pp. 556-557.

9. *Pravda,* 23 September 1946.

Mikhail Mikhailovich Zoshchenko (1895-1958) was a popular satirical writer and playwright. The scathing criticism to which he was subjected in 1946 led to his being deprived of the right to publish. After Stalin's death he was given work writing for magazines but was still a target of discrimination. The 1946 decree criticizing Zoshchenko and Akhmatova was rescinded only in the late 1980s during Gorbachev's perestroika.

Anna Andreevna Akhmatova (1889-1966) was among Russia's most important poets. Under Stalin, she was subjected to ongoing persecution. Her first husband was shot and the second died in a labor camp, and her only son spent many years in a camp. A number of anti-Stalinist works by Akhmatova are famous, her poetic cycle *Requiem* first and foremost.

10. RGASPI, f. 558, op. 11, d. 732, ll. 1-19.

11. Nikolai Krementsov, *Stalinist Science* (Princeton, 1997); V. D. Esakov and E. S. Levina, *Stalinskie "sudy chesti": "Delo KR"* (Moscow, 2005).

12. Cited in V. Pechatnov, *Stalin, Ruzvel't, Trumen: SSSR i SShA v 1940-kh gg.* (Moscow, 2006), pp. 392-393.

13. RGASPI, f. 558, op. 11, d. 382, l. 45; Pechatnov, *Stalin, Ruzvel't, Trumen,* p. 421.

14. G. Procacci and G. Adibekov et al., eds., *The Cominform: Minutes of the Three Conferences, 1947/1948/1949* (Milan, 1994), pp. 225-226.

15. Eugene Zaleski, *Stalinist Planning for Economic Growth, 1933-1952* (Chapel Hill, 1980), pp. 347-348.

16. N. Vert and S. V. Mironenko, eds., *Istoriia stalinskogo Gulaga. Konets 1920-kh-pervaia polovina 1950-kh godov,* vol. 1: *Massovye repressii v SSSR* (Moscow, 2004), p. 610.

17. A. I. Kokurin and N. V. Petrov, comps., *GULAG. 1917-1960* (Moscow, 2000), pp. 435, 447; V. N. Zemskov, *Spetsposelentsy v SSSR, 1930-1960* (Moscow, 2003), p. 225.

18. The total population of the USSR at the beginning of 1953 was 188 million; V. P. Popov, *Ekonomicheskaia politika sovetskogo gosudarstva. 1946-1953 gg.* (Moscow and Tambov, 2000), p. 16.

19. V. A. Kozlov and S. V. Mironenko, eds., *"Osobaia papka" Stalina. Iz materialov Sekretariata NKVD-MVD SSSR. 1944-1953* (Moscow, 1994).

20. E. Iu. Zubkova, *Pribaltika i Kreml'* (Moscow, 2008), p. 256; V. Naumov and Iu. Sigachev, comps., *Lavrentii Beriia. 1953. Stenogramma iul'skogo plenuma TsK KPSS i drugie dokumenty* (Moscow, 1999), p. 47.

21. RGASPI, f. 558, op. 11, d. 1481, l. 45.

22. Ibid., d. 97, ll. 35-36.

23. Ibid., ll. 96-99.

24. V. O. Pechatnov, "'The Allies Are Pressing on You to Break Your Will. . . .' Foreign Policy Correspondence between Stalin and Molotov and Other Politburo Members, September 1945-December 1946," Cold War International History Project, Working Paper No. 26 (September 1999).

25. Ibid., p. 2.

26. Cited in ibid., p. 4.

27. O. V. Khlevniuk et al., comps., *Politbiuro TsK VKP(b) i Sovet Ministrov SSSR. 1945–1953* (Moscow, 2002), pp. 198–199.

28. RGASPI, f. 558, op. 11, d. 771, ll. 9–10.

29. Khlevniuk et al., *Politbiuro TsK VKP(b) i Sovet Ministrov SSSR,* pp. 195, 196.

30. RGASPI, f. 558, op. 11, d. 771, l. 11.

31. Ibid., ll. 7–8.

32. Khlevniuk et al., *Politbiuro TsK VKP(b) i Sovet Ministrov SSSR,* p. 195. This conflict is also described in Pechatnov, "'The Allies Are Pressing on You to Break Your Will,'" pp. 8–15.

33. Khlevniuk et al., *Politbiuro TsK VKP(b) i Sovet Ministrov SSSR,* pp. 196–197.

34. Cited in ibid., pp. 197–198.

35. Ibid., pp. 198–199.

36. Ibid., p. 200.

37. Ibid., pp. 24–25, 38.

38. Vsevolod Nikolaevich Merkulov (1895–1953) was a longtime aid to Beria who had come with him to Moscow in 1938 and was appointed his first deputy at the NKVD. In 1943 Merkulov was in charge of the State Security Commissariat, which had been made into a separate agency outside of the internal affairs commissariat (the NKVD). After being removed from this post amid scandal, he still held high-level positions and during Stalin's final years headed the State Control Ministry. As a client of Beria, he was arrested and shot in late 1953 after Beria himself.

39. Viktor Semenovich Abakumov (1908–1954) rose through the state security ranks and during the war served as Stalin's deputy at the defense commissariat in charge of military counterintelligence. In 1946–1951 he served as state security minister before being arrested in 1951. Even after Stalin's death he was shot rather than being released from prison.

40. Memorandum from Merkulov dated 23 July 1953; cited in V. A. Kozlov, ed., *Neizvestnaia Rossiia XX vek,* vol. 3 (Moscow, 1993), p. 73.

41. RGASPI, f. 558, op. 11, d. 442, ll. 202–206; V. Naumov et al., comps., *Georgii Zhukov. Stenogramma oktiabr'skogo (1957 g.) plenuma TsK KPSS i drugie dokumenty* (Moscow, 2001), pp. 16–17.

42. A. G. Zverev, *Zapiski ministra* (Moscow, 1973), pp. 231–234.

43. Iu. I. Kashin, comp., *Po stranitsam arkhivnykh fondov Tsentral'nogo banka Rossiiskoi Federatsii,* vol. 3 (Moscow, 2007), pp. 31–32.

44. Popov, *Ekonomicheskaia politika sovetskogo gosudarstva,* pp. 83–88. A key memorandum by Zverev dated 8 October 1946 and providing an overview of the experience of the 1922–1924 Soviet currency reform, including notations by Stalin, has been published in *Istochnik,* no. 5 (2001): 21–47. The memorandum is held in the APRF.

45. A. A. Chernobaev, ed., *Na prieme u Stalina. Tetradi (zhurnaly) zapisei lits, priniatykh I. V. Stalinym (1924–1953 gg.)* (Moscow, 2008), p. 617.

46. RGASPI, f. 17, op. 163, d. 1506, l. 22.

47. Kashin, *Po stranitsam arkhivnykh fondov Tsentral'nogo banka,* vol. 3, pp. 96–97.

48. E. Iu. Zavadskaia and T. V. Tsarevskaia, "Denezhnaia reforma 1947 goda: Reaktsiia naseleniia. Po dokumentam iz 'osobykh papok' Stalina," *Otechestvennaia istoriia,* no. 6 (1997): 135–137.

49. Zubkova et al., *Sovetskaia zhizn',* pp. 561–564.

50. Ibid., p. 564–567.

51. Iu. Aksenov and A. Uliukaev, "O prostykh resheniiakh neprostykh problem. Denezhnaia reforma 1947 goda," *Kommunist,* no. 6 (1990): 83.

52. Chernobaev, *Na prieme u Stalina,* pp. 495–496.

53. *Istochnik,* no. 5 (2001): 51.

54. Zubkova et al., *Sovetskaia zhizn',* p. 529.

55. "On Per Person Norms for Sales of Food and Manufactured Goods"; USSR Council of Ministers Resolution No. 3867, dated 14 December 1947; GARF, f. R-5446, op. 1, d. 316, ll. 288–289. These limits remained in effect until 1958.

56. Aksenov and Uliukaev, "O prostykh resheniiakh neprostykh problem," pp. 84–85.

57. Julie Hessler, *A Social History of Soviet Trade: Trade Policy, Retail Practices, and Consumption, 1917–1953* (Princeton, 2004), p. 314.

58. Zubkova et al., *Sovetskaia zhizn',* p. 578.

59. RGASPI, f. 17, op. 122, d. 308, l. 183.

60. Ibid., op. 88, d. 900, l. 178.

61. Donald Filtzer, *Soviet Workers and Late Stalinism: Labour and the Restoration of the Stalinist System after World War II* (Cambridge, 2002), pp. 77–116.

62. In recent years a huge number of documents pertaining to the sovietization of Eastern Europe and Stalin's role in this process has been published. For a multifaceted study of these questions, see T. V. Volokitina et al., *Moskva i Vostochnaia Evropa. Stanovlenie politicheskikh rezhimov sovetskogo tipa (1949–1953)* (Moscow, 2008).

63. Ibid., pp. 430–550.

64. For a more in-depth account, see Yoram Gorlizki and Oleg Khlevniuk, *Cold Peace: Stalin and the Soviet Ruling Circle, 1945–1953* (New York, 2004), pp. 79–89.

65. Khlevniuk et al., *Politbiuro TsK VKP(b) i Sovet Ministrov SSSR,* p. 67.

66. For an interpretation of the Leningrad Affair as Stalin's response to the spread and strengthening of patron-client relations within the Soviet nomenklatura, see Benjamin Tromly, "The Leningrad Affair and Soviet Patronage Politics, 1949–1950," *Europe-Asia Studies* 56, no. 5 (July 2004): 707–729.

67. Cited in F. Chuev, *Sto sorok besed s Molotovym* (Moscow, 1991), p. 475.

68. Voting was carried out by *opros* (polling); in other words, members voted remotely, not while they were seated together in a Politburo meeting. According to the tally compiled by Poskrebyshev, who handled most of the clerical aspects of Politburo resolutions, Stalin, Bulganin, Voroshilov, Voznesensky, Shvernik, Kaganovich, Mikoyan, Andreev, Beria, Malenkov, and Kosygin voted in favor of expelling Zhemchuzhina from the party. "Com. Molotov abstained"; RGASPI, f. 17, op. 163, d. 1518, l. 162.

69. Ibid., l. 164; Khlevniuk et al., *Politbiuro TsK VKP(b) i Sovet Ministrov SSSR*, p. 313.

70. Joshua Rubenstein and Vladimir P. Naumov, eds., *Stalin's Secret Pogrom: The Postwar Inquisition of the Jewish Anti-Fascist Committee* (New Haven, 2001).

71. Cited in *Vestnik arkhiva prezidenta Rossiiskoi Federatsii. Voina 1941–1945* (Moscow, 2010), p. 333.

72. Letter from Gorbenko, a member of the military, dated 15 July 1945; RGASPI, f. 558, op. 11, d. 863, ll. 79–86.

73. Yuri Slezkine, *The Jewish Century* (Princeton, 2004), p. 297.

74. Letter from military journalist S. A. Lifshits dated March 1949; RGASPI, f. 558, op. 11, d. 876, l. 15; f. 17, op. 132, d. 118, ll. 1–3.

75. From the diary of People's Commissar V. A. Malyshev, who was present at the meeting; cited in *Istochnik*, no. 5 (1997): 140–141.

76. This and subsequent excerpts from documents pertaining to preparations for Mao's visit are quoted, with minor modifications, from Sergey Radchenko and David Wolff, "To the Summit via Proxy-Summits: New Evidence from Soviet and Chinese Archives on Mao's Long March to Moscow, 1949," *Cold War International History Project Bulletin*, no 16. (Spring 2008): 118–129.

77. A. M. Ledovskii, *SSSR i Stalin v sud'bakh Kitaia. Dokumenty i svidetel'stva uchastnika sobytii. 1937–1952* (Moscow, 1999), p. 55.

78. Chen Jian, "The Sino-Soviet Alliance and China's Entry into the Korean War," Cold War International History Project, Working Paper No. 1 (June 1992), p. 19.

79. A. V. Pantsov, *Mao Tzedun* (Moscow, 2007), p. 47.

80. Cited in A. V. Pantsov, comp., *Mao Tzedun. Avtobiografiia. Stikhi* (Moscow, 2008), p. 166.

81. A. M. Ledovskii, "Stalin, Mao Tzedun i koreiskaia voina 1950–1953," *Novaia i noveishaia istoriia*, no. 5 (2005): 106.

82. RGASPI, f. 558, op. 11, d. 329, ll. 10–17; Chen Jian et al., eds., "Stalin's Conversations: Talks with Mao Zedong, December 1949–January 1950, and with Zhou Enlai, August–September 1952," *Cold War International History Project Bulletin*, nos. 6–7 (Winter 1995–1996): 5–7.

83. From the memoirs of Matyas Rakosi; cited in *Istoricheskii arkhiv*, no. 3 (1997): 142–143.

84. Odd Arne Westad, "Fighting for Friendship: Mao, Stalin, and the Sino-Soviet Treaty of 1950," *Cold War International History Project Bulletin*, nos. 8–9 (Winter 1996–1997): 227–228; Dieter Heinzig, *The Soviet Union and Communist China, 1945–1950: The Arduous Road to the Alliance* (London, 2003), pp. 281–282, 286–289.

85. Ledovskii, *SSSR i Stalin v sud'bakh Kitaia*, p. 143.

86. Cited in N. Fedorenko, "Nochnye besedy," *Pravda*, 23 October 1988, p. 4.

87. RGASPI, f. 558, op. 11, d. 329, l. 51.

88. Fedorenko, "Nochnye besedy."

89. For a detailed examination of Stalin's role in the Soviet nuclear project, see David Holloway, *Stalin and the Bomb: The Soviet Union and Atomic Energy, 1939–1956* (New Haven, 1996).

90. Letter written to the members of the Soviet leadership by Beria from prison, 1 July 1953; cited in Naumov and Sigachev, *Lavrentii Beriia*, p. 75.

91. Cited in A. V. Torkunov, *Zagadochnaia voina: Koreiskii konflikt 1950–1953* (Moscow, 2000), pp. 6–8.
92. Kathryn Weathersby, "To Attack, or Not to Attack? Stalin, Kim Il Sung, and the Prelude to War," *International History Project Bulletin,* no 5. (Spring 1995): 7–8.
93. Ibid., p. 9; Chernobaev, *Na prieme u Stalina,* p. 533.
94. K. Vezersbi [Weathersby], "Sovetskie tseli v Koree, 1945–1950 gg.," in *Kholodnaia voina. Novye podkhody, novye dokumenty,* ed. M. M. Narinskii (Moscow, 1995), p. 316.
95. In January 1950 the USSR was boycotting the United Nations, demanding that the new Communist government of China be allowed representation. Starting the war in Korea at a time when the Soviet representative to the Security Council was absent was a clear blunder by Stalin, one of which the United States took full advantage.
96. Cited in Kathryn Weathersby (introduction and translations), "New Russian Documents on the Korean War," *Cold War International History Project Bulletin,* nos. 6–7 (Winter 1995–1996): 40.
97. Cited in Torkunov, *Zagadochnaia voina,* p. 97.
98. Cited in Alexandre Y. Mansourov, "Stalin, Mao, Kim, and China's Decision to Enter the Korean War," *Cold War International History Project Bulletin,* nos. 6–7 (Winter 1995–1996): 118. (Bracketed insertion is Mansourov's.)
99. Cited in Ledovskii, "Stalin, Mao Tzedun i koreiskaia voina," p. 106.
100. From the memoirs of Matyas Rakosi; cited in *Istoricheskii arkhiv,* nos. 5–6 (1997): 7–8. The fact that this meeting took place is also confirmed by the defense minister of Czechoslovakia, Alexeje Čepička; *Voprosy istorii,* no. 10 (1999): 85–86.
101. Zaleski, *Stalinist Planning for Economic Growth,* pp. 668–669.
102. Russian State Archive of the Economy (RGAE), f. 4372, op. 11, d. 677, ll. 9–10. Figures for military expenditures are for four ministries created after Stalin's death: defense (which brought together the former defense and naval ministries), defense industry (an updated version of the former armaments ministry), the aviation industry, and medium-machine building. These ministries accounted for the lion's share (although not all) of military spending.
103. N. S. Simonov, *Voenno-promyshlennyi kompleks SSSR v 1920–1950-e gody* (Moscow, 1996), pp. 210–266.
104. Council of Ministers resolutions dated 9 and 19 February 1953; A. A. Danilov and A. V. Pryzhikov, *Rozhdenie sverkhderzhavy. SSSR v pervye poslevoennye gody* (Moscow, 2001), pp. 92–93.
105. RGASPI, f. 558, op. 11, d. 329, ll. 66; Ledovskii, *SSSR i Stalin v sud'bakh Kitaia,* p. 160.
106. A. I. Kokurin and Iu. N. Morukov, *Stalinskie stroiki GULAGA. 1930–1953* (Moscow, 2005).
107. RGAE, f. 4372, op. 11, d. 282, l. 66.
108. *Narodnoe khoziastvo SSSR. Statisticheskii sbornik* (Moscow, 1956), p. 118.
109. RGASPI, f. 558, op. 11, d. 882, ll. 57–58.
110. Letter dated 1 November 1952; RGASPI, f. 558, op. 11, d. 903, ll. 42–46.
111. This undated letter was sent from Stalin's secretariat for Malenkov to deal with on 4 November 1952; RGASPI, f. 558, op. 11, d. 901, ll. 39–40.

112. Chernobaev, *Na prieme u Stalina*, p. 551; N. Kovaleva et al., comps., *Molotov, Malenkov, Kaganovich. 1957. Stenogramma iiun'skogo plenuma TsK KPSS i drugie dokumenty* (Moscow, 1998), pp. 193–194.

113. On the works of this commission and Stalin's position on the subject, see Gorlizki and Khlevniuk, *Cold Peace*, pp. 139–140.

114. A. I. Mikoian, *Tak bylo. Razmyshleniia o minuvshem* (Moscow, 1999), p. 578.

115. RGAE, f. 4372, op. 11, d. 459, ll. 164–170.

116. Kokurin and Petrov, *GULAG. 1917–1960*, pp. 788–791; RGAE, f. 4372, op. 11, d. 677, l. 9.

117. The inventories did not specify the agency originating the coded telegrams. RGASPI, f. 558, op. 11, d. 117, ll. 1–173.

118. Ignatiev told this story in testimony given 27 March 1953; N. V. Petrov, *Palachi* (Moscow, 2011), p. 307.

119. K. A. Stoliarov, *Palachi i zhertvy* (Moscow, 1998), p. 163.

120. Ibid., pp. 225–226.

121. Ibid., pp. 167–168.

122. Naumov and Sigachev, *Lavrentii Beriia*, pp. 34–35.

123. For more details, see Timothy Blauvelt, "Abkhazia: Patronage and Power in the Stalin Era," *Nationalities Papers* 35, no. 2 (2007): 220, 222–223.

124. Naumov and Sigachev, *Lavrentii Beriia*, pp. 29–40.

125. It was at the Nineteenth Party Congress that the party's name was officially changed from the All-Union Communist Party of Bolsheviks, commonly referred to by the acronym VKP(b), to simply the Communist Party of the Soviet Union or KPSS. This name endured until the party and country were abolished in 1991.

126. Mikoian, *Tak bylo*, p. 573.

127. Ibid., pp. 574–576; Chuev, *Sto sorok besed s Molotovym*, p. 469; L. N. Efremov, *Dorogami bor'by i truda* (Stavropol, 1998), pp. 12–16.

128. N. Mukhitdinov, *Reka vremeni. Ot Stalina do Gorbacheva. Vospominaniia* (Moscow, 1995), pp. 88–89.

129. Volokitina et al., *Moskva i Vostochnaia Evropa*, pp. 558–566.

130. Explanatory memorandum from Ignatiev to Beria dated 27 March 1953; cited in Petrov, *Palachi*, p. 297.

131. Ibid., pp. 287, 299–300.

132. Cited in V. N. Khaustov et al., comps. *Lubianka. Stalin i MGB SSSR. Mart 1946–mart 1953* (Moscow, 2007), pp. 522–523.

133. Cited in N. V. Petrov, *Pervyi predsedatel' KGB Ivan Serov* (Moscow, 2005), p. 124.

134. From a transcript of remarks by Stalin to a commission on reorganizing the Ministry of State Security's intelligence service, November–December 1952; cited in *Istochnik*, no. 5 (2001): 132.

135. These press items were edited by Stalin. RGASPI, f. 558, op. 11, d. 157, ll. 9–14, 29–33; Khlevniuk et al., *Politbiuro TsK VKP(b) i Sovet Ministrov SSSR*, pp. 392–397.

136. For a detailed examination of this theory about the deportation of Jews, see G. V. Kostyrchenko, *Stalin protiv "kosmopolitov". Vlast' i evreiskaia intelligentsiia v SSSR* (Moscow, 2009), pp. 329–380.

137. B. S. Klein, "Politika SShA i 'delo vrachei,'" *Voprosy istorii*, no. 6 (2006): 35–47.

The Dictatorship Collapses

1. A. A. Chernobaev, ed., *Na prieme u Stalina. Tetradi (zhurnaly) zapisei lits, prini-atykh I. V. Stalinym (1924–1953 gg.)* (Moscow, 2008), p. 553; O. V. Khlevniuk et al., comps., *Politbiuro TsK VKP(b) i Sovet Ministrov SSSR. 1945–1953* (Moscow, 2002), p. 436. When the log of visitors to Stalin's office was published, Tkachev's name was mistakenly given as Tolkachev.
2. Chernobaev, *Na prieme u Stalina,* p. 553; Khlevniuk et al., *Politbiuro TsK VKP(b) i Sovet Ministrov SSSR,* p. 436.
3. A. L. Miasnikov, *Ia lechil Stalina* (Moscow, 2011), p. 295.
4. Khlevniuk et al., *TsK VKP(b) i Sovet Ministrov SSSR,* pp. 436–437.
5. N. Kovaleva et al., comps., *Molotov, Malenkov, Kaganovich. 1957. Stenogramma iiun'skogo plenuma TsK KPSS i drugie dokumenty* (Moscow, 1998), pp. 42, 45. The papers were removed when Malenkov's assistant was arrested.
6. The decisions were recorded in the minutes of the 5 March 1953 joint meeting of the Central Committee plenum, the Council of Ministers, and the Presidium of the Supreme Soviet. *Istochnik,* no. 1 (1994): 107–111.
7. K. M. Simonov, *Glazami cheloveka moego pokoleniia* (Moscow, 1989), pp. 257–258.
8. Ibid., p. 260.
9. Svetlana Alliluyeva, *Twenty Letters to a Friend,* trans. Priscilla Johnson McMillan (New York, 1967), p. 10.
10. Chernobaev, *Na prieme u Stalina,* p. 553.
11. From Shepilov's memoirs; cited in *Voprosy istorii,* no. 3 (1998): 15.
12. A. N. Artizov et al., comps., *Reabilitatsiia: Kak eto bylo,* vol. 1 (Moscow, 2000), p. 19.
13. V. Naumov and Iu. Sigachev, comps., *Lavrentii Beriia. 1953. Stenogramma iul'skogo plenuma TsK KPSS i drugie dokumenty* (Moscow, 1999), pp. 28–29.
14. Oleg Khlevniuk, "The Economy of the OGPU, NKVD and MVD of the USSR, 1930–1953: The Scale, Structure and Trends of Development," in *The Economics of Forced Labor: The Soviet Gulag,* ed. Paul R. Gregory and Valery Lazarev (Stanford, CA, 2003), pp. 54–55.
15. According to official statistics, between 1 January and 1 October 1953 the number of cows increased from 24.3 million to 26 million, and almost 1 million of that increase took place outside of the collective and state farm system. During that same period the number of pigs increased from 28.5 to 47.6 million, including an increase of 12 million in private herds; *Narodnoe khoziastvo SSSR. Statisticheskii sbornik* (Moscow, 1956), pp. 119–120. Even with the consideration of possible seasonal fluctuations, these numbers are significant and surely attributable to lower taxes and higher procurement prices.
16. A. V. Torkunov, *Zagadochnaia voina: Koreiskii konflikt 1950–1953* (Moscow, 2000), pp. 272–279.
17. This directive was largely in response to the large number of defections from East Germany to the West. See Naumov and Sigachev, *Lavrentii Beriia,* pp. 55–59.

The Funeral

1. Speech by Khrushchev at a dinner in the Bulgarian city of Varna during an official visit on 16 May 1962; cited in *Istochnik,* no. 6 (2003): 130.

2. Letter dated 10 March 1953 from a group of citizens to the Central Committee and the Supreme Soviet; GARF, f. R-7523, op. 52, d. 18, ll. 94–95.

3. Anonymous letter addressed to Georgy Malenkov, dated 6 March 1953; RGASPI, f. 558, op. 11, d. 1486, l. 157.

4. Ibid., d. 1487, l. 55.

5. Ibid., ll. 66–71.

6. Cited in V. A. Kozlov, *Neizvestnaia Rossiia XX vek,* vol. 2 (Moscow, 1992), pp. 254–258.

7. Cited in V. A. Kozlov and S. V. Mironenko, *58-10. Nadzornye proizvodstva Prokuratury SSSR po delam ob antisovetskoi agitatsii i propagande. Annotirovannyi katalog. Mart 1953–1991* (Moscow, 1999), pp. 13, 21, 23, 32.

8. There is a long list of published documents and studies on the public mood and mechanisms used to shape it and on social adaptation and the particular mindset that Stalinism strove to shape. Studies vary in terms of their authors' viewpoints and the aspect of reality they emphasize. See, for example, the following: Sheila Fitzpatrick: *The Cultural Front: Power and Culture in Revolutionary Russia* (Ithaca, NY, 1992), and *Tear off the Masks! Identity and Imposture in Twentieth-Century Russia* (Princeton, 2005); Stephen Kotkin, *Magnetic Mountain: Stalinism as a Civilization* (Berkeley and Los Angeles, 1995); Sarah Davies, *Popular Opinion in Stalin's Russia: Terror, Propaganda and Dissent, 1934–1941* (Cambridge, 1997); Elena Zubkova, *Russia after the War: Hopes, Illusions, and Disappointments, 1945–1957* (New York, 1998); Jochen Hellbeck, *Revolution on My Mind: Writing a Diary under Stalin* (Cambridge, MA, 2006).

9. Yoram Gorlizki, "Political Reform and Local Party Interventions under Khrushchev," in *Reforming Justice in Russia, 1864–1996,* ed. Peter H. Solomon (New York and London, 1997), pp. 259–260.

10. Letter from Stakhanov to Stalin in May 1945; RGASPI, f. 558, op. 11, d. 891, l. 128. For a similar letter sent to Molotov before the war, see GARF, f. R-5446, op. 82, d. 108, l. 145; d. 120, l. 74.

11. According to official statistics, at the start of 1953 more than 40 percent of the country's population lived in cities. It should be kept in mind, however, that this figure included residents of small cities and settlements where the standard of living was close to that of the peasants.

12. In 1952, out of the 443,000 tons of meat sold through state and cooperative outlets across the USSR, 110,000 were sent to Moscow and 57,400 were sent to Leningrad; GARF, f. R-5446, op. 87, d. 1162, l. 171.

13. A. I. Mikoian, *Tak bylo. Razmyshleniia o minuvshem* (Moscow, 1999), p. 355.

14. Amir Weiner, *Making Sense of War: The Second World War and the Fate of the Bolshevik Revolution* (Princeton, 2000).

15. Golfo Alexopoulos, *Stalin's Outcasts: Aliens, Citizens, and the Soviet State, 1926–1936* (Ithaca, NY, and London, 2003).

16. Lynne Viola, *Peasant Rebels under Stalin: Collectivization and the Culture of Peasant Resistance* (New York and Oxford, 1996); Lynne Viola, ed., *Contending with Stalinism: Soviet Power and Popular Resistance in the 1930s* (Ithaca, NY, 2002); Jef-

frey J. Rossman, *Worker Resistance under Stalin: Class and Revolution on the Shop Floor* (Cambridge, MA, and London, 2005).

17. In recent years historians have produced several valuable studies on this problem. See, for example, the following: Sheila Fitzpatrick, *Everyday Stalinism: Ordinary Life in Extraordinary Times: Soviet Russia in the 1930s* (New York, 1999); Elena Osokina, *Our Daily Bread: Socialist Distribution and the Art of Survival in Stalin's Russia, 1927-1941* (New York and London, 2001); Donald Filtzer, *The Hazards of Urban Life in Late Stalinist Russia: Health, Hygiene, and Living Standards, 1943-1953* (Cambridge, 2010).

18. Calculations based on E. Iu. Zubkova et al., comps., *Sovetskaia zhizn'. 1945-1953* (Moscow, 2003), pp. 102-103; O. V. Khlevniuk et al., comps., *Politbiuro TsK VKP(b) i Sovet Ministrov SSSR, 1945-1953* (Moscow, 2002), pp. 388-389. For comparison, see A. I. Kokurin and N. V. Petrov, *GULAG. 1917-1960* (Moscow, 2000), pp. 543-551.

19. This letter was given to Malenkov to read; RGASPI, f. 558, op. 11, d. 901, l. 37.

20. Zubkova et al., *Sovetskaia zhizn'*, p. 107.

21. Cited in ibid., p. 263.

22. Figures for state and private urban housing are from RGAE, f. 1562, op. 41, d. 56, ll. 30-33. Figures for the urban population as of early 1953 are from V. P. Popov, *Ekonomicheskaia politika Sovetskogo gosudarstva. 1946-1953 gg.* (Moscow and Tambov, 2000), p. 16.

23. RGAE, f. 1562, op. 41, d. 56, ll. 30-33. The inventory of publicly owned residential buildings included the best-built ones, which belonged to local government councils (soviets) and agencies. A significant proportion of urban housing was in private hands. These buildings were in much worse shape.

24. Zubkova et al., *Sovetskaia zhizn'*, p. 179.

25. N. Vert and S. V. Mironenko, eds., *Istoriia stalinskogo Gulaga. Konets 1920-kh-pervaia polovina 1950-kh godov*, vol. 1: *Massovye repressii v SSSR* (Moscow, 2004), pp. 623-624.

26. B. V. Zhiromskaia, I. N. Kiselev, and Iu. A. Poliakov, *Polveka pod grifom "sekretno": Vsesoiuznaia perepis' naseleniia 1937 goda* (Moscow, 1996), pp. 98, 100.

27. Terry Martin, *The Affirmative Action Empire: Nations and Nationalism in the Soviet Union, 1923-1939* (Ithaca, NY, and London, 2001).

28. See one recent study: Timothy Snyder, *Bloodlands: Europe between Hitler and Stalin* (New York, 2010).

29. For documents and letters characterizing inter-ethnic conflicts during the final period of Stalin's rule, see L. P. Kosheleva et al., comps., *Sovetskaia natsional'naia politika. Ideologiia i praktiki realizatsii* (Moscow, 2013).

30. Geoffrey Hosking, *Rulers and Victims: The Russians in the Soviet Union* (Cambridge, MA, and London, 2006).

31. E. Khodzha [Enver Hoxha], *So Stalinym. Vospominaniia* (Tirana, 1984), p. 90.

32. RGASPI, f. 558, op. 11, d. 1479, ll. 14-18.

33. A. Berelovich and V. Danilov, eds., *Sovetskaia derevnia glazami VChK-OGPU-NKVD: 1918-1939 gg.*, vols. 1-4 (Moscow, 1998-2012); G. N. Sevost'ianov et al., eds., *"Sovershenno sekretno": Lubianka-Stalinu o polozhenii v strane (1922-1934)*, vols. 1-9 (Moscow, 2001-2013).

34. GARF, f. R-9401, op. 12, d. 100, ll. 91–92.

35. When the apparat of the Special Sector was being reorganized in 1939, provisions were made for the creation of fifteen staff positions for people reading letters addressed to Stalin. Their duties included familiarizing themselves with the letters and sorting them (APRF, f. 3, op. 22, d. 65, l. 37). If we assume that each reader spent an average of ten minutes per letter, in working an eight-hour day, all fifteen readers would be able to review 720 letters per day or approximately 260,000 per year. Probably the number was higher. Experienced readers would process letters quickly, especially as many letters were short. Furthermore, using a shift system, the apparat worked essentially around the clock, and shifts were not strictly limited to eight hours.

36. APRF, f. 3, op. 22, d. 65, l. 51. The Special Sector's Fifth Section also took care of Stalin's library.

37. The letters shown to the Special Sector leadership during 1945–1953 have been preserved. See RGASPI, f. 558, op. 11, dd. 888–904.

38. Letters selected to be shown to Stalin were accompanied by a list entitled "Letters and Petitions Received Addressed to Com. Stalin." In addition to the letters presented to Stalin, this list included certain letters sent for review by other Soviet leaders. Apparently these were letters it was felt Stalin did not need to see but about which he would be interested in knowing. Stalin's personal archive contains a rather complete set of such lists of letters only for 1945–1952 (but lacks those received while he was vacationing in the south); RGASPI, f. 558, op. 11, dd. 862–882.

39. Jan Plamper, *The Stalin Cult: A Study in the Alchemy of Power* (New Haven, 2012).

ACKNOWLEDGMENTS

When Jonathan Brent and Vadim Staklo—then the editorial director and project manager for Yale University Press's Annals of Communism series respectively—suggested that I write a biography of Stalin, I was more puzzled than glad. But now that the book has been completed, I am truly thankful to them.

Few know more about the Stalin era than my friends Yoram Gorlizki, Andrea Graziosi, Jan Plamper, and David Shearer, and I am grateful to them for reading the manuscript and making valuable comments. This work also greatly benefited from the skillful editing of William Frucht, the press's executive editor, the keen eye and remarkable memory of the manuscript's copy editor, Bojana Ristich, and the expertise of production editor Margaret Otzel. A critical role was played by the book's translator, Nora Favorov, my most attentive and demanding reader.

This biography is the culmination of long years of studying Soviet history. These years brought collaboration and friendship with many knowledgeable colleagues. My interactions with all of them have helped prepare me to produce this work.

To start with those no longer living, I learned a great deal from Moshe Lewin, Viktor Petrovich Danilov, Victor Zaslavsky, and Derek Watson—all prominent historians and wonderful human beings.

Next, this book would not have been possible without decades of work alongside my friends and fellow archival researchers. At RGASPI, I have been fortunate to work with Andrei Sorokin, Lyudmila Kosheleva, Marina Astakhova, Galina Gorskaia, and Elena Kirillova. My work at GARF would have been impossible without the constant support of Sergei Mironenko, Larisa Rogovaya, Larisa Malashenko, Dina Nokhotovich, Sofia Somonova, Galina Kuznetsova, and Tatiana Zhukova. Together we compiled a number of collections of historical documents.

For twenty-five years now I have been a proud member of the Robert Davies team. His dedication to the study of history and his amazing productivity are an example for us all.

Collaboration, interaction, and friendship with a number of historians have greatly contributed to my work. I would like to express my sincere gratitude to Golfo Alexopoulos, Jörg Baberowski, Alain Blum, Yves Cohen, Marta Craveri, Victor Dönninghaus, Michael David-Fox, Mark Elie, Benno Ennker, Klaus Gestwa, Mark Harrison, Jana Howlett, Melanie Ilic, Nicolaus Katzer, Vladimir Kozlov, Sergei Kudryashov, Hiroaki Kuromiya, Terry Martin, Silvio Pons, Valeri Pozner, Arfon Rees, Andrea Romano, Ingrid Schierle, Robert Service, Jeremy Smith, Takeshi Tomita, Aleksandr Vatlin, Lynne Viola, Amir Weiner, Nicolas Werth, Stephen Wheatcroft, and Elena Zubkova.

Paul Gregory, Ron Suny, Sheila Fitzpatrick, Piter Solomon, and Dietrich Beyrau have been attentive and patient conversation partners for many years.

I would also like to express gratitude to the German Historical Institute in Moscow, Fondation Maison des Sciences de l'Homme, and the Ukrainian Studies Fund for their support.

As always, I would not miss this opportunity to wish success to my daughter Dasha.

As fate would have it, when I began work on this project my wife Katya fell ill. By the time I completed the manuscript, she was no longer with us.

To her, I dedicate this book.

INDEX

Illustrations are indicated by Gallery number

Borisov, Mikhail, 128, 132, 133

Britain: appeasement of Hitler, 163, 167; Chur-chill-Stalin meetings, 224, 230, 244; and Polish invasion, 169–170; in postwar settlement, 270; second front plan, 223–224, 228, 229; wartime aid to Stalin, 211, 212

Budenny, Semen, 202, 361n21

Bukharin, Nikolai Ivanovich: 68, 90, 94, Gallery 6; on anti-Trotsky coalition, 81–82; biography of, 343n55; execution of, 140; -Kamenev secret meeting, 107; as oppositionist, 105, 106, 108; in power struggle, 75–76, 77, 78, 80

Bukovina, 173

Bulgakov, Mikhail Afanasyevich, 96, 346n10

Bulganin, Nikolai Aleksandrovich, 2; biography of, 333n1; in interregnum period, 312; in Mao's Moscow visit, 289; at Stalin's deathbed, 142, 189, 312; Stalin's promotion of, 303; in wartime leadership, 241

Bulgaria, in Communist bloc, 281

Cannibalism, in famine of 1932–1933, 119

Capital investment, postwar, 299, 322

Capture by enemy provisions (Order No. 270), 210

Caucasus region, culture of violence in, 21–22

Central Committee: February-March 1937 ple-num, 154–155; majority faction, 80; Presidium, 305–306, 312; Presidium Bureau, 306, 311, 312; Special Sector, 329; Stalin's reorganization of, 178

Chadaev, Yakov, 181, 202, 221

Chamberlain, Austen, 88

Chamberlain, Neville, 163

Chapaev (film), 96

Charkviani, Khristofor, 14

Chechens, forced relocation of, 233

Chiang Kai-shek, 288

"Children's literature," xiv–xv

China-Soviet relations: collective leadership debate on, 90; in Korean War, 294, 296; Mao's Soviet visit, 149, 287–288, 289–293; non-aggression pact of 1937, 156; treaty of 1945, 91, 288, 290; treaty of 1950, 291–292

Chinese civil war, 286, 288

Chizhikov, Petr, 251

Chochia, Grigory, 25

Chubar, Vlas, 177

Chuikov, Vasily, 171–172

Churchill, Winston, 269; Iron Curtain speech of, 267; and second front plan, 223–224, 228, 229; -Stalin meetings, 224, 230, 244, Gallery 12

Civil War: casualties of, 54; opponents of Bolshe-viks in, 53; Polish front, 59–61; Stalin's missions during, 54–56; Stalin-Trotsky conflict, 61–63; Tsaritsyn terror campaign during, 56–59

Clausewitz, Carl von, 95

Cold War, origins of, 266–267

Collaborators with Nazi occupation, prosecution of, 232

Collective leadership, Gallery, 6, 7; anti-Trotsky coalition in, 80, 81–82; division of functions, 80–81; expulsion of leftist opposition, 83–86, 90, 100; and foreign threats campaign, 88–89; and New Economic Policy (NEP), 81, 82, 87, 88, 110; opponents of Stalin's rise to power, 82–83, 104–105, 106, 108; policy debates within, 89–91; purge of oppositionists, 137–139; Stalin faction in, 105, 106; after Stalin's death, 310–313; Stalin's resignation offer, 79–80, 91; Stalin's restructuring of NEP, 100–106; victory of Stalin faction, 106–108

Collectivization, agricultural, 110–113, 115–116, 299, 300, 322

Cominform, creation of, 267

Conquest, Robert, 150

Constitution, liberalization of, 134–135

Consumer goods: price of, 321–322, 324; short-ages of, 276–278

Corruption, and currency reform, 278–279

Cosmopolitanism campaign, 284, 286

Crimea: ethnic deportations from, 232, 233; Soviet-German Front in, 220, 221, 228; Yalta Conference, 244–246, 289, Gallery 12

Currency reform, 274–280, 321

Czechoslovakia: in Communist bloc, 280; German invasion of, 164; Munich Agreement on, 163–164; Slansky trial, 307; -Soviet mutual assistance treaty, 135

Dacha ("near dacha"): Gallery 10; landscaping of, 4–5; library at, 93–96, 346n5; renovations of, 3–4; security personnel at, 33, 36, 92, 142–143, 189, 338n2; social gatherings at, 5–7, 93, 196; Stalin's death at, 33, 92, 142–144, 338n1

Dachas, southern, 191, 193, 359n42

Daily Herald, 270–271

Daladier, Édouard, 163

Danilov, V. P., 348n19

Deikina, V. F., 300–301

Denunciations, 328

Dimitrov, Georgy, 171

Disease epidemics, 119

"Dizzy with Success" (Stalin), 114

Djilas, Milovan, 5, 196, 235
Doctors' Plot, 196, 307–309, 314
Draule, Milda, 130
Dureiko, N. M., 132–133
Dzerzhinsky, Feliks Edmundovich, 71, 73, 344n66

Eastern Europe: Berlin blockade, 281; liberalization in interregnum period, 316; military buildup in, 297; sovietization of, 266, 267, 270, 280, 370n62; Stalin's enemies campaign in, 281; and Titoism, 280–281
Eastern Front. *See* Soviet-German Front
Economy: and capital investment, 299, 302; and currency reform, 274–280, 321; interregnum period reforms, 302, 315; postwar recovery, 279–280; and price reduction, 321–322; Sovnarkom Bureau oversight of, 178–179; standard of living, 262; Terror's impact on, 161; urbanite advantages in, 321; and war mobilization, 184–185, 274; wartime leadership of, 240–241. *See also* Agriculture; Famine; Industrialization; New Economic Policy (NEP)
Edinonachalie, in Red Army, 238
Eikhe, Robert, 177
Ellman, Michael, 332n10
Engels, Friedrich, 94
Erenburg, Ilya, 236
Erickson, John, 201
Espionage, Soviet, 357–358n76
Estonia: and German-Soviet non-aggression pact, 166; postwar repression in, 268; forced resettlement campaign in, 174; sovietization of, 170–171, 173
Ethnic groups: forced resettlement of, 232–234; and russification policy, 325. *See also* Jews, Soviet

Famine: of 1921–1922, 64, 118; of 1931–1933, 3, 7, 38, 116, 117–122; of 1936, 124; as political weapon, 38; postwar, 261, 267; preferential treatment of urbanites, 321
Fedorenko, Nikolai, 292
Feuchtwanger, Lion, 162
Fifth column, Stalin's suspicions of, 155–157, 162
Film screenings, 2–3, 93, 96–97, 347n12
Filtzer, Donald, 280
Finland: and German-Soviet non-aggression pact, 166; Soviet invasion of (Winter War), 172–173, 186
"Five" (ruling group), 1
Five-Year Plan: First, 109, 116, 117, 123; Second, 124
Food shortages, 184–185, 278, 300–301, 323–324

Foreign intelligence, Stalin's suspicions of, 155–157, 162
Foreign policy: arms race, 297–298; Baltic states occupation, 170–171; breakdown in relations with West, 266–267; China (*See* China-Soviet relations); under collective leadership, 88–89; Doctors' Plot as tool of, 309; and European alliances, 123, 135, 163; Finland invasion (Winter War), 172–173, 186; German-Soviet non-aggression pact, 164–169, 170, 174; Hitler-Molotov four-way alliance negotiations, 174–176; in interregnum period, 315–316; and Japanese border clashes, 163, 168–169; and Japanese postwar settlement, 248–249, 270; and Japanese threat, 123, 153, 156; and Korean War, 294–296, 298, 316; "kowtowing to the West" campaign, 265–266, 285, 286; and Munich Agreement, 163–164; and nuclear capability, 293; Polish occupation, 170; postwar challenges for, 261–262; preemptive strike plan, 182–183; sovietization of postwar Eastern Europe, 266, 267, 270, 280, 370n62; sovietization under Molotov–Ribbentrop pact, 171, 173–174; and Spanish civil war, 153–154; and spheres of influence, 171, 244; Stalin's caution and pragmatism in, 298; Terror's consequences for, 162; and Titoism, 280–281; United Nations boycott, 372n95; war readiness in, 153, 164, 183–188
Foreign press, rumors of power struggle in, 269, 270–271
France, Anatole, 95
France: appeasement of Hitler, 163, 167; fall of, 173; and Polish invasion, 169–170; -Soviet mutual assistance treaty, 135
Franco, Francisco, 153

Genghis Khan, 138
Georgia: ethnic deportations from, 233; Mingrelian Affair, 304–305, 314–315; in Transcaucasian Federation dispute, 71–72, 73, 74, 75
Georgian language, Stalin's use of, 97
German-Soviet Front. *See* Soviet-German Front
Germany: Berlin blockade, 281; Politburo plan for revolution in, 77–78; Red Army crimes against civilians, 234–235; Weimar, 123. *See also* Nazi Germany
Goebbels, Joseph, xiv
Golovanov, Aleksandr, 214, 230
Gomulka, Wladyslaw, 281
Gorbachev, M., 192
Gori, Stalin's birth in, 11

173; in interregnum period, 312, 314; in Kirov murder investigation, 128; memoirs of, xiv, 333n1; Politburo appointment of, 177; Stalin characterized by, 5; on Stalin's ceremonial farewell, 317; at Stalin's deathbed, 142, 143, 189, 312, 338n1; on Stalin's exile, 30; Stalin's promotion of, 303; at Stalin's social gatherings, 2, 5, 6; in wartime leadership, 221; and Zhukov, 360n2

Kibirov, I. I., 31

Kiev: fall of, 212–213; liberation of, 228

Kiev Theological Seminary, 18

Kim Il Sung, 294, 295, 296

Kirov, Sergei Mironovich, Gallery 7; biography of, 339n7; bodyguards of, 133; and collective leadership, 83; motive for murder of, 130–131; murder of, 34, 127–129; and plot against Stalin, 127; Stalin's involvement in murder of, 131–134; vacation with Stalin, 193, 194

Kirponos, Mikhail, 212, 213

Kliueva, Nina, 265

Kolkhozes (collective farms), 110–113, 299, 300

Korean War, 294–296, 298, 316

Kornilov, Lavr, 49

Kosarev, Aleksandr Vasilyevich, 131, 351n66

Kosior, Stanislav, 177

Kostov, Traicho, 281

Kosygin, Gallery 14

Kovalev, I. V., 361n27

"Kowtowing to the West" campaign, 265–266, 285, 286

Kremlin: German bombing of, 218; movie theater in, 2–3, 96–97; purge of staff, 139; Stalin's office in, 2, 242, 311

Kremlin Affair, 139

Kronstadt rebellion, 64

Kruglov, Sergei, 276

Krupskaia, Nadezhda, 70, 72, 82

Kulaks: collectivization campaign against, 111–113; executions of, 116, 150; grain requisitions from, 101, 102–104, 105, 110; forced resettlement of, 38, 112, 116

Kulik, Grigory Ivanovich: biography of, 340n20; murder of wife, 40; as Stalin's emissary to front, 201

Kulik-Simonich, Kira, 40

Kuomintang, 286, 288

Kuperin, I. I., 311

Kurile Islands, 248, 249, 290

Kuromiya, Hiroaki, 120

Kursk, Battle of, 226–227, 228

Kutuzov, Mikhail, 2, 242, 264

Kuzakova, M. P., 251

Kuznetsov, Aleksi Aleksandrovich, Gallery 14; biography of, 353n6; in leadership reorganization, 282; in Leningrad Affair, 144, 282–283

Kuznetsov, Nikolai Gerasimovich, 202, 213, 361n22

Labor camps, 38, 268, 325

Lake Khasan, Battle of, 163

Lakoba, Nestor, Gallery 10

Lashevich, Mikhail, 84

Latvia: and German-Soviet non-aggression pact, 166; postwar repression in, 268; forced resettlement campaign in, 174; sovietization of, 170–171, 173

League of Nations, 123, 173

Lend-Lease aid, 212

Lenin, Vladimir Ilyich: assassination attempt on, 57, 128; death of, 79; death mask of, 2; evacuation of sarcophagus of, 203; federation proposal of, 68–69; health of, 65, 68, 70, 74; as military leader, 264; New Economic Policy (NEP) of, 7, 64–65; and invasion of Poland, 59–60; in Provisional Government crackdown, 48, 49; return from Switzerland, 45; revolutionary action plan of, 44–47; revolutionary teachings of, 24; and seizure of power, 50–51, 52; Stalin attacked by, 72–74, 79; –Stalin relationship, 25, 28, 46, 54, 64–65, 67–68, 69–75; Stalin's correspondence with, 32, 60; Stalin's support for revolutionary agenda of, 47–49, 52–53; Stalin as student of, 24, 53, 93–94; and Stalin-Trotsky conflict, 62–63; "testament" of, 73, 79, 91, 137; –Trotsky relationship, 51–52, 65–66, 70; on Tsaritsyn terror campaign, 58

Leningrad Affair, 144, 282–283, 310

Leningrad Blockade, 213, 225

Leningrad magazine, 265

Letter writing, citizen, 300–301, 327–329, 377n35, n38

Lewin, Moshe, 74

Liberalization policy, 124–125

Literature: censorship of, 96; in Stalin's library, 95; Stalin's taste in, 17, 93, 95–96

Lithuania: and German-Soviet non-aggression pact, 166; postwar repression in, 268; forced resettlement campaign from, 174; sovietization of, 170–171, 173

Litvinov, Maksim Maksimovich, 164, 356n37

Liushkov, Genrikh, 162

Livestock production, postwar, 299–300, 374n15
Lozgachev, P. V., 4
Ludwig, Emil, 16

Main Guard Directorate, 33–34, 35–36
Makhrovsky, Konstantin, 56–57
Malenkov, Georgy Maksimillianovich: 2, Gallery 14; biography of, 332n1; capital investment reduction under, 302; in interregnum period, 312; in leadership reorganizations, 178, 181, 272–273, 282, 303; and Molotov scandal, 271, 272; Politburo appointment of, 177; at Stalin's deathbed, 143, 189, 311, 312; on Timoshenko, 222; in wartime leadership, 200, 204, 205, 207, 214, 216, 222, 225, 240, 269
Malinovsky, Roman, 28, 29, 32, 337n48
Malinovsky, S. V., 14–15
Mao Zedong, 286; and Korean War, 296; Moscow visit of, 149, 287–288, 289–293
Marshall Plan, 267
Martin, Terry, 325
Martov, Yuly Osipovich, 85, 86, 345n95
Mekhlis, Lev Zakharovich, 199, 220, 221, 360n9
Mensheviks: opposition to armed robberies, 26; in party congresses, 25; in Petrograd Soviet, 43, 44; and Provisional Government, 50; revolutionary agenda of, 24
Menshikov, Mikhail, 144
Merkulov, Vsevolod Nikolaevich, 273, 369n38
Merzliakov, M. A., 31
Meyerhold, Vsevolod Emilyevich, 97, 347n13
Mgeladze, Akaky, 359n42
Miasnikov, Aleksandr, 189, 197, 311
Mikhail, Grand Duke, 42
Mikhoels, Solomon Mikhailovich, 40, 284, 340n23
Mikoyan (Mikoian), Anastas Ivanovich, Gallery 7; on agricultural policy, 302; assassination attempt on, 35; biography of, 334n2; China visit of, 288; dismissal of, 144, 283; in interregnum period, 311; in leadership reorganizations, 178–179, 306–307; and Leningrad Affair, 283; memoirs of, xiv, 332n10; and Molotov scandal, 271, 272; on Moscow evacuation, 214; on Presidium makeup, 306; on price reduction, 321–322; in Stalin faction, 105; at Stalin's social gatherings, 6; Stalin's threat to, 144; Stalin's vacation with, 192; in wartime leadership, 204, 205, 206, 207, 225, 240, 241, 269
Mikoyan (Mikoian), Sergo, 206, 332n10

Military. See Air Force; Soviet-German Front; Red Army
Military production: German, 186–187; Soviet, 183–184, 297–298
Mingrelian Affair, 304–305, 314–315
Mola, Emilio, 153
Molotov, Vyacheslav Mikhailovich: 192, Gallery 14; in Baltic states negotiations, 171; biography of, 333–334n2; on collective leadership, 89–90; dismissal of, 144, 284; in foreign affairs post, 164–165, 180; foreign press rumors blamed on, 269, 270–271; and German invasion, 199, 200–201; on grain expropriation, 101; -Hitler four-way alliance negotiations, 174–176; and Hitler-Stalin non-aggression pact, 166; in interregnum period, 311, 312; on Kaganovich, 147; in leadership reorganizations, 178, 179–180, 181, 306–307; in Mao's Moscow visit, 289; negotiations with West, 267; and postwar settlement, 269–270; purge of wife, 283–284, 314; in Stalin faction, 105; Stalin's attacks on, 181–182, 270–272, 283; on Stalin's mental state, 197, 204–205; on Stalin's security, 34; Stalin's threat to, 144, 146; on Trotsky, 154; in wartime leadership, 202, 204, 205, 206, 214, 216, 225, 240, 269; Western allies visited by, 223
Monetary reform, 274–280, 321
Montefiore, Simon Sebag, ix
Moscow Conference, 212
Moscow, Siege of: defenses in, 217; and evacuation plans, 214–216; October Revolution anniversary celebrations in, 217–219; political stability during, 216; popular uprisings during, 216–217; Stalin's presence during, 227–228
Movie screenings, 2–3, 93, 96–97, 347n12
Munich Agreement, 163–164, 167
Munitions industry, 183–184, 185–186
Murphy, David, 357–358n76
Music, Stalin's taste in, 97

Nakhimov, Pavel, 242
Nationalities. See Ethnic groups
Nationalities commission, 65
NATO, 281, 297
Nazaretian, Amaiak, 66–67
Nazi Germany: in Anti-Comintern Pact, 154; collaborators in occupied territories, 232; collapse of, 231, 247; invasion of Czechoslovakia, 164; invasion of Poland, 169–170; invasion of Soviet Union, 173, 176, 187–188, 198–202; military production of, 186–187; in Munich Agreement,

163–164, 167; occupation of Europe, 173, 174; -Soviet non-aggression pact, 165–169, 174; Stalin's overtures to, 164–166; in Tripartite Pact, 174. *See also* Soviet-German Front

Nevsky, Aleksandr, 242

New Economic Policy (NEP): under collective leadership, 81, 82, 110; under Lenin, 7, 64–65; party infighting over, 87, 88; Stalin's restructuring of, 100–104

New York Times, 271

Nicholas II, abdication of, 42

Nicolaevsky, Boris, 22

Nikolaev, Leonid: background of, 129–130; execution of relatives, 351n68; motives for Kirov's murder, 130–131; murder of Kirov, 128–129, 131–132, 351n68; prior detentions by NKVD, 132

NKVD: fabricated evidence of, 140; formation of, 125; in Kirov murder investigation, 131–133; in Kremlin Affair, 139; Order No.00447, 150; purge of, 140, 160; in Trotsky murder, 174; Yezhov's direction of Terror, 157, 158–159

Nomenklatura: new stock, 147; privileged lifestyle of, 320; purge of, 139–140, 144, 150, 282–283, 304, 320; Stalin's control over, 36–37, 147–148; Stalin's reorganization of, 178

Norway, German occupation of, 174

Nuclear development, 293, 297

October Revolution, 8, 50–53; anniversary of, 217–219

Onufrieva, Pelageia, 251–252

Order No. 227, 223

Order No. 270, 210

Ordzhonikidze, Grigory Konstantinovich: 66, 82, 192, Gallery 7; biography of, 343n55; on Central Committee expulsion of left opposition, 90; on factional disputes, 106–107; and "Georgian Affair," 71, 73; health of, 102; on industrialization, 109; and Lenin-Stalin conflict, 73; on peasant uprisings, 115; in power struggle, 76; in Stalin faction, 105; suicide of, 140, 177

Ordzhonikidze, Zinaida, 253

Orlov, A. Ya., 289

Osinsky, Valerian Valerianovich, 85–86, 345n92

Ostrovskii, Aleksandr, 19

Panic-mongers and cowards, campaign against, 223

Parade of Our Troops on Moscow's Red Square on 7 November 1941 (film), 218–219

Party apparat. *See* Nomenklatura

Patricide, The (Kazbegi), 17

Paulus, Friedrich, 225, 258

Pavlov, Dmitry, 208

Peasants: currency reform impact on, 278; and famines, 38, 116, 117–122; income of, 353n16; postwar discontent of, 262; forced resettlement of, 38, 322; revolts of, 110, 113–115, 323; taxation of, 302; working conditions of, 324–325. *See also* Agriculture; Kulaks

Penal colonies, 38

Penalty battalions, 223, 237, 242

Pereprygina, Lidiia, 30, 31, 252, 338n60

Peter the Great, Stalin's view of, 94, 95

Petrograd Soviet, 43, 44, 52

Petrovskaia, Stefaniia, 251

Petrovsky, Grigory, 177

Plato, 95

Plekhanov, Georgy, 94

Poland: Civil War campaign in, 59–61; in Communist bloc, 281, 297; German invasion of, 169–170; and German-Soviet non-aggression pact, 166; Katyn massacre, 170; postwar settlement in, 245, 248; Warsaw uprising, 244

Politburo: abolition of, 305–306; eavesdropping on members, 145, 353n10; execution of members, 144, 177; expulsion of leftist opposition, 84–86; independence in day-to-day work, 310–311; power struggle in, 75–81, 86–87; reorganizations of leadership, 66, 177–179, 303; replaced during Great Terror, 177–178; Stalin's appointment to, 54; Stalin's dictatorial powers approved by, 180–181; Stalin's domination of, 144–147, 176–177, 241; voting process in, 370n66; wartime domestic duties of, 240–241; and wartime leadership, 203, 204, 205, 206, 207, 238, 241; and world revolution, 77–78; young generation in, 177, 181. *See also* Collective leadership

Popular front against fascism, 135

Poskrebyshev, Aleksandr, 255, 329

Postyshev, Pavel, 177

Pravda, 44, 51, 79, 89, 93, 113, 155, 193, 236, 308, 314

Presidential Archive of the Russian Federation (APRF), xiv

Presidium, of Central Committee, 305–306, 312

Presidium Bureau, of Central Committee, 306, 311, 312

Preventive war theory, 183, 184

Prisoners of war: German, 231; Soviet, 210

Private peasant plots, 7, 111, 112, 124, 278

Prosveshchenie (*Enlightenment*) (magazine), 94

Provisional Government: crackdown on Bolsheviks, 48–49; formation of, 42; and Kornilov mutiny, 49–50; overthrow of, 45, 50–53; socialist support for, 43

Purges: during Civil War, 56–59; under collective leadership, 89; Doctors' Plot, 196, 307–309, 314; Leningrad Affair, 144, 282–283, 310; Mingrelian Affair, 304–305, 314–315; of Molotov's wife, 283–284, 314; of nomenklatura, 139–140, 144, 150, 282–283, 304, 320; rehabilitation of victims, 314–315; Shakhty Affair, 107; of state security, 34–35, 36, 40, 303–304. *See also* Terror

Radzinsky, Edvard, ix, 338n1
Rajk, Laszlo, 281
Rakosi, Matyas, 196, 290, 297
Rape, by Red Army, 234–235
Rationing, abolition of, 275, 278
Razin, Ye. A., 264, 265
Reconciliation campaign, 135–136
Red Army: anti-government sentiment of peasant recruits, 105; in Baltic states, 170–171; Berlin operation of, 246–247; in Civil War, 55–56, 59–61; crimes against civilians, 234–236; in Eastern Europe, 244; in Finland (Winter War), 172–173, 186; growth of, 185–186; in Japanese border clashes, 163; modernization of, 183–184; in Poland, 170; postwar buildup, 297–298; purge of, 155, 161, 162–163, 186, 355n31; Stalin's critique of command, 186, 219, 236–237; Stalin's reorganizations of command, 237–239, 273–274; Stalin-Trotsky conflict over, 61–63. *See also* Soviet-German Front
Religion, 242–243, 325
Retail prices, and currency reform, 277, 278
Revolution of 1905, 24–25
Revolution of 1917: Bolshevik seizure of power, 50–53; escalation of, 47; Lenin's radical action plan, 44–46; Lenin-Stalin collaboration during, 46, 47–49, 50; moderate (rightist) Bolshevik faction in, 43–44, 46–47, 50, 51; outbreak of, 42. *See also* Provisional Government
Rhee, Syngman, 294
Ribbentrop, Joachim von, 165, 166, 174
Rieber, Alfred, 21
Robins, Raymond, 120–121
Rokossovsky, Konstantin Konstantinovich, 222–223, 297, 364n94
Roosevelt, Franklin: 269, Gallery 12; correspondence with Stalin, 228, 246; and Hopkins mission to Moscow, 211; and Red Army criminal behavior, 235–236; representatives at Moscow

Conference, 212; and second front plan, 223, 228, 229, 230
Roskin, Grigory, 265
Rozengolts, Arkady, 152
Rudzutak, Yan Ernestovich: biography of, 345n100; compromising evidence against, 106; execution of, 177; as oppositionist, 90
Rukhadze, Nikolai, 304–305
Russian Federation, proposals for, 68–69
Russian language proficiency, Stalin's, 97–98
Russian Orthodox Church, reconciliation with, 242–243
Russification policy, 325
Russo-Japanese War of 1905, 248
Rybalko, R. S., 319
Rykov, Aleksei Ivanovich: 80, 191, Gallery 6; biography of, 344n80; execution of, 140; expulsion of, 108; and left opposition, 90; as oppositionist, 105, 106, 108

Sakhalin: oil pipeline, 179; and postwar settlement, 248, 289
Salaries, 35, 353n16
Saltykov-Shchedrin, Mikhail, 95
Sapronov, Timofei Vladimirovich, 85, 345n94
Savings bank deposits, and currency reform, 275, 277, 279
Schulenburg, Friedrich von der, 199
Second front plan, 223–224, 228, 229, 230
"Secret Five" group, 177–178
Security system. *See* NKVD; State security
Seliavkin, Aleksei, 126, 350n58
Sevastopol, siege of, 221
Shakhty Affair, 107
Shakhurin, Aleksei, 187, 215–216
Shaposhnikov, Boris Mikhailovich, 201, 361n14
Shcherbakov, Aleksandr Sergeevich: biography of, 356–357n57; Politburo appointment of, 177; in wartime leadership, 214, 216
Shepilov, Dmitry, 314
Shkiriatov, Matvei, Gallery 14, 311
Sholokhov, Mikhail Aleksandrovich, 119, 121–122, 349n39
Shostakovich, Dmitry Dmitryevich, 97, 347n14
Shtemenko, Sergei, 229–230, 247, 297
Shumiatsky, Boris, 2, 3, 347n12
Shvernik, Nikolai, 311
Siberia: grain expropriation in, 101, 102–104; Stalin's exile in, 23, 29–32, 190
Simonov, Konstantin, 144–145, 213, 313
Slansky, Rudolf, 307
Smirnov, Vladimir Mikhailovich, 85, 345n93

Smolensk, Battle of, 210–211

Smolny Institute, Kirov's murder at, 128–129

Social Democratic movement: in Baku, 26–27; European congresses of, 25; factions of, 24; radical wing of, 21; in revolution of 1905, 24–25; Stalin's involvement in, 18, 19, 21, 22–24. *See also* Bolsheviks; Mensheviks

Socialist Revolutionaries (SRs), 43, 50, 158

Sokolnikov, Grigory Yakovlevich, 87, 345n97

Soviet-German Front: capture by enemy provisions (Order No. 270), 210; casualties of, 208, 220, 222, 224, 232, 261, 263; in Crimea, 220, 221, 228; crimes against civilians, 234–236; defeats in early stages of war, 208, 209–210, 222, 238, 263–265; final battles, 243–244; first days of combat, 201–205; Kharkov, Battle of, 221, 222; Kursk, Battle of, 226–227, 228; Lend-Lease aid, 212; Leningrad Blockade, 213, 225; Moscow Siege, 213–219, 227–228; penalty battalions/anti-retreat units, 223, 237, 242; physical destruction in, 232, 261; popular uprisings/disturbances in, 216–217; ratio of forces, 231; repressive measures in, 209–210, 223, 237, 242; Smolensk, Battle of, 210–211; Stalingrad, Battle of, 224–225, 228, 238; Stalin's emissaries at, 201, 208–209; Stalin's strategic directives in, 208, 210, 212–213, 217, 219–221, 225, 226–227, 239–240; Stalin's visits to, 227–228; in Ukraine, 212–213, 221, 222, 228; victories of 1944, 230–231; Zhukov's commands, 212, 213, 214, 360n2. *See also* Stalin, Joseph, wartime leadership of

Sovnarkom Bureau of the USSR: Commission on Current Issues, 365n136; formation of, 178–179; function of, 181

Spain, repression of foreign espionage, 156

Spanish Civil War, 153–154, 163

Special Sector, 329, 377nn35–37

Spheres of influence in Europe, 244

Stakhanov, Aleksei, 320–321

Stakhanovites, 320–321

Stalin, Joseph, Gallery 3, 13, 15; "agree and ignore" approach of, 105–106; in airplane flight, 229–230; anti-Semitism of, 284–285, 286; apologists for, ix, x–xi ; arrests of, 23, 27, 28, Gallery 4; biographies of, ix–x, 149, 331n2; birth of, 11; bodyguards of, 33–36, 92, 189, 338–339n5; and Bolshevik armed robbery, 26; in car crash, 34; and Caucasian culture of violence, 21–22; childhood and youth of, 11–14; in Civil War Southwestern Front, 59–61; in Civil War Tsaritsyn command, 54–56, Gallery 5; Civil War Tsaritsyn terror campaign of, 56–59; in

collective leadership (*See* Collective leadership); collectivization policy of, 110–113, 115–116, 299, 300; conflict with Bolshevik colleagues, 63; consolidation of power, 176–181; constitutional liberalization by, 134–135; dachas of, 3–7, 191, 193, Gallery 10; death of, 313–314; dictatorial powers of, 36–39, 180–181, 303; "Dizzy with Success," 114; double agent rumors about, 27; economy under (*See* Economy); editor of *Pravda*, 44, 51; education of, 12, 13, 14–20, Gallery 2; on espionage threat, 154–155; at European party congresses, 25; exile of, 23, 27, 29–32, 42, 98, 190, 251; family life/relations with children, 253, 254, 256–260, Gallery 9, 11; famine explanation of, 120–122; federation proposal of, 69; film favorites of, 96–97; final days of, 33, 92, 142–144, 189, 310–313, 338n1; on foreign intelligence threat, 155–157, 162, 284; foreign policy of (*See* Foreign policy); and foreign press rumors of leadership struggle, 269, 270–271; funeral and ceremonial farewells, 314, 317–318; generalissimo rank of, 225–226, 261; as general secretary of party, 66–67, 108; grain expropriation policy of, 101, 102–104, 105, 110, 119–120; health of, 145, 189–197, 303; historical interests of, 94–95; -Hitler non-aggression pact, 165–169, 174; ideological influences on, 7, 93–94; industrialization policy of, 108–109, 117, 124–125, 267, 298, 299; inner circle of (*See* Inner circle); and Kirov's murder, 128, 129, 130–134; Kremlin office of, 2, 242, 311; languages, knowledge of, 97–98, 289; Lenin cited in speeches of, 93; -Lenin relationship, 25, 28, 46, 54, 64–65, 67–68, 69–75, Gallery 5; Lenin's attack on, 72–74, 79; Lenin's ideological influence on, 24, 53, 93–94; Lenin's revolutionary agenda supported by, 47–49, 50, 52–53; letters from public sent to, 300–301, 327–329, 377n35, n38; libraries of, 93–96, 138, 346n5; literary tastes of, 17, 93, 95–96; Mao's visit to, 149, 287–288, 289–293; marriage to Nadezhda Allilueva, 49, 252–256, Gallery 8; marriage to Yekaterina Svanidze, 25, 27, 250–251; marshal rank of, 226; medical care of, 189, 192, 196–197, 309; mental state of, 151–153, 197, 204–205; on military professionals, 59; modest facade of, 148–149; -Molotov relationship, 181–182, 269, 270–272; musical tastes of, 97; name change of, 28; official trips of, 102; oratory of, 97; parents of, 11, 13, Gallery 1; personality of, 7, 21–22, 40–41, 149, 181, 197, 270, 289; physical defects of, 13–14, 190; plot against, 127; poetry of, 17; postwar challenges to,

Stalin, Joseph (*continued*)
262–263; power over subordinates, 1, 144–149; in power struggle for leadership, 75–81, 86–87; on preemptive strike, 182–183; and private agriculture, 7, 112, 124; promotion of younger generation leaders, 177, 181, 196; public appearances of, 136–137, 326; public image of, 329–330; public sentiment at death of, 318–319; radicalization during seminary years, 18–20, 21; reading materials/information sources of, 92–96, 327; reconciliation campaign of, 135–136; reorganization of leadership, 178–179, 272–274, 303, 306–307; reorganization of military command, 237–239, 273–274; reorganization of political structure, 305–306; research on (*See* Archival sources); in revolution of 1905, 24–25; in revolutionary movement, 42, 43–44, 46–47, 51; rise in Bolshevik leadership ranks, 28, 54, 65–66; romantic relationships of, 30, 251–252, 255; seats of power, 1–2; and "Secret Five" leadership group, 177–178; seventieth birthday celebration, 290; Siberian visit of 1928, 102–104, 326; in Social Democratic movement, 18, 19, 21, 22–24; social gatherings of, 5–7, 196; sovietization goal of, 171–172; and Spanish Civil War, 154; state security controlled by, 39–40, 145, 158; succession to, 310–316; theatrical tastes of, 97; in Tiflis weather station job, 21; -Trotsky conflict over Polish Front, 61–63; as tsarist heir, 8–9; vacations in south, 191–194, 268–269, 303–304, Gallery 8, 10; under Vlasik, 35; war preparations of, 183–187; world-view of, 7–8, 98–99; writings of, 320, Gallery 16; writing style of, 97; *See also* Purges; Stalinist system; Terror

Stalin, Joseph, wartime leadership of: Gallery 11; at Berlin Conference, 247–248; in Churchill meetings, 224, 230; and collaborators with Nazi occupation, 232; combat operation directives in, 208, 210, 212–213, 217, 219–221, 225, 226–227, 239–240; Command Headquarters in, 202; defeats blamed on subordinates, 221–223; and domestic policy, 240–241; emissaries to front, 201, 208–209; ethnic deportations policy, 232–234; explanation of Red Army retreat, 263–265; in first days of war, 203–205; front line visit of, 227–228; and German invasion, reaction to, 187–188, 198–202; and health problems, 194–196, 214; in Japanese war, 248–249; and Lend-Lease aid, 211–212; and mental health problem, 204–205; and military command structure, 237–239; and military leadership

reorganization, 241–242; and military staffing decisions, 220–221; mistrust of Western Allies, 246, 248, 266; and Moscow evacuation, 214–216; and prisoners of war procession, 231; propaganda campaign, 217–219; radio address (3 July 1942), 207; and Red Army crimes against civilians, 234–236; Red Army criticized by, 186, 219, 236–237; and religious reconciliation, 242–243; repressive measures in, 209–210, 223, 237, 242; and second front plan, 223–224, 229, 230; State Defense Committee in, 205–207; at Tehran Conference, 229–230; at Yalta Conference, 244–246, Gallery 12

Stalin, Nadezhda Allilueva (second wife): Gallery 8; biography of, 334n8; career of, 252–253; and Khrushchev, 333n1; marriage of, 49, 252, 254–255; suicide of, 3, 255–256

Stalin, Svetlana (daughter). *See* Allilueva (Allilu-yeva), Svetlana

Stalin, Vasily (son): Gallery 11; birth of, 152; childhood of, 254, 256; death of, 260; public appearance of, 136–137; relationship with father, 257, 258, 259–260; at Stalin's deathbed, 250

Stalin, Yakov (son): Gallery 11; birth of, 250–251; childhood and youth of, 25, 27, 252–253; as prisoner of war, 258; relationship with father, 253, 257

Stalin, Yekaterina Svanidze (first wife), 25, 27, 250–251

Stalin Collection of the Russian State Archive of Social and Political History (RGASPI), xiii–xiv

Stalingrad, Battle of, 224–225, 228, 238

Stalingrad (Tsaritsyn), in Civil War, 54–59

Stalinist system: beneficiaries of, 320–322; campaigns and counter-campaigns of, 39; "inevitable Stalinism" theory, xi; modernization as justification for, x–xi; nostalgia for, 330; public mood under, 319–330; victims of, 37–38, 322–323

Standard of living, 262, 323–324

State Defense Committee, 205–207, 240

State security: under Beria, 181, 332–333n1; formation of NKVD, 125; interregnum period reform of, 315; investigation of secret police abuses, 125–126; party opposition suppressed by, 83–85; purges of, 34–35, 36, 40, 303–304; reorganization of, 340n19; reports/summaries as information source, 327; Stalin's control of, 39–40, 145, 158; Stalin's guards, 33–34, 35–36; torture by, 38; in wartime, 216; at Yalta Conference, 245–246. *See also* NKVD

Sudoplatov, Pavel, 353n10